More Boot Sector Games

Deep secrets of 8086/8088 programming

Óscar Toledo Gutiérrez

More Boot Sector Games

Copyright © 2020 Óscar Toledo Gutiérrez

ISBN: 978-1-67817-744-7

Official website: **http://nanochess.org/**

The author welcomes your comments, suggestions and errata reports. Please send them to: **biyubi@gmail.com**

You can also follow him on Twitter as **@nanochess**

First published in 2020.

Dedicated to my beloved wife Rosa Nely and our little fairies Myriam Sofia and Samantha.

For Elisa, keep smiling.

For my mother and my father, thanks for all.

Contents

The Book

Chapter 7

Appendix A

Appendix B

Appendix C

Appendix D

Appendix E

Foreword

Bearded old men

As far back as I can remember, I always wanted to be a programmer. When I was little I was lucky enough to be exposed to the world of personal computers and computer games in then almost-ready-to-collapse Soviet Union. I wanted to be just like those bearded old men (who were in their thirties at most) hiding away in dark offices of a local scientific research university. Sadly, that dream did not come true, and I never became a programmer professionally, but I still very much enjoy programming just for fun.

What did end up happening though is I immersed myself into the world of IBM PC compatibles, and games released for them. The collapse of the USSR and subsequent economic hardships actually helped me in my quest of playing as many MS-DOS games as possible because new hardware was often near impossible to acquire for regular citizens, with older machines sticking around for much longer than expected, and lack of any kind of copyright law and legal publishing led to lots and lots of games being available for not a lot of money. But eventually all of it came to an end. Computers became affordable even in Russia, along with latest game releases, and most people stopped caring about games from the DOS era. But I held on.

The early 2000s when I moved to the United States, weren't too kind to old computer games. Not a lot of people remembered them, and even less talked about them. I knew that there must have been other people out there who, like me, remembered old PC games fondly, but I haven't met many of them in person. After a while when broadband internet started making its way into most homes, there was a gradual rise of interest in retro videogames. I waited for DOS gaming's turn. I waited. And waited. Eventually I realized that if I wanted to see something I enjoyed covered, I had to do it myself, and that's when I started DOS Nostalgia, my project dedicated to retro PC gaming. At the time there was very little coverage of DOS gaming in general. Being a retro PC enthusiast felt pretty lonely, and it didn't look like it was about to change.

But I'm happy to report that I was wrong! A decade has passed, and all kinds of wonderful things happened. I'm sure part of it was just waiting. When a game is 5 years old, it's just old. But when it's 25 years old, it's retro! And retro is cool. And the other part is nostalgia. People grew up, got careers and families, and now fondly looked back at simpler times when they were kids. They remembered games in 16 colors in big cardboard boxes with fat manuals, and the smell of freshly manufactured floppy disks. Now there are many fantastic YouTube channels dedicated to retro IBM PC gaming, each year brings more and more modern hardware to use in vintage machines, and, of course, there are books.

I try to keep my finger on the pulse of everything that might interest a retro PC gaming enthusiast these days, but when I saw a listing of Óscar's book, I could barely believe it. It felt so incredibly niche, as if someone wrote a book just for me. Boot sector stuff was always interesting to me, and I already needed a reason to brush up on my barely existent Assembler skills. The premise of having each game fit into just 512 *bytes* was fascinating. I absolutely had to get the book. And then I was pleasantly surprised once again. The book was written in a very approachable manner, and all the examples turned out to be fairly sophisticated for something that small. Everything was perfect for my skill as a programmer, and the whole process was a lot of fun. It also turned out that I was wrong again! I've seen many people all over the world express interest in the book, and it's incredibly satisfying to know that there are so many other enthusiasts who also care about something like a Basic interpreter that fits neatly into a boot sector.

I'm glad to know that the book was successful enough for Óscar to write a followup. I thought the programs in the first book were as sophisticated as it was going to get, but the ones in this book have really knocked my socks off. I hope all of you dear readers will have as much fun with it as I did. Books like this one are the reason I am no longer pessimistic about the future of retro PC gaming. I see many works that unite us in our journey of common interest, and I know there are going be many more along the way (and I still can't believe that this foreword is nine times bigger than the compiled code of the largest program discussed in this book).

Anatoly Shashkin

@dosnostalgic

http://www.dosnostalgia.com

January 30, 2020.

Preface

Why this book?

I'm very humbled by the success of my previous book "Programming Boot Sector Games". I was pretty surprised that people around the world praised it, recommended it, took pictures of it proudly on social networks, and told me that a book like it was greatly needed. Also I got some new friends with the same passion!

I'm amazed by the coincidences around its publication, like the 40-year anniversary of the 8086 processor, the resurgence of the popularity of PC/XT machines like the elegant yet expensive NuXT processor board, and the endless-looking parade of vintage PC computer restorations on Youtube channels like LGR and The 8-Bit Guy.

I had just finished writing the previous book when an idea came to my mind: "What about a launcher for all these games?" And then the most crazy one "What if it is a small operating system in 512 bytes?" And thus bootOS was born.

bootOS broke my personal marks on Github, with so far more than one thousand starrings.

Don't worry if you understand little to no 8086/8088 assembly language, because all the programs in this book are heavily commented in an easy-to-understand language. You can always refer to my previous book "Programming Boot Sector Games" for a crash course on 8086/8088 assembly language! But again, no example exceeds 512 bytes of machine code!

This time the examples include: Follow the Lights, a lights game; bootOS, an operating system in 510 bytes of x86 machine code; bootRogue, a small RPG reminiscent of the well-known Rogue developed for UNIX™ operating system and later for MS-DOS; Bricks, a paddle/ball/wall game with full-color and sound effects; and CubicDoom, a ray-casting game à la Wolfenstein-3D.

I've included again the 8086/8088 instruction set, but this time sorted alphabetically, because it's very useful to find an instruction by name to code it directly for self-modifying code, or for using it to create one-byte jump tricks.

For this book I assume you have previous knowledge of programming in any high-level language that includes hexadecimal numbers, like C, C++, PHP, Java, Javascript, etc., and how to use command-line on Windows, Linux or Mac OS X.

I strongly recommend to enter each program using the keyboard, because it's a great practice to read the instructions as you type them. No real warrior can learn only from copy & paste.[1]

Welcome to a world of creativity.

Óscar Toledo G.
November 2019

---

[1] Although if you get stuck, all the programs are available for download at my git: https://github.com/nanochess/

Acknowledgments

The friends are the treasure

Although this became a cliché in almost every movie and cartoon, I really feel like this has been true all my life. I've learned many things from every person I've known along my life, and also made great friendships along the way.

I want to give special thanks to Michael Hayes (Zendocon) for volunteering again as proofreader for this book.

Eric Davisson @XlogicX made suggestions for the optimization chapter, and authorized to use some messages we interchanged about bootRogue. Travis Goodspeed @travisgoodspeed asked me to do an old-style advertisement of my book Programming Boot Sector Games for PoC||GTFO issue 20,[2] and I greatly enjoyed doing it without using clip art! Even the cake was real.

Sending greetings to @foone who fills my timeline with interesting history of retrocomputing (and pictures!) and has suffered unboxing his old IBM PC 5150 to test my boot sector craziness, Mikko Hyppönen @mikko superhero and master of reverse engineering (though he still says he is a supervillain), Binni Shah @binitamshah who publishes the most interesting hacks for every platform, Jim Leonard @mobygamer who keeps me updated on old gaming, Clint @lazygamereviews for covering old PC hardware, and Anatoly Shashkin @dosnostalgic whose game-of-the-day

---

[2] International Journal of Proof-of-Concept or Get The Fuck Out. https://www.alchemistowl.org/pocorgtfo/

pictures make my day and graciously contributed the foreword for this book.

I'm deeply grateful to Peter Ferrie (qkumba) who contributed the foreword to my previous book and optimizations for my boot sector programs.

To HellMood who suggested translating Toledo Atomchess to *nasm* syntax and gave me some optimization suggestions. This fact helped a lot of people to assemble the game into their machines all around the world.

Also want to say hello to @ThomasFuchs. I took an online course with him (it was one of the prizes for winning the 2nd place of JS1K in 2010). I was nicely surprised when saw a picture with "Programming Boot Sector Games" in his bookshelf along his omnipresent cat.

Chapter 1

We said yesterday

In the previous book we did a crash course on 8086/8088 programming, yet we had to leave certain things at the side of the road.

However to understand the programs in this new book, we need to dive deeper into the processor's instructions, and of course, add some further information for your enjoyment.

I'll start refreshing the information about tools setup.

1.1 Tools setup.

Let us download the Netwide Assembler (NASM) from *www.nasm.us*. This is a command-line utility.

Uncompress it to some directory where you can work. My suggestion for Windows: *My documents/nasm/*

For Linux and Mac OS X, I suggest to create a *nasm* directory under your home directory.

You must edit your source code somehow. I typically use EDIT from MS-DOS under Windows XP (not included with it, but easy to search and download), but you can resort to your daily editor, like *Notepad++*, *emacs*, *vi*, *vim*, *nano* or even the original *Notepad* included with Windows.

Testing your programs will require some extra tools. If you are using Windows 10 or Mac OS X, then you'll need DosBox available from *http://*

www.dosbox.com or VirtualBox from *http://www.virtualbox.org* to test your programs.

Notice that the Netwide Assembler works on any modern PC with Windows, Linux, and also under Mac OS X. It has the advantage that its syntax for the 8086/8088 processor is similar to the recommended one by Intel. Other free assemblers like *gas* (from the GNU toolchain) use the AT&T syntax, which unfortunately is too complicated for our learning purposes.

The documentation for *nasm* is available online at the following address: *https://nasm.us/docs.php*

1.2 Practice.

Create your first assembler program. Name it anything like *first.asm* and put it inside the same directory as *nasm*:

```
    org 0x0100
start:
    cld
    mov si,string
repeat:
    lodsb
    test al,al
    je end
    push si
    mov ah,0x0e
    mov bx,0x000f
    int 0x10
    pop si
    jmp repeat

end:
    int 0x20

string:
    db "I am your father",0
```

Then using the command-line (*cmd.exe* in Windows, or your current shell in Linux or Mac OS X), go to *nasm* directory/folder and assemble the program with this command (where ↵ appears I mean to press the Enter key):

```
nasm -f bin first.asm -o first.com↵
```

If everything went right, it should assemble without an error, and no message will be output to command-line. It simply will end and you now should have a file in your current directory named *first.com* that is 36 bytes in size. And you can run it using (MS-DOS/Windows only; for the other platforms you need an emulator as previously described):

```
first↵
```

The message "I am your father" will appear in the console.

I would suggest changing the message (just make sure to stay within the double quotes), so you can get a grasp of how things change once you start continuously assembling a program.

1.3 Using the boot sector.

You can have the amazing feeling of running a game without an operating system (and of course obliged for the chapter 6 related to bootOS).

How to try a boot sector program:

1. Writing it to the boot sector of a real floppy disk.[3] This means that you have a floppy disk drive installed in your computer (probably of the 3 ½" variety, although Windows 98 still supports 5 ¼" ones, but don't forget to put the write protection tab because Windows has the bad taste of rewriting the boot

---

[3] The first floppy disk for IBM PC had the size 5 ¼" and could keep the amazing quantity of 180K bytes (single density), and then it became double density for 360K bytes. There also appeared 3 ½" floppy disks with 720K bytes, and later a mixture of 5 ¼" at 1.2 MB and 3 ½" at 1.44 MB. There even appeared briefly a 2" floppy disk with a capacity of 2.88 MB but it never grew popular.

sector or recommending a full format of the disk if it doesn't recognize the boot sector as standard). I recommend using *Rawrite32* for Windows.[4] Or Linux command-line: `sudo dd if=boot.img of=/dev/fd0 count=1 bs=512`

2. Creating a file filled with zeroes of length 1474560 (1.44 MB), put `boot.img` at the start of the file and record an empty CD with El Torito specification.[5] For Windows, Nero and EasyCD support the option for creating a bootable CD. For Linux see: `https://www.tldp.org/HOWTO/Bootdisk-HOWTO/cd-roms.html`

3. Writing it to the boot sector of a USB memory stick, same as step 1 but replacing target device with the USB drive (Windows) or the device file (Linux). But beware that you will destroy the important partition information of the USB memory, so you need a means to read the boot sector and save it so you can reuse the USB memory later. Saving the boot record with Linux would be (don't forget to replace */dev/fd0* with the correct one for the USB memory): `dd if=/dev/fd0 of=saved.img count=1 bs=512`

4. Feeding an emulator or virtual machine with the *boot.img* file as bootable disk. *VirtualBox* allows you to set up a floppy disk drive with a file as the image (applies for Windows, Mac OS X and Linux). While *qemu* can be run from the Linux command line: `qemu-system-x86_64 -fda boot.img`

Intel plans to remove altogether the support for boot sector by 2020, but this still means every PC manufactured before that year continues to support boot sectors the same way since 1981.

---

[4] https://www.netbsd.org/~martin/rawrite32/

[5] As CD-ROM was created and standardized, it came up El Torito specification in 1995. It made it possible to embed a 1.44 MB. boot image inside a CD-ROM.

1.4 The int instruction.

Our first insight will be into the **int** instruction. It has been used for calling the services available at the PC BIOS. However the way it goes into the BIOS wasn't documented, yet.

In fact the first kilobyte of RAM memory available on a PC machine (0x00000-0x003ff) is reserved for a table of 256 entries or interruption vectors. Each entry has a width of 4 bytes, or more correctly, two 16-bit words.

The first one is a value for the IP (Instruction Pointer) register, and the second one is a value for the CS (Code Segment) register.

0x00000	Target IP	Target CS	**int 0x00**
0x00004	Target IP	Target CS	**int 0x01**
0x00008	Target IP	Target CS	**int 0x02**
0x0000c	Target IP	Target CS	**int 0x03**
...	...		
0x003fc	Target IP	Target CS	**int 0xff**

Table 1-1. Structure of table for **int** vectors.

Once the processor finds the **int** instruction, it multiplies the service number by four and indexes it into the first kilobyte of RAM for getting the target address of the service call. So when a **int 0x10** instruction appears, the processor reads the addresses 0x00040-0x00043 to retrieve the destination CS:IP address. Given both registers are loaded, the processor is free to access any of the 1 MB of memory.[6]

Before calling the new address, the processor saves the Flags register into the stack, followed by the current value of the CS register, and then the address of the next instruction from the IP register.

---

[6] As a side note, you could be confused about the 1 MB limit, but even the 80386, Pentium or higher processors are limited to addressing the first 1 MB of memory when working in 16-bit mode.

5

SP+0	Caller IP
SP+2	Caller CS
SP+4	Caller Flags

Table 1-2. Stack pointer state after the processor executed the **int** instruction.

Once the service is called and finished doing its work, it should finish with an **iret** instruction. This instruction forces the processor to retrieve the return address (CS:IP) and the old value of Flags register. It cannot be a **ret** instruction (it only retrieves the previous IP address), nor a **retf** instruction (it only retrieves the IP and CS registers, and would leave dangling data on stack: the old Flags value).

Note it depends on the programmer whether the processor registers are saved. For example, **int 0x10** on most PC BIOS will save all registers, except the register BP on some buggy VGA BIOS (graphics cards).

The best example of **int** usage appears in chapter 6, related to bootOS, an operating system that fits inside a boot sector.

Notice there are two one-byte versions of **int**: **into**, and **int 3**. These call respectively the vector 0x04 and 0x03.

The **int 3** instruction is typically used by debuggers to insert breakpoints at strategic points of programs, in order to debug the state of the processor when reaching these. As this is a one-byte instruction, it can be inserted anywhere without being afraid of damaging the next instruction. For example, remember the **xchg ax,bx** instruction that uses only one byte. In this case if a two-byte **int** instruction needed to be used, then the next instruction would be corrupted.

1.5 Hardware interruptions.

The interruption vectors 0x08-0x0f are reserved for hardware interruptions or Interrupt ReQuests (IRQ).

Don't ever use these for your purposes because their handling depends on the hardware these are supporting, and setting a routine in the vectors without proper handling of hardware will definitely cause a crash of the system.

- 0x08 - IRQ0 - System timer. Called 18.2 times per second. Also is in charge of turning off the floppy disk motor.
- 0x09 - IRQ1 - Keyboard interruption. Called for every scancode generated by the keyboard. This includes both pressing and depressing keys. Not commonly used because the handling varies between PC XT, PC AT and modern hardware.
- 0x0a - IRQ2 - Vertical retrace interrupt / Printer 2 (also known as LPT2).
- 0x0b - IRQ3 - Serial communications 2 (also known as COM2).
- 0x0c - IRQ4 - Serial communications 1 (also known as COM1).
- 0x0d - IRQ5 - Fixed disk interrupt.
- 0x0e - IRQ6 - Floppy disk interrupt.
- 0x0f - IRQ7 - Printer 1 (also known as LPT1).

Starting on PC AT machines, circa 1984, you should also avoid interruption vectors 0x70-0x77 (IRQ8-IRQ15) because these are redirected from a second set of hardware interruptions.[7]

1.6 Exceptions.

When something goes weird with some instructions, even if somewhat simple, the 8086 processor has exceptions.

This means it will invoke some services when very special cases happen like:

- Division by zero. It goes to interruption vector 0x00. It happens when the divisor for the **div** or **idiv** instructions is zero, but it's

---

[7] As a side note, the interrupt vectors allowed the IBM PC from the start to have more advanced operating systems as the hardware didn't have to wait for peripherals to complete its execution (CP/M 8-bit machines typically didn't have these facilities). It was specially useful for UNIX-like operating systems, like XENIX that appeared in 1983, Minix in 1987, and later Linux in 1991.

also invoked when the resulting value is bigger than the destination register.

- Step-by-step debugging. It goes to interruption vector 0x01 after each instruction. It is enabled by bit 8 (T or Trap) of the Flags register. Typically it is saved as a specially formed stack frame with the Flags register bit T set, and an **iret** instruction executed, causing a trap **int 0x01** to be generated immediately after execution of the instruction. Of course, this depends on saving the complete registers of the processor so the debugged program can continue its course.[8]

- Non-maskable interrupt. It goes to interruption vector 0x02, typically generated by hardware.

- Breakpoint. It goes to interruption vector 0x03. It's generated by the **int 3** instruction.

- Overflow. It goes to interruption vector 0x04. It's generated by the **into** instruction.

These exceptions or traps save the Flags register and the CS:IP address of the instruction triggering the exception just as if an **int** instruction was executed.

Notice that later processors like 80286 and 80386 added exceptions of their own.

1.7 Bigger programs.

The 8086 processor also has the **jmp far** and **call far** instructions that loads both CS and IP registers at the same time (**call far** saves the old values into the stack), and the **retf** instruction that retrieves the previous values of CS and IP in order to return correctly.

These instructions are required if your programs reach more than 64K of code.

---

[8] On a side note, most viruses disabled vector 0x01 or checked for traces of the utility DEBUG.COM in order to avoid being debugged. Even modern malware also does some of this detection with vector 0x03 (Breakpoint).

The MS-DOS operating system (and Windows until version 8) included support for the 16-bit EXE file format that includes a table of relocations, because these **jmp far** and **call far** instructions use absolute values for the target addresses, and need to be relocated per the available RAM memory.

The difference of speed on these instructions made C compilers to include different "models" for compilation like these examples taken from Watcom C:

- Small (64k code + 64k data). This is representable with a COM file.[9]
- Medium (big code + 64k data). Only EXE file.
- Compact (64k code + big data). Only EXE file.
- Big (big code + big data). Only EXE file.
- Huge (big code + big data + pointers adjusted whenever 64k frontiers were exceeded). Only EXE file.

These models hindered C code compatibility between different compilers for many years, made porting jobs from UNIX code and vice versa very difficult, and essentially limited the software running on PC machines for many years until the appearance of linear memory handling inside Windows 95/98, or for MS-DOS with 386 extenders like DOS/4GW that was popularized with the Doom game and the Watcom C compiler.

1.8 High-level language interfacing.

Even if the 8086/8088 processors were launched in 1978, they included a very important register for high-level language support: the BP register.

The high-level languages, like C or Pascal, have the concept of a stack frame. And BP allows to keep track of the current stack frame, and it

---

[9] Even though it is similar to the 8080/Z80 representation of code, the old 8-bit processor were limited to combined code and data on less than 64k due to addressing limits.

is a welcome benefit as the SP register cannot be used to access memory (except via **push** and **pop** instructions).

We'll give an example of C language here (don't worry, I'll try to not fry your brain).

The whole concept of the C language are the functions. The functions are basically subroutines with input parameters (the names for these parameters are *local* to the function), and a single result.[10] We'll set up our example only on integers.

```c
int add_numbers(int a, int b, int c)
{
    return a + b + c;
}

int main(void)
{
    int a;

    a = add_numbers(5, 6, 7);
}
```

We'll do a hypothetical compilation of this code for your enjoyment:

```
add_numbers:
    push bp
    mov bp,sp
    mov ax,[bp+4]
    add ax,[bp+6]
    add ax,[bp+8]
    pop bp
    ret
```

The input parameters are passed on the stack, and *add_numbers* saves the previous value of BP before setting a new Base Pointer. As this function actually doesn't have any local variables, SP stays unchanged.

---

[10] This was a difficult concept to understand for a programmer coming from a BASIC language environment like me. In BASIC all variables were global! In the C language, almost every name declared is local, except the global variables put outside the functions.

The function reads its 3 input parameters and adds them, the result is returned on the register AX, and it will always be on that register.

Remember we did a **push bp**. The old value of BP is at the top of the stack [bp+0], then the next value on stack is the return address [bp+2], and the [bp+4] is the first argument of the function.

Now the *main* function; this is the function where every C program starts. Of course we won't show the required setup before entering into the program, like setting segment registers and stack pointer.

```
main:
    push bp
    mov bp,sp
    sub sp,2
    mov ax,7
    push ax
    mov ax,6
    push ax
    mov ax,5
    push ax
    call add_numbers
    add sp,6
    mov [bp-2],ax
    mov sp,bp
    pop bp
    ret
```

Our *main* function has an integer local variable, so after setting the BP register, it subtracts 2 from SP to make space (we could also make it a **push** instruction with any value).

Then it pushes the parameters for the *add_numbers* function, in *reverse order* so the function sees the input parameters in the right order.

After the call it must remove the three input parameters from the stack, so it uses **add sp,6**. Finally the result is saved into the local variable, located at [bp-2]. Why? Because we subtracted 2 from SP, so there is space just to the left.

Let us show it graphically:

add_numbers

[BP+0]	Old BP value	BP pointer for *add_numbers*
[BP+2]	Return address	
[BP+4]	5	
[BP+6]	6	
[BP+8]	7	
main [BP-2]	Local variable *a*	
[BP+0]	Old BP value	BP pointer for *main*
[BP+2]	Return address	

The top of this diagram is at lower addresses, the bottom of the diagram is at higher addresses. The real address doesn't matter.

Remember each **call** and **push** instruction makes the SP register go to lower addresses (decrement by 2), while each **ret** and **pop** instruction makes the SP register go to higher addresses (increment by 2).

This register BP alone made the 8086/8088 processors more competitive with high-level languages, and made the 8-bit processors like the Z80 or 6502 bite the dust, because the frame supporting code used just too many instructions/space on 8-bit processors and made them slow.

Chapter 2

Boot sector game design

The boot sector games are contained in 512 bytes. This means we have very little space, but even then it doesn't mean there's no planning. In fact, the scarce space makes it more important to do some planning ahead before coding anything.

Some of the important things are pretty basic, like: doing a preliminary analysis to see if a game idea can fit the size, separating the defining parts, choosing between text or graphics mode, or seeing what changes are needed in a game to make it recognizable after the "crunch" to make it small.

An advanced part of design is the redesign: the fact of taking your code and applying a completely different way of thinking in order to fit in the available space. Redesign isn't feasible for big games, but we are talking about 512 bytes. I had to make a note of this because I don't want you to be fooled thinking that everything applies on scale. Things that are perfectly valid when developing small programs (like early optimization or putting global variables into main registers), aren't good for big programs as they would drive development directly to hell.

2.1 Initialization / Core

The most important part of the game design for a boot sector game (and technically for any game), is the creation of the core game.

The core game is the part of the game that does all the basic operations for your game.

Here is a basic guide to recognize the basic operations on your game:

1. Use paper and write a label for each moving thing in your game. Be sure to leave a big space between labels because you'll be adding text.

2. Put a label to the background (if it interacts with the other thingies).

3. Add a list of things that each label should do (for example, an enemy should pursue the player, or the player can move and shoot, or the thingie should appear at certain points of the game).

4. Make sure these are all the things that can happen inside your game loop. Also define the victory and defeat conditions.

Don't be afraid to add other things that you like, for example, a victory dance of the player when he wins the game. But mark it clearly as *not basic* for having a working game.

If you are going to have more than 2 computer-controlled enemies on screen, then you should consider an initialization loop, a process loop, and a drawing loop. This way adding enemies will use relatively the *same* program space, only increasing the memory used—and it typically isn't included inside the boot sector so it doesn't count toward the byte limit.

If your initialization pattern requires fixed positions for enemies, consider calculating the start position by setting an initial value, and adding an offset value, instead of creating a start position table (typically using too many bytes).

If the initial positions for enemies aren't fixed, try using a random function.

Once you have labels for the moving things in your game, proceed to polish their definitions:

1. Take note of the data these need to work (like the X and Y coordinates, or a status byte, or a sprite number byte).

2. Take note of the data that needs to be initialized.

3. Take note of the keyboard information that needs to be processed.

At this point you'll have the game basically ready to be coded. If you are unable to translate your design document to code, it means you still haven't fully defined the core, and you should repeat your analysis to find the missing parts.

Once this limited game is coded, you can start adding the graphics and polishing required.

And then when the game is fully working, you can proceed to add the non-basic things, if you still have space on the boot sector.

At a certain point of the steep curve of experience, you'll be able to estimate mentally if the game in mind can fit on a boot sector (or whatever space you are going to use).

Given the limitations, most of the time we won't be considering the ability to exit from the boot game (the only way would be to call **int 0x19** to boot again the machine, or **int 0x20** if you are under an MS-DOS operating system or bootOS).

2.2 How much memory for graphics.

Anything that depends heavily on graphics will be more difficult to implement than, for example, text graphics.

A recognizable graphic requires typically a minimum of 8x8 pixels (8 bytes), and having eight different graphics means using 64 bytes of space; that's an eighth of the available space.

If your game is going to use more than eight different graphics, then it is better that your game core isn't too complex (see my previous book "Programming Boot Sector Games" for the difficulties encountered in Pillman or Invaders).

Interestingly CubicDoom doesn't use any "bitmapped" graphic; all is pseudo-3D visualization.

If you want your game or demo to run smoothly on old PC/XT machines then you should test with an emulator like DosBox which allows to slow down the execution speed.

2.3 Graphic cards.

On all the examples of my books, I've been using the video mode 0x13 allowing 320x200 pixels with 256 colors; this is known as a common VGA mode. This is a video mode that isn't available on old PC machines, except if you add a video graphics card, as VGA cards started appearing in 1988.

The most basic video mode is CGA at 320x200x4 colors, but unfortunately most VGA cards (and *all* the modern machines) are incompatible with that video mode.

If working on an ultra-old PC machine is your objective, I would recommend to use a common text mode.

2.4 How much memory for sound.

We can use the PC Speaker for generating sound, and it requires a minimum of 19 bytes to setup a tone on speaker as a subroutine, and 7 bytes to turn off the speaker, also as a subroutine.

Also you need to call the subroutine (setting frequency value and calling it), so you need 6 bytes each time to put a tone.

As the inner core is more important, you should consider sound a secondary objective unless your game depends completely on sound.

On a side note, some emulators fail to implement PC speaker emulation, like VirtualBox that only supports it on Linux platforms.

2.5 How much memory for steady framerate.

Our boot sector game should work on a wide variety of PC platforms, counting in the tens of millions. It can even be run on an original PC machine.

In order to keep a steady framerate, or the same speed on all machines, you'll need to use the clock services to find the tick change in order to synchronize your game to 18.2 hz.

At least 14 bytes are required each time.

Although a BIOS memory location can be read to get the current number of ticks, it's preferable to use **int 0x1a**, because some emulators fail to implement it, like VirtualBox.

2.6 How many bytes for keyboard handling.

The keyboard handling should use **int 0x16**. It has the advantage that it will work on all PC machines, instead of using port numbers, because these only work on PC/XT or PC/AT machines, and also sometimes prevent a USB keyboard from working.

A minimum of 10 bytes is used to read the keyboard when a key is available without stopping the game. Or a minimum of 4 bytes to read modifier keys. All this plus the code size of input comparisons.

The common comparison code for arrow keys uses 16 bytes and looks like this:

```
            cmp al,0x48    ; Up arrow?
            je go_up
            cmp al,0x4b    ; Left arrow?
            je go_left
            cmp al,0x4d    ; Right arrow?
            je go_right
            cmp al,0x50    ; Down arrow?
            je go_down

go_up:         ; your code

go_left:       ; your code

go_right:      ; your code

go_down:       ; your code

```

2.7 Are my registers touched or not?

You cannot be sure of the state of the registers at the start of your program, specially at start of a boot sector, but here are some clues:

- The D (Direction) flag state cannot be assumed, important for **movs, stos, lods,** and all other string instructions. Clear it, or set it as you require it.

- The values of AX, BX, CX, DX, SI, DI, BP, and SP aren't guaranteed across platforms.

- You can be sure SS:SP are initialized and have space for around 256 bytes at some place in RAM between 0x000400 and 0x07c00.

- You cannot be sure of the values of CS, DS, and ES. Most probably CS is 0x0000, but *some*[11] BIOS loaders are crazy!

Calling the BIOS services with the **int** instruction will also typically save most of the registers.

Courtesy of Internet whispers, we know some VGA BIOS destroy the BP register while calling **int 0x10**.

If you are using **int 0x16** (keyboard services) and **int 0x1a** (clock/ time services), you can be sure only the input and output registers are used, and all other registers are preserved. This is more than enough knowledge when writing your games or applications.

2.8 What if it doesn't fit the boot sector size.

You are coding the best-ever application, demo, or game for a boot sector, and you discover in awe that your beautiful code doesn't fit into 510 bytes.

There are several solutions for your ordeal:

- Are you using the shortest algorithms? Or are you trying to fit a complex sophisticated algorithm that will make strong men cry?

---

[11] Scarce, very rare. We hope, but many people still say that some undocumented BIOS boots via **jmp 0x07c0:0x0000**, meaning CS will be 0x07c0 and IP will be 0x0000.

- Are you using too many graphics? Are you sure you need all the animation frames?

- Do you have too many items on screen handled independently? Consider reducing it to a single loop if all these share data. Consider optimization for comparison lists.

- Did you insert bells & whistles before getting it to work? Like sound, flashes, status bar, title screen, ending screen, credits screen, etc.

- Are you still using direct memory access instead of **[BP+n]** idiom?

- Have you tried to use registers as global variables?

- Do you have an exit key? Consider making the game to restart when a game is finished.

- Are you considering the values of registers as your game progresses sequentially? Most of the time, you can reuse values on registers if there aren't multiple code paths going into the same instruction.

- Have you considered relocating register usage? It's shortest to use AX and AL for arithmetic operations.

- Have you considered using special instructions? If you are using **mov ah,0** and AL never exceeds 127 then you can safely use **cbw**.

- Changing values of segment registers is costly and cumbersome. Try to stay with fixed values for these.

2.9 Case study: Follow the Lights.

I could simply write about game development, but I had (for the purpose of this book) to test my own words, so I coded a Follow the Lights game in a couple of hours and rushed to write this section remembering the development order I discussed earlier.[12]

The game has four big color buttons that are illuminated, and has some switches and buttons to set modes and replay sequences, and also generates sounds for each light.

This game was pretty popular at the start of the 1980s. It proposes a random sequence of lights to the player, and the player should enter the same sequence in order; if the player is successful, the game adds another light to the sequence, and continues until the player makes a mistake.

For details about the lights, sound frequencies, and timing, I found invaluable help at https://www.waitingforfriday.com/?p=586

Given the algorithm is already known, the parts (the labels) of our game will be:

1. The buttons "user interface".
2. The sound interface.
3. Add one light to the sequence.
4. Show the lights on the sequence.
5. Wait for player to enter the sequence of lights.
6. Defeat tone.
7. Victory tones.

The design went in this order:

1. Copy&Paste the speaker routines from my previous F-Bird game (see my book "Programming Boot Sector Games" chapter 6), or Bricks on this book on chapter 4.
2. Develop the "user interface" to show the four buttons. Given these can be illuminated at any time, also check if any is pressed

---

[12] The blessing (or curse) of being an experienced programmer means that lots of times I refuse to write paper documents because I go to code the program from my brain directly onto the computer. This approach fails completely if you are interrupted, or doing multiple tasks at the same time, or it takes more than 24 hours to complete the program. Then restarting the development can be a nightmare if you didn't make any notes.

in order to "illuminate" it. Also add the corresponding number to each color, so the player knows what key to press.

3. If a button is illuminated, generate the respective sound tone. At this point I had made a mistake, because if the button wasn't illuminated it would turn off the speaker, but it so happened the four buttons were drawn one after another, so if one is illuminated and playing sound, the "unilluminated" ones prevented it from sounding. The solution was simple: Turn off the speaker outside the routine.

4. Generate a random number in order to add a light to the sequence. The random seed is kept on the SI register, multiplied, and a small constant is added. But only the top 8 bits are used to generate more "pseudo-randomness".

5. The variables, including the memory for the sequence of lights, are preserved on the stack, using the register BP as base. A counter keeps the length of the sequence, plus a timing counter for a faster light show as the sequence length grows.

6. Showing the light sequence, and expecting the light sequence share the same basic architecture, using the DI register to count the light number, read the memory, show the light (or wait for the keyboard and do a comparison), and keep advancing until the full sequence has been processed.

7. Repeat the game loop. Plus the defeat tone. The last thing added was the victory tune.

Being a small game, there were no complications making it fit in the boot sector size.

2.10 Initialization.

The code starts with the definitions:

```
;
; Follow the lights
;
; by Oscar Toledo G.
;
; Creation date: Jan/16/2020.
; Revision date: Jan/17/2020.
;    Added victory tune after 31 good lights.
;


;
; Very useful info gathered from:
; https://www.waitingforfriday.com/?p=586
;
cpu 8086

%ifdef com_file
org 0x0100
%else
org 0x7c00
%endif

old_time:       equ 0x00 ; Old ticks
button:         equ 0x02 ; Button pressed
next_seq:       equ 0x04 ; Next seq. number
timing:         equ 0x06 ; Current timing
memory:         equ 0x08 ; Start of memory
memory_end:     equ 0x28 ; End of memory
```

This game uses 40 bytes of variables (indicated by *memory_end*). The variables are *old_time* for keeping the current tick number from the BIOS, *button* for keeping the current button pressed, *next_seq* the length of the sequence (or the position for putting the next random light), *timing* for keeping the speed of the lights, and *memory* for saving the lights sequence.

```
start:
    xor ax,ax
    mov cx,memory_end/2
.0:
    push ax             ; Zero word initialize
    loop .0             ; Repeat until completed

    mov al,0x02         ; Text mode 80x25
    int 0x10            ; Set up video mode
```

```
        mov bp,sp              ; Setup BP (Base Pointer)

        in al,0x40             ; Get a pseudorandom number
        xchg ax,si             ; Put into SI

        cld                    ; Clear Direction flag.
        mov ax,0xb800          ; Point to video segment
        mov ds,ax
        mov es,ax

        call show_buttons  ; Show buttons

restart_game:
        xor ax,ax              ; Restart sequence
        mov [bp+next_seq],ax
```

The game initialization sets AX to zero, and loads CX with the value
of *memory_end* divided by 2; this is because it will be using **push ax** to
initialize the variables, and each **push** instruction introduces *two bytes* onto
the stack.

When the stack is filled with all these zero variables, the current
Stack Pointer address (SP register) is copied to the Base Pointer register in
order to use it for accessing the variables. But first it sets up the video mode
of 80x25 characters in color using **int 0x10**. As you remember this is done
because this BIOS interrupt could destroy the content of the BP register
(see section 2.7). Notice also how it loads only the AL register with 2 for the
video mode, taking advantage of AH already being zero.

It reads the timer counter chip and puts the value onto the register
SI; the high byte doesn't matter.

It resets the D flag (remember we don't know its initial state), and sets
up the DS and ES registers to the screen memory segment.

The final step of the initialization is to show the user interface by
calling *show_buttons*, and set the sequence length to zero.

23

2.11 Adding a light to the sequence.

The game loop starts by doing a small wait in order to give time to the player to "recover" from entering the last lights sequence.

And then it adds a new pseudo-random light to the sequence.

```
game_loop:
        mov cl,15                 ; Wait 0.8 seconds.
        call wait_ticks

        ;
        ; Add a new light to sequence
        ;
        mov di,[bp+next_seq]      ; Curr. position.

        mov ax,97                 ; Generate random number
        mul si
        add ax,23
        xchg ax,si                ; SI = next seed.

                                  ; Notice it uses the
                                  ; high byte because the
                                  ; random period is
                                  ; longer.

        and ah,0x03               ; Extract random from AH
        add ah,0x31               ; Add ASCII 1
        mov [bp+di+memory],ah     ; Save into memory

        mov ax,8                  ; 8 approx 0.42 secs.
        cmp di,5                  ; For 5 or fewer lights.
        jb .2
        mov al,6                  ; 6 approx 0.32 secs.
        cmp di,13                 ; For 13 or fewer lights.
        jb .2
        mov al,4                  ; 4 approx 0.22 secs.
.2:
        mov [bp+timing],ax
        cmp di,31                 ; Doing the 31st light?
        je victory                ; Yes, jump to victory.
        inc byte [bp+next_seq]
```

The register DI contains the next position available in the sequence, and generates the random number using the current value of SI. The old value of SI gets into AX and the high-byte is used to select one of four lights, and saves it into the sequence memory by means of **mov [bp+di +memory],ah**. Notice how BP is the Base Pointer to variables, *memory* is the offset to the sequence array, and DI is the index into the sequence.

Given we are using BP to access the variables, it automatically instructs the processor to use the SS register to access memory. So it doesn't access the video memory, but the stack memory.

The sequence length selects the timing for lights: 5 or fewer lights use 0.42 seconds approximately, 0.32 seconds for more lights up to 13, and 0.22 seconds for more lights. This value is saved onto the *timing* variable.

Finally before incrementing the sequence size, it checks if it added the 32nd light and in that case it jumps to *victory*.

2.12 Show the current lights sequence.

Showing the current light sequence is just a matter of stepping over the sequence array.

```
    ;
    ; Show current sequence
    ;
    xor di,di             ; Restart counter
.1: mov al,[bp+di+memory]  ; Read light
    push di
    mov [bp+button],al     ; Push button
    call show_buttons      ; Show
    mov cx,[bp+timing]     ; Wait
    call wait_ticks
    call speaker_off       ; Turn off

    mov byte [bp+button],0
    call show_buttons      ; Depress button
    call wait_tick
    pop di
    inc di                 ; Increase counter
    cmp di,[bp+next_seq]
    jne .1
```

The DI register contains the index onto the array, and starts from zero. It reads the array on the register AL, and puts it as the current pressed *button*, then calls *show_buttons* to illuminate the button and play the tone, waits the required time, and turns off the speaker, turns off the button (setting *button* variable to zero), and waits a tick so the user can notice the change between tones.

Finally it increases the index and does a comparison to see if it reached the sequence length.

2.13 The player's turn.

Once the lights have been displayed, it's the player's turn. Given we are on a computer, the player could have cheated and pressed the keyboard as soon as each light is shown, so we empty the keyboard buffer before doing anything else.

```
        ;
        ; Empty keyboard buffer
        ;
.9:
        mov ah,0x01         ; Check for key pressed.
        int 0x16
        je .8               ; No, jump.
        mov ah,0x00         ; Read key.
        int 0x16
        jmp .9              ; Repeat loop
.8:
```

It works by checking for a key pressed, and if pressed reads it from the buffer, and repeats the loop until no keys are on the buffer.

```
        ;
        ; Comparison of player input with
        ; sequence.
        ;
        xor di,di           ; Restart counter
.4:     mov ah,0x00         ; Wait for a key
        int 0x16
        cmp al,0x1b         ; Esc pressed?
        je exit_game        ; Yes, jump.
        cmp al,0x31         ; Less than ASCII 1?
```

26

```
jb .4                          ; Yes, jump.
cmp al,0x35                    ; Higher than ASCII 4?
jnb .4                         ; Yes, jump.
push ax
push di
mov [bp+button],al             ; Push button
call show_buttons              ; Show
mov cx,[bp+timing]             ; Wait
call wait_ticks
call speaker_off               ; Turn off

mov byte [bp+button],0
call show_buttons              ; Depress button
call wait_tick
pop di
pop ax
cmp al,[bp+di+memory]          ; Good hit?
jne wrong                      ; No, jump

inc di                         ; Increase counter
cmp di,[bp+next_seq]
jne .4
jmp game_loop
```

Again the DI register is used as an index into the sequence array.

It waits for a key to be pressed like Esc to exit the game, and ignores anything outside the 1, 2, 3, or 4 keys. Once a number key is hit, it saves it into the *button* variable and illuminates the button (and generates the sound tone), waits a little and then deactivates the button (again loading zero onto *button*).

Notice how it saves the registers AX and DI, and restores them afterward in order to do the comparison with the sequence buffer. If the comparison is unsuccessful, then it jumps to *wrong*, or else it increases DI and repeats the loop until the whole sequence has been entered by the player.

The final step is to repeat the game loop, adding another light, and so on.

2.14 Player's defeat and victory.

If the player makes a mistake, a defeat tone is played for 1.5 seconds, pauses for 1.5 seconds, and then restarts the game.

```
        ;
        ; Player defeat by wrong button
        ;
wrong:
        mov cx,28409            ; 1193180 / 42
        call speaker            ; Failure tone
        mov cl,27               ; 1.5 secs
        call wait_ticks
        call speaker_off        ; Turn off
        mov cl,27               ; 1.5 secs
        call wait_ticks
        jmp restart_game        ; Restart game
```

But if the player is able enough to remember a sequence of 31 lights, then he/she is rewarded with a small victory tune that sarcastically is finished with the defeat tone.

```
        ;
        ; Victory
        ;
victory:
        mov al,'2'              ; Victory tune
        mov cx,14 ; 14 notes
.1: push cx
        push ax
        mov byte [bp+button],al
        call show_buttons       ; Play
        mov cl,2 ; Wait 0.1 secs.
        call wait_ticks
        mov byte [bp+button],0  ; Depress
        call show_buttons
        pop ax
        inc ax                  ; Next note
        cmp al,'5'              ; If goes to 5...
        jne .2
        mov al,'1'              ; ...go back to 1.
.2:
        pop cx
        loop .1
        jmp wrong               ; Finish and restart
```

The tune is played fast and the note sequence is 2,3,4,1, 2,3,4,1, 2,3,4,1, 2,3 for a total of 14 notes. Instead of keeping a table, it simply keeps an ASCII 2 on the AL register, and increments it wrapping around to ASCII 1 once it reaches ASCII 5.

The code is pretty similar to the lights show. It illuminates the button, waits, and deactivates the button.

```
;
; Exit game
;
exit_game:
    mov ax,0x0002        ; Clear screen by...
    int 0x10             ; ...mode setup.
    int 0x20             ; Exit to DOS / bootOS.
```

The exit routine clears the screen before returning to the parent operating system (MS-DOS, DR-DOS, Windows or bootOS).

2.15 User interface.

The user interface are the four buttons being displayed on the center of the screen.

```
;
; Show game buttons
;
show_buttons:
    mov di,0x0166        ; Top left on screen
    mov bx,0x312f        ; ASCII 1, white on green
    mov cx,2873          ; 1193180 / 415.305 hz
    call show_button

    mov di,0x0192        ; Top right on screen
    mov bx,0x324f        ; ASCII 2, white on red
    mov cx,3835          ; 1193180 / 311.127 hz
    call show_button

    mov di,0x0846        ; Bottom left on screen
    mov bx,0x336f        ; ASCII 3, white on brown
    mov cx,4812          ; 1193180 / 247.942 hz
    call show_button
```

```
        mov di,0x0872          ; Bottom right on screen
        mov bx,0x343f          ; ASCII 4, white on turquoise
        mov cx,5746            ; 1193180 / 207.652 hz

        ; Fall-through

show_button:
        mov al,0x20           ; Fill with spaces
        cmp bh,[bp+button]    ; Is it pressed?
        jne .0                ; No, jump.
        call speaker          ; Yes, play sound.
        mov al,0xb0           ; Semi-filled block
.0:
        mov cx,10             ; 10 rows high.
.1:     push cx
        mov ah,bl             ; Set attribute byte.
        mov cl,20             ; 20 columns width.
        rep stosw             ; Fill on screen
        add di,160-20*2       ; Go to next row
        pop cx
        loop .1               ; Repeat until filled
        mov al,bh             ; Get button number
        mov [di+20-5*160],ax  ; Put on center
        ret                   ; Return
```

The *show_buttons* routine calls the *show_button* routine four times, but it saves 4 bytes by simply falling to the *show_button* routine (avoiding a final **call/ret** instruction).

The position of each button is kept on the DI register, BH contains the ASCII number to be shown at the center of each button, BL contains the attribute code for color, and CX contains the value for the timer counter that generates the sound tone.

The *show_button* routine sets AL to 0x20 (ASCII space), but if it is drawing a pressed button then it calls *speaker* to play the sound tone contained on CX, and sets AL to 0xb0 (filled block) so the button gets "illuminated".

The button drawing code is relatively straightforward, drawing a button of 20 columns by 10 rows at the DI address, filling using **rep/stosw**, incrementing DI by a whole row each time, and finally putting the number on the center of the button (**mov al,bh**).

2.16 Time control.

The timing control is done with **int 0x1a** (clock/time services), waiting for the clock chip to increase ticks by one. This happens 18.2 times per second.

```
    ;
    ; Wait for one tick
    ;
wait_tick:
    mov cl,1


    ;
    ; Wait for several ticks
    ;
    ; Input:
    ; CL = Number of ticks
    ;
wait_ticks:
    mov ch,0
.0:
    push cx                     ; Save counter
.1:
    mov ah,0x00                 ; Read ticks
    int 0x1a                    ; Call BIOS
    cmp dx,[bp+old_time]        ; Wait for tick change
    je .1
    mov [bp+old_time],dx        ; Save new tick
    pop cx                      ; Restore counter
    loop .0                     ; Loop until complete
    ret                         ; Return
```

There are two variants: *wait_tick* waits for a tick to lapse, and *wait_ticks* that waits for several ticks to lapse (using the CL value as the count of ticks).

Essentially it calls the interrupt 0x1a, service 0x00, and waits for DX to be different from the current value of *old_time*, and then it updates *old_time* for the next time it is called.

31

2.17 Sound.

The sound is generated by using the timer counter 2 integrated on PC machines. Interestingly this is not very well supported by some emulators like VirtualBox. I've tested using DosBox.

```
    ;
    ; Generate sound on PC speaker
    ;
    ; Input:
    ; CX = Frequency value.
    ;       (calculate 1193180/freq = req. value)
    ;
speaker:
    mov al,0xb6         ; Setup timer 2
    out 0x43,al
    mov al,cl           ; Low byte of timer count
    out 0x42,al
    mov al,ch           ; High byte of timer count
    out 0x42,al
    in al,0x61
    or al,0x03          ; Wire PC speaker to timer 2
    out 0x61,al
    ret
```

Generating a sound is a matter of doing a mode setup on timer 2, and writing the low-byte and high-byte values of the frequency counter, also setting up a further port to "wire" the timer 2 output to the PC speaker.

```
    ;
    ; Turn speaker off
    ;
speaker_off:
    in al,0x61
    and al,0xfc         ; Turn off
    out 0x61,al
    ret
```

The other very much needed function is a way to turn off the speaker.

```
        ;
        ; Boot sector signature
        ;
%ifdef com_file
%else
        times 510-($-$$) db 0x4f
        db 0x55,0xaa   ; Make it a bootable sector
%endif
```

Finally this is the bootable signature required for the BIOS.

Chapter 3

bootRogue

This a small RPG game where you are an adventurer looking for the long
lost Amulet of Yendor inside dungeons filled with monsters.

The original Rogue game was developed in 1980 by Michael Toy,
Glenn Wichman, and Ken Arnold for UNIX-based mainframe systems
while studying at the University of California, Santa Cruz. It became so
popular that even Dennis Ritchie, the creator of the C language, claimed
that it "wasted more CPU time than anything in history".

It is a text-based game where everything is shown as letters; in
particular the monsters are represented with the letters A to Z, and the
player with the @ character.

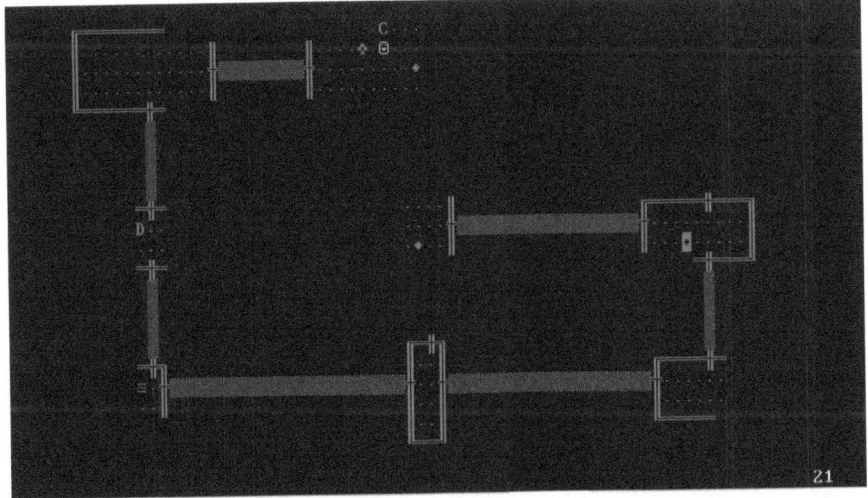

But the first time I saw this game was as an executable file on a floppy disk for MS-DOS. It had some color and used predefined characters for the player (a happy face), the rooms and items. And yes, it also got me glued to the computer for many, many hours.

It inspired a whole generation of game programmers.

3.1 Development decisions.

This section concentrates on the design decisions that directed the development of bootRogue.

The main design decisions were:

- It should look like the MS-DOS version of Rogue.

- There should be combat by rounds like in Rogue (after each clash, the new HP is shown—this can be addictive because essentially you see how the monster is overcoming you when having around the same strength as you because it's pseudo-random).

With some constraints, these were the decisions that guided all the development. At the end only the graphic characters are the same, as the color didn't fit into the final version of bootRogue.

The first prototype[13] with 357 bytes only drew the rooms and allowed to move the player around them. Like I recommended at the beginning of chapter 2, it implemented the basic core of the game. I felt confident when I saw there was still much space available. Around this I built the remainder of the game.

The second prototype with 467 bytes added the ability to go down deeper into the dungeon, showed the Amulet of Yendor, allowed to reach the "outside", and integrated the circle-of-light feature.

Finally the third prototype added the monsters, weapons, and battles. Essentially it was the game I wanted to do, but it was too big for a boot sector at a size of 829 bytes.

---

[13] You can see the prototype history at https://github.com/nanochess/bootRogue/tree/master/backup

We can say I was too enthusiastic about the project, and simply went ahead implementing the features. But I was very careful to not add badly-done code, or ugly "hacks", because I knew that it would make the game harder to optimize.

Then it took me 10 iterations (or prototypes) to reduce it to a boot sector size.

These optimizations were made:

- 4th prototype (rogue3.asm), 70 bytes saved (759 bytes). Removed direct memory initialization, and used **stosw**. Removed the random connection generator for rooms, and used a table for connections. Moving variables into registers. Optimization of number display for HP (Health Points).

- 5th prototype (rogue4.asm), 89 bytes saved (670 bytes). Reuse of values on registers. Removing monsters table à la original Rogue. Used the BP register to contain the address of an often-used random function, and doing call to register (saves one byte per call). Optimized battle function.

- 6th prototype (rogue5.asm), 18 bytes saved (652 bytes). Number output routine rewritten. Arithmetic optimization (like instead of putting -1 into a variable whose value was 1, it simply negates it, saving one byte). Notice how the number of bytes saved is reduced because the optimization starts to become difficult.

- 7th prototype (rogue6.asm), 9 bytes saved (643 bytes). Avoids comparison of non-revealed room square, and instead creates monsters and items while drawing the rooms.

- 8th prototype (rogue7.asm), 13 bytes saved (630 bytes). Moved all variables to the stack pointer, and the different addressing mode saves bytes (saving one byte for each variable operation).

- 9th prototype (rogue8.asm), 28 bytes saved (602 bytes). Reusing of values inside registers. Uses 8-bit operations instead of 16-bit operations when using constants (immediate values). Removed table of items found on screen to use a comparison table.

- 10th prototype (rogue9.asm), 6 bytes saved (596 bytes). Small register related optimizations (again using 8-bit operations to load 16-bit constant where low byte isn't important). Relocation of registers in battle code. Removal of key direction table.

- 11th prototype (rogue10.asm), 20 bytes saved (576 bytes). Relocation of variables in order to use values contained on register AX, also reuse of AX value. Comparison of items now is optimized. Avoid saving monster's HP on memory, and instead use register.

- 12th prototype (rogue11.asm), 23 bytes saved (553 bytes). Removed table of mazes and instead generate connection maze using a random number with a mask. Saved register movement by changing AX to BX, allowing to write the ladder character directly to memory; same for AX to DI on room drawing. Removed jump instruction by tying respective routine. Simplified room filling code.

- 13th prototype (rogue12.asm), 43 bytes saved (510 bytes). Removed experience leveling (exp). This was a last measure needed to fit the game into the desired size.

I lost some features, like monsters letters compatible with those on original Rogue, because the table was too big (26 letters + 26 values for characteristics = 52 bytes that I needed desperately). This table still can be seen on 2nd and 3rd prototype (rogue1.asm and rogue2.asm respectively).

Notice how the game lost very few of the original features and it's easily recognizable as a rogue-like game.

At the end the whole game was created over a period of nine days of coding frenzy.

3.2 The look.

There are many constraints when you are working with 510 bytes of space, but one thing had to be done: it should look like the MS-DOS version of the game, because it is iconic and recognizable anywhere.

It also creates dungeons in a pseudo-random fashion and connects them to create a maze.

```
;
; bootRogue game in 512 bytes (boot sector)
;
; by Oscar Toledo G.
; http://nanochess.org/
;
; (c) Copyright 2019 Oscar Toledo G.
;
; Creation date: Sep/19/2019. Generates room boxes.
; Revision date: Sep/27/2019.
;

    CPU 8086

ROW_WIDTH:       EQU 0x00A0   ; Width in bytes of each video row
BOX_MAX_WIDTH:   EQU 23       ; Max width of a room box
BOX_MAX_HEIGHT:  EQU 6        ; Max height of a room box
BOX_WIDTH:       EQU 26       ; Width of box area in screen
BOX_HEIGHT:      EQU 8        ; Height of box area in screen
```

The text screen is 80 columns wide, and each character word includes an attribute (or color) byte, so *ROW_WIDTH* accounts for 160-byte rows.

The screen is divided into 3x3 areas for rooms (each area sizes up to *BOX_WIDTH*BOX_HEIGHT*).

Inside this area the maximum width and height of a box (room) cannot be bigger than *BOX_MAX_WIDTH* and *BOX_MAX_HEIGHT*, otherwise the rooms would touch.

```
        ; See page 45 of my book Programming Boot Sector Games
LIGHT_COLOR:    EQU 0x06     ; Light color (brown)
HERO_COLOR:     EQU 0x0e     ; Hero color (yellow)

        ; See page 179 of my book Programming Boot Sector Games
GR_VERT:        EQU 0xba     ; Vertical line graphic
GR_TOP_RIGHT:   EQU 0xbb     ; Top right graphic
GR_BOT_RIGHT:   EQU 0xbc     ; Bottom right graphic
GR_BOT_LEFT:    EQU 0xc8     ; Bottom left graphic
```

```
GR_TOP_LEFT:     EQU 0xc9         ; Top left graphic
GR_HORIZ:        EQU 0xcd         ; Horizontal line graphic

GR_TUNNEL:       EQU 0xb1         ; Tunnel graphic (shaded block)
GR_DOOR:         EQU 0xce         ; Door graphic (crosshair graphic)
GR_FLOOR:        EQU 0xfa         ; Floor graphic (middle point)

GR_HERO:         EQU 0x01         ; Hero graphic (smiling face)

GR_LADDER:       EQU 0xf0         ; Ladder graphic
GR_TRAP:         EQU 0x04         ; Trap graphic (diamond)
GR_FOOD:         EQU 0x05         ; Food graphic (clover)
GR_ARMOR:        EQU 0x08         ; Armor graphic (square with hole)
GR_YENDOR:       EQU 0x0c         ; Amulet of Yendor graphic
GR_GOLD:         EQU 0x0f         ; Gold graphic (asterisk)
GR_WEAPON:       EQU 0x18         ; Weapon graphic (up arrow)

YENDOR_LEVEL:    EQU 26           ; Level of appearance for Amulet
```

The original Rogue game draws the rooms on a 3x3 arrangement, where each room would have a different size and location over the grid. For the purposes of bootRogue, each room has a different size but each one is centered on the grid.

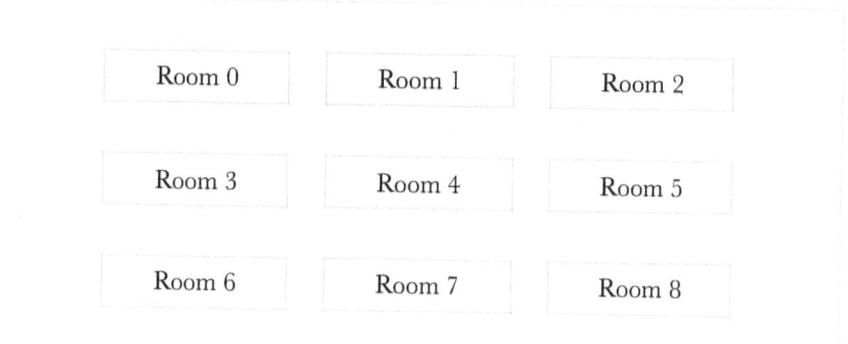

Figure 3-1. bootRogue screen format.

Then tunnels bring together the rooms:

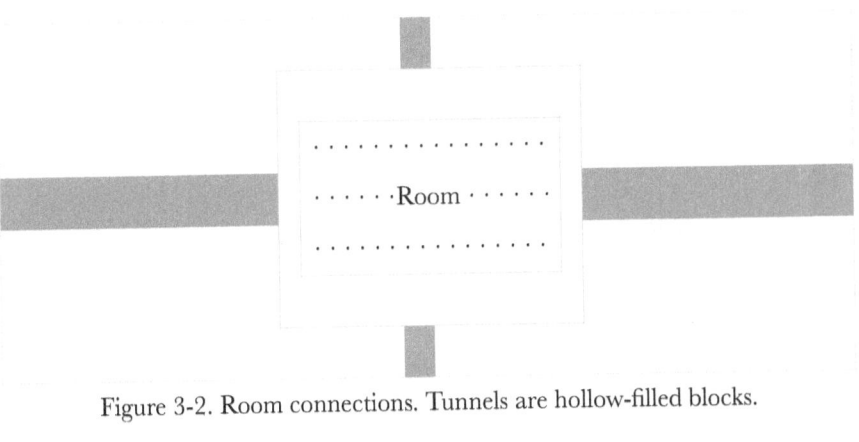

Figure 3-2. Room connections. Tunnels are hollow-filled blocks.

And items are filled afterwards:

Figure 3-3. Room after being filled.

Finally, the label *YENDOR_LEVEL* contains the depth level where the Amulet of Yendor will be shown.

3.3 Initialization.

Very few variables are required for this game, and some are preserved on registers used globally.

```
%ifdef com_file
    org 0x0100
%else
    org 0x7c00
%endif
```

```
            ;
            ; Sorted by order of PUSH instructions
            ;
rnd:        equ 0x0008      ; Random seed
starve:     equ 0x0006      ; Starve counter
hp:         equ 0x0004      ; Current HP
level:      equ 0x0003      ; Current level (starting at 0x01)
yendor:     equ 0x0002      ; 0x01 = Not found. 0xff = Found.
armor:      equ 0x0001      ; Armor level
weapon:     equ 0x0000      ; Weapon level


            ;
            ; Start of the adventure!
            ;
start:
            in ax,0x40      ; Read timer counter
            push ax         ; Setup pseudorandom number generator
            mov ax,16
            push ax         ; starve
            push ax         ; hp
            mov al,1
            push ax         ; yendor (low byte) + level (high byte)
            push ax         ; weapon (low byte) + armor (high byte)
            inc ax          ; ax = 0x0002 (it was 0x0001)
            int 0x10
            mov ax,0xb800   ; Text video segment
            mov ds,ax
            mov es,ax

            mov si,random   ; SI as a space saver for CALL

            mov bp,sp       ; Using BP because it implies SS
```

The initialization of the variables is done using **push** instructions, instead of **mov [var],ax** instructions. It saves 2 bytes per variable. To later retrieve these variables, it uses the BP register. The BP register has the advantage that it is accessed by the SS register (a separate data segment register for stack data).

The game doesn't care about the initial state of both SS and SP, because all data is accessed relative to BP. This also saves bytes as the Stack Pointer register and the Stack Segment register don't need to be initialized.

bootRogue depends on a pseudo-random number generator, and it is reset using the content of the internal Timer Counter 0.

Then both the *starve* counter and the *hp* variable (Health Points) are set to 16. Then four 8-bit variables are initialized with two **push** instructions: *yendor* = 1, *level* = 0, *weapon* = 1, *armor* = 0. It uses the fact that the AX register is set to 0x0001 (AH contains zero and AL contains one).

It sets the text mode display increasing AX by one to make it 0x0002 (AH = 0x00, video mode setup, AL = 0x02, text mode number) and doing **int 0x10**.

Finally it sets the DS and ES registers to point to the video memory at 0xb8000, the SI register to contain the address of the *random* pseudo-random generator function, and the BP register as a pointer to the variables.

bp+0	weapon	armor	Last **push** (current SP address)
bp+2	yendor	level	
bp+4	hp		
bp+6	starve		
bp+8	rnd		First **push**

Table 3-4. Stack frame used by bootRogue.

3.4 Generating the maze.

The maze generation of bootRogue is relatively straightforward.

```
generate_dungeon:

        ;
        ; Advance to next level (can go deeper or higher)
        ;
        mov bl,[bp+yendor]
        add [bp+level],bl
    %ifdef com_file
        jne .0
        jmp quit        ; Stop if level zero is reached
  .0:
    %else
        je $            ; Stop if level zero is reached
    %endif
```

The first step is to increase or decrease the current level. It reads the *yendor* variable to know which way (it can be 0x01 or 0xff, equivalent to 1 or -1), and adds it to the *level* variable (it is initialized as zero at start, so the first level always ends up being 1).

If the level becomes zero, it means the variable *yendor* is 255 (or -1) and also that the player came out of the dungeons, or game won. The game only stops in that case.

```
;
; Select a maze for the dungeon
;
; There are many combinations of values that generate at
; least 16 mazes in order to avoid a table.
;
mov ax,[bp+rnd]
and ax,0x4182
or ax,0x1a6d
xchg ax,dx
```

Using the 16-bit seed of the random number generator, it generates a connection map for rooms that is saved into the **DX** register.

Each two bits indicate a connection to right or downwards. But not all connections are valid. For example, having a downward connection on the bottom three rooms would be a bug.

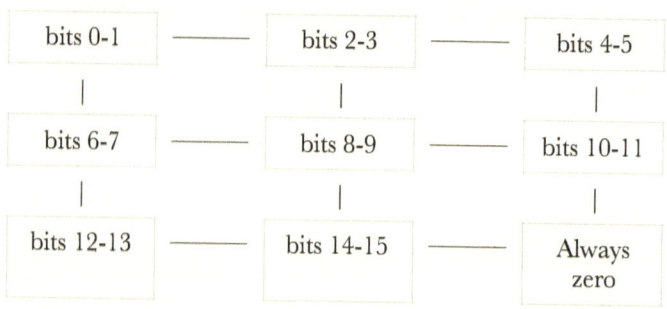

Figure 3-5. Room map and DX connection bits on the screen.

The pseudo-magic constants were calculated with an automatized program to generate all possible values (see Appendix D), and made sure that generated the most possible different room connections. Although at the end it generated several constants that only can generate 16 different connection maps.

Let us see an example; if the *rnd* variable contains 0x6417, then it does: $DX = (rnd$ & $0x4182)$ | $0x1a6d$, for a result of 0x5a6f. This value creates the following connection map for the rooms.

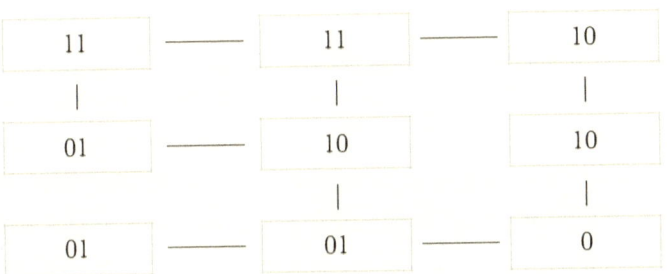

Figure 3-6. Room map for DX equal to 0x5a6f.

The beauty of this bitmap is that it can be extracted from the **DX** register by shifting it right by one bit each time.

```
;
; Clean the screen to black over black (it hides the maze)
;
xor ax,ax
xor di,di
mov ch,0x08
rep stosw
```

The original Rogue game for **MS-DOS** kept the player in the dark, and the maze would slowly be revealed as the player walked over the map. The game manages this same effect by filling the whole screen with zero attribute, and this means each letter is black foreground on black background, making the maze invisible.

```
;
; Draw the nine rooms
;
.7:
```

```
        push ax
        call fill_room
        pop ax
        add ax,BOX_WIDTH*2
        cmp al,0x9c              ; Finished drawing three rooms?
        jne .6                   ; No, jump
                                 ; Yes, go to following row
        add ax,ROW_WIDTH*BOX_HEIGHT-BOX_WIDTH*3*2
    .6:
        cmp ax,ROW_WIDTH*BOX_HEIGHT*3
        jb .7
```

The register AX is set up to point to the top left of the screen, because it was already zero (from filling the screen with black). Then it calls the *fill_room* function and after restoring AX, it adds the *BOX_WIDTH*2* value in order to advance to the next adjacent room at the right. If the lower part contains 0x9c, it means it is located at a border, and adds a further offset to go to the next row.

Finally it repeats all this until the nine rooms are complete.

```
        ;
        ; Put the ladder at a random corner room
        ;
        shl word [bp+rnd],1
        mov ax,3*ROW_WIDTH+12*2
        mov bx,19*ROW_WIDTH+12*2
        jnc .2
        xchg ax,bx
    .2: jns .8
        add ax,BOX_WIDTH*2*2
    .8:
        xchg ax,di

        mov byte [di],GR_LADDER
```

Each level needs to have a ladder so the player can descend further into the dungeon. Doing a **shl** instruction over the random seed generates two bits (one in the Carry flag, and another in the Sign flag, bit 15 and bit 14 respectively). These two bits are used to choose one of the four corner rooms.

The AX register is set up to contain the coordinate of the top left room, and the BX register is prepared to contain the coordinate of the bottom left room. If the Carry flag is set, both values are exchanged.

Then if the Sign flag is set, an offset is added to AX to point to the rightmost room. The value of AX is moved onto DI and a ladder is put there (*GR_LADDER*).

```
        ;
        ; Put the Amulet of Yendor
        ;
        cmp byte [bp+level],YENDOR_LEVEL
        jb .1
        mov byte [bx],GR_YENDOR
.1:
```

Finally, the maze setup is complete by putting the Amulet of Yendor on the position contained on the register BX, only if the *level* variable is equal or greater than *YENDOR_LEVEL*.

3.5 Circle of light and hero.

The hero is made to appear at the center of the dungeon, from where he can start exploring the map. As a side note, in the original Rogue game, the player could appear anywhere on the screen.

```
          ;
          ; Setup hero start
          ;
          mov di,11*ROW_WIDTH+38*2
          ;
          ; Main game loop
          ;
game_loop:
          mov ax,game_loop        ; Force to repeat, the whole loop...
          push ax                 ; ...ends with ret.

          ;
          ; Circle of light around the player (3x3)
          ;
          mov bx,0x0005           ; BX values
.1:       dec bx
```

```
dec bx                          ; -1 1 3 -0x00a0
mov al,LIGHT_COLOR
mov [bx+di-ROW_WIDTH],al        ; -1(1)3
mov [bx+di],al
mov [bx+di+ROW_WIDTH],al        ; -1 1 3 +0x00a0
jns .1
```

During the game loop, the DI register contains the actual position of the player on the screen.

It saves the address of the *game_loop* label onto the stack, because the game returns to it using the **ret** instruction. This saves many bytes of code, because the shortest **jmp** instruction uses two bytes, while **ret** uses only one byte.

Then it draws the revealing circle of light around the player. It isn't a circle, but a square of 3x3 characters. Basically it only changes the black on black attribute for a *LIGHT_COLOR* byte.

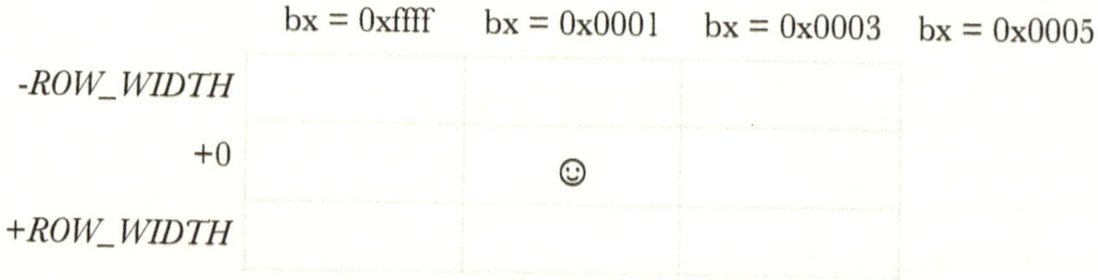

	bx = 0xffff	bx = 0x0001	bx = 0x0003	bx = 0x0005
-ROW_WIDTH				
+0		☺		
+ROW_WIDTH				

Figure 3-7. Circle of light around the player.

```
        ;
        ; Show our hero
        ;
        push word [di]          ; Save character and attribute under
        mov word [di],HERO_COLOR*256+GR_HERO
        add byte [bp+starve],2
        sbb ax,ax               ; HP down 1 every 128 steps
        call add_hp             ; Update stats
    ;   mov ah,0x00             ; Comes here with ah = 0
        int 0x16                ; Read keyboard
        pop word [di]           ; Restore character and attribute
```

It shows the hero putting a 16-bit word on screen containing the *GR_HERO* graphic (the smiling face) and the *HERO_COLOR* attribute. Before showing the player, it saves the content under the player, because it could have been a floor, door or tunnel; everything else will be taken out and replaced with a *GR_FLOOR* graphic later in the game.

After doing this, it adds 2 to the variable *starve*, to generate a 0 or -1 value on the register AX by using the Carry flag to detect overflow (going from 255 to 0), with the effect that it will subtract 1 from the Health Points every 128 walking steps (256 divided by 2).

```
        mov al,ah
    %ifdef com_file
        cmp al,0x01
        je quit             ; Exit if Esc key is pressed
    %endif

        sub al,0x4c
        mov ah,0x02         ; Left/right multiplies by 2
        cmp al,0xff         ; Going left (scancode 0x4b)
        je .2
        cmp al,0x01         ; Going right (scancode 0x4d)
        je .2
        cmp al,0xfc         ; Going up (scancode 0x48)
        je .3
        cmp al,0x04         ; Going down (scancode 0x50)
        jne move_cancel
    .3:
        mov ah,0x28         ; Up/down multiplies by 40
    .2:
        imul ah             ; Signed multiplication

        xchg ax,bx          ; bx = displacement offset
        mov al,[di+bx]      ; Read the target contents
```

The player movement is done using the arrow keys. The game reads the scan codes using **int 0x16** service 0x01.

This is translated to a displacement offset on the register BX and the target character is read into AL.

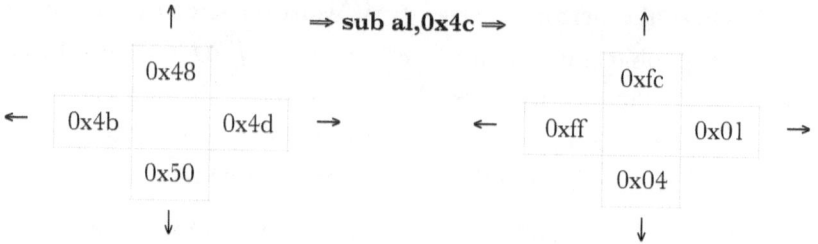

Figure 3-8. Scan codes and result values. Upward
and downward values are before the multiplication.

3.6 Taking items.

The RPG (Role Playing Games) series of games depends on taking objects
and using them.

So far all the *GR_** graphics (17 things) can be walked over by the
hero. But of course, it will never find *GR_HERO* because the only time it is
used is to show the hero and then it is removed, so this leaves 16 things to
check for.

It could do a comparison for each of the 16 values, but it would take
4 bytes for each comparison. Instead it does comparison with intermediate
values and can "deduct" the existence of other values through comparison
with a single value, and using the less-than or greater-than conditions.

```
;
; Things that exist on screen start with GR_* (17 things)
; So no need to account for all cases. We won't ever
; find GR_HERO so there are 16 things to look for.
;
cmp al,GR_LADDER        ; GR_LADDER?
je ladder_found
```

The first thing checked is *GR_LADDER*, and if found it jumps to
ladder_found.

```
; 15 things to look for (plus zero and monsters)
; Anything > GR_TUNNEL and < GR_DOOR is a wall
cmp al,GR_DOOR          ; GR_DOOR?
jnc .4
```

50

```
        cmp al,GR_TUNNEL          ; GR_TUNNEL?
        ja move_cancel
 .4:
```

Now if it finds a value greater than or equal to *GR_TUNNEL* (0xb1) and less than *GR_DOOR* (0xce) then it is a room border (*GR_VERT*, *GR_HORIZ*, *GR_TOP_RIGHT*, *GR_BOT_RIGHT*, *GR_TOP_LEFT*, or *GR_BOT_LEFT*) and cannot be walked over, so the movement is canceled by jumping to *move_cancel*.

```
        ; 9 things to look for (plus zero and monsters)
        cmp al,GR_TRAP            ; GR_TRAP?
        jb move_cancel           ; < it must be blank, cancel mov.
        ; Move player
        lea di,[di+bx]           ; Do move.
        mov bh,0x06              ; Random range for GR_FOOD & GR_TRAP
        je trap_found           ; = Yes, went over trap
```

If the value found is less than *GR_TRAP* then it means it is the background (for example, around a tunnel) and cannot be walked over, so it jumps to *move_cancel*.

Now the move is done by updating the DI register because the remaining things are to be walked over. As the Flags registers haven't changed since the **cmp** instruction, now it uses the **je** instruction (Jump if Equal) to jump if a trap has been found.

```
        ; 8 things to look for (plus monsters)
        cmp al,GR_TUNNEL         ; GR_TUNNEL+GR_DOOR+GR_FLOOR ?
        jnc move_cancel         ; Yes, jump.
```

Then if the value is greater than or equal to *GR_TUNNEL* it jumps to *move_cancel*, but as this is only a **ret** instruction and DI has already been updated, it actually makes the player move if the character is *GR_TUNNEL*, *GR_DOOR*, or *GR_FLOOR*.

```
        cmp al,GR_WEAPON         ; GR_WEAPON?
        ja battle               ; > it's a monster, so go to battle
        ; Only items at this part of code, so clean floor
        mov byte [di],GR_FLOOR  ; Delete item from floor
```

```
        je weapon_found              ; = weapon found
```

If the character value is greater than *GR_WEAPON*, it means a monster letter has been found, and jumps (**ja**) to *battle*. If the value was equal then it jumps (**je**) to *weapon_found* but first erases the object from the floor overwriting *GR_FLOOR*.

Now there only remain values below *GR_WEAPON* (0x18).

```
            ; 4 things to look for
            cmp al,GR_ARMOR          ; GR_ARMOR?
            je armor_found           ; Yes, increase armor
            jb food_found            ; < it's GR_FOOD, increase hp
            ; 2 things to look for
            cmp al,GR_GOLD           ; GR_GOLD?
            je move_cancel           ; Yes, simply take it.
            ; At this point 'al' can only be GR_YENDOR
            ; Amulet of Yendor found!
            neg byte [bp+yendor]     ; Now player goes upwards.
move_cancel:
            ret                      ; Return to main loop.

    %ifdef com_file
quit:
            int 0x20
    %endif
```

It does a comparison with *GR_ARMOR*, and if it is equal then it jumps to *armor_found*, or else if less than it jumps to *food_found*. Notice how a single comparison serves to do *two comparisons*, because it already processed all other possible values.

The final comparison is against *GR_GOLD*, and if equal it simply returns to the game loop by means of *move_cancel*, as the gold was already erased from the screen. Because of the lack of space, it doesn't account for the gold, but it is there for a better gaming experience.

If it wasn't *GR_GOLD* it could be only *GR_YENDOR* by process of elimination, and it negates the *yendor* variable, so now the player goes up instead of down when taking a ladder.

3.7 Effects of taking items.

The routines that handle the taking of items are relatively simple.

```
;       I--
;     I--
;   I--
;
ladder_found:
        jmp generate_dungeon
```

The *ladder_found* routine simply jumps to *generate_dungeon* to create the next dungeon level.

```
;    _____
; I       I
; I #X I
; I X# I
;   \__/
;
armor_found:
        inc byte [bp+armor]     ; Increase armor level
        ret
```

Finding armor increments the *armor* variable by one.

```
;
;           /|  _____
; (|===|oo>_____>
;           \|
;
weapon_found:
        inc byte [bp+weapon]    ; Increase weapon level
        ret
```

Finding a weapon item increases the *weapon* variable by one.

```
;
; Aaaarghhhh!
;
trap_found:
        call si                 ; Random 1-6
sub_hp: neg ax                  ; Make it negative
        db 0xbb                 ; MOV BX to jump two bytes
```

Finding a trap generates a random number (notice in section 3.5 how BH was loaded with 6 before jumping into *trap_found*) into AX, then it negates the number, and falls through to *add_hp* by jumping two bytes using a **mov bx** instruction (**db 0xbb**). The effect of this instruction is to load two bytes into BX that aren't used, but these bytes are the **call si** instruction, so this way it effectively jumps two bytes.

```
        ;
        ;     /--\
        ; ====     I
        ;     \--/
        ;
food_found:
        call si                  ; Random 1-6
```

Same as before, finding food generates a random number (also notice in section 3.5 how BH was loaded with 6 before jumping here). But this time it isn't negated, so it is added to the Health Points (HP).

```
add_hp: add ax,[bp+hp]           ; Add to current HP
    %ifdef com_file
        js quit                  ; Exit if Esc key is pressed
    %else
        js $                     ; Stall if dead
    %endif
        mov [bp+hp],ax           ; Update HP.
```

The *add_hp* function adds the value of **AX** to the *hp* variable. If the result is negative it means the player is now dead and it stops the game, or else it updates the *hp* variable.

```
        ;
        ; Update screen indicator
        ;
        mov bx,0x0f98            ; Point to bottom right corner
        call .1
    %ifdef com_file
        mov al,[bp+weapon]
        call .1
        mov al,[bp+armor]
        call .1
    %endif
```

```
        mov al,[bp+level]
.1:
        xor cx,cx                ; CX = Quotient
.2:     inc cx
        sub ax,10                ; Division by subtraction
        jnc .2
        add ax,0x0a3a            ; Remainder to ASCII digit + color
        call .3                  ; Put on screen
        xchg ax,cx
        dec ax                   ; Quotient is zero?
        jnz .1                   ; No, jump to show more digits.

.3:     mov [bx],ax
        dec bx
        dec bx
        ret
```

Now it updates the screen indicator located at the bottom right corner of the screen. Using the current value in AX, it calls *.1* to show a decimal number, and also shows together the current *level* number.

The division routine to show the decimal number doesn't use the **div** instruction because that would mean the DX register content would be lost. So it does a division by means of successive subtraction by ten. The result comes into CX, while AX contains the remainder that is used to display a digit.

As the value out of the loop is negative, it adds 0x3a to AL to get an ASCII digit in the range 0x30-0x39. It also adds fully to AX to integrate the bright green color attribute.

When the quotient isn't zero, it continues with the division procedure, or else it exits the loop with AX equal to zero, and it is used to add a space to the left of the number.

3.8 Let's battle!

The battle section is the most important in RPGs. However in this game it is relatively simple.

```
        ;
        ; Let's battle!!!
        ;
battle:
        and al,0x1f      ; Separate number of monster (1-26)
        shl al,1         ; Make it slightly harder
        mov ah,al        ; Use also as its HP
        xchg ax,dx       ; Its attack is equivalent to its number
```

The number of the monster (1-26) is multiplied by 2 to make it its attack number (saved into DL), and also its health points (saved into DH).

```
        ; Player's attack
.2:
        mov bh,[bp+weapon]       ; Use current weapon level as dice
        call si
        sub dh,al        ; Subtract from monster's HP
        jc .3            ; Killed? yes, jump
```

The player attacks first, and BH is loaded with the *weapon* variable. So the player attack number is a value between 1 and *weapon*.

The resulting random number is subtracted from DH. If the Carry flag gets set it means the monster is now dead (its HP became negative) and jumps to *.3*.

```
        ; Monster's attack
        mov bh,dl        ; Use monster number as dice
        call si
        sub al,[bp+armor]        ; Subtract armor from attack
        jc .4
        call sub_hp      ; Subtract from player's HP
.4:
```

Now the monster attacks to the player. Its number is multiplied by 2 and used as dice, so its attack is 1 to 52 for the toughest monster. The *armor* variable is subtracted from the result and the total subtracted from the player's HP.

This simple implementation means that collecting enough armor will nullify almost all monster attacks.

```
        ;   mov ah,0x00      ; Comes here with ah = 0
            int 0x16         ; Wait for a key.
            jmp .2           ; Another battle round.
```

Now it does a classical Rogue thing: it waits for a key before continuing to the next round of battle (remember the subroutine *sub_hp* updated the health points on screen).

```
            ;
            ; Monster is dead
            ;
    .3:
            mov byte [di],GR_FLOOR  ; Remove from screen
            ret
```

When the battle is over, and the player isn't dead (otherwise the game would stop before), then it erases the monster from the screen, replacing it with a *GR_FLOOR* tile.

3.9 Fill the dungeon with gold.

The work of filling rooms with gold, items, and enemies uses an important part of the space dedicated to the game.

```
            ;
            ; Fill a room
            ;
    fill_room:
            add ax,(BOX_HEIGHT/2-1)*ROW_WIDTH+(BOX_WIDTH/2)*2
            push ax
            xchg ax,di
            shr dx,1                  ; Obtain bit of right connection
            mov ax,0x0000+GR_TUNNEL
            mov cx,BOX_WIDTH
            jnc .3
            push di
            rep stosw                 ; Horizontal tunnel
            pop di
    .3:
```

Even though the room width and height are pseudo-random, it draws tunnels from the center of the room to the center of the connecting room, so the size doesn't matter.

The first step is to get a pointer to the center of the room by adding a constant to the register AX and putting it into DI.

Now it extracts a bit from the DX connection bitmap using **shr**.

If the Carry flag is set, it uses **rep stosw** to draw a horizontal tunnel (AX loaded with *GR_TUNNEL* and black-on-black attribute, and CX loaded with *BOX_WIDTH* to reach the adjacent room). Notice DI is saved to be used again.

```
        shr dx,1                    ; Obtain bit of down connection
        jnc .5
        mov cl,BOX_HEIGHT
.4:
        stosb                       ; Vertical tunnel
        add di,ROW_WIDTH-1
        loop .4
.5:
```

Then it extracts another bit from the DX connection bitmap using **shr**. The fact it is using **shr** implies it is filling the DX register with zeroes, and this is important for the ninth room because it never has connection with anything and DX will be zero.

Now if the Carry flag is set, it does a loop to draw a vertical tunnel using the combination **stosb/add**. Notice how the added constant is one less than *ROW_WIDTH* because **stosb** increments the DI register by one.

```
        mov bh,BOX_MAX_WIDTH-2
        call si                     ; Get a random width for room.
        xchg ax,cx
        mov bh,BOX_MAX_HEIGHT-2
        call si                     ; Get a random height for room.
        mov ch,al
```

Now it gets a random width and height for the room. The width is saved onto CL, and the height onto CH.

```
        shr al,1               ;
        inc ax
        mov ah,ROW_WIDTH
        mul ah
        add ax,cx              ; Now it has a centering offset
        sub ah,ch              ; Better than "mov bx,cx mov bh,0"
        and al,0xfe
        add al,0x04
        pop di
        sub di,ax              ; Subtract from room center
```

Then it divides the height by two, adds one, multiplies by
ROW_WIDTH and now it has a centering offset in the vertical side. Notice
how it adds the width of the box to AX, and removes CH from the
equation, so the combination **add ax,cx/sub ah,ch** technically is
equivalent to **add ax,cl**.

Because each character on the PC screen is equivalent to two bytes,
it already did the division by two for the width of the box, so all that
remains is to clear bit 0 (otherwise it would write on attribute bytes instead
of character bytes), and adjust the horizontal offset.

Finally the resulting value is subtracted from the center of the box to
get the top left corner of the room.

```
        mov al,GR_TOP_LEFT        ; Draw top row of room
        mov bx,GR_TOP_RIGHT*256+GR_HORIZ
        call fill
.9:
        mov al,GR_VERT            ; Draw intermediate row of room
        mov bx,GR_VERT*256+GR_FLOOR
        call fill
        dec ch
        jns .9
        mov al,GR_BOT_LEFT        ; Draw bottom row of room
        mov bx,GR_BOT_RIGHT*256+GR_HORIZ

        ;
        ; Fill a row on screen for a room
        ;
fill:   push cx                  ; Save CX because it needs CL value
        push di                  ; Save video position
        call door                ; Left border
.1:     mov al,bl                ; Filler
```

```
        call door
        dec cl
        jns .1
        mov al,bh              ; Right border
        call door
        pop di                 ; Restore video position
        pop cx                 ; Restore CX
        add di,0x00a0          ; Goes to next row on screen
        ret
```

The room is drawn in three steps: top border, interior (repeated multiple times), and bottom border.

Figure 3-9. Empty room being drawn.

The left character is put into AL for immediate drawing with a call to *door*, then the BL character is drawn several times (indicated by register CL), and finally the BH character is drawn at the right. Then it goes to the next video line.

```
        ;
        ; Draw a room character on screen
        ;
door:
        cmp al,GR_FLOOR        ; Drawing floor?
        jne .3                 ; No, jump
```

If the character being drawn for the room isn't *GR_FLOOR* then it simply jumps to draw it.

```
        call si                 ; Get a random number (BH=GR_VERT)
        cmp al,6                ; Chance of creating a monster
        jnc .11
        add al,[bp+level]       ; More diff. monsters as more level
.9:
        sub al,0x05
        cmp al,0x17             ; Fit inside ASCII letters
        jge .9
        add al,0x44             ; Offset into ASCII letters
        jmp short .12
```

If it is *GR_FLOOR*, it generates a random number, and any number below 6 creates a monster. This number between 1 and 5 is added to *level*, and then limited to the range -3..22, so when we add 68, it becomes an ASCII letter between A and Z (0x41-0x5a).

```
.11:
        cmp al,11               ; Chance of creating an item
        xchg ax,bx
        cs mov bl,[si+bx+(items-random-6)]
        xchg ax,bx
        jb .12
        mov al,GR_FLOOR         ; Show only floor.
.12:
```

A number between 6 and 10 creates an item. It is indexed into the *items* table, using the SI register as reference (remember it points to the *random* function), minus the base 6.

Any other number simply shows the floor (*GR_FLOOR*).

```
.3:
        cmp al,GR_HORIZ
        je .1
        cmp al,GR_VERT
        jne .2
.1:     cmp byte [di],GR_TUNNEL
        jne .2
        mov al,GR_DOOR
.2:     stosb
        inc di
        ret
```

The final trick of the *door* function is to detect if it is going to draw a wall (*GR_HORIZ* or *GR_VERT*), then it checks if a tunnel is below, and changes the character to *GR_DOOR*.

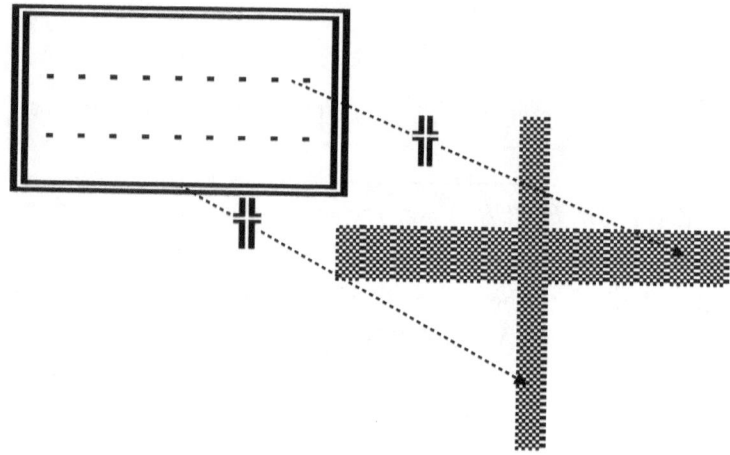

Figure 3-10. Replacement character for sides of room. Anywhere where it crosses a tunnel (drawn previously).

Finally it draws the character to the screen using **stosb** and then increments DI to avoid the attribute byte.

3.10 Random function.

The random function needs to be small, yet needs to generate numbers in a requested range for the dice functions required by battle.

```
random:
        mov al,251
        mul byte [bp+rnd]
        add al,83
        mov [bp+rnd],ax

;       rdtsc           ; Would make it dependent on Pentium II

;       in al,(0x40)    ; Only works for slow requirements.

        xor ah,ah
        div bh
```

```
        mov al,ah
        cbw
        inc ax
        ret
```

It works by multiplying the random seed (*rnd*) by 251 and adding 83. Other functions available for generating random numbers are the **rdtsc** instruction of the Pentium II, but I wanted this game to work on an old PC XT. We also could have read the Timer Counter value as in my other games, but it doesn't "move" fast enough, so if read continuously it isn't really random.

Then the resulting number is limited to 0-255 (using XOR AH,AH, same as MOV AH,0) and then divides by BH. The remainder in AH is converted to a 16-bit number in AX, and incremented. So if BH contained 6 at entry, then the generated number is between 1 and 6.

These are the items used to fill the rooms:

```
        ;
        ; Items
        ;
items:
        db GR_FOOD
        db GR_GOLD
        db GR_TRAP
        db GR_WEAPON
        db GR_ARMOR
```

And the required signature to make this a bootable sector:

```
%ifdef com_file
%else
        times 510-($-$$) db 0x4f
        db 0x55,0xaa            ; Make it a bootable sector
%endif
```

3.11 Explorations on bootRogue.

bootRogue had an amazing response from the public. Many people praised how I managed to keep the spirit and feeling of the original Rogue.

I even got an interesting message by Eric Davisson (XlogicX) who surprised me with this header "Please keep Rogue.asm as it is, it's perfect!".

I'm including portions of his messages with his authorization because I feel these are very interesting:

If you could, please don't change your random algorithm or how it's called, including how many times each function may call it (like how generating a dungeon may call it around 200 times). The game is absolutely perfect they way it is! I'll explain.

First of all, I love the hunger system added, though, it could be more challenging if 'add byte [bp+starve],1' were changed to be 3 or 4. I have legit beaten it on 3, possibly 4. But with an insight that I gained, I can set it to 32 (meaning you lose an HP every 8 moves) and still beat the game.

This game, as it stands now, has an amazing amount of potential for making a game guide. Even simple hints/tips like: if you see a piece of armor, there's a good chance you'll see some food 2 spots to the right. Or, if you need an exit, check one of the corners. But as you'll read below, there are some more way more intense tricks.

Being that you are using more of a mathy pseudo random this time, I suspected that there might be some noticeable patterns or emergent behavior (you probably suspected the same). I just wanted to go down this rabbit hole. So I tapped and logged the random values coming out of the generator you have. I used a scripting (python) technique with gdb, that if you haven't tried this kind of thing before, then now you know; it can be super useful. Here's the script I used:

```
python
import re
def pex(arg):
  try:
    return gdb.execute(arg, to_string=True)
  except:
    return("error")

i = 0
```

```
pex("target remote | qemu-system-i386 -S -gdb stdio -m 16 -boot c -
hda rogue")
pex("set architecture i8086")
pex("display /i ($cs*16)+$pc")
pex("stepi 11")
pex("br *0x7de5")

f = open('log.txt', 'w')
f.close
while i < 1000000:
  pex("cont")
  result = pex("info register ax")
  if 'error' not in result and '""' not in result:
    matches = re.match(r'^ax\s+(\S+)', result)
    result = matches.group(1)
    f = open('log.txt', 'a')
    f.write('{}\n'.format(result))
    f.close

f.close
pex("quit")
```

Execute it with: gdb -x script.s rogue

I noticed that after about 400-500 iterations of random, a pattern does start to emerge where it starts repeating 128 distinct values in a loop. If any one of those 128 values gets entered into by random, then the loop will start. So this clued me into the possibility that I might see some patterns when playing, but only after a couple of dungeons into the game. Again, not surprising to either of us that there would be a loop when doing random like this.

You were already aware there were about 16 dungeon types, as you put in your comments. After a lot of testing, I found that there are fortunately quite a bit more. I used my magic lantern cheat/patch to really see the patterns and have finer control of what I was doing. I noticed that if I just went straight for the exit (when possible), that the same 2-4 maps would cycle over and over in order. Now, having the insight that this is all based on random, I knew that if I picked up some food, hit a trap, or fought an enemy, this would affect which map I get next, and it does. Not only does it, it happens predictably/consistently (with exception to fighting enemies, as this COULD make more than one call to random). So this means that to some degree, not only can I know which dungeons exist, but even have some degree of control to actually pick the next dungeon I want!

As an example (the one I used to beet the game with 8 move hunger), I cycle between 3 maps. One of the maps (I have been internally calling map 13), has food and armor to the side of you as you come up the entrance of the top center room. The exit is in the top left, but I also get the food and armor found at the top of this room. This makes for 2 items (food) that affect random, which brings me to the next map.

This next map is simple, I go straight up again, get the sword blocking the entrance of the top center room, and go right to the top left room for the exit.

For the next room, I take the same path as the one before it, but this time no sword, but there is an armor and a food in the path to the exit on the exit room. After doing this (exactly), you end up back in 'room 13' to repeat the cycle. This is enough food to 'tread water' and not starve even when losing 1 HP every 8 moves. When playing, if I noticed that I'm in any of these 3 maps, I now know I'm also in the cycle of them.

Knowing how to get to any of these 3 maps is a different story, but I'm mapping it all out and already have a lot of variety. And there is a lot of variety for each single-serving random calling item, if I run out of food items, I can just jump on a trap a few times to get more dungeon options. The funny thing is that the more HP you have, the more choice you get for getting your pick of a dungeon.

Chapter 4

Bricks

The evolution of the original Pong game by Nolan Bushnell, it added a wall of bricks. Instead of two players, now there is one against a brick wall. It was called Breakout. Interestingly the original arcade artwork said that the player is actually playing as a prison inmate attempting to knock a ball and chain into the prison wall with a mallet. If the player successfully destroys the wall, the inmate escapes with others following.[14]

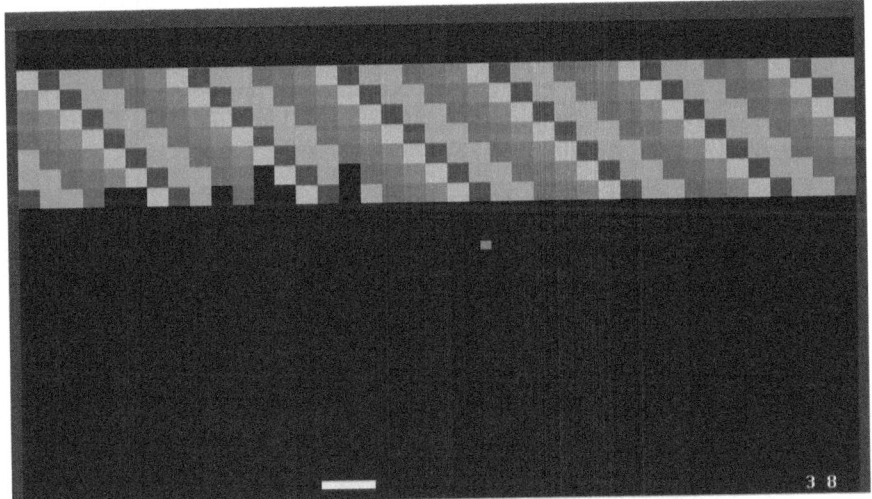

[14] https://en.wikipedia.org/wiki/Breakout_(video_game)

Atari trademarked the names Pong and Breakout, but the concept spread widely among every computer and game console ever manufactured, although with different names.

4.1 Implementation design.

The game consists of a paddle, a ball, borders on the screen, and the brick wall.

For this game, I have used the **int 0x16** BIOS service 0x02 (Read Modifier Keys). This service allows us to read the pressed or depressed state of some keys: Left Shift, Right Shift, Left Alt, Right Alt, Left Ctrl, Right Ctrl, Caps Lock, Num Lock, and Scroll Lock.

As you may remember, the BIOS can tell us if a key has been pressed and wait to read a key, but it cannot tell us if a key has been *depressed*. This means that we don't have a way to stop the player from moving unless we limit its input to the keys listed above.

As a side note, the Scroll Lock key was never too popular and disappeared slowly by late 1990s along with its light on the keyboard. Num Lock also has disappeared on laptop keyboards. So both are pretty useless if you want to have wide compatibility with the available PC machines.

Also the ball will have variables using 8.8 fraction (8 bits of integer part and 8 bits of fraction part) in order to allow smooth movement and angle-like displacement.

4.2 Definitions.

The code starts with the **org** directive to setup the start position of the executable.

```
;
; Bricks game in one boot sector
;
; by Oscar Toledo G.
;
; Creation date: Nov/02/2019.
;
```

```
    cpu 8086


    ;
    ; Press Left Shift to start the game
    ; Press Left Ctrl to move the paddle to the left
    ; Press Left Alt to move the paddle to the right
    ;

    %ifdef com_file
        org 0x0100
    %else
        org 0x7c00
    %endif

old_time:   equ 0x0fa0; Old time
ball_x:   equ 0x0fa2   ; X-coordinate of ball (8.8 fraction)
ball_y:   equ 0x0fa4   ; Y-coordinate of ball (8.8 fraction)
ball_xs: equ 0x0fa6   ; X-speed of ball (8.8 fraction)
ball_ys: equ 0x0fa8   ; Y-speed of ball (8.8 fraction)
beep:     equ 0x0faa   ; Frame count to turn off sound
bricks:   equ 0x0fac   ; Remaining bricks
balls:    equ 0x0fae   ; Remaining balls
score:    equ 0x0fb0   ; Current score
```

Several variables are defined inside the video memory to avoid changing segment registers on the fly (see appendix A.1).

The *old_time* variable contains the old value of the timer counter for frame synchronization, while *ball_x* and *ball_y* contain the current x,y coordinate of the ball. Furthermore *ball_xs* and *ball_ys* contain the fractional x and y speed of the ball, although it could also be called a movement vector.

There is a *beep* variable that is used as a counter to disable the beeper sounds that are generated. The *bricks* variable contains a count of the number of bricks on the screen, so it can trigger another level when all the bricks are cleared.

The *balls* variable is a lives counter, so the player has several chances of clearing the wall after losing the ball. And finally the *score* variable will contain the current score of the game.

4.3 Variables setup.

The first step is to set the display video mode.

```
        ;
        ; Start of the game
        ;
start:
        mov ax,0x0002       ; Text mode 80x25x16 colors
        int 0x10            ; Setup
        mov ax,0xb800       ; Address of video screen
        mov ds,ax           ; Setup DS
        mov es,ax           ; Setup ES
        mov word [score],0  ; Reset score
        mov byte [balls],4  ; Balls remaining
```

Only the *score* and *balls* variables are initialized at this time, to set the score to zero, and chances to four respectively.

4.4 Starting a level.

Starting a level is a matter of creating a border around the play field (except the bottom side), and drawing the wall on screen.

```
        ;
        ; Start another level
        ;
another_level:
        mov word [bricks],273   ; 273 bricks on screen
        xor di,di
        mov ax,0x01b1           ; Draw top border
        mov cx,80
        cld
        rep stosw
```

It sets up the remaining *bricks* variable to 273, and draws the top border using a blue dithered block from the video ROM character set.

```
        mov cx,24           ; 24 rows
    .1:
        stosw               ; Draw left border
        mov ax,0x20         ; No bricks on this row
        push cx
```

```
        cmp cx,23
        jae .2
        sub cx,15
        jbe .2
        mov al,0xdb              ; Bricks on this row
        mov ah,cl
.2:
        mov cx,39               ; 39 bricks per row
.3:
        stosw
        stosw
        inc ah                  ; Increase attribute color
        cmp ah,0x08
        jne .4
        mov ah,0x01
.4:
        loop .3
        pop cx

        mov ax,0x01b1           ; Draw right border
        stosw
        loop .1
```

Then it starts drawing 24 rows; the common thing for all these rows is that they have left and right borders. The 1st and 2nd row doesn't have bricks, but the 3rd to 9th rows have bricks (comparison being done with **cmp cx,23** and **cmp cx,15**).

As seven rows have bricks, the row number is used as the starting color for the brick. Each brick of the 39 shown per row is two characters wide and drawn by using a pair of **stosw** instructions. Each time the color is increased, if it reaches 0x08 then it cycles back to 0x01 (blue).

4.5 Starting a ball.

The paddle position is set up to the bottom center of the screen before starting a ball.

```
        ;
        ; Start another ball
        ;
        mov di,0x0f4a           ; Position of paddle
another_ball:
```

```
        mov byte [ball_x+1],0x28      ; Center X
        mov byte [ball_y+1],0x14      ; Center Y
        xor ax,ax
        mov [ball_xs],ax              ; Static on screen
        mov [ball_ys],ax
        mov byte [beep],0x01
```

The ball starts at row 20 and column 40 (x = 40, y =20). The game keeps both the x,y coordinates as 8.8 fractions (8 bits of integer part, and 8 bits of fractional part).

Then it initializes the ball speed to zero. This avoids movement of the ball until the player triggers it.

It also resets the *beep* variable to zero to keep silent.

4.6 Game loop.

The game loop comprises the main core of the bricks game. Before entering the game loop it sets up the SI register to point off screen so it doesn't erase any part of the screen before moving the ball for the first time.

```
        mov si,0x0ffe                 ; Don't erase ball yet
game_loop:
        call wait_frame               ; Wait 1/18.2 secs.

        mov word [si],0x0000          ; Erase ball

        call update_score             ; Update score
```

The first step of the game loop is to wait for a clock tick to happen, then it erases the ball from screen, and updates the current score being shown.

```
        mov ah,0x02                   ; Read modifier keys
        int 0x16
        test al,0x04                  ; Left ctrl
        je .1
        mov byte [di+6],0             ; Erase right side of paddle
        mov byte [di+8],0
```

```
        sub di,byte 4              ; Move paddle to left
        cmp di,0x0f02              ; Limit
        ja .1
        mov di,0x0f02
.1:
        test al,0x08               ; Left alt
        je .2
        xor ax,ax                  ; Erase left side of paddle
        stosw
        stosw                      ; DI increased automatically
        cmp di,0x0f94              ; Limit
        jb .2
        mov di,0x0f94
.2:
        test al,0x02               ; Left shift
        je .15
        mov ax,[ball_xs]           ; Ball moving?
        add ax,[ball_ys]
        jne .15                    ; Yes, jump
                                   ; Setup movement of ball
        mov word [ball_xs],0xff40
        mov word [ball_ys],0xff80
.15:
        mov ax,0x0adf              ; Paddle graphic and color
        push di
        stosw                      ; Draw paddle
        stosw
        stosw
        stosw
        stosw
        pop di
```

It reads the modifier keys to detect if the player wants to move the paddle:

- The left Ctrl key moves the paddle to the left and it is detected by **test al,0x04**. It erases two characters from the right side of the paddle and then moves the paddle to the left. It also limits the value of the DI register to avoid going off screen.

- The left Alt key moves the paddle to the right and it is detected by **test al,0x08**. It erases two characters from the left side of the paddle and then moves the paddle to the right. It also limits the value of the DI register to avoid going off screen.

- The left Shift key is detected by **test al,0x02** and by adding both ball speeds (*ball_xs* and *ball_ys*). It detects if both are zero, in which case it initializes the start speed for the ball.

In all cases remember the **test** instruction is equivalent to the **and** instruction, except it doesn't change the register being tested, so we can keep testing bits on the same register (of course if we don't modify the register), and it sets the Z Flag if the resulting value is zero.

The end of the code for paddle movement redraws the paddle using a half-filled block in green color on the screen, while preserving the DI register as **stosw** increments it.

4.7 Ball movement.

The ball movement is relatively complex because we are using fractional coordinates to move it and a trick to make it smoother: it uses the top-half of the character block or the bottom-half of the character block per the y-coordinate fraction, in order to double the vertical resolution of drawing.

This is nice because the screen has 80 characters width, but only 25 characters height. Using half of the character box makes it look like 80x50 pixels.

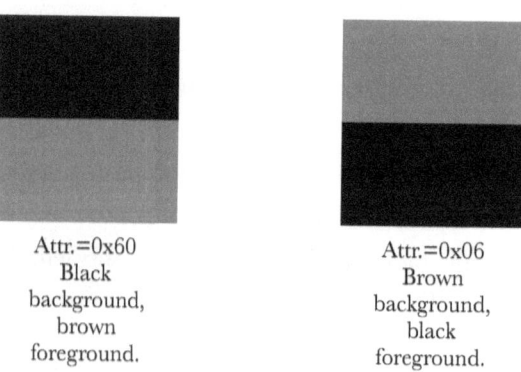

Attr.=0x60
Black
background,
brown
foreground.

Attr.=0x06
Brown
background,
black
foreground.

Figure 4-1. Using same character code (0xdc) with two different colors to get double Y resolution.

74

```
        mov bx,[ball_x]              ; Draw ball
        mov ax,[ball_y]
        call locate_ball             ; Locate on screen
        test byte [ball_y],0x80       ; Y-coordinate half fraction?
        mov ah,0x60              ; Interchange colors for smooth mov.
        je .12
        mov ah,0x06
.12:    mov al,0xdc                  ; Graphic
        mov [bx],ax                  ; Draw
        push bx
        pop si
```

The first step is to get the coordinates of the ball into **BX** and **AX**, then call *locate_ball* in order to get its memory screen position.

It tests for half-row and sets the color for the ball instead of changing the graphic for the ball, because we are using the character codes for testing collisions. Remember the paddle uses the 0xdf graphic code (top-half of character box filled), while the ball uses the 0xdc graphic code (bottom-half of character box filled). The game would behave wrong if it were to find a 0xdf code, because it would confuse the ball with the paddle.

If we use the 0xdc graphics code, then the color 0x60 means the background is brown, while the foreground is black. This causes the top-half of the character box to be brown. Still using the 0xdc graphics code, the color 0x06 now means the foreground is brown, while the background is black. This causes the bottom-half of the character box to be brown. See figure 7-1 for a visual example.

Finally it copies the ball position contained in **BX** to the **SI** register.

```
.14:
        mov bx,[ball_x]             ; Ball position
        mov ax,[ball_y]
        add bx,[ball_xs]            ; Add movement speed
        add ax,[ball_ys]
        push ax
        push bx
        call locate_ball           ; Locate on screen
        mov al,[bx]
        cmp al,0xb1                ; Touching borders
        jne .3
        mov cx,5423               ; 1193180 / 220
```

75

```
        call speaker              ; Generate sound
        pop bx
        pop ax
        cmp bh,0x4f
        je .8
        test bh,bh
        jne .7
.8:
        neg word [ball_xs]        ; Negate X-speed if it touches a side
.7:
        cmp ah,0x00
        jne .9
        neg word [ball_ys]        ; Negate Y-speed if it touches a side
.9: jmp .14
```

For the ball movement, it adds the x and y speed to the current position, then locates the screen character, and reads it. The graphic code 0xb1 represents the play field border, and hitting it generates a 220 hz. tone (1193180 / 220 hz = counter 5423 for timer 0). If it hits the left or right side border then it negates the X speed, and for the top border it negates the Y speed.

4.8 Paddle hit.

We already accounted for hits against the borders. Now it is time for the paddle.

```
.3:
        cmp al,0xdf               ; Touching paddle
        jne .4
        sub bx,di                 ; Subtract paddle position
        sub bx,byte 4
        mov cl,6                  ; Multiply by 64
        shl bx,cl
        mov [ball_xs],bx          ; New X speed for ball
        mov word [ball_ys],0xff80   ; Update Y speed for ball
        mov cx,2711               ; 1193180 / 440
        call speaker              ; Generate sound
        pop bx
        pop ax
        jmp .14
```

It detects a paddle hit by looking for the character code 0xdf. Then it takes the paddle position relative to the ball for generating the X speed, and sets the Y speed to -1.0 (up). It also generates a 440 hz. tone on the speaker.

Notice that this allows the player to have slight control over ball direction.

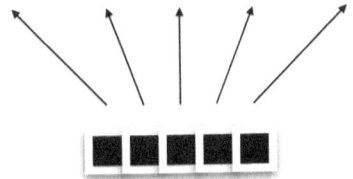

Figure 4-2. Ball directions per paddle character.

```
.4:
        cmp al,0xdb             ; Touching brick
        jne .5
        mov cx,1355             ; 1193180 / 880
        call speaker            ; Generate sound
        test bl,2               ; Aligned with brick?
        jne .10                 ; Yes, jump
        dec bx                  ; Align
        dec bx
.10:    xor ax,ax               ; Erase brick
        mov [bx],ax
        mov [bx+2],ax
        inc word [score]        ; Increase score
        neg word [ball_ys]      ; Negate Y speed (rebound)
        pop bx
        pop ax
        dec word [bricks]       ; One brick less on screen
        jne .14                 ; Fully completed? No, jump.
        jmp another_level       ; Start another level
```

If the ball touches a brick (represented by code 0xdb), it generates a 880hz. tone on the speaker. As each brick is made by two characters, it sometimes needs to center the screen position by doing a comparison with **test bl,2** and correcting with a pair of **dec bx**.

It can happen that a streak of bricks is destroyed by the ball, because only the Y speed of the ball is reversed when hitting a brick, but the X speed remains unchanged, so it can alternatively hit bricks on a line.

It increases the current *score*, negates the Y speed (rebounds the ball), decrements the number of bricks on the screen, and if it becomes zero then starts another level.

```
.5:
    pop bx
    pop ax
.6:
    mov [ball_x],bx          ; Update ball position
    mov [ball_y],ax
    cmp ah,0x19              ; Ball exited through bottom?
    je ball_lost            ; Yes, jump
    jmp game_loop           ; No, repeat game loop
```

Finally, if nothing is hit then it saves the new ball position, and if the Y coordinate goes to 0x19 it means the ball has exit through the bottom and jumps to *ball_lost*, or else it jumps to *game_loop*.

```
    ;
    ; Ball lost
    ;
ball_lost:
    mov cx,10846            ; 1193180 / 110
    call speaker            ; Generate sound

    mov word [si],0         ; Erase ball
    dec byte [balls]        ; One ball less
    js .1                   ; All finished? Yes, jump
    jmp another_ball        ; Start another ball

.1: call wait_frame.2       ; Turn off sound
    int 0x20                ; Exit to DOS / bootOS
```

When a ball is lost, it generates a very low frequency sound of 110 hz, and then erases the ball from the screen. It also decrements the number of available balls, and if all balls are gone it returns to the operating system (or bootOS) while silencing the sound.

4.9 Supporting subroutines.

There are four supporting subroutines:

```
wait_frame:
.0:
      mov ah,0x00               ; Read ticks
      int 0x1a                  ; Call BIOS
      cmp dx,[old_time]         ; Wait for change
      je .0
      mov [old_time],dx

      dec byte [beep]           ; Decrease time to turn off beep
      jne .1
.2:
      in al,0x61
      and al,0xfc               ; Turn off
      out 0x61,al
.1:

      ret
```

The subroutine *wait_frame* waits for a clock tick to pass. It calls the BIOS to read the clock, and does a continuous comparison of DX against *old_time* until it changes value.

Then it decrements the *beep* counter, and if it becomes zero silences the PC speaker.

```
      ;
      ; Generate sound on PC speaker
      ;
speaker:
      mov al,0xb6               ; Setup timer 2
      out 0x43,al
      mov al,cl                 ; Low byte of timer count
      out 0x42,al
      mov al,ch                 ; High byte of timer count
      out 0x42,al
      in al,0x61
      or al,0x03                ; Connect PC speaker to timer 2
      out 0x61,al
      mov byte [beep],3         ; Duration
      ret
```

To generate sound on the PC speaker, it sets up timer 2 and loads the 16-bit frequency counter. Then it internally "links" the output of timer 2 and the PC speaker. Finally, it sets the *beep* variable to 3, so the sound keeps playing for two frames.

```
        ;
        ; Locate ball on screen
        ;
locate_ball:
        mov al,0xa0
        mul ah                  ; AH = Y coordinate (row)
        mov bl,bh               ; BH = X coordinate (column)
        mov bh,0
        shl bx,1
        add bx,ax
        ret
```

The subroutine *locate_ball* takes the Y coordinate of ball on AH and the X coordinate on BH, and then it returns the screen position on BX.

```
        ;
        ; Update score indicator (from bootRogue)
        ;
update_score:
        mov bx,0x0f98           ; Point to bottom right corner
        mov ax,[score]
        call .1
        mov al,[balls]
.1:
        xor cx,cx               ; CX = Quotient
.2:     inc cx
        sub ax,10               ; Division by subtraction
        jnc .2
        add ax,0x0a3a           ; Convert remainder to ASCII digit + color
        call .3                 ; Put on screen
        xchg ax,cx
        dec ax                  ; Quotient is zero?
        jnz .1                  ; No, jump to show more digits.

.3:     mov [bx],ax
        dec bx
        dec bx
        ret
```

The *update_score* subroutine comes from bootRogue and it is in charge of showing the current player score along with the number of balls remaining.

4.10 Bootable signature.

This completes the game for working with a boot sector.

```
%ifdef com_file
%else
times 510-($-$$) db 0x4f
db 0x55,0xaa                ; Make it a bootable sector
%endif
```

Chapter 5

CubicDoom

The year was 1992, and many new games were starting to come with support for the VGA mode of 320x200x256 colors. Among these games the newest thing was Wolfenstein 3D by a small company named ID Software.

You started at a prison cell, just after killing a soldier, and now have his gun. Pressing a key you advance towards the door, and pressing another key would open it with a clanky metallic sound, and you could see more doors of other cells. If you explore some of these, you could find the bones

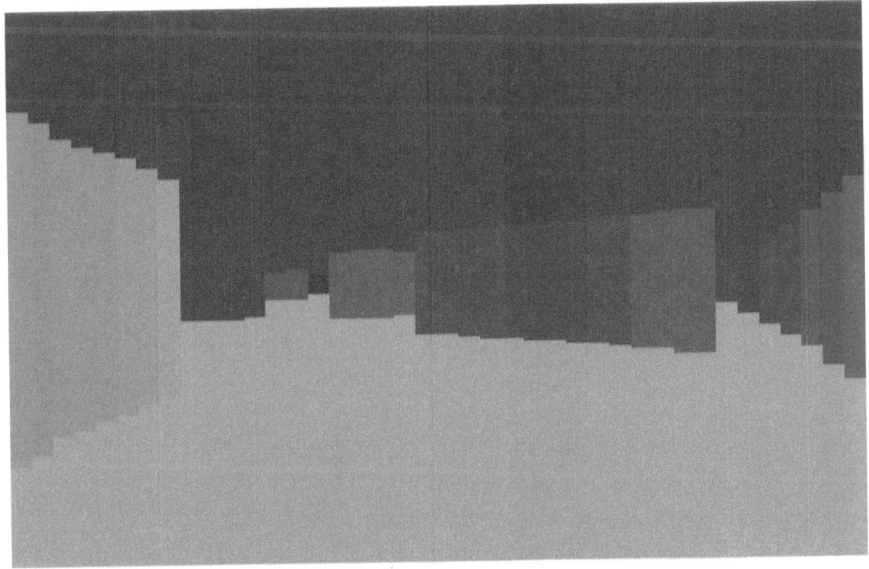

of poor allied prisoners. No other souls, then you would see a food plate, and as you went for it you would hear "Achtung!" and a gunshot, then you franticly tried to turn around to see who was shooting you, and nervously pressed the shoot key while the soldier moved getting nearer to you, until a blood curtain descended over your view. And you were dead.

Was it the novelty? Or the gore? Maybe the surprise, the action, or the fear? Whatever it was, Wolfenstein 3D rose to the stars and paved the way for another iconic game: Doom.

5.1 The challenge.

Wolfenstein was designed in a year when the 80286 machines still dominated the market, better known as PC/AT machines. These were replacing the old PC/XT computers, had more speed, better graphics, and finally sound cards replacing the beepers.

But the 80286 processor couldn't do high-speed mathematics, so John Carmack (creator of the Wolfenstein engine) had to resort to precalculated tables for the pseudo-3d display, and devised an algorithm that would be known as ray-casting.

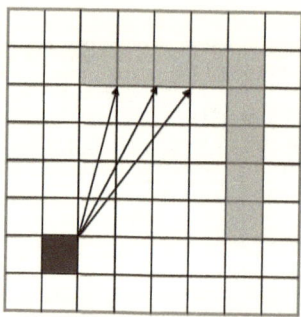

Figure 5-1. Ray-casting from the player's position being "drawn" until a wall is touched. In this case each cell of the map will be represented by a byte inside the 16x16 map on memory.

Ray-casting is the process of drawing a line from the observer (the player) through the scenario until hitting a wall, then it calculates the height of the wall based on the distance, and column by column it draws the scene. It also kept a Z-buffer (an array of wall distances) so it can later draw the game sprites while maintaining visual priority.

Ray-casting is a simplification of another algorithm known as Ray-tracing, where every pixel on screen is drawn by tracing lines from the observer (instead of drawing only columns). But in ray-tracing the intersection of lines is calculated by very complicated mathematics,[15] while in ray-casting only integers are used to draw block-by-block the viewing line, advancing through the map until it finds a collision.

But could a game of this complexity be made within the size of a boot sector? It was a tough challenge. I started by drawing a fixed maze of 16x16, where a bit set to one would be a wall, and a bit cleared would be an empty space, so it used 32 bytes (16 words). Also it wasn't designed to be easy to modify.

My first iteration of the code required a 360-degree sine table compressed onto 64 values with 6 bits of precision, but I discovered very soon that it wasn't enough for drawing a screen projection with reasonable resolution. So I had to increase the sine table size to 128 values.

A ray-casting core was ready by day 2 using all the space available in the boot sector, and it looked very nice!

Later I added the enemies (cubes moving towards you), and then I had to start the optimization to fit everything.

5.2 Definitions.

The CubicDoom game starts with some constant definitions, and assignment of space for variables.

---

[15] One of the easiest figures to calculate on a ray tracer is a sphere; the intersection is solved by a quadratic equation. One of the most difficult ones is the torus, requiring a 4th degree polynomial. Notice I'm only talking about the intersection equation—doing a calculation of the normal at the point of intersection, and/or the respective texture mapping is a highly complex discussion. Modern games are now using ray tracing for rendering scenes in real-time. This amazing accomplishment is due to the powerful GPU (Graphic Processing Units) that are available on modern gaming consoles.

```
;
; CubicDoom
;
; by Oscar Toledo G.
;
; Creation date: Nov/21/2019.
; Revision date: Nov/22/2019. Now working.
; Revision date: Nov/23/2019. Optimized.
; Revision date: Nov/24/2019. Builds a world. Added evil cubes,
;                             and can shoot them. 517 bytes.
; Revision date: Nov/25/2019. Optimized last bytes. 509 bytes.
; Revision date: Nov/26/2019. Smaller extract. 508 bytes
;                             (Peter Ferrie).
;
;

        cpu 8086

EMPTY:  equ 0x00        ; Code for empty space
WALL:   equ 0x80        ; Code for wall
ENEMY:  equ 0xc0        ; Code for enemy, includes shot count

    %ifdef com_file
        org 0x0100
    %else
        org 0x7c00
    %endif

down:   equ 0x000b      ; Enemies down
shot:   equ 0x000a      ; Shot made
rnd:    equ 0x0008      ; Random number
px:     equ 0x0006      ; Current X position (4.12)
py:     equ 0x0004      ; Current Y position (4.12)
pa:     equ 0x0002      ; Current screen angle
oldtim: equ 0x0000      ; Old time

maze:   equ 0xff00      ; Location of maze (16x16)
```

It's amazing that this game, being complex, uses so few variables and data. Almost everything is visual.

There are a few constants: *EMPTY* for empty spaces on the maze, *WALL* for walls on the maze, and *ENEMY* which is a special moving wall representing the enemies.

The variables are kept on the stack and are: *oldtim* for keeping the latest tick count from the **PC** internal clock, *pa* containing the current viewing angle (only the lowest 7 bits are used for a value of 0-127), *px* and *py* for keeping the current x,y position (4 integer bits and 12 fraction bits), *rnd* for a pseudo-random number generator (same as bootRogue—see section 3.9), *shot* to signal when player shoots, and *down* to count enemies down so the game can go to the next level.

The *maze* array is kept on the video memory. It is a 16x16 byte array for a total of 256 bytes. Given it is at the highest possible address of video memory (0xff00), adding 256 to its address will make the number zero (allowing use of the Z Flag as a trigger to detect if the whole maze has been searched). Also as the length is 256 bytes, it's easy to load only the high byte of the address, and put the index location in the low byte, so this way it saves the bytes of an **add** instruction.

5.3 Start of the game.

Like any well-behaved game, CubicDoom starts by setting the VGA screen mode of 320x200x256 colors, and sets up the DS and ES registers to point to the screen memory.

```
        ;
        ; Start of the game
        ;
start:
        mov ax,0x0013   ; Graphics mode 320x200x256 colors
        int 0x10        ; Setup video mode
        mov ax,0xa000   ; Point to video memory.
        mov ds,ax
        mov es,ax
restart:
        cld
        xor cx,cx
        push cx         ; shot+down
        in ax,0x40
        push ax         ; rnd
        mov ah,0x18     ; Start point at maze
        push ax         ; px
        push ax         ; py
        mov cl,0x04
```

```
        push cx          ; pa
        push cx          ; oldtim
        mov bp,sp        ; Setup BP to access variables
```

The variables are also reset at this moment using the method of **push**ing them into the stack, and later it makes BP to point to the first variable. The access method will be by means of the **[bp+offset]** addressing mode.

5.4 Creating the maze.

The process of creating our virtual world is relatively simple. It initializes a 16x16 maze with a wall border surrounding it, and fills the interior with empty space.

```
        mov bx,maze      ; Point to maze
.0:     mov al,bl
        add al,0x11      ; Right and bottom borders at zero
        cmp al,0x22      ; Inside any border?
        jb .5            ; Yes, jump
        and al,0x0e      ; Inside left/right border?
        mov al,EMPTY
        jne .4           ; No, jump
.5:     mov al,WALL
.4:     mov [bx],al      ; Put into maze
        inc bx           ; Next square
        jne .0           ; If BX is zero, maze completed
```

By means of the **add al,0x11** instruction, it moves the bottom and right border 0xef-0xff values to 0x00-0x10. So the comparison instruction detects them.

Also anything on the right border, like 0x1f or 0x2f, is translated into 0x20 and 0x30, being detected by the **and al,0x0e** instruction. Why? Due to the left border, for example, 0x10 and 0x20 is translated to 0x21 and 0x31 respectively.

After this routine runs, the maze will be filled with *EMPTY* bytes, and there will be surrounding border composed of *WALL* bytes.

0x00	0x01	0x02	...		0x0d	0x0e	0x0f
0x10							0x1f
0x20							0x2f
0xd0							0xdf
0xe0							0xef
0xf0	0xf1	0xf2	...		0xfd	0xfe	0xff

Table 5-2. Index locations of the maze for the borders.

0x11	0x12	0x13	...		0x1e	0x1f	0x20
0x21							0x30
0x31							0x40
0xe1							0xf0
0xf1							0x00
0x01	0x02	0x03	...		0x0e	0x0f	0x10

Table 5-3. Index locations after doing **add al,0x11**. Notice how the top and bottom rows are less than 0x22. Also notice how the left and right columns have the lower nibble equal to 0 or 1, easily detected by means of **and al,0x0e**.

```
            mov cl,12        ; 12 walls and enemies
            mov [bp+down],cl        ; Take note of enemies down
            mov di,maze+34   ; Point to center of maze
            mov dl,12        ; Modulo 12 for random number
    .2:
            call random
            mov byte [di+bx],WALL    ; Setup a wall
            call random
            mov byte [di+bx],ENEMY   ; Setup an enemy
            add di,byte 16   ; Go to next row of maze
            loop .2          ; Repeat until filled
```

The inner 12x12 area of the maze is then filled with one wall and one enemy per row. Before starting the loop, it saves the "enemy alive" number on the variable *down*.

One call to *random* generates a value 0-11 on BX, and it is used to put a wall inside the maze.

Another call to *random* generates a value 0-11 on BX, and it is used to put an enemy inside the maze. Notice it can overlap a wall, but we don't have enough space to check for it, so we allow it to happen.

It repeats the loop, going to the next row to fill, until it has filled the twelve enemies.

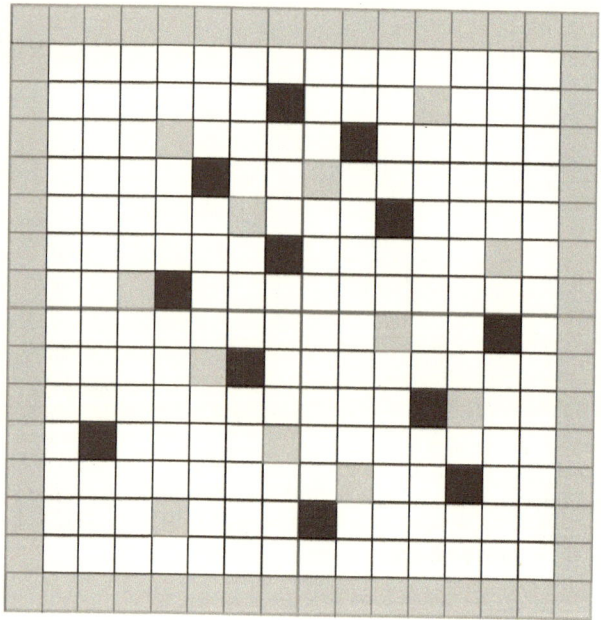

Figure 5-4. A possible initial configuration of the maze, where gray are the walls, while black are the enemy cubes.

5.5 Main game loop.

As tradition requires, the game loop starts by synchronizing the game with the clock ticks of the PC by calling *wait_frame*. This allows it to run at the same speed on any PC machine.

```
game_loop:
        call wait_frame ; Wait a frame

        and dl,31        ; 32 frames have passed?
        jnz .16          ; No, jump
        ;
        ; Move cubes
        ;
        call get_dir     ; Get player position, also SI=0
        call get_pos     ; Convert position to maze address
        mov cx,bx        ; Save into CX

        mov bl,0         ; BH already ready, start at corner

.17:    cmp byte [bx],ENEMY
        jb .18
        cmp bx,cx        ; Cube over player?
        jne .25          ; No, jump
        ;
        ; Handle death
        ;
.22:
        mov byte [si],0x0c       ; Blood pixel
        add si,byte 23   ; Advance by prime number
.23:
        je restart       ; Zero = full loop, restart game.
        jnb .22          ; Carry = one fill complete.
        push si
        call wait_frame ; Wait a frame (for fast machines)
        pop si
        jmp .22          ; Continue


.25:
        mov di,bx
        mov al,bl
        mov ah,cl
        mov dx,0x0f0f    ; Extract columns
        and dx,ax
        xor ax,dx        ; Extract rows
        cmp ah,al        ; Same row?
        je .19           ; Yes, jump
        lea di,[bx+0x10]        ; Cube moves down
        jnb .19
        lea di,[bx-0x10]        ; Cube moves up
.19:    cmp dh,dl        ; Same column?
        je .20           ; Yes, jump
        dec di           ; Cube goes left
        jb .20
```

```
           inc di          ; Cube goes right
           inc di
    .20:   cmp byte [di],0  ; Can move?
           jne .18          ; No, jump.
           mov al,[bx]      ; Take cube
           mov byte [bx],0  ; Erase origin
           stosb            ; Put into new place
    .18:
           inc bx           ; Continue searching the maze...
           jne .17          ; ...until the end

    .16:
```

When 32 frames have elapsed (**and dl,31** checks for it), it tries to move all the enemy cubes towards the player.

First it obtains the current position of the player by calling *get_dir*, and the maze location by calling *get_pos*, saving the result onto CX.

Then it starts searching the maze starting at the top-left corner (**mov bl,0**). If an enemy is not found inside the square, then it jumps to *.18* where it goes onto the next square of the maze. The loop is complete when BX goes to zero. Remember the maze is located at 0xff00, so 0xff00 + 256 = 0x10000, and wraps around to zero because the registers are 16-bit.

If the enemy is over the player, then it starts the death sequence. Fortunately *get_dir* already reset SI to zero, so it draws a red pixel (value 0x0c, defined by the video to be red) on the screen, and adds a prime number (23) to SI. Given the properties of prime numbers, SI will become zero *once the screen is completely filled with red*, and the game will restart. This is an homage to Wolfenstein 3-D.

At some point SI will wrap around the video memory, detected by means of the Carry Flag, and then it waits for a clock tick to happen before continuing with the loop. This way the red sequence is slowed down on fast machines.

The new position for a moving cube is contained in the DI register; it is copied from the current maze position preserved in the BX register.

The AH register gets a copy of the player position (CL register; it was set up before entering the loop), and the AL register gets a copy of the enemy position (BL register; it is being used to explore the maze).

Now it extracts the column numbers on the DX register (loading DX with 0x0f0f and doing a logical AND operation). Using the value on the DX register, it XORs it with AX, so the columns are removed from AX and only the row numbers remain. This saves one byte in comparison to using **and ax,0xf0f0**.[16]

So now AX contains the enemy and player row numbers, while DX contains the enemy and player column numbers.

Now comes the chase algorithm, pretty simple by today standards, but the most fitting for the small space we have for working.

It does a comparison of AH and AL (row numbers): If both are equal, it means the cube is horizontally aligned with the player and jumps; else if the cube is below the player, it goes one row up using **lea di, [bx-0x10]**; or if the cube is above the player, it goes one row down by means of **lea di,[bx+0x10]**.

Now it does a comparison of DH and DL (column numbers): If both are equal, it means the cube is vertically aligned with the player and jumps; else if the cube is at the right of the player, it goes to the left using **dec di**; else it goes to the right using a pair of **inc di** (notice it already subtracted one from DI, so it needs to add two to go to the right).

The cube can only move if the target square is empty (because a wall could be blocking it), and then it copies the cube from the origin BX to the target DI, and erases the origin square. It copies the cube value because it could have been incremented per shots received from the player.

5.6 Interlude.

As a kid I discovered the chase algorithm on the Chase game shown in "More BASIC Computer Games" edited by David Ahl and published in

---

[16] This trick was contributed by Peter Ferrie to the git repository.

1979. The game is credited to be originally created by Mac Oglesby. By the way, each game in the book was accompanied by a nice and imaginative drawing of a robot doing some action.

This game was also published in a Z80 machine code version in the May, 1977 issue of Dr. Dobb's Journal of Computer Calisthenics & Orthodontia.[17]

I've been very lucky and able to touch both pieces of history (the book and a compiled book of Dr. Dobb's Journal).

In the old times, not having a book or magazine meant you couldn't learn! But now you can access all these older magazines at the website *archive.org*

Thanks to the people running *archive.org* you can also access an even older version of the Chase game on the Creative Computing magazine from January/February 1976, where the original author was listed as unknown. I was surprised and pretty humbled to be able to see this piece of history on the Internet while writing this book.

The main difference of the CubicDoom implementation is that the walls are solid, while in the Chase game the walls supposedly are electrified and destroy both you and the robots, so you need only to stay between walls to destroy the robots. On other versions of Chase, the walls are mines.

5.7 The 3D view.

The 3D view is the most complex portion of the game, and it is where the simple internal maze is translated to an interesting display.

---

[17] Dr. Dobb's Journal was a highly influential magazine that started by publishing Tiny BASIC versions for the hobbyists. It also introduced the C language by means of Small-C, and several other languages like Forth and PILOT. It had great contributors like Steve Wozniak (his floating point subroutines for 6502 still raise surprised eyebrows), Jef Raskin (later developer of the Apple Macintosh ROM), and Gary Kildall (creator of the CP/M operating system). Before the Internet, a magazine or book was the only way to get access to important source code. It should be mentioned that it came from People Computer Company, a tiny nonprofit educational corporation founded by Bob Albrecht.

```
        ;
        ; Draw 3D view
        ;
        mov di,39        ; Column number is 39
.2:
        lea ax,[di-20]   ; Almost 60 degrees to the left
        add ax,[bp+pa]   ; Get vision angle
        call get_dir     ; Get position and direction
.3:
        call read_maze   ; Verify wall hit
        jnc .3           ; Continue if it was open space
```

The ray-casting algorithm works in columns. A big game would draw columns pixel-by-pixel in order to have detailed scenery, but it would need a big sine table. The sine table for this game handles 128 values for 360 degrees, so index 64 is equivalent to 90°, and index 128 is equivalent to 180°.

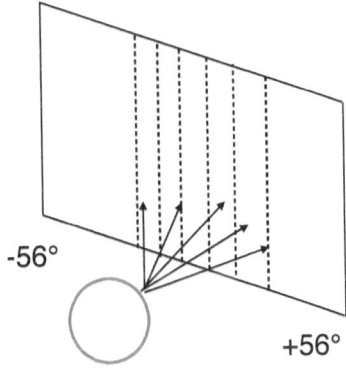

-56°   +56°

Figure 5-5. How the projected screen is drawn. The current viewing angle is subtracted 20 while drawing; this is more or less equivalent to 56 degrees, so the viewing area encompasses 112 degrees.

The game is designed to handle 40 columns on viewing, and this is reflected on the starting value for the DI register equal to 39. Each column will be 8 pixels wide for filling the whole screen 40 * 8 = 320 pixels horizontally.

The rays are generated from the position of the player in angles. The current column angle is taken from DI minus 20 and added to the current viewing angle, then it calls *get_dir* to get the player position on registers DX and BX, and the ray-casting fractional vector on registers CX and AX. The subroutine also initializes the SI register to zero.

An inner loop calls *read_maze* continuously (it also increases ray coordinates) until it hits a wall (Carry Flag will be set). Also the subroutine increases the SI register to calculate the ray distance. The *read_maze* subroutine also sets the Z flag if it hit a normal wall, or clears it if hit an enemy.

```
.4:
        mov cx,0x1204    ; Add grayscale color set...
                         ; ...also load CL with 4. (division by 16)
        jz .24           ; Jump if normal wall
        mov ch,32        ; Rainbow

        cmp di,byte 20
        jne .24          ; Jump if not at center
        cmp byte [bp+shot],1
        je .24           ; Jump if not shooting
        call get_pos
        inc byte [bx]    ; Increase cube hits
        cmp byte [bx],ENEMY+3   ; 3 hits?
        jne .24          ; No, jump
        mov byte [bx],0 ; Yes, remove.
        dec byte [bp+down]      ; One cube less
        je .23           ; Zero means to get another level
.24:
```

The wall color is chosen per the Z flag, where a normal wall loads CH with 0x12 (the color code for a gray palette gamut), or an enemy cube loads CH with 0x20 for a rainbow palette gamut.

Notice the side-load of CL with 4 for a division by 16 later.

If it is drawing an enemy (rainbow), it checks if it is drawing at the center of the screen (DI equals 20) if the player pressed the shoot key (*bp +shot*), and then it gets the position on the maze array, increases the hits on enemy, and if it reaches 3 (*ENEMY+3*) then the game removes the cube from the screen. While doing this it also decreases the number of enemies on screen, and if it becomes zero, it starts another game level by jumping to *.23*.

Nothing visual is done at this point, only removal of the cube from the maze array. The display code will be in charge later of removing it from the screen.

```
lea ax,[di+12]   ; Get cos(-30) to cos(30)
call get_sin     ; Get cos (8 bit fraction)
mul si           ; Correct wall distance to...
mov bl,ah        ; ...avoid fishbowl effect
mov bh,dl        ; Divide by 256
inc bx           ; Avoid zero value
```

The ray-casting algorithm causes a fishbowl effect that must be corrected using the values of *cos(-30)* to *cos(30)* (our vision angle is 60 degrees). But the game only has a *sin* function, so it adds 32 to get a 90° deviation that get us a *cos* function, so -20 + 32 = 12, the value used in the **lea** instruction. It reads the fractional value using *get_sin*, and does this using integer arithmetic:

$$BX = (get\_sin() * SI) / 256 + 1$$

```
      mov ax,0x0800   ; Constant for projection plane
      cwd
      div bx          ; Divide
      cmp ax,198      ; Limit to screen height
      jb .14
      mov ax,198
.14:  mov si,ax       ; Height of wall
```

This part of the code is in charge of getting the wall height, using a simplified projection plane according to this formula:

$$SI = max(2048 / BX, 198)$$

```
shr ax,cl    ; Divide distance by 16
add al,ch    ; Add palette index
xchg ax,bx   ; Put into BX
```

And then it adds depth shadows to the CH color. It uses the wall height divided by 16 (right shift by CL=4), and puts the resulting value into BL (the AH/BH contents doesn't matter).

```
push di
dec cx              ; CL=3. Multiply column by 8 pixels
shl di,cl

mov ax,200          ; Height of screen...
sub ax,si           ; ...minus wall height
shr ax,1            ; Divide by 2

push ax
push si
xchg ax,cx
mov al,[bp+shot]         ; Ceiling color
call fill_column
xchg ax,bx          ; Wall color
pop cx
call fill_column
mov al,0x03         ; Floor color (a la Wolfenstein)
pop cx
call fill_column
pop di
dec di              ; Decrease column
jns .2              ; Completed? No, jump.
```

The column number is multiplied by 8 (remember DI contains the current column number) by means of a shift to left. CL already contained 4, so it decrements CX to get CL equal to 3.

We know the height of the wall, but we also need to fill on screen the ceiling and floor. So it calculates the height of the screen in pixels minus the height of the wall, and divides the result by two. The resulting value is saved onto the stack using **push ax**, and then moved onto CX, getting the color for ceiling from the variable *shot* (it can be blue or white), and draws it by calling *fill_column*.

Now it moves BL (wall color) back to AL, copies SI (wall height) onto CX, and calls *fill_column* for drawing the wall column.

Finally it restores the ceiling height with **pop cx** to use it for the floor, and draws the floor using color 0x03, and it happens to be pretty similar to the color used by Wolfenstein 3-D.

Now the column rendering is complete, and it decrements DI to go to the next column to the left. If the register DI becomes negative, then it has finished drawing the whole screen.

5.8 Player movement.

The player movements are done with the modifier keys of the PC keyboard (Ctrl, Shift, and Alt). This is because these are the only keys that can tell us if they are pressed or depressed.

```
        mov ah,0x02        ; Service 0x02 = Read modifier keys
        int 0x16           ; Call BIOS

        mov bx,[bp+pa]     ; Get current angle
        test al,0x04       ; Left Ctrl pressed?
        je .8
        dec bx             ; Decrease angle
        dec bx
.8:
        test al,0x08       ; Left Alt pressed?
        je .9
        inc bx             ; Increase angle
        inc bx
.9:
        mov ah,1           ; No shot
        test al,0x01       ; Right shift pressed?
        je .11
        test bh,0x01       ; But not before?
        jne .11
        mov ah,7           ; Indicate shot

.11:    mov [bp+shot],ah
        mov bh,al
        mov [bp+pa],bx     ; Update angle
```

Turning to the left is done with the left Ctrl key, and it decreases the viewing angle by two. Turning to the right is done with the left Alt key, and it increases the viewing angle by two.

By default, the ceiling color is blue (**mov ah,1**) but if a shot is made, it changes briefly to white (**mov ah,7**). The color also signals to look for collision against an enemy and it is saved on the *shot* variable. The right Shift key shoots—it saves the previous state of this key, so it only accepts a shoot command when the key wasn't pressed previously; this prevents the player from keeping the shoot key pressed. The old state is saved as the high byte of the angle, because only the lower seven bits are used.

```
        test al,0x02     ; Left shift pressed?
        je .10
        xchg ax,bx       ; Put angle into AX
        call get_dir     ; Get position and direction
.5:     call read_maze   ; Move and check for wall hit
        jc .10           ; Hit, jump without updating position.
        cmp si,byte 4    ; Four times (the speed)
        jne .5

        mov [bp+px],dx   ; Update X position
        mov [bp+py],bx   ; Update Y position
.10:
        jmp game_loop    ; Repeat game loop
```

When the left Shift key is pressed, it moves the viewing angle into AX and uses it to get the direction vector on CX,AX (it also puts zero onto the SI register), and advances four times on the given direction calling *read_maze*.

If it hits a wall, it means the movement isn't possible and doesn't update the player position, or else it finishes the routine by updating *px* and *py*, the position of the player.

5.9 Mathematical functions.

The mathematical functions are based on the sine function returning an 8-bit fraction.

```
        ;
        ; Get a direction vector
        ;
get_dir:
        xor si,si        ; Wall distance = 0
```

```
            mov dx,[bp+px]   ; Get X position
            push ax
            call get_sin     ; Get sine
            xchg ax,cx       ; Onto DX
            pop ax
            add al,32        ; Add 90 degrees to get cosine
            ;
            ; Get sine
            ;
get_sin:
            test al,64       ; Angle >= 180 degrees?
            pushf
            test al,32       ; Angle 90-179 or 270-359 degrees?
            je .2
            xor al,31        ; Invert bits (reduces table)
    .2:
            and ax,31        ; Only 90 degrees in table
            mov bx,sin_table
            cs xlat          ; Get fraction
            popf
            je .1            ; Jump if angle less than 180
            neg ax           ; Else negate result
    .1:
            mov bx,[bp+py]   ; Get Y position
            ret
```

Getting the direction vector starts by putting zero into SI (the distance counter), saving the X position of the player onto DX, and then getting the sine for the current angle given by AX. The sine value goes onto CX.

Then it adds 32 to the current angle (90 degrees) and calls again the sine function to get a cosine. The result is put onto AX, while BX is loaded with the Y position of the player.

So the registers are like this on return:

- DX = X position (4.12).

- BX = Y position (4.12).

- CX = X vector (sine of the angle).

- AX = Y vector (cosine of the angle).

The *get_sin* subroutine works with a table of 90 degrees, so it has to be slightly complex in order to cover the 360 degrees. The first **test** instruction checks if the angle is in the range of 180 to 359 degrees (values 64-127), so it negates the result on exit.

The second **test** instruction checks if the angle is in the range of 90-179 or 270-359 degrees, so it reverses the angle slightly deviated. For example, sin(1) equals 0.0174 and sin(179) also equals 0.174. But in this case, taking in account our circle of 360 degrees translated to 128 values: sin(1) is equal to sin(62)—it should have been 63, but we are O.K. with this.

```
            ;
            ; Read maze
            ;
read_maze:
            inc si          ; Count distance to wall
            add dx,cx       ; Move X
            add bx,ax       ; Move Y
            push bx
            push cx
            call get_pos
            mov bl,[bx]     ; Read maze byte
            shl bl,1        ; Carry = 1 = wall, Zero = Wall 0 / 1
            pop cx
            pop bx
            ret             ; Return
```

The *read_maze* subroutine increments the SI register, counting the distance to the wall, adds the x,y vector to the current x,y position, and then reads the maze under the new position.

By shifting the maze byte by one bit position to the left, the Carry Flag is set if there is a wall, and the Zero Flag is clear or set depending on if it is a wall or enemy.

```
            ;
            ; Convert coordinates to position
            ;
get_pos:
            mov bl,dh       ; X-coordinate
            mov cl,0x04     ; Divide by 4096
            shr bl,cl
            and bh,0xf0     ; Y-coordinate / 4096 * 16
            or bl,bh        ; Translate to maze array
            mov bh,maze>>8
            ret
```

Getting the maze contents of the current position is done by means of two divisions by 4096; both X and Y are divided and used as indexes into the maze.

$$maze\_pos = (y\ /\ 4096 * 16) + (x\ /\ 4096)$$

5.10 Utility subroutines.

A few other utility subroutines are required by cubicDoom: fill a column, generate a random number, and wait for a clock tick.

```
        ;
        ; Fill a screen column
        ;
fill_column:
        mov ah,al      ; Duplicate pixel value
.1:     stosw          ; Draw 2 pixels
        stosw          ; Draw 2 pixels
        stosw          ; Draw 2 pixels
        stosw          ; Draw 2 pixels
        add di,0x0138  ; Go to next row
        loop .1        ; Repeat until fully drawn
        ret            ; Return
```

As we said before, each ray-casting column is 8 pixels wide. In order to save code space, the pixel value on AL is copied into AH, and then **stosw** is used four times to draw the eight pixels.

Then it adds 312 to the DI register to go to the next row, and repeats the loop until the full column height is drawn.

```
        ;
        ; Generate a pseudo-random number (from bootRogue)
        ;
random:
        mov al,251
        mul byte [bp+rnd]
        add al,83
        mov [bp+rnd],al
        mov ah,0
        div dl
        mov bl,ah
        mov bh,0
        ret
```

The random function comes from bootRogue with the same values for the generator, except it doesn't extend sign on result. It is used only two times by the game.

```
        ;
        ; Wait a frame (18.2 hz)
        ;
wait_frame:
.1:
        mov ah,0x00      ; Get ticks
        int 0x1a         ; Call BIOS time service
        cmp dx,[bp+oldtim]   ; Same as old time?
        je .1                ; Yes, wait.
        mov [bp+oldtim],dx
        ret
```

The *wait_frame* subroutine is called two times to wait for one tick of the clock. It does this by waiting for a change of the tick value calling the BIOS service 0x1a function 0x00. This synchronizes the game on fast machines.

5.11 Boot signature.

Finally, the game is completed with a boot signature, but not before including the sine table for the first 90 degrees of the circle. The table gives an 8-bit fractional result; this is enough precision for the game.

Remember the remaining degrees of the sine table are calculated by means of extra code (see section 5.9).

```
        ;
        ; Sine table (0.8 format)
        ;
        ; 32 bytes are 90 degrees.
        ;
sin_table:
        db 0x00,0x09,0x16,0x24,0x31,0x3e,0x47,0x53
        db 0x60,0x6c,0x78,0x80,0x8b,0x96,0xa1,0xab
        db 0xb5,0xbb,0xc4,0xcc,0xd4,0xdb,0xe0,0xe6
        db 0xec,0xf1,0xf5,0xf7,0xfa,0xfd,0xff,0xff

    %ifdef com_file
```

```
%else
    times 510-($-$$) db 0x4f
    db 0x55,0xaa              ; Make it a bootable sector
%endif
```

Chapter 6

bootOS

One thing that happens when you have several boot sector programs is that you are changing floppy disks continuously, or (on your emulator) selecting different boot images each time.

Just after sending the "Programming Boot Sector Games" book to press, I wondered: Could there be made a launcher program? This rapidly evolved as an operating system.

```
bootOS
$dir
fbird
pillman
invaders
basic
textmode
counter
data.bin
bootslide
atomchess
tetranglix
snake
mine
rogue
bricks
cubicdoom
sokoban
$_
```

6.1 Memory management.

In the good old times when personal computers were young and their processors were 8-bit, a young Gary Kildall created in 1974 the Control Program/Monitor for Intel 8080 microprocessors (and later 8085 and Zilog Z80), later renamed to Control Program for Microcomputers, although the initials remained the same as CP/M.

Already there were a lot of books on operating systems, but Kildall made something so cleverly simple: no memory management. The only fixed location was 0x0000 as a cold restart, 0x0005 for calling CP/M (with the C register containing the service code requested), and all programs started at 0x0100, the very same address that would be used for COM files and MS-DOS!

The programs furthermore could read address 0x0006 as a 16-bit word to determine the maximum RAM memory available. And that's all![18]

Digital Research, Inc., as Kildall's company was called, went to sell 250,000 licenses of CP/M by September, 1981. And unfortunately it went down very quickly with the creation of IBM PC and MS-DOS.

Of course, any CP/M program with bugs would crash the system, probably also deleting some files in the process.[19]

So I followed the same "good behavior" approach for bootOS. I decided from the start that every program would be loaded into address 0x07c00 as a normal boot sector (avoiding relocation). The area 0x07a00 - 0x07bff would contain bootOS, the area 0x07800 - 0x79ff would contain a directory buffer, and the Stack Pointer would be set up at 0x07800 (remember it grows toward lower addresses).

---

[18] If you are curious about more details of the CP/M memory map, here is more information: http://www.gaby.de/cpm/manuals/archive/cpm22htm/ch5.htm

[19] And by Murphy's law, if some file is deleted, it will be an important one!

0x00000-0x003ff	Interruption table
0x00400-0x077ff	BIOS or otherwise
	Area for SP growth
0x07800	Stack Pointer start
0x07800-0x079ff	Directory buffer
0x07a00-0x07bff	bootOS code
0x07c00-0x07dff	User's programs
0x07e00-0x9ffff	Free for programs

Table 2-1. Memory map for bootOS.

6.2 File system.

The file system is the way that files are saved into the storage media (a floppy disk or its emulated version for the purposes of this program).

The first **IBM PC** came out with 5 ¼" 180 **KB** floppy drives. The floppy disks physically look like this:

Figure 2-2. 5 ¼" floppy disk. The top left label was provided by the manufacturer, and the top right label was added by the user. There is also a square hole that can be covered for write-protection. The center hole is for the motor, the long hole is for the head, and the small hole is for the index synchronization (start of track).

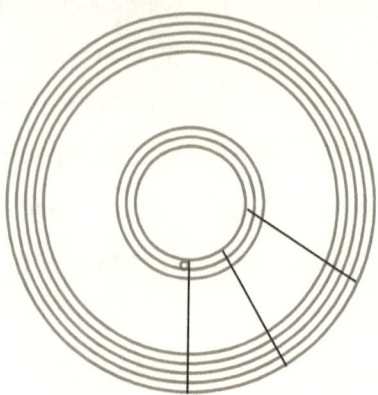

Figure 2-3. Track disposition inside the floppy disk. The outer track is the zero track where the floppy disk head starts. The inner track is the track number 39. Each track is divided in sectors marked by the index hole (small circle). Not all tracks and sectors shown, nor at scale.

The head of the floppy drive moves over the disk starting from the outer tracks and going into the center. It synchronizes the start of a track using the index hole on the disk (detected by means of a photosensor). There are 40 tracks on a 180 KB floppy drive, and each track contains 9 sectors of 512 bytes.

Then came the 360 KB floppy drive. It looked the same physically but the read/write head works also from below, effectively using *both* sides for data (you also needed 360 KB floppy disks because the 180 KB ones only had magnetic coating on one side). Also there are 40 tracks on a 360 KB floppy disk, but there are *two sides*.

The bootOS program doesn't care about the size of the disk as it only uses the first sector and side 0 of each track, plus the second sector of track 0, side 0.

The first sector of the disk is devoted to bootOS so the PC can boot it, and the second sector is dedicated to the directory of files. This is an example directory sector.

0x0000	fbird	Track 1
0x0020	pillman	Track 2
0x0040	invaders	Track 3
...	...	...
0x01e0	*zero filled*	Track 32

Table 2-4. Example of directory sector. Each entry contains the ASCII name of each file, and the remaining is filled with zero bytes. An empty entry is all filled with zero bytes.

And this is the real representation inside the directory sector. The offsets shown are the offset inside the sector, and it should be added to 0x7800 for the final memory address after reading it:

```
0000:  66 62 69 72  64 00 00 00   fbird...
0008:  00 00 00 00  00 00 00 00   ........
0010:  70 69 6c 6c  6d 61 6e 00   pillman.
0018:  00 00 00 00  00 00 00 00   ........
0020:  69 6e 76 61  64 65 72 73   invaders
0028:  00 00 00 00  00 00 00 00   ........
0030:  62 61 73 69  63 00 00 00   basic...
0038:  00 00 00 00  00 00 00 00   ........
0040:  74 65 78 74  6d 6f 64 65   textmode
0048:  00 00 00 00  00 00 00 00   ........
0050:  63 6f 75 6e  74 65 72 00   counter.
0058:  00 00 00 00  00 00 00 00   ........
0060:  64 61 74 61  2e 62 69 6e   data.bin
0068:  00 00 00 00  00 00 00 00   ........
0070:  62 6f 6f 74  73 6c 69 64   bootslid
0078:  65 00 00 00  00 00 00 00   e.......
0080:  61 74 6f 6d  63 68 65 73   atomches
0088:  73 00 00 00  00 00 00 00   s.......
0090:  74 65 74 72  61 6e 67 6c   tetrangl
0098:  69 78 00 00  00 00 00 00   ix......
00a0:  73 6e 61 6b  65 00 00 00   snake...
00a8:  00 00 00 00  00 00 00 00   ........
00b0:  6d 69 6e 65  00 00 00 00   mine....
00b8:  00 00 00 00  00 00 00 00   ........
00c0:  72 6f 67 75  65 00 00 00   rogue...
00c8:  00 00 00 00  00 00 00 00   ........
00d0:  62 72 69 63  6b 73 00 00   bricks..
00d8:  00 00 00 00  00 00 00 00   ........
00e0:  63 75 62 69  63 64 6f 6f   cubicdoo
00e8:  6d 00 00 00  00 00 00 00   m.......
```

```
00f0:  00 00 00 00   00 00 00 00    ........
00f8:  00 00 00 00   00 00 00 00    ........
0100:  00 00 00 00   00 00 00 00    ........
0108:  00 00 00 00   00 00 00 00    ........
0110:  00 00 00 00   00 00 00 00    ........
0118:  00 00 00 00   00 00 00 00    ........
0120:  00 00 00 00   00 00 00 00    ........
0128:  00 00 00 00   00 00 00 00    ........
0130:  00 00 00 00   00 00 00 00    ........
0138:  00 00 00 00   00 00 00 00    ........
0140:  00 00 00 00   00 00 00 00    ........
0148:  00 00 00 00   00 00 00 00    ........
0150:  00 00 00 00   00 00 00 00    ........
0158:  00 00 00 00   00 00 00 00    ........
0160:  00 00 00 00   00 00 00 00    ........
0168:  00 00 00 00   00 00 00 00    ........
0170:  00 00 00 00   00 00 00 00    ........
0178:  00 00 00 00   00 00 00 00    ........
0180:  00 00 00 00   00 00 00 00    ........
0188:  00 00 00 00   00 00 00 00    ........
0190:  00 00 00 00   00 00 00 00    ........
0198:  00 00 00 00   00 00 00 00    ........
01a0:  00 00 00 00   00 00 00 00    ........
01a8:  00 00 00 00   00 00 00 00    ........
01b0:  00 00 00 00   00 00 00 00    ........
01b8:  00 00 00 00   00 00 00 00    ........
01c0:  00 00 00 00   00 00 00 00    ........
01c8:  00 00 00 00   00 00 00 00    ........
01d0:  00 00 00 00   00 00 00 00    ........
01d8:  00 00 00 00   00 00 00 00    ........
01e0:  00 00 00 00   00 00 00 00    ........
01e8:  00 00 00 00   00 00 00 00    ........
01f0:  00 00 00 00   00 00 00 00    ........
01f8:  00 00 00 00   00 00 00 00    ........
```

Notice the ASCII bytes for file names that are represented on the third column (see Appendix B).

Getting the location of a file is a matter of getting the position of the filename inside the directory. The first file in the directory is saved at track 1, the second file in the directory is saved at track 2, and successively the last file in the directory is saved at track 32.

6.3 System services.

User programs shouldn't need to know the internal design of the operating system, but must use a few "known" services to load files, save files, read keyboard, output to screen, and return to operating system.

bootOS assigns the following interruption vectors for these services:

- **int 0x20.** Restart. It returns to the bootOS prompt, and it should be the final call in any bootOS user program.

- **int 0x21.** Input key. It waits for a key to be pressed, and returns the ASCII code inside the AL register.

- **int 0x22.** Output character. It outputs to screen the ASCII character code contained inside the AL register.

- **int 0x23.** Load file. It loads a file from the disk. DS:BX should point to the ASCII file name finished with a zero byte. ES:DI should point to the 512 byte buffer for reading the file. It will return the Carry flag set if the file isn't found, or else the Carry flag will be clear.

- **int 0x24.** Save file. It saves a file onto the disk. DS:BX should point to the ASCII file name finished with a zero byte. ES:DI should point to the 512 byte buffer containing the data for the file. It will return the Carry flag set if the file couldn't be created.

- **int 0x25.** Delete file. It deletes a file from the disk. DS:BX should point to the ASCII file name finished with a zero byte. It will return the Carry flag set if the file couldn't be found.

Given everything is integrated in bootOS, it's a monolithic operating system.

6.4 bootOS cold boot.

Now we can follow the bootOS source code.

```
        ;
        ; bootOS, an operating system in 512 bytes
        ;
        ; by Oscar Toledo G.
        ; http://nanochess.org/
        ;
        ; Creation date: Jul/21/2019. 6pm 10pm
        ;

        cpu 8086

stack:  equ 0x7700      ; Stack pointer (grows to lower addresses)
line:   equ 0x7780      ; Buffer for line input
sector: equ 0x7800      ; Sector data for directory
osbase: equ 0x7a00      ; bootOS location
boot:   equ 0x7c00      ; Boot sector location

entry_size:     equ 16  ; Directory entry size
sector_size:    equ 512 ; Sector size
max_entries:    equ sector_size/entry_size
```

The first step is to define a few labels with important constants used by bootOS. The *stack* label contains the base address for the Stack Pointer register. The *line* label points to the address for the line buffer where commands entered by the user are saved. The *sector* label points to the address where the directory sector will be preserved. And finally *osbase* contains the base address of bootOS, while *boot* contains the base address from where it is booted.

The label *sector_size* indicates the size of one sector of the floppy disk, while *entry_size* indicates the length in bytes of each entry into the directory, and finally *max_entries* is equivalent to the number of entries fitting in one disk sector.

```
        ;
        ; Cold start of bootOS
        ;
        ; Notice it is loaded at 0x7c00 (boot) and needs to
        ; relocate itself to 0x7a00 (osbase). The instructions
        ; between 'start' and 'ver_command' shouldn't depend
        ; on the assembly location (osbase) because these
        ; are running at boot location (boot).
```

```
        ;
        org osbase
start:
        xor ax,ax        ; Set all segments to zero
        mov ds,ax
        mov es,ax
        mov ss,ax
        mov sp,stack     ; Set stack to guarantee data safety

        cld              ; Clear D flag.
        mov si,boot      ; Copy bootOS boot sector...
        mov di,osbase    ; ...into osbase
        mov cx,sector_size
        rep movsb
```

The cold start of bootOS is when it boots for the first time. It sets all segment registers to zero in order to point to the first 64K of RAM memory, and initializes the Stack Pointer base address. It then clears the D flag (so **movsb** increments the SI and DI registers), and copies bootOS into its base address (from 0x7c00 to 0x7a00).

```
        mov si,int_0x20 ; SI now points to int_0x20
        mov di,0x0020*4 ; Address of service for int 0x20
        mov cl,6
.load_vec:
        movsw            ; Copy IP address
        stosw            ; Copy CS address
        loop .load_vec
```

Then it sets up the interruption vectors with the addresses of internal bootOS services. Notice how two 16-bit words are loaded for each vector. One is copied using **movsw** from the table *int_0x20*, and the other is written to using **stosw since** it copies the zero value still contained inside the register AX.

```
        ;
        ; 'ver' command
        ;
ver_command:
        mov si,intro
        call output_string
        int int_restart ; Restart bootOS
```

It shows the bootOS welcome message that says "bootOS". This same code is used for the "ver" command. Finally it uses the restart vector to enter itself into the operating system.

6.5 Warm start.

The warm start is when an operating system is already loaded into memory, and the user only needs to go back to the command prompt.

```
        ;
        ; Warm start of bootOS
        ;
restart:
        cld             ; Clear D flag.
        push cs         ; Reinit all segment registers
        push cs
        push cs
        pop ds
        pop es
        pop ss
        mov sp,stack    ; Restart stack

        mov al,'$'      ; Command prompt
        call input_line ; Input line

        cmp byte [si],0x00  ; Empty line?
        je restart          ; Yes, get another line
```

It doesn't know the status of the segment registers, nor the Direction flag, so it resets all these to known values (again to zero for the first 64K of RAM memory). Then it also has to reset the Stack Pointer register.

Once ready it shows the $ command prompt, and waits for a line from keyboard using *input_line*. If the line is empty, then it repeats the loop.

```
        mov di,commands ; Point to commands list

        ; Notice that filenames starting with same characters
        ; won't be recognized as such (so file dirab cannot be
        ; executed).
os11:
        mov al,[di]      ; Read length of command in chars
        inc di
        and ax,0x00ff    ; Is it zero?
        je os12          ; Yes, jump
        xchg ax,cx
        push si          ; Save current position
        rep cmpsb        ; Compare statement
        jne os14         ; Equal? No, jump
        call word [di]   ; Call command process
        jmp restart      ; Go to expect another command

os14:   add di,cx        ; Advance the list pointer
        inc di           ; Avoid the address
        inc di
        pop si
        jmp os11         ; Compare another statement
```

If the line is non-empty, then it sets up the DI register to point to the list of commands allowed by bootOS.

The comparison starts by reading the length of the command in characters. If it is zero then the list of commands has been fully explored and it exits jumping to *os12*, or else it copies the length into register CX.

Then it does a comparison of the full string using **rep cmpsb** (comparison of the strings pointed by registers SI and DI, with length contained in the CX register).

If the comparison is successful then the Z flag will be set, and DI will be pointing to the address of the command. It is called using **call word [di]** that reads a 16-bit word pointed by DI and jumps to that address (of course, it automatically saves the return address into the stack).

117

If the comparison wasn't successful then DI will be at some point in the middle of the string, and we advance it using **add di,cx** with the effect that the remaining count contained in the register CX will cause it to point to the 16-bit address of the command. That is avoided by using a pair of instructions **inc di**. Then it repeats the loop until the whole command list has been compared.

```
os12:    mov bx,si         ; Input pointer
         mov di,boot       ; Location to read data
         int int_load_file      ; Load file
         jc os7            ; Jump if error
         jmp bx


         ;
         ; File not found error
         ;
os7:
         mov si,error_message
         call output_string
         int int_restart ; Go to expect another command
```

If the command isn't implemented, then it copies the contents of register SI (still pointing to the line buffer) into BX (the parameter for Load File service), loads the register DI with the address of the boot sector, and calls the Load File service. If the Carry flag is set, then it means an error happened and it jumps to *os7* to show an error message, or else it jumps to the newly-loaded program using **jmp bx** (BX contains the start of the loaded program).

6.6 The 'del' command.

The command "del" is implemented by bootOS to delete files contained on the disk

```
         ;
         ; >> COMMAND <<
         ; del filename
         ;
del_command:
```

```
os22:
        mov bx,si          ; Copy SI (buffer pointer) to BX
        lodsb
        cmp al,0x20        ; Avoid spaces
        je os22
        int int_delete_file
        jc os7
        ret
```

On input, the SI register contains the pointer to the line buffer just after the "del" letters. It needs to avoid the spaces following the command, so it uses **lodsb** to read the following character, and repeats the loop if a space character is found. Notice each time it copies the new value of SI onto BX, so when it finds a non-space character, then BX contains the location of it (remember **lodsb** increments the SI register, so SI ends pointing ahead).

It calls the Delete File service of bootOS, and if the Carry flag is set, then it jumps to *os7* to show an error message.

The **ret** instruction returns the flow control to show the command prompt again.

6.7 The 'dir' command.

One vital command of bootOS is the 'dir' command. It shows the directory of files contained on the floppy disk, and it is the only way the user can see what files can be executed.[20]

_____

[20] The other possible way would be to write the filenames on the disk label yourself.

```
        ;
        ; 'dir' command
        ;
dir_command:
        call read_dir           ; Read the directory
        mov di,bx
os18:
        cmp byte [di],0         ; Empty entry?
        je os17                 ; Yes, jump
        mov si,di               ; Point to data
        call output_string      ; Show name
os17:   call next_entry
        jne os18                ; No, jump
        ret                     ; Return
```

It calls *read_dir* to read the directory into the memory address allocated for that purpose. The call also sets the BX register with the memory address that is copied onto the DI register.

If the byte is zero then the entry is free and it isn't displayed, or else it copies the address from DI onto the SI register and calls *output_string* to show the filename.

Now it calls *next_entry* to advance the directory pointer to the next entry, and also does a comparison with the end of directory.

6.8 Calculating the file name length.

At some point, bootOS needs to know the length in characters of a file name, in order to copy the right quantity of bytes.

```
        ;
        ; Get filename length and prepare for directory lookup
        ; Entry:
        ;   si = pointer to string
        ; Output:
        ;   si = unaffected
        ;   di = pointer to start of directory
        ;   cx = length of filename including zero terminator
        ;
filename_length:
        push si
        xor cx,cx       ; cx = 0
```

120

```
.loop:
        lodsb           ; Read character.
        inc cx          ; Count character.
        cmp al,0        ; Is it zero (end character)?
        jne .loop       ; No, jump.

        pop si
        mov di,sector   ; Point to start of directory.
        ret
```

Notice the comments are documenting the purpose of the subroutine (or function) *filename_length*.

It should be called with the SI register pointing to the address containing the file name. This pointer can be provided by the internal line buffer or externally from user programs calling bootOS.

The register CX will contain the size in bytes and it is initialized to zero. It loads each byte of the string and increases CX accordingly, and also repeats the loop until a zero byte is found (**cmp al,0** does the comparison).

Finally, it restores the original SI value and sets up DI to point to the start of the directory sector.

6.9 Loading a file.

The main core of bootOS is the Load File service. It calls several functions in sequence: Find File, Read File, and return an error flag.

```
        ;
        ; >> SERVICE <<
        ; Load file
        ;
        ; Entry:
        ;   ds:bx = Pointer to filename ended with zero byte.
        ;   es:di = Destination.
        ; Output:
        ;   Carry flag = Set = not found, clear = successful.
        ;
load_file:
        push di         ; Save destination
        push es
```

```
        call find_file   ; Find the file (sanitizes ES)
        mov ah,0x02      ; Read sector
shared_file:
        pop es
        pop bx           ; Restore destination on BX
        jc ret_cf        ; Jump if error
        call disk        ; Do operation with disk
                         ; Carry guaranteed to be clear.
ret_cf:
        mov bp,sp
        rcl byte [bp+4],1    ; Insert Carry flag in Flags (uses SS)
        iret
```

First, it saves the contents of DI and ES, both making the target address for the file being read. Then it calls the *find_file* function, and if the file isn't found it jumps to *ret_cf* with the Carry flag set, or else it reads the disk (notice **mov ah,0x02** to set up the BIOS Disk Read service), and the *disk* function will also clear the Carry flag.

Section 1.4 described how the **int** instruction works, and now it's time to use the positions of the stack frame to be able to return an error code using the Carry flag, since the following **iret** instruction will restore the Flags register from the content on stack (erasing the current Carry flag state unless it does something).

There aren't any 8086/8088 instructions that can directly read memory using the SP register, so it copies its content onto the BP register.

Then it inserts the current Carry flag into the [BP+4] memory position using **rcl** (Rotate-Carry-Left). This instruction moves all bits one place to the left and inserts the Carry bit into the lowest bit (bit 0). It fits the position of the Carry flag exactly inside the Flags register, and after the **iret** instruction the user will be able to test the Carry flag for errors. All the other flags are meaningless.

6.10 Saving a file.

Saving a file requires exactly the same parameters as loading a file, but it writes over the floppy disk. Also it can replace an existing file, or create a new one on the directory sector.

```
            ;
            ; >> SERVICE <<
            ; Save file
            ;
            ; Entry:
            ;    ds:bx = Pointer to filename ended with zero byte.
            ;    es:di = Source.
            ; Output:
            ;    Carry flag = Set = error, clear = good.
            ;
save_file:
            push di                  ; Save origin
            push es
            push bx                  ; Save filename pointer
            int int_delete_file      ; Delete previous file (sanitizes
ES)
            pop bx                   ; Restore filename pointer
            call filename_length     ; Prepare for lookup

.find:  es cmp byte [di],0           ; Found empty directory entry?
            je .empty                ; Yes, jump and fill it.
            call next_entry
            jne .find
            jmp shared_file

.empty: push di
            rep movsb                ; Copy full name into directory
            call write_dir           ; Save directory
            pop di
            call get_location        ; Get location of file
            mov ah,0x03              ; Write sector
            jmp shared_file
```

The first step is to delete any existing file with the same name. It simplifies the work by calling the Delete File service of bootOS. Fortunately it has a "standard" convention for passing file names using DS:BX, so it doesn't need to copy data between registers. It doesn't need to check for error flag because it doesn't matter if the file doesn't exist.

Then it gets the file name length in bytes in order to be ready for the next step. Remember it sets the DI register to point to the start of the directory sector (there's no need to read it again, as the Delete File service already read the sector).

It reads the first byte of the entry, and if it is zero then it has found an empty entry inside the directory and jumps to .*empty*. Otherwise it goes to the next directory entry calling *next_entry* and repeats the loop if it hasn't finished, or else it jumps to *shared_file* to report an error.

Inside .*empty* it copies the file name onto the directory using **rep movsb**. Notice the Delete File service copied the contents of the BX registers to the SI register (the pointer to the file name), while it has been searching for empty entries using the DI registers, and already filled the CX register with the size in bytes of the file name (including the 0x00 terminator).

It writes the updated directory sector calling to *write_dir*.

Finally it gets the location of the new file with a call to *get_location* (notice the saved/restored DI register because the pointer to directory also is used for getting the position of the file on the floppy disk), and then writes the file data jumping to *shared_file* with the AH register properly loaded with 0x03 (BIOS Disk Service for Writing Disk).

6.11 Deleting a file.

The process of deleting a file is as follows: read the directory, find the file, return an error flag if it doesn't exist, otherwise fill the directory entry with zero, and write the directory to the floppy disk.

Notice it doesn't delete the file data; it only marks the directory entry as free.

```
        ;
        ; >> SERVICE <<
        ; Delete file
        ;
        ; Entry:
        ;    ds:bx = Pointer to filename ended with zero byte.
        ; Output:
        ;    Carry flag = Set = not found, clear = deleted.
        ;
delete_file:
        call find_file          ; Find file (sanitizes ES)
        jc ret_cf               ; If carry set then not found, jump.
```

```
        mov cx,entry_size
        call write_zero_dir      ; Fill whole entry with zero. Write
directory.
        jmp ret_cf
```

It's short because it uses portions of other bootOS functions.

6.12 Finding a file.

Finding a file is a central part of bootOS, as it is used for everything:
loading a file, saving a file, and deleting a file.

```
        ;
        ; Find file
        ;
        ; Entry:
        ;   ds:bx = Pointer to filename ended with zero byte.
        ; Result:
        ;   es:di = Pointer to directory entry
        ;   Carry flag = Clear if found, set if not found.
find_file:
        push bx
        call read_dir    ; Read directory (sanitizes ES)
        pop si
        call filename_length    ; Get filename length and setup DI
os6:
        push si
        push di
        push cx
        repe cmpsb       ; Compare name with entry
        pop cx
        pop di
        pop si
        je get_location ; Jump if equal.
        call next_entry
        jne os6          ; No, jump
        ret              ; Return

next_entry:
        add di,byte entry_size        ; Go to next entry.
        cmp di,sector+sector_size     ; Complete directory?
        stc                           ; Error, not found.
        ret
```

125

```
;
; Get location of file on disk
;
; Entry:
;    DI = Pointer to entry in directory.
;
; Output:
;    CH = Track number in disk.
;    CL = Sector (always 0x01).
;
; The position of a file inside the disk depends on its
; position in the directory. The first entry goes to
; track 1, the second entry to track 2 and so on.
;
get_location:
        lea ax,[di-(sector-entry_size)] ; Get entry pointer into
directory
                            ; Plus one entry (files start on track 1)
        mov cl,4            ; 2^(8-4) = entry_size
        shl ax,cl           ; Shift left and clear Carry flag
        inc ax              ; AL = Sector 1
        xchg ax,cx          ; CH = Track, CL = Sector
        ret
```

The first step is to read the directory sector from the floppy disk. This is accomplished by means of calling *read_dir*. Then it calls *filename_length* to get the file name size in characters on register CX and sets up DI to point to the start of the directory sector.

Then it compares the file name with the current entry of the directory (notice how it saves the values of the registers CX, SI, and DI for further usage). If the comparison is successful it jumps to *get_location* where it gets the location of the file on the floppy disk.

If the comparison is unsuccessful, it goes to the next entry of directory by calling *next_entry* and if it hasn't finished searching the directory then it loops back for another comparison, or else it returns with the Carry flag set to signal that the file wasn't found.

The *next_entry* function moves the DI register pointer to the next entry into the directory by means of an **add** instruction, and then does a comparison with the end of the directory. In any case it sets the Carry flag for further error indication (it is reset for a successful operation result by other paths of code execution).

Finally the *get_location* function is in charge of calculating the track, side and sector location for the file. Instead of having a FAT (File Allocation Table) on the disk, it is simplified so the position of the file name in the directory also gives the position of the file over the floppy disk.

So the first directory entry will be on track 1, the second at track 2, and continues successively.

For doing this calculation it uses the instruction **lea** (Load Effective Address). It loads the calculated operand address into a register, but instead it is used for doing arithmetic. The register DI contains the pointer to the directory entry, so the **lea** instruction subtracts the *sector* label minus the size of a directory entry. This means that AX will contain a value of *entry_size* if the register DI was pointing at the start of the directory.

Then it multiplies AX by 16 by means of shifting it to the left by 4 bits. This is a trick because to get the track number it should have divided the AX value by 16 (the value of *entry_size*) to get the track number into AL, but instead we need the track number in the AH register for the BIOS Disk Routines, so by multiplying it by 16, the track number gets into AH.

So if DI is pointing to the first directory entry, then AX will get filled with 0x10 (16 decimal). It multiplies AX by 16, so it becomes 0x0100 (256 decimal). So AH contains 0x01 and AL contains 0x00.

Finally it does **inc ax** to put AL to 0x01 using one single byte instruction (setting a request for sector 1), and moves it to the CX register using **xchg ax,cx** for BIOS Disk Routines usage.

6.13 Formatting a disk.

In the good old times, every disk needed to be formatted before being used. This was because the disks were manufactured only with the coating and got packed immediately for sale. The formatting made sure the disk controller filled the disk with meaningful data so it could be read and written to.

The formatting is the process of going through all the tracks of the floppy disk, writing all the sectors and internal headers. In fact this is achieved by a special **BIOS Disk Routines** service that is outside of the scope of this book.

The sectors were filled with a constant byte; it was 0xe5 in the CP/M times, and it was 0xf6 in the **MS-DOS** times.

So each time you read a sector completely filled with one of these values, it meant (most of the time) the sector was unused.

But later companies started selling pre-formatted disks; this meant you wouldn't need to format the floppy disk before using it. So I expect you to use pre-formatted disks with bootOS.

```
        ;
        ; >> COMMAND <<
        ; format
        ;
format_command:
        mov di,sector    ; Fill whole sector to zero
        mov cx,sector_size
        call write_zero_dir
        mov bx,osbase    ; Copy bootOS onto first sector
        dec cx
        jmp short disk
```

The "format" command fills the whole directory sector to zero, and writes it to the disk, and then copies bootOS to the first sector of the disk (**BX** is loaded with *osbase*, and **CX** is decremented to set it up to 0x0001, meaning track 0, sector 1).

The method would be: extract the current disk, insert a new pre-formatted disk, enter the "format" command, and now you have a new bootable bootOS disk.

It's almost magic.

6.14 Disk routines.

The core of the disk routines of bootOS handles the directory access, and the global access to the disk. It doesn't check for write-protected disks, and faulty disks will cause it to stall.

```
        ;
        ; Read the directory from disk
        ;
read_dir:
        push cs          ; bootOS code segment...
        pop es           ; ...to sanitize ES register
        mov ah,0x02
        jmp short disk_dir

write_zero_dir:
        mov al,0
        rep stosb


        ;
        ; Write the directory to disk
        ;
write_dir:
        mov ah,0x03
disk_dir:
        mov bx,sector
        mov cx,0x0002
        ;
        ; Do disk operation.
        ;
        ; Input:
        ;   AH = 0x02 read disk, 0x03 write disk
        ;   ES:BX = data source/target
        ;   CH = Track number
        ;   CL = Sector number
        ;
disk:
        push ax
        push bx
        push cx
        push es
        mov al,0x01      ; AL = 1 sector
        xor dx,dx        ; DH = Drive A. DL = Head 0.
        int 0x13
        pop es
        pop cx
        pop bx
```

```
        pop ax
        jc disk        ; Retry
        ret
```

The *read_dir* function "sanitizes" the ES register. What does that mean? It means the ES register is reset to point to the first 64K of RAM where the directory sector buffer is located. Then it loads the AH register with 0x02 for the BIOS Disk Read service, and jumps to *disk_dir* (shared with the *write_dir* function).

The *write_zero_dir* is a helper function that fills a buffer with zero (provided with the DI register pointing to the target, and the CX register with the size in bytes of the target). Remember it is used by the "format" command (zeroing a whole sector) and the Delete File service (zeroing a directory entry).

The *write_dir* function assumes the ES register points to the right location, and it loads the AH register with 0x03 for the BIOS Disk Write service, then it loads BX to point to the directory sector buffer, and CX with 0x0002 for track 0, sector 2, where the directory sector is located on the floppy disk.

Finally the *disk* function calls the BIOS using **int 0x13** and retries the operation continuously until it has success. It can repeat at first because the motor of the floppy drive is turning on, but it also can stall because it tries to write and the floppy disk is protected, or the floppy disk is unreadable because of a physical error.

Notice how DX is reset to zero, because DH signals the floppy drive (0x00 means the first floppy drive, most known as A: for MS-DOS users), and DL signals the side of the disk (always 0x00; this means side 1 is unused). Finally AL is loaded with one, so the BIOS only reads or writes one sector.

6.15 Reading a line from the keyboard.

To interact with the user, bootOS requires a routine able to read a line from the keyboard. It expects it to be finished by means of the user pressing Enter.

```
            ;
            ; Input line from keyboard
            ; Entry:
            ;   al = prompt character
            ; Output:
            ;   buffer 'line' contains line, finished with CR
            ;   SI points to 'line'.
            ;
input_line:
            int int_output_char ; Output prompt character
            mov si,line    ; Setup SI and DI to start of line buffer
            mov di,si      ; Target for writing line
os1:        cmp al,0x08    ; Backspace?
            jne os2
            dec di         ; Undo the backspace write
            dec di         ; Erase a character
os2:        int int_input_key  ; Read keyboard
            cmp al,0x0d    ; CR pressed?
            jne os10
            mov al,0x00
os10:       stosb          ; Save key in buffer
            jne os1        ; No, wait another key
            ret            ; Yes, return
```

The prompt character comes as an ASCII code inside the AL register, and it's displayed immediately by using an **int** instruction calling bootOS service.

Then it sets up the SI and DI registers to point to the *line* buffer.

As a trick to save space, it does a comparison with the Backspace character and moves back the buffer pointer by two positions (because the **stosb** instruction saved the Backspace code 0x08 into the buffer and incremented the DI register).

It reads the keyboard by using an **int** instruction calling the right bootOS service (it also displays the key pressed).

131

If the Enter key is pressed, its code 0x0d is converted to 0x00 (the preferred way of ending strings inside bootOS) and it will exit the routine after saving it with **stosb** (because the Z Flag is set), or else it will loop back to wait for another character from the keyboard.

6.16 Input/output core.

The bootOS program continuously requests input from the keyboard and outputs results to screen, and also provides these services to user programs.

```
            ;
            ; Read a key into al
            ; Also outputs it to screen
            ;
input_key:
        mov ah,0x00
        int 0x16
            ;
            ; Screen output of character contained in al
            ; Expands 0x0d (CR) into 0x0a 0x0d (LF CR)
            ;
output_char:
        cmp al,0x0d
        jne os3
        mov al,0x0a
        int int_output_char
        mov al,0x0d
os3:
        mov ah,0x0e      ; Output character to TTY
        mov bx,0x0007    ; Gray. Required for graphic modes
        int 0x10         ; BIOS int 0x10 = Video
        iret
```

The *input_key* service reads the keyboard by calling the BIOS services, and then immediately displays it, falling through to *output_char*.

The *output_char* service displays the ASCII code contained in the AL register, and if the code is 0x0d (Enter key), it also generates a 0x0a code to change the cursor line. The original ASCII specification lists 0x0d as CR (Carriage Return), and 0x0a as LF (Line Feed).

Finally it displays the letter on screen, and since it doesn't know the display mode it needs to set up BX to point to text page 0 (BH) and color 7 (BL) for graphic modes.

```
;
; Output string
;
; Entry:
;   SI = address
;
; Implementation:
;   It assumes that SI never points to a zero length string.
;
output_string:
        lodsb                   ; Read character
        int int_output_char     ; Output to screen
        cmp al,0x00             ; Is it 0x00 (terminator)?
        jne output_string       ; No, the loop continues
        mov al,0x0d
        int int_output_char
        ret
```

Finally, the *output_string* function outputs a string to the screen (it is used by the bootOS welcome message, the error message, and the disk directory display).

It loads each letter using the instruction **lodsb**, calls the Output Char service of bootOS, and if it hasn't reached the terminator (0x00 byte) it will loop displaying the string.

Once it finds the terminator, it sends a 0x0d character to the screen to force a change of line.

6.17 Creating files.

Without a way to create bootOS files, it is not very useful. So I've included the "enter" command, that allows to copy files and to enter new files using hexadecimal codes. You can also think of it as a very primitive debugger or monitor program that only allows to enter hexadecimal codes.

```
            ;
            ; 'enter' command
            ;
enter_command:
            mov di,boot             ; Point to boot sector
os23:       push di
            mov al,'h'              ; Prompt character
            call input_line         ; Input line
            pop di
            cmp byte [si],0         ; Empty line?
            je os20                 ; Yes, jump
os19:       call xdigit             ; Get a hexadecimal digit
            jnc os23
            mov cl,4
            shl al,cl
            xchg ax,cx
            call xdigit             ; Get a hexadecimal digit
            or al,cl
            stosb                   ; Write one byte
            jmp os19                ; Repeat loop to complete line
os20:
            mov al,'*'              ; Prompt character
            call input_line         ; Input line with filename
            push si
            pop bx
            mov di,boot             ; Point to data entered
            int int_save_file       ; Save new file
            ret


            ;
            ; Convert ASCII letter to hexadecimal digit
            ;
xdigit:
            lodsb
            cmp al,0x00             ; Zero character marks end of line
            je os15
            sub al,0x30             ; Avoid spaces (anything below ASCII
0x30)
            jc xdigit
            cmp al,0x0a
            jc os15
            sub al,0x07
            and al,0x0f
            stc
os15:
            ret
```

Once the "enter" command is entered, it shows a "h" prompt and waits for a line from the keyboard.

The user then should enter hexadecimal bytes over multiple lines until finishing with an empty line.

The routine sets up the DI register to point to the boot sector at 0x07c00. Notice that if the user immediately enters an empty line, then *the current content of memory at 0x07c00 can be saved as a new file*, effectively copying it to a new file.

If the line isn't empty and there is a valid hexadecimal digit, it builds a byte from two hexadecimal digits (0-9, A-F or a-f) using two calls to *xdigit* and then it saves the byte using **stosb**. It repeats the operation until the full input line is processed and then jumps to wait for another line.

After an empty line is entered, an asterisk prompt is shown and the user can enter a file name, again calling *input_line*, then it copies the SI value (pointing to the line buffer) to BX (file name), sets up DI to point again to the boot sector, and calls the bootOS service for saving the file to the floppy disk.

Here is an example of creating a file (the arrow means the Enter key):

```
$enter↵
hbb 17 7c 8a 07 84 c0 74 0c 53 b4 0e bb 0f 00 cd↵
h10 5b 43 eb ee cd 20 48 65 6c 6c 6f 2c 20 77 6f↵
h72 6c 64 0d 0a 00↵
h↵
*hello↵
$dir↵
hello
$hello↵
Hello, world
$_
```

6.18 Tables and messages.

The tables and messages used by bootOS are very few. For example the welcome message and the error message account for 12 bytes:

```
        ;
        ; Our amazing presentation line
        ;
intro:
        db "bootOS",0

error_message:
        db "Oops",0
```

The command list is somewhat longer. Each command is started by a length byte followed by the command, and then by the address of the function. The list is finished with a zero byte.

```
        ;
        ; Commands supported by bootOS
        ;
commands:
        db 3,"dir"
        dw dir_command
        db 6,"format"
        dw format_command
        db 5,"enter"
        dw enter_command
        db 3,"del"
        dw del_command
        db 3,"ver"
        dw ver_command
        db 0
```

Finally the service list is present so bootOS can fill the interruption vector table for **int 0x20-0x25**.

```
int_restart:            equ 0x20
int_input_key:          equ 0x21
int_output_char:        equ 0x22
int_load_file:          equ 0x23
int_save_file:          equ 0x24
int_delete_file:        equ 0x25
```

```
int_0x20:
        dw restart         ; int 0x20
        dw input_key       ; int 0x21
        dw output_char     ; int 0x22
        dw load_file       ; int 0x23
        dw save_file       ; int 0x24
        dw delete_file     ; int 0x25
```

And the obligatory boot sector signature:

```
        times 510-($-$$) db 0x4f
        db 0x55,0xaa              ; Make it a bootable sector
```

6.19 Compatibility.

I did some small modifications to previous boot sector games to allow for exiting to the bootOS interface. You can find these changes on my Git at https://github.com/nanochess/

There is also available a prebuilt 360K disk image that you can test immediately, or even load onto a real floppy disk.

Some other boot games available on the Internet collected by Eric Davisson (twitter @XlogicX) were adapted or included in the boot image, like a Tetris and a Snake game.

bootOS has been tested over a modern PC XT machine based on NuXT motherboard courtesy of @bison42 (Twitter account).

Chapter 7

Optimization tricks

Throughout my books I've shown several games and talked about optimization tricks. But of course, these can pass "unnoticed" because of the description of the games' inner workings.

So this appendix recollects most of these optimization tips.

7.1 Keeping segment registers static.

In many of my games, I've set up the segment registers value to a constant number just after video setup.

There are two common setups: graphic mode and text mode.

The text mode initialization code goes like this:

```
; Setup text mode 80 columns by 25 rows.
mov ax,0x0002
int 0x10
mov ax,0xb800
mov ds,ax
mov es,ax
; Now you can write to the screen at 0x0000-0x0f9f.
; There is guaranteed free space at 0x0fa0-0x3fff.
```

Notice it guarantees around 12 kilobytes of free space to save variables. Why 12 kilobytes if the whole segment is 32K? (at segment 0xc000 starts the video BIOS of EGA/VGA cards). It happens because the old PC machines in 1981 had only 16K of video memory for CGA video cards, the first ones that allowed color text mode.

The graphics mode initialization goes like this:

```
; Setup graphics mode 320x200x256 colors.
mov ax,0x0013
int 0x10
mov ax,0xa000
mov ds,ax
mov es,ax
; Now you can write to screen at 0x0000-0xf9ff.
; There is guaranteed free space at 0xfa00-0xffff.
```

The 320x200x256 colors video mode has a 64K RAM segment starting at 0xa0000.

Notice that changing a segment register requires 5 bytes (**mov** immediate and **mov** to segment register) and 7 bytes if two segments registers are changed. ES isn't required sometimes if you aren't going to use **stosb**, **scasb**, **cmpsb**, or the word versions of these instructions. There's probably also **push/pop** for saving previous values of segment registers.

So the mere fact of fixing your segment registers to video memory saves you around 5 to 11 bytes on your code (supposing you change the segment registers to access the screen).

If you are using tables inside your code, you can always add the CS modifier before the instruction (per *nasm* syntax) to access your tables (meaning it will access the code segment). Of course, you should calculate how many segment prefixes you'll be adding to see if you're saving bytes (remember each segment prefix uses one extra byte).

```
mov ax,[bx+table]    ; If you use the DS register

cs mov ax,[bx+table] ; If you take advantage of the CS register
```

Also at initialization, you can consider reusing a zero on the AL register with your own code, so the loading of AX can be **mov ah,0xa0** or **mov ah,0xb8**. It saves yet another byte.

7.2 Saving on memory variable access.

The addressing used by all the instructions of the 8086/8088 processors is 16-bit. For direct access to memory, only AX can be loaded/saved using 3-byte instructions. All other registers require 4-byte instructions.

Also almost all arithmetic operations require 4-byte instructions.

There is another option: using the stack. The stack has the advantage of being located in its own segment, and this segment is controlled by the SS register (Stack Segment).

For a boot sector game, we can be sure the BIOS located the stack pointer and stack segment at a place with enough space for 256 bytes. This means we don't need to set up the SP register or the SS register.

Also, we can prepare the variable space by using **push**. This instruction uses only one byte, instead of the 3 bytes required to write AX to a memory address.

If the space is going to be uninitialized, we can use **sub sp,imm** where *imm* means the number of bytes required on the stack.

Then the final value of SP (Stack Pointer) must be copied onto BP (Base Pointer). Why is this? Because if we use **call/ret** then this would move the SP position, so we keep it fixed by accessing BP, and also there are no addressing modes that can use SP.

The variables then can be loaded or written to by using the idiom **[bp+imm]**, where *imm* is the offset location of the required variable. This addressing mode has the advantage that the processor chooses by itself the SS register to load or write the data, so we avoid an extra prefix byte.

Also you can use **push/pop** to access the top variable (the one at bp address or bp+0), saving a further byte because the addressing mode cannot optimize access to **[bp]** as a two-byte instruction, because that addressing code is already used by direct address access. You can see it easily in this example with both the BX and BP registers; while the BX register has the two-byte direct access, the BP register doesn't have it (watch the second byte of each instruction):

```
8B 07           MOV AX,[BX]
8B 47 02        MOV AX,[BX+2]
8B 87 34 12     MOV AX,[BX+0x1234]

8B 06 AA 55     MOV AX,[0x55aa]
8B 46 02        MOV AX,[BP+2]
8B 86 34 12     MOV AX,[BP+0x1234]
```

This trick has been extensively used on CubicDoom, bootRogue, and Bricks.

7.3 Moving variables onto registers.

The registers SI, DI, and BP can be used to keep variables or addresses, saving a great deal of bytes on a program.

There are several ways of using registers:

• For keeping global variables.

• Being reused for keeping local variables (for example, inside a loop)

• For keeping addresses to optimize repeated calls.

For example, the bricks game uses the register SI to keep the previous screen position of the ball, and the register DI to keep the current position of the paddle. Accessing a register uses only two bytes on the vast majority of 8086/8088 instructions, while memory accesses tend to use three to four bytes. Plus the initialization can be done using a single **mov** instruction, reducing the code from 6 bytes to 3 bytes (16-bit value) or 2 bytes (8-bit value).

You can see an example of local variables on registers being used on CubicDoom in the column drawing loop.

The optimization of repeated calls is used in bootRogue, where the register SI is loaded with the address of the random number generator function, and then called several times using **call si**. This adds 3 bytes overhead to initialize SI, and then saves one byte in each **call** instruction.

7.4 Operations by copying AL.

Sometimes a result kept in register AL is copied to another register to do an operation over the value. A common idiom could be like this one:

```
mov ah,al     ; 2 bytes. Copy AL onto AH
and ah,0x07   ; 3 bytes. Logical AND of AH with 0x07.
...           ; ... Code continues ...
```

Instead it can be optimized like this:

```
mov ah,0x07   ; 2 bytes. Load mask onto AH
and ah,al     ; 2 bytes. Logical AND of AH with AL's value.
```

It saves one byte. Same can be applied to all other 8-bit registers (BH, BL, CH, CL, DH, and DL), because the immediate arithmetic operations with registers outside of AL take 3 bytes.

This trick was used on Toledo Atomchess for reducing the byte count.

7.5 CX going to zero.

The instruction **loop** always exits with the register CX equal to zero. You can use this to your advantage to avoid doing immediate operations with zero and instead using the value of CX, CH, or CL registers.

The same applies after the instructions **rep/movsb**, **rep/stosb**, or its word variants.

7.6 Comparisons with multiple values.

For a boot sector game, doing a comparison with values spread over a wide range cannot be optimized with a table. So instead we need to resort to common **cmp** instructions.

However, you can optimize these. The first step is to make a table of the values you are going to compare.

The most simple table could be like this:

```
cmp al,0x01
je do_work_1
cmp al,0x03
je do_work_3
cmp al,0x05
je do_work_5
cmp al,0x09
je do_work_9
jmp do_nothing      ; Code might never reach here.
```

One question we need to ask is whether only valid values will ever appear, in the above example, after comparison of 1, 3 and 5, then it's obvious it must be 9, *or* there's open exit.

For optimization we'll assume there are no other values apart from 1, 3, 5, and 9.

```
cmp al,0x03      ; Comparison with 3
jb do_work_1     ; If less than then it's 1
je do_work_3     ; If equal then it's 3
cmp al,0x09      ; Comparison with 9
jb do_work_5     ; If less than then it's 5
jmp do_work_9
```

From Toledo Atomchess comes this example about looking for values 1 to 6.

```
dec ax           ; 0 becomes 255
cmp al,0x06      ; Now anything starting on 6 is invalid.
jnb .1           ; Jump if not in range
```

A more complex example comes from bootRogue, with values over a wide range of 8-bit values.

```
GR_VERT:         EQU 0xba      ; Vertical line graphic
GR_TOP_RIGHT:    EQU 0xbb      ; Top right graphic
GR_BOT_RIGHT:    EQU 0xbc      ; Bottom right graphic
GR_BOT_LEFT:     EQU 0xc8      ; Bottom left graphic
GR_TOP_LEFT:     EQU 0xc9      ; Top left graphic
GR_HORIZ:        EQU 0xcd      ; Horizontal line graphic
```

```
GR_TUNNEL:      EQU 0xb1        ; Tunnel graphic (shaded block)
GR_DOOR:        EQU 0xce        ; Door graphic (crosshair graphic)
GR_FLOOR:       EQU 0xfa        ; Floor graphic (middle point)

GR_HERO:        EQU 0x01        ; Hero graphic (smiling face)

GR_LADDER:      EQU 0xf0        ; Ladder graphic
GR_TRAP:        EQU 0x04        ; Trap graphic (diamond)
GR_FOOD:        EQU 0x05        ; Food graphic (clover)
GR_ARMOR:       EQU 0x08        ; Armor graphic (square with hole)
GR_YENDOR:      EQU 0x0c        ; Amulet of Yendor graphic
GR_GOLD:        EQU 0x0f        ; Gold graphic (asterisk)
GR_WEAPON:      EQU 0x18        ; Weapon graphic (up arrow)
```

It's guaranteed that all these 17 values can appear over the screen, plus zero for empty spaces, and the range 0x41-0x5a for monsters. It has a small optimization: The hero cannot move over another hero, so it's a comparison that doesn't have to be made. Even with so many cases, the comparison code manages to be small enough:

```
        mov al,[di+bx]          ; Read the target contents

        cmp al,GR_LADDER        ; GR_LADDER?
        je ladder_found

        ; 15 things to look for (plus zero and monsters)
        ; Anything > GR_TUNNEL and < GR_DOOR is a wall
        cmp al,GR_DOOR          ; GR_DOOR?
        jnc .4
        cmp al,GR_TUNNEL        ; GR_TUNNEL?
        ja move_cancel
.4:
        ; 9 things to look for (plus zero and monsters)
        cmp al,GR_TRAP          ; GR_TRAP?
        jb move_cancel          ; < it must be blank, cancel move.
        ; Move player
        lea di,[di+bx]          ; Do move.
        mov bh,0x06             ; Random range
        je trap_found           ; = Yes, went over trap
        ; 8 things to look for (plus monsters)
        cmp al,GR_TUNNEL        ; GR_TUNNEL+GR_DOOR+GR_FLOOR ?
        jnc move_cancel         ; Yes, jump.
        cmp al,GR_WEAPON        ; GR_WEAPON?
        ja battle               ; > it's a monster, go to battle
        ; Only items at this part of code, so clean floor
```

```
mov byte [di],GR_FLOOR  ; Delete item from floor
je weapon_found         ; = weapon found
; 4 things to look for
cmp al,GR_ARMOR         ; GR_ARMOR?
je armor_found          ; Yes, increase armor
jb food_found           ; < it's GR_FOOD, increase hp
; 2 things to look for
cmp al,GR_GOLD          ; GR_GOLD?
je move_cancel          ; Yes, simply take it.
; At this point 'al' can only be GR_YENDOR
; Amulet of Yendor found!
```

If you have difficulties following this source code, try replacing the *GR_** label names with the real values.

7.7 Incomplete constants.

Sometimes we don't need the full constant to do an operation. For example, when filling the text screen to zero to clear it:

```
xor di,di      ; Setup DI pointer to start of text page
mov ch,0x08    ; Erase 4096 bytes or more (CL value undef.)
xor ax,ax
stosw
```

This will work just fine for erasing the text screen, and it's okay if it erases a little more. This can also work for memory buffers if you're careful. And you don't need to use the full 3-byte instruction **mov cx,n**.

7.8 Reuse register values.

Once a program is complete, it's easy to deduct the values that registers have at each point by following the program sequence.

Labels certainly don't introduce too much complexity, as we can consider multiple sets of values while following the code.

By experience, I can follow code visually and have in my memory the values of registers as code advances.

But for novices, I would recommend to annotate your instructions on square paper, and put the registers' values to the right.

Notice a register could enter a loop with a value, and *be modified inside the loop*, so take in account each loop label in the assembly listing to see if a register indeed will be preserving the value you intend to reuse.

Sometimes the internal program logic can be rearranged to get access to a constant in a register. For example:

```
mov ax,0x0101
push ax          ; level + yendor
push ax          ; weapon + armor
mov ah,0
push ax          ; exp
mov al,16
push ax          ; n_exp
push ax          ; hp
push ax          ; max_hp
mov al,0x02      ; ah already is zero.
int 0x10
```

Now the optimized version saving two bytes:

```
xor ax,ax
push ax          ; exp
inc ax
push ax          ; yendor (low byte) + level (high byte)
push ax          ; weapon (low byte) + armor (high byte)
mov al,16
push ax          ; n_exp
push ax          ; hp
push ax          ; max_hp
mov al,0x02      ; ah already is zero
int 0x10
```

Both of these examples come from a prototype bootRogue version. Only half of this code ended up being used in the released version, but it still gives you a good idea of how to optimize your code by reorganizing variable location, or even code logic.

7.9 Fall-through subroutines.

Some bytes can be saved at the end of subroutines. The basic thing is that a subroutine is called with **call** and should return with **ret**.

For example, here is a simplified example taken from the Follow the Lights game on chapter 2:

```
show_buttons:
    ; data 1
    call show_button
    ; data 2
    call show_button
    ; data 3
    call show_button
    ; data 4
    call show_button
    ret

show_button:
    ret
```

The last call to *show_button* can be rewritten like this:

```
show_buttons:
    ; data 1
    call show_button
    ; data 2
    call show_button
    ; data 3
    call show_button
    ; data 4
    jmp show_button

show_button:
    ret
```

This saves one byte, because jumping onto *show_button* causes the **ret** to return to the original routine calling *show_buttons*. Remember to think of **call** and **ret** like stacking dishes, so the **jmp** instruction avoids stacking another dish, and when reaching the **ret** instruction it returns correctly.

But if the code is together in memory, the code can be rewritten like this:

```
show_buttons:
    ; data 1
    call show_button
    ; data 2
    call show_button
    ; data 3
    call show_button
    ; data 4
    ; fall-through
show_button:
    ret
```

Because the **jmp** instruction only changes the Instruction Pointer (IP register), it can be safely removed if jumping to the following instruction, as was the case.

7.10 Secondary effects.

Some instructions have secondary effects that are important to know in order to get more optimization:

- **cbw**, it will always initialize AH to zero if AL is less than 0x80. So it can save one byte instead of using **mov ah,0x00**.

- **cwd**, it will always initialize DX to zero if AX is less than 0x8000. So it can save two bytes instead of using **xor dx,dx** or three bytes if using **mov dx,0**.

- **loop**, after the loop the register CX will be always zero.

7.11 Keep the conditional jumps short.

Be sure to give a look at the generated *lst* file, because you'll be able to see when a conditional jump is extended automatically by the assembler with a **jmp** instruction if the target address is beyond the range of -128 bytes to +127 bytes.

The typical solution is to move portions of the code nearer to the conditional jump, or move the conditional jump close to its target, or remove it altogether by a redesign.

149

7.12 One-byte instructions.

There are many one-byte instructions that can be useful instead of using equivalents of two or three bytes.

This is the list of instructions.

```
06          PUSH ES
07          POP ES
0e          PUSH CS
16          PUSH SS
17          POP SS
1e          PUSH DS
1f          POP DS
26          ES:
27          DAA
2e          CS:
2f          DAS
36          SS:
37          AAA
3e          DS:
3f          AAS
40          INC AX   ; Instead of INC AL
41          INC CX   ; Instead of INC CL
42          INC DX   ; Instead of INC DL
43          INC BX   ; Instead of INC BL
44          INC SP
45          INC BP
46          INC SI
47          INC DI
48          DEC AX   ; Instead of DEC AL
49          DEC CX   ; Instead of DEC CL
4a          DEC DX   ; Instead of DEC DL
4b          DEC BX   ; Instead of DEC BL
4c          DEC SP
4d          DEC BP
4e          DEC SI
4f          DEC DI
50          PUSH AX
51          PUSH CX
52          PUSH DX
53          PUSH BX
54          PUSH SP
55          PUSH BP
56          PUSH SI
57          PUSH DI
58          POP AX
59          POP CX
```

5a	POP DX
5b	POP BX
5c	POP SP
5d	POP BP
5e	POP SI
5f	POP DI
90	NOP
91	XCHG AX,CX
92	XCHG AX,DX
93	XCHG AX,BX
94	XCHG AX,SP
95	XCHG AX,BP
96	XCHG AX,SI
97	XCHG AX,DI
98	CBW
99	CWD
9b	WAIT
9c	PUSHF
9d	POPF
9e	SAHF
9f	LAHF
a4	MOVSB
a5	MOVSW
a6	CMPSB
a7	CMPSW
aa	STOSB
ab	STOSW
ac	LODSB
ad	LODSW
ae	SCASB
af	SCASW
c3	RET
cb	RETF
cc	INT 3
ce	INTO
cf	IRET
d7	XLAT
ec	IN AL,DX
ed	IN AX,DX
ee	OUT DX,AL
ef	OUT DX,AX
f0	LOCK
f2	REPNZ
f3	REPZ
f4	HLT
f5	CMC
f8	CLC
f9	STC

```
fa              CLI
fb              STI
fc              STD
fd              CLD
```

There are some suggested optimizations for **inc/dec** instructions, but these only work with the following caveats:

- Be sure your register doesn't change from 0xff to 0x00 (**inc**), or 0x00 to 0xff (**dec**) due to the carry over.

- The flags won't be the same because these will come from the full 16-bit register instead of the 8-bit one.

7.13 Replacing jumps with a single byte.

Replacing jumps with a single byte is possible when the following conditions are met:

- The **jmp** instruction jumps over a one-byte instruction, or the **jmp** instruction jumps over a two-byte instruction.

- If it's a one-byte instruction, an 8-bit register is free. If it's a two-byte instruction, a 16-bit register is free.

The replacement instruction for the **jmp** is a single byte in the range 0xb8-0xbf for jumping over two-byte instructions, or 0xb0-0xb7 for jumping over one-byte instructions.

```
MOV AL,0x55         ;b0 55
MOV CL,0x55         ;b1 55
MOV DL,0x55         ;b2 55
MOV BL,0x55         ;b3 55
MOV AH,0x55         ;b4 55
MOV CH,0x55         ;b5 55
MOV DH,0x55         ;b6 55
MOV BH,0x55         ;b7 55

MOV AX,0x5566       ;b8 66 55
MOV CX,0x5566       ;b9 66 55
MOV DX,0x5566       ;ba 66 55
MOV BX,0x5566       ;bb 66 55
MOV SP,0x5566       ;bc 66 55
```

```
        MOV BP,0x5566        ;bd 66 55
        MOV SI,0x5566        ;be 66 55
        MOV DI,0x5566        ;bf 66 55
```

The selected byte is chosen per the unused register available. So the register effectively is loaded with trash and serves as a one-byte jump.

See an example of this optimization where one byte is saved:

```
          cmp al,5                        cmp al,5
          jb less                         jb less
          mov ah,4                        mov ah,4
          jmp continue                    db 0xb9    ; MOV CX=2 bytes jump
less:                          less:
          mov ah,7                        mov ah,7   ; 2 bytes instruction
continue:
```

153

Appendix A

Small BIOS reference

The BIOS provides several services and several subfunctions for each one. We don't intend to cover everything but we will cover the most essential ones. If you are interested in diving more into INT services, you can always search INT 0x10, INT 0x13 or INT 0x16 in any Internet search engine.

A.1 INT 0x10 Video services.

INT 0x10 covers video services. It preserves all registers, except BP in some buggy BIOS.

A.1.1 Set video mode (AH = 0x00)

Sets the current video mode:

AL = Video mode.

The recommended modes are:

- AL = 0x02 = Text 80x25 color. Data segment 0xb800.
- AL = 0x12 = VGA 640x480x16 colors. Data segment 0xa000.
- AL = 0x13 = VGA 320x200x256 colors. Data segment 0xa000.

A.1.2 Display letter in terminal (AH = 0x0e)

Display letter contained in AL to terminal. BH must contain the page number (use 0x00 always) and BL the text color (use 0x0f, only used in graphic modes).

It handles special codes:

- 0x0d = Returns cursor to start of line.
- 0x0a = Advances cursor to next line.
- 0x08 = Cursor back one character.
- 0x07 = Bell.

A.2 INT 0x13 Disk services.

INT 0x13 covers disk services. The registers will probably be trashed.

A.2.1 Read sector (AH = 0x02)

Reads a sector from the floppy disk or hard drive. The floppy drive can be trapped by emulation of floppy disk from CD-ROM.

- AL = Number of sectors to read.
- CH = Low byte of cylinder number.
- CL = Sector number (bits 5-0) and high two bits of cylinder (bits 7-6).
- DH = Head number.
- DL = Drive number (0x00 disk drive A, 0x01 disk drive B, 0x80 hard disk 1, 0x81 hard disk 2).
- ES:BX = Data buffer.

On return, if the Carry flag is set, it indicates there was an error (it may be the floppy disk wasn't ready or there is no floppy disk). You can retry the operation.

This service is useful for reading bigger programs from the boot sector.

A.2.2 Write sector (AH = 0x03)

Writes a sector in floppy disk or hard drive.

- AL = Number of sectors to write.
- CH = Low byte of cylinder number.
- CL = Sector number (bits 5-0) and high two bits of cylinder (bits 7-6).
- DH = Head number.
- DL = Drive number (0x00 disk drive A, 0x01 disk drive B, 0x80 hard disk 1, 0x81 hard disk 2).
- ES:BX = Data buffer.

On return, if the Carry flag is set, it indicates there was an error (it may be the floppy disk wasn't ready, was write protected, or there is no floppy disk). You can retry the operation. Guess what's the most-used service by old virus programs.

A.3 INT 0x16 Keyboard services.

It provides keyboard services. All registers are preserved except for AX and Flags.

A.3.1 AH = 0x00 Get key.

If no key is available then it waits for a key to be pressed. It will discard Shift, Alt, Caps and Ctrl keys.

It will return AH = BIOS scan code, AL = ASCII character.

A.3.2 AH = 0x01 Check for available key.

If no key is available then it returns the Z flag set, or else it returns the Z flag clear.

If a key is available, it will return the key available without emptying the buffer. AH = BIOS scan code, AL = ASCII character.

A.3.3 AH = 0x02 Get keyboard flags.

It returns the register AL filled with the following flags:

- bit 0 : 1 = Right shift key pressed.
- bit 1 : 1 = Left shift key pressed.
- bit 2 : 1 = Ctrl key pressed.
- bit 3 : 1 = Alt key pressed.
- bit 4 : 1 = Scroll Lock down.
- bit 5 : 1 = Num Lock down.
- bit 6 : 1 = Caps Lock down.
- bit 7 : 1 = Insert on.

A.4 INT 0x19 Bootstrap loader.

This interrupt causes the BIOS to reboot (it reloads the first boot sector that it can find).

A.5 INT 0x1A Time services.

It provides time services.

A.5.1 AH = 0x00 Get system time.

It returns the number of clock ticks since midnight into CX:DX.

The number of clock ticks per second is approximately 18.2, so every second the value will increase roughly by 18.

A.6 INT 0x20 Terminate program.

This interrupt causes the operating system to terminate the current program. This only works with MS-DOS, DR-DOS, FreeDOS or the command-line of Windows 7 and previous versions. It's also implemented in bootOS.

Appendix B

ASCII charset

The ASCII charset available by default on booting up a common PC.

```
00-      18- ↑    30- 0    48- H    60- `    78- x    90- É    A8- ¿    C0- └    D8- ╪    F0- ≡
01- ☺    19- ↓    31- 1    49- I    61- a    79- y    91- æ    A9- ⌐    C1- ┴    D9- ┘    F1- ±
02- ☻    1A- →    32- 2    4A- J    62- b    7A- z    92- Æ    AA- ¬    C2- ┬    DA- ┌    F2- ≥
03- ♥    1B- ←    33- 3    4B- K    63- c    7B- {    93- ô    AB- ½    C3- ├    DB- █    F3- ≤
04- ♦    1C- ∟    34- 4    4C- L    64- d    7C- |    94- ö    AC- ¼    C4- ─    DC- ▄    F4- ⌠
05- ♠    1D- ↔    35- 5    4D- M    65- e    7D- }    95- ò    AD- ¡    C5- ┼    DD- ▌    F5- ⌡
06- ♣    1E- ▲    36- 6    4E- N    66- f    7E- ~    96- û    AE- «    C6- ╞    DE- ▐    F6- ÷
07- •    1F- ▼    37- 7    4F- O    67- g    7F- ⌂    97- ù    AF- »    C7- ╟    DF- ▀    F7- ≈
08- ◘    20-      38- 8    50- P    68- h    80- Ç    98- ÿ    B0- ░    C8- ╚    E0- α    F8- °
09- ○    21- !    39- 9    51- Q    69- i    81- ü    99- Ö    B1- ▒    C9- ╔    E1- ß    F9- ·
0A- ◙    22- "    3A- :    52- R    6A- j    82- é    9A- Ü    B2- ▓    CA- ╩    E2- Γ    FA- ·
0B- ♂    23- #    3B- ;    53- S    6B- k    83- â    9B- ¢    B3- │    CB- ╦    E3- π    FB- √
0C- ♀    24- $    3C- <    54- T    6C- l    84- ä    9C- £    B4- ┤    CC- ╠    E4- Σ    FC- ⁿ
0D- ♪    25- %    3D- =    55- U    6D- m    85- à    9D- ¥    B5- ╡    CD- ═    E5- σ    FD- ²
0E- ♫    26- &    3E- >    56- V    6E- n    86- å    9E- ₧    B6- ╢    CE- ╬    E6- µ    FE- ■
0F- ☼    27- '    3F- ?    57- W    6F- o    87- ç    9F- ƒ    B7- ╖    CF- ╧    E7- τ    FF-
10- ►    28- (    40- @    58- X    70- p    88- ê    A0- á    B8- ╕    D0- ╨    E8- Φ
11- ◄    29- )    41- A    59- Y    71- q    89- ë    A1- í    B9- ╣    D1- ╤    E9- Θ
12- ↕    2A- *    42- B    5A- Z    72- r    8A- è    A2- ó    BA- ║    D2- ╥    EA- Ω
13- ‼    2B- +    43- C    5B- [    73- s    8B- ï    A3- ú    BB- ╗    D3- ╙    EB- δ
14- ¶    2C- ,    44- D    5C- \    74- t    8C- î    A4- ñ    BC- ╝    D4- ╘    EC- ∞
15- §    2D- -    45- E    5D- ]    75- u    8D- ì    A5- Ñ    BD- ╜    D5- ╒    ED- φ
16- ▬    2E- .    46- F    5E- ^    76- v    8E- Ä    A6- ª    BE- ╛    D6- ╓    EE- ε
17- ↨    2F- /    47- G    5F- _    77- w    8F- Å    A7- º    BF- ┐    D7- ╫    EF- ∩
```

The ASCII charset is comprised by the symbols 0x20-0x7f. The remaining are known as PC-850 charset. Don't trust the characters in the range 0x80-0xff when running under DOS or Windows command-line, because these can change with the codepage for the default language. Typically the characters almost always available are the bottom set (0x00-0x1f), the single line bars (0xbe-0xc6, 0xcd and 0xd4), and the filler blocks (0xdb-0xdf).

This chart has been generated by booting this program under VirtualBox and doing a screenshot:

```
        ;
        ; Create an ASCII chart
        ; by Oscar Toledo G.
        ; Creation date: Jun/27/2019.
        ;

        cpu 8086

        org 0x7c00      ; Start for boot sector

        mov ax,0x0002   ; Text mode 80x25
        int 0x10        ; Set video mode

        mov ax,0xb800   ; Screen segment
        mov ds,ax       ; Load for using it
        mov es,ax

        xor di,di       ; DI = 0x0000
        mov cx,0x07d0   ; CX = 2000 characters
        mov ax,0xf020   ; AX = Black on white
        rep stosw       ; Fill the screen

        mov di,0x00a4   ; Point to row 1, column 2
        mov al,0x00     ; AL = Character 0x00
a1:
        push di         ; Save current address
        push ax         ; Save current letter
        mov cl,4        ; Take high nibble
        shr al,cl
        add al,0x30     ; Convert to ASCII
        cmp al,0x3a     ; Higher than 9?
        jb a3           ; No, jump
        add al,0x07     ; Add 7 to make it a letter
a3:     stosb           ; Put on screen
        inc di          ; Avoid attribute

        pop ax
        push ax
        and al,0x0f     ; Take lower nibble
        add al,0x30     ; Convert to ASCII
        cmp al,0x3a     ; Higher than 9?
        jb a4           ; No, jump
        add al,0x07     ; Add 7 to make it a letter
a4:     stosb           ; Put on screen
        inc di          ; Avoid attribute
```

160

```
        mov al,0x2d    ; Hyphen
        stosb          ; Put on screen
        inc di         ; Avoid attribute

        inc di         ; Jump one letter
        inc di
        pop ax
        stosb          ; Put current letter
        pop di         ; Restore address
        inc al         ; Next letter
        jz a2          ; Jump if zero (ending)

        add di,0x00a0 ; Go to next line
        cmp di,0x0fa0 ; Reached end of screen?
        jb a1          ; No, jump.
        sub di,0x0f00-14  ; Go back 24 lines
                       ; and move 7 columns to right.
        jmp a1         ; Repeat cycle.

a2:     jmp $          ; Completed.

        times 510-($-$$) db 0x4f   ; Fill boot sector

        db 0x55,0xaa   ; Make it bootable
```

Appendix C

8088 instruction set

This is the full 8088 processor instruction set. Instead of including an abbreviated opcode list with R/M fields, I preferred to show the whole instruction set without some repeated opcodes. This allows you to see the bytes used for each instruction in order to optimize your code, and also to inspire yourself to reorganize your code using the possible variations for addressing and registers.

The list has been generated by an automated tool and verified with *nasm* to make sure each instruction is valid. It accounts for 12485 different instructions! I'm sure some repeated instructions are present, but the opcode is different.

This is the 8088/8086 Flags register with its bits separated:

15	14	13	12	11	10	9	8	7	6	5	4	3	2	1	0
				O	D	I	T	S	Z		A		P		C

O means Overflow: it happens when the result of an operation exceeds the signed capacity of an 8-bit or 16-bit register. D is the Direction flag: it's used for the string operations (MOVS and related). I is the Interruption flag: it's used for low-level hardware. T is the Trap flag: it's enabled when a trap is taken. S is the Sign flag: it takes a copy of the highest bit of the operation. Z is the Zero flag: it is set when the result is zero. A is the Auxiliary Carry: it is set when half of the result sets Carry (not useful because it isn't accessible directly). P is the Parity flag: it is set when the number of bits set to 1 in the result are even. C is the Carry flag: it is set when the result exceeds the capacity of the register.

The other information needed for developing are the flags affected by each instruction:

- SAHF stores the AH register into bits 7-0 of Flags register, while LAHF loads the Flags register bits 7-0 into the AH register.

- ADD, SUB, ADC, SBC, AND, OR, XOR, CMP, TEST, ROL, ROR, RCL, RCR, SHL, SHR, SAR, NEG, MUL, DIV, IMUL, IDIV, CMPS, SCAS, DAA, DAS, AAA, AAS, AAM and AAD. These affect the O, S, Z, A, P and C flags.

- INC, DEC. These affect the O, S, Z, A and P flags, but not the C flag.

- CLC, sets C flag to 0, SEC sets C flag to 1, CMC complements the C flag.

- MOV/LEA/LDS/LES instructions don't affect the flags.

C.1 Instruction set ordered by mnemonic.

```
AAA .............................;37
AAD .............................;d5 0a
AAM .............................;d4 0a
AAS .............................;3f
ADC AH,0x88 .....................;80 d4 88
ADC AH,AH .......................;10 e4
ADC AH,AL .......................;10 c4
ADC AH,BH .......................;10 fc
ADC AH,BL .......................;10 dc
ADC AH,CH .......................;10 ec
ADC AH,CL .......................;10 cc
ADC AH,DH .......................;10 f4
ADC AH,DL .......................;10 d4
ADC AH,[0x5566] .................;12 26 66 55
ADC AH,[BP+0x5566] ..............;12 a6 66 55
ADC AH,[BP+0x55] ................;12 66 55
ADC AH,[BP+DI+0x5566] ...........;12 a3 66 55
ADC AH,[BP+DI+0x55] .............;12 63 55
ADC AH,[BP+DI] ..................;12 23
ADC AH,[BP+SI+0x5566] ...........;12 a2 66 55
ADC AH,[BP+SI+0x55] .............;12 62 55
ADC AH,[BP+SI] ..................;12 22
ADC AH,[BX+0x5566] ..............;12 a7 66 55
ADC AH,[BX+0x55] ................;12 67 55
ADC AH,[BX+DI+0x5566] ...........;12 a1 66 55
ADC AH,[BX+DI+0x55] .............;12 61 55
ADC AH,[BX+DI] ..................;12 21
ADC AH,[BX+SI+0x5566] ...........;12 a0 66 55
ADC AH,[BX+SI+0x55] .............;12 60 55
ADC AH,[BX+SI] ..................;12 20
ADC AH,[BX] .....................;12 27
ADC AH,[DI+0x5566] ..............;12 a5 66 55
ADC AH,[DI+0x55] ................;12 65 55
ADC AH,[DI] .....................;12 25
ADC AH,[SI+0x5566] ..............;12 a4 66 55
ADC AH,[SI+0x55] ................;12 64 55
ADC AH,[SI] .....................;12 24
ADC AL,0x55 .....................;14 55
ADC AL,0x88 .....................;80 d0 88
ADC AL,AH .......................;10 e0
ADC AL,AL .......................;10 c0
ADC AL,BH .......................;10 f8
ADC AL,BL .......................;10 d8
ADC AL,CH .......................;10 e8
ADC AL,CL .......................;10 c8
ADC AL,DH .......................;10 f0
ADC AL,DL .......................;10 d0
ADC AL,[0x5566] .................;12 06 66 55
ADC AL,[BP+0x5566] ..............;12 86 66 55
ADC AL,[BP+0x55] ................;12 46 55
ADC AL,[BP+DI+0x5566] ...........;12 83 66 55
ADC AL,[BP+DI+0x55] .............;12 43 55
ADC AL,[BP+DI] ..................;12 03
ADC AL,[BP+SI+0x5566] ...........;12 82 66 55
ADC AL,[BP+SI+0x55] .............;12 42 55
ADC AL,[BP+SI] ..................;12 02
ADC AL,[BX+0x5566] ..............;12 87 66 55
ADC AL,[BX+0x55] ................;12 47 55
ADC AL,[BX+DI+0x5566] ...........;12 81 66 55
ADC AL,[BX+DI+0x55] .............;12 41 55
ADC AL,[BX+DI] ..................;12 01
ADC AL,[BX+SI+0x5566] ...........;12 80 66 55
ADC AL,[BX+SI+0x55] .............;12 40 55
ADC AL,[BX+SI] ..................;12 00
ADC AL,[BX] .....................;12 07
ADC AL,[DI+0x5566] ..............;12 85 66 55
ADC AL,[DI+0x55] ................;12 45 55
ADC AL,[DI] .....................;12 05
ADC AL,[SI+0x5566] ..............;12 84 66 55
ADC AL,[SI+0x55] ................;12 44 55
ADC AL,[SI] .....................;12 04
ADC AX,0x5566 ...................;15 66 55
```

```
ADC AX,0x77 ....................... ;83 d0 77
ADC AX,0x7788 ..................... ;81 d0 88 77
ADC AX,AX ......................... ;11 c0
ADC AX,BP ......................... ;11 e8
ADC AX,BX ......................... ;11 d8
ADC AX,CX ......................... ;11 c8
ADC AX,DI ......................... ;11 f8
ADC AX,DX ......................... ;11 d0
ADC AX,SI ......................... ;11 f0
ADC AX,SP ......................... ;11 e0
ADC AX,[0x5566] ................... ;13 06 66 55
ADC AX,[BP+0x5566] ................ ;13 86 66 55
ADC AX,[BP+0x55] .................. ;13 46 55
ADC AX,[BP+DI+0x5566] ............. ;13 83 66 55
ADC AX,[BP+DI+0x55] ............... ;13 43 55
ADC AX,[BP+DI] .................... ;13 03
ADC AX,[BP+SI+0x5566] ............. ;13 82 66 55
ADC AX,[BP+SI+0x55] ............... ;13 42 55
ADC AX,[BP+SI] .................... ;13 02
ADC AX,[BX+0x5566] ................ ;13 87 66 55
ADC AX,[BX+0x55] .................. ;13 47 55
ADC AX,[BX+DI+0x5566] ............. ;13 81 66 55
ADC AX,[BX+DI+0x55] ............... ;13 41 55
ADC AX,[BX+DI] .................... ;13 01
ADC AX,[BX+SI+0x5566] ............. ;13 80 66 55
ADC AX,[BX+SI+0x55] ............... ;13 40 55
ADC AX,[BX+SI] .................... ;13 00
ADC AX,[BX] ....................... ;13 07
ADC AX,[DI+0x5566] ................ ;13 85 66 55
ADC AX,[DI+0x55] .................. ;13 45 55
ADC AX,[DI] ....................... ;13 05
ADC AX,[SI+0x5566] ................ ;13 84 66 55
ADC AX,[SI+0x55] .................. ;13 44 55
ADC AX,[SI] ....................... ;13 04
ADC BH,0x88 ....................... ;80 d7 88
ADC BH,AH ......................... ;10 e7
ADC BH,AL ......................... ;10 c7
ADC BH,BH ......................... ;10 ff
ADC BH,BL ......................... ;10 df
ADC BH,CH ......................... ;10 ef
ADC BH,CL ......................... ;10 cf
ADC BH,DH ......................... ;10 f7
ADC BH,DL ......................... ;10 d7
ADC BH,[0x5566] ................... ;12 3e 66 55
ADC BH,[BP+0x5566] ................ ;12 be 66 55
ADC BH,[BP+0x55] .................. ;12 7e 55
ADC BH,[BP+DI+0x5566] ............. ;12 bb 66 55
ADC BH,[BP+DI+0x55] ............... ;12 7b 55
ADC BH,[BP+DI] .................... ;12 3b
ADC BH,[BP+SI+0x5566] ............. ;12 ba 66 55
ADC BH,[BP+SI+0x55] ............... ;12 7a 55
ADC BH,[BP+SI] .................... ;12 3a
ADC BH,[BX+0x5566] ................ ;12 bf 66 55
ADC BH,[BX+0x55] .................. ;12 7f 55
ADC BH,[BX+DI+0x5566] ............. ;12 b9 66 55
ADC BH,[BX+DI+0x55] ............... ;12 79 55
ADC BH,[BX+DI] .................... ;12 39
ADC BH,[BX+SI+0x5566] ............. ;12 b8 66 55
ADC BH,[BX+SI+0x55] ............... ;12 78 55
ADC BH,[BX+SI] .................... ;12 38
ADC BH,[BX] ....................... ;12 3f
ADC BH,[DI+0x5566] ................ ;12 bd 66 55
ADC BH,[DI+0x55] .................. ;12 7d 55
ADC BH,[DI] ....................... ;12 3d
ADC BH,[SI+0x5566] ................ ;12 bc 66 55
ADC BH,[SI+0x55] .................. ;12 7c 55
ADC BH,[SI] ....................... ;12 3c
ADC BL,0x88 ....................... ;80 d3 88
ADC BL,AH ......................... ;10 e3
ADC BL,AL ......................... ;10 c3
ADC BL,BH ......................... ;10 fb
ADC BL,BL ......................... ;10 db
ADC BL,CH ......................... ;10 eb
ADC BL,CL ......................... ;10 cb
ADC BL,DH ......................... ;10 f3
ADC BL,DL ......................... ;10 d3
ADC BL,[0x5566] ................... ;12 1e 66 55
ADC BL,[BP+0x5566] ................ ;12 9e 66 55
ADC BL,[BP+0x55] .................. ;12 5e 55
ADC BL,[BP+DI+0x5566] ............. ;12 9b 66 55
ADC BL,[BP+DI+0x55] ............... ;12 5b 55
ADC BL,[BP+DI] .................... ;12 1b
ADC BL,[BP+SI+0x5566] ............. ;12 9a 66 55
ADC BL,[BP+SI+0x55] ............... ;12 5a 55
ADC BL,[BP+SI] .................... ;12 1a
ADC BL,[BX+0x5566] ................ ;12 9f 66 55
ADC BL,[BX+0x55] .................. ;12 5f 55
ADC BL,[BX+DI+0x5566] ............. ;12 99 66 55
ADC BL,[BX+DI+0x55] ............... ;12 59 55
ADC BL,[BX+DI] .................... ;12 19
ADC BL,[BX+SI+0x5566] ............. ;12 98 66 55
ADC BL,[BX+SI+0x55] ............... ;12 58 55
ADC BL,[BX+SI] .................... ;12 18
ADC BL,[BX] ....................... ;12 1f
ADC BL,[DI+0x5566] ................ ;12 9d 66 55
ADC BL,[DI+0x55] .................. ;12 5d 55
ADC BL,[DI] ....................... ;12 1d
ADC BL,[SI+0x5566] ................ ;12 9c 66 55
ADC BL,[SI+0x55] .................. ;12 5c 55
ADC BL,[SI] ....................... ;12 1c
ADC BP,0x77 ....................... ;83 d5 77
ADC BP,0x7788 ..................... ;81 d5 88 77
ADC BP,AX ......................... ;11 c5
ADC BP,BP ......................... ;11 ed
ADC BP,BX ......................... ;11 dd
ADC BP,CX ......................... ;11 cd
ADC BP,DI ......................... ;11 fd
ADC BP,DX ......................... ;11 d5
ADC BP,SI ......................... ;11 f5
ADC BP,SP ......................... ;11 e5
ADC BP,[0x5566] ................... ;13 2e 66 55
ADC BP,[BP+0x5566] ................ ;13 ae 66 55
ADC BP,[BP+0x55] .................. ;13 6e 55
ADC BP,[BP+DI+0x5566] ............. ;13 ab 66 55
ADC BP,[BP+DI+0x55] ............... ;13 6b 55
ADC BP,[BP+DI] .................... ;13 2b
ADC BP,[BP+SI+0x5566] ............. ;13 aa 66 55
ADC BP,[BP+SI+0x55] ............... ;13 6a 55
ADC BP,[BP+SI] .................... ;13 2a
ADC BP,[BX+0x5566] ................ ;13 af 66 55
ADC BP,[BX+0x55] .................. ;13 6f 55
ADC BP,[BX+DI+0x5566] ............. ;13 a9 66 55
ADC BP,[BX+DI+0x55] ............... ;13 69 55
ADC BP,[BX+DI] .................... ;13 29
ADC BP,[BX+SI+0x5566] ............. ;13 a8 66 55
ADC BP,[BX+SI+0x55] ............... ;13 68 55
ADC BP,[BX+SI] .................... ;13 28
ADC BP,[BX] ....................... ;13 2f
ADC BP,[DI+0x5566] ................ ;13 ad 66 55
ADC BP,[DI+0x55] .................. ;13 6d 55
ADC BP,[DI] ....................... ;13 2d
ADC BP,[SI+0x5566] ................ ;13 ac 66 55
ADC BP,[SI+0x55] .................. ;13 6c 55
ADC BP,[SI] ....................... ;13 2c
ADC BX,0x77 ....................... ;83 d3 77
ADC BX,0x7788 ..................... ;81 d3 88 77
ADC BX,AX ......................... ;11 c3
ADC BX,BP ......................... ;11 eb
ADC BX,BX ......................... ;11 db
ADC BX,CX ......................... ;11 cb
ADC BX,DI ......................... ;11 fb
ADC BX,DX ......................... ;11 d3
ADC BX,SI ......................... ;11 f3
ADC BX,SP ......................... ;11 e3
ADC BX,[0x5566] ................... ;13 1e 66 55
ADC BX,[BP+0x5566] ................ ;13 9e 66 55
ADC BX,[BP+0x55] .................. ;13 5e 55
ADC BX,[BP+DI+0x5566] ............. ;13 9b 66 55
ADC BX,[BP+DI+0x55] ............... ;13 5b 55
ADC BX,[BP+DI] .................... ;13 1b
ADC BX,[BP+SI+0x5566] ............. ;13 9a 66 55
ADC BX,[BP+SI+0x55] ............... ;13 5a 55
ADC BX,[BP+SI] .................... ;13 1a
ADC BX,[BX+0x5566] ................ ;13 9f 66 55
ADC BX,[BX+0x55] .................. ;13 5f 55
ADC BX,[BX+DI+0x5566] ............. ;13 99 66 55
ADC BX,[BX+DI+0x55] ............... ;13 59 55
ADC BX,[BX+DI] .................... ;13 19
ADC BX,[BX+SI+0x5566] ............. ;13 98 66 55
ADC BX,[BX+SI+0x55] ............... ;13 58 55
ADC BX,[BX+SI] .................... ;13 18
ADC BX,[BX] ....................... ;13 1f
ADC BX,[DI+0x5566] ................ ;13 9d 66 55
ADC BX,[DI+0x55] .................. ;13 5d 55
ADC BX,[DI] ....................... ;13 1d
ADC BX,[SI+0x5566] ................ ;13 9c 66 55
ADC BX,[SI+0x55] .................. ;13 5c 55
ADC BX,[SI] ....................... ;13 1c
ADC BYTE [0x5566],0x88 ........... ;80 16 66 55 88
ADC BYTE [BP+0x5566],0x88 ........ ;80 96 66 55 88
ADC BYTE [BP+0x55],0x88 .......... ;80 56 55 88
ADC BYTE [BP+DI+0x5566],0x88 ..... ;80 93 66 55 88
ADC BYTE [BP+DI+0x55],0x88 ....... ;80 53 55 88
ADC BYTE [BP+DI],0x88 ............ ;80 13 88
ADC BYTE [BP+SI+0x5566],0x88 ..... ;80 92 66 55 88
ADC BYTE [BP+SI+0x55],0x88 ....... ;80 52 55 88
ADC BYTE [BP+SI],0x88 ............ ;80 12 88
ADC BYTE [BX+0x5566],0x88 ........ ;80 97 66 55 88
```

165

```
ADC BYTE [BX+0x55],0x88 ........ ;80 57 55 88
ADC BYTE [BX+DI+0x5566],0x88 ... ;80 91 66 55 88
ADC BYTE [BX+DI+0x55],0x88 ..... ;80 51 55 88
ADC BYTE [BX+DI],0x88 .......... ;80 11 88
ADC BYTE [BX+SI+0x5566],0x88 ... ;80 90 66 55 88
ADC BYTE [BX+SI+0x55],0x88 ..... ;80 50 55 88
ADC BYTE [BX+SI],0x88 .......... ;80 10 88
ADC BYTE [BX],0x88 ............. ;80 17 88
ADC BYTE [DI+0x5566],0x88 ...... ;80 95 66 55 88
ADC BYTE [DI+0x55],0x88 ........ ;80 55 55 88
ADC BYTE [DI],0x88 ............. ;80 15 88
ADC BYTE [SI+0x5566],0x88 ...... ;80 94 66 55 88
ADC BYTE [SI+0x55],0x88 ........ ;80 54 55 88
ADC BYTE [SI],0x88 ............. ;80 14 88
ADC CH,0x88 ................... ;80 d5 88
ADC CH,AH .................... ;10 e5
ADC CH,AL .................... ;10 c5
ADC CH,BH .................... ;10 fd
ADC CH,BL .................... ;10 dd
ADC CH,CH .................... ;10 ed
ADC CH,CL .................... ;10 cd
ADC CH,DH .................... ;10 f5
ADC CH,DL .................... ;10 d5
ADC CH,[0x5566] ............... ;12 2e 66 55
ADC CH,[BP+0x5566] ............ ;12 ae 66 55
ADC CH,[BP+0x55] .............. ;12 6e 55
ADC CH,[BP+DI+0x5566] ......... ;12 ab 66 55
ADC CH,[BP+DI+0x55] ........... ;12 6b 55
ADC CH,[BP+DI] ................ ;12 2b
ADC CH,[BP+SI+0x5566] ......... ;12 aa 66 55
ADC CH,[BP+SI+0x55] ........... ;12 6a 55
ADC CH,[BP+SI] ................ ;12 2a
ADC CH,[BX+0x5566] ............ ;12 af 66 55
ADC CH,[BX+0x55] .............. ;12 6f 55
ADC CH,[BX+DI+0x5566] ......... ;12 a9 66 55
ADC CH,[BX+DI+0x55] ........... ;12 69 55
ADC CH,[BX+DI] ................ ;12 29
ADC CH,[BX+SI+0x5566] ......... ;12 a8 66 55
ADC CH,[BX+SI+0x55] ........... ;12 68 55
ADC CH,[BX+SI] ................ ;12 28
ADC CH,[BX] ................... ;12 2f
ADC CH,[DI+0x5566] ............ ;12 ad 66 55
ADC CH,[DI+0x55] .............. ;12 6d 55
ADC CH,[DI] ................... ;12 2d
ADC CH,[SI+0x5566] ............ ;12 ac 66 55
ADC CH,[SI+0x55] .............. ;12 6c 55
ADC CH,[SI] ................... ;12 2c
ADC CL,0x88 ................... ;80 d1 88
ADC CL,AH .................... ;10 e1
ADC CL,AL .................... ;10 c1
ADC CL,BH .................... ;10 f9
ADC CL,BL .................... ;10 d9
ADC CL,CH .................... ;10 e9
ADC CL,CL .................... ;10 c9
ADC CL,DH .................... ;10 f1
ADC CL,DL .................... ;10 d1
ADC CL,[0x5566] ............... ;12 0e 66 55
ADC CL,[BP+0x5566] ............ ;12 8e 66 55
ADC CL,[BP+0x55] .............. ;12 4e 55
ADC CL,[BP+DI+0x5566] ......... ;12 8b 66 55
ADC CL,[BP+DI+0x55] ........... ;12 4b 55
ADC CL,[BP+DI] ................ ;12 0b
ADC CL,[BP+SI+0x5566] ......... ;12 8a 66 55
ADC CL,[BP+SI+0x55] ........... ;12 4a 55
ADC CL,[BP+SI] ................ ;12 0a
ADC CL,[BX+0x5566] ............ ;12 8f 66 55
ADC CL,[BX+0x55] .............. ;12 4f 55
ADC CL,[BX+DI+0x5566] ......... ;12 89 66 55
ADC CL,[BX+DI+0x55] ........... ;12 49 55
ADC CL,[BX+DI] ................ ;12 09
ADC CL,[BX+SI+0x5566] ......... ;12 88 66 55
ADC CL,[BX+SI+0x55] ........... ;12 48 55
ADC CL,[BX+SI] ................ ;12 08
ADC CL,[BX] ................... ;12 0f
ADC CL,[DI+0x5566] ............ ;12 8d 66 55
ADC CL,[DI+0x55] .............. ;12 4d 55
ADC CL,[DI] ................... ;12 0d
ADC CL,[SI+0x5566] ............ ;12 8c 66 55
ADC CL,[SI+0x55] .............. ;12 4c 55
ADC CL,[SI] ................... ;12 0c
ADC CX,0x77 ................... ;83 d1 77
ADC CX,0x7788 ................. ;81 d1 88 77
ADC CX,AX .................... ;11 c1
ADC CX,BP .................... ;11 e9
ADC CX,BX .................... ;11 d9
ADC CX,CX .................... ;11 c9
ADC CX,DI .................... ;11 f9
ADC CX,DX .................... ;11 d1
ADC CX,SI .................... ;11 f1
```

```
ADC CX,SP .................... ;11 e1
ADC CX,[0x5566] ............... ;13 0e 66 55
ADC CX,[BP+0x5566] ............ ;13 8e 66 55
ADC CX,[BP+0x55] .............. ;13 4e 55
ADC CX,[BP+DI+0x5566] ......... ;13 8b 66 55
ADC CX,[BP+DI+0x55] ........... ;13 4b 55
ADC CX,[BP+DI] ................ ;13 0b
ADC CX,[BP+SI+0x5566] ......... ;13 8a 66 55
ADC CX,[BP+SI+0x55] ........... ;13 4a 55
ADC CX,[BP+SI] ................ ;13 0a
ADC CX,[BX+0x5566] ............ ;13 8f 66 55
ADC CX,[BX+0x55] .............. ;13 4f 55
ADC CX,[BX+DI+0x5566] ......... ;13 89 66 55
ADC CX,[BX+DI+0x55] ........... ;13 49 55
ADC CX,[BX+DI] ................ ;13 09
ADC CX,[BX+SI+0x5566] ......... ;13 88 66 55
ADC CX,[BX+SI+0x55] ........... ;13 48 55
ADC CX,[BX+SI] ................ ;13 08
ADC CX,[BX] ................... ;13 0f
ADC CX,[DI+0x5566] ............ ;13 8d 66 55
ADC CX,[DI+0x55] .............. ;13 4d 55
ADC CX,[DI] ................... ;13 0d
ADC CX,[SI+0x5566] ............ ;13 8c 66 55
ADC CX,[SI+0x55] .............. ;13 4c 55
ADC CX,[SI] ................... ;13 0c
ADC DH,0x88 ................... ;80 d6 88
ADC DH,AH .................... ;10 e6
ADC DH,AL .................... ;10 c6
ADC DH,BH .................... ;10 fe
ADC DH,BL .................... ;10 de
ADC DH,CH .................... ;10 ee
ADC DH,CL .................... ;10 ce
ADC DH,DH .................... ;10 f6
ADC DH,DL .................... ;10 d6
ADC DH,[0x5566] ............... ;12 36 66 55
ADC DH,[BP+0x5566] ............ ;12 b6 66 55
ADC DH,[BP+0x55] .............. ;12 76 55
ADC DH,[BP+DI+0x5566] ......... ;12 b3 66 55
ADC DH,[BP+DI+0x55] ........... ;12 73 55
ADC DH,[BP+DI] ................ ;12 33
ADC DH,[BP+SI+0x5566] ......... ;12 b2 66 55
ADC DH,[BP+SI+0x55] ........... ;12 72 55
ADC DH,[BP+SI] ................ ;12 32
ADC DH,[BX+0x5566] ............ ;12 b7 66 55
ADC DH,[BX+0x55] .............. ;12 77 55
ADC DH,[BX+DI+0x5566] ......... ;12 b1 66 55
ADC DH,[BX+DI+0x55] ........... ;12 71 55
ADC DH,[BX+DI] ................ ;12 31
ADC DH,[BX+SI+0x5566] ......... ;12 b0 66 55
ADC DH,[BX+SI+0x55] ........... ;12 70 55
ADC DH,[BX+SI] ................ ;12 30
ADC DH,[BX] ................... ;12 37
ADC DH,[DI+0x5566] ............ ;12 b5 66 55
ADC DH,[DI+0x55] .............. ;12 75 55
ADC DH,[DI] ................... ;12 35
ADC DH,[SI+0x5566] ............ ;12 b4 66 55
ADC DH,[SI+0x55] .............. ;12 74 55
ADC DH,[SI] ................... ;12 34
ADC DI,0x77 ................... ;83 d7 77
ADC DI,0x7788 ................. ;81 d7 88 77
ADC DI,AX .................... ;11 c7
ADC DI,BP .................... ;11 ef
ADC DI,BX .................... ;11 df
ADC DI,CX .................... ;11 cf
ADC DI,DI .................... ;11 ff
ADC DI,DX .................... ;11 d7
ADC DI,SI .................... ;11 f7
ADC DI,SP .................... ;11 e7
ADC DI,[0x5566] ............... ;13 3e 66 55
ADC DI,[BP+0x5566] ............ ;13 be 66 55
ADC DI,[BP+0x55] .............. ;13 7e 55
ADC DI,[BP+DI+0x5566] ......... ;13 bb 66 55
ADC DI,[BP+DI+0x55] ........... ;13 7b 55
ADC DI,[BP+DI] ................ ;13 3b
ADC DI,[BP+SI+0x5566] ......... ;13 ba 66 55
ADC DI,[BP+SI+0x55] ........... ;13 7a 55
ADC DI,[BP+SI] ................ ;13 3a
ADC DI,[BX+0x5566] ............ ;13 bf 66 55
ADC DI,[BX+0x55] .............. ;13 7f 55
ADC DI,[BX+DI+0x5566] ......... ;13 b9 66 55
ADC DI,[BX+DI+0x55] ........... ;13 79 55
ADC DI,[BX+DI] ................ ;13 39
ADC DI,[BX+SI+0x5566] ......... ;13 b8 66 55
ADC DI,[BX+SI+0x55] ........... ;13 78 55
ADC DI,[BX+SI] ................ ;13 38
ADC DI,[BX] ................... ;13 3f
ADC DI,[DI+0x5566] ............ ;13 bd 66 55
ADC DI,[DI+0x55] .............. ;13 7d 55
ADC DI,[DI] ................... ;13 3d
```

```
ADC DI,[SI+0x5566] .............;13 bc 66 55       ADC SI,[BX+0x5566] .............;13 b7 66 55
ADC DI,[SI+0x55] ...............;13 7c 55          ADC SI,[BX+0x55] ...............;13 77 55
ADC DI,[SI] ....................;13 3c             ADC SI,[BX+DI+0x5566] ..........;13 b1 66 55
ADC DL,0x88 ....................;80 d2 88          ADC SI,[BX+DI+0x55] ............;13 71 55
ADC DL,AH ......................;10 e2             ADC SI,[BX+DI] .................;13 31
ADC DL,AL ......................;10 c2             ADC SI,[BX+SI+0x5566] ..........;13 b0 66 55
ADC DL,BH ......................;10 fa             ADC SI,[BX+SI+0x55] ............;13 70 55
ADC DL,BL ......................;10 da             ADC SI,[BX+SI] .................;13 30
ADC DL,CH ......................;10 ea             ADC SI,[BX] ....................;13 37
ADC DL,CL ......................;10 ca             ADC SI,[DI+0x5566] .............;13 b5 66 55
ADC DL,DH ......................;10 f2             ADC SI,[DI+0x55] ...............;13 75 55
ADC DL,DL ......................;10 d2             ADC SI,[DI] ....................;13 35
ADC DL,[0x5566] ................;12 16 66 55       ADC SI,[SI+0x5566] .............;13 b4 66 55
ADC DL,[BP+0x5566] .............;12 96 66 55       ADC SI,[SI+0x55] ...............;13 74 55
ADC DL,[BP+0x55] ...............;12 56 55          ADC SI,[SI] ....................;13 34
ADC DL,[BP+DI+0x5566] ..........;12 93 66 55       ADC SP,0x77 ....................;83 d4 77
ADC DL,[BP+DI+0x55] ............;12 53 55          ADC SP,0x7788 ..................;81 d4 88 77
ADC DL,[BP+DI] .................;12 13             ADC SP,AX ......................;11 c4
ADC DL,[BP+SI+0x5566] ..........;12 92 66 55       ADC SP,BP ......................;11 ec
ADC DL,[BP+SI+0x55] ............;12 52 55          ADC SP,BX ......................;11 dc
ADC DL,[BP+SI] .................;12 12             ADC SP,CX ......................;11 cc
ADC DL,[BX+0x5566] .............;12 97 66 55       ADC SP,DI ......................;11 fc
ADC DL,[BX+0x55] ...............;12 57 55          ADC SP,DX ......................;11 d4
ADC DL,[BX+DI+0x5566] ..........;12 91 66 55       ADC SP,SI ......................;11 f4
ADC DL,[BX+DI+0x55] ............;12 51 55          ADC SP,SP ......................;11 e4
ADC DL,[BX+DI] .................;12 11             ADC SP,[0x5566] ................;13 26 66 55
ADC DL,[BX+SI+0x5566] ..........;12 90 66 55       ADC SP,[BP+0x5566] .............;13 a6 66 55
ADC DL,[BX+SI+0x55] ............;12 50 55          ADC SP,[BP+0x55] ...............;13 66 55
ADC DL,[BX+SI] .................;12 10             ADC SP,[BP+DI+0x5566] ..........;13 a3 66 55
ADC DL,[BX] ....................;12 17             ADC SP,[BP+DI+0x55] ............;13 63 55
ADC DL,[DI+0x5566] .............;12 95 66 55       ADC SP,[BP+DI] .................;13 23
ADC DL,[DI+0x55] ...............;12 55 55          ADC SP,[BP+SI+0x5566] ..........;13 a2 66 55
ADC DL,[DI] ....................;12 15             ADC SP,[BP+SI+0x55] ............;13 62 55
ADC DL,[SI+0x5566] .............;12 94 66 55       ADC SP,[BP+SI] .................;13 22
ADC DL,[SI+0x55] ...............;12 54 55          ADC SP,[BX+0x5566] .............;13 a7 66 55
ADC DL,[SI] ....................;12 14             ADC SP,[BX+0x55] ...............;13 67 55
ADC DX,0x77 ....................;83 d2 77          ADC SP,[BX+DI+0x5566] ..........;13 a1 66 55
ADC DX,0x7788 ..................;81 d2 88 77       ADC SP,[BX+DI+0x55] ............;13 61 55
ADC DX,AX ......................;11 c2             ADC SP,[BX+DI] .................;13 21
ADC DX,BP ......................;11 ea             ADC SP,[BX+SI+0x5566] ..........;13 a0 66 55
ADC DX,BX ......................;11 da             ADC SP,[BX+SI+0x55] ............;13 60 55
ADC DX,CX ......................;11 ca             ADC SP,[BX+SI] .................;13 20
ADC DX,DI ......................;11 fa             ADC SP,[BX] ....................;13 27
ADC DX,DX ......................;11 d2             ADC SP,[DI+0x5566] .............;13 a5 66 55
ADC DX,SI ......................;11 f2             ADC SP,[DI+0x55] ...............;13 65 55
ADC DX,SP ......................;11 e2             ADC SP,[DI] ....................;13 25
ADC DX,[0x5566] ................;13 16 66 55       ADC SP,[SI+0x5566] .............;13 a4 66 55
ADC DX,[BP+0x5566] .............;13 96 66 55       ADC SP,[SI+0x55] ...............;13 64 55
ADC DX,[BP+0x55] ...............;13 56 55          ADC SP,[SI] ....................;13 24
ADC DX,[BP+DI+0x5566] ..........;13 93 66 55       ADC WORD [0x5566],0x77 .........;83 16 66 55 77
ADC DX,[BP+DI+0x55] ............;13 53 55          ADC WORD [0x5566],0x7788 .......;81 16 66 55 88 77
ADC DX,[BP+DI] .................;13 13             ADC WORD [BP+0x5566],0x77 ......;83 96 66 55 77
ADC DX,[BP+SI+0x5566] ..........;13 92 66 55       ADC WORD [BP+0x5566],0x7788 ....;81 96 66 55 88 77
ADC DX,[BP+SI+0x55] ............;13 52 55          ADC WORD [BP+0x55],0x77 ........;83 56 55 77
ADC DX,[BP+SI] .................;13 12             ADC WORD [BP+0x55],0x7788 ......;81 56 55 88 77
ADC DX,[BX+0x5566] .............;13 97 66 55       ADC WORD [BP+DI+0x5566],0x77 ...;83 93 66 55 77
ADC DX,[BX+0x55] ...............;13 57 55          ADC WORD [BP+DI+0x5566],0x7788 .;81 93 66 55 88 77
ADC DX,[BX+DI+0x5566] ..........;13 91 66 55       ADC WORD [BP+DI+0x55],0x77 .....;83 53 55 77
ADC DX,[BX+DI+0x55] ............;13 51 55          ADC WORD [BP+DI+0x55],0x7788 ...;81 53 55 88 77
ADC DX,[BX+DI] .................;13 11             ADC WORD [BP+DI],0x77 ..........;83 13 77
ADC DX,[BX+SI+0x5566] ..........;13 90 66 55       ADC WORD [BP+DI],0x7788 ........;81 13 88 77
ADC DX,[BX+SI+0x55] ............;13 50 55          ADC WORD [BP+SI+0x5566],0x77 ...;83 92 66 55 77
ADC DX,[BX+SI] .................;13 10             ADC WORD [BP+SI+0x5566],0x7788 .;81 92 66 55 88 77
ADC DX,[BX] ....................;13 17             ADC WORD [BP+SI+0x55],0x77 .....;83 52 55 77
ADC DX,[DI+0x5566] .............;13 95 66 55       ADC WORD [BP+SI+0x55],0x7788 ...;81 52 55 88 77
ADC DX,[DI+0x55] ...............;13 55 55          ADC WORD [BP+SI],0x77 ..........;83 12 77
ADC DX,[DI] ....................;13 15             ADC WORD [BP+SI],0x7788 ........;81 12 88 77
ADC DX,[SI+0x5566] .............;13 94 66 55       ADC WORD [BX+0x5566],0x77 ......;83 97 66 55 77
ADC DX,[SI+0x55] ...............;13 54 55          ADC WORD [BX+0x5566],0x7788 ....;81 97 66 55 88 77
ADC DX,[SI] ....................;13 14             ADC WORD [BX+0x55],0x77 ........;83 57 55 77
ADC SI,0x77 ....................;83 d6 77          ADC WORD [BX+0x55],0x7788 ......;81 57 55 88 77
ADC SI,0x7788 ..................;81 d6 88 77       ADC WORD [BX+DI+0x5566],0x77 ...;83 91 66 55 77
ADC SI,AX ......................;11 c6             ADC WORD [BX+DI+0x5566],0x7788 .;81 91 66 55 88 77
ADC SI,BP ......................;11 ee             ADC WORD [BX+DI+0x55],0x77 .....;83 51 55 77
ADC SI,BX ......................;11 de             ADC WORD [BX+DI+0x55],0x7788 ...;81 51 55 88 77
ADC SI,CX ......................;11 ce             ADC WORD [BX+DI],0x77 ..........;83 11 77
ADC SI,DI ......................;11 fe             ADC WORD [BX+DI],0x7788 ........;81 11 88 77
ADC SI,DX ......................;11 d6             ADC WORD [BX+SI+0x5566],0x77 ...;83 90 66 55 77
ADC SI,SI ......................;11 f6             ADC WORD [BX+SI+0x5566],0x7788 .;81 90 66 55 88 77
ADC SI,SP ......................;11 e6             ADC WORD [BX+SI+0x55],0x77 .....;83 50 55 77
ADC SI,[0x5566] ................;13 36 66 55       ADC WORD [BX+SI+0x55],0x7788 ...;81 50 55 88 77
ADC SI,[BP+0x5566] .............;13 b6 66 55       ADC WORD [BX+SI],0x77 ..........;83 10 77
ADC SI,[BP+0x55] ...............;13 76 55          ADC WORD [BX+SI],0x7788 ........;81 10 88 77
ADC SI,[BP+DI+0x5566] ..........;13 b3 66 55       ADC WORD [BX],0x77 .............;83 17 77
ADC SI,[BP+DI+0x55] ............;13 73 55          ADC WORD [BX],0x7788 ...........;81 17 88 77
ADC SI,[BP+DI] .................;13 33             ADC WORD [DI+0x5566],0x77 ......;83 95 66 55 77
ADC SI,[BP+SI+0x5566] ..........;13 b2 66 55       ADC WORD [DI+0x5566],0x7788 ....;81 95 66 55 88 77
ADC SI,[BP+SI+0x55] ............;13 72 55          ADC WORD [DI+0x55],0x77 ........;83 55 55 77
ADC SI,[BP+SI] .................;13 32             ADC WORD [DI+0x55],0x7788 ......;81 55 55 88 77
```

167

```
ADC WORD [DI],0x77 ...........;83 15 77          ADC [BP+DI],AL ...............;10 03
ADC WORD [DI],0x7788 .........;81 15 88 77       ADC [BP+DI],AX ...............;11 03
ADC WORD [SI+0x5566],0x77 ....;83 94 66 55 77    ADC [BP+DI],BH ...............;10 3b
ADC WORD [SI+0x5566],0x7788 ..;81 94 66 55 88 77 ADC [BP+DI],BL ...............;10 1b
ADC WORD [SI+0x55],0x77 ......;83 54 55 77       ADC [BP+DI],BP ...............;11 2b
ADC WORD [SI+0x55],0x7788 ....;81 54 55 88 77    ADC [BP+DI],BX ...............;11 1b
ADC WORD [SI],0x77 ...........;83 14 77          ADC [BP+DI],CH ...............;10 2b
ADC WORD [SI],0x7788 .........;81 14 88 77       ADC [BP+DI],CL ...............;10 0b
ADC [0x5566],AH ..............;10 26 66 55       ADC [BP+DI],CX ...............;11 0b
ADC [0x5566],AL ..............;10 06 66 55       ADC [BP+DI],DH ...............;10 33
ADC [0x5566],AX ..............;11 06 66 55       ADC [BP+DI],DI ...............;11 3b
ADC [0x5566],BH ..............;10 3e 66 55       ADC [BP+DI],DL ...............;10 13
ADC [0x5566],BL ..............;10 1e 66 55       ADC [BP+DI],DX ...............;11 13
ADC [0x5566],BP ..............;11 2e 66 55       ADC [BP+DI],SI ...............;11 33
ADC [0x5566],BX ..............;11 1e 66 55       ADC [BP+DI],SP ...............;11 23
ADC [0x5566],CH ..............;10 2e 66 55       ADC [BP+SI+0x5566],AH ........;10 a2 66 55
ADC [0x5566],CL ..............;10 0e 66 55       ADC [BP+SI+0x5566],AL ........;10 82 66 55
ADC [0x5566],CX ..............;11 0e 66 55       ADC [BP+SI+0x5566],AX ........;11 82 66 55
ADC [0x5566],DH ..............;10 36 66 55       ADC [BP+SI+0x5566],BH ........;10 ba 66 55
ADC [0x5566],DI ..............;11 3e 66 55       ADC [BP+SI+0x5566],BL ........;10 9a 66 55
ADC [0x5566],DL ..............;10 16 66 55       ADC [BP+SI+0x5566],BP ........;11 aa 66 55
ADC [0x5566],DX ..............;11 16 66 55       ADC [BP+SI+0x5566],BX ........;11 9a 66 55
ADC [0x5566],SI ..............;11 36 66 55       ADC [BP+SI+0x5566],CH ........;10 aa 66 55
ADC [0x5566],SP ..............;11 26 66 55       ADC [BP+SI+0x5566],CL ........;10 8a 66 55
ADC [BP+0x5566],AH ...........;10 a6 66 55       ADC [BP+SI+0x5566],CX ........;11 8a 66 55
ADC [BP+0x5566],AL ...........;10 86 66 55       ADC [BP+SI+0x5566],DH ........;10 b2 66 55
ADC [BP+0x5566],AX ...........;11 86 66 55       ADC [BP+SI+0x5566],DI ........;11 ba 66 55
ADC [BP+0x5566],BH ...........;10 be 66 55       ADC [BP+SI+0x5566],DL ........;10 92 66 55
ADC [BP+0x5566],BL ...........;10 9e 66 55       ADC [BP+SI+0x5566],DX ........;11 92 66 55
ADC [BP+0x5566],BP ...........;11 ae 66 55       ADC [BP+SI+0x5566],SI ........;11 b2 66 55
ADC [BP+0x5566],BX ...........;11 9e 66 55       ADC [BP+SI+0x5566],SP ........;11 a2 66 55
ADC [BP+0x5566],CH ...........;10 ae 66 55       ADC [BP+SI+0x55],AH ..........;10 62 55
ADC [BP+0x5566],CL ...........;10 8e 66 55       ADC [BP+SI+0x55],AL ..........;10 42 55
ADC [BP+0x5566],CX ...........;11 8e 66 55       ADC [BP+SI+0x55],AX ..........;11 42 55
ADC [BP+0x5566],DH ...........;10 b6 66 55       ADC [BP+SI+0x55],BH ..........;10 7a 55
ADC [BP+0x5566],DI ...........;11 be 66 55       ADC [BP+SI+0x55],BL ..........;10 5a 55
ADC [BP+0x5566],DL ...........;10 96 66 55       ADC [BP+SI+0x55],BP ..........;11 6a 55
ADC [BP+0x5566],DX ...........;11 96 66 55       ADC [BP+SI+0x55],BX ..........;11 5a 55
ADC [BP+0x5566],SI ...........;11 b6 66 55       ADC [BP+SI+0x55],CH ..........;10 6a 55
ADC [BP+0x5566],SP ...........;11 a6 66 55       ADC [BP+SI+0x55],CL ..........;10 4a 55
ADC [BP+0x55],AH .............;10 66 55          ADC [BP+SI+0x55],CX ..........;11 4a 55
ADC [BP+0x55],AL .............;10 46 55          ADC [BP+SI+0x55],DH ..........;10 72 55
ADC [BP+0x55],AX .............;11 46 55          ADC [BP+SI+0x55],DI ..........;11 7a 55
ADC [BP+0x55],BH .............;10 7e 55          ADC [BP+SI+0x55],DL ..........;10 52 55
ADC [BP+0x55],BL .............;10 5e 55          ADC [BP+SI+0x55],DX ..........;11 52 55
ADC [BP+0x55],BP .............;11 6e 55          ADC [BP+SI+0x55],SI ..........;11 72 55
ADC [BP+0x55],BX .............;11 5e 55          ADC [BP+SI+0x55],SP ..........;11 62 55
ADC [BP+0x55],CH .............;10 6e 55          ADC [BP+SI],AH ...............;10 22
ADC [BP+0x55],CL .............;10 4e 55          ADC [BP+SI],AL ...............;10 02
ADC [BP+0x55],CX .............;11 4e 55          ADC [BP+SI],AX ...............;11 02
ADC [BP+0x55],DH .............;10 76 55          ADC [BP+SI],BH ...............;10 3a
ADC [BP+0x55],DI .............;11 7e 55          ADC [BP+SI],BL ...............;10 1a
ADC [BP+0x55],DL .............;10 56 55          ADC [BP+SI],BP ...............;11 2a
ADC [BP+0x55],DX .............;11 56 55          ADC [BP+SI],BX ...............;11 1a
ADC [BP+0x55],SI .............;11 76 55          ADC [BP+SI],CH ...............;10 2a
ADC [BP+0x55],SP .............;11 66 55          ADC [BP+SI],CL ...............;10 0a
ADC [BP+DI+0x5566],AH ........;10 a3 66 55       ADC [BP+SI],CX ...............;11 0a
ADC [BP+DI+0x5566],AL ........;10 83 66 55       ADC [BP+SI],DH ...............;10 32
ADC [BP+DI+0x5566],AX ........;11 83 66 55       ADC [BP+SI],DI ...............;11 3a
ADC [BP+DI+0x5566],BH ........;10 bb 66 55       ADC [BP+SI],DL ...............;10 12
ADC [BP+DI+0x5566],BL ........;10 9b 66 55       ADC [BP+SI],DX ...............;11 12
ADC [BP+DI+0x5566],BP ........;11 ab 66 55       ADC [BP+SI],SI ...............;11 32
ADC [BP+DI+0x5566],BX ........;11 9b 66 55       ADC [BP+SI],SP ...............;11 22
ADC [BP+DI+0x5566],CH ........;10 ab 66 55       ADC [BX+0x5566],AH ...........;10 a7 66 55
ADC [BP+DI+0x5566],CL ........;10 8b 66 55       ADC [BX+0x5566],AL ...........;10 87 66 55
ADC [BP+DI+0x5566],CX ........;11 8b 66 55       ADC [BX+0x5566],AX ...........;11 87 66 55
ADC [BP+DI+0x5566],DH ........;10 b3 66 55       ADC [BX+0x5566],BH ...........;10 bf 66 55
ADC [BP+DI+0x5566],DI ........;11 bb 66 55       ADC [BX+0x5566],BL ...........;10 9f 66 55
ADC [BP+DI+0x5566],DL ........;10 93 66 55       ADC [BX+0x5566],BP ...........;11 af 66 55
ADC [BP+DI+0x5566],DX ........;11 93 66 55       ADC [BX+0x5566],BX ...........;11 9f 66 55
ADC [BP+DI+0x5566],SI ........;11 b3 66 55       ADC [BX+0x5566],CH ...........;10 af 66 55
ADC [BP+DI+0x5566],SP ........;11 a3 66 55       ADC [BX+0x5566],CL ...........;10 8f 66 55
ADC [BP+DI+0x55],AH ..........;10 63 55          ADC [BX+0x5566],CX ...........;11 8f 66 55
ADC [BP+DI+0x55],AL ..........;10 43 55          ADC [BX+0x5566],DH ...........;10 b7 66 55
ADC [BP+DI+0x55],AX ..........;11 43 55          ADC [BX+0x5566],DI ...........;11 bf 66 55
ADC [BP+DI+0x55],BH ..........;10 7b 55          ADC [BX+0x5566],DL ...........;10 97 66 55
ADC [BP+DI+0x55],BL ..........;10 5b 55          ADC [BX+0x5566],DX ...........;11 97 66 55
ADC [BP+DI+0x55],BP ..........;11 6b 55          ADC [BX+0x5566],SI ...........;11 b7 66 55
ADC [BP+DI+0x55],BX ..........;11 5b 55          ADC [BX+0x5566],SP ...........;11 a7 66 55
ADC [BP+DI+0x55],CH ..........;10 6b 55          ADC [BX+0x55],AH .............;10 67 55
ADC [BP+DI+0x55],CL ..........;10 4b 55          ADC [BX+0x55],AL .............;10 47 55
ADC [BP+DI+0x55],CX ..........;11 4b 55          ADC [BX+0x55],AX .............;11 47 55
ADC [BP+DI+0x55],DH ..........;10 73 55          ADC [BX+0x55],BH .............;10 7f 55
ADC [BP+DI+0x55],DI ..........;11 7b 55          ADC [BX+0x55],BP .............;10 5f 55
ADC [BP+DI+0x55],DL ..........;10 53 55          ADC [BX+0x55],BX .............;11 5f 55
ADC [BP+DI+0x55],DX ..........;11 53 55          ADC [BX+0x55],CH .............;10 6f 55
ADC [BP+DI+0x55],SI ..........;11 73 55          ADC [BX+0x55],CL .............;10 4f 55
ADC [BP+DI+0x55],SP ..........;11 63 55          ADC [BX+0x55],CX .............;11 4f 55
ADC [BP+DI],AH ...............;10 23
```

```
ADC [BX+0x55],DH ...............;10 77 55
ADC [BX+0x55],DI ...............;11 7f 55
ADC [BX+0x55],DL ...............;10 57 55
ADC [BX+0x55],DX ...............;11 57 55
ADC [BX+0x55],SI ...............;11 77 55
ADC [BX+0x55],SP ...............;11 67 55
ADC [BX+DI+0x5566],AH ..........;10 a1 66 55
ADC [BX+DI+0x5566],AL ..........;10 81 66 55
ADC [BX+DI+0x5566],AX ..........;11 81 66 55
ADC [BX+DI+0x5566],BH ..........;10 b9 66 55
ADC [BX+DI+0x5566],BL ..........;10 99 66 55
ADC [BX+DI+0x5566],BP ..........;11 a9 66 55
ADC [BX+DI+0x5566],BX ..........;11 99 66 55
ADC [BX+DI+0x5566],CH ..........;10 a9 66 55
ADC [BX+DI+0x5566],CL ..........;10 89 66 55
ADC [BX+DI+0x5566],CX ..........;11 89 66 55
ADC [BX+DI+0x5566],DH ..........;10 b1 66 55
ADC [BX+DI+0x5566],DI ..........;11 b9 66 55
ADC [BX+DI+0x5566],DL ..........;10 91 66 55
ADC [BX+DI+0x5566],DX ..........;11 91 66 55
ADC [BX+DI+0x5566],SI ..........;11 b1 66 55
ADC [BX+DI+0x5566],SP ..........;11 a1 66 55
ADC [BX+DI+0x55],AH ............;10 61 55
ADC [BX+DI+0x55],AL ............;10 41 55
ADC [BX+DI+0x55],AX ............;11 41 55
ADC [BX+DI+0x55],BH ............;10 79 55
ADC [BX+DI+0x55],BL ............;10 59 55
ADC [BX+DI+0x55],BP ............;11 69 55
ADC [BX+DI+0x55],BX ............;11 59 55
ADC [BX+DI+0x55],CH ............;10 69 55
ADC [BX+DI+0x55],CL ............;10 49 55
ADC [BX+DI+0x55],CX ............;11 49 55
ADC [BX+DI+0x55],DH ............;10 71 55
ADC [BX+DI+0x55],DI ............;11 79 55
ADC [BX+DI+0x55],DL ............;10 51 55
ADC [BX+DI+0x55],DX ............;11 51 55
ADC [BX+DI+0x55],SI ............;11 71 55
ADC [BX+DI+0x55],SP ............;11 61 55
ADC [BX+DI],AH .................;10 21
ADC [BX+DI],AL .................;10 01
ADC [BX+DI],AX .................;11 01
ADC [BX+DI],BH .................;10 39
ADC [BX+DI],BL .................;10 19
ADC [BX+DI],BP .................;11 29
ADC [BX+DI],BX .................;11 19
ADC [BX+DI],CH .................;10 29
ADC [BX+DI],CL .................;10 09
ADC [BX+DI],CX .................;11 09
ADC [BX+DI],DH .................;10 31
ADC [BX+DI],DI .................;11 39
ADC [BX+DI],DL .................;10 11
ADC [BX+DI],DX .................;11 11
ADC [BX+DI],SI .................;11 31
ADC [BX+DI],SP .................;11 21
ADC [BX+SI+0x5566],AH ..........;10 a0 66 55
ADC [BX+SI+0x5566],AL ..........;10 80 66 55
ADC [BX+SI+0x5566],AX ..........;11 80 66 55
ADC [BX+SI+0x5566],BH ..........;10 b8 66 55
ADC [BX+SI+0x5566],BL ..........;10 98 66 55
ADC [BX+SI+0x5566],BP ..........;11 a8 66 55
ADC [BX+SI+0x5566],BX ..........;11 98 66 55
ADC [BX+SI+0x5566],CH ..........;10 a8 66 55
ADC [BX+SI+0x5566],CL ..........;10 88 66 55
ADC [BX+SI+0x5566],CX ..........;11 88 66 55
ADC [BX+SI+0x5566],DH ..........;10 b0 66 55
ADC [BX+SI+0x5566],DI ..........;11 b8 66 55
ADC [BX+SI+0x5566],DL ..........;10 90 66 55
ADC [BX+SI+0x5566],DX ..........;11 90 66 55
ADC [BX+SI+0x5566],SI ..........;11 b0 66 55
ADC [BX+SI+0x5566],SP ..........;11 a0 66 55
ADC [BX+SI+0x55],AH ............;10 40 55
ADC [BX+SI+0x55],AL ............;10 40 55
ADC [BX+SI+0x55],AX ............;11 40 55
ADC [BX+SI+0x55],BH ............;10 78 55
ADC [BX+SI+0x55],BL ............;10 58 55
ADC [BX+SI+0x55],BP ............;11 68 55
ADC [BX+SI+0x55],BX ............;11 58 55
ADC [BX+SI+0x55],CH ............;10 68 55
ADC [BX+SI+0x55],CL ............;10 48 55
ADC [BX+SI+0x55],CX ............;11 48 55
ADC [BX+SI+0x55],DH ............;10 70 55
ADC [BX+SI+0x55],DI ............;11 78 55
ADC [BX+SI+0x55],DL ............;10 50 55
ADC [BX+SI+0x55],DX ............;11 50 55
ADC [BX+SI+0x55],SI ............;11 70 55
ADC [BX+SI+0x55],SP ............;11 60 55
ADC [BX+SI],AH .................;10 20
ADC [BX+SI],AL .................;10 00
ADC [BX+SI],AX .................;11 00
ADC [BX+SI],BH .................;10 38
ADC [BX+SI],BL .................;10 18
ADC [BX+SI],BP .................;11 28
ADC [BX+SI],BX .................;11 18
ADC [BX+SI],CH .................;10 28
ADC [BX+SI],CL .................;10 08
ADC [BX+SI],CX .................;11 08
ADC [BX+SI],DH .................;10 30
ADC [BX+SI],DI .................;11 38
ADC [BX+SI],DL .................;10 10
ADC [BX+SI],DX .................;11 10
ADC [BX+SI],SI .................;11 30
ADC [BX+SI],SP .................;11 20
ADC [BX],AH ....................;10 27
ADC [BX],AL ....................;10 07
ADC [BX],AX ....................;11 07
ADC [BX],BH ....................;10 3f
ADC [BX],BL ....................;10 1f
ADC [BX],BP ....................;11 2f
ADC [BX],BX ....................;11 1f
ADC [BX],CH ....................;10 2f
ADC [BX],CL ....................;10 0f
ADC [BX],CX ....................;11 0f
ADC [BX],DH ....................;10 37
ADC [BX],DI ....................;11 3f
ADC [BX],DL ....................;10 17
ADC [BX],DX ....................;11 17
ADC [BX],SI ....................;11 37
ADC [BX],SP ....................;11 27
ADC [DI+0x5566],AH .............;10 a5 66 55
ADC [DI+0x5566],AL .............;10 85 66 55
ADC [DI+0x5566],AX .............;11 85 66 55
ADC [DI+0x5566],BH .............;10 bd 66 55
ADC [DI+0x5566],BL .............;10 9d 66 55
ADC [DI+0x5566],BP .............;11 ad 66 55
ADC [DI+0x5566],BX .............;11 9d 66 55
ADC [DI+0x5566],CH .............;10 ad 66 55
ADC [DI+0x5566],CL .............;10 8d 66 55
ADC [DI+0x5566],CX .............;11 8d 66 55
ADC [DI+0x5566],DH .............;10 b5 66 55
ADC [DI+0x5566],DI .............;11 bd 66 55
ADC [DI+0x5566],DL .............;10 95 66 55
ADC [DI+0x5566],DX .............;11 95 66 55
ADC [DI+0x5566],SI .............;11 b5 66 55
ADC [DI+0x5566],SP .............;11 a5 66 55
ADC [DI+0x55],AH ...............;10 65 55
ADC [DI+0x55],AL ...............;10 45 55
ADC [DI+0x55],AX ...............;11 45 55
ADC [DI+0x55],BH ...............;10 7d 55
ADC [DI+0x55],BL ...............;10 5d 55
ADC [DI+0x55],BP ...............;11 6d 55
ADC [DI+0x55],BX ...............;11 5d 55
ADC [DI+0x55],CH ...............;10 6d 55
ADC [DI+0x55],CL ...............;10 4d 55
ADC [DI+0x55],CX ...............;11 4d 55
ADC [DI+0x55],DH ...............;10 75 55
ADC [DI+0x55],DI ...............;11 7d 55
ADC [DI+0x55],DL ...............;10 55 55
ADC [DI+0x55],DX ...............;11 55 55
ADC [DI+0x55],SI ...............;11 75 55
ADC [DI+0x55],SP ...............;11 65 55
ADC [DI],AH ....................;10 25
ADC [DI],AL ....................;10 05
ADC [DI],AX ....................;11 05
ADC [DI],BH ....................;10 3d
ADC [DI],BL ....................;10 1d
ADC [DI],BP ....................;11 2d
ADC [DI],BX ....................;11 1d
ADC [DI],CH ....................;10 2d
ADC [DI],CL ....................;10 0d
ADC [DI],CX ....................;11 0d
ADC [DI],DH ....................;10 35
ADC [DI],DI ....................;11 3d
ADC [DI],DL ....................;10 15
ADC [DI],DX ....................;11 15
ADC [DI],SI ....................;11 35
ADC [DI],SP ....................;11 25
ADC [SI+0x5566],AH .............;10 a4 66 55
ADC [SI+0x5566],AL .............;10 84 66 55
ADC [SI+0x5566],AX .............;11 84 66 55
ADC [SI+0x5566],BH .............;10 bc 66 55
ADC [SI+0x5566],BL .............;10 9c 66 55
ADC [SI+0x5566],BP .............;11 ac 66 55
ADC [SI+0x5566],BX .............;11 9c 66 55
ADC [SI+0x5566],CH .............;10 ac 66 55
ADC [SI+0x5566],CL .............;10 8c 66 55
ADC [SI+0x5566],CX .............;11 8c 66 55
ADC [SI+0x5566],DH .............;10 b4 66 55
ADC [SI+0x5566],DI .............;11 bc 66 55
```

```
ADC [SI+0x5566],DL ..............;10 94 66 55
ADC [SI+0x5566],DX ..............;11 94 66 55
ADC [SI+0x5566],SI ..............;11 b4 66 55
ADC [SI+0x5566],SP ..............;11 a4 66 55
ADC [SI+0x55],AH ................;10 64 55
ADC [SI+0x55],AL ................;10 44 55
ADC [SI+0x55],AX ................;11 44 55
ADC [SI+0x55],BH ................;10 7c 55
ADC [SI+0x55],BL ................;10 5c 55
ADC [SI+0x55],BP ................;11 6c 55
ADC [SI+0x55],BX ................;11 5c 55
ADC [SI+0x55],CH ................;10 6c 55
ADC [SI+0x55],CL ................;10 4c 55
ADC [SI+0x55],CX ................;11 4c 55
ADC [SI+0x55],DH ................;10 74 55
ADC [SI+0x55],DI ................;11 7c 55
ADC [SI+0x55],DL ................;10 54 55
ADC [SI+0x55],DX ................;11 54 55
ADC [SI+0x55],SI ................;11 74 55
ADC [SI+0x55],SP ................;11 64 55
ADC [SI],AH .....................;10 24
ADC [SI],AL .....................;10 04
ADC [SI],AX .....................;11 04
ADC [SI],BH .....................;10 3c
ADC [SI],BL .....................;10 1c
ADC [SI],BP .....................;11 2c
ADC [SI],BX .....................;11 1c
ADC [SI],CH .....................;10 2c
ADC [SI],CL .....................;10 0c
ADC [SI],CX .....................;11 0c
ADC [SI],DH .....................;10 34
ADC [SI],DI .....................;11 3c
ADC [SI],DL .....................;10 14
ADC [SI],DX .....................;11 14
ADC [SI],SI .....................;11 34
ADC [SI],SP .....................;11 24
ADD AH,0x88 .....................;80 c4 88
ADD AH,AH .......................;00 e4
ADD AH,AL .......................;00 c4
ADD AH,BH .......................;00 fc
ADD AH,BL .......................;00 dc
ADD AH,CH .......................;00 ec
ADD AH,CL .......................;00 cc
ADD AH,DH .......................;00 f4
ADD AH,DL .......................;00 d4
ADD AH,[0x5566] .................;02 26 66 55
ADD AH,[BP+0x5566] ..............;02 a6 66 55
ADD AH,[BP+0x55] ................;02 66 55
ADD AH,[BP+DI+0x5566] ...........;02 a3 66 55
ADD AH,[BP+DI+0x55] .............;02 63 55
ADD AH,[BP+DI] ..................;02 23
ADD AH,[BP+SI+0x5566] ...........;02 a2 66 55
ADD AH,[BP+SI+0x55] .............;02 62 55
ADD AH,[BP+SI] ..................;02 22
ADD AH,[BX+0x5566] ..............;02 a7 66 55
ADD AH,[BX+0x55] ................;02 67 55
ADD AH,[BX+DI+0x5566] ...........;02 a1 66 55
ADD AH,[BX+DI+0x55] .............;02 61 55
ADD AH,[BX+DI] ..................;02 21
ADD AH,[BX+SI+0x5566] ...........;02 a0 66 55
ADD AH,[BX+SI+0x55] .............;02 60 55
ADD AH,[BX+SI] ..................;02 20
ADD AH,[BX] .....................;02 27
ADD AH,[DI+0x5566] ..............;02 a5 66 55
ADD AH,[DI+0x55] ................;02 65 55
ADD AH,[DI] .....................;02 25
ADD AH,[SI+0x5566] ..............;02 a4 66 55
ADD AH,[SI+0x55] ................;02 64 55
ADD AH,[SI] .....................;02 24
ADD AL,0x55 .....................;04 55
ADD AL,0x88 .....................;80 c0 88
ADD AL,AH .......................;00 e0
ADD AL,AL .......................;00 c0
ADD AL,BH .......................;00 f8
ADD AL,BL .......................;00 d8
ADD AL,CH .......................;00 e8
ADD AL,CL .......................;00 c8
ADD AL,DH .......................;00 f0
ADD AL,DL .......................;00 d0
ADD AL,[0x5566] .................;02 06 66 55
ADD AL,[BP+0x5566] ..............;02 86 66 55
ADD AL,[BP+0x55] ................;02 46 55
ADD AL,[BP+DI+0x5566] ...........;02 83 66 55
ADD AL,[BP+DI+0x55] .............;02 43 55
ADD AL,[BP+DI] ..................;02 03
ADD AL,[BP+SI+0x5566] ...........;02 82 66 55
ADD AL,[BP+SI+0x55] .............;02 42 55
ADD AL,[BP+SI] ..................;02 02
ADD AL,[BX+0x5566] ..............;02 87 66 55

ADD AL,[BX+0x55] ................;02 47 55
ADD AL,[BX+DI+0x5566] ...........;02 81 66 55
ADD AL,[BX+DI+0x55] .............;02 41 55
ADD AL,[BX+DI] ..................;02 01
ADD AL,[BX+SI+0x5566] ...........;02 80 66 55
ADD AL,[BX+SI+0x55] .............;02 40 55
ADD AL,[BX+SI] ..................;02 00
ADD AL,[BX] .....................;02 07
ADD AL,[DI+0x5566] ..............;02 85 66 55
ADD AL,[DI+0x55] ................;02 45 55
ADD AL,[DI] .....................;02 05
ADD AL,[SI+0x5566] ..............;02 84 66 55
ADD AL,[SI+0x55] ................;02 44 55
ADD AL,[SI] .....................;02 04
ADD AX,0x5566 ...................;05 66 55
ADD AX,0x77 .....................;83 c0 77
ADD AX,0x7788 ...................;81 c0 88 77
ADD AX,AX .......................;01 c0
ADD AX,BP .......................;01 e8
ADD AX,BX .......................;01 d8
ADD AX,CX .......................;01 c8
ADD AX,DI .......................;01 f8
ADD AX,DX .......................;01 d0
ADD AX,SI .......................;01 f0
ADD AX,SP .......................;01 e0
ADD AX,[0x5566] .................;03 06 66 55
ADD AX,[BP+0x5566] ..............;03 86 66 55
ADD AX,[BP+0x55] ................;03 46 55
ADD AX,[BP+DI+0x5566] ...........;03 83 66 55
ADD AX,[BP+DI+0x55] .............;03 43 55
ADD AX,[BP+DI] ..................;03 03
ADD AX,[BP+SI+0x5566] ...........;03 82 66 55
ADD AX,[BP+SI+0x55] .............;03 42 55
ADD AX,[BP+SI] ..................;03 02
ADD AX,[BX+0x5566] ..............;03 87 66 55
ADD AX,[BX+0x55] ................;03 47 55
ADD AX,[BX+DI+0x5566] ...........;03 81 66 55
ADD AX,[BX+DI+0x55] .............;03 41 55
ADD AX,[BX+DI] ..................;03 01
ADD AX,[BX+SI+0x5566] ...........;03 80 66 55
ADD AX,[BX+SI+0x55] .............;03 40 55
ADD AX,[BX+SI] ..................;03 00
ADD AX,[BX] .....................;03 07
ADD AX,[DI+0x5566] ..............;03 85 66 55
ADD AX,[DI+0x55] ................;03 45 55
ADD AX,[DI] .....................;03 05
ADD AX,[SI+0x5566] ..............;03 84 66 55
ADD AX,[SI+0x55] ................;03 44 55
ADD AX,[SI] .....................;03 04
ADD BH,0x88 .....................;80 c7 88
ADD BH,AH .......................;00 e7
ADD BH,AL .......................;00 c7
ADD BH,BH .......................;00 ff
ADD BH,BL .......................;00 df
ADD BH,CH .......................;00 ef
ADD BH,CL .......................;00 cf
ADD BH,DH .......................;00 f7
ADD BH,DL .......................;00 d7
ADD BH,[0x5566] .................;02 3e 66 55
ADD BH,[BP+0x5566] ..............;02 be 66 55
ADD BH,[BP+0x55] ................;02 7e 55
ADD BH,[BP+DI+0x5566] ...........;02 bb 66 55
ADD BH,[BP+DI+0x55] .............;02 7b 55
ADD BH,[BP+DI] ..................;02 3b
ADD BH,[BP+SI+0x5566] ...........;02 ba 66 55
ADD BH,[BP+SI+0x55] .............;02 7a 55
ADD BH,[BP+SI] ..................;02 3a
ADD BH,[BX+0x5566] ..............;02 bf 66 55
ADD BH,[BX+0x55] ................;02 7f 55
ADD BH,[BX+DI+0x5566] ...........;02 b9 66 55
ADD BH,[BX+DI+0x55] .............;02 79 55
ADD BH,[BX+DI] ..................;02 39
ADD BH,[BX+SI+0x5566] ...........;02 b8 66 55
ADD BH,[BX+SI+0x55] .............;02 78 55
ADD BH,[BX+SI] ..................;02 38
ADD BH,[BX] .....................;02 3f
ADD BH,[DI+0x5566] ..............;02 bd 66 55
ADD BH,[DI+0x55] ................;02 7d 55
ADD BH,[DI] .....................;02 3d
ADD BH,[SI+0x5566] ..............;02 bc 66 55
ADD BH,[SI+0x55] ................;02 7c 55
ADD BH,[SI] .....................;02 3c
ADD BL,0x88 .....................;80 c3 88
ADD BL,AH .......................;00 e3
ADD BL,AL .......................;00 c3
ADD BL,BH .......................;00 fb
ADD BL,BL .......................;00 db
ADD BL,CH .......................;00 eb
ADD BL,CL .......................;00 cb
```

```
ADD BL,DH .......................:00 f3
ADD BL,DL .......................:00 d3
ADD BL,[0x5566] .................:02 1e 66 55
ADD BL,[BP+0x5566] ..............:02 9e 66 55
ADD BL,[BP+0x55] ................:02 5e 55
ADD BL,[BP+DI+0x5566] ...........:02 9b 66 55
ADD BL,[BP+DI+0x55] .............:02 5b 55
ADD BL,[BP+DI] ..................:02 1b
ADD BL,[BP+SI+0x5566] ...........:02 9a 66 55
ADD BL,[BP+SI+0x55] .............:02 5a 55
ADD BL,[BP+SI] ..................:02 1a
ADD BL,[BX+0x5566] ..............:02 9f 66 55
ADD BL,[BX+0x55] ................:02 5f 55
ADD BL,[BX+DI+0x5566] ...........:02 99 66 55
ADD BL,[BX+DI+0x55] .............:02 59 55
ADD BL,[BX+DI] ..................:02 19
ADD BL,[BX+SI+0x5566] ...........:02 98 66 55
ADD BL,[BX+SI+0x55] .............:02 58 55
ADD BL,[BX+SI] ..................:02 18
ADD BL,[BX] .....................:02 1f
ADD BL,[DI+0x5566] ..............:02 9d 66 55
ADD BL,[DI+0x55] ................:02 5d 55
ADD BL,[DI] .....................:02 1d
ADD BL,[SI+0x5566] ..............:02 9c 66 55
ADD BL,[SI+0x55] ................:02 5c 55
ADD BL,[SI] .....................:02 1c
ADD BP,0x77 .....................:83 c5 77
ADD BP,0x7788 ...................:81 c5 88 77
ADD BP,AX .......................:01 c5
ADD BP,BP .......................:01 ed
ADD BP,BX .......................:01 dd
ADD BP,CX .......................:01 cd
ADD BP,DI .......................:01 fd
ADD BP,DX .......................:01 d5
ADD BP,SI .......................:01 f5
ADD BP,SP .......................:01 e5
ADD BP,[0x5566] .................:03 2e 66 55
ADD BP,[BP+0x5566] ..............:03 ae 66 55
ADD BP,[BP+0x55] ................:03 6e 55
ADD BP,[BP+DI+0x5566] ...........:03 ab 66 55
ADD BP,[BP+DI+0x55] .............:03 6b 55
ADD BP,[BP+DI] ..................:03 2b
ADD BP,[BP+SI+0x5566] ...........:03 aa 66 55
ADD BP,[BP+SI+0x55] .............:03 6a 55
ADD BP,[BP+SI] ..................:03 2a
ADD BP,[BX+0x5566] ..............:03 af 66 55
ADD BP,[BX+0x55] ................:03 6f 55
ADD BP,[BX+DI+0x5566] ...........:03 a9 66 55
ADD BP,[BX+DI+0x55] .............:03 69 55
ADD BP,[BX+DI] ..................:03 29
ADD BP,[BX+SI+0x5566] ...........:03 a8 66 55
ADD BP,[BX+SI+0x55] .............:03 68 55
ADD BP,[BX+SI] ..................:03 28
ADD BP,[BX] .....................:03 2f
ADD BP,[DI+0x5566] ..............:03 ad 66 55
ADD BP,[DI+0x55] ................:03 6d 55
ADD BP,[DI] .....................:03 2d
ADD BP,[SI+0x5566] ..............:03 ac 66 55
ADD BP,[SI+0x55] ................:03 6c 55
ADD BP,[SI] .....................:03 2c
ADD BX,0x77 .....................:83 c3 77
ADD BX,0x7788 ...................:81 c3 88 77
ADD BX,AX .......................:01 c3
ADD BX,BP .......................:01 eb
ADD BX,BX .......................:01 db
ADD BX,CX .......................:01 cb
ADD BX,DI .......................:01 fb
ADD BX,DX .......................:01 d3
ADD BX,SI .......................:01 f3
ADD BX,SP .......................:01 e3
ADD BX,[0x5566] .................:03 1e 66 55
ADD BX,[BP+0x5566] ..............:03 9e 66 55
ADD BX,[BP+0x55] ................:03 5e 55
ADD BX,[BP+DI+0x5566] ...........:03 9b 66 55
ADD BX,[BP+DI+0x55] .............:03 5b 55
ADD BX,[BP+DI] ..................:03 1b
ADD BX,[BP+SI+0x5566] ...........:03 9a 66 55
ADD BX,[BP+SI+0x55] .............:03 5a 55
ADD BX,[BP+SI] ..................:03 1a
ADD BX,[BX+0x5566] ..............:03 9f 66 55
ADD BX,[BX+0x55] ................:03 5f 55
ADD BX,[BX+DI+0x5566] ...........:03 99 66 55
ADD BX,[BX+DI+0x55] .............:03 59 55
ADD BX,[BX+DI] ..................:03 19
ADD BX,[BX+SI+0x5566] ...........:03 98 66 55
ADD BX,[BX+SI+0x55] .............:03 58 55
ADD BX,[BX+SI] ..................:03 18
ADD BX,[BX] .....................:03 1f
ADD BX,[DI+0x5566] ..............:03 9d 66 55
```

```
ADD BX,[DI+0x55] ................:03 5d 55
ADD BX,[DI] .....................:03 1d
ADD BX,[SI+0x5566] ..............:03 9c 66 55
ADD BX,[SI+0x55] ................:03 5c 55
ADD BX,[SI] .....................:03 1c
ADD BYTE [0x5566],0x88 ..........:80 06 66 55 88
ADD BYTE [BP+0x5566],0x88 .......:80 86 66 55 88
ADD BYTE [BP+0x55],0x88 .........:80 46 55 88
ADD BYTE [BP+DI+0x5566],0x88 ....:80 83 66 55 88
ADD BYTE [BP+DI+0x55],0x88 ......:80 43 55 88
ADD BYTE [BP+DI],0x88 ...........:80 03 88
ADD BYTE [BP+SI+0x5566],0x88 ....:80 82 66 55 88
ADD BYTE [BP+SI+0x55],0x88 ......:80 42 55 88
ADD BYTE [BP+SI],0x88 ...........:80 02 88
ADD BYTE [BX+0x5566],0x88 .......:80 87 66 55 88
ADD BYTE [BX+0x55],0x88 .........:80 47 55 88
ADD BYTE [BX+DI+0x5566],0x88 ....:80 81 66 55 88
ADD BYTE [BX+DI+0x55],0x88 ......:80 41 55 88
ADD BYTE [BX+DI],0x88 ...........:80 01 88
ADD BYTE [BX+SI+0x5566],0x88 ....:80 80 66 55 88
ADD BYTE [BX+SI+0x55],0x88 ......:80 40 55 88
ADD BYTE [BX+SI],0x88 ...........:80 00 88
ADD BYTE [BX],0x88 ..............:80 07 88
ADD BYTE [DI+0x5566],0x88 .......:80 85 66 55 88
ADD BYTE [DI+0x55],0x88 .........:80 45 55 88
ADD BYTE [DI],0x88 ..............:80 05 88
ADD BYTE [SI+0x5566],0x88 .......:80 84 66 55 88
ADD BYTE [SI+0x55],0x88 .........:80 44 55 88
ADD BYTE [SI],0x88 ..............:80 04 88
ADD CH,0x88 .....................:80 c5 88
ADD CH,AH .......................:00 e5
ADD CH,AL .......................:00 c5
ADD CH,BH .......................:00 fd
ADD CH,BL .......................:00 dd
ADD CH,CH .......................:00 ed
ADD CH,CL .......................:00 cd
ADD CH,DH .......................:00 f5
ADD CH,DL .......................:00 d5
ADD CH,[0x5566] .................:02 2e 66 55
ADD CH,[BP+0x5566] ..............:02 ae 66 55
ADD CH,[BP+0x55] ................:02 6e 55
ADD CH,[BP+DI+0x5566] ...........:02 ab 66 55
ADD CH,[BP+DI+0x55] .............:02 6b 55
ADD CH,[BP+DI] ..................:02 2b
ADD CH,[BP+SI+0x5566] ...........:02 aa 66 55
ADD CH,[BP+SI+0x55] .............:02 6a 55
ADD CH,[BP+SI] ..................:02 2a
ADD CH,[BX+0x5566] ..............:02 af 66 55
ADD CH,[BX+0x55] ................:02 6f 55
ADD CH,[BX+DI+0x5566] ...........:02 a9 66 55
ADD CH,[BX+DI+0x55] .............:02 69 55
ADD CH,[BX+DI] ..................:02 29
ADD CH,[BX+SI+0x5566] ...........:02 a8 66 55
ADD CH,[BX+SI+0x55] .............:02 68 55
ADD CH,[BX+SI] ..................:02 28
ADD CH,[BX] .....................:02 2f
ADD CH,[DI+0x5566] ..............:02 ad 66 55
ADD CH,[DI+0x55] ................:02 6d 55
ADD CH,[DI] .....................:02 2d
ADD CH,[SI+0x5566] ..............:02 ac 66 55
ADD CH,[SI+0x55] ................:02 6c 55
ADD CH,[SI] .....................:02 2c
ADD CL,0x88 .....................:80 c1 88
ADD CL,AH .......................:00 e1
ADD CL,AL .......................:00 c1
ADD CL,BH .......................:00 f9
ADD CL,BL .......................:00 d9
ADD CL,CH .......................:00 e9
ADD CL,CL .......................:00 c9
ADD CL,DH .......................:00 f1
ADD CL,DL .......................:00 d1
ADD CL,[0x5566] .................:02 0e 66 55
ADD CL,[BP+0x5566] ..............:02 8e 66 55
ADD CL,[BP+0x55] ................:02 4e 55
ADD CL,[BP+DI+0x5566] ...........:02 8b 66 55
ADD CL,[BP+DI+0x55] .............:02 4b 55
ADD CL,[BP+DI] ..................:02 0b
ADD CL,[BP+SI+0x5566] ...........:02 8a 66 55
ADD CL,[BP+SI+0x55] .............:02 4a 55
ADD CL,[BP+SI] ..................:02 0a
ADD CL,[BX+0x5566] ..............:02 8f 66 55
ADD CL,[BX+0x55] ................:02 4f 55
ADD CL,[BX+DI+0x5566] ...........:02 89 66 55
ADD CL,[BX+DI+0x55] .............:02 49 55
ADD CL,[BX+DI] ..................:02 09
ADD CL,[BX+SI+0x5566] ...........:02 88 66 55
ADD CL,[BX+SI+0x55] .............:02 48 55
ADD CL,[BX+SI] ..................:02 08
ADD CL,[BX] .....................:02 0f
```

171

```
ADD CL,[DI+0x5566] .............;02 8d 66 55
ADD CL,[DI+0x55] ...............;02 4d 55
ADD CL,[DI] ....................;02 0d
ADD CL,[SI+0x5566] .............;02 8c 66 55
ADD CL,[SI+0x55] ...............;02 4c 55
ADD CL,[SI] ....................;02 0c
ADD CX,0x77 ....................;83 c1 77
ADD CX,0x7788 ..................;81 c1 88 77
ADD CX,AX ......................;01 c1
ADD CX,BP ......................;01 e9
ADD CX,BX ......................;01 d9
ADD CX,CX ......................;01 c9
ADD CX,DI ......................;01 f9
ADD CX,DX ......................;01 d1
ADD CX,SI ......................;01 f1
ADD CX,SP ......................;01 e1
ADD CX,[0x5566] ................;03 0e 66 55
ADD CX,[BP+0x5566] .............;03 8e 66 55
ADD CX,[BP+0x55] ...............;03 4e 55
ADD CX,[BP+DI+0x5566] ..........;03 8b 66 55
ADD CX,[BP+DI+0x55] ............;03 4b 55
ADD CX,[BP+DI] .................;03 0b
ADD CX,[BP+SI+0x5566] ..........;03 8a 66 55
ADD CX,[BP+SI+0x55] ............;03 4a 55
ADD CX,[BP+SI] .................;03 0a
ADD CX,[BX+0x5566] .............;03 8f 66 55
ADD CX,[BX+0x55] ...............;03 4f 55
ADD CX,[BX+DI+0x5566] ..........;03 89 66 55
ADD CX,[BX+DI+0x55] ............;03 49 55
ADD CX,[BX+DI] .................;03 09
ADD CX,[BX+SI+0x5566] ..........;03 88 66 55
ADD CX,[BX+SI+0x55] ............;03 48 55
ADD CX,[BX+SI] .................;03 08
ADD CX,[BX] ....................;03 0f
ADD CX,[DI+0x5566] .............;03 8d 66 55
ADD CX,[DI+0x55] ...............;03 4d 55
ADD CX,[DI] ....................;03 0d
ADD CX,[SI+0x5566] .............;03 8c 66 55
ADD CX,[SI+0x55] ...............;03 4c 55
ADD CX,[SI] ....................;03 0c
ADD DH,0x88 ....................;80 c6 88
ADD DH,AH ......................;00 e6
ADD DH,AL ......................;00 c6
ADD DH,BH ......................;00 fe
ADD DH,BL ......................;00 de
ADD DH,CH ......................;00 ee
ADD DH,CL ......................;00 ce
ADD DH,DH ......................;00 f6
ADD DH,DL ......................;00 d6
ADD DH,[0x5566] ................;02 36 66 55
ADD DH,[BP+0x5566] .............;02 b6 66 55
ADD DH,[BP+0x55] ...............;02 76 55
ADD DH,[BP+DI+0x5566] ..........;02 b3 66 55
ADD DH,[BP+DI+0x55] ............;02 73 55
ADD DH,[BP+DI] .................;02 33
ADD DH,[BP+SI+0x5566] ..........;02 b2 66 55
ADD DH,[BP+SI+0x55] ............;02 72 55
ADD DH,[BP+SI] .................;02 32
ADD DH,[BX+0x5566] .............;02 b7 66 55
ADD DH,[BX+0x55] ...............;02 77 55
ADD DH,[BX+DI+0x5566] ..........;02 b1 66 55
ADD DH,[BX+DI+0x55] ............;02 71 55
ADD DH,[BX+DI] .................;02 31
ADD DH,[BX+SI+0x5566] ..........;02 b0 66 55
ADD DH,[BX+SI+0x55] ............;02 70 55
ADD DH,[BX+SI] .................;02 30
ADD DH,[BX] ....................;02 37
ADD DH,[DI+0x5566] .............;02 b5 66 55
ADD DH,[DI+0x55] ...............;02 75 55
ADD DH,[DI] ....................;02 35
ADD DH,[SI+0x5566] .............;02 b4 66 55
ADD DH,[SI+0x55] ...............;02 74 55
ADD DH,[SI] ....................;02 34
ADD DI,0x77 ....................;83 c7 77
ADD DI,0x7788 ..................;81 c7 88 77
ADD DI,AX ......................;01 c7
ADD DI,BP ......................;01 ef
ADD DI,BX ......................;01 df
ADD DI,CX ......................;01 cf
ADD DI,DI ......................;01 ff
ADD DI,DX ......................;01 d7
ADD DI,SI ......................;01 f7
ADD DI,SP ......................;01 e7
ADD DI,[0x5566] ................;03 3e 66 55
ADD DI,[BP+0x5566] .............;03 be 66 55
ADD DI,[BP+0x55] ...............;03 7e 55
ADD DI,[BP+DI+0x5566] ..........;03 bb 66 55
ADD DI,[BP+DI+0x55] ............;03 7b 55
ADD DI,[BP+DI] .................;03 3b

ADD DI,[BP+SI+0x5566] ..........;03 ba 66 55
ADD DI,[BP+SI+0x55] ............;03 7a 55
ADD DI,[BP+SI] .................;03 3a
ADD DI,[BX+0x5566] .............;03 bf 66 55
ADD DI,[BX+0x55] ...............;03 7f 55
ADD DI,[BX+DI+0x5566] ..........;03 b9 66 55
ADD DI,[BX+DI+0x55] ............;03 79 55
ADD DI,[BX+DI] .................;03 39
ADD DI,[BX+SI+0x5566] ..........;03 b8 66 55
ADD DI,[BX+SI+0x55] ............;03 78 55
ADD DI,[BX+SI] .................;03 38
ADD DI,[BX] ....................;03 3f
ADD DI,[DI+0x5566] .............;03 bd 66 55
ADD DI,[DI+0x55] ...............;03 7d 55
ADD DI,[DI] ....................;03 3d
ADD DI,[SI+0x5566] .............;03 bc 66 55
ADD DI,[SI+0x55] ...............;03 7c 55
ADD DI,[SI] ....................;03 3c
ADD DL,0x88 ....................;80 c2 88
ADD DL,AH ......................;00 e2
ADD DL,AL ......................;00 c2
ADD DL,BH ......................;00 fa
ADD DL,BL ......................;00 da
ADD DL,CH ......................;00 ea
ADD DL,CL ......................;00 ca
ADD DL,DH ......................;00 f2
ADD DL,DL ......................;00 d2
ADD DL,[0x5566] ................;02 16 66 55
ADD DL,[BP+0x5566] .............;02 96 66 55
ADD DL,[BP+0x55] ...............;02 56 55
ADD DL,[BP+DI+0x5566] ..........;02 93 66 55
ADD DL,[BP+DI+0x55] ............;02 53 55
ADD DL,[BP+DI] .................;02 13
ADD DL,[BP+SI+0x5566] ..........;02 92 66 55
ADD DL,[BP+SI+0x55] ............;02 52 55
ADD DL,[BP+SI] .................;02 12
ADD DL,[BX+0x5566] .............;02 97 66 55
ADD DL,[BX+0x55] ...............;02 57 55
ADD DL,[BX+DI+0x5566] ..........;02 91 66 55
ADD DL,[BX+DI+0x55] ............;02 51 55
ADD DL,[BX+DI] .................;02 11
ADD DL,[BX+SI+0x5566] ..........;02 90 66 55
ADD DL,[BX+SI+0x55] ............;02 50 55
ADD DL,[BX+SI] .................;02 10
ADD DL,[BX] ....................;02 17
ADD DL,[DI+0x5566] .............;02 95 66 55
ADD DL,[DI+0x55] ...............;02 55 55
ADD DL,[DI] ....................;02 15
ADD DL,[SI+0x5566] .............;02 94 66 55
ADD DL,[SI+0x55] ...............;02 54 55
ADD DL,[SI] ....................;02 14
ADD DX,0x77 ....................;83 c2 77
ADD DX,0x7788 ..................;81 c2 88 77
ADD DX,AX ......................;01 c2
ADD DX,BP ......................;01 ea
ADD DX,BX ......................;01 da
ADD DX,CX ......................;01 ca
ADD DX,DI ......................;01 fa
ADD DX,DX ......................;01 d2
ADD DX,SI ......................;01 f2
ADD DX,SP ......................;01 e2
ADD DX,[0x5566] ................;03 16 66 55
ADD DX,[BP+0x5566] .............;03 96 66 55
ADD DX,[BP+0x55] ...............;03 56 55
ADD DX,[BP+DI+0x5566] ..........;03 93 66 55
ADD DX,[BP+DI+0x55] ............;03 53 55
ADD DX,[BP+DI] .................;03 13
ADD DX,[BP+SI+0x5566] ..........;03 92 66 55
ADD DX,[BP+SI+0x55] ............;03 52 55
ADD DX,[BP+SI] .................;03 12
ADD DX,[BX+0x5566] .............;03 97 66 55
ADD DX,[BX+0x55] ...............;03 57 55
ADD DX,[BX+DI+0x5566] ..........;03 91 66 55
ADD DX,[BX+DI+0x55] ............;03 51 55
ADD DX,[BX+DI] .................;03 11
ADD DX,[BX+SI+0x5566] ..........;03 90 66 55
ADD DX,[BX+SI+0x55] ............;03 50 55
ADD DX,[BX+SI] .................;03 10
ADD DX,[BX] ....................;03 17
ADD DX,[DI+0x5566] .............;03 95 66 55
ADD DX,[DI+0x55] ...............;03 55 55
ADD DX,[DI] ....................;03 15
ADD DX,[SI+0x5566] .............;03 94 66 55
ADD DX,[SI+0x55] ...............;03 54 55
ADD DX,[SI] ....................;03 14
ADD SI,0x77 ....................;83 c6 77
ADD SI,0x7788 ..................;81 c6 88 77
ADD SI,AX ......................;01 c6
ADD SI,BP ......................;01 ee
```

```
ADD SI,BX .....................;01 de
ADD SI,CX .....................;01 ce
ADD SI,DI .....................;01 fe
ADD SI,DX .....................;01 d6
ADD SI,SI .....................;01 f6
ADD SI,SP .....................;01 e6
ADD SI,[0x5566] ...............;03 36 66 55
ADD SI,[BP+0x5566] ............;03 b6 66 55
ADD SI,[BP+0x55] ..............;03 76 55
ADD SI,[BP+DI+0x5566] .........;03 b3 66 55
ADD SI,[BP+DI+0x55] ...........;03 73 55
ADD SI,[BP+DI] ................;03 33
ADD SI,[BP+SI+0x5566] .........;03 b2 66 55
ADD SI,[BP+SI+0x55] ...........;03 72 55
ADD SI,[BP+SI] ................;03 32
ADD SI,[BX+0x5566] ............;03 b7 66 55
ADD SI,[BX+0x55] ..............;03 77 55
ADD SI,[BX+DI+0x5566] .........;03 b1 66 55
ADD SI,[BX+DI+0x55] ...........;03 71 55
ADD SI,[BX+DI] ................;03 31
ADD SI,[BX+SI+0x5566] .........;03 b0 66 55
ADD SI,[BX+SI+0x55] ...........;03 70 55
ADD SI,[BX+SI] ................;03 30
ADD SI,[BX] ...................;03 37
ADD SI,[DI+0x5566] ............;03 b5 66 55
ADD SI,[DI+0x55] ..............;03 75 55
ADD SI,[DI] ...................;03 35
ADD SI,[SI+0x5566] ............;03 b4 66 55
ADD SI,[SI+0x55] ..............;03 74 55
ADD SI,[SI] ...................;03 34
ADD SP,0x77 ...................;83 c4 77
ADD SP,0x7788 .................;81 c4 88 77
ADD SP,AX .....................;01 c4
ADD SP,BP .....................;01 ec
ADD SP,BX .....................;01 dc
ADD SP,CX .....................;01 cc
ADD SP,DI .....................;01 fc
ADD SP,DX .....................;01 d4
ADD SP,SI .....................;01 f4
ADD SP,SP .....................;01 e4
ADD SP,[0x5566] ...............;03 26 66 55
ADD SP,[BP+0x5566] ............;03 a6 66 55
ADD SP,[BP+0x55] ..............;03 66 55
ADD SP,[BP+DI+0x5566] .........;03 a3 66 55
ADD SP,[BP+DI+0x55] ...........;03 63 55
ADD SP,[BP+DI] ................;03 23
ADD SP,[BP+SI+0x5566] .........;03 a2 66 55
ADD SP,[BP+SI+0x55] ...........;03 62 55
ADD SP,[BP+SI] ................;03 22
ADD SP,[BX+0x5566] ............;03 a7 66 55
ADD SP,[BX+0x55] ..............;03 67 55
ADD SP,[BX+DI+0x5566] .........;03 a1 66 55
ADD SP,[BX+DI+0x55] ...........;03 61 55
ADD SP,[BX+DI] ................;03 21
ADD SP,[BX+SI+0x5566] .........;03 a0 66 55
ADD SP,[BX+SI+0x55] ...........;03 60 55
ADD SP,[BX+SI] ................;03 20
ADD SP,[BX] ...................;03 27
ADD SP,[DI+0x5566] ............;03 a5 66 55
ADD SP,[DI+0x55] ..............;03 65 55
ADD SP,[DI] ...................;03 25
ADD SP,[SI+0x5566] ............;03 a4 66 55
ADD SP,[SI+0x55] ..............;03 64 55
ADD SP,[SI] ...................;03 24
ADD WORD [0x5566],0x77 ........;83 06 66 55 77
ADD WORD [0x5566],0x7788 ......;81 06 66 55 88 77
ADD WORD [BP+0x5566],0x77 .....;83 86 66 55 77
ADD WORD [BP+0x5566],0x7788 ...;81 86 66 55 88 77
ADD WORD [BP+0x55],0x77 .......;83 46 55 77
ADD WORD [BP+0x55],0x7788 .....;81 46 55 88 77
ADD WORD [BP+DI+0x5566],0x77 ..;83 83 66 55 77
ADD WORD [BP+DI+0x5566],0x7788 .;81 83 66 55 88 77
ADD WORD [BP+DI+0x55],0x77 ....;83 43 55 77
ADD WORD [BP+DI+0x55],0x7788 ...;81 43 55 88 77
ADD WORD [BP+DI],0x77 .........;83 03 77
ADD WORD [BP+DI],0x7788 .......;81 03 88 77
ADD WORD [BP+SI+0x5566],0x77 ..;83 82 66 55 77
ADD WORD [BP+SI+0x5566],0x7788 .;81 82 66 55 88 77
ADD WORD [BP+SI+0x55],0x77 ....;83 42 55 77
ADD WORD [BP+SI+0x55],0x7788 ...;81 42 55 88 77
ADD WORD [BP+SI],0x77 .........;83 02 77
ADD WORD [BP+SI],0x7788 .......;81 02 88 77
ADD WORD [BX+0x5566],0x77 .....;83 87 66 55 77
ADD WORD [BX+0x5566],0x7788 ...;81 87 66 55 88 77
ADD WORD [BX+0x55],0x77 .......;83 47 55 77
ADD WORD [BX+0x55],0x7788 .....;81 47 55 88 77
ADD WORD [BX+DI+0x5566],0x77 ..;83 81 66 55 77
ADD WORD [BX+DI+0x5566],0x7788 .;81 81 66 55 88 77
ADD WORD [BX+DI+0x55],0x77 ....;83 41 55 77

ADD WORD [BX+DI+0x55],0x7788 ...;81 41 55 88 77
ADD WORD [BX+DI],0x77 .........;83 01 77
ADD WORD [BX+DI],0x7788 .......;81 01 88 77
ADD WORD [BX+SI+0x5566],0x77 ..;83 80 66 55 77
ADD WORD [BX+SI+0x5566],0x7788 ;81 80 66 55 88 77
ADD WORD [BX+SI+0x55],0x77 ....;83 40 55 77
ADD WORD [BX+SI+0x55],0x7788 ...;81 40 55 88 77
ADD WORD [BX+SI],0x77 .........;83 00 77
ADD WORD [BX+SI],0x7788 .......;81 00 88 77
ADD WORD [BX],0x77 ............;83 07 77
ADD WORD [BX],0x7788 ..........;81 07 88 77
ADD WORD [DI+0x5566],0x77 .....;83 85 66 55 77
ADD WORD [DI+0x5566],0x7788 ...;81 85 66 55 88 77
ADD WORD [DI+0x55],0x77 .......;83 45 55 77
ADD WORD [DI+0x55],0x7788 .....;81 45 55 88 77
ADD WORD [DI],0x77 ............;83 05 77
ADD WORD [DI],0x7788 ..........;81 05 88 77
ADD WORD [SI+0x5566],0x77 .....;83 84 66 55 77
ADD WORD [SI+0x5566],0x7788 ...;81 84 66 55 88 77
ADD WORD [SI+0x55],0x77 .......;83 44 55 77
ADD WORD [SI+0x55],0x7788 .....;81 44 55 88 77
ADD WORD [SI],0x77 ............;83 04 77
ADD WORD [SI],0x7788 ..........;81 04 88 77
ADD [0x5566],AH ...............;00 26 66 55
ADD [0x5566],AL ...............;00 06 66 55
ADD [0x5566],AX ...............;01 06 66 55
ADD [0x5566],BH ...............;00 3e 66 55
ADD [0x5566],BL ...............;00 1e 66 55
ADD [0x5566],BP ...............;01 2e 66 55
ADD [0x5566],BX ...............;01 1e 66 55
ADD [0x5566],CH ...............;00 2e 66 55
ADD [0x5566],CL ...............;00 0e 66 55
ADD [0x5566],CX ...............;01 0e 66 55
ADD [0x5566],DH ...............;00 36 66 55
ADD [0x5566],DI ...............;01 3e 66 55
ADD [0x5566],DL ...............;00 16 66 55
ADD [0x5566],DX ...............;01 16 66 55
ADD [0x5566],SI ...............;01 36 66 55
ADD [0x5566],SP ...............;01 26 66 55
ADD [BP+0x5566],AH ............;00 a6 66 55
ADD [BP+0x5566],AL ............;00 86 66 55
ADD [BP+0x5566],AX ............;01 86 66 55
ADD [BP+0x5566],BH ............;00 be 66 55
ADD [BP+0x5566],BL ............;00 9e 66 55
ADD [BP+0x5566],BP ............;01 ae 66 55
ADD [BP+0x5566],BX ............;01 9e 66 55
ADD [BP+0x5566],CH ............;00 ae 66 55
ADD [BP+0x5566],CL ............;00 8e 66 55
ADD [BP+0x5566],CX ............;01 8e 66 55
ADD [BP+0x5566],DH ............;00 b6 66 55
ADD [BP+0x5566],DI ............;01 be 66 55
ADD [BP+0x5566],DL ............;00 96 66 55
ADD [BP+0x5566],DX ............;01 96 66 55
ADD [BP+0x5566],SI ............;01 b6 66 55
ADD [BP+0x5566],SP ............;01 a6 66 55
ADD [BP+0x55],AH ..............;00 66 55
ADD [BP+0x55],AL ..............;00 46 55
ADD [BP+0x55],AX ..............;01 46 55
ADD [BP+0x55],BH ..............;00 7e 55
ADD [BP+0x55],BL ..............;00 5e 55
ADD [BP+0x55],BP ..............;01 6e 55
ADD [BP+0x55],BX ..............;01 5e 55
ADD [BP+0x55],CH ..............;00 6e 55
ADD [BP+0x55],CL ..............;00 4e 55
ADD [BP+0x55],CX ..............;01 4e 55
ADD [BP+0x55],DH ..............;00 76 55
ADD [BP+0x55],DI ..............;01 7e 55
ADD [BP+0x55],DL ..............;00 56 55
ADD [BP+0x55],DX ..............;01 56 55
ADD [BP+0x55],SI ..............;01 76 55
ADD [BP+0x55],SP ..............;01 66 55
ADD [BP+DI+0x5566],AH .........;00 a3 66 55
ADD [BP+DI+0x5566],AL .........;00 83 66 55
ADD [BP+DI+0x5566],AX .........;01 83 66 55
ADD [BP+DI+0x5566],BH .........;00 bb 66 55
ADD [BP+DI+0x5566],BL .........;00 9b 66 55
ADD [BP+DI+0x5566],BP .........;01 ab 66 55
ADD [BP+DI+0x5566],BX .........;01 9b 66 55
ADD [BP+DI+0x5566],CH .........;00 ab 66 55
ADD [BP+DI+0x5566],CL .........;00 8b 66 55
ADD [BP+DI+0x5566],CX .........;01 8b 66 55
ADD [BP+DI+0x5566],DH .........;00 b3 66 55
ADD [BP+DI+0x5566],DI .........;01 bb 66 55
ADD [BP+DI+0x5566],DL .........;00 93 66 55
ADD [BP+DI+0x5566],DX .........;01 93 66 55
ADD [BP+DI+0x5566],SI .........;01 b3 66 55
ADD [BP+DI+0x5566],SP .........;01 a3 66 55
ADD [BP+DI+0x55],AH ...........;00 63 55
ADD [BP+DI+0x55],AL ...........;00 43 55
```

```
ADD [BP+DI+0x55],AX ...........;01 43 55
ADD [BP+DI+0x55],BH ...........;00 7b 55
ADD [BP+DI+0x55],BL ...........;00 5b 55
ADD [BP+DI+0x55],BP ...........;01 6b 55
ADD [BP+DI+0x55],BX ...........;01 5b 55
ADD [BP+DI+0x55],CH ...........;00 6b 55
ADD [BP+DI+0x55],CL ...........;00 4b 55
ADD [BP+DI+0x55],CX ...........;01 4b 55
ADD [BP+DI+0x55],DH ...........;00 73 55
ADD [BP+DI+0x55],DI ...........;01 7b 55
ADD [BP+DI+0x55],DL ...........;00 53 55
ADD [BP+DI+0x55],DX ...........;01 53 55
ADD [BP+DI+0x55],SI ...........;01 73 55
ADD [BP+DI+0x55],SP ...........;01 63 55
ADD [BP+DI],AH ................;00 23
ADD [BP+DI],AL ................;00 03
ADD [BP+DI],AX ................;01 03
ADD [BP+DI],BH ................;00 3b
ADD [BP+DI],BL ................;00 1b
ADD [BP+DI],BP ................;01 2b
ADD [BP+DI],BX ................;01 1b
ADD [BP+DI],CH ................;00 2b
ADD [BP+DI],CL ................;00 0b
ADD [BP+DI],CX ................;01 0b
ADD [BP+DI],DH ................;00 33
ADD [BP+DI],DI ................;01 3b
ADD [BP+DI],DL ................;00 13
ADD [BP+DI],DX ................;01 13
ADD [BP+DI],SI ................;01 33
ADD [BP+DI],SP ................;01 23
ADD [BP+SI+0x5566],AH .........;00 a2 66 55
ADD [BP+SI+0x5566],AL .........;00 82 66 55
ADD [BP+SI+0x5566],AX .........;01 82 66 55
ADD [BP+SI+0x5566],BH .........;00 ba 66 55
ADD [BP+SI+0x5566],BL .........;00 9a 66 55
ADD [BP+SI+0x5566],BP .........;01 aa 66 55
ADD [BP+SI+0x5566],BX .........;01 9a 66 55
ADD [BP+SI+0x5566],CH .........;00 aa 66 55
ADD [BP+SI+0x5566],CL .........;00 8a 66 55
ADD [BP+SI+0x5566],CX .........;01 8a 66 55
ADD [BP+SI+0x5566],DH .........;00 b2 66 55
ADD [BP+SI+0x5566],DI .........;01 ba 66 55
ADD [BP+SI+0x5566],DL .........;00 92 66 55
ADD [BP+SI+0x5566],DX .........;01 92 66 55
ADD [BP+SI+0x5566],SI .........;01 b2 66 55
ADD [BP+SI+0x5566],SP .........;01 a2 66 55
ADD [BP+SI+0x55],AH ...........;00 62 55
ADD [BP+SI+0x55],AL ...........;00 42 55
ADD [BP+SI+0x55],AX ...........;01 42 55
ADD [BP+SI+0x55],BH ...........;00 7a 55
ADD [BP+SI+0x55],BL ...........;00 5a 55
ADD [BP+SI+0x55],BP ...........;01 6a 55
ADD [BP+SI+0x55],BX ...........;01 5a 55
ADD [BP+SI+0x55],CH ...........;00 6a 55
ADD [BP+SI+0x55],CL ...........;00 4a 55
ADD [BP+SI+0x55],CX ...........;01 4a 55
ADD [BP+SI+0x55],DH ...........;00 72 55
ADD [BP+SI+0x55],DI ...........;01 7a 55
ADD [BP+SI+0x55],DL ...........;00 52 55
ADD [BP+SI+0x55],DX ...........;01 52 55
ADD [BP+SI+0x55],SI ...........;01 72 55
ADD [BP+SI+0x55],SP ...........;01 62 55
ADD [BP+SI],AH ................;00 22
ADD [BP+SI],AL ................;00 02
ADD [BP+SI],AX ................;01 02
ADD [BP+SI],BH ................;00 3a
ADD [BP+SI],BL ................;00 1a
ADD [BP+SI],BP ................;01 2a
ADD [BP+SI],BX ................;01 1a
ADD [BP+SI],CH ................;00 2a
ADD [BP+SI],CL ................;00 0a
ADD [BP+SI],CX ................;01 0a
ADD [BP+SI],DH ................;00 32
ADD [BP+SI],DI ................;01 3a
ADD [BP+SI],DL ................;00 12
ADD [BP+SI],DX ................;01 12
ADD [BP+SI],SI ................;01 32
ADD [BP+SI],SP ................;01 22
ADD [BX+0x5566],AH ............;00 a7 66 55
ADD [BX+0x5566],AL ............;00 87 66 55
ADD [BX+0x5566],AX ............;01 87 66 55
ADD [BX+0x5566],BH ............;00 bf 66 55
ADD [BX+0x5566],BL ............;00 9f 66 55
ADD [BX+0x5566],BP ............;01 af 66 55
ADD [BX+0x5566],BX ............;01 9f 66 55
ADD [BX+0x5566],CH ............;00 af 66 55
ADD [BX+0x5566],CL ............;00 8f 66 55
ADD [BX+0x5566],CX ............;01 8f 66 55
ADD [BX+0x5566],DH ............;00 b7 66 55

ADD [BX+0x5566],DI ............;01 bf 66 55
ADD [BX+0x5566],DL ............;00 97 66 55
ADD [BX+0x5566],DX ............;01 97 66 55
ADD [BX+0x5566],SI ............;01 b7 66 55
ADD [BX+0x5566],SP ............;01 a7 66 55
ADD [BX+0x55],AH ..............;00 67 55
ADD [BX+0x55],AL ..............;00 47 55
ADD [BX+0x55],AX ..............;01 47 55
ADD [BX+0x55],BH ..............;00 7f 55
ADD [BX+0x55],BL ..............;00 5f 55
ADD [BX+0x55],BP ..............;01 6f 55
ADD [BX+0x55],BX ..............;01 5f 55
ADD [BX+0x55],CH ..............;00 6f 55
ADD [BX+0x55],CL ..............;00 4f 55
ADD [BX+0x55],CX ..............;01 4f 55
ADD [BX+0x55],DH ..............;00 77 55
ADD [BX+0x55],DI ..............;01 7f 55
ADD [BX+0x55],DL ..............;00 57 55
ADD [BX+0x55],DX ..............;01 57 55
ADD [BX+0x55],SI ..............;01 77 55
ADD [BX+0x55],SP ..............;01 67 55
ADD [BX+DI+0x5566],AH .........;00 a1 66 55
ADD [BX+DI+0x5566],AL .........;00 81 66 55
ADD [BX+DI+0x5566],AX .........;01 81 66 55
ADD [BX+DI+0x5566],BH .........;00 b9 66 55
ADD [BX+DI+0x5566],BL .........;00 99 66 55
ADD [BX+DI+0x5566],BP .........;01 a9 66 55
ADD [BX+DI+0x5566],BX .........;01 99 66 55
ADD [BX+DI+0x5566],CH .........;00 a9 66 55
ADD [BX+DI+0x5566],CL .........;00 89 66 55
ADD [BX+DI+0x5566],CX .........;01 89 66 55
ADD [BX+DI+0x5566],DH .........;00 b1 66 55
ADD [BX+DI+0x5566],DI .........;01 b9 66 55
ADD [BX+DI+0x5566],DL .........;00 91 66 55
ADD [BX+DI+0x5566],DX .........;01 91 66 55
ADD [BX+DI+0x5566],SI .........;01 b1 66 55
ADD [BX+DI+0x5566],SP .........;01 a1 66 55
ADD [BX+DI+0x55],AH ...........;00 61 55
ADD [BX+DI+0x55],AL ...........;00 41 55
ADD [BX+DI+0x55],AX ...........;01 41 55
ADD [BX+DI+0x55],BH ...........;00 79 55
ADD [BX+DI+0x55],BL ...........;00 59 55
ADD [BX+DI+0x55],BP ...........;01 69 55
ADD [BX+DI+0x55],BX ...........;01 59 55
ADD [BX+DI+0x55],CH ...........;00 69 55
ADD [BX+DI+0x55],CL ...........;00 49 55
ADD [BX+DI+0x55],CX ...........;01 49 55
ADD [BX+DI+0x55],DH ...........;00 71 55
ADD [BX+DI+0x55],DI ...........;01 79 55
ADD [BX+DI+0x55],DL ...........;00 51 55
ADD [BX+DI+0x55],DX ...........;01 51 55
ADD [BX+DI+0x55],SI ...........;01 71 55
ADD [BX+DI+0x55],SP ...........;01 61 55
ADD [BX+DI],AH ................;00 21
ADD [BX+DI],AL ................;00 01
ADD [BX+DI],AX ................;01 01
ADD [BX+DI],BH ................;00 39
ADD [BX+DI],BL ................;00 19
ADD [BX+DI],BP ................;01 29
ADD [BX+DI],BX ................;01 19
ADD [BX+DI],CH ................;00 29
ADD [BX+DI],CL ................;00 09
ADD [BX+DI],CX ................;01 09
ADD [BX+DI],DH ................;00 31
ADD [BX+DI],DI ................;01 39
ADD [BX+DI],DL ................;00 11
ADD [BX+DI],DX ................;01 11
ADD [BX+DI],SI ................;01 31
ADD [BX+DI],SP ................;01 21
ADD [BX+SI+0x5566],AH .........;00 a0 66 55
ADD [BX+SI+0x5566],AL .........;00 80 66 55
ADD [BX+SI+0x5566],AX .........;01 80 66 55
ADD [BX+SI+0x5566],BH .........;00 b8 66 55
ADD [BX+SI+0x5566],BL .........;00 98 66 55
ADD [BX+SI+0x5566],BP .........;01 a8 66 55
ADD [BX+SI+0x5566],BX .........;01 98 66 55
ADD [BX+SI+0x5566],CH .........;00 a8 66 55
ADD [BX+SI+0x5566],CL .........;00 88 66 55
ADD [BX+SI+0x5566],CX .........;01 88 66 55
ADD [BX+SI+0x5566],DH .........;00 b0 66 55
ADD [BX+SI+0x5566],DI .........;01 b8 66 55
ADD [BX+SI+0x5566],DL .........;00 90 66 55
ADD [BX+SI+0x5566],DX .........;01 90 66 55
ADD [BX+SI+0x5566],SI .........;01 b0 66 55
ADD [BX+SI+0x5566],SP .........;01 a0 66 55
ADD [BX+SI+0x55],AH ...........;00 60 55
ADD [BX+SI+0x55],AL ...........;00 40 55
ADD [BX+SI+0x55],AX ...........;01 40 55
ADD [BX+SI+0x55],BH ...........;00 78 55
```

```
ADD [BX+SI+0x55],BL .............;00 58 55        ADD [DI],DX ....................;01 15
ADD [BX+SI+0x55],BP .............;01 68 55        ADD [DI],SI ....................;01 35
ADD [BX+SI+0x55],BX .............;01 58 55        ADD [DI],SP ....................;01 25
ADD [BX+SI+0x55],CH .............;00 68 55        ADD [SI+0x5566],AH .............;00 a4 66 55
ADD [BX+SI+0x55],CL .............;00 48 55        ADD [SI+0x5566],AL .............;00 84 66 55
ADD [BX+SI+0x55],CX .............;01 48 55        ADD [SI+0x5566],AX .............;01 84 66 55
ADD [BX+SI+0x55],DH .............;00 70 55        ADD [SI+0x5566],BH .............;00 bc 66 55
ADD [BX+SI+0x55],DI .............;01 78 55        ADD [SI+0x5566],BL .............;00 9c 66 55
ADD [BX+SI+0x55],DL .............;00 50 55        ADD [SI+0x5566],BP .............;01 ac 66 55
ADD [BX+SI+0x55],DX .............;01 50 55        ADD [SI+0x5566],BX .............;01 9c 66 55
ADD [BX+SI+0x55],SI .............;01 70 55        ADD [SI+0x5566],CH .............;00 ac 66 55
ADD [BX+SI+0x55],SP .............;01 60 55        ADD [SI+0x5566],CL .............;00 8c 66 55
ADD [BX+SI],AH ..................;00 20           ADD [SI+0x5566],CX .............;01 8c 66 55
ADD [BX+SI],AL ..................;00 00           ADD [SI+0x5566],DH .............;00 b4 66 55
ADD [BX+SI],AX ..................;01 00           ADD [SI+0x5566],DI .............;01 bc 66 55
ADD [BX+SI],BH ..................;00 38           ADD [SI+0x5566],DL .............;00 94 66 55
ADD [BX+SI],BL ..................;00 18           ADD [SI+0x5566],DX .............;01 94 66 55
ADD [BX+SI],BP ..................;01 28           ADD [SI+0x5566],SI .............;01 b4 66 55
ADD [BX+SI],BX ..................;01 18           ADD [SI+0x5566],SP .............;01 a4 66 55
ADD [BX+SI],CH ..................;00 28           ADD [SI+0x55],AH ...............;00 64 55
ADD [BX+SI],CL ..................;00 08           ADD [SI+0x55],AL ...............;00 44 55
ADD [BX+SI],CX ..................;01 08           ADD [SI+0x55],AX ...............;01 44 55
ADD [BX+SI],DH ..................;00 30           ADD [SI+0x55],BH ...............;00 7c 55
ADD [BX+SI],DI ..................;01 38           ADD [SI+0x55],BL ...............;00 5c 55
ADD [BX+SI],DL ..................;00 10           ADD [SI+0x55],BP ...............;01 6c 55
ADD [BX+SI],DX ..................;01 10           ADD [SI+0x55],BX ...............;01 5c 55
ADD [BX+SI],SI ..................;01 30           ADD [SI+0x55],CH ...............;00 6c 55
ADD [BX+SI],SP ..................;01 20           ADD [SI+0x55],CL ...............;00 4c 55
ADD [BX],AH .....................;00 27           ADD [SI+0x55],CX ...............;01 4c 55
ADD [BX],AL .....................;00 07           ADD [SI+0x55],DH ...............;00 74 55
ADD [BX],AX .....................;01 07           ADD [SI+0x55],DI ...............;01 7c 55
ADD [BX],BH .....................;00 3f           ADD [SI+0x55],DL ...............;00 54 55
ADD [BX],BL .....................;00 1f           ADD [SI+0x55],DX ...............;01 54 55
ADD [BX],BP .....................;01 2f           ADD [SI+0x55],SI ...............;01 74 55
ADD [BX],BX .....................;01 1f           ADD [SI+0x55],SP ...............;01 64 55
ADD [BX],CH .....................;00 2f           ADD [SI],AH ....................;00 24
ADD [BX],CL .....................;00 0f           ADD [SI],AL ....................;00 04
ADD [BX],CX .....................;01 0f           ADD [SI],AX ....................;01 04
ADD [BX],DH .....................;00 37           ADD [SI],BH ....................;00 3c
ADD [BX],DI .....................;01 3f           ADD [SI],BL ....................;00 1c
ADD [BX],DL .....................;00 17           ADD [SI],BP ....................;01 2c
ADD [BX],DX .....................;01 17           ADD [SI],BX ....................;01 1c
ADD [BX],SI .....................;01 37           ADD [SI],CH ....................;00 2c
ADD [BX],SP .....................;01 27           ADD [SI],CL ....................;00 0c
ADD [DI+0x5566],AH .............;00 a5 66 55      ADD [SI],CX ....................;01 0c
ADD [DI+0x5566],AL .............;00 85 66 55      ADD [SI],DH ....................;00 34
ADD [DI+0x5566],AX .............;01 85 66 55      ADD [SI],DI ....................;01 3c
ADD [DI+0x5566],BH .............;00 bd 66 55      ADD [SI],DL ....................;00 14
ADD [DI+0x5566],BL .............;00 9d 66 55      ADD [SI],DX ....................;01 14
ADD [DI+0x5566],BP .............;01 ad 66 55      ADD [SI],SI ....................;01 34
ADD [DI+0x5566],BX .............;01 9d 66 55      ADD [SI],SP ....................;01 24
ADD [DI+0x5566],CH .............;00 ad 66 55      AND AH,0x88 ....................;80 e4 88
ADD [DI+0x5566],CL .............;00 8d 66 55      AND AH,AH ......................;20 e4
ADD [DI+0x5566],CX .............;01 8d 66 55      AND AH,AL ......................;20 c4
ADD [DI+0x5566],DH .............;00 b5 66 55      AND AH,BH ......................;20 fc
ADD [DI+0x5566],DI .............;01 bd 66 55      AND AH,BL ......................;20 dc
ADD [DI+0x5566],DL .............;00 95 66 55      AND AH,CH ......................;20 ec
ADD [DI+0x5566],DX .............;01 95 66 55      AND AH,CL ......................;20 cc
ADD [DI+0x5566],SI .............;01 b5 66 55      AND AH,DH ......................;20 f4
ADD [DI+0x5566],SP .............;01 a5 66 55      AND AH,DL ......................;20 d4
ADD [DI+0x55],AH ...............;00 65 55         AND AH,[0x5566] ................;22 26 66 55
ADD [DI+0x55],AL ...............;00 45 55         AND AH,[BP+0x5566] .............;22 a6 66 55
ADD [DI+0x55],AX ...............;01 45 55         AND AH,[BP+0x55] ...............;22 66 55
ADD [DI+0x55],BH ...............;00 7d 55         AND AH,[BP+DI+0x5566] ..........;22 a3 66 55
ADD [DI+0x55],BL ...............;00 5d 55         AND AH,[BP+DI+0x55] ............;22 63 55
ADD [DI+0x55],BP ...............;01 6d 55         AND AH,[BP+DI] .................;22 23
ADD [DI+0x55],BX ...............;01 5d 55         AND AH,[BP+SI+0x5566] ..........;22 a2 66 55
ADD [DI+0x55],CH ...............;00 6d 55         AND AH,[BP+SI+0x55] ............;22 62 55
ADD [DI+0x55],CL ...............;00 4d 55         AND AH,[BP+SI] .................;22 22
ADD [DI+0x55],CX ...............;01 4d 55         AND AH,[BX+0x5566] .............;22 a7 66 55
ADD [DI+0x55],DH ...............;00 75 55         AND AH,[BX+0x55] ...............;22 67 55
ADD [DI+0x55],DI ...............;01 7d 55         AND AH,[BX+DI+0x5566] ..........;22 a1 66 55
ADD [DI+0x55],DL ...............;00 55 55         AND AH,[BX+DI+0x55] ............;22 61 55
ADD [DI+0x55],DX ...............;01 55 55         AND AH,[BX+DI] .................;22 21
ADD [DI+0x55],SI ...............;01 75 55         AND AH,[BX+SI+0x5566] ..........;22 a0 66 55
ADD [DI+0x55],SP ...............;01 65 55         AND AH,[BX+SI+0x55] ............;22 60 55
ADD [DI],AH .....................;00 25           AND AH,[BX+SI] .................;22 20
ADD [DI],AL .....................;00 05           AND AH,[BX] ....................;22 27
ADD [DI],AX .....................;01 05           AND AH,[DI+0x5566] .............;22 a5 66 55
ADD [DI],BH .....................;00 3d           AND AH,[DI+0x55] ...............;22 65 55
ADD [DI],BL .....................;00 1d           AND AH,[DI] ....................;22 25
ADD [DI],BP .....................;01 2d           AND AH,[SI+0x5566] .............;22 a4 66 55
ADD [DI],BX .....................;01 1d           AND AH,[SI+0x55] ...............;22 64 55
ADD [DI],CH .....................;00 2d           AND AH,[SI] ....................;22 24
ADD [DI],CL .....................;00 0d           AND AL,0x55 ....................;24 55
ADD [DI],CX .....................;01 0d           AND AL,0x88 ....................;80 e0 88
ADD [DI],DH .....................;00 35           AND AL,AH ......................;20 e0
ADD [DI],DI .....................;01 3d           AND AL,AL ......................;20 c0
ADD [DI],DL .....................;00 15           AND AL,BH ......................;20 f8
```

175

```
AND AL,BL .....................;20 d8
AND AL,CH .....................;20 e8
AND AL,CL .....................;20 c8
AND AL,DH .....................;20 f0
AND AL,DL .....................;20 d0
AND AL,[0x5566] ...............;22 06 66 55
AND AL,[BP+0x5566] ............;22 86 66 55
AND AL,[BP+0x55] ..............;22 46 55
AND AL,[BP+DI+0x5566] .........;22 83 66 55
AND AL,[BP+DI+0x55] ...........;22 43 55
AND AL,[BP+DI] ................;22 03
AND AL,[BP+SI+0x5566] .........;22 82 66 55
AND AL,[BP+SI+0x55] ...........;22 42 55
AND AL,[BP+SI] ................;22 02
AND AL,[BX+0x5566] ............;22 87 66 55
AND AL,[BX+0x55] ..............;22 47 55
AND AL,[BX+DI+0x5566] .........;22 81 66 55
AND AL,[BX+DI+0x55] ...........;22 41 55
AND AL,[BX+DI] ................;22 01
AND AL,[BX+SI+0x5566] .........;22 80 66 55
AND AL,[BX+SI+0x55] ...........;22 40 55
AND AL,[BX+SI] ................;22 00
AND AL,[BX] ...................;22 07
AND AL,[DI+0x5566] ............;22 85 66 55
AND AL,[DI+0x55] ..............;22 45 55
AND AL,[DI] ...................;22 05
AND AL,[SI+0x5566] ............;22 84 66 55
AND AL,[SI+0x55] ..............;22 44 55
AND AL,[SI] ...................;22 04
AND AX,0x5566 .................;25 66 55
AND AX,0x77 ...................;83 e0 77
AND AX,0x7788 .................;81 e0 88 77
AND AX,AX .....................;21 c0
AND AX,BP .....................;21 e8
AND AX,BX .....................;21 d8
AND AX,CX .....................;21 c8
AND AX,DI .....................;21 f8
AND AX,DX .....................;21 d0
AND AX,SI .....................;21 f0
AND AX,SP .....................;21 e0
AND AX,[0x5566] ...............;23 06 66 55
AND AX,[BP+0x5566] ............;23 86 66 55
AND AX,[BP+0x55] ..............;23 46 55
AND AX,[BP+DI+0x5566] .........;23 83 66 55
AND AX,[BP+DI+0x55] ...........;23 43 55
AND AX,[BP+DI] ................;23 03
AND AX,[BP+SI+0x5566] .........;23 82 66 55
AND AX,[BP+SI+0x55] ...........;23 42 55
AND AX,[BP+SI] ................;23 02
AND AX,[BX+0x5566] ............;23 87 66 55
AND AX,[BX+0x55] ..............;23 47 55
AND AX,[BX+DI+0x5566] .........;23 81 66 55
AND AX,[BX+DI+0x55] ...........;23 41 55
AND AX,[BX+DI] ................;23 01
AND AX,[BX+SI+0x5566] .........;23 80 66 55
AND AX,[BX+SI+0x55] ...........;23 40 55
AND AX,[BX+SI] ................;23 00
AND AX,[BX] ...................;23 07
AND AX,[DI+0x5566] ............;23 85 66 55
AND AX,[DI+0x55] ..............;23 45 55
AND AX,[DI] ...................;23 05
AND AX,[SI+0x5566] ............;23 84 66 55
AND AX,[SI+0x55] ..............;23 44 55
AND AX,[SI] ...................;23 04
AND BH,0x88 ...................;80 e7 88
AND BH,AH .....................;20 e7
AND BH,AL .....................;20 c7
AND BH,BH .....................;20 ff
AND BH,BL .....................;20 df
AND BH,CH .....................;20 ef
AND BH,CL .....................;20 cf
AND BH,DH .....................;20 f7
AND BH,DL .....................;20 d7
AND BH,[0x5566] ...............;22 3e 66 55
AND BH,[BP+0x5566] ............;22 be 66 55
AND BH,[BP+0x55] ..............;22 7e 55
AND BH,[BP+DI+0x5566] .........;22 bb 66 55
AND BH,[BP+DI+0x55] ...........;22 7b 55
AND BH,[BP+DI] ................;22 3b
AND BH,[BP+SI+0x5566] .........;22 ba 66 55
AND BH,[BP+SI+0x55] ...........;22 7a 55
AND BH,[BP+SI] ................;22 3a
AND BH,[BX+0x5566] ............;22 bf 66 55
AND BH,[BX+0x55] ..............;22 7f 55
AND BH,[BX+DI+0x5566] .........;22 b9 66 55
AND BH,[BX+DI+0x55] ...........;22 79 55
AND BH,[BX+DI] ................;22 39
AND BH,[BX+SI+0x5566] .........;22 b8 66 55
AND BH,[BX+SI+0x55] ...........;22 78 55
```

```
AND BH,[BX+SI] ................;22 38
AND BH,[BX] ...................;22 3f
AND BH,[DI+0x5566] ............;22 bd 66 55
AND BH,[DI+0x55] ..............;22 7d 55
AND BH,[DI] ...................;22 3d
AND BH,[SI+0x5566] ............;22 bc 66 55
AND BH,[SI+0x55] ..............;22 7c 55
AND BH,[SI] ...................;22 3c
AND BL,0x88 ...................;80 e3 88
AND BL,AH .....................;20 e3
AND BL,AL .....................;20 c3
AND BL,BH .....................;20 fb
AND BL,BL .....................;20 db
AND BL,CH .....................;20 eb
AND BL,CL .....................;20 cb
AND BL,DH .....................;20 f3
AND BL,DL .....................;20 d3
AND BL,[0x5566] ...............;22 1e 66 55
AND BL,[BP+0x5566] ............;22 9e 66 55
AND BL,[BP+0x55] ..............;22 5e 55
AND BL,[BP+DI+0x5566] .........;22 9b 66 55
AND BL,[BP+DI+0x55] ...........;22 5b 55
AND BL,[BP+DI] ................;22 1b
AND BL,[BP+SI+0x5566] .........;22 9a 66 55
AND BL,[BP+SI+0x55] ...........;22 5a 55
AND BL,[BP+SI] ................;22 1a
AND BL,[BX+0x5566] ............;22 9f 66 55
AND BL,[BX+0x55] ..............;22 5f 55
AND BL,[BX+DI+0x5566] .........;22 99 66 55
AND BL,[BX+DI+0x55] ...........;22 59 55
AND BL,[BX+DI] ................;22 19
AND BL,[BX+SI+0x5566] .........;22 98 66 55
AND BL,[BX+SI+0x55] ...........;22 58 55
AND BL,[BX+SI] ................;22 18
AND BL,[BX] ...................;22 1f
AND BL,[DI+0x5566] ............;22 9d 66 55
AND BL,[DI+0x55] ..............;22 5d 55
AND BL,[DI] ...................;22 1d
AND BL,[SI+0x5566] ............;22 9c 66 55
AND BL,[SI+0x55] ..............;22 5c 55
AND BL,[SI] ...................;22 1c
AND BP,0x77 ...................;83 e5 77
AND BP,0x7788 .................;81 e5 88 77
AND BP,AX .....................;21 c5
AND BP,BP .....................;21 ed
AND BP,BX .....................;21 dd
AND BP,CX .....................;21 cd
AND BP,DI .....................;21 fd
AND BP,DX .....................;21 d5
AND BP,SI .....................;21 f5
AND BP,SP .....................;21 e5
AND BP,[0x5566] ...............;23 2e 66 55
AND BP,[BP+0x5566] ............;23 ae 66 55
AND BP,[BP+0x55] ..............;23 6e 55
AND BP,[BP+DI+0x5566] .........;23 ab 66 55
AND BP,[BP+DI+0x55] ...........;23 6b 55
AND BP,[BP+DI] ................;23 2b
AND BP,[BP+SI+0x5566] .........;23 aa 66 55
AND BP,[BP+SI+0x55] ...........;23 6a 55
AND BP,[BP+SI] ................;23 2a
AND BP,[BX+0x5566] ............;23 af 66 55
AND BP,[BX+0x55] ..............;23 6f 55
AND BP,[BX+DI+0x5566] .........;23 a9 66 55
AND BP,[BX+DI+0x55] ...........;23 69 55
AND BP,[BX+DI] ................;23 29
AND BP,[BX+SI+0x5566] .........;23 a8 66 55
AND BP,[BX+SI+0x55] ...........;23 68 55
AND BP,[BX+SI] ................;23 28
AND BP,[BX] ...................;23 2f
AND BP,[DI+0x5566] ............;23 ad 66 55
AND BP,[DI+0x55] ..............;23 6d 55
AND BP,[DI] ...................;23 2d
AND BP,[SI+0x5566] ............;23 ac 66 55
AND BP,[SI+0x55] ..............;23 6c 55
AND BP,[SI] ...................;23 2c
AND BX,0x77 ...................;83 e3 77
AND BX,0x7788 .................;81 e3 88 77
AND BX,AX .....................;21 c3
AND BX,BP .....................;21 eb
AND BX,BX .....................;21 db
AND BX,CX .....................;21 cb
AND BX,DI .....................;21 fb
AND BX,DX .....................;21 d3
AND BX,SI .....................;21 f3
AND BX,SP .....................;21 e3
AND BX,[0x5566] ...............;23 1e 66 55
AND BX,[BP+0x5566] ............;23 9e 66 55
AND BX,[BP+0x55] ..............;23 5e 55
AND BX,[BP+DI+0x5566] .........;23 9b 66 55
```

```
AND BX,[BP+DI+0x55] .............;23 5b 55
AND BX,[BP+DI] .................;23 1b
AND BX,[BP+SI+0x5566] ..........;23 9a 66 55
AND BX,[BP+SI+0x55] ............;23 5a 55
AND BX,[BP+SI] .................;23 1a
AND BX,[BX+0x5566] .............;23 9f 66 55
AND BX,[BX+0x55] ...............;23 5f 55
AND BX,[BX+DI+0x5566] ..........;23 99 66 55
AND BX,[BX+DI+0x55] ............;23 59 55
AND BX,[BX+DI] .................;23 19
AND BX,[BX+SI+0x5566] ..........;23 98 66 55
AND BX,[BX+SI+0x55] ............;23 58 55
AND BX,[BX+SI] .................;23 18
AND BX,[BX] ....................;23 1f
AND BX,[DI+0x5566] .............;23 9d 66 55
AND BX,[DI+0x55] ...............;23 5d 55
AND BX,[DI] ....................;23 1d
AND BX,[SI+0x5566] .............;23 9c 66 55
AND BX,[SI+0x55] ...............;23 5c 55
AND BX,[SI] ....................;23 1c
AND BYTE [0x5566],0x88 .........;80 26 66 55 88
AND BYTE [BP+0x5566],0x88 ......;80 a6 66 55 88
AND BYTE [BP+0x55],0x88 ........;80 66 55 88
AND BYTE [BP+DI+0x5566],0x88 ...;80 a3 66 55 88
AND BYTE [BP+DI+0x55],0x88 .....;80 63 55 88
AND BYTE [BP+DI],0x88 ..........;80 23 88
AND BYTE [BP+SI+0x5566],0x88 ...;80 a2 66 55 88
AND BYTE [BP+SI+0x55],0x88 .....;80 62 55 88
AND BYTE [BP+SI],0x88 ..........;80 22 88
AND BYTE [BX+0x5566],0x88 ......;80 a7 66 55 88
AND BYTE [BX+0x55],0x88 ........;80 67 55 88
AND BYTE [BX+DI+0x5566],0x88 ...;80 a1 66 55 88
AND BYTE [BX+DI+0x55],0x88 .....;80 61 55 88
AND BYTE [BX+DI],0x88 ..........;80 21 88
AND BYTE [BX+SI+0x5566],0x88 ...;80 a0 66 55 88
AND BYTE [BX+SI+0x55],0x88 .....;80 60 55 88
AND BYTE [BX+SI],0x88 ..........;80 20 88
AND BYTE [BX],0x88 .............;80 27 88
AND BYTE [DI+0x5566],0x88 ......;80 a5 66 55 88
AND BYTE [DI+0x55],0x88 ........;80 65 55 88
AND BYTE [DI],0x88 .............;80 25 88
AND BYTE [SI+0x5566],0x88 ......;80 a4 66 55 88
AND BYTE [SI+0x55],0x88 ........;80 64 55 88
AND BYTE [SI],0x88 .............;80 24 88
AND CH,0x88 ....................;80 e5 88
AND CH,AH ......................;20 e5
AND CH,AL ......................;20 c5
AND CH,BH ......................;20 fd
AND CH,BL ......................;20 dd
AND CH,CH ......................;20 ed
AND CH,CL ......................;20 cd
AND CH,DH ......................;20 f5
AND CH,DL ......................;20 d5
AND CH,[0x5566] ................;22 2e 66 55
AND CH,[BP+0x5566] .............;22 ae 66 55
AND CH,[BP+0x55] ...............;22 6e 55
AND CH,[BP+DI+0x5566] ..........;22 ab 66 55
AND CH,[BP+DI+0x55] ............;22 6b 55
AND CH,[BP+DI] .................;22 2b
AND CH,[BP+SI+0x5566] ..........;22 aa 66 55
AND CH,[BP+SI+0x55] ............;22 6a 55
AND CH,[BP+SI] .................;22 2a
AND CH,[BX+0x5566] .............;22 af 66 55
AND CH,[BX+0x55] ...............;22 6f 55
AND CH,[BX+DI+0x5566] ..........;22 a9 66 55
AND CH,[BX+DI+0x55] ............;22 69 55
AND CH,[BX+DI] .................;22 29
AND CH,[BX+SI+0x5566] ..........;22 a8 66 55
AND CH,[BX+SI+0x55] ............;22 68 55
AND CH,[BX+SI] .................;22 28
AND CH,[BX] ....................;22 2f
AND CH,[DI+0x5566] .............;22 ad 66 55
AND CH,[DI+0x55] ...............;22 6d 55
AND CH,[DI] ....................;22 2d
AND CH,[SI+0x5566] .............;22 ac 66 55
AND CH,[SI+0x55] ...............;22 6c 55
AND CH,[SI] ....................;22 2c
AND CL,0x88 ....................;80 e1 88
AND CL,AH ......................;20 e1
AND CL,AL ......................;20 c1
AND CL,BH ......................;20 f9
AND CL,BL ......................;20 d9
AND CL,CH ......................;20 e9
AND CL,CL ......................;20 c9
AND CL,DH ......................;20 f1
AND CL,DL ......................;20 d1
AND CL,[0x5566] ................;22 0e 66 55
AND CL,[BP+0x5566] .............;22 8e 66 55
AND CL,[BP+0x55] ...............;22 4e 55

AND CL,[BP+DI+0x5566] ..........;22 8b 66 55
AND CL,[BP+DI+0x55] ............;22 4b 55
AND CL,[BP+DI] .................;22 0b
AND CL,[BP+SI+0x5566] ..........;22 8a 66 55
AND CL,[BP+SI+0x55] ............;22 4a 55
AND CL,[BP+SI] .................;22 0a
AND CL,[BX+0x5566] .............;22 8f 66 55
AND CL,[BX+0x55] ...............;22 4f 55
AND CL,[BX+DI+0x5566] ..........;22 89 66 55
AND CL,[BX+DI+0x55] ............;22 49 55
AND CL,[BX+DI] .................;22 09
AND CL,[BX+SI+0x5566] ..........;22 88 66 55
AND CL,[BX+SI+0x55] ............;22 48 55
AND CL,[BX+SI] .................;22 08
AND CL,[BX] ....................;22 0f
AND CL,[DI+0x5566] .............;22 8d 66 55
AND CL,[DI+0x55] ...............;22 4d 55
AND CL,[DI] ....................;22 0d
AND CL,[SI+0x5566] .............;22 8c 66 55
AND CL,[SI+0x55] ...............;22 4c 55
AND CL,[SI] ....................;22 0c
AND CX,0x77 ....................;83 e1 77
AND CX,0x7788 ..................;81 e1 88 77
AND CX,AX ......................;21 c1
AND CX,BP ......................;21 e9
AND CX,BX ......................;21 d9
AND CX,CX ......................;21 c9
AND CX,DI ......................;21 f9
AND CX,DX ......................;21 d1
AND CX,SI ......................;21 f1
AND CX,SP ......................;21 e1
AND CX,[0x5566] ................;23 0e 66 55
AND CX,[BP+0x5566] .............;23 8e 66 55
AND CX,[BP+0x55] ...............;23 4e 55
AND CX,[BP+DI+0x5566] ..........;23 8b 66 55
AND CX,[BP+DI+0x55] ............;23 4b 55
AND CX,[BP+DI] .................;23 0b
AND CX,[BP+SI+0x5566] ..........;23 8a 66 55
AND CX,[BP+SI+0x55] ............;23 4a 55
AND CX,[BP+SI] .................;23 0a
AND CX,[BX+0x5566] .............;23 8f 66 55
AND CX,[BX+0x55] ...............;23 4f 55
AND CX,[BX+DI+0x5566] ..........;23 89 66 55
AND CX,[BX+DI+0x55] ............;23 49 55
AND CX,[BX+DI] .................;23 09
AND CX,[BX+SI+0x5566] ..........;23 88 66 55
AND CX,[BX+SI+0x55] ............;23 48 55
AND CX,[BX+SI] .................;23 08
AND CX,[BX] ....................;23 0f
AND CX,[DI+0x5566] .............;23 8d 66 55
AND CX,[DI+0x55] ...............;23 4d 55
AND CX,[DI] ....................;23 0d
AND CX,[SI+0x5566] .............;23 8c 66 55
AND CX,[SI+0x55] ...............;23 4c 55
AND CX,[SI] ....................;23 0c
AND DH,0x88 ....................;80 e6 88
AND DH,AH ......................;20 e6
AND DH,AL ......................;20 c6
AND DH,BH ......................;20 fe
AND DH,BL ......................;20 de
AND DH,CH ......................;20 ee
AND DH,CL ......................;20 ce
AND DH,DH ......................;20 f6
AND DH,DL ......................;20 d6
AND DH,[0x5566] ................;22 36 66 55
AND DH,[BP+0x5566] .............;22 b6 66 55
AND DH,[BP+0x55] ...............;22 76 55
AND DH,[BP+DI+0x5566] ..........;22 b3 66 55
AND DH,[BP+DI+0x55] ............;22 73 55
AND DH,[BP+DI] .................;22 33
AND DH,[BP+SI+0x5566] ..........;22 b2 66 55
AND DH,[BP+SI+0x55] ............;22 72 55
AND DH,[BP+SI] .................;22 32
AND DH,[BX+0x5566] .............;22 b7 66 55
AND DH,[BX+0x55] ...............;22 77 55
AND DH,[BX+DI+0x5566] ..........;22 b1 66 55
AND DH,[BX+DI+0x55] ............;22 71 55
AND DH,[BX+DI] .................;22 31
AND DH,[BX+SI+0x5566] ..........;22 b0 66 55
AND DH,[BX+SI+0x55] ............;22 70 55
AND DH,[BX+SI] .................;22 30
AND DH,[BX] ....................;22 37
AND DH,[DI+0x5566] .............;22 b5 66 55
AND DH,[DI+0x55] ...............;22 75 55
AND DH,[DI] ....................;22 35
AND DH,[SI+0x5566] .............;22 b4 66 55
AND DH,[SI+0x55] ...............;22 74 55
AND DH,[SI] ....................;22 34
AND DI,0x77 ....................;83 e7 77
```

177

```
AND DI,0x7788 ...............;81 e7 88 77
AND DI,AX ...................;21 c7
AND DI,BP ...................;21 ef
AND DI,BX ...................;21 df
AND DI,CX ...................;21 cf
AND DI,DI ...................;21 ff
AND DI,DX ...................;21 d7
AND DI,SI ...................;21 f7
AND DI,SP ...................;21 e7
AND DI,[0x5566] .............;23 3e 66 55
AND DI,[BP+0x5566] ..........;23 be 66 55
AND DI,[BP+0x55] ............;23 7e 55
AND DI,[BP+DI+0x5566] .......;23 bb 66 55
AND DI,[BP+DI+0x55] .........;23 7b 55
AND DI,[BP+DI] ..............;23 3b
AND DI,[BP+SI+0x5566] .......;23 ba 66 55
AND DI,[BP+SI+0x55] .........;23 7a 55
AND DI,[BP+SI] ..............;23 3a
AND DI,[BX+0x5566] ..........;23 bf 66 55
AND DI,[BX+0x55] ............;23 7f 55
AND DI,[BX+DI+0x5566] .......;23 b9 66 55
AND DI,[BX+DI+0x55] .........;23 79 55
AND DI,[BX+DI] ..............;23 39
AND DI,[BX+SI+0x5566] .......;23 b8 66 55
AND DI,[BX+SI+0x55] .........;23 78 55
AND DI,[BX+SI] ..............;23 38
AND DI,[BX] .................;23 3f
AND DI,[DI+0x5566] ..........;23 bd 66 55
AND DI,[DI+0x55] ............;23 7d 55
AND DI,[DI] .................;23 3d
AND DI,[SI+0x5566] ..........;23 bc 66 55
AND DI,[SI+0x55] ............;23 7c 55
AND DI,[SI] .................;23 3c
AND DL,0x88 .................;80 e2 88
AND DL,AH ...................;20 e2
AND DL,AL ...................;20 c2
AND DL,BH ...................;20 fa
AND DL,BL ...................;20 da
AND DL,CH ...................;20 ea
AND DL,CL ...................;20 ca
AND DL,DH ...................;20 f2
AND DL,DL ...................;20 d2
AND DL,[0x5566] .............;22 16 66 55
AND DL,[BP+0x5566] ..........;22 96 66 55
AND DL,[BP+0x55] ............;22 56 55
AND DL,[BP+DI+0x5566] .......;22 93 66 55
AND DL,[BP+DI+0x55] .........;22 53 55
AND DL,[BP+DI] ..............;22 13
AND DL,[BP+SI+0x5566] .......;22 92 66 55
AND DL,[BP+SI+0x55] .........;22 52 55
AND DL,[BP+SI] ..............;22 12
AND DL,[BX+0x5566] ..........;22 97 66 55
AND DL,[BX+0x55] ............;22 57 55
AND DL,[BX+DI+0x5566] .......;22 91 66 55
AND DL,[BX+DI+0x55] .........;22 51 55
AND DL,[BX+DI] ..............;22 11
AND DL,[BX+SI+0x5566] .......;22 90 66 55
AND DL,[BX+SI+0x55] .........;22 50 55
AND DL,[BX+SI] ..............;22 10
AND DL,[BX] .................;22 17
AND DL,[DI+0x5566] ..........;22 95 66 55
AND DL,[DI+0x55] ............;22 55 55
AND DL,[DI] .................;22 15
AND DL,[SI+0x5566] ..........;22 94 66 55
AND DL,[SI+0x55] ............;22 54 55
AND DL,[SI] .................;22 14
AND DX,0x77 .................;83 e2 77
AND DX,0x7788 ...............;81 e2 88 77
AND DX,AX ...................;21 c2
AND DX,BP ...................;21 ea
AND DX,BX ...................;21 da
AND DX,CX ...................;21 ca
AND DX,DI ...................;21 fa
AND DX,DX ...................;21 d2
AND DX,SI ...................;21 f2
AND DX,SP ...................;21 e2
AND DX,[0x5566] .............;23 16 66 55
AND DX,[BP+0x5566] ..........;23 96 66 55
AND DX,[BP+0x55] ............;23 56 55
AND DX,[BP+DI+0x5566] .......;23 93 66 55
AND DX,[BP+DI+0x55] .........;23 53 55
AND DX,[BP+DI] ..............;23 13
AND DX,[BP+SI+0x5566] .......;23 92 66 55
AND DX,[BP+SI+0x55] .........;23 52 55
AND DX,[BP+SI] ..............;23 12
AND DX,[BX+0x5566] ..........;23 97 66 55
AND DX,[BX+0x55] ............;23 57 55
AND DX,[BX+DI+0x5566] .......;23 91 66 55
AND DX,[BX+DI+0x55] .........;23 51 55

AND DX,[BX+DI] ..............;23 11
AND DX,[BX+SI+0x5566] .......;23 90 66 55
AND DX,[BX+SI+0x55] .........;23 50 55
AND DX,[BX+SI] ..............;23 10
AND DX,[BX] .................;23 17
AND DX,[DI+0x5566] ..........;23 95 66 55
AND DX,[DI+0x55] ............;23 55 55
AND DX,[DI] .................;23 15
AND DX,[SI+0x5566] ..........;23 94 66 55
AND DX,[SI+0x55] ............;23 54 55
AND DX,[SI] .................;23 14
AND SI,0x77 .................;83 e6 77
AND SI,0x7788 ...............;81 e6 88 77
AND SI,AX ...................;21 c6
AND SI,BP ...................;21 ee
AND SI,BX ...................;21 de
AND SI,CX ...................;21 ce
AND SI,DI ...................;21 fe
AND SI,DX ...................;21 d6
AND SI,SI ...................;21 f6
AND SI,SP ...................;21 e6
AND SI,[0x5566] .............;23 36 66 55
AND SI,[BP+0x5566] ..........;23 b6 66 55
AND SI,[BP+0x55] ............;23 76 55
AND SI,[BP+DI+0x5566] .......;23 b3 66 55
AND SI,[BP+DI+0x55] .........;23 73 55
AND SI,[BP+DI] ..............;23 33
AND SI,[BP+SI+0x5566] .......;23 b2 66 55
AND SI,[BP+SI+0x55] .........;23 72 55
AND SI,[BP+SI] ..............;23 32
AND SI,[BX+0x5566] ..........;23 b7 66 55
AND SI,[BX+0x55] ............;23 77 55
AND SI,[BX+DI+0x5566] .......;23 b1 66 55
AND SI,[BX+DI+0x55] .........;23 71 55
AND SI,[BX+DI] ..............;23 31
AND SI,[BX+SI+0x5566] .......;23 b0 66 55
AND SI,[BX+SI+0x55] .........;23 70 55
AND SI,[BX+SI] ..............;23 30
AND SI,[BX] .................;23 37
AND SI,[DI+0x5566] ..........;23 b5 66 55
AND SI,[DI+0x55] ............;23 75 55
AND SI,[DI] .................;23 35
AND SI,[SI+0x5566] ..........;23 b4 66 55
AND SI,[SI+0x55] ............;23 74 55
AND SI,[SI] .................;23 34
AND SP,0x77 .................;83 e4 77
AND SP,0x7788 ...............;81 e4 88 77
AND SP,AX ...................;21 c4
AND SP,BP ...................;21 ec
AND SP,BX ...................;21 dc
AND SP,CX ...................;21 cc
AND SP,DI ...................;21 fc
AND SP,DX ...................;21 d4
AND SP,SI ...................;21 f4
AND SP,SP ...................;21 e4
AND SP,[0x5566] .............;23 26 66 55
AND SP,[BP+0x5566] ..........;23 a6 66 55
AND SP,[BP+0x55] ............;23 66 55
AND SP,[BP+DI+0x5566] .......;23 a3 66 55
AND SP,[BP+DI+0x55] .........;23 63 55
AND SP,[BP+DI] ..............;23 23
AND SP,[BP+SI+0x5566] .......;23 a2 66 55
AND SP,[BP+SI+0x55] .........;23 62 55
AND SP,[BP+SI] ..............;23 22
AND SP,[BX+0x5566] ..........;23 a7 66 55
AND SP,[BX+0x55] ............;23 67 55
AND SP,[BX+DI+0x5566] .......;23 a1 66 55
AND SP,[BX+DI+0x55] .........;23 61 55
AND SP,[BX+DI] ..............;23 21
AND SP,[BX+SI+0x5566] .......;23 a0 66 55
AND SP,[BX+SI+0x55] .........;23 60 55
AND SP,[BX+SI] ..............;23 20
AND SP,[BX] .................;23 27
AND SP,[DI+0x5566] ..........;23 a5 66 55
AND SP,[DI+0x55] ............;23 65 55
AND SP,[DI] .................;23 25
AND SP,[SI+0x5566] ..........;23 a4 66 55
AND SP,[SI+0x55] ............;23 64 55
AND SP,[SI] .................;23 24
AND WORD [0x5566],0x77 ......;83 26 66 55 77
AND WORD [0x5566],0x7788 ....;81 26 66 55 88 77
AND WORD [BP+0x5566],0x77 ...;83 a6 66 55 77
AND WORD [BP+0x5566],0x7788 .;81 a6 66 55 88 77
AND WORD [BP+0x55],0x77 .....;83 66 55 77
AND WORD [BP+0x55],0x7788 ...;81 66 55 88 77
AND WORD [BP+DI+0x5566],0x77 ;83 a3 66 55 77
AND WORD [BP+DI+0x5566],0x7788 .;81 a3 66 55 88 77
AND WORD [BP+DI+0x55],0x77 ...;83 63 55 77
AND WORD [BP+DI+0x55],0x7788 ...;81 63 55 88 77
```

```
AND WORD [BP+DI],0x77 ...........;83 23 77                    AND [BP+DI+0x5566],BH ..........;20 bb 66 55
AND WORD [BP+DI],0x7788 .........;81 23 88 77                 AND [BP+DI+0x5566],BL ..........;20 9b 66 55
AND WORD [BP+SI+0x5566],0x77 ....;83 a2 66 55 77             AND [BP+DI+0x5566],BP ..........;21 ab 66 55
AND WORD [BP+SI+0x5566],0x7788 ..;81 a2 66 55 88 77         AND [BP+DI+0x5566],BX ..........;21 9b 66 55
AND WORD [BP+SI+0x55],0x77 ......;83 62 55 77               AND [BP+DI+0x5566],CH ..........;20 ab 66 55
AND WORD [BP+SI+0x55],0x7788 ....;81 62 55 88 77           AND [BP+DI+0x5566],CL ..........;20 8b 66 55
AND WORD [BP+SI],0x77 ...........;83 22 77                   AND [BP+DI+0x5566],CX ..........;21 8b 66 55
AND WORD [BP+SI],0x7788 .........;81 22 88 77               AND [BP+DI+0x5566],DH ..........;20 b3 66 55
AND WORD [BX+0x5566],0x77 .......;83 a7 66 55 77           AND [BP+DI+0x5566],DI ..........;21 bb 66 55
AND WORD [BX+0x5566],0x7788 .....;81 a7 66 55 88 77       AND [BP+DI+0x5566],DL ..........;20 93 66 55
AND WORD [BX+0x55],0x77 .........;83 67 55 77               AND [BP+DI+0x5566],DX ..........;21 93 66 55
AND WORD [BX+0x55],0x7788 .......;81 67 55 88 77           AND [BP+DI+0x5566],SI ..........;21 b3 66 55
AND WORD [BX+DI+0x5566],0x77 ....;83 a1 66 55 77           AND [BP+DI+0x5566],SP ..........;21 a3 66 55
AND WORD [BX+DI+0x5566],0x7788 ..;81 a1 66 55 88 77       AND [BP+DI+0x55],AH .............;20 63 55
AND WORD [BX+DI+0x55],0x77 ......;83 61 55 77               AND [BP+DI+0x55],AX .............;20 43 55
AND WORD [BX+DI+0x55],0x7788 ....;81 61 55 88 77           AND [BP+DI+0x55],AX .............;21 43 55
AND WORD [BX+DI],0x77 ...........;83 21 77                   AND [BP+DI+0x55],BH .............;20 7b 55
AND WORD [BX+DI],0x7788 .........;81 21 88 77               AND [BP+DI+0x55],BL .............;20 5b 55
AND WORD [BX+SI+0x5566],0x77 ....;83 a0 66 55 77           AND [BP+DI+0x55],BP .............;21 6b 55
AND WORD [BX+SI+0x5566],0x7788 ..;81 a0 66 55 88 77       AND [BP+DI+0x55],BX .............;21 5b 55
AND WORD [BX+SI+0x55],0x77 ......;83 60 55 77               AND [BP+DI+0x55],CH .............;20 6b 55
AND WORD [BX+SI+0x55],0x7788 ....;81 60 55 88 77           AND [BP+DI+0x55],CL .............;20 4b 55
AND WORD [BX+SI],0x77 ...........;83 20 77                   AND [BP+DI+0x55],CX .............;21 4b 55
AND WORD [BX+SI],0x7788 .........;81 20 88 77               AND [BP+DI+0x55],DH .............;20 73 55
AND WORD [BX],0x77 ..............;83 27 77                   AND [BP+DI+0x55],DI .............;21 7b 55
AND WORD [BX],0x7788 ............;81 27 88 77               AND [BP+DI+0x55],DL .............;20 53 55
AND WORD [DI+0x5566],0x77 .......;83 a5 66 55 77           AND [BP+DI+0x55],DX .............;21 53 55
AND WORD [DI+0x5566],0x7788 .....;81 a5 66 55 88 77       AND [BP+DI+0x55],SI .............;21 73 55
AND WORD [DI+0x55],0x77 .........;83 65 55 77               AND [BP+DI+0x55],SP .............;21 63 55
AND WORD [DI+0x55],0x7788 .......;81 65 55 88 77           AND [BP+DI],AH .................;20 23
AND WORD [DI],0x77 ..............;83 25 77                   AND [BP+DI],AL .................;20 03
AND WORD [DI],0x7788 ............;81 25 88 77               AND [BP+DI],AX .................;21 03
AND WORD [SI+0x5566],0x77 .......;83 a4 66 55 77           AND [BP+DI],BH .................;20 3b
AND WORD [SI+0x5566],0x7788 .....;81 a4 66 55 88 77       AND [BP+DI],BL .................;20 1b
AND WORD [SI+0x55],0x77 .........;83 64 55 77               AND [BP+DI],BP .................;21 2b
AND WORD [SI+0x55],0x7788 .......;81 64 55 88 77           AND [BP+DI],BX .................;21 1b
AND WORD [SI],0x77 ..............;83 24 77                   AND [BP+DI],CH .................;20 2b
AND WORD [SI],0x7788 ............;81 24 88 77               AND [BP+DI],CL .................;20 0b
AND [0x5566],AH .................;20 26 66 55               AND [BP+DI],CX .................;21 0b
AND [0x5566],AL .................;20 06 66 55               AND [BP+DI],DH .................;20 33
AND [0x5566],AX .................;21 06 66 55               AND [BP+DI],DI .................;21 3b
AND [0x5566],BH .................;20 3e 66 55               AND [BP+DI],DL .................;20 13
AND [0x5566],BL .................;20 1e 66 55               AND [BP+DI],DX .................;21 13
AND [0x5566],BP .................;21 2e 66 55               AND [BP+DI],SI .................;21 33
AND [0x5566],BX .................;21 1e 66 55               AND [BP+DI],SP .................;21 23
AND [0x5566],CH .................;20 2e 66 55               AND [BP+SI+0x5566],AH ..........;20 a2 66 55
AND [0x5566],CL .................;20 0e 66 55               AND [BP+SI+0x5566],AL ..........;20 82 66 55
AND [0x5566],CX .................;21 0e 66 55               AND [BP+SI+0x5566],AX ..........;21 82 66 55
AND [0x5566],DH .................;20 36 66 55               AND [BP+SI+0x5566],BH ..........;20 ba 66 55
AND [0x5566],DI .................;21 3e 66 55               AND [BP+SI+0x5566],BL ..........;20 9a 66 55
AND [0x5566],DL .................;20 16 66 55               AND [BP+SI+0x5566],BP ..........;21 aa 66 55
AND [0x5566],DX .................;21 16 66 55               AND [BP+SI+0x5566],BX ..........;21 9a 66 55
AND [0x5566],SI .................;21 36 66 55               AND [BP+SI+0x5566],CH ..........;20 aa 66 55
AND [0x5566],SP .................;21 26 66 55               AND [BP+SI+0x5566],CL ..........;20 8a 66 55
AND [BP+0x5566],AH ..............;20 a6 66 55               AND [BP+SI+0x5566],CX ..........;21 8a 66 55
AND [BP+0x5566],AL ..............;20 86 66 55               AND [BP+SI+0x5566],DH ..........;20 b2 66 55
AND [BP+0x5566],AX ..............;21 86 66 55               AND [BP+SI+0x5566],DI ..........;21 ba 66 55
AND [BP+0x5566],BH ..............;20 be 66 55               AND [BP+SI+0x5566],DL ..........;20 92 66 55
AND [BP+0x5566],BL ..............;20 9e 66 55               AND [BP+SI+0x5566],DX ..........;21 92 66 55
AND [BP+0x5566],BP ..............;21 ae 66 55               AND [BP+SI+0x5566],SI ..........;21 b2 66 55
AND [BP+0x5566],BX ..............;21 9e 66 55               AND [BP+SI+0x5566],SP ..........;21 a2 66 55
AND [BP+0x5566],CH ..............;20 ae 66 55               AND [BP+SI+0x55],AH ............;20 62 55
AND [BP+0x5566],CL ..............;20 8e 66 55               AND [BP+SI+0x55],AL ............;20 42 55
AND [BP+0x5566],CX ..............;21 8e 66 55               AND [BP+SI+0x55],AX ............;21 42 55
AND [BP+0x5566],DH ..............;20 b6 66 55               AND [BP+SI+0x55],BH ............;20 7a 55
AND [BP+0x5566],DI ..............;21 be 66 55               AND [BP+SI+0x55],BL ............;20 5a 55
AND [BP+0x5566],DL ..............;20 96 66 55               AND [BP+SI+0x55],BP ............;21 6a 55
AND [BP+0x5566],DX ..............;21 96 66 55               AND [BP+SI+0x55],BX ............;21 5a 55
AND [BP+0x5566],SI ..............;21 b6 66 55               AND [BP+SI+0x55],CH ............;20 6a 55
AND [BP+0x5566],SP ..............;21 a6 66 55               AND [BP+SI+0x55],CL ............;20 4a 55
AND [BP+0x55],AH ................;20 66 55                   AND [BP+SI+0x55],CX ............;21 4a 55
AND [BP+0x55],AL ................;20 46 55                   AND [BP+SI+0x55],DH ............;20 72 55
AND [BP+0x55],AX ................;21 46 55                   AND [BP+SI+0x55],DI ............;21 7a 55
AND [BP+0x55],BH ................;20 7e 55                   AND [BP+SI+0x55],DL ............;20 52 55
AND [BP+0x55],BL ................;20 5e 55                   AND [BP+SI+0x55],DX ............;21 52 55
AND [BP+0x55],BP ................;21 6e 55                   AND [BP+SI+0x55],SI ............;21 72 55
AND [BP+0x55],BX ................;21 5e 55                   AND [BP+SI+0x55],SP ............;21 62 55
AND [BP+0x55],CH ................;20 6e 55                   AND [BP+SI],AH .................;20 22
AND [BP+0x55],CL ................;20 4e 55                   AND [BP+SI],AL .................;20 02
AND [BP+0x55],CX ................;21 4e 55                   AND [BP+SI],AX .................;21 02
AND [BP+0x55],DH ................;20 76 55                   AND [BP+SI],BH .................;20 3a
AND [BP+0x55],DI ................;21 7e 55                   AND [BP+SI],BL .................;20 1a
AND [BP+0x55],DL ................;20 56 55                   AND [BP+SI],BP .................;21 2a
AND [BP+0x55],DX ................;21 56 55                   AND [BP+SI],BX .................;21 1a
AND [BP+0x55],SI ................;21 76 55                   AND [BP+SI],CH .................;20 2a
AND [BP+0x55],SP ................;21 66 55                   AND [BP+SI],CL .................;20 0a
AND [BP+DI+0x5566],AH ..........;20 a3 66 55               AND [BP+SI],CX .................;21 0a
AND [BP+DI+0x5566],AL ..........;20 83 66 55               AND [BP+SI],DH .................;20 32
AND [BP+DI+0x5566],AX ..........;21 83 66 55               AND [BP+SI],DI .................;21 3a
```

179

```
AND [BP+SI],DL ................;20 12
AND [BP+SI],DX ................;21 12
AND [BP+SI],SI ................;21 32
AND [BP+SI],SP ................;21 22
AND [BX+0x5566],AH ...........;20 a7 66 55
AND [BX+0x5566],AL ...........;20 87 66 55
AND [BX+0x5566],AX ...........;21 87 66 55
AND [BX+0x5566],BH ...........;20 bf 66 55
AND [BX+0x5566],BL ...........;20 9f 66 55
AND [BX+0x5566],BP ...........;21 af 66 55
AND [BX+0x5566],BX ...........;21 9f 66 55
AND [BX+0x5566],CH ...........;20 af 66 55
AND [BX+0x5566],CL ...........;20 8f 66 55
AND [BX+0x5566],CX ...........;21 8f 66 55
AND [BX+0x5566],DH ...........;20 b7 66 55
AND [BX+0x5566],DI ...........;21 bf 66 55
AND [BX+0x5566],DL ...........;20 97 66 55
AND [BX+0x5566],DX ...........;21 97 66 55
AND [BX+0x5566],SI ...........;21 b7 66 55
AND [BX+0x5566],SP ...........;21 a7 66 55
AND [BX+0x55],AH ..............;20 67 55
AND [BX+0x55],AL ..............;20 47 55
AND [BX+0x55],AX ..............;21 47 55
AND [BX+0x55],BH ..............;20 7f 55
AND [BX+0x55],BL ..............;20 5f 55
AND [BX+0x55],BP ..............;21 6f 55
AND [BX+0x55],BX ..............;21 5f 55
AND [BX+0x55],CH ..............;20 6f 55
AND [BX+0x55],CL ..............;20 4f 55
AND [BX+0x55],CX ..............;21 4f 55
AND [BX+0x55],DH ..............;20 77 55
AND [BX+0x55],DI ..............;21 7f 55
AND [BX+0x55],DL ..............;20 57 55
AND [BX+0x55],DX ..............;21 57 55
AND [BX+0x55],SI ..............;21 77 55
AND [BX+0x55],SP ..............;21 67 55
AND [BX+DI+0x5566],AH ........;20 a1 66 55
AND [BX+DI+0x5566],AL ........;20 81 66 55
AND [BX+DI+0x5566],AX ........;21 81 66 55
AND [BX+DI+0x5566],BH ........;20 b9 66 55
AND [BX+DI+0x5566],BL ........;20 99 66 55
AND [BX+DI+0x5566],BP ........;21 a9 66 55
AND [BX+DI+0x5566],BX ........;21 99 66 55
AND [BX+DI+0x5566],CH ........;20 a9 66 55
AND [BX+DI+0x5566],CL ........;20 89 66 55
AND [BX+DI+0x5566],CX ........;21 89 66 55
AND [BX+DI+0x5566],DH ........;20 b1 66 55
AND [BX+DI+0x5566],DI ........;21 b9 66 55
AND [BX+DI+0x5566],DL ........;20 91 66 55
AND [BX+DI+0x5566],DX ........;21 91 66 55
AND [BX+DI+0x5566],SI ........;21 b1 66 55
AND [BX+DI+0x5566],SP ........;21 a1 66 55
AND [BX+DI+0x55],AH ..........;20 61 55
AND [BX+DI+0x55],AL ..........;20 41 55
AND [BX+DI+0x55],AX ..........;21 41 55
AND [BX+DI+0x55],BH ..........;20 79 55
AND [BX+DI+0x55],BL ..........;20 59 55
AND [BX+DI+0x55],BP ..........;21 69 55
AND [BX+DI+0x55],BX ..........;21 59 55
AND [BX+DI+0x55],CH ..........;20 69 55
AND [BX+DI+0x55],CL ..........;20 49 55
AND [BX+DI+0x55],CX ..........;21 49 55
AND [BX+DI+0x55],DH ..........;20 71 55
AND [BX+DI+0x55],DI ..........;21 79 55
AND [BX+DI+0x55],DL ..........;20 51 55
AND [BX+DI+0x55],DX ..........;21 51 55
AND [BX+DI+0x55],SI ..........;21 71 55
AND [BX+DI+0x55],SP ..........;21 61 55
AND [BX+DI],AH ................;20 21
AND [BX+DI],AL ................;20 01
AND [BX+DI],AX ................;21 01
AND [BX+DI],BH ................;20 39
AND [BX+DI],BL ................;20 19
AND [BX+DI],BP ................;21 29
AND [BX+DI],BX ................;21 19
AND [BX+DI],CH ................;20 29
AND [BX+DI],CL ................;20 09
AND [BX+DI],CX ................;21 09
AND [BX+DI],DH ................;20 31
AND [BX+DI],DI ................;21 39
AND [BX+DI],DL ................;20 11
AND [BX+DI],DX ................;21 11
AND [BX+DI],SI ................;21 31
AND [BX+DI],SP ................;21 21
AND [BX+SI+0x5566],AH ........;20 a0 66 55
AND [BX+SI+0x5566],AL ........;20 80 66 55
AND [BX+SI+0x5566],AX ........;21 80 66 55
AND [BX+SI+0x5566],BH ........;20 b8 66 55
AND [BX+SI+0x5566],BL ........;20 98 66 55

AND [BX+SI+0x5566],BP .........;21 a8 66 55
AND [BX+SI+0x5566],BX .........;21 98 66 55
AND [BX+SI+0x5566],CH .........;20 a8 66 55
AND [BX+SI+0x5566],CL .........;20 88 66 55
AND [BX+SI+0x5566],CX .........;21 88 66 55
AND [BX+SI+0x5566],DH .........;20 b0 66 55
AND [BX+SI+0x5566],DI .........;21 b8 66 55
AND [BX+SI+0x5566],DL .........;20 90 66 55
AND [BX+SI+0x5566],DX .........;21 90 66 55
AND [BX+SI+0x5566],SI .........;21 b0 66 55
AND [BX+SI+0x5566],SP .........;21 a0 66 55
AND [BX+SI+0x55],AH ...........;20 60 55
AND [BX+SI+0x55],AL ...........;20 40 55
AND [BX+SI+0x55],AX ...........;21 40 55
AND [BX+SI+0x55],BH ...........;20 78 55
AND [BX+SI+0x55],BL ...........;20 58 55
AND [BX+SI+0x55],BP ...........;21 68 55
AND [BX+SI+0x55],BX ...........;21 58 55
AND [BX+SI+0x55],CH ...........;20 68 55
AND [BX+SI+0x55],CL ...........;20 48 55
AND [BX+SI+0x55],CX ...........;21 48 55
AND [BX+SI+0x55],DH ...........;20 70 55
AND [BX+SI+0x55],DI ...........;21 78 55
AND [BX+SI+0x55],DL ...........;20 50 55
AND [BX+SI+0x55],DX ...........;21 50 55
AND [BX+SI+0x55],SI ...........;21 70 55
AND [BX+SI+0x55],SP ...........;21 60 55
AND [BX+SI],AH ................;20 20
AND [BX+SI],AL ................;20 00
AND [BX+SI],AX ................;21 00
AND [BX+SI],BH ................;20 38
AND [BX+SI],BL ................;20 18
AND [BX+SI],BP ................;21 28
AND [BX+SI],BX ................;21 18
AND [BX+SI],CH ................;20 28
AND [BX+SI],CL ................;20 08
AND [BX+SI],CX ................;21 08
AND [BX+SI],DH ................;20 30
AND [BX+SI],DI ................;21 38
AND [BX+SI],DL ................;20 10
AND [BX+SI],DX ................;21 10
AND [BX+SI],SI ................;21 30
AND [BX+SI],SP ................;21 20
AND [BX],AH ...................;20 27
AND [BX],AL ...................;20 07
AND [BX],AX ...................;21 07
AND [BX],BH ...................;20 3f
AND [BX],BL ...................;20 1f
AND [BX],BP ...................;21 2f
AND [BX],BX ...................;21 1f
AND [BX],CH ...................;20 2f
AND [BX],CL ...................;20 0f
AND [BX],CX ...................;21 0f
AND [BX],DH ...................;20 37
AND [BX],DI ...................;21 3f
AND [BX],DL ...................;20 17
AND [BX],DX ...................;21 17
AND [BX],SI ...................;21 37
AND [BX],SP ...................;21 27
AND [DI+0x5566],AH ...........;20 a5 66 55
AND [DI+0x5566],AL ...........;20 85 66 55
AND [DI+0x5566],AX ...........;21 85 66 55
AND [DI+0x5566],BH ...........;20 bd 66 55
AND [DI+0x5566],BL ...........;20 9d 66 55
AND [DI+0x5566],BP ...........;21 ad 66 55
AND [DI+0x5566],BX ...........;21 9d 66 55
AND [DI+0x5566],CH ...........;20 ad 66 55
AND [DI+0x5566],CL ...........;20 8d 66 55
AND [DI+0x5566],CX ...........;21 8d 66 55
AND [DI+0x5566],DH ...........;20 b5 66 55
AND [DI+0x5566],DI ...........;21 bd 66 55
AND [DI+0x5566],DL ...........;20 95 66 55
AND [DI+0x5566],DX ...........;21 95 66 55
AND [DI+0x5566],SI ...........;21 b5 66 55
AND [DI+0x5566],SP ...........;21 a5 66 55
AND [DI+0x55],AH ..............;20 65 55
AND [DI+0x55],AL ..............;20 45 55
AND [DI+0x55],AX ..............;21 45 55
AND [DI+0x55],BH ..............;20 7d 55
AND [DI+0x55],BL ..............;20 5d 55
AND [DI+0x55],BP ..............;21 6d 55
AND [DI+0x55],BX ..............;21 5d 55
AND [DI+0x55],CH ..............;20 6d 55
AND [DI+0x55],CL ..............;20 4d 55
AND [DI+0x55],CX ..............;21 4d 55
AND [DI+0x55],DH ..............;20 75 55
AND [DI+0x55],DI ..............;21 7d 55
AND [DI+0x55],DL ..............;20 55 55
AND [DI+0x55],DX ..............;21 55 55
```

```
AND [DI+0x55],SI .............;21 75 55
AND [DI+0x55],SP .............;21 65 55
AND [DI],AH ..................;20 25
AND [DI],AL ..................;20 05
AND [DI],AX ..................;21 05
AND [DI],BH ..................;20 3d
AND [DI],BL ..................;20 1d
AND [DI],BP ..................;21 2d
AND [DI],BX ..................;21 1d
AND [DI],CH ..................;20 2d
AND [DI],CL ..................;20 0d
AND [DI],CX ..................;21 0d
AND [DI],DH ..................;20 35
AND [DI],DI ..................;21 3d
AND [DI],DL ..................;20 15
AND [DI],DX ..................;21 15
AND [DI],SI ..................;21 35
AND [DI],SP ..................;21 25
AND [SI+0x5566],AH ...........;20 a4 66 55
AND [SI+0x5566],AL ...........;20 84 66 55
AND [SI+0x5566],AX ...........;21 84 66 55
AND [SI+0x5566],BH ...........;20 bc 66 55
AND [SI+0x5566],BL ...........;20 9c 66 55
AND [SI+0x5566],BP ...........;21 ac 66 55
AND [SI+0x5566],BX ...........;21 9c 66 55
AND [SI+0x5566],CH ...........;20 ac 66 55
AND [SI+0x5566],CL ...........;20 8c 66 55
AND [SI+0x5566],CX ...........;21 8c 66 55
AND [SI+0x5566],DH ...........;20 b4 66 55
AND [SI+0x5566],DI ...........;21 bc 66 55
AND [SI+0x5566],DL ...........;20 94 66 55
AND [SI+0x5566],DX ...........;21 94 66 55
AND [SI+0x5566],SI ...........;21 b4 66 55
AND [SI+0x5566],SP ...........;21 a4 66 55
AND [SI+0x55],AH .............;20 64 55
AND [SI+0x55],AL .............;20 44 55
AND [SI+0x55],AX .............;21 44 55
AND [SI+0x55],BH .............;20 7c 55
AND [SI+0x55],BL .............;20 5c 55
AND [SI+0x55],BP .............;21 6c 55
AND [SI+0x55],BX .............;21 5c 55
AND [SI+0x55],CH .............;20 6c 55
AND [SI+0x55],CL .............;20 4c 55
AND [SI+0x55],CX .............;21 4c 55
AND [SI+0x55],DH .............;20 74 55
AND [SI+0x55],DI .............;21 7c 55
AND [SI+0x55],DL .............;20 54 55
AND [SI+0x55],DX .............;21 54 55
AND [SI+0x55],SI .............;21 74 55
AND [SI+0x55],SP .............;21 64 55
AND [SI],AH ..................;20 24
AND [SI],AL ..................;20 04
AND [SI],AX ..................;21 04
AND [SI],BH ..................;20 3c
AND [SI],BL ..................;20 1c
AND [SI],BP ..................;21 2c
AND [SI],BX ..................;21 1c
AND [SI],CH ..................;20 2c
AND [SI],CL ..................;20 0c
AND [SI],CX ..................;21 0c
AND [SI],DH ..................;20 34
AND [SI],DI ..................;21 3c
AND [SI],DL ..................;20 14
AND [SI],DX ..................;21 14
AND [SI],SI ..................;21 34
AND [SI],SP ..................;21 24
CALL 0x5566 ..................;e8 66 55
CALL 0x5566:0x7788 ...........;9a 66 55 88 77
CALL FAR [0x5566] ............;ff 1e 66 55
CALL FAR [BP+0x5566] .........;ff 9e 66 55
CALL FAR [BP+0x55] ...........;ff 5e 55
CALL FAR [BP+DI+0x5566] ......;ff 9b 66 55
CALL FAR [BP+DI+0x55] ........;ff 5b 55
CALL FAR [BP+DI] .............;ff 1b
CALL FAR [BP+SI+0x5566] ......;ff 9a 66 55
CALL FAR [BP+SI+0x55] ........;ff 5a 55
CALL FAR [BP+SI] .............;ff 1a
CALL FAR [BX+0x5566] .........;ff 9f 66 55
CALL FAR [BX+0x55] ...........;ff 5f 55
CALL FAR [BX+DI+0x5566] ......;ff 99 66 55
CALL FAR [BX+DI+0x55] ........;ff 59 55
CALL FAR [BX+DI] .............;ff 19
CALL FAR [BX+SI+0x5566] ......;ff 98 66 55
CALL FAR [BX+SI+0x55] ........;ff 58 55
CALL FAR [BX+SI] .............;ff 18
CALL FAR [BX] ................;ff 1f
CALL FAR [DI+0x5566] .........;ff 9d 66 55
CALL FAR [DI+0x55] ...........;ff 5d 55
CALL FAR [DI] ................;ff 1d

CALL FAR [SI+0x5566] .........;ff 9c 66 55
CALL FAR [SI+0x55] ...........;ff 5c 55
CALL FAR [SI] ................;ff 1c
CALL [0x5566] ................;ff 16 66 55
CALL [BP+0x5566] .............;ff 96 66 55
CALL [BP+0x55] ...............;ff 56 55
CALL [BP+DI+0x5566] ..........;ff 93 66 55
CALL [BP+DI+0x55] ............;ff 53 55
CALL [BP+DI] .................;ff 13
CALL [BP+SI+0x5566] ..........;ff 92 66 55
CALL [BP+SI+0x55] ............;ff 52 55
CALL [BP+SI] .................;ff 12
CALL [BX+0x5566] .............;ff 97 66 55
CALL [BX+0x55] ...............;ff 57 55
CALL [BX+DI+0x5566] ..........;ff 91 66 55
CALL [BX+DI+0x55] ............;ff 51 55
CALL [BX+DI] .................;ff 11
CALL [BX+SI+0x5566] ..........;ff 90 66 55
CALL [BX+SI+0x55] ............;ff 50 55
CALL [BX+SI] .................;ff 10
CALL [BX] ....................;ff 17
CALL [DI+0x5566] .............;ff 95 66 55
CALL [DI+0x55] ...............;ff 55 55
CALL [DI] ....................;ff 15
CALL [SI+0x5566] .............;ff 94 66 55
CALL [SI+0x55] ...............;ff 54 55
CALL [SI] ....................;ff 14
CBW ..........................;98
CLC ..........................;f8
CLD ..........................;fc
CLI ..........................;fa
CMC ..........................;f5
CMP AH,0x88 ..................;80 fc 88
CMP AH,AH ....................;38 e4
CMP AH,AL ....................;38 c4
CMP AH,BH ....................;38 fc
CMP AH,BL ....................;38 dc
CMP AH,CH ....................;38 ec
CMP AH,CL ....................;38 cc
CMP AH,DH ....................;38 f4
CMP AH,DL ....................;38 d4
CMP AH,[0x5566] ..............;3a 26 66 55
CMP AH,[BP+0x5566] ...........;3a a6 66 55
CMP AH,[BP+0x55] .............;3a 66 55
CMP AH,[BP+DI+0x5566] ........;3a a3 66 55
CMP AH,[BP+DI+0x55] ..........;3a 63 55
CMP AH,[BP+DI] ...............;3a 23
CMP AH,[BP+SI+0x5566] ........;3a a2 66 55
CMP AH,[BP+SI+0x55] ..........;3a 62 55
CMP AH,[BP+SI] ...............;3a 22
CMP AH,[BX+0x5566] ...........;3a a7 66 55
CMP AH,[BX+0x55] .............;3a 67 55
CMP AH,[BX+DI+0x5566] ........;3a a1 66 55
CMP AH,[BX+DI+0x55] ..........;3a 61 55
CMP AH,[BX+DI] ...............;3a 21
CMP AH,[BX+SI+0x5566] ........;3a a0 66 55
CMP AH,[BX+SI+0x55] ..........;3a 60 55
CMP AH,[BX+SI] ...............;3a 20
CMP AH,[BX] ..................;3a 27
CMP AH,[DI+0x5566] ...........;3a a5 66 55
CMP AH,[DI+0x55] .............;3a 65 55
CMP AH,[DI] ..................;3a 25
CMP AH,[SI+0x5566] ...........;3a a4 66 55
CMP AH,[SI+0x55] .............;3a 64 55
CMP AH,[SI] ..................;3c 55
CMP AL,0x55 ..................;3c 55
CMP AL,0x88 ..................;80 f8 88
CMP AL,AH ....................;38 e0
CMP AL,AL ....................;38 c0
CMP AL,BH ....................;38 f8
CMP AL,BL ....................;38 d8
CMP AL,CH ....................;38 e8
CMP AL,CL ....................;38 c8
CMP AL,DH ....................;38 f0
CMP AL,DL ....................;38 d0
CMP AL,[0x5566] ..............;3a 06 66 55
CMP AL,[BP+0x5566] ...........;3a 86 66 55
CMP AL,[BP+0x55] .............;3a 46 55
CMP AL,[BP+DI+0x5566] ........;3a 83 66 55
CMP AL,[BP+DI+0x55] ..........;3a 43 55
CMP AL,[BP+DI] ...............;3a 03
CMP AL,[BP+SI+0x5566] ........;3a 82 66 55
CMP AL,[BP+SI+0x55] ..........;3a 42 55
CMP AL,[BP+SI] ...............;3a 02
CMP AL,[BX+0x5566] ...........;3a 87 66 55
CMP AL,[BX+0x55] .............;3a 47 55
CMP AL,[BX+DI+0x5566] ........;3a 81 66 55
CMP AL,[BX+DI+0x55] ..........;3a 41 55
CMP AL,[BX+DI] ...............;3a 01
```

```
CMP AL,[BX+SI+0x5566] ..........;3a 80 66 55
CMP AL,[BX+SI+0x55] ...........;3a 40 55
CMP AL,[BX+SI] .............;3a 00
CMP AL,[BX] .............;3a 07
CMP AL,[DI+0x5566] ...........;3a 85 66 55
CMP AL,[DI+0x55] ...........;3a 45 55
CMP AL,[DI] .............;3a 05
CMP AL,[SI+0x5566] ...........;3a 84 66 55
CMP AL,[SI+0x55] ...........;3a 44 55
CMP AL,[SI] .............;3a 04
CMP AX,0x5566 .............;3d 66 55
CMP AX,0x77 .............;83 f8 77
CMP AX,0x7788 .............;81 f8 88 77
CMP AX,AX .............;39 c0
CMP AX,BP .............;39 e8
CMP AX,BX .............;39 d8
CMP AX,CX .............;39 c8
CMP AX,DI .............;39 f8
CMP AX,DX .............;39 d0
CMP AX,SI .............;39 f0
CMP AX,SP .............;39 e0
CMP AX,[0x5566] ...........;3b 06 66 55
CMP AX,[BP+0x5566] ........;3b 86 66 55
CMP AX,[BP+0x55] ...........;3b 46 55
CMP AX,[BP+DI+0x5566] ....;3b 83 66 55
CMP AX,[BP+DI+0x55] ......;3b 43 55
CMP AX,[BP+DI] ...........;3b 03
CMP AX,[BP+SI+0x5566] ....;3b 82 66 55
CMP AX,[BP+SI+0x55] ......;3b 42 55
CMP AX,[BP+SI] ...........;3b 02
CMP AX,[BX+0x5566] ........;3b 87 66 55
CMP AX,[BX+0x55] ...........;3b 47 55
CMP AX,[BX+DI+0x5566] ....;3b 81 66 55
CMP AX,[BX+DI+0x55] ......;3b 41 55
CMP AX,[BX+DI] ...........;3b 01
CMP AX,[BX+SI+0x5566] ....;3b 80 66 55
CMP AX,[BX+SI+0x55] ......;3b 40 55
CMP AX,[BX+SI] ...........;3b 00
CMP AX,[BX] ...........;3b 07
CMP AX,[DI+0x5566] ........;3b 85 66 55
CMP AX,[DI+0x55] ...........;3b 45 55
CMP AX,[DI] ...........;3b 05
CMP AX,[SI+0x5566] ........;3b 84 66 55
CMP AX,[SI+0x55] ...........;3b 44 55
CMP AX,[SI] ...........;3b 04
CMP BH,0x88 .............;80 ff 88
CMP BH,AH .............;38 e7
CMP BH,AL .............;38 c7
CMP BH,BH .............;38 ff
CMP BH,BL .............;38 df
CMP BH,CH .............;38 ef
CMP BH,CL .............;38 cf
CMP BH,DH .............;38 f7
CMP BH,DL .............;38 d7
CMP BH,[0x5566] ...........;3a 3e 66 55
CMP BH,[BP+0x5566] ........;3a be 66 55
CMP BH,[BP+0x55] ...........;3a 7e 55
CMP BH,[BP+DI+0x5566] ....;3a bb 66 55
CMP BH,[BP+DI+0x55] ......;3a 7b 55
CMP BH,[BP+DI] ...........;3a 3b
CMP BH,[BP+SI+0x5566] ....;3a ba 66 55
CMP BH,[BP+SI+0x55] ......;3a 7a 55
CMP BH,[BP+SI] ...........;3a 3a
CMP BH,[BX+0x5566] ........;3a bf 66 55
CMP BH,[BX+0x55] ...........;3a 7f 55
CMP BH,[BX+DI+0x5566] ....;3a b9 66 55
CMP BH,[BX+DI+0x55] ......;3a 79 55
CMP BH,[BX+DI] ...........;3a 39
CMP BH,[BX+SI+0x5566] ....;3a b8 66 55
CMP BH,[BX+SI+0x55] ......;3a 78 55
CMP BH,[BX+SI] ...........;3a 38
CMP BH,[BX] ...........;3a 3f
CMP BH,[DI+0x5566] ........;3a bd 66 55
CMP BH,[DI+0x55] ...........;3a 7d 55
CMP BH,[DI] ...........;3a 3d
CMP BH,[SI+0x5566] ........;3a bc 66 55
CMP BH,[SI+0x55] ...........;3a 7c 55
CMP BH,[SI] ...........;3a 3c
CMP BL,0x88 .............;80 fb 88
CMP BL,AH .............;38 e3
CMP BL,AL .............;38 c3
CMP BL,BH .............;38 fb
CMP BL,BL .............;38 db
CMP BL,CH .............;38 eb
CMP BL,CL .............;38 cb
CMP BL,DH .............;38 f3
CMP BL,DL .............;38 d3
CMP BL,[0x5566] ...........;3a 1e 66 55
CMP BL,[BP+0x5566] ........;3a 9e 66 55

CMP BL,[BP+0x55] ...........;3a 5e 55
CMP BL,[BP+DI+0x5566] ....;3a 9b 66 55
CMP BL,[BP+DI+0x55] ......;3a 5b 55
CMP BL,[BP+DI] ...........;3a 1b
CMP BL,[BP+SI+0x5566] ....;3a 9a 66 55
CMP BL,[BP+SI+0x55] ......;3a 5a 55
CMP BL,[BP+SI] ...........;3a 1a
CMP BL,[BX+0x5566] ........;3a 9f 66 55
CMP BL,[BX+0x55] ...........;3a 5f 55
CMP BL,[BX+DI+0x5566] ....;3a 99 66 55
CMP BL,[BX+DI+0x55] ......;3a 59 55
CMP BL,[BX+DI] ...........;3a 19
CMP BL,[BX+SI+0x5566] ....;3a 98 66 55
CMP BL,[BX+SI+0x55] ......;3a 58 55
CMP BL,[BX+SI] ...........;3a 18
CMP BL,[BX] ...........;3a 1f
CMP BL,[DI+0x5566] ........;3a 9d 66 55
CMP BL,[DI+0x55] ...........;3a 5d 55
CMP BL,[DI] ...........;3a 1d
CMP BL,[SI+0x5566] ........;3a 9c 66 55
CMP BL,[SI+0x55] ...........;3a 5c 55
CMP BL,[SI] ...........;3a 1c
CMP BP,0x77 .............;83 fd 77
CMP BP,0x7788 .............;81 fd 88 77
CMP BP,AX .............;39 c5
CMP BP,BP .............;39 ed
CMP BP,BX .............;39 dd
CMP BP,CX .............;39 cd
CMP BP,DI .............;39 fd
CMP BP,DX .............;39 d5
CMP BP,SI .............;39 f5
CMP BP,SP .............;39 e5
CMP BP,[0x5566] ...........;3b 2e 66 55
CMP BP,[BP+0x5566] ........;3b ae 66 55
CMP BP,[BP+0x55] ...........;3b 6e 55
CMP BP,[BP+DI+0x5566] ....;3b ab 66 55
CMP BP,[BP+DI+0x55] ......;3b 6b 55
CMP BP,[BP+DI] ...........;3b 2b
CMP BP,[BP+SI+0x5566] ....;3b aa 66 55
CMP BP,[BP+SI+0x55] ......;3b 6a 55
CMP BP,[BP+SI] ...........;3b 2a
CMP BP,[BX+0x5566] ........;3b af 66 55
CMP BP,[BX+0x55] ...........;3b 6f 55
CMP BP,[BX+DI+0x5566] ....;3b a9 66 55
CMP BP,[BX+DI+0x55] ......;3b 69 55
CMP BP,[BX+DI] ...........;3b 29
CMP BP,[BX+SI+0x5566] ....;3b a8 66 55
CMP BP,[BX+SI+0x55] ......;3b 68 55
CMP BP,[BX+SI] ...........;3b 28
CMP BP,[BX] ...........;3b 2f
CMP BP,[DI+0x5566] ........;3b ad 66 55
CMP BP,[DI+0x55] ...........;3b 6d 55
CMP BP,[DI] ...........;3b 2d
CMP BP,[SI+0x5566] ........;3b ac 66 55
CMP BP,[SI+0x55] ...........;3b 6c 55
CMP BP,[SI] ...........;3b 2c
CMP BX,0x77 .............;83 fb 77
CMP BX,0x7788 .............;81 fb 88 77
CMP BX,AX .............;39 c3
CMP BX,BP .............;39 eb
CMP BX,BX .............;39 db
CMP BX,CX .............;39 cb
CMP BX,DI .............;39 fb
CMP BX,DX .............;39 d3
CMP BX,SI .............;39 f3
CMP BX,SP .............;39 e3
CMP BX,[0x5566] ...........;3b 1e 66 55
CMP BX,[BP+0x5566] ........;3b 9e 66 55
CMP BX,[BP+0x55] ...........;3b 5e 55
CMP BX,[BP+DI+0x5566] ....;3b 9b 66 55
CMP BX,[BP+DI+0x55] ......;3b 5b 55
CMP BX,[BP+DI] ...........;3b 1b
CMP BX,[BP+SI+0x5566] ....;3b 9a 66 55
CMP BX,[BP+SI+0x55] ......;3b 5a 55
CMP BX,[BP+SI] ...........;3b 1a
CMP BX,[BX+0x5566] ........;3b 9f 66 55
CMP BX,[BX+0x55] ...........;3b 5f 55
CMP BX,[BX+DI+0x5566] ....;3b 99 66 55
CMP BX,[BX+DI+0x55] ......;3b 59 55
CMP BX,[BX+DI] ...........;3b 19
CMP BX,[BX+SI+0x5566] ....;3b 98 66 55
CMP BX,[BX+SI+0x55] ......;3b 58 55
CMP BX,[BX+SI] ...........;3b 18
CMP BX,[BX] ...........;3b 1f
CMP BX,[DI+0x5566] ........;3b 9d 66 55
CMP BX,[DI+0x55] ...........;3b 5d 55
CMP BX,[DI] ...........;3b 1d
CMP BX,[SI+0x5566] ........;3b 9c 66 55
CMP BX,[SI+0x55] ...........;3b 5c 55
```

```
CMP BX,[SI] .....................;3b 1c
CMP BYTE [0x5566],0x88 ..........;80 3e 66 55 88
CMP BYTE [BP+0x5566],0x88 .......;80 be 66 55 88
CMP BYTE [BP+0x55],0x88 .........;80 7e 55 88
CMP BYTE [BP+DI+0x5566],0x88 ....;80 bb 66 55 88
CMP BYTE [BP+DI+0x55],0x88 ......;80 7b 55 88
CMP BYTE [BP+DI],0x88 ...........;80 3b 88
CMP BYTE [BP+SI+0x5566],0x88 ....;80 ba 66 55 88
CMP BYTE [BP+SI+0x55],0x88 ......;80 7a 55 88
CMP BYTE [BP+SI],0x88 ...........;80 3a 88
CMP BYTE [BX+0x5566],0x88 .......;80 bf 66 55 88
CMP BYTE [BX+0x55],0x88 .........;80 7f 55 88
CMP BYTE [BX+DI+0x5566],0x88 ....;80 b9 66 55 88
CMP BYTE [BX+DI+0x55],0x88 ......;80 79 55 88
CMP BYTE [BX+DI],0x88 ...........;80 39 88
CMP BYTE [BX+SI+0x5566],0x88 ....;80 b8 66 55 88
CMP BYTE [BX+SI+0x55],0x88 ......;80 78 55 88
CMP BYTE [BX+SI],0x88 ...........;80 38 88
CMP BYTE [BX],0x88 ..............;80 3f 88
CMP BYTE [DI+0x5566],0x88 .......;80 bd 66 55 88
CMP BYTE [DI+0x55],0x88 .........;80 7d 55 88
CMP BYTE [DI],0x88 ..............;80 3d 88
CMP BYTE [SI+0x5566],0x88 .......;80 bc 66 55 88
CMP BYTE [SI+0x55],0x88 .........;80 7c 55 88
CMP BYTE [SI],0x88 ..............;80 3c 88
CMP CH,0x88 .....................;80 fd 88
CMP CH,AH .......................;38 e5
CMP CH,AL .......................;38 c5
CMP CH,BH .......................;38 fd
CMP CH,BL .......................;38 dd
CMP CH,CH .......................;38 ed
CMP CH,CL .......................;38 cd
CMP CH,DH .......................;38 f5
CMP CH,DL .......................;38 d5
CMP CH,[0x5566] .................;3a 2e 66 55
CMP CH,[BP+0x5566] ..............;3a ae 66 55
CMP CH,[BP+0x55] ................;3a 6e 55
CMP CH,[BP+DI+0x5566] ...........;3a ab 66 55
CMP CH,[BP+DI+0x55] .............;3a 6b 55
CMP CH,[BP+DI] ..................;3a 2b
CMP CH,[BP+SI+0x5566] ...........;3a aa 66 55
CMP CH,[BP+SI+0x55] .............;3a 6a 55
CMP CH,[BP+SI] ..................;3a 2a
CMP CH,[BX+0x5566] ..............;3a af 66 55
CMP CH,[BX+0x55] ................;3a 6f 55
CMP CH,[BX+DI+0x5566] ...........;3a a9 66 55
CMP CH,[BX+DI+0x55] .............;3a 69 55
CMP CH,[BX+DI] ..................;3a 29
CMP CH,[BX+SI+0x5566] ...........;3a a8 66 55
CMP CH,[BX+SI+0x55] .............;3a 68 55
CMP CH,[BX+SI] ..................;3a 28
CMP CH,[BX] .....................;3a 2f
CMP CH,[DI+0x5566] ..............;3a ad 66 55
CMP CH,[DI+0x55] ................;3a 6d 55
CMP CH,[DI] .....................;3a 2d
CMP CH,[SI+0x5566] ..............;3a ac 66 55
CMP CH,[SI+0x55] ................;3a 6c 55
CMP CH,[SI] .....................;3a 2c
CMP CL,0x88 .....................;80 f9 88
CMP CL,AH .......................;38 e1
CMP CL,AL .......................;38 c1
CMP CL,BH .......................;38 f9
CMP CL,BL .......................;38 d9
CMP CL,CH .......................;38 e9
CMP CL,CL .......................;38 c9
CMP CL,DH .......................;38 f1
CMP CL,DL .......................;38 d1
CMP CL,[0x5566] .................;3a 0e 66 55
CMP CL,[BP+0x5566] ..............;3a 8e 66 55
CMP CL,[BP+0x55] ................;3a 4e 55
CMP CL,[BP+DI+0x5566] ...........;3a 8b 66 55
CMP CL,[BP+DI+0x55] .............;3a 4b 55
CMP CL,[BP+DI] ..................;3a 0b
CMP CL,[BP+SI+0x5566] ...........;3a 8a 66 55
CMP CL,[BP+SI+0x55] .............;3a 4a 55
CMP CL,[BP+SI] ..................;3a 0a
CMP CL,[BX+0x5566] ..............;3a 8f 66 55
CMP CL,[BX+0x55] ................;3a 4f 55
CMP CL,[BX+DI+0x5566] ...........;3a 89 66 55
CMP CL,[BX+DI+0x55] .............;3a 49 55
CMP CL,[BX+DI] ..................;3a 09
CMP CL,[BX+SI+0x5566] ...........;3a 88 66 55
CMP CL,[BX+SI+0x55] .............;3a 48 55
CMP CL,[BX+SI] ..................;3a 08
CMP CL,[BX] .....................;3a 0f
CMP CL,[DI+0x5566] ..............;3a 8d 66 55
CMP CL,[DI+0x55] ................;3a 4d 55
CMP CL,[DI] .....................;3a 0d
CMP CL,[SI+0x5566] ..............;3a 8c 66 55

CMP CL,[SI+0x55] ................;3a 4c 55
CMP CL,[SI] .....................;3a 0c
CMP CX,0x77 .....................;83 f9 77
CMP CX,0x7788 ...................;81 f9 88 77
CMP CX,AX .......................;39 c1
CMP CX,BP .......................;39 e9
CMP CX,BX .......................;39 d9
CMP CX,CX .......................;39 c9
CMP CX,DI .......................;39 f9
CMP CX,DX .......................;39 d1
CMP CX,SI .......................;39 f1
CMP CX,SP .......................;39 e1
CMP CX,[0x5566] .................;3b 0e 66 55
CMP CX,[BP+0x5566] ..............;3b 8e 66 55
CMP CX,[BP+0x55] ................;3b 4e 55
CMP CX,[BP+DI+0x5566] ...........;3b 8b 66 55
CMP CX,[BP+DI+0x55] .............;3b 4b 55
CMP CX,[BP+DI] ..................;3b 0b
CMP CX,[BP+SI+0x5566] ...........;3b 8a 66 55
CMP CX,[BP+SI+0x55] .............;3b 4a 55
CMP CX,[BP+SI] ..................;3b 0a
CMP CX,[BX+0x5566] ..............;3b 8f 66 55
CMP CX,[BX+0x55] ................;3b 4f 55
CMP CX,[BX+DI+0x5566] ...........;3b 89 66 55
CMP CX,[BX+DI+0x55] .............;3b 49 55
CMP CX,[BX+DI] ..................;3b 09
CMP CX,[BX+SI+0x5566] ...........;3b 88 66 55
CMP CX,[BX+SI+0x55] .............;3b 48 55
CMP CX,[BX+SI] ..................;3b 08
CMP CX,[BX] .....................;3b 0f
CMP CX,[DI+0x5566] ..............;3b 8d 66 55
CMP CX,[DI+0x55] ................;3b 4d 55
CMP CX,[DI] .....................;3b 0d
CMP CX,[SI+0x5566] ..............;3b 8c 66 55
CMP CX,[SI+0x55] ................;3b 4c 55
CMP CX,[SI] .....................;3b 0c
CMP DH,0x88 .....................;80 fe 88
CMP DH,AH .......................;38 e6
CMP DH,AL .......................;38 c6
CMP DH,BH .......................;38 fe
CMP DH,BL .......................;38 de
CMP DH,CH .......................;38 ee
CMP DH,CL .......................;38 ce
CMP DH,DH .......................;38 f6
CMP DH,DL .......................;38 d6
CMP DH,[0x5566] .................;3a 36 66 55
CMP DH,[BP+0x5566] ..............;3a b6 66 55
CMP DH,[BP+0x55] ................;3a 76 55
CMP DH,[BP+DI+0x5566] ...........;3a b3 66 55
CMP DH,[BP+DI+0x55] .............;3a 73 55
CMP DH,[BP+DI] ..................;3a 33
CMP DH,[BP+SI+0x5566] ...........;3a b2 66 55
CMP DH,[BP+SI+0x55] .............;3a 72 55
CMP DH,[BP+SI] ..................;3a 32
CMP DH,[BX+0x5566] ..............;3a b7 66 55
CMP DH,[BX+0x55] ................;3a 77 55
CMP DH,[BX+DI+0x5566] ...........;3a b1 66 55
CMP DH,[BX+DI+0x55] .............;3a 71 55
CMP DH,[BX+DI] ..................;3a 31
CMP DH,[BX+SI+0x5566] ...........;3a b0 66 55
CMP DH,[BX+SI+0x55] .............;3a 70 55
CMP DH,[BX+SI] ..................;3a 30
CMP DH,[BX] .....................;3a 37
CMP DH,[DI+0x5566] ..............;3a b5 66 55
CMP DH,[DI+0x55] ................;3a 75 55
CMP DH,[DI] .....................;3a 35
CMP DH,[SI+0x5566] ..............;3a b4 66 55
CMP DH,[SI+0x55] ................;3a 74 55
CMP DH,[SI] .....................;3a 34
CMP DI,0x77 .....................;83 ff 77
CMP DI,0x7788 ...................;81 ff 88 77
CMP DI,AX .......................;39 c7
CMP DI,BP .......................;39 ef
CMP DI,BX .......................;39 df
CMP DI,CX .......................;39 cf
CMP DI,DI .......................;39 ff
CMP DI,DX .......................;39 d7
CMP DI,SI .......................;39 f7
CMP DI,SP .......................;39 e7
CMP DI,[0x5566] .................;3b 3e 66 55
CMP DI,[BP+0x5566] ..............;3b be 66 55
CMP DI,[BP+0x55] ................;3b 7e 55
CMP DI,[BP+DI+0x5566] ...........;3b bb 66 55
CMP DI,[BP+DI+0x55] .............;3b 7b 55
CMP DI,[BP+DI] ..................;3b 3b
CMP DI,[BP+SI+0x5566] ...........;3b ba 66 55
CMP DI,[BP+SI+0x55] .............;3b 7a 55
CMP DI,[BP+SI] ..................;3b 3a
CMP DI,[BX+0x5566] ..............;3b bf 66 55
```

```
CMP DI,[BX+0x55] ................;3b 7f 55
CMP DI,[BX+DI+0x5566] ..........;3b b9 66 55
CMP DI,[BX+DI+0x55] ............;3b 79 55
CMP DI,[BX+DI] .................;3b 39
CMP DI,[BX+SI+0x5566] ..........;3b b8 66 55
CMP DI,[BX+SI+0x55] ............;3b 78 55
CMP DI,[BX+SI] .................;3b 38
CMP DI,[BX] ....................;3b 3f
CMP DI,[DI+0x5566] .............;3b bd 66 55
CMP DI,[DI+0x55] ...............;3b 7d 55
CMP DI,[DI] ....................;3b 3d
CMP DI,[SI+0x5566] .............;3b bc 66 55
CMP DI,[SI+0x55] ...............;3b 7c 55
CMP DI,[SI] ....................;3b 3c
CMP DL,0x88 ....................;80 fa 88
CMP DL,AH ......................;38 e2
CMP DL,AL ......................;38 c2
CMP DL,BH ......................;38 fa
CMP DL,BL ......................;38 da
CMP DL,CH ......................;38 ea
CMP DL,CL ......................;38 ca
CMP DL,DH ......................;38 f2
CMP DL,DL ......................;38 d2
CMP DL,[0x5566] ................;3a 16 66 55
CMP DL,[BP+0x5566] .............;3a 96 66 55
CMP DL,[BP+0x55] ...............;3a 56 55
CMP DL,[BP+DI+0x5566] ..........;3a 93 66 55
CMP DL,[BP+DI+0x55] ............;3a 53 55
CMP DL,[BP+DI] .................;3a 13
CMP DL,[BP+SI+0x5566] ..........;3a 92 66 55
CMP DL,[BP+SI+0x55] ............;3a 52 55
CMP DL,[BP+SI] .................;3a 12
CMP DL,[BX+0x5566] .............;3a 97 66 55
CMP DL,[BX+0x55] ...............;3a 57 55
CMP DL,[BX+DI+0x5566] ..........;3a 91 66 55
CMP DL,[BX+DI+0x55] ............;3a 51 55
CMP DL,[BX+DI] .................;3a 11
CMP DL,[BX+SI+0x5566] ..........;3a 90 66 55
CMP DL,[BX+SI+0x55] ............;3a 50 55
CMP DL,[BX+SI] .................;3a 10
CMP DL,[BX] ....................;3a 17
CMP DL,[DI+0x5566] .............;3a 95 66 55
CMP DL,[DI+0x55] ...............;3a 55 55
CMP DL,[DI] ....................;3a 15
CMP DL,[SI+0x5566] .............;3a 94 66 55
CMP DL,[SI+0x55] ...............;3a 54 55
CMP DL,[SI] ....................;3a 14
CMP DX,0x77 ....................;83 fa 77
CMP DX,0x7788 ..................;81 fa 88 77
CMP DX,AX ......................;39 c2
CMP DX,BP ......................;39 ea
CMP DX,BX ......................;39 da
CMP DX,CX ......................;39 ca
CMP DX,DI ......................;39 fa
CMP DX,DX ......................;39 d2
CMP DX,SI ......................;39 f2
CMP DX,SP ......................;39 e2
CMP DX,[0x5566] ................;3b 16 66 55
CMP DX,[BP+0x5566] .............;3b 96 66 55
CMP DX,[BP+0x55] ...............;3b 56 55
CMP DX,[BP+DI+0x5566] ..........;3b 93 66 55
CMP DX,[BP+DI+0x55] ............;3b 53 55
CMP DX,[BP+DI] .................;3b 13
CMP DX,[BP+SI+0x5566] ..........;3b 92 66 55
CMP DX,[BP+SI+0x55] ............;3b 52 55
CMP DX,[BP+SI] .................;3b 12
CMP DX,[BX+0x5566] .............;3b 97 66 55
CMP DX,[BX+0x55] ...............;3b 57 55
CMP DX,[BX+DI+0x5566] ..........;3b 91 66 55
CMP DX,[BX+DI+0x55] ............;3b 51 55
CMP DX,[BX+DI] .................;3b 11
CMP DX,[BX+SI+0x5566] ..........;3b 90 66 55
CMP DX,[BX+SI+0x55] ............;3b 50 55
CMP DX,[BX+SI] .................;3b 10
CMP DX,[BX] ....................;3b 17
CMP DX,[DI+0x5566] .............;3b 95 66 55
CMP DX,[DI+0x55] ...............;3b 55 55
CMP DX,[DI] ....................;3b 15
CMP DX,[SI+0x5566] .............;3b 94 66 55
CMP DX,[SI+0x55] ...............;3b 54 55
CMP DX,[SI] ....................;3b 14
CMP SI,0x77 ....................;83 fe 77
CMP SI,0x7788 ..................;81 fe 88 77
CMP SI,AX ......................;39 c6
CMP SI,BP ......................;39 ee
CMP SI,BX ......................;39 de
CMP SI,CX ......................;39 ce
CMP SI,DI ......................;39 fe
CMP SI,DX ......................;39 d6

CMP SI,SI ......................;39 f6
CMP SI,SP ......................;39 e6
CMP SI,[0x5566] ................;3b 36 66 55
CMP SI,[BP+0x5566] .............;3b b6 66 55
CMP SI,[BP+0x55] ...............;3b 76 55
CMP SI,[BP+DI+0x5566] ..........;3b b3 66 55
CMP SI,[BP+DI+0x55] ............;3b 73 55
CMP SI,[BP+DI] .................;3b 33
CMP SI,[BP+SI+0x5566] ..........;3b b2 66 55
CMP SI,[BP+SI+0x55] ............;3b 72 55
CMP SI,[BP+SI] .................;3b 32
CMP SI,[BX+0x5566] .............;3b b7 66 55
CMP SI,[BX+0x55] ...............;3b 77 55
CMP SI,[BX+DI+0x5566] ..........;3b b1 66 55
CMP SI,[BX+DI+0x55] ............;3b 71 55
CMP SI,[BX+DI] .................;3b 31
CMP SI,[BX+SI+0x5566] ..........;3b b0 66 55
CMP SI,[BX+SI+0x55] ............;3b 70 55
CMP SI,[BX+SI] .................;3b 30
CMP SI,[BX] ....................;3b 37
CMP SI,[DI+0x5566] .............;3b b5 66 55
CMP SI,[DI+0x55] ...............;3b 75 55
CMP SI,[DI] ....................;3b 35
CMP SI,[SI+0x5566] .............;3b b4 66 55
CMP SI,[SI+0x55] ...............;3b 74 55
CMP SI,[SI] ....................;3b 34
CMP SP,0x77 ....................;83 fc 77
CMP SP,0x7788 ..................;81 fc 88 77
CMP SP,AX ......................;39 c4
CMP SP,BP ......................;39 ec
CMP SP,BX ......................;39 dc
CMP SP,CX ......................;39 cc
CMP SP,DI ......................;39 fc
CMP SP,DX ......................;39 d4
CMP SP,SI ......................;39 f4
CMP SP,SP ......................;39 e4
CMP SP,[0x5566] ................;3b 26 66 55
CMP SP,[BP+0x5566] .............;3b a6 66 55
CMP SP,[BP+0x55] ...............;3b 66 55
CMP SP,[BP+DI+0x5566] ..........;3b a3 66 55
CMP SP,[BP+DI+0x55] ............;3b 63 55
CMP SP,[BP+DI] .................;3b 23
CMP SP,[BP+SI+0x5566] ..........;3b a2 66 55
CMP SP,[BP+SI+0x55] ............;3b 62 55
CMP SP,[BP+SI] .................;3b 22
CMP SP,[BX+0x5566] .............;3b a7 66 55
CMP SP,[BX+0x55] ...............;3b 67 55
CMP SP,[BX+DI+0x5566] ..........;3b a1 66 55
CMP SP,[BX+DI+0x55] ............;3b 61 55
CMP SP,[BX+DI] .................;3b 21
CMP SP,[BX+SI+0x5566] ..........;3b a0 66 55
CMP SP,[BX+SI+0x55] ............;3b 60 55
CMP SP,[BX+SI] .................;3b 20
CMP SP,[BX] ....................;3b 27
CMP SP,[DI+0x5566] .............;3b a5 66 55
CMP SP,[DI+0x55] ...............;3b 65 55
CMP SP,[DI] ....................;3b 25
CMP SP,[SI+0x5566] .............;3b a4 66 55
CMP SP,[SI+0x55] ...............;3b 64 55
CMP SP,[SI] ....................;3b 24
CMP WORD [0x5566],0x77 .........;83 3e 66 55 77
CMP WORD [0x5566],0x7788 .......;81 3e 66 55 88 77
CMP WORD [BP+0x5566],0x77 ......;83 be 66 55 77
CMP WORD [BP+0x5566],0x7788 ....;81 be 66 55 88 77
CMP WORD [BP+0x55],0x77 ........;83 7e 55 77
CMP WORD [BP+0x55],0x7788 ......;81 7e 55 88 77
CMP WORD [BP+DI+0x5566],0x77 ...;83 bb 66 55 77
CMP WORD [BP+DI+0x5566],0x7788 .;81 bb 66 55 88 77
CMP WORD [BP+DI+0x55],0x77 .....;83 7b 55 77
CMP WORD [BP+DI+0x55],0x7788 ...;81 7b 55 88 77
CMP WORD [BP+DI],0x77 ..........;83 3b 77
CMP WORD [BP+DI],0x7788 ........;81 3b 88 77
CMP WORD [BP+SI+0x5566],0x77 ...;83 ba 66 55 77
CMP WORD [BP+SI+0x5566],0x7788 .;81 ba 66 55 88 77
CMP WORD [BP+SI+0x55],0x77 .....;83 7a 55 77
CMP WORD [BP+SI+0x55],0x7788 ...;81 7a 55 88 77
CMP WORD [BP+SI],0x77 ..........;83 3a 77
CMP WORD [BP+SI],0x7788 ........;81 3a 88 77
CMP WORD [BX+0x5566],0x77 ......;83 bf 66 55 77
CMP WORD [BX+0x5566],0x7788 ....;81 bf 66 55 88 77
CMP WORD [BX+0x55],0x77 ........;83 7f 55 77
CMP WORD [BX+0x55],0x7788 ......;81 7f 55 88 77
CMP WORD [BX+DI+0x5566],0x77 ...;83 b9 66 55 77
CMP WORD [BX+DI+0x5566],0x7788 .;81 b9 66 55 88 77
CMP WORD [BX+DI+0x55],0x77 .....;83 79 55 77
CMP WORD [BX+DI+0x55],0x7788 ...;81 79 55 88 77
CMP WORD [BX+DI],0x77 ..........;83 39 77
CMP WORD [BX+DI],0x7788 ........;81 39 88 77
CMP WORD [BX+SI+0x5566],0x77 ...;83 b8 66 55 77
```

```
CMP WORD [BX+SI+0x5566],0x7788 .;81 b8 66 55 88 77   CMP [BP+DI+0x55],BX .............;39 5b 55
CMP WORD [BX+SI+0x55],0x77 ....;83 78 55 77           CMP [BP+DI+0x55],CH .............;38 6b 55
CMP WORD [BX+SI+0x55],0x7788 ...;81 78 55 88 77       CMP [BP+DI+0x55],CL .............;38 4b 55
CMP WORD [BX+SI],0x77 .........;83 38 77              CMP [BP+DI+0x55],CX .............;39 4b 55
CMP WORD [BX+SI],0x7788 .......;81 38 88 77           CMP [BP+DI+0x55],DH .............;38 73 55
CMP WORD [BX],0x77 ............;83 3f 77              CMP [BP+DI+0x55],DI .............;39 7b 55
CMP WORD [BX],0x7788 ..........;81 3f 88 77           CMP [BP+DI+0x55],DL .............;38 53 55
CMP WORD [DI+0x5566],0x77 .....;83 bd 66 55 77        CMP [BP+DI+0x55],DX .............;39 53 55
CMP WORD [DI+0x5566],0x7788 ...;81 bd 66 55 88 77     CMP [BP+DI+0x55],SI .............;39 73 55
CMP WORD [DI+0x55],0x77 .......;83 7d 55 77           CMP [BP+DI+0x55],SP .............;39 63 55
CMP WORD [DI+0x55],0x7788 .....;81 7d 55 88 77        CMP [BP+DI],AH .................;38 23
CMP WORD [DI],0x77 ............;83 3d 77              CMP [BP+DI],AL .................;38 03
CMP WORD [DI],0x7788 ..........;81 3d 88 77           CMP [BP+DI],AX .................;39 03
CMP WORD [SI+0x5566],0x77 .....;83 bc 66 55 77        CMP [BP+DI],BH .................;38 3b
CMP WORD [SI+0x5566],0x7788 ...;81 bc 66 55 88 77     CMP [BP+DI],BL .................;38 1b
CMP WORD [SI+0x55],0x77 .......;83 7c 55 77           CMP [BP+DI],BP .................;39 2b
CMP WORD [SI+0x55],0x7788 .....;81 7c 55 88 77        CMP [BP+DI],BX .................;39 1b
CMP WORD [SI],0x77 ............;83 3c 77              CMP [BP+DI],CH .................;38 2b
CMP WORD [SI],0x7788 ..........;81 3c 88 77           CMP [BP+DI],CL .................;38 0b
CMP [0x5566],AH ...............;38 26 66 55           CMP [BP+DI],CX .................;39 0b
CMP [0x5566],AL ...............;38 06 66 55           CMP [BP+DI],DH .................;38 33
CMP [0x5566],AX ...............;39 06 66 55           CMP [BP+DI],DI .................;39 3b
CMP [0x5566],BH ...............;38 3e 66 55           CMP [BP+DI],DL .................;38 13
CMP [0x5566],BL ...............;38 1e 66 55           CMP [BP+DI],DX .................;39 13
CMP [0x5566],BP ...............;39 2e 66 55           CMP [BP+DI],SI .................;39 33
CMP [0x5566],BX ...............;39 1e 66 55           CMP [BP+DI],SP .................;39 23
CMP [0x5566],CH ...............;38 2e 66 55           CMP [BP+SI+0x5566],AH ..........;38 a2 66 55
CMP [0x5566],CL ...............;38 0e 66 55           CMP [BP+SI+0x5566],AL ..........;38 82 66 55
CMP [0x5566],CX ...............;39 0e 66 55           CMP [BP+SI+0x5566],AX ..........;39 82 66 55
CMP [0x5566],DH ...............;38 36 66 55           CMP [BP+SI+0x5566],BH ..........;38 ba 66 55
CMP [0x5566],DI ...............;39 3e 66 55           CMP [BP+SI+0x5566],BL ..........;38 9a 66 55
CMP [0x5566],DL ...............;38 16 66 55           CMP [BP+SI+0x5566],BP ..........;39 aa 66 55
CMP [0x5566],DX ...............;39 16 66 55           CMP [BP+SI+0x5566],BX ..........;39 9a 66 55
CMP [0x5566],SI ...............;39 36 66 55           CMP [BP+SI+0x5566],CH ..........;38 aa 66 55
CMP [0x5566],SP ...............;39 26 66 55           CMP [BP+SI+0x5566],CL ..........;38 8a 66 55
CMP [BP+0x5566],AH ............;38 a6 66 55           CMP [BP+SI+0x5566],CX ..........;39 8a 66 55
CMP [BP+0x5566],AL ............;38 86 66 55           CMP [BP+SI+0x5566],DH ..........;38 b2 66 55
CMP [BP+0x5566],AX ............;39 86 66 55           CMP [BP+SI+0x5566],DI ..........;39 ba 66 55
CMP [BP+0x5566],BH ............;38 be 66 55           CMP [BP+SI+0x5566],DL ..........;38 92 66 55
CMP [BP+0x5566],BL ............;38 9e 66 55           CMP [BP+SI+0x5566],DX ..........;39 92 66 55
CMP [BP+0x5566],BP ............;39 ae 66 55           CMP [BP+SI+0x5566],SI ..........;39 b2 66 55
CMP [BP+0x5566],BX ............;39 9e 66 55           CMP [BP+SI+0x5566],SP ..........;39 a2 66 55
CMP [BP+0x5566],CH ............;38 ae 66 55           CMP [BP+SI+0x55],AH ............;38 62 55
CMP [BP+0x5566],CL ............;38 8e 66 55           CMP [BP+SI+0x55],AL ............;38 42 55
CMP [BP+0x5566],CX ............;39 8e 66 55           CMP [BP+SI+0x55],AX ............;39 42 55
CMP [BP+0x5566],DH ............;38 b6 66 55           CMP [BP+SI+0x55],BH ............;38 7a 55
CMP [BP+0x5566],DI ............;39 be 66 55           CMP [BP+SI+0x55],BL ............;38 5a 55
CMP [BP+0x5566],DL ............;38 96 66 55           CMP [BP+SI+0x55],BP ............;39 6a 55
CMP [BP+0x5566],DX ............;39 96 66 55           CMP [BP+SI+0x55],BX ............;39 5a 55
CMP [BP+0x5566],SI ............;39 b6 66 55           CMP [BP+SI+0x55],CH ............;38 6a 55
CMP [BP+0x5566],SP ............;39 a6 66 55           CMP [BP+SI+0x55],CL ............;38 4a 55
CMP [BP+0x55],AH ..............;38 66 55              CMP [BP+SI+0x55],CX ............;39 4a 55
CMP [BP+0x55],AL ..............;38 46 55              CMP [BP+SI+0x55],DH ............;38 72 55
CMP [BP+0x55],AX ..............;39 46 55              CMP [BP+SI+0x55],DI ............;39 7a 55
CMP [BP+0x55],BH ..............;38 7e 55              CMP [BP+SI+0x55],DL ............;38 52 55
CMP [BP+0x55],BL ..............;38 5e 55              CMP [BP+SI+0x55],DX ............;39 52 55
CMP [BP+0x55],BP ..............;39 6e 55              CMP [BP+SI+0x55],SI ............;39 72 55
CMP [BP+0x55],BX ..............;39 5e 55              CMP [BP+SI+0x55],SP ............;39 62 55
CMP [BP+0x55],CH ..............;38 6e 55              CMP [BP+SI],AH .................;38 22
CMP [BP+0x55],CL ..............;38 4e 55              CMP [BP+SI],AL .................;38 02
CMP [BP+0x55],CX ..............;39 4e 55              CMP [BP+SI],AX .................;39 02
CMP [BP+0x55],DH ..............;38 76 55              CMP [BP+SI],BH .................;38 3a
CMP [BP+0x55],DI ..............;39 7e 55              CMP [BP+SI],BL .................;38 1a
CMP [BP+0x55],DL ..............;38 56 55              CMP [BP+SI],BP .................;39 2a
CMP [BP+0x55],DX ..............;39 56 55              CMP [BP+SI],BX .................;39 1a
CMP [BP+0x55],SI ..............;39 76 55              CMP [BP+SI],CH .................;38 2a
CMP [BP+0x55],SP ..............;39 66 55              CMP [BP+SI],CL .................;38 0a
CMP [BP+DI+0x5566],AH .........;38 a3 66 55           CMP [BP+SI],CX .................;39 0a
CMP [BP+DI+0x5566],AL .........;38 83 66 55           CMP [BP+SI],DH .................;38 32
CMP [BP+DI+0x5566],AX .........;39 83 66 55           CMP [BP+SI],DI .................;39 3a
CMP [BP+DI+0x5566],BH .........;38 bb 66 55           CMP [BP+SI],DL .................;38 12
CMP [BP+DI+0x5566],BL .........;38 9b 66 55           CMP [BP+SI],DX .................;39 12
CMP [BP+DI+0x5566],BP .........;39 ab 66 55           CMP [BP+SI],SI .................;39 32
CMP [BP+DI+0x5566],BX .........;39 9b 66 55           CMP [BP+SI],SP .................;39 22
CMP [BP+DI+0x5566],CH .........;38 ab 66 55           CMP [BX+0x5566],AH .............;38 a7 66 55
CMP [BP+DI+0x5566],CL .........;38 8b 66 55           CMP [BX+0x5566],AL .............;38 87 66 55
CMP [BP+DI+0x5566],CX .........;39 8b 66 55           CMP [BX+0x5566],AX .............;39 87 66 55
CMP [BP+DI+0x5566],DH .........;38 b3 66 55           CMP [BX+0x5566],BH .............;38 bf 66 55
CMP [BP+DI+0x5566],DI .........;39 bb 66 55           CMP [BX+0x5566],BL .............;38 9f 66 55
CMP [BP+DI+0x5566],DL .........;38 93 66 55           CMP [BX+0x5566],BP .............;39 af 66 55
CMP [BP+DI+0x5566],DX .........;39 93 66 55           CMP [BX+0x5566],BX .............;39 9f 66 55
CMP [BP+DI+0x5566],SI .........;39 b3 66 55           CMP [BX+0x5566],CH .............;38 af 66 55
CMP [BP+DI+0x5566],SP .........;39 a3 66 55           CMP [BX+0x5566],CL .............;38 8f 66 55
CMP [BP+DI+0x55],AH ...........;38 63 55              CMP [BX+0x5566],CX .............;39 8f 66 55
CMP [BP+DI+0x55],AL ...........;38 43 55              CMP [BX+0x5566],DH .............;38 b7 66 55
CMP [BP+DI+0x55],AX ...........;39 43 55              CMP [BX+0x5566],DI .............;39 bf 66 55
CMP [BP+DI+0x55],BH ...........;38 7b 55              CMP [BX+0x5566],DL .............;38 97 66 55
CMP [BP+DI+0x55],BL ...........;38 5b 55              CMP [BX+0x5566],DX .............;39 97 66 55
CMP [BP+DI+0x55],BP ...........;39 6b 55              CMP [BX+0x5566],SI .............;39 b7 66 55
```

```
CMP [BX+0x5566],SP .............;39 a7 66 55        CMP [BX+SI+0x55],CL .........;38 48 55
CMP [BX+0x55],AH .............;38 67 55            CMP [BX+SI+0x55],CX .........;39 48 55
CMP [BX+0x55],AL .............;38 47 55            CMP [BX+SI+0x55],DH .........;38 70 55
CMP [BX+0x55],AX .............;39 47 55            CMP [BX+SI+0x55],DI .........;39 78 55
CMP [BX+0x55],BH .............;38 7f 55            CMP [BX+SI+0x55],DL .........;38 50 55
CMP [BX+0x55],BL .............;38 5f 55            CMP [BX+SI+0x55],DX .........;39 50 55
CMP [BX+0x55],BP .............;39 6f 55            CMP [BX+SI+0x55],SI .........;39 70 55
CMP [BX+0x55],BX .............;39 5f 55            CMP [BX+SI+0x55],SP .........;39 60 55
CMP [BX+0x55],CH .............;38 6f 55            CMP [BX+SI],AH ..............;38 20
CMP [BX+0x55],CL .............;38 4f 55            CMP [BX+SI],AL ..............;38 00
CMP [BX+0x55],CX .............;39 4f 55            CMP [BX+SI],AX ..............;39 00
CMP [BX+0x55],DH .............;38 77 55            CMP [BX+SI],BH ..............;38 38
CMP [BX+0x55],DI .............;39 7f 55            CMP [BX+SI],BL ..............;38 18
CMP [BX+0x55],DL .............;38 57 55            CMP [BX+SI],BP ..............;39 28
CMP [BX+0x55],DX .............;39 57 55            CMP [BX+SI],BX ..............;39 18
CMP [BX+0x55],SI .............;39 77 55            CMP [BX+SI],CH ..............;38 28
CMP [BX+0x55],SP .............;39 67 55            CMP [BX+SI],CL ..............;38 08
CMP [BX+DI+0x5566],AH .......;38 a1 66 55          CMP [BX+SI],CX ..............;39 08
CMP [BX+DI+0x5566],AL .......;38 81 66 55          CMP [BX+SI],DH ..............;38 30
CMP [BX+DI+0x5566],AX .......;39 81 66 55          CMP [BX+SI],DI ..............;39 38
CMP [BX+DI+0x5566],BH .......;38 b9 66 55          CMP [BX+SI],DL ..............;38 10
CMP [BX+DI+0x5566],BL .......;38 99 66 55          CMP [BX+SI],DX ..............;39 10
CMP [BX+DI+0x5566],BP .......;39 a9 66 55          CMP [BX+SI],SI ..............;39 30
CMP [BX+DI+0x5566],BX .......;39 99 66 55          CMP [BX+SI],SP ..............;39 20
CMP [BX+DI+0x5566],CH .......;38 a9 66 55          CMP [BX],AH .................;38 27
CMP [BX+DI+0x5566],CL .......;38 89 66 55          CMP [BX],AL .................;38 07
CMP [BX+DI+0x5566],CX .......;39 89 66 55          CMP [BX],AX .................;39 07
CMP [BX+DI+0x5566],DH .......;38 b1 66 55          CMP [BX],BH .................;38 3f
CMP [BX+DI+0x5566],DI .......;39 b9 66 55          CMP [BX],BL .................;38 1f
CMP [BX+DI+0x5566],DL .......;38 91 66 55          CMP [BX],BP .................;39 2f
CMP [BX+DI+0x5566],DX .......;39 91 66 55          CMP [BX],BX .................;39 1f
CMP [BX+DI+0x5566],SI .......;39 b1 66 55          CMP [BX],CH .................;38 2f
CMP [BX+DI+0x5566],SP .......;39 a1 66 55          CMP [BX],CL .................;38 0f
CMP [BX+DI+0x55],AH .........;38 61 55             CMP [BX],CX .................;39 0f
CMP [BX+DI+0x55],AL .........;38 41 55             CMP [BX],DH .................;38 37
CMP [BX+DI+0x55],AX .........;39 41 55             CMP [BX],DI .................;39 3f
CMP [BX+DI+0x55],BH .........;38 79 55             CMP [BX],DL .................;38 17
CMP [BX+DI+0x55],BL .........;38 59 55             CMP [BX],DX .................;39 17
CMP [BX+DI+0x55],BP .........;39 69 55             CMP [BX],SI .................;39 37
CMP [BX+DI+0x55],BX .........;39 59 55             CMP [BX],SP .................;39 27
CMP [BX+DI+0x55],CH .........;38 69 55             CMP [DI+0x5566],AH ..........;38 a5 66 55
CMP [BX+DI+0x55],CL .........;38 49 55             CMP [DI+0x5566],AL ..........;38 85 66 55
CMP [BX+DI+0x55],CX .........;39 49 55             CMP [DI+0x5566],AX ..........;39 85 66 55
CMP [BX+DI+0x55],DH .........;38 71 55             CMP [DI+0x5566],BH ..........;38 bd 66 55
CMP [BX+DI+0x55],DI .........;39 79 55             CMP [DI+0x5566],BL ..........;38 9d 66 55
CMP [BX+DI+0x55],DL .........;38 51 55             CMP [DI+0x5566],BP ..........;39 ad 66 55
CMP [BX+DI+0x55],DX .........;39 51 55             CMP [DI+0x5566],BX ..........;39 9d 66 55
CMP [BX+DI+0x55],SI .........;39 71 55             CMP [DI+0x5566],CH ..........;38 ad 66 55
CMP [BX+DI+0x55],SP .........;39 61 55             CMP [DI+0x5566],CL ..........;38 8d 66 55
CMP [BX+DI],AH ..............;38 21               CMP [DI+0x5566],CX ..........;39 8d 66 55
CMP [BX+DI],AL ..............;38 01               CMP [DI+0x5566],DH ..........;38 b5 66 55
CMP [BX+DI],AX ..............;39 01               CMP [DI+0x5566],DI ..........;39 bd 66 55
CMP [BX+DI],BH ..............;38 39               CMP [DI+0x5566],DL ..........;38 95 66 55
CMP [BX+DI],BL ..............;38 19               CMP [DI+0x5566],DX ..........;39 95 66 55
CMP [BX+DI],BP ..............;39 29               CMP [DI+0x5566],SI ..........;39 b5 66 55
CMP [BX+DI],BX ..............;39 19               CMP [DI+0x5566],SP ..........;39 a5 66 55
CMP [BX+DI],CH ..............;38 29               CMP [DI+0x55],AH ............;38 65 55
CMP [BX+DI],CL ..............;38 09               CMP [DI+0x55],AL ............;38 45 55
CMP [BX+DI],CX ..............;39 09               CMP [DI+0x55],AX ............;39 45 55
CMP [BX+DI],DH ..............;38 31               CMP [DI+0x55],BH ............;38 7d 55
CMP [BX+DI],DI ..............;39 39               CMP [DI+0x55],BL ............;38 5d 55
CMP [BX+DI],DL ..............;38 11               CMP [DI+0x55],BP ............;39 6d 55
CMP [BX+DI],DX ..............;39 11               CMP [DI+0x55],BX ............;39 5d 55
CMP [BX+DI],SI ..............;39 31               CMP [DI+0x55],CH ............;38 6d 55
CMP [BX+DI],SP ..............;39 21               CMP [DI+0x55],CL ............;38 4d 55
CMP [BX+SI+0x5566],AH .......;38 a0 66 55          CMP [DI+0x55],CX ............;39 4d 55
CMP [BX+SI+0x5566],AL .......;38 80 66 55          CMP [DI+0x55],DH ............;38 75 55
CMP [BX+SI+0x5566],AX .......;39 80 66 55          CMP [DI+0x55],DI ............;39 7d 55
CMP [BX+SI+0x5566],BH .......;38 b8 66 55          CMP [DI+0x55],DL ............;38 55 55
CMP [BX+SI+0x5566],BL .......;38 98 66 55          CMP [DI+0x55],DX ............;39 55 55
CMP [BX+SI+0x5566],BP .......;39 a8 66 55          CMP [DI+0x55],SI ............;39 75 55
CMP [BX+SI+0x5566],BX .......;39 98 66 55          CMP [DI+0x55],SP ............;39 65 55
CMP [BX+SI+0x5566],CH .......;38 a8 66 55          CMP [DI],AH .................;38 25
CMP [BX+SI+0x5566],CL .......;38 88 66 55          CMP [DI],AL .................;38 05
CMP [BX+SI+0x5566],CX .......;39 88 66 55          CMP [DI],AX .................;39 05
CMP [BX+SI+0x5566],DH .......;38 b0 66 55          CMP [DI],BH .................;38 3d
CMP [BX+SI+0x5566],DI .......;39 b8 66 55          CMP [DI],BL .................;38 1d
CMP [BX+SI+0x5566],DL .......;38 90 66 55          CMP [DI],BP .................;39 2d
CMP [BX+SI+0x5566],DX .......;39 90 66 55          CMP [DI],BX .................;39 1d
CMP [BX+SI+0x5566],SI .......;39 b0 66 55          CMP [DI],CH .................;38 2d
CMP [BX+SI+0x5566],SP .......;39 a0 66 55          CMP [DI],CL .................;38 0d
CMP [BX+SI+0x55],AH .........;38 60 55             CMP [DI],CX .................;39 0d
CMP [BX+SI+0x55],AL .........;38 40 55             CMP [DI],DH .................;38 35
CMP [BX+SI+0x55],AX .........;39 40 55             CMP [DI],DI .................;39 3d
CMP [BX+SI+0x55],BH .........;38 78 55             CMP [DI],DL .................;38 15
CMP [BX+SI+0x55],BL .........;38 58 55             CMP [DI],DX .................;39 15
CMP [BX+SI+0x55],BP .........;39 68 55             CMP [DI],SI .................;39 35
CMP [BX+SI+0x55],BX .........;39 58 55             CMP [DI],SP .................;39 25
CMP [BX+SI+0x55],CH .........;38 68 55             CMP [SI+0x5566],AH ..........;38 a4 66 55
```

186

```
CMP [SI+0x5566],AL ............;38 84 66 55
CMP [SI+0x5566],AX ............;39 84 66 55
CMP [SI+0x5566],BH ............;38 bc 66 55
CMP [SI+0x5566],BL ............;38 9c 66 55
CMP [SI+0x5566],BP ............;39 ac 66 55
CMP [SI+0x5566],BX ............;39 9c 66 55
CMP [SI+0x5566],CH ............;38 ac 66 55
CMP [SI+0x5566],CL ............;38 8c 66 55
CMP [SI+0x5566],CX ............;39 8c 66 55
CMP [SI+0x5566],DH ............;38 b4 66 55
CMP [SI+0x5566],DI ............;39 bc 66 55
CMP [SI+0x5566],DL ............;38 94 66 55
CMP [SI+0x5566],DX ............;39 94 66 55
CMP [SI+0x5566],SI ............;39 b4 66 55
CMP [SI+0x5566],SP ............;39 a4 66 55
CMP [SI+0x55],AH ..............;38 64 55
CMP [SI+0x55],AL ..............;38 44 55
CMP [SI+0x55],AX ..............;39 44 55
CMP [SI+0x55],BH ..............;38 7c 55
CMP [SI+0x55],BL ..............;38 5c 55
CMP [SI+0x55],BP ..............;39 6c 55
CMP [SI+0x55],BX ..............;39 5c 55
CMP [SI+0x55],CH ..............;38 6c 55
CMP [SI+0x55],CL ..............;38 4c 55
CMP [SI+0x55],CX ..............;39 4c 55
CMP [SI+0x55],DH ..............;38 74 55
CMP [SI+0x55],DI ..............;39 7c 55
CMP [SI+0x55],DL ..............;38 54 55
CMP [SI+0x55],DX ..............;39 54 55
CMP [SI+0x55],SI ..............;39 74 55
CMP [SI+0x55],SP ..............;39 64 55
CMP [SI],AH ...................;38 24
CMP [SI],AL ...................;38 04
CMP [SI],AX ...................;39 04
CMP [SI],BH ...................;38 3c
CMP [SI],BL ...................;38 1c
CMP [SI],BP ...................;39 2c
CMP [SI],BX ...................;39 1c
CMP [SI],CH ...................;38 2c
CMP [SI],CL ...................;38 0c
CMP [SI],CX ...................;39 0c
CMP [SI],DH ...................;38 34
CMP [SI],DI ...................;39 3c
CMP [SI],DL ...................;38 14
CMP [SI],DX ...................;39 14
CMP [SI],SI ...................;39 34
CMP [SI],SP ...................;39 24
CMPSB .........................;a6
CMPSW .........................;a7
CS ............................;2e
CWD ...........................;99
DAA ...........................;27
DAS ...........................;2f
DEC AX ........................;48
DEC BP ........................;4d
DEC BX ........................;4b
DEC BYTE [0x5566] .............;fe 0e 66 55
DEC BYTE [BP+0x5566] ..........;fe 8e 66 55
DEC BYTE [BP+0x55] ............;fe 4e 55
DEC BYTE [BP+DI+0x5566] .......;fe 8b 66 55
DEC BYTE [BP+DI+0x55] .........;fe 4b 55
DEC BYTE [BP+DI] ..............;fe 0b
DEC BYTE [BP+SI+0x5566] .......;fe 8a 66 55
DEC BYTE [BP+SI+0x55] .........;fe 4a 55
DEC BYTE [BP+SI] ..............;fe 0a
DEC BYTE [BX+0x5566] ..........;fe 8f 66 55
DEC BYTE [BX+0x55] ............;fe 4f 55
DEC BYTE [BX+DI+0x5566] .......;fe 89 66 55
DEC BYTE [BX+DI+0x55] .........;fe 49 55
DEC BYTE [BX+DI] ..............;fe 09
DEC BYTE [BX+SI+0x5566] .......;fe 88 66 55
DEC BYTE [BX+SI+0x55] .........;fe 48 55
DEC BYTE [BX+SI] ..............;fe 08
DEC BYTE [BX] .................;fe 0f
DEC BYTE [DI+0x5566] ..........;fe 8d 66 55
DEC BYTE [DI+0x55] ............;fe 4d 55
DEC BYTE [DI] .................;fe 0d
DEC BYTE [SI+0x5566] ..........;fe 8c 66 55
DEC BYTE [SI+0x55] ............;fe 4c 55
DEC BYTE [SI] .................;fe 0c
DEC CX ........................;49
DEC DI ........................;4f
DEC DX ........................;4a
DEC SI ........................;4e
DEC SP ........................;4c
DEC WORD [0x5566] .............;ff 0e 66 55
DEC WORD [BP+0x5566] ..........;ff 8e 66 55
DEC WORD [BP+0x55] ............;ff 4e 55
DEC WORD [BP+DI+0x5566] .......;ff 8b 66 55

DEC WORD [BP+DI+0x55] .........;ff 4b 55
DEC WORD [BP+DI] ..............;ff 0b
DEC WORD [BP+SI+0x5566] .......;ff 8a 66 55
DEC WORD [BP+SI+0x55] .........;ff 4a 55
DEC WORD [BP+SI] ..............;ff 0a
DEC WORD [BX+0x5566] ..........;ff 8f 66 55
DEC WORD [BX+0x55] ............;ff 4f 55
DEC WORD [BX+DI+0x5566] .......;ff 89 66 55
DEC WORD [BX+DI+0x55] .........;ff 49 55
DEC WORD [BX+DI] ..............;ff 09
DEC WORD [BX+SI+0x5566] .......;ff 88 66 55
DEC WORD [BX+SI+0x55] .........;ff 48 55
DEC WORD [BX+SI] ..............;ff 08
DEC WORD [BX] .................;ff 0f
DEC WORD [DI+0x5566] ..........;ff 8d 66 55
DEC WORD [DI+0x55] ............;ff 4d 55
DEC WORD [DI] .................;ff 0d
DEC WORD [SI+0x5566] ..........;ff 8c 66 55
DEC WORD [SI+0x55] ............;ff 4c 55
DEC WORD [SI] .................;ff 0c
DIV AH ........................;f6 f4
DIV AL ........................;f6 f0
DIV AX ........................;f7 f0
DIV BH ........................;f6 f7
DIV BL ........................;f6 f3
DIV BP ........................;f7 f5
DIV BX ........................;f7 f3
DIV BYTE [0x5566] .............;f6 36 66 55
DIV BYTE [BP+0x5566] ..........;f6 b6 66 55
DIV BYTE [BP+0x55] ............;f6 76 55
DIV BYTE [BP+DI+0x5566] .......;f6 b3 66 55
DIV BYTE [BP+DI+0x55] .........;f6 73 55
DIV BYTE [BP+DI] ..............;f6 33
DIV BYTE [BP+SI+0x5566] .......;f6 b2 66 55
DIV BYTE [BP+SI+0x55] .........;f6 72 55
DIV BYTE [BP+SI] ..............;f6 32
DIV BYTE [BX+0x5566] ..........;f6 b7 66 55
DIV BYTE [BX+0x55] ............;f6 77 55
DIV BYTE [BX+DI+0x5566] .......;f6 b1 66 55
DIV BYTE [BX+DI+0x55] .........;f6 71 55
DIV BYTE [BX+DI] ..............;f6 31
DIV BYTE [BX+SI+0x5566] .......;f6 b0 66 55
DIV BYTE [BX+SI+0x55] .........;f6 70 55
DIV BYTE [BX+SI] ..............;f6 30
DIV BYTE [BX] .................;f6 37
DIV BYTE [DI+0x5566] ..........;f6 b5 66 55
DIV BYTE [DI+0x55] ............;f6 75 55
DIV BYTE [DI] .................;f6 35
DIV BYTE [SI+0x5566] ..........;f6 b4 66 55
DIV BYTE [SI+0x55] ............;f6 74 55
DIV BYTE [SI] .................;f6 34
DIV CH ........................;f6 f5
DIV CL ........................;f6 f1
DIV CX ........................;f7 f1
DIV DH ........................;f6 f6
DIV DI ........................;f7 f7
DIV DL ........................;f6 f2
DIV DX ........................;f7 f2
DIV SI ........................;f7 f6
DIV SP ........................;f7 f4
DIV WORD [0x5566] .............;f7 36 66 55
DIV WORD [BP+0x5566] ..........;f7 b6 66 55
DIV WORD [BP+0x55] ............;f7 76 55
DIV WORD [BP+DI+0x5566] .......;f7 b3 66 55
DIV WORD [BP+DI+0x55] .........;f7 73 55
DIV WORD [BP+DI] ..............;f7 33
DIV WORD [BP+SI+0x5566] .......;f7 b2 66 55
DIV WORD [BP+SI+0x55] .........;f7 72 55
DIV WORD [BP+SI] ..............;f7 32
DIV WORD [BX+0x5566] ..........;f7 b7 66 55
DIV WORD [BX+0x55] ............;f7 77 55
DIV WORD [BX+DI+0x5566] .......;f7 b1 66 55
DIV WORD [BX+DI+0x55] .........;f7 71 55
DIV WORD [BX+DI] ..............;f7 31
DIV WORD [BX+SI+0x5566] .......;f7 b0 66 55
DIV WORD [BX+SI+0x55] .........;f7 70 55
DIV WORD [BX+SI] ..............;f7 30
DIV WORD [BX] .................;f7 37
DIV WORD [DI+0x5566] ..........;f7 b5 66 55
DIV WORD [DI+0x55] ............;f7 75 55
DIV WORD [DI] .................;f7 35
DIV WORD [SI+0x5566] ..........;f7 b4 66 55
DIV WORD [SI+0x55] ............;f7 74 55
DIV WORD [SI] .................;f7 34
DS ............................;3e
ES ............................;26
HLT ...........................;f4
IDIV AH .......................;f6 fc
IDIV AL .......................;f6 f8
```

```
IDIV AX ...........................;f7 f8
IDIV BH ...........................;f6 ff
IDIV BL ...........................;f6 fb
IDIV BP ...........................;f7 fd
IDIV BX ...........................;f7 fb
IDIV BYTE [0x5566] ................;f6 3e 66 55
IDIV BYTE [BP+0x5566] .............;f6 be 66 55
IDIV BYTE [BP+0x55] ...............;f6 7e 55
IDIV BYTE [BP+DI+0x5566] ..........;f6 bb 66 55
IDIV BYTE [BP+DI+0x55] ............;f6 7b 55
IDIV BYTE [BP+DI] .................;f6 3b
IDIV BYTE [BP+SI+0x5566] ..........;f6 ba 66 55
IDIV BYTE [BP+SI+0x55] ............;f6 7a 55
IDIV BYTE [BP+SI] .................;f6 3a
IDIV BYTE [BX+0x5566] .............;f6 bf 66 55
IDIV BYTE [BX+0x55] ...............;f6 7f 55
IDIV BYTE [BX+DI+0x5566] ..........;f6 b9 66 55
IDIV BYTE [BX+DI+0x55] ............;f6 79 55
IDIV BYTE [BX+DI] .................;f6 39
IDIV BYTE [BX+SI+0x5566] ..........;f6 b8 66 55
IDIV BYTE [BX+SI+0x55] ............;f6 78 55
IDIV BYTE [BX+SI] .................;f6 38
IDIV BYTE [BX] ....................;f6 3f
IDIV BYTE [DI+0x5566] .............;f6 bd 66 55
IDIV BYTE [DI+0x55] ...............;f6 7d 55
IDIV BYTE [DI] ....................;f6 3d
IDIV BYTE [SI+0x5566] .............;f6 bc 66 55
IDIV BYTE [SI+0x55] ...............;f6 7c 55
IDIV BYTE [SI] ....................;f6 3c
IDIV CH ...........................;f6 fd
IDIV CL ...........................;f6 f9
IDIV CX ...........................;f7 f9
IDIV DH ...........................;f6 fe
IDIV DI ...........................;f7 ff
IDIV DL ...........................;f6 fa
IDIV DX ...........................;f7 fa
IDIV SI ...........................;f7 fe
IDIV SP ...........................;f7 fc
IDIV WORD [0x5566] ................;f7 3e 66 55
IDIV WORD [BP+0x5566] .............;f7 be 66 55
IDIV WORD [BP+0x55] ...............;f7 7e 55
IDIV WORD [BP+DI+0x5566] ..........;f7 bb 66 55
IDIV WORD [BP+DI+0x55] ............;f7 7b 55
IDIV WORD [BP+DI] .................;f7 3b
IDIV WORD [BP+SI+0x5566] ..........;f7 ba 66 55
IDIV WORD [BP+SI+0x55] ............;f7 7a 55
IDIV WORD [BP+SI] .................;f7 3a
IDIV WORD [BX+0x5566] .............;f7 bf 66 55
IDIV WORD [BX+0x55] ...............;f7 7f 55
IDIV WORD [BX+DI+0x5566] ..........;f7 b9 66 55
IDIV WORD [BX+DI+0x55] ............;f7 79 55
IDIV WORD [BX+DI] .................;f7 39
IDIV WORD [BX+SI+0x5566] ..........;f7 b8 66 55
IDIV WORD [BX+SI+0x55] ............;f7 78 55
IDIV WORD [BX+SI] .................;f7 38
IDIV WORD [BX] ....................;f7 3f
IDIV WORD [DI+0x5566] .............;f7 bd 66 55
IDIV WORD [DI+0x55] ...............;f7 7d 55
IDIV WORD [DI] ....................;f7 3d
IDIV WORD [SI+0x5566] .............;f7 bc 66 55
IDIV WORD [SI+0x55] ...............;f7 7c 55
IDIV WORD [SI] ....................;f7 3c
IMUL AH ...........................;f6 ec
IMUL AL ...........................;f6 e8
IMUL AX ...........................;f7 e8
IMUL BH ...........................;f6 ef
IMUL BL ...........................;f6 eb
IMUL BP ...........................;f7 ed
IMUL BX ...........................;f7 eb
IMUL BYTE [0x5566] ................;f6 2e 66 55
IMUL BYTE [BP+0x5566] .............;f6 ae 66 55
IMUL BYTE [BP+0x55] ...............;f6 6e 55
IMUL BYTE [BP+DI+0x5566] ..........;f6 ab 66 55
IMUL BYTE [BP+DI+0x55] ............;f6 6b 55
IMUL BYTE [BP+DI] .................;f6 2b
IMUL BYTE [BP+SI+0x5566] ..........;f6 aa 66 55
IMUL BYTE [BP+SI+0x55] ............;f6 6a 55
IMUL BYTE [BP+SI] .................;f6 2a
IMUL BYTE [BX+0x5566] .............;f6 af 66 55
IMUL BYTE [BX+0x55] ...............;f6 6f 55
IMUL BYTE [BX+DI+0x5566] ..........;f6 a9 66 55
IMUL BYTE [BX+DI+0x55] ............;f6 69 55
IMUL BYTE [BX+DI] .................;f6 29
IMUL BYTE [BX+SI+0x5566] ..........;f6 a8 66 55
IMUL BYTE [BX+SI+0x55] ............;f6 68 55
IMUL BYTE [BX+SI] .................;f6 28
IMUL BYTE [BX] ....................;f6 2f
IMUL BYTE [DI+0x5566] .............;f6 ad 66 55
IMUL BYTE [DI+0x55] ...............;f6 6d 55
IMUL BYTE [DI] ....................;f6 2d
IMUL BYTE [SI+0x5566] .............;f6 ac 66 55
IMUL BYTE [SI+0x55] ...............;f6 6c 55
IMUL BYTE [SI] ....................;f6 2c
IMUL CH ...........................;f6 ed
IMUL CL ...........................;f6 e9
IMUL CX ...........................;f7 e9
IMUL DH ...........................;f6 ee
IMUL DI ...........................;f7 ef
IMUL DL ...........................;f6 ea
IMUL DX ...........................;f7 ea
IMUL SI ...........................;f7 ee
IMUL SP ...........................;f7 ec
IMUL WORD [0x5566] ................;f7 2e 66 55
IMUL WORD [BP+0x5566] .............;f7 ae 66 55
IMUL WORD [BP+0x55] ...............;f7 6e 55
IMUL WORD [BP+DI+0x5566] ..........;f7 ab 66 55
IMUL WORD [BP+DI+0x55] ............;f7 6b 55
IMUL WORD [BP+DI] .................;f7 2b
IMUL WORD [BP+SI+0x5566] ..........;f7 aa 66 55
IMUL WORD [BP+SI+0x55] ............;f7 6a 55
IMUL WORD [BP+SI] .................;f7 2a
IMUL WORD [BX+0x5566] .............;f7 af 66 55
IMUL WORD [BX+0x55] ...............;f7 6f 55
IMUL WORD [BX+DI+0x5566] ..........;f7 a9 66 55
IMUL WORD [BX+DI+0x55] ............;f7 69 55
IMUL WORD [BX+DI] .................;f7 29
IMUL WORD [BX+SI+0x5566] ..........;f7 a8 66 55
IMUL WORD [BX+SI+0x55] ............;f7 68 55
IMUL WORD [BX+SI] .................;f7 28
IMUL WORD [BX] ....................;f7 2f
IMUL WORD [DI+0x5566] .............;f7 ad 66 55
IMUL WORD [DI+0x55] ...............;f7 6d 55
IMUL WORD [DI] ....................;f7 2d
IMUL WORD [SI+0x5566] .............;f7 ac 66 55
IMUL WORD [SI+0x55] ...............;f7 6c 55
IMUL WORD [SI] ....................;f7 2c
IN AL,(0x55) ......................;e4 55
IN AL,DX ..........................;ec
IN AX,(0x55) ......................;e5 55
IN AX,DX ..........................;ed
INC AX ............................;40
INC BP ............................;45
INC BX ............................;43
INC BYTE [0x5566] .................;fe 06 66 55
INC BYTE [BP+0x5566] ..............;fe 86 66 55
INC BYTE [BP+0x55] ................;fe 46 55
INC BYTE [BP+DI+0x5566] ...........;fe 83 66 55
INC BYTE [BP+DI+0x55] .............;fe 43 55
INC BYTE [BP+DI] ..................;fe 03
INC BYTE [BP+SI+0x5566] ...........;fe 82 66 55
INC BYTE [BP+SI+0x55] .............;fe 42 55
INC BYTE [BP+SI] ..................;fe 02
INC BYTE [BX+0x5566] ..............;fe 87 66 55
INC BYTE [BX+0x55] ................;fe 47 55
INC BYTE [BX+DI+0x5566] ...........;fe 81 66 55
INC BYTE [BX+DI+0x55] .............;fe 41 55
INC BYTE [BX+DI] ..................;fe 01
INC BYTE [BX+SI+0x5566] ...........;fe 80 66 55
INC BYTE [BX+SI+0x55] .............;fe 40 55
INC BYTE [BX+SI] ..................;fe 00
INC BYTE [BX] .....................;fe 07
INC BYTE [DI+0x5566] ..............;fe 85 66 55
INC BYTE [DI+0x55] ................;fe 45 55
INC BYTE [DI] .....................;fe 05
INC BYTE [SI+0x5566] ..............;fe 84 66 55
INC BYTE [SI+0x55] ................;fe 44 55
INC BYTE [SI] .....................;fe 04
INC CX ............................;41
INC DI ............................;47
INC DX ............................;42
INC SI ............................;46
INC SP ............................;44
INC WORD [0x5566] .................;ff 06 66 55
INC WORD [BP+0x5566] ..............;ff 86 66 55
INC WORD [BP+0x55] ................;ff 46 55
INC WORD [BP+DI+0x5566] ...........;ff 83 66 55
INC WORD [BP+DI+0x55] .............;ff 43 55
INC WORD [BP+DI] ..................;ff 03
INC WORD [BP+SI+0x5566] ...........;ff 82 66 55
INC WORD [BP+SI+0x55] .............;ff 42 55
INC WORD [BP+SI] ..................;ff 02
INC WORD [BX+0x5566] ..............;ff 87 66 55
INC WORD [BX+0x55] ................;ff 47 55
INC WORD [BX+DI+0x5566] ...........;ff 81 66 55
INC WORD [BX+DI+0x55] .............;ff 41 55
INC WORD [BX+DI] ..................;ff 01
INC WORD [BX+SI+0x5566] ...........;ff 80 66 55
INC WORD [BX+SI+0x55] .............;ff 40 55
```

```
INC WORD [BX+SI] ...............:ff 00
INC WORD [BX] ..................:ff 07
INC WORD [DI+0x5566] ...........:ff 85 66 55
INC WORD [DI+0x55] .............:ff 45 55
INC WORD [DI] ..................:ff 05
INC WORD [SI+0x5566] ...........:ff 84 66 55
INC WORD [SI+0x55] .............:ff 44 55
INC WORD [SI] ..................:ff 04
INT 0x55 .......................:cd 55
INT3 ...........................:cc
INTO ...........................:ce
IRET ...........................:cf
JA 0x55 ........................:77 55
JB 0x55 ........................:72 55
JBE 0x55 .......................:76 55
JCXZ 0x55 ......................:e3 55
JG 0x55 ........................:7f 55
JGE 0x55 .......................:7d 55
JL 0x55 ........................:7c 55
JLE 0x55 .......................:7e 55
JMP 0x55 .......................:eb 55
JMP 0x5566 .....................:e9 66 55
JMP 0x5566:0x7788 ..............:ea 66 55 88 77
JMP FAR [0x5566] ...............:ff 2e 66 55
JMP FAR [BP+0x5566] ............:ff ae 66 55
JMP FAR [BP+0x55] ..............:ff 6e 55
JMP FAR [BP+DI+0x5566] .........:ff ab 66 55
JMP FAR [BP+DI+0x55] ...........:ff 6b 55
JMP FAR [BP+DI] ................:ff 2b
JMP FAR [BP+SI+0x5566] .........:ff aa 66 55
JMP FAR [BP+SI+0x55] ...........:ff 6a 55
JMP FAR [BP+SI] ................:ff 2a
JMP FAR [BX+0x5566] ............:ff af 66 55
JMP FAR [BX+0x55] ..............:ff 6f 55
JMP FAR [BX+DI+0x5566] .........:ff a9 66 55
JMP FAR [BX+DI+0x55] ...........:ff 69 55
JMP FAR [BX+DI] ................:ff 29
JMP FAR [BX+SI+0x5566] .........:ff a8 66 55
JMP FAR [BX+SI+0x55] ...........:ff 68 55
JMP FAR [BX+SI] ................:ff 28
JMP FAR [BX] ...................:ff 2f
JMP FAR [DI+0x5566] ............:ff ad 66 55
JMP FAR [DI+0x55] ..............:ff 6d 55
JMP FAR [DI] ...................:ff 2d
JMP FAR [SI+0x5566] ............:ff ac 66 55
JMP FAR [SI+0x55] ..............:ff 6c 55
JMP FAR [SI] ...................:ff 2c
JMP [0x5566] ...................:ff 26 66 55
JMP [BP+0x5566] ................:ff a6 66 55
JMP [BP+0x55] ..................:ff 66 55
JMP [BP+DI+0x5566] .............:ff a3 66 55
JMP [BP+DI+0x55] ...............:ff 63 55
JMP [BP+DI] ....................:ff 23
JMP [BP+SI+0x5566] .............:ff a2 66 55
JMP [BP+SI+0x55] ...............:ff 62 55
JMP [BP+SI] ....................:ff 22
JMP [BX+0x5566] ................:ff a7 66 55
JMP [BX+0x55] ..................:ff 67 55
JMP [BX+DI+0x5566] .............:ff a1 66 55
JMP [BX+DI+0x55] ...............:ff 61 55
JMP [BX+DI] ....................:ff 21
JMP [BX+SI+0x5566] .............:ff a0 66 55
JMP [BX+SI+0x55] ...............:ff 60 55
JMP [BX+SI] ....................:ff 20
JMP [BX] .......................:ff 27
JMP [DI+0x5566] ................:ff a5 66 55
JMP [DI+0x55] ..................:ff 65 55
JMP [DI] .......................:ff 25
JMP [SI+0x5566] ................:ff a4 66 55
JMP [SI+0x55] ..................:ff 64 55
JMP [SI] .......................:ff 24
JNB 0x55 .......................:73 55
JNO 0x55 .......................:71 55
JNS 0x55 .......................:79 55
JNZ 0x55 .......................:75 55
JO 0x55 ........................:70 55
JPE 0x55 .......................:7a 55
JPO 0x55 .......................:7b 55
JS 0x55 ........................:78 55
JZ 0x55 ........................:74 55
LAHF ...........................:9f
LDS AX,[0x5566] ................:c5 06 66 55
LDS AX,[BP+0x5566] .............:c5 86 66 55
LDS AX,[BP+0x55] ...............:c5 46 55
LDS AX,[BP+DI+0x5566] ..........:c5 83 66 55
LDS AX,[BP+DI+0x55] ............:c5 43 55
LDS AX,[BP+DI] .................:c5 03
LDS AX,[BP+SI+0x5566] ..........:c5 82 66 55
LDS AX,[BP+SI+0x55] ............:c5 42 55

LDS AX,[BP+SI] .................:c5 02
LDS AX,[BX+0x5566] .............:c5 87 66 55
LDS AX,[BX+0x55] ...............:c5 47 55
LDS AX,[BX+DI+0x5566] ..........:c5 81 66 55
LDS AX,[BX+DI+0x55] ............:c5 41 55
LDS AX,[BX+DI] .................:c5 01
LDS AX,[BX+SI+0x5566] ..........:c5 80 66 55
LDS AX,[BX+SI+0x55] ............:c5 40 55
LDS AX,[BX+SI] .................:c5 00
LDS AX,[BX] ....................:c5 07
LDS AX,[DI+0x5566] .............:c5 85 66 55
LDS AX,[DI+0x55] ...............:c5 45 55
LDS AX,[DI] ....................:c5 05
LDS AX,[SI+0x5566] .............:c5 84 66 55
LDS AX,[SI+0x55] ...............:c5 44 55
LDS AX,[SI] ....................:c5 04
LDS BP,[0x5566] ................:c5 2e 66 55
LDS BP,[BP+0x5566] .............:c5 ae 66 55
LDS BP,[BP+0x55] ...............:c5 6e 55
LDS BP,[BP+DI+0x5566] ..........:c5 ab 66 55
LDS BP,[BP+DI+0x55] ............:c5 6b 55
LDS BP,[BP+DI] .................:c5 2b
LDS BP,[BP+SI+0x5566] ..........:c5 aa 66 55
LDS BP,[BP+SI+0x55] ............:c5 6a 55
LDS BP,[BP+SI] .................:c5 2a
LDS BP,[BX+0x5566] .............:c5 af 66 55
LDS BP,[BX+0x55] ...............:c5 6f 55
LDS BP,[BX+DI+0x5566] ..........:c5 a9 66 55
LDS BP,[BX+DI+0x55] ............:c5 69 55
LDS BP,[BX+DI] .................:c5 29
LDS BP,[BX+SI+0x5566] ..........:c5 a8 66 55
LDS BP,[BX+SI+0x55] ............:c5 68 55
LDS BP,[BX+SI] .................:c5 28
LDS BP,[BX] ....................:c5 2f
LDS BP,[DI+0x5566] .............:c5 ad 66 55
LDS BP,[DI+0x55] ...............:c5 6d 55
LDS BP,[DI] ....................:c5 2d
LDS BP,[SI+0x5566] .............:c5 ac 66 55
LDS BP,[SI+0x55] ...............:c5 6c 55
LDS BP,[SI] ....................:c5 2c
LDS BX,[0x5566] ................:c5 1e 66 55
LDS BX,[BP+0x5566] .............:c5 9e 66 55
LDS BX,[BP+0x55] ...............:c5 5e 55
LDS BX,[BP+DI+0x5566] ..........:c5 9b 66 55
LDS BX,[BP+DI+0x55] ............:c5 5b 55
LDS BX,[BP+DI] .................:c5 1b
LDS BX,[BP+SI+0x5566] ..........:c5 9a 66 55
LDS BX,[BP+SI+0x55] ............:c5 5a 55
LDS BX,[BP+SI] .................:c5 1a
LDS BX,[BX+0x5566] .............:c5 9f 66 55
LDS BX,[BX+0x55] ...............:c5 5f 55
LDS BX,[BX+DI+0x5566] ..........:c5 99 66 55
LDS BX,[BX+DI+0x55] ............:c5 59 55
LDS BX,[BX+DI] .................:c5 19
LDS BX,[BX+SI+0x5566] ..........:c5 98 66 55
LDS BX,[BX+SI+0x55] ............:c5 58 55
LDS BX,[BX+SI] .................:c5 18
LDS BX,[BX] ....................:c5 1f
LDS BX,[DI+0x5566] .............:c5 9d 66 55
LDS BX,[DI+0x55] ...............:c5 5d 55
LDS BX,[DI] ....................:c5 1d
LDS BX,[SI+0x5566] .............:c5 9c 66 55
LDS BX,[SI+0x55] ...............:c5 5c 55
LDS BX,[SI] ....................:c5 1c
LDS CX,[0x5566] ................:c5 0e 66 55
LDS CX,[BP+0x5566] .............:c5 8e 66 55
LDS CX,[BP+0x55] ...............:c5 4e 55
LDS CX,[BP+DI+0x5566] ..........:c5 8b 66 55
LDS CX,[BP+DI+0x55] ............:c5 4b 55
LDS CX,[BP+DI] .................:c5 0b
LDS CX,[BP+SI+0x5566] ..........:c5 8a 66 55
LDS CX,[BP+SI+0x55] ............:c5 4a 55
LDS CX,[BP+SI] .................:c5 0a
LDS CX,[BX+0x5566] .............:c5 8f 66 55
LDS CX,[BX+0x55] ...............:c5 4f 55
LDS CX,[BX+DI+0x5566] ..........:c5 89 66 55
LDS CX,[BX+DI+0x55] ............:c5 49 55
LDS CX,[BX+DI] .................:c5 09
LDS CX,[BX+SI+0x5566] ..........:c5 88 66 55
LDS CX,[BX+SI+0x55] ............:c5 48 55
LDS CX,[BX+SI] .................:c5 08
LDS CX,[BX] ....................:c5 0f
LDS CX,[DI+0x5566] .............:c5 8d 66 55
LDS CX,[DI+0x55] ...............:c5 4d 55
LDS CX,[DI] ....................:c5 0d
LDS CX,[SI+0x5566] .............:c5 8c 66 55
LDS CX,[SI+0x55] ...............:c5 4c 55
LDS CX,[SI] ....................:c5 0c
LDS DI,[0x5566] ................:c5 3e 66 55
```

```
LDS DI,[BP+0x5566] ............. ;c5 be 66 55
LDS DI,[BP+0x55] ............... ;c5 7e 55
LDS DI,[BP+DI+0x5566] .......... ;c5 bb 66 55
LDS DI,[BP+DI+0x55] ............ ;c5 7b 55
LDS DI,[BP+DI] ................. ;c5 3b
LDS DI,[BP+SI+0x5566] .......... ;c5 ba 66 55
LDS DI,[BP+SI+0x55] ............ ;c5 7a 55
LDS DI,[BP+SI] ................. ;c5 3a
LDS DI,[BX+0x5566] ............. ;c5 bf 66 55
LDS DI,[BX+0x55] ............... ;c5 7f 55
LDS DI,[BX+DI+0x5566] .......... ;c5 b9 66 55
LDS DI,[BX+DI+0x55] ............ ;c5 79 55
LDS DI,[BX+DI] ................. ;c5 39
LDS DI,[BX+SI+0x5566] .......... ;c5 b8 66 55
LDS DI,[BX+SI+0x55] ............ ;c5 78 55
LDS DI,[BX+SI] ................. ;c5 38
LDS DI,[BX] .................... ;c5 3f
LDS DI,[DI+0x5566] ............. ;c5 bd 66 55
LDS DI,[DI+0x55] ............... ;c5 7d 55
LDS DI,[DI] .................... ;c5 3d
LDS DI,[SI+0x5566] ............. ;c5 bc 66 55
LDS DI,[SI+0x55] ............... ;c5 7c 55
LDS DI,[SI] .................... ;c5 3c
LDS DX,[0x5566] ................ ;c5 16 66 55
LDS DX,[BP+0x5566] ............. ;c5 96 66 55
LDS DX,[BP+0x55] ............... ;c5 56 55
LDS DX,[BP+DI+0x5566] .......... ;c5 93 66 55
LDS DX,[BP+DI+0x55] ............ ;c5 53 55
LDS DX,[BP+DI] ................. ;c5 13
LDS DX,[BP+SI+0x5566] .......... ;c5 92 66 55
LDS DX,[BP+SI+0x55] ............ ;c5 52 55
LDS DX,[BP+SI] ................. ;c5 12
LDS DX,[BX+0x5566] ............. ;c5 97 66 55
LDS DX,[BX+0x55] ............... ;c5 57 55
LDS DX,[BX+DI+0x5566] .......... ;c5 91 66 55
LDS DX,[BX+DI+0x55] ............ ;c5 51 55
LDS DX,[BX+DI] ................. ;c5 11
LDS DX,[BX+SI+0x5566] .......... ;c5 90 66 55
LDS DX,[BX+SI+0x55] ............ ;c5 50 55
LDS DX,[BX+SI] ................. ;c5 10
LDS DX,[BX] .................... ;c5 17
LDS DX,[DI+0x5566] ............. ;c5 95 66 55
LDS DX,[DI+0x55] ............... ;c5 55 55
LDS DX,[DI] .................... ;c5 15
LDS DX,[SI+0x5566] ............. ;c5 94 66 55
LDS DX,[SI+0x55] ............... ;c5 54 55
LDS DX,[SI] .................... ;c5 14
LDS SI,[0x5566] ................ ;c5 36 66 55
LDS SI,[BP+0x5566] ............. ;c5 b6 66 55
LDS SI,[BP+0x55] ............... ;c5 76 55
LDS SI,[BP+DI+0x5566] .......... ;c5 b3 66 55
LDS SI,[BP+DI+0x55] ............ ;c5 73 55
LDS SI,[BP+DI] ................. ;c5 33
LDS SI,[BP+SI+0x5566] .......... ;c5 b2 66 55
LDS SI,[BP+SI+0x55] ............ ;c5 72 55
LDS SI,[BP+SI] ................. ;c5 32
LDS SI,[BX+0x5566] ............. ;c5 b7 66 55
LDS SI,[BX+0x55] ............... ;c5 77 55
LDS SI,[BX+DI+0x5566] .......... ;c5 b1 66 55
LDS SI,[BX+DI+0x55] ............ ;c5 71 55
LDS SI,[BX+DI] ................. ;c5 31
LDS SI,[BX+SI+0x5566] .......... ;c5 b0 66 55
LDS SI,[BX+SI+0x55] ............ ;c5 70 55
LDS SI,[BX+SI] ................. ;c5 30
LDS SI,[BX] .................... ;c5 37
LDS SI,[DI+0x5566] ............. ;c5 b5 66 55
LDS SI,[DI+0x55] ............... ;c5 75 55
LDS SI,[DI] .................... ;c5 35
LDS SI,[SI+0x5566] ............. ;c5 b4 66 55
LDS SI,[SI+0x55] ............... ;c5 74 55
LDS SI,[SI] .................... ;c5 34
LDS SP,[0x5566] ................ ;c5 26 66 55
LDS SP,[BP+0x5566] ............. ;c5 a6 66 55
LDS SP,[BP+0x55] ............... ;c5 66 55
LDS SP,[BP+DI+0x5566] .......... ;c5 a3 66 55
LDS SP,[BP+DI+0x55] ............ ;c5 63 55
LDS SP,[BP+DI] ................. ;c5 23
LDS SP,[BP+SI+0x5566] .......... ;c5 a2 66 55
LDS SP,[BP+SI+0x55] ............ ;c5 62 55
LDS SP,[BP+SI] ................. ;c5 22
LDS SP,[BX+0x5566] ............. ;c5 a7 66 55
LDS SP,[BX+0x55] ............... ;c5 67 55
LDS SP,[BX+DI+0x5566] .......... ;c5 a1 66 55
LDS SP,[BX+DI+0x55] ............ ;c5 61 55
LDS SP,[BX+DI] ................. ;c5 21
LDS SP,[BX+SI+0x5566] .......... ;c5 a0 66 55
LDS SP,[BX+SI+0x55] ............ ;c5 60 55
LDS SP,[BX+SI] ................. ;c5 20
LDS SP,[BX] .................... ;c5 27
```

```
LDS SP,[DI+0x5566] ............. ;c5 a5 66 55
LDS SP,[DI+0x55] ............... ;c5 65 55
LDS SP,[DI] .................... ;c5 25
LDS SP,[SI+0x5566] ............. ;c5 a4 66 55
LDS SP,[SI+0x55] ............... ;c5 64 55
LDS SP,[SI] .................... ;c5 24
LEA AX,[0x5566] ................ ;8d 06 66 55
LEA AX,[BP+0x5566] ............. ;8d 86 66 55
LEA AX,[BP+0x55] ............... ;8d 46 55
LEA AX,[BP+DI+0x5566] .......... ;8d 83 66 55
LEA AX,[BP+DI+0x55] ............ ;8d 43 55
LEA AX,[BP+DI] ................. ;8d 03
LEA AX,[BP+SI+0x5566] .......... ;8d 82 66 55
LEA AX,[BP+SI+0x55] ............ ;8d 42 55
LEA AX,[BP+SI] ................. ;8d 02
LEA AX,[BX+0x5566] ............. ;8d 87 66 55
LEA AX,[BX+0x55] ............... ;8d 47 55
LEA AX,[BX+DI+0x5566] .......... ;8d 81 66 55
LEA AX,[BX+DI+0x55] ............ ;8d 41 55
LEA AX,[BX+DI] ................. ;8d 01
LEA AX,[BX+SI+0x5566] .......... ;8d 80 66 55
LEA AX,[BX+SI+0x55] ............ ;8d 40 55
LEA AX,[BX+SI] ................. ;8d 00
LEA AX,[BX] .................... ;8d 07
LEA AX,[DI+0x5566] ............. ;8d 85 66 55
LEA AX,[DI+0x55] ............... ;8d 45 55
LEA AX,[DI] .................... ;8d 05
LEA AX,[SI+0x5566] ............. ;8d 84 66 55
LEA AX,[SI+0x55] ............... ;8d 44 55
LEA AX,[SI] .................... ;8d 04
LEA BP,[0x5566] ................ ;8d 2e 66 55
LEA BP,[BP+0x5566] ............. ;8d ae 66 55
LEA BP,[BP+0x55] ............... ;8d 6e 55
LEA BP,[BP+DI+0x5566] .......... ;8d ab 66 55
LEA BP,[BP+DI+0x55] ............ ;8d 6b 55
LEA BP,[BP+DI] ................. ;8d 2b
LEA BP,[BP+SI+0x5566] .......... ;8d aa 66 55
LEA BP,[BP+SI+0x55] ............ ;8d 6a 55
LEA BP,[BP+SI] ................. ;8d 2a
LEA BP,[BX+0x5566] ............. ;8d af 66 55
LEA BP,[BX+0x55] ............... ;8d 6f 55
LEA BP,[BX+DI+0x5566] .......... ;8d a9 66 55
LEA BP,[BX+DI+0x55] ............ ;8d 69 55
LEA BP,[BX+DI] ................. ;8d 29
LEA BP,[BX+SI+0x5566] .......... ;8d a8 66 55
LEA BP,[BX+SI+0x55] ............ ;8d 68 55
LEA BP,[BX+SI] ................. ;8d 28
LEA BP,[BX] .................... ;8d 2f
LEA BP,[DI+0x5566] ............. ;8d ad 66 55
LEA BP,[DI+0x55] ............... ;8d 6d 55
LEA BP,[DI] .................... ;8d 2d
LEA BP,[SI+0x5566] ............. ;8d ac 66 55
LEA BP,[SI+0x55] ............... ;8d 6c 55
LEA BP,[SI] .................... ;8d 2c
LEA BX,[0x5566] ................ ;8d 1e 66 55
LEA BX,[BP+0x5566] ............. ;8d 9e 66 55
LEA BX,[BP+0x55] ............... ;8d 5e 55
LEA BX,[BP+DI+0x5566] .......... ;8d 9b 66 55
LEA BX,[BP+DI+0x55] ............ ;8d 5b 55
LEA BX,[BP+DI] ................. ;8d 1b
LEA BX,[BP+SI+0x5566] .......... ;8d 9a 66 55
LEA BX,[BP+SI+0x55] ............ ;8d 5a 55
LEA BX,[BP+SI] ................. ;8d 1a
LEA BX,[BX+0x5566] ............. ;8d 9f 66 55
LEA BX,[BX+0x55] ............... ;8d 5f 55
LEA BX,[BX+DI+0x5566] .......... ;8d 99 66 55
LEA BX,[BX+DI+0x55] ............ ;8d 59 55
LEA BX,[BX+DI] ................. ;8d 19
LEA BX,[BX+SI+0x5566] .......... ;8d 98 66 55
LEA BX,[BX+SI+0x55] ............ ;8d 58 55
LEA BX,[BX+SI] ................. ;8d 18
LEA BX,[BX] .................... ;8d 1f
LEA BX,[DI+0x5566] ............. ;8d 9d 66 55
LEA BX,[DI+0x55] ............... ;8d 5d 55
LEA BX,[DI] .................... ;8d 1d
LEA BX,[SI+0x5566] ............. ;8d 9c 66 55
LEA BX,[SI+0x55] ............... ;8d 5c 55
LEA BX,[SI] .................... ;8d 1c
LEA CX,[0x5566] ................ ;8d 0e 66 55
LEA CX,[BP+0x5566] ............. ;8d 8e 66 55
LEA CX,[BP+0x55] ............... ;8d 4e 55
LEA CX,[BP+DI+0x5566] .......... ;8d 8b 66 55
LEA CX,[BP+DI+0x55] ............ ;8d 4b 55
LEA CX,[BP+DI] ................. ;8d 0b
LEA CX,[BP+SI+0x5566] .......... ;8d 8a 66 55
LEA CX,[BP+SI+0x55] ............ ;8d 4a 55
LEA CX,[BP+SI] ................. ;8d 0a
LEA CX,[BX+0x5566] ............. ;8d 8f 66 55
LEA CX,[BX+0x55] ............... ;8d 4f 55
```

```
LEA CX,[BX+DI+0x5566] .......... ;8d 89 66 55
LEA CX,[BX+DI+0x55] ............ ;8d 49 55
LEA CX,[BX+DI] ................. ;8d 09
LEA CX,[BX+SI+0x5566] .......... ;8d 88 66 55
LEA CX,[BX+SI+0x55] ............ ;8d 48 55
LEA CX,[BX+SI] ................. ;8d 08
LEA CX,[BX] .................... ;8d 0f
LEA CX,[DI+0x5566] ............. ;8d 8d 66 55
LEA CX,[DI+0x55] ............... ;8d 4d 55
LEA CX,[DI] .................... ;8d 0d
LEA CX,[SI+0x5566] ............. ;8d 8c 66 55
LEA CX,[SI+0x55] ............... ;8d 4c 55
LEA CX,[SI] .................... ;8d 0c
LEA DI,[0x5566] ................ ;8d 3e 66 55
LEA DI,[BP+0x5566] ............. ;8d be 66 55
LEA DI,[BP+0x55] ............... ;8d 7e 55
LEA DI,[BP+DI+0x5566] .......... ;8d bb 66 55
LEA DI,[BP+DI+0x55] ............ ;8d 7b 55
LEA DI,[BP+DI] ................. ;8d 3b
LEA DI,[BP+SI+0x5566] .......... ;8d ba 66 55
LEA DI,[BP+SI+0x55] ............ ;8d 7a 55
LEA DI,[BP+SI] ................. ;8d 3a
LEA DI,[BX+0x5566] ............. ;8d bf 66 55
LEA DI,[BX+0x55] ............... ;8d 7f 55
LEA DI,[BX+DI+0x5566] .......... ;8d b9 66 55
LEA DI,[BX+DI+0x55] ............ ;8d 79 55
LEA DI,[BX+DI] ................. ;8d 39
LEA DI,[BX+SI+0x5566] .......... ;8d b8 66 55
LEA DI,[BX+SI+0x55] ............ ;8d 78 55
LEA DI,[BX+SI] ................. ;8d 38
LEA DI,[BX] .................... ;8d 3f
LEA DI,[DI+0x5566] ............. ;8d bd 66 55
LEA DI,[DI+0x55] ............... ;8d 7d 55
LEA DI,[DI] .................... ;8d 3d
LEA DI,[SI+0x5566] ............. ;8d bc 66 55
LEA DI,[SI+0x55] ............... ;8d 7c 55
LEA DI,[SI] .................... ;8d 3c
LEA DX,[0x5566] ................ ;8d 16 66 55
LEA DX,[BP+0x5566] ............. ;8d 96 66 55
LEA DX,[BP+0x55] ............... ;8d 56 55
LEA DX,[BP+DI+0x5566] .......... ;8d 93 66 55
LEA DX,[BP+DI+0x55] ............ ;8d 53 55
LEA DX,[BP+DI] ................. ;8d 13
LEA DX,[BP+SI+0x5566] .......... ;8d 92 66 55
LEA DX,[BP+SI+0x55] ............ ;8d 52 55
LEA DX,[BP+SI] ................. ;8d 12
LEA DX,[BX+0x5566] ............. ;8d 97 66 55
LEA DX,[BX+0x55] ............... ;8d 57 55
LEA DX,[BX+DI+0x5566] .......... ;8d 91 66 55
LEA DX,[BX+DI+0x55] ............ ;8d 51 55
LEA DX,[BX+DI] ................. ;8d 11
LEA DX,[BX+SI+0x5566] .......... ;8d 90 66 55
LEA DX,[BX+SI+0x55] ............ ;8d 50 55
LEA DX,[BX+SI] ................. ;8d 10
LEA DX,[BX] .................... ;8d 17
LEA DX,[DI+0x5566] ............. ;8d 95 66 55
LEA DX,[DI+0x55] ............... ;8d 55 55
LEA DX,[DI] .................... ;8d 15
LEA DX,[SI+0x5566] ............. ;8d 94 66 55
LEA DX,[SI+0x55] ............... ;8d 54 55
LEA DX,[SI] .................... ;8d 14
LEA SI,[0x5566] ................ ;8d 36 66 55
LEA SI,[BP+0x5566] ............. ;8d b6 66 55
LEA SI,[BP+0x55] ............... ;8d 76 55
LEA SI,[BP+DI+0x5566] .......... ;8d b3 66 55
LEA SI,[BP+DI+0x55] ............ ;8d 73 55
LEA SI,[BP+DI] ................. ;8d 33
LEA SI,[BP+SI+0x5566] .......... ;8d b2 66 55
LEA SI,[BP+SI+0x55] ............ ;8d 72 55
LEA SI,[BP+SI] ................. ;8d 32
LEA SI,[BX+0x5566] ............. ;8d b7 66 55
LEA SI,[BX+0x55] ............... ;8d 77 55
LEA SI,[BX+DI+0x5566] .......... ;8d b1 66 55
LEA SI,[BX+DI+0x55] ............ ;8d 71 55
LEA SI,[BX+DI] ................. ;8d 31
LEA SI,[BX+SI+0x5566] .......... ;8d b0 66 55
LEA SI,[BX+SI+0x55] ............ ;8d 70 55
LEA SI,[BX+SI] ................. ;8d 30
LEA SI,[BX] .................... ;8d 37
LEA SI,[DI+0x5566] ............. ;8d b5 66 55
LEA SI,[DI+0x55] ............... ;8d 75 55
LEA SI,[DI] .................... ;8d 35
LEA SI,[SI+0x5566] ............. ;8d b4 66 55
LEA SI,[SI+0x55] ............... ;8d 74 55
LEA SI,[SI] .................... ;8d 34
LEA SP,[0x5566] ................ ;8d 26 66 55
LEA SP,[BP+0x5566] ............. ;8d a6 66 55
LEA SP,[BP+0x55] ............... ;8d 66 55
LEA SP,[BP+DI+0x5566] .......... ;8d a3 66 55
```

```
LEA SP,[BP+DI+0x55] ............ ;8d 63 55
LEA SP,[BP+DI] ................. ;8d 23
LEA SP,[BP+SI+0x5566] .......... ;8d a2 66 55
LEA SP,[BP+SI+0x55] ............ ;8d 62 55
LEA SP,[BP+SI] ................. ;8d 22
LEA SP,[BX+0x5566] ............. ;8d a7 66 55
LEA SP,[BX+0x55] ............... ;8d 67 55
LEA SP,[BX+DI+0x5566] .......... ;8d a1 66 55
LEA SP,[BX+DI+0x55] ............ ;8d 61 55
LEA SP,[BX+DI] ................. ;8d 21
LEA SP,[BX+SI+0x5566] .......... ;8d a0 66 55
LEA SP,[BX+SI+0x55] ............ ;8d 60 55
LEA SP,[BX+SI] ................. ;8d 20
LEA SP,[BX] .................... ;8d 27
LEA SP,[DI+0x5566] ............. ;8d a5 66 55
LEA SP,[DI+0x55] ............... ;8d 65 55
LEA SP,[DI] .................... ;8d 25
LEA SP,[SI+0x5566] ............. ;8d a4 66 55
LEA SP,[SI+0x55] ............... ;8d 64 55
LEA SP,[SI] .................... ;8d 24
LES AX,[0x5566] ................ ;c4 06 66 55
LES AX,[BP+0x5566] ............. ;c4 86 66 55
LES AX,[BP+0x55] ............... ;c4 46 55
LES AX,[BP+DI+0x5566] .......... ;c4 83 66 55
LES AX,[BP+DI+0x55] ............ ;c4 43 55
LES AX,[BP+DI] ................. ;c4 03
LES AX,[BP+SI+0x5566] .......... ;c4 82 66 55
LES AX,[BP+SI+0x55] ............ ;c4 42 55
LES AX,[BP+SI] ................. ;c4 02
LES AX,[BX+0x5566] ............. ;c4 87 66 55
LES AX,[BX+0x55] ............... ;c4 47 55
LES AX,[BX+DI+0x5566] .......... ;c4 81 66 55
LES AX,[BX+DI+0x55] ............ ;c4 41 55
LES AX,[BX+DI] ................. ;c4 01
LES AX,[BX+SI+0x5566] .......... ;c4 80 66 55
LES AX,[BX+SI+0x55] ............ ;c4 40 55
LES AX,[BX+SI] ................. ;c4 00
LES AX,[BX] .................... ;c4 07
LES AX,[DI+0x5566] ............. ;c4 85 66 55
LES AX,[DI+0x55] ............... ;c4 45 55
LES AX,[DI] .................... ;c4 05
LES AX,[SI+0x5566] ............. ;c4 84 66 55
LES AX,[SI+0x55] ............... ;c4 44 55
LES AX,[SI] .................... ;c4 04
LES BP,[0x5566] ................ ;c4 2e 66 55
LES BP,[BP+0x5566] ............. ;c4 ae 66 55
LES BP,[BP+0x55] ............... ;c4 6e 55
LES BP,[BP+DI+0x5566] .......... ;c4 ab 66 55
LES BP,[BP+DI+0x55] ............ ;c4 6b 55
LES BP,[BP+DI] ................. ;c4 2b
LES BP,[BP+SI+0x5566] .......... ;c4 aa 66 55
LES BP,[BP+SI+0x55] ............ ;c4 6a 55
LES BP,[BP+SI] ................. ;c4 2a
LES BP,[BX+0x5566] ............. ;c4 af 66 55
LES BP,[BX+0x55] ............... ;c4 6f 55
LES BP,[BX+DI+0x5566] .......... ;c4 a9 66 55
LES BP,[BX+DI+0x55] ............ ;c4 69 55
LES BP,[BX+DI] ................. ;c4 29
LES BP,[BX+SI+0x5566] .......... ;c4 a8 66 55
LES BP,[BX+SI+0x55] ............ ;c4 68 55
LES BP,[BX+SI] ................. ;c4 28
LES BP,[BX] .................... ;c4 2f
LES BP,[DI+0x5566] ............. ;c4 ad 66 55
LES BP,[DI+0x55] ............... ;c4 6d 55
LES BP,[DI] .................... ;c4 2d
LES BP,[SI+0x5566] ............. ;c4 ac 66 55
LES BP,[SI+0x55] ............... ;c4 6c 55
LES BP,[SI] .................... ;c4 2c
LES BX,[0x5566] ................ ;c4 1e 66 55
LES BX,[BP+0x5566] ............. ;c4 9e 66 55
LES BX,[BP+0x55] ............... ;c4 5e 55
LES BX,[BP+DI+0x5566] .......... ;c4 9b 66 55
LES BX,[BP+DI+0x55] ............ ;c4 5b 55
LES BX,[BP+DI] ................. ;c4 1b
LES BX,[BP+SI+0x5566] .......... ;c4 9a 66 55
LES BX,[BP+SI+0x55] ............ ;c4 5a 55
LES BX,[BP+SI] ................. ;c4 1a
LES BX,[BX+0x5566] ............. ;c4 9f 66 55
LES BX,[BX+0x55] ............... ;c4 5f 55
LES BX,[BX+DI+0x5566] .......... ;c4 99 66 55
LES BX,[BX+DI+0x55] ............ ;c4 59 55
LES BX,[BX+DI] ................. ;c4 19
LES BX,[BX+SI+0x5566] .......... ;c4 98 66 55
LES BX,[BX+SI+0x55] ............ ;c4 58 55
LES BX,[BX+SI] ................. ;c4 18
LES BX,[BX] .................... ;c4 1f
LES BX,[DI+0x5566] ............. ;c4 9d 66 55
LES BX,[DI+0x55] ............... ;c4 5d 55
LES BX,[DI] .................... ;c4 1d
```

```
LES BX,[SI+0x5566] .............;c4 9c 66 55
LES BX,[SI+0x55] ..............;c4 5c 55
LES BX,[SI] ...................;c4 1c
LES CX,[0x5566] ...............;c4 0e 66 55
LES CX,[BP+0x5566] ............;c4 8e 66 55
LES CX,[BP+0x55] ..............;c4 4e 55
LES CX,[BP+DI+0x5566] .........;c4 8b 66 55
LES CX,[BP+DI+0x55] ...........;c4 4b 55
LES CX,[BP+DI] ................;c4 0b
LES CX,[BP+SI+0x5566] .........;c4 8a 66 55
LES CX,[BP+SI+0x55] ...........;c4 4a 55
LES CX,[BP+SI] ................;c4 0a
LES CX,[BX+0x5566] ............;c4 8f 66 55
LES CX,[BX+0x55] ..............;c4 4f 55
LES CX,[BX+DI+0x5566] .........;c4 89 66 55
LES CX,[BX+DI+0x55] ...........;c4 49 55
LES CX,[BX+DI] ................;c4 09
LES CX,[BX+SI+0x5566] .........;c4 88 66 55
LES CX,[BX+SI+0x55] ...........;c4 48 55
LES CX,[BX+SI] ................;c4 08
LES CX,[BX] ...................;c4 0f
LES CX,[DI+0x5566] ............;c4 8d 66 55
LES CX,[DI+0x55] ..............;c4 4d 55
LES CX,[DI] ...................;c4 0d
LES CX,[SI+0x5566] ............;c4 8c 66 55
LES CX,[SI+0x55] ..............;c4 4c 55
LES CX,[SI] ...................;c4 0c
LES DI,[0x5566] ...............;c4 3e 66 55
LES DI,[BP+0x5566] ............;c4 be 66 55
LES DI,[BP+0x55] ..............;c4 7e 55
LES DI,[BP+DI+0x5566] .........;c4 bb 66 55
LES DI,[BP+DI+0x55] ...........;c4 7b 55
LES DI,[BP+DI] ................;c4 3b
LES DI,[BP+SI+0x5566] .........;c4 ba 66 55
LES DI,[BP+SI+0x55] ...........;c4 7a 55
LES DI,[BP+SI] ................;c4 3a
LES DI,[BX+0x5566] ............;c4 bf 66 55
LES DI,[BX+0x55] ..............;c4 7f 55
LES DI,[BX+DI+0x5566] .........;c4 b9 66 55
LES DI,[BX+DI+0x55] ...........;c4 79 55
LES DI,[BX+DI] ................;c4 39
LES DI,[BX+SI+0x5566] .........;c4 b8 66 55
LES DI,[BX+SI+0x55] ...........;c4 78 55
LES DI,[BX+SI] ................;c4 38
LES DI,[BX] ...................;c4 3f
LES DI,[DI+0x5566] ............;c4 bd 66 55
LES DI,[DI+0x55] ..............;c4 7d 55
LES DI,[DI] ...................;c4 3d
LES DI,[SI+0x5566] ............;c4 bc 66 55
LES DI,[SI+0x55] ..............;c4 7c 55
LES DI,[SI] ...................;c4 3c
LES DX,[0x5566] ...............;c4 16 66 55
LES DX,[BP+0x5566] ............;c4 96 66 55
LES DX,[BP+0x55] ..............;c4 56 55
LES DX,[BP+DI+0x5566] .........;c4 93 66 55
LES DX,[BP+DI+0x55] ...........;c4 53 55
LES DX,[BP+DI] ................;c4 13
LES DX,[BP+SI+0x5566] .........;c4 92 66 55
LES DX,[BP+SI+0x55] ...........;c4 52 55
LES DX,[BP+SI] ................;c4 12
LES DX,[BX+0x5566] ............;c4 97 66 55
LES DX,[BX+0x55] ..............;c4 57 55
LES DX,[BX+DI+0x5566] .........;c4 91 66 55
LES DX,[BX+DI+0x55] ...........;c4 51 55
LES DX,[BX+DI] ................;c4 11
LES DX,[BX+SI+0x5566] .........;c4 90 66 55
LES DX,[BX+SI+0x55] ...........;c4 50 55
LES DX,[BX+SI] ................;c4 10
LES DX,[BX] ...................;c4 17
LES DX,[DI+0x5566] ............;c4 95 66 55
LES DX,[DI+0x55] ..............;c4 55 55
LES DX,[DI] ...................;c4 15
LES DX,[SI+0x5566] ............;c4 94 66 55
LES DX,[SI+0x55] ..............;c4 54 55
LES DX,[SI] ...................;c4 14
LES SI,[0x5566] ...............;c4 36 66 55
LES SI,[BP+0x5566] ............;c4 b6 66 55
LES SI,[BP+0x55] ..............;c4 76 55
LES SI,[BP+DI+0x5566] .........;c4 b3 66 55
LES SI,[BP+DI+0x55] ...........;c4 73 55
LES SI,[BP+DI] ................;c4 33
LES SI,[BP+SI+0x5566] .........;c4 b2 66 55
LES SI,[BP+SI+0x55] ...........;c4 72 55
LES SI,[BP+SI] ................;c4 32
LES SI,[BX+0x5566] ............;c4 b7 66 55
LES SI,[BX+0x55] ..............;c4 77 55
LES SI,[BX+DI+0x5566] .........;c4 b1 66 55
LES SI,[BX+DI+0x55] ...........;c4 71 55
LES SI,[BX+DI] ................;c4 31

LES SI,[BX+SI+0x5566] .........;c4 b0 66 55
LES SI,[BX+SI+0x55] ...........;c4 70 55
LES SI,[BX+SI] ................;c4 30
LES SI,[BX] ...................;c4 37
LES SI,[DI+0x5566] ............;c4 b5 66 55
LES SI,[DI+0x55] ..............;c4 75 55
LES SI,[DI] ...................;c4 35
LES SI,[SI+0x5566] ............;c4 b4 66 55
LES SI,[SI+0x55] ..............;c4 74 55
LES SI,[SI] ...................;c4 34
LES SP,[0x5566] ...............;c4 26 66 55
LES SP,[BP+0x5566] ............;c4 a6 66 55
LES SP,[BP+0x55] ..............;c4 66 55
LES SP,[BP+DI+0x5566] .........;c4 a3 66 55
LES SP,[BP+DI+0x55] ...........;c4 63 55
LES SP,[BP+DI] ................;c4 23
LES SP,[BP+SI+0x5566] .........;c4 a2 66 55
LES SP,[BP+SI+0x55] ...........;c4 62 55
LES SP,[BP+SI] ................;c4 22
LES SP,[BX+0x5566] ............;c4 a7 66 55
LES SP,[BX+0x55] ..............;c4 67 55
LES SP,[BX+DI+0x5566] .........;c4 a1 66 55
LES SP,[BX+DI+0x55] ...........;c4 61 55
LES SP,[BX+DI] ................;c4 21
LES SP,[BX+SI+0x5566] .........;c4 a0 66 55
LES SP,[BX+SI+0x55] ...........;c4 60 55
LES SP,[BX+SI] ................;c4 20
LES SP,[BX] ...................;c4 27
LES SP,[DI+0x5566] ............;c4 a5 66 55
LES SP,[DI+0x55] ..............;c4 65 55
LES SP,[DI] ...................;c4 25
LES SP,[SI+0x5566] ............;c4 a4 66 55
LES SP,[SI+0x55] ..............;c4 64 55
LES SP,[SI] ...................;c4 24
LOCK ..........................;f0
LODSB .........................;ac
LODSW .........................;ad
LOOP 0x55 .....................;e2 55
LOOPNZ 0x55 ...................;e0 55
LOOPZ 0x55 ....................;e1 55
MOV AH,0x55 ...................;b4 55
MOV AH,AH .....................;88 e4
MOV AH,AL .....................;88 c4
MOV AH,BH .....................;88 fc
MOV AH,BL .....................;88 dc
MOV AH,CH .....................;88 ec
MOV AH,CL .....................;88 cc
MOV AH,DH .....................;88 f4
MOV AH,DL .....................;88 d4
MOV AH,[0x5566] ...............;8a 26 66 55
MOV AH,[BP+0x5566] ............;8a a6 66 55
MOV AH,[BP+0x55] ..............;8a 66 55
MOV AH,[BP+DI+0x5566] .........;8a a3 66 55
MOV AH,[BP+DI+0x55] ...........;8a 63 55
MOV AH,[BP+DI] ................;8a 23
MOV AH,[BP+SI+0x5566] .........;8a a2 66 55
MOV AH,[BP+SI+0x55] ...........;8a 62 55
MOV AH,[BP+SI] ................;8a 22
MOV AH,[BX+0x5566] ............;8a a7 66 55
MOV AH,[BX+0x55] ..............;8a 67 55
MOV AH,[BX+DI+0x5566] .........;8a a1 66 55
MOV AH,[BX+DI+0x55] ...........;8a 61 55
MOV AH,[BX+DI] ................;8a 21
MOV AH,[BX+SI+0x5566] .........;8a a0 66 55
MOV AH,[BX+SI+0x55] ...........;8a 60 55
MOV AH,[BX+SI] ................;8a 20
MOV AH,[BX] ...................;8a 27
MOV AH,[DI+0x5566] ............;8a a5 66 55
MOV AH,[DI+0x55] ..............;8a 65 55
MOV AH,[DI] ...................;8a 25
MOV AH,[SI+0x5566] ............;8a a4 66 55
MOV AH,[SI+0x55] ..............;8a 64 55
MOV AH,[SI] ...................;8a 24
MOV AL,0x55 ...................;b0 55
MOV AL,AH .....................;88 e0
MOV AL,AL .....................;88 c0
MOV AL,BH .....................;88 f8
MOV AL,BL .....................;88 d8
MOV AL,CH .....................;88 e8
MOV AL,CL .....................;88 c8
MOV AL,DH .....................;88 f0
MOV AL,DL .....................;88 d0
MOV AL,[0x5566] ...............;8a 06 66 55
MOV AL,[0x5566] ...............;a0 66 55
MOV AL,[BP+0x5566] ............;8a 86 66 55
MOV AL,[BP+0x55] ..............;8a 46 55
MOV AL,[BP+DI+0x5566] .........;8a 83 66 55
MOV AL,[BP+DI+0x55] ...........;8a 43 55
MOV AL,[BP+DI] ................;8a 03
```

192

```
MOV AL,[BP+SI+0x5566] .........;8a 82 66 55
MOV AL,[BP+SI+0x55] ...........;8a 42 55
MOV AL,[BP+SI] ................;8a 02
MOV AL,[BX+0x5566] ............;8a 87 66 55
MOV AL,[BX+0x55] ..............;8a 47 55
MOV AL,[BX+DI+0x5566] .........;8a 81 66 55
MOV AL,[BX+DI+0x55] ...........;8a 41 55
MOV AL,[BX+DI] ................;8a 01
MOV AL,[BX+SI+0x5566] .........;8a 80 66 55
MOV AL,[BX+SI+0x55] ...........;8a 40 55
MOV AL,[BX+SI] ................;8a 00
MOV AL,[BX] ...................;8a 07
MOV AL,[DI+0x5566] ............;8a 85 66 55
MOV AL,[DI+0x55] ..............;8a 45 55
MOV AL,[DI] ...................;8a 05
MOV AL,[SI+0x5566] ............;8a 84 66 55
MOV AL,[SI+0x55] ..............;8a 44 55
MOV AL,[SI] ...................;8a 04
MOV AX,0x5566 .................;b8 66 55
MOV AX,AX .....................;89 c0
MOV AX,BP .....................;89 e8
MOV AX,BX .....................;89 d8
MOV AX,CS .....................;8c c8
MOV AX,CX .....................;89 c8
MOV AX,DI .....................;89 f8
MOV AX,DS .....................;8c d8
MOV AX,DX .....................;89 d0
MOV AX,ES .....................;8c c0
MOV AX,SI .....................;89 f0
MOV AX,SP .....................;89 e0
MOV AX,SS .....................;8c d0
MOV AX,[0x5566] ...............;8b 06 66 55
MOV AX,[0x5566] ...............;a1 66 55
MOV AX,[BP+0x5566] ............;8b 86 66 55
MOV AX,[BP+0x55] ..............;8b 46 55
MOV AX,[BP+DI+0x5566] .........;8b 83 66 55
MOV AX,[BP+DI+0x55] ...........;8b 43 55
MOV AX,[BP+DI] ................;8b 03
MOV AX,[BP+SI+0x5566] .........;8b 82 66 55
MOV AX,[BP+SI+0x55] ...........;8b 42 55
MOV AX,[BP+SI] ................;8b 02
MOV AX,[BX+0x5566] ............;8b 87 66 55
MOV AX,[BX+0x55] ..............;8b 47 55
MOV AX,[BX+DI+0x5566] .........;8b 81 66 55
MOV AX,[BX+DI+0x55] ...........;8b 41 55
MOV AX,[BX+DI] ................;8b 01
MOV AX,[BX+SI+0x5566] .........;8b 80 66 55
MOV AX,[BX+SI+0x55] ...........;8b 40 55
MOV AX,[BX+SI] ................;8b 00
MOV AX,[BX] ...................;8b 07
MOV AX,[DI+0x5566] ............;8b 85 66 55
MOV AX,[DI+0x55] ..............;8b 45 55
MOV AX,[DI] ...................;8b 05
MOV AX,[SI+0x5566] ............;8b 84 66 55
MOV AX,[SI+0x55] ..............;8b 44 55
MOV AX,[SI] ...................;8b 04
MOV BH,0x55 ...................;b7 55
MOV BH,AH .....................;88 e7
MOV BH,AL .....................;88 c7
MOV BH,BH .....................;88 ff
MOV BH,BL .....................;88 df
MOV BH,CH .....................;88 ef
MOV BH,CL .....................;88 cf
MOV BH,DH .....................;88 f7
MOV BH,DL .....................;88 d7
MOV BH,[0x5566] ...............;8a 3e 66 55
MOV BH,[BP+0x5566] ............;8a be 66 55
MOV BH,[BP+0x55] ..............;8a 7e 55
MOV BH,[BP+DI+0x5566] .........;8a bb 66 55
MOV BH,[BP+DI+0x55] ...........;8a 7b 55
MOV BH,[BP+DI] ................;8a 3b
MOV BH,[BP+SI+0x5566] .........;8a ba 66 55
MOV BH,[BP+SI+0x55] ...........;8a 7a 55
MOV BH,[BP+SI] ................;8a 3a
MOV BH,[BX+0x5566] ............;8a bf 66 55
MOV BH,[BX+0x55] ..............;8a 7f 55
MOV BH,[BX+DI+0x5566] .........;8a b9 66 55
MOV BH,[BX+DI+0x55] ...........;8a 79 55
MOV BH,[BX+DI] ................;8a 39
MOV BH,[BX+SI+0x5566] .........;8a b8 66 55
MOV BH,[BX+SI+0x55] ...........;8a 78 55
MOV BH,[BX+SI] ................;8a 38
MOV BH,[BX] ...................;8a 3f
MOV BH,[DI+0x5566] ............;8a bd 66 55
MOV BH,[DI+0x55] ..............;8a 7d 55
MOV BH,[DI] ...................;8a 3d
MOV BH,[SI+0x5566] ............;8a bc 66 55
MOV BH,[SI+0x55] ..............;8a 7c 55
MOV BH,[SI] ...................;8a 3c

MOV BL,0x55 ...................;b3 55
MOV BL,AH .....................;88 e3
MOV BL,AL .....................;88 c3
MOV BL,BH .....................;88 fb
MOV BL,BL .....................;88 db
MOV BL,CH .....................;88 eb
MOV BL,CL .....................;88 cb
MOV BL,DH .....................;88 f3
MOV BL,DL .....................;88 d3
MOV BL,[0x5566] ...............;8a 1e 66 55
MOV BL,[BP+0x5566] ............;8a 9e 66 55
MOV BL,[BP+0x55] ..............;8a 5e 55
MOV BL,[BP+DI+0x5566] .........;8a 9b 66 55
MOV BL,[BP+DI+0x55] ...........;8a 5b 55
MOV BL,[BP+DI] ................;8a 1b
MOV BL,[BP+SI+0x5566] .........;8a 9a 66 55
MOV BL,[BP+SI+0x55] ...........;8a 5a 55
MOV BL,[BP+SI] ................;8a 1a
MOV BL,[BX+0x5566] ............;8a 9f 66 55
MOV BL,[BX+0x55] ..............;8a 5f 55
MOV BL,[BX+DI+0x5566] .........;8a 99 66 55
MOV BL,[BX+DI+0x55] ...........;8a 59 55
MOV BL,[BX+DI] ................;8a 19
MOV BL,[BX+SI+0x5566] .........;8a 98 66 55
MOV BL,[BX+SI+0x55] ...........;8a 58 55
MOV BL,[BX+SI] ................;8a 18
MOV BL,[BX] ...................;8a 1f
MOV BL,[DI+0x5566] ............;8a 9d 66 55
MOV BL,[DI+0x55] ..............;8a 5d 55
MOV BL,[DI] ...................;8a 1d
MOV BL,[SI+0x5566] ............;8a 9c 66 55
MOV BL,[SI+0x55] ..............;8a 5c 55
MOV BL,[SI] ...................;8a 1c
MOV BP,0x5566 .................;bd 66 55
MOV BP,AX .....................;89 c5
MOV BP,BP .....................;89 ed
MOV BP,BX .....................;89 dd
MOV BP,CS .....................;8c cd
MOV BP,CX .....................;89 cd
MOV BP,DI .....................;89 fd
MOV BP,DS .....................;8c dd
MOV BP,DX .....................;89 d5
MOV BP,ES .....................;8c c5
MOV BP,SI .....................;89 f5
MOV BP,SP .....................;89 e5
MOV BP,SS .....................;8c d5
MOV BP,[0x5566] ...............;8b 2e 66 55
MOV BP,[BP+0x5566] ............;8b ae 66 55
MOV BP,[BP+0x55] ..............;8b 6e 55
MOV BP,[BP+DI+0x5566] .........;8b ab 66 55
MOV BP,[BP+DI+0x55] ...........;8b 6b 55
MOV BP,[BP+DI] ................;8b 2b
MOV BP,[BP+SI+0x5566] .........;8b aa 66 55
MOV BP,[BP+SI+0x55] ...........;8b 6a 55
MOV BP,[BP+SI] ................;8b 2a
MOV BP,[BX+0x5566] ............;8b af 66 55
MOV BP,[BX+0x55] ..............;8b 6f 55
MOV BP,[BX+DI+0x5566] .........;8b a9 66 55
MOV BP,[BX+DI+0x55] ...........;8b 69 55
MOV BP,[BX+DI] ................;8b 29
MOV BP,[BX+SI+0x5566] .........;8b a8 66 55
MOV BP,[BX+SI+0x55] ...........;8b 68 55
MOV BP,[BX+SI] ................;8b 28
MOV BP,[BX] ...................;8b 2f
MOV BP,[DI+0x5566] ............;8b ad 66 55
MOV BP,[DI+0x55] ..............;8b 6d 55
MOV BP,[DI] ...................;8b 2d
MOV BP,[SI+0x5566] ............;8b ac 66 55
MOV BP,[SI+0x55] ..............;8b 6c 55
MOV BP,[SI] ...................;8b 2c
MOV BX,0x5566 .................;bb 66 55
MOV BX,AX .....................;89 c3
MOV BX,BP .....................;89 eb
MOV BX,BX .....................;89 db
MOV BX,CS .....................;8c cb
MOV BX,CX .....................;89 cb
MOV BX,DI .....................;89 fb
MOV BX,DS .....................;8c db
MOV BX,DX .....................;89 d3
MOV BX,ES .....................;8c c3
MOV BX,SI .....................;89 f3
MOV BX,SP .....................;89 e3
MOV BX,SS .....................;8c d3
MOV BX,[0x5566] ...............;8b 1e 66 55
MOV BX,[BP+0x5566] ............;8b 9e 66 55
MOV BX,[BP+0x55] ..............;8b 5e 55
MOV BX,[BP+DI+0x5566] .........;8b 9b 66 55
MOV BX,[BP+DI+0x55] ...........;8b 5b 55
MOV BX,[BP+DI] ................;8b 1b
```

```
MOV BX,[BP+SI+0x5566] ..........;8b 9a 66 55
MOV BX,[BP+SI+0x55] ...........;8b 5a 55
MOV BX,[BP+SI] ................;8b 1a
MOV BX,[BX+0x5566] ............;8b 9f 66 55
MOV BX,[BX+0x55] ..............;8b 5f 55
MOV BX,[BX+DI+0x5566] .........;8b 99 66 55
MOV BX,[BX+DI+0x55] ...........;8b 59 55
MOV BX,[BX+DI] ................;8b 19
MOV BX,[BX+SI+0x5566] .........;8b 98 66 55
MOV BX,[BX+SI+0x55] ...........;8b 58 55
MOV BX,[BX+SI] ................;8b 18
MOV BX,[BX] ...................;8b 1f
MOV BX,[DI+0x5566] ............;8b 9d 66 55
MOV BX,[DI+0x55] ..............;8b 5d 55
MOV BX,[DI] ...................;8b 1d
MOV BX,[SI+0x5566] ............;8b 9c 66 55
MOV BX,[SI+0x55] ..............;8b 5c 55
MOV BX,[SI] ...................;8b 1c
MOV BYTE [0x5566],0x88 ........;c6 06 66 55 88
MOV BYTE [BP+0x5566],0x88 .....;c6 86 66 55 88
MOV BYTE [BP+0x55],0x88 .......;c6 46 55 88
MOV BYTE [BP+DI+0x5566],0x88 ..;c6 83 66 55 88
MOV BYTE [BP+DI+0x55],0x88 ....;c6 43 55 88
MOV BYTE [BP+DI],0x88 .........;c6 03 88
MOV BYTE [BP+SI+0x5566],0x88 ..;c6 82 66 55 88
MOV BYTE [BP+SI+0x55],0x88 ....;c6 42 55 88
MOV BYTE [BP+SI],0x88 .........;c6 02 88
MOV BYTE [BX+0x5566],0x88 .....;c6 87 66 55 88
MOV BYTE [BX+0x55],0x88 .......;c6 47 55 88
MOV BYTE [BX+DI+0x5566],0x88 ..;c6 81 66 55 88
MOV BYTE [BX+DI+0x55],0x88 ....;c6 41 55 88
MOV BYTE [BX+DI],0x88 .........;c6 01 88
MOV BYTE [BX+SI+0x5566],0x88 ..;c6 80 66 55 88
MOV BYTE [BX+SI+0x55],0x88 ....;c6 40 55 88
MOV BYTE [BX+SI],0x88 .........;c6 00 88
MOV BYTE [BX],0x88 ............;c6 07 88
MOV BYTE [DI+0x5566],0x88 .....;c6 85 66 55 88
MOV BYTE [DI+0x55],0x88 .......;c6 45 55 88
MOV BYTE [DI],0x88 ............;c6 05 88
MOV BYTE [SI+0x5566],0x88 .....;c6 84 66 55 88
MOV BYTE [SI+0x55],0x88 .......;c6 44 55 88
MOV BYTE [SI],0x88 ............;c6 04 88
MOV CH,0x55 ...................;b5 55
MOV CH,AH .....................;88 e5
MOV CH,AL .....................;88 c5
MOV CH,BH .....................;88 fd
MOV CH,BL .....................;88 dd
MOV CH,CH .....................;88 ed
MOV CH,CL .....................;88 cd
MOV CH,DH .....................;88 f5
MOV CH,DL .....................;88 d5
MOV CH,[0x5566] ...............;8a 2e 66 55
MOV CH,[BP+0x5566] ............;8a ae 66 55
MOV CH,[BP+0x55] ..............;8a 6e 55
MOV CH,[BP+DI+0x5566] .........;8a ab 66 55
MOV CH,[BP+DI+0x55] ...........;8a 6b 55
MOV CH,[BP+DI] ................;8a 2b
MOV CH,[BP+SI+0x5566] .........;8a aa 66 55
MOV CH,[BP+SI+0x55] ...........;8a 6a 55
MOV CH,[BP+SI] ................;8a 2a
MOV CH,[BX+0x5566] ............;8a af 66 55
MOV CH,[BX+0x55] ..............;8a 6f 55
MOV CH,[BX+DI+0x5566] .........;8a a9 66 55
MOV CH,[BX+DI+0x55] ...........;8a 69 55
MOV CH,[BX+DI] ................;8a 29
MOV CH,[BX+SI+0x5566] .........;8a a8 66 55
MOV CH,[BX+SI+0x55] ...........;8a 68 55
MOV CH,[BX+SI] ................;8a 28
MOV CH,[BX] ...................;8a 2f
MOV CH,[DI+0x5566] ............;8a ad 66 55
MOV CH,[DI+0x55] ..............;8a 6d 55
MOV CH,[DI] ...................;8a 2d
MOV CH,[SI+0x5566] ............;8a ac 66 55
MOV CH,[SI+0x55] ..............;8a 6c 55
MOV CH,[SI] ...................;8a 2c
MOV CL,0x55 ...................;b1 55
MOV CL,AH .....................;88 e1
MOV CL,AL .....................;88 c1
MOV CL,BH .....................;88 f9
MOV CL,BL .....................;88 d9
MOV CL,CH .....................;88 e9
MOV CL,CL .....................;88 c9
MOV CL,DH .....................;88 f1
MOV CL,DL .....................;88 d1
MOV CL,[0x5566] ...............;8a 0e 66 55
MOV CL,[BP+0x5566] ............;8a 8e 66 55
MOV CL,[BP+0x55] ..............;8a 4e 55
MOV CL,[BP+DI+0x5566] .........;8a 8b 66 55
MOV CL,[BP+DI+0x55] ...........;8a 4b 55

MOV CL,[BP+DI] ................;8a 0b
MOV CL,[BP+SI+0x5566] .........;8a 8a 66 55
MOV CL,[BP+SI+0x55] ...........;8a 4a 55
MOV CL,[BP+SI] ................;8a 0a
MOV CL,[BX+0x5566] ............;8a 8f 66 55
MOV CL,[BX+0x55] ..............;8a 4f 55
MOV CL,[BX+DI+0x5566] .........;8a 89 66 55
MOV CL,[BX+DI+0x55] ...........;8a 49 55
MOV CL,[BX+DI] ................;8a 09
MOV CL,[BX+SI+0x5566] .........;8a 88 66 55
MOV CL,[BX+SI+0x55] ...........;8a 48 55
MOV CL,[BX+SI] ................;8a 08
MOV CL,[BX] ...................;8a 0f
MOV CL,[DI+0x5566] ............;8a 8d 66 55
MOV CL,[DI+0x55] ..............;8a 4d 55
MOV CL,[DI] ...................;8a 0d
MOV CL,[SI+0x5566] ............;8a 8c 66 55
MOV CL,[SI+0x55] ..............;8a 4c 55
MOV CL,[SI] ...................;8a 0c
MOV CS,AX .....................;8e c8
MOV CS,BP .....................;8e cd
MOV CS,BX .....................;8e cb
MOV CS,CX .....................;8e c9
MOV CS,DI .....................;8e cf
MOV CS,DX .....................;8e ca
MOV CS,SI .....................;8e ce
MOV CS,SP .....................;8e cc
MOV CS,[0x5566] ...............;8e 0e 66 55
MOV CS,[BP+0x5566] ............;8e 8e 66 55
MOV CS,[BP+0x55] ..............;8e 4e 55
MOV CS,[BP+DI+0x5566] .........;8e 8b 66 55
MOV CS,[BP+DI+0x55] ...........;8e 4b 55
MOV CS,[BP+DI] ................;8e 0b
MOV CS,[BP+SI+0x5566] .........;8e 8a 66 55
MOV CS,[BP+SI+0x55] ...........;8e 4a 55
MOV CS,[BP+SI] ................;8e 0a
MOV CS,[BX+0x5566] ............;8e 8f 66 55
MOV CS,[BX+0x55] ..............;8e 4f 55
MOV CS,[BX+DI+0x5566] .........;8e 89 66 55
MOV CS,[BX+DI+0x55] ...........;8e 49 55
MOV CS,[BX+DI] ................;8e 09
MOV CS,[BX+SI+0x5566] .........;8e 88 66 55
MOV CS,[BX+SI+0x55] ...........;8e 48 55
MOV CS,[BX+SI] ................;8e 08
MOV CS,[BX] ...................;8e 0f
MOV CS,[DI+0x5566] ............;8e 8d 66 55
MOV CS,[DI+0x55] ..............;8e 4d 55
MOV CS,[DI] ...................;8e 0d
MOV CS,[SI+0x5566] ............;8e 8c 66 55
MOV CS,[SI+0x55] ..............;8e 4c 55
MOV CS,[SI] ...................;8e 0c
MOV CX,0x5566 .................;b9 66 55
MOV CX,AX .....................;89 c1
MOV CX,BP .....................;89 e9
MOV CX,BX .....................;89 d9
MOV CX,CS .....................;8c c9
MOV CX,CX .....................;89 c9
MOV CX,DI .....................;89 f9
MOV CX,DS .....................;8c d9
MOV CX,DX .....................;89 d1
MOV CX,ES .....................;8c c1
MOV CX,SI .....................;89 f1
MOV CX,SP .....................;89 e1
MOV CX,SS .....................;8c d1
MOV CX,[0x5566] ...............;8b 0e 66 55
MOV CX,[BP+0x5566] ............;8b 8e 66 55
MOV CX,[BP+0x55] ..............;8b 4e 55
MOV CX,[BP+DI+0x5566] .........;8b 8b 66 55
MOV CX,[BP+DI+0x55] ...........;8b 4b 55
MOV CX,[BP+DI] ................;8b 0b
MOV CX,[BP+SI+0x5566] .........;8b 8a 66 55
MOV CX,[BP+SI+0x55] ...........;8b 4a 55
MOV CX,[BP+SI] ................;8b 0a
MOV CX,[BX+0x5566] ............;8b 8f 66 55
MOV CX,[BX+0x55] ..............;8b 4f 55
MOV CX,[BX+DI+0x5566] .........;8b 89 66 55
MOV CX,[BX+DI+0x55] ...........;8b 49 55
MOV CX,[BX+DI] ................;8b 09
MOV CX,[BX+SI+0x5566] .........;8b 88 66 55
MOV CX,[BX+SI+0x55] ...........;8b 48 55
MOV CX,[BX+SI] ................;8b 08
MOV CX,[BX] ...................;8b 0f
MOV CX,[DI+0x5566] ............;8b 8d 66 55
MOV CX,[DI+0x55] ..............;8b 4d 55
MOV CX,[DI] ...................;8b 0d
MOV CX,[SI+0x5566] ............;8b 8c 66 55
MOV CX,[SI+0x55] ..............;8b 4c 55
MOV CX,[SI] ...................;8b 0c
MOV DH,0x55 ...................;b6 55
```

```
MOV DH,AH .......................;88 e6        MOV DL,[BX+DI+0x5566] ..........;8a 91 66 55
MOV DH,AL .......................;88 c6        MOV DL,[BX+DI+0x55] ............;8a 51 55
MOV DH,BH .......................;88 fe        MOV DL,[BX+DI] .................;8a 11
MOV DH,BL .......................;88 de        MOV DL,[BX+SI+0x5566] ..........;8a 90 66 55
MOV DH,CH .......................;88 ee        MOV DL,[BX+SI+0x55] ............;8a 50 55
MOV DH,CL .......................;88 ce        MOV DL,[BX+SI] .................;8a 10
MOV DH,DH .......................;88 f6        MOV DL,[BX] ....................;8a 17
MOV DH,DL .......................;88 d6        MOV DL,[DI+0x5566] .............;8a 95 66 55
MOV DH,[0x5566] .................;8a 36 66 55  MOV DL,[DI+0x55] ...............;8a 55 55
MOV DH,[BP+0x5566] .............;8a b6 66 55   MOV DL,[DI] ....................;8a 15
MOV DH,[BP+0x55] ...............;8a 76 55      MOV DL,[SI+0x5566] .............;8a 94 66 55
MOV DH,[BP+DI+0x5566] ..........;8a b3 66 55   MOV DL,[SI+0x55] ...............;8a 54 55
MOV DH,[BP+DI+0x55] ............;8a 73 55      MOV DL,[SI] ....................;8a 14
MOV DH,[BP+DI] .................;8a 33         MOV DS,AX ......................;8e d8
MOV DH,[BP+SI+0x5566] ..........;8a b2 66 55   MOV DS,BP ......................;8e dd
MOV DH,[BP+SI+0x55] ............;8a 72 55      MOV DS,BX ......................;8e db
MOV DH,[BP+SI] .................;8a 32         MOV DS,CX ......................;8e d9
MOV DH,[BX+0x5566] .............;8a b7 66 55   MOV DS,DI ......................;8e df
MOV DH,[BX+0x55] ...............;8a 77 55      MOV DS,DX ......................;8e da
MOV DH,[BX+DI+0x5566] ..........;8a b1 66 55   MOV DS,SI ......................;8e de
MOV DH,[BX+DI+0x55] ............;8a 71 55      MOV DS,SP ......................;8e dc
MOV DH,[BX+DI] .................;8a 31         MOV DS,[0x5566] ................;8e 1e 66 55
MOV DH,[BX+SI+0x5566] ..........;8a b0 66 55   MOV DS,[BP+0x5566] .............;8e 9e 66 55
MOV DH,[BX+SI+0x55] ............;8a 70 55      MOV DS,[BP+0x55] ...............;8e 5e 55
MOV DH,[BX+SI] .................;8a 30         MOV DS,[BP+DI+0x5566] ..........;8e 9b 66 55
MOV DH,[BX] ....................;8a 37         MOV DS,[BP+DI+0x55] ............;8e 5b 55
MOV DH,[DI+0x5566] .............;8a b5 66 55   MOV DS,[BP+DI] .................;8e 1b
MOV DH,[DI+0x55] ...............;8a 75 55      MOV DS,[BP+SI+0x5566] ..........;8e 9a 66 55
MOV DH,[DI] ....................;8a 35         MOV DS,[BP+SI+0x55] ............;8e 5a 55
MOV DH,[SI+0x5566] .............;8a b4 66 55   MOV DS,[BP+SI] .................;8e 1a
MOV DH,[SI+0x55] ...............;8a 74 55      MOV DS,[BX+0x5566] .............;8e 9f 66 55
MOV DH,[SI] ....................;8a 34         MOV DS,[BX+0x55] ...............;8e 5f 55
MOV DI,0x5566 ..................;bf 66 55      MOV DS,[BX+DI+0x5566] ..........;8e 99 66 55
MOV DI,AX ......................;89 c7         MOV DS,[BX+DI+0x55] ............;8e 59 55
MOV DI,BP ......................;89 ef         MOV DS,[BX+DI] .................;8e 19
MOV DI,BX ......................;89 df         MOV DS,[BX+SI+0x5566] ..........;8e 98 66 55
MOV DI,CS ......................;8c cf         MOV DS,[BX+SI+0x55] ............;8e 58 55
MOV DI,CX ......................;89 cf         MOV DS,[BX+SI] .................;8e 18
MOV DI,DI ......................;89 ff         MOV DS,[BX] ....................;8e 1f
MOV DI,DS ......................;8c df         MOV DS,[DI+0x5566] .............;8e 9d 66 55
MOV DI,DX ......................;89 d7         MOV DS,[DI+0x55] ...............;8e 5d 55
MOV DI,ES ......................;8c c7         MOV DS,[DI] ....................;8e 1d
MOV DI,SI ......................;89 f7         MOV DS,[SI+0x5566] .............;8e 9c 66 55
MOV DI,SP ......................;89 e7         MOV DS,[SI+0x55] ...............;8e 5c 55
MOV DI,SS ......................;8c d7         MOV DS,[SI] ....................;8e 1c
MOV DI,[0x5566] .................;8b 3e 66 55  MOV DX,0x5566 ..................;ba 66 55
MOV DI,[BP+0x5566] .............;8b be 66 55   MOV DX,AX ......................;89 c2
MOV DI,[BP+0x55] ...............;8b 7e 55      MOV DX,BP ......................;89 ea
MOV DI,[BP+DI+0x5566] ..........;8b bb 66 55   MOV DX,BX ......................;89 da
MOV DI,[BP+DI+0x55] ............;8b 7b 55      MOV DX,CS ......................;8c ca
MOV DI,[BP+DI] .................;8b 3b         MOV DX,CX ......................;89 ca
MOV DI,[BP+SI+0x5566] ..........;8b ba 66 55   MOV DX,DI ......................;89 fa
MOV DI,[BP+SI+0x55] ............;8b 7a 55      MOV DX,DS ......................;8c da
MOV DI,[BP+SI] .................;8b 3a         MOV DX,DX ......................;89 d2
MOV DI,[BX+0x5566] .............;8b bf 66 55   MOV DX,ES ......................;8c c2
MOV DI,[BX+0x55] ...............;8b 7f 55      MOV DX,SI ......................;89 f2
MOV DI,[BX+DI+0x5566] ..........;8b b9 66 55   MOV DX,SP ......................;89 e2
MOV DI,[BX+DI+0x55] ............;8b 79 55      MOV DX,SS ......................;8c d2
MOV DI,[BX+DI] .................;8b 39         MOV DX,[0x5566] ................;8b 16 66 55
MOV DI,[BX+SI+0x5566] ..........;8b b8 66 55   MOV DX,[BP+0x5566] .............;8b 96 66 55
MOV DI,[BX+SI+0x55] ............;8b 78 55      MOV DX,[BP+0x55] ...............;8b 56 55
MOV DI,[BX+SI] .................;8b 38         MOV DX,[BP+DI+0x5566] ..........;8b 93 66 55
MOV DI,[BX] ....................;8b 3f         MOV DX,[BP+DI+0x55] ............;8b 53 55
MOV DI,[DI+0x5566] .............;8b bd 66 55   MOV DX,[BP+DI] .................;8b 13
MOV DI,[DI+0x55] ...............;8b 7d 55      MOV DX,[BP+SI+0x5566] ..........;8b 92 66 55
MOV DI,[DI] ....................;8b 3d         MOV DX,[BP+SI+0x55] ............;8b 52 55
MOV DI,[SI+0x5566] .............;8b bc 66 55   MOV DX,[BP+SI] .................;8b 12
MOV DI,[SI+0x55] ...............;8b 7c 55      MOV DX,[BX+0x5566] .............;8b 97 66 55
MOV DI,[SI] ....................;8b 3c         MOV DX,[BX+0x55] ...............;8b 57 55
MOV DL,0x55 ....................;b2 55         MOV DX,[BX+DI+0x5566] ..........;8b 91 66 55
MOV DL,AH ......................;88 e2         MOV DX,[BX+DI+0x55] ............;8b 51 55
MOV DL,AL ......................;88 c2         MOV DX,[BX+DI] .................;8b 11
MOV DL,BH ......................;88 fa         MOV DX,[BX+SI+0x5566] ..........;8b 90 66 55
MOV DL,BL ......................;88 da         MOV DX,[BX+SI+0x55] ............;8b 50 55
MOV DL,CH ......................;88 ea         MOV DX,[BX+SI] .................;8b 10
MOV DL,CL ......................;88 ca         MOV DX,[BX] ....................;8b 17
MOV DL,DH ......................;88 f2         MOV DX,[DI+0x5566] .............;8b 95 66 55
MOV DL,DL ......................;88 d2         MOV DX,[DI+0x55] ...............;8b 55 55
MOV DL,[0x5566] .................;8a 16 66 55  MOV DX,[DI] ....................;8b 15
MOV DL,[BP+0x5566] .............;8a 96 66 55   MOV DX,[SI+0x5566] .............;8b 94 66 55
MOV DL,[BP+0x55] ...............;8a 56 55      MOV DX,[SI+0x55] ...............;8b 54 55
MOV DL,[BP+DI+0x5566] ..........;8a 93 66 55   MOV DX,[SI] ....................;8b 14
MOV DL,[BP+DI+0x55] ............;8a 53 55      MOV ES,AX ......................;8e c0
MOV DL,[BP+DI] .................;8a 13         MOV ES,BP ......................;8e c5
MOV DL,[BP+SI+0x5566] ..........;8a 92 66 55   MOV ES,BX ......................;8e c3
MOV DL,[BP+SI+0x55] ............;8a 52 55      MOV ES,CX ......................;8e c1
MOV DL,[BP+SI] .................;8a 12         MOV ES,DI ......................;8e c7
MOV DL,[BX+0x5566] .............;8a 97 66 55   MOV ES,DX ......................;8e c2
MOV DL,[BX+0x55] ...............;8a 57 55      MOV ES,SI ......................;8e c6
```

195

```
MOV ES,SP .....................;8e c4
MOV ES,[0x5566] ...............;8e 06 66 55
MOV ES,[BP+0x5566] ............;8e 86 66 55
MOV ES,[BP+0x55] ..............;8e 46 55
MOV ES,[BP+DI+0x5566] .........;8e 83 66 55
MOV ES,[BP+DI+0x55] ...........;8e 43 55
MOV ES,[BP+DI] ................;8e 03
MOV ES,[BP+SI+0x5566] .........;8e 82 66 55
MOV ES,[BP+SI+0x55] ...........;8e 42 55
MOV ES,[BP+SI] ................;8e 02
MOV ES,[BX+0x5566] ............;8e 87 66 55
MOV ES,[BX+0x55] ..............;8e 47 55
MOV ES,[BX+DI+0x5566] .........;8e 81 66 55
MOV ES,[BX+DI+0x55] ...........;8e 41 55
MOV ES,[BX+DI] ................;8e 01
MOV ES,[BX+SI+0x5566] .........;8e 80 66 55
MOV ES,[BX+SI+0x55] ...........;8e 40 55
MOV ES,[BX+SI] ................;8e 00
MOV ES,[BX] ...................;8e 07
MOV ES,[DI+0x5566] ............;8e 85 66 55
MOV ES,[DI+0x55] ..............;8e 45 55
MOV ES,[DI] ...................;8e 05
MOV ES,[SI+0x5566] ............;8e 84 66 55
MOV ES,[SI+0x55] ..............;8e 44 55
MOV ES,[SI] ...................;8e 04
MOV SI,0x5566 .................;be 66 55
MOV SI,AX .....................;89 c6
MOV SI,BP .....................;89 ee
MOV SI,BX .....................;89 de
MOV SI,CS .....................;8c ce
MOV SI,CX .....................;89 ce
MOV SI,DI .....................;89 fe
MOV SI,DS .....................;8c de
MOV SI,DX .....................;89 d6
MOV SI,ES .....................;8c c6
MOV SI,SI .....................;89 f6
MOV SI,SP .....................;89 e6
MOV SI,SS .....................;8c d6
MOV SI,[0x5566] ...............;8b 36 66 55
MOV SI,[BP+0x5566] ............;8b b6 66 55
MOV SI,[BP+0x55] ..............;8b 76 55
MOV SI,[BP+DI+0x5566] .........;8b b3 66 55
MOV SI,[BP+DI+0x55] ...........;8b 73 55
MOV SI,[BP+DI] ................;8b 33
MOV SI,[BP+SI+0x5566] .........;8b b2 66 55
MOV SI,[BP+SI+0x55] ...........;8b 72 55
MOV SI,[BP+SI] ................;8b 32
MOV SI,[BX+0x5566] ............;8b b7 66 55
MOV SI,[BX+0x55] ..............;8b 77 55
MOV SI,[BX+DI+0x5566] .........;8b b1 66 55
MOV SI,[BX+DI+0x55] ...........;8b 71 55
MOV SI,[BX+DI] ................;8b 31
MOV SI,[BX+SI+0x5566] .........;8b b0 66 55
MOV SI,[BX+SI+0x55] ...........;8b 70 55
MOV SI,[BX+SI] ................;8b 30
MOV SI,[BX] ...................;8b 37
MOV SI,[DI+0x5566] ............;8b b5 66 55
MOV SI,[DI+0x55] ..............;8b 75 55
MOV SI,[DI] ...................;8b 35
MOV SI,[SI+0x5566] ............;8b b4 66 55
MOV SI,[SI+0x55] ..............;8b 74 55
MOV SI,[SI] ...................;8b 34
MOV SP,0x5566 .................;bc 66 55
MOV SP,AX .....................;89 c4
MOV SP,BP .....................;89 ec
MOV SP,BX .....................;89 dc
MOV SP,CS .....................;8c cc
MOV SP,CX .....................;89 cc
MOV SP,DI .....................;89 fc
MOV SP,DS .....................;8c dc
MOV SP,DX .....................;89 d4
MOV SP,ES .....................;8c c4
MOV SP,SI .....................;89 f4
MOV SP,SP .....................;89 e4
MOV SP,SS .....................;8c d4
MOV SP,[0x5566] ...............;8b 26 66 55
MOV SP,[BP+0x5566] ............;8b a6 66 55
MOV SP,[BP+0x55] ..............;8b 66 55
MOV SP,[BP+DI+0x5566] .........;8b a3 66 55
MOV SP,[BP+DI+0x55] ...........;8b 63 55
MOV SP,[BP+DI] ................;8b 23
MOV SP,[BP+SI+0x5566] .........;8b a2 66 55
MOV SP,[BP+SI+0x55] ...........;8b 62 55
MOV SP,[BP+SI] ................;8b 22
MOV SP,[BX+0x5566] ............;8b a7 66 55
MOV SP,[BX+0x55] ..............;8b 67 55
MOV SP,[BX+DI+0x5566] .........;8b a1 66 55
MOV SP,[BX+DI+0x55] ...........;8b 61 55
MOV SP,[BX+DI] ................;8b 21
MOV SP,[BX+SI+0x5566] .........;8b a0 66 55
MOV SP,[BX+SI+0x55] ...........;8b 60 55
MOV SP,[BX+SI] ................;8b 20
MOV SP,[BX] ...................;8b 27
MOV SP,[DI+0x5566] ............;8b a5 66 55
MOV SP,[DI+0x55] ..............;8b 65 55
MOV SP,[DI] ...................;8b 25
MOV SP,[SI+0x5566] ............;8b a4 66 55
MOV SP,[SI+0x55] ..............;8b 64 55
MOV SP,[SI] ...................;8b 24
MOV SS,AX .....................;8e d0
MOV SS,BP .....................;8e d5
MOV SS,BX .....................;8e d3
MOV SS,CX .....................;8e d1
MOV SS,DI .....................;8e d7
MOV SS,DX .....................;8e d2
MOV SS,SI .....................;8e d6
MOV SS,SP .....................;8e d4
MOV SS,[0x5566] ...............;8e 16 66 55
MOV SS,[BP+0x5566] ............;8e 96 66 55
MOV SS,[BP+0x55] ..............;8e 56 55
MOV SS,[BP+DI+0x5566] .........;8e 93 66 55
MOV SS,[BP+DI+0x55] ...........;8e 53 55
MOV SS,[BP+DI] ................;8e 13
MOV SS,[BP+SI+0x5566] .........;8e 92 66 55
MOV SS,[BP+SI+0x55] ...........;8e 52 55
MOV SS,[BP+SI] ................;8e 12
MOV SS,[BX+0x5566] ............;8e 97 66 55
MOV SS,[BX+0x55] ..............;8e 57 55
MOV SS,[BX+DI+0x5566] .........;8e 91 66 55
MOV SS,[BX+DI+0x55] ...........;8e 51 55
MOV SS,[BX+DI] ................;8e 11
MOV SS,[BX+SI+0x5566] .........;8e 90 66 55
MOV SS,[BX+SI+0x55] ...........;8e 50 55
MOV SS,[BX+SI] ................;8e 10
MOV SS,[BX] ...................;8e 17
MOV SS,[DI+0x5566] ............;8e 95 66 55
MOV SS,[DI+0x55] ..............;8e 55 55
MOV SS,[DI] ...................;8e 15
MOV SS,[SI+0x5566] ............;8e 94 66 55
MOV SS,[SI+0x55] ..............;8e 54 55
MOV SS,[SI] ...................;8e 14
MOV WORD [0x5566],0x7788 ......;c7 06 66 55 88 77
MOV WORD [BP+0x5566],0x7788 ...;c7 86 66 55 88 77
MOV WORD [BP+0x55],0x7788 .....;c7 46 55 88 77
MOV WORD [BP+DI+0x5566],0x7788 .;c7 83 66 55 88 77
MOV WORD [BP+DI+0x55],0x7788 ...;c7 43 55 88 77
MOV WORD [BP+DI],0x7788 .......;c7 03 88 77
MOV WORD [BP+SI+0x5566],0x7788 .;c7 82 66 55 88 77
MOV WORD [BP+SI+0x55],0x7788 ...;c7 42 55 88 77
MOV WORD [BP+SI],0x7788 .......;c7 02 88 77
MOV WORD [BX+0x5566],0x7788 ...;c7 87 66 55 88 77
MOV WORD [BX+0x55],0x7788 .....;c7 47 55 88 77
MOV WORD [BX+DI+0x5566],0x7788 .;c7 81 66 55 88 77
MOV WORD [BX+DI+0x55],0x7788 ...;c7 41 55 88 77
MOV WORD [BX+DI],0x7788 .......;c7 01 88 77
MOV WORD [BX+SI+0x5566],0x7788 .;c7 80 66 55 88 77
MOV WORD [BX+SI+0x55],0x7788 ...;c7 40 55 88 77
MOV WORD [BX+SI],0x7788 .......;c7 00 88 77
MOV WORD [BX],0x7788 ..........;c7 07 88 77
MOV WORD [DI+0x5566],0x7788 ...;c7 85 66 55 88 77
MOV WORD [DI+0x55],0x7788 .....;c7 45 55 88 77
MOV WORD [DI],0x7788 ..........;c7 05 88 77
MOV WORD [SI+0x5566],0x7788 ...;c7 84 66 55 88 77
MOV WORD [SI+0x55],0x7788 .....;c7 44 55 88 77
MOV WORD [SI],0x7788 ..........;c7 04 88 77
MOV [0x5566],AH ...............;88 26 66 55
MOV [0x5566],AL ...............;88 06 66 55
MOV [0x5566],AL ...............;a2 66 55
MOV [0x5566],AX ...............;89 06 66 55
MOV [0x5566],AX ...............;a3 66 55
MOV [0x5566],BH ...............;88 3e 66 55
MOV [0x5566],BL ...............;88 1e 66 55
MOV [0x5566],BP ...............;89 2e 66 55
MOV [0x5566],BX ...............;89 1e 66 55
MOV [0x5566],CH ...............;88 2e 66 55
MOV [0x5566],CL ...............;88 0e 66 55
MOV [0x5566],CS ...............;8c 0e 66 55
MOV [0x5566],CX ...............;89 0e 66 55
MOV [0x5566],DH ...............;88 36 66 55
MOV [0x5566],DI ...............;89 3e 66 55
MOV [0x5566],DL ...............;88 16 66 55
MOV [0x5566],DS ...............;8c 1e 66 55
MOV [0x5566],DX ...............;89 16 66 55
MOV [0x5566],ES ...............;8c 06 66 55
MOV [0x5566],SI ...............;89 36 66 55
MOV [0x5566],SP ...............;89 26 66 55
MOV [0x5566],SS ...............;8c 16 66 55
MOV [BP+0x5566],AH ............;88 a6 66 55
```

```
MOV [BP+0x5566],AL         ;88 86 66 55
MOV [BP+0x5566],AX         ;89 86 66 55
MOV [BP+0x5566],BH         ;88 be 66 55
MOV [BP+0x5566],BL         ;88 9e 66 55
MOV [BP+0x5566],BP         ;89 ae 66 55
MOV [BP+0x5566],BX         ;89 9e 66 55
MOV [BP+0x5566],CH         ;88 ae 66 55
MOV [BP+0x5566],CL         ;88 8e 66 55
MOV [BP+0x5566],CS         ;8c 8e 66 55
MOV [BP+0x5566],CX         ;89 8e 66 55
MOV [BP+0x5566],DH         ;88 b6 66 55
MOV [BP+0x5566],DI         ;89 be 66 55
MOV [BP+0x5566],DL         ;88 96 66 55
MOV [BP+0x5566],DS         ;8c 9e 66 55
MOV [BP+0x5566],DX         ;89 96 66 55
MOV [BP+0x5566],ES         ;8c 86 66 55
MOV [BP+0x5566],SI         ;89 b6 66 55
MOV [BP+0x5566],SP         ;89 a6 66 55
MOV [BP+0x5566],SS         ;8c 96 66 55
MOV [BP+0x55],AH           ;88 66 55
MOV [BP+0x55],AL           ;88 46 55
MOV [BP+0x55],AX           ;89 46 55
MOV [BP+0x55],BH           ;88 7e 55
MOV [BP+0x55],BL           ;88 5e 55
MOV [BP+0x55],BP           ;89 6e 55
MOV [BP+0x55],BX           ;89 5e 55
MOV [BP+0x55],CH           ;88 6e 55
MOV [BP+0x55],CL           ;88 4e 55
MOV [BP+0x55],CS           ;8c 4e 55
MOV [BP+0x55],CX           ;89 4e 55
MOV [BP+0x55],DH           ;88 76 55
MOV [BP+0x55],DI           ;89 7e 55
MOV [BP+0x55],DL           ;88 56 55
MOV [BP+0x55],DS           ;8c 5e 55
MOV [BP+0x55],DX           ;89 56 55
MOV [BP+0x55],ES           ;8c 46 55
MOV [BP+0x55],SI           ;89 76 55
MOV [BP+0x55],SP           ;89 66 55
MOV [BP+0x55],SS           ;8c 56 55
MOV [BP+DI+0x5566],AH      ;88 a3 66 55
MOV [BP+DI+0x5566],AL      ;88 83 66 55
MOV [BP+DI+0x5566],AX      ;89 83 66 55
MOV [BP+DI+0x5566],BH      ;88 bb 66 55
MOV [BP+DI+0x5566],BL      ;88 9b 66 55
MOV [BP+DI+0x5566],BP      ;89 ab 66 55
MOV [BP+DI+0x5566],BX      ;89 9b 66 55
MOV [BP+DI+0x5566],CH      ;88 ab 66 55
MOV [BP+DI+0x5566],CL      ;88 8b 66 55
MOV [BP+DI+0x5566],CS      ;8c 8b 66 55
MOV [BP+DI+0x5566],CX      ;89 8b 66 55
MOV [BP+DI+0x5566],DH      ;88 b3 66 55
MOV [BP+DI+0x5566],DI      ;89 bb 66 55
MOV [BP+DI+0x5566],DL      ;88 93 66 55
MOV [BP+DI+0x5566],DS      ;8c 9b 66 55
MOV [BP+DI+0x5566],DX      ;89 93 66 55
MOV [BP+DI+0x5566],ES      ;8c 83 66 55
MOV [BP+DI+0x5566],SI      ;89 b3 66 55
MOV [BP+DI+0x5566],SP      ;89 a3 66 55
MOV [BP+DI+0x5566],SS      ;8c 93 66 55
MOV [BP+DI+0x55],AH        ;88 63 55
MOV [BP+DI+0x55],AL        ;88 43 55
MOV [BP+DI+0x55],AX        ;89 43 55
MOV [BP+DI+0x55],BH        ;88 7b 55
MOV [BP+DI+0x55],BL        ;88 5b 55
MOV [BP+DI+0x55],BP        ;89 6b 55
MOV [BP+DI+0x55],BX        ;89 5b 55
MOV [BP+DI+0x55],CH        ;88 6b 55
MOV [BP+DI+0x55],CL        ;88 4b 55
MOV [BP+DI+0x55],CS        ;8c 4b 55
MOV [BP+DI+0x55],CX        ;89 4b 55
MOV [BP+DI+0x55],DH        ;88 73 55
MOV [BP+DI+0x55],DI        ;89 7b 55
MOV [BP+DI+0x55],DL        ;88 53 55
MOV [BP+DI+0x55],DS        ;8c 5b 55
MOV [BP+DI+0x55],DX        ;89 53 55
MOV [BP+DI+0x55],ES        ;8c 43 55
MOV [BP+DI+0x55],SI        ;89 73 55
MOV [BP+DI+0x55],SP        ;89 63 55
MOV [BP+DI+0x55],SS        ;8c 53 55
MOV [BP+DI],AH             ;88 23
MOV [BP+DI],AL             ;88 03
MOV [BP+DI],AX             ;89 03
MOV [BP+DI],BH             ;88 3b
MOV [BP+DI],BL             ;88 1b
MOV [BP+DI],BP             ;89 2b
MOV [BP+DI],BX             ;89 1b
MOV [BP+DI],CH             ;88 2b
MOV [BP+DI],CL             ;88 0b
MOV [BP+DI],CS             ;8c 0b

MOV [BP+DI],CX             ;89 0b
MOV [BP+DI],DH             ;88 33
MOV [BP+DI],DI             ;89 3b
MOV [BP+DI],DL             ;88 13
MOV [BP+DI],DS             ;8c 1b
MOV [BP+DI],DX             ;89 13
MOV [BP+DI],ES             ;8c 03
MOV [BP+DI],SI             ;89 33
MOV [BP+DI],SP             ;89 23
MOV [BP+DI],SS             ;8c 13
MOV [BP+SI+0x5566],AH      ;88 a2 66 55
MOV [BP+SI+0x5566],AL      ;88 82 66 55
MOV [BP+SI+0x5566],AX      ;89 82 66 55
MOV [BP+SI+0x5566],BH      ;88 ba 66 55
MOV [BP+SI+0x5566],BL      ;88 9a 66 55
MOV [BP+SI+0x5566],BP      ;89 aa 66 55
MOV [BP+SI+0x5566],BX      ;89 9a 66 55
MOV [BP+SI+0x5566],CH      ;88 aa 66 55
MOV [BP+SI+0x5566],CL      ;88 8a 66 55
MOV [BP+SI+0x5566],CS      ;8c 8a 66 55
MOV [BP+SI+0x5566],CX      ;89 8a 66 55
MOV [BP+SI+0x5566],DH      ;88 b2 66 55
MOV [BP+SI+0x5566],DI      ;89 ba 66 55
MOV [BP+SI+0x5566],DL      ;88 92 66 55
MOV [BP+SI+0x5566],DS      ;8c 9a 66 55
MOV [BP+SI+0x5566],DX      ;89 92 66 55
MOV [BP+SI+0x5566],ES      ;8c 82 66 55
MOV [BP+SI+0x5566],SI      ;89 b2 66 55
MOV [BP+SI+0x5566],SP      ;89 a2 66 55
MOV [BP+SI+0x5566],SS      ;8c 92 66 55
MOV [BP+SI+0x55],AH        ;88 62 55
MOV [BP+SI+0x55],AL        ;88 42 55
MOV [BP+SI+0x55],AX        ;89 42 55
MOV [BP+SI+0x55],BH        ;88 7a 55
MOV [BP+SI+0x55],BL        ;88 5a 55
MOV [BP+SI+0x55],BP        ;89 6a 55
MOV [BP+SI+0x55],BX        ;89 5a 55
MOV [BP+SI+0x55],CH        ;88 6a 55
MOV [BP+SI+0x55],CL        ;88 4a 55
MOV [BP+SI+0x55],CS        ;8c 4a 55
MOV [BP+SI+0x55],CX        ;89 4a 55
MOV [BP+SI+0x55],DH        ;88 72 55
MOV [BP+SI+0x55],DI        ;89 7a 55
MOV [BP+SI+0x55],DL        ;88 52 55
MOV [BP+SI+0x55],DS        ;8c 5a 55
MOV [BP+SI+0x55],DX        ;89 52 55
MOV [BP+SI+0x55],ES        ;8c 42 55
MOV [BP+SI+0x55],SI        ;89 72 55
MOV [BP+SI+0x55],SP        ;89 62 55
MOV [BP+SI+0x55],SS        ;8c 52 55
MOV [BP+SI],AH             ;88 22
MOV [BP+SI],AL             ;88 02
MOV [BP+SI],AX             ;89 02
MOV [BP+SI],BH             ;88 3a
MOV [BP+SI],BL             ;88 1a
MOV [BP+SI],BP             ;89 2a
MOV [BP+SI],BX             ;89 1a
MOV [BP+SI],CH             ;88 2a
MOV [BP+SI],CL             ;88 0a
MOV [BP+SI],CS             ;8c 0a
MOV [BP+SI],CX             ;89 0a
MOV [BP+SI],DH             ;88 32
MOV [BP+SI],DI             ;89 3a
MOV [BP+SI],DL             ;88 12
MOV [BP+SI],DS             ;8c 1a
MOV [BP+SI],DX             ;89 12
MOV [BP+SI],ES             ;8c 02
MOV [BP+SI],SI             ;89 32
MOV [BP+SI],SP             ;89 22
MOV [BP+SI],SS             ;8c 12
MOV [BX+0x5566],AH         ;88 a7 66 55
MOV [BX+0x5566],AL         ;88 87 66 55
MOV [BX+0x5566],AX         ;89 87 66 55
MOV [BX+0x5566],BH         ;88 bf 66 55
MOV [BX+0x5566],BL         ;88 9f 66 55
MOV [BX+0x5566],BP         ;89 af 66 55
MOV [BX+0x5566],BX         ;89 9f 66 55
MOV [BX+0x5566],CH         ;88 af 66 55
MOV [BX+0x5566],CL         ;88 8f 66 55
MOV [BX+0x5566],CS         ;8c 8f 66 55
MOV [BX+0x5566],CX         ;89 8f 66 55
MOV [BX+0x5566],DH         ;88 b7 66 55
MOV [BX+0x5566],DI         ;89 bf 66 55
MOV [BX+0x5566],DL         ;88 97 66 55
MOV [BX+0x5566],DS         ;8c 9f 66 55
MOV [BX+0x5566],DX         ;89 97 66 55
MOV [BX+0x5566],ES         ;8c 87 66 55
MOV [BX+0x5566],SI         ;89 b7 66 55
MOV [BX+0x5566],SP         ;89 a7 66 55
```

```
MOV [BX+0x5566],SS         ;8c 97 66 55
MOV [BX+0x55],AH           ;88 67 55
MOV [BX+0x55],AL           ;88 47 55
MOV [BX+0x55],AX           ;89 47 55
MOV [BX+0x55],BH           ;88 7f 55
MOV [BX+0x55],BL           ;88 5f 55
MOV [BX+0x55],BP           ;89 6f 55
MOV [BX+0x55],BX           ;89 5f 55
MOV [BX+0x55],CH           ;88 6f 55
MOV [BX+0x55],CL           ;88 4f 55
MOV [BX+0x55],CS           ;8c 4f 55
MOV [BX+0x55],CX           ;89 4f 55
MOV [BX+0x55],DH           ;88 77 55
MOV [BX+0x55],DI           ;89 7f 55
MOV [BX+0x55],DL           ;88 57 55
MOV [BX+0x55],DS           ;8c 5f 55
MOV [BX+0x55],DX           ;89 57 55
MOV [BX+0x55],ES           ;8c 47 55
MOV [BX+0x55],SI           ;89 77 55
MOV [BX+0x55],SP           ;89 67 55
MOV [BX+0x55],SS           ;8c 57 55
MOV [BX+DI+0x5566],AH      ;88 a1 66 55
MOV [BX+DI+0x5566],AL      ;88 81 66 55
MOV [BX+DI+0x5566],AX      ;89 81 66 55
MOV [BX+DI+0x5566],BH      ;88 b9 66 55
MOV [BX+DI+0x5566],BL      ;88 99 66 55
MOV [BX+DI+0x5566],BP      ;89 a9 66 55
MOV [BX+DI+0x5566],BX      ;89 99 66 55
MOV [BX+DI+0x5566],CH      ;88 a9 66 55
MOV [BX+DI+0x5566],CL      ;88 89 66 55
MOV [BX+DI+0x5566],CS      ;8c 89 66 55
MOV [BX+DI+0x5566],CX      ;89 89 66 55
MOV [BX+DI+0x5566],DH      ;88 b1 66 55
MOV [BX+DI+0x5566],DI      ;89 b9 66 55
MOV [BX+DI+0x5566],DL      ;88 91 66 55
MOV [BX+DI+0x5566],DS      ;8c 99 66 55
MOV [BX+DI+0x5566],DX      ;89 91 66 55
MOV [BX+DI+0x5566],ES      ;8c 81 66 55
MOV [BX+DI+0x5566],SI      ;89 b1 66 55
MOV [BX+DI+0x5566],SP      ;89 a1 66 55
MOV [BX+DI+0x5566],SS      ;8c 91 66 55
MOV [BX+DI+0x55],AH        ;88 61 55
MOV [BX+DI+0x55],AL        ;88 41 55
MOV [BX+DI+0x55],AX        ;89 41 55
MOV [BX+DI+0x55],BH        ;88 79 55
MOV [BX+DI+0x55],BL        ;88 59 55
MOV [BX+DI+0x55],BP        ;89 69 55
MOV [BX+DI+0x55],BX        ;89 59 55
MOV [BX+DI+0x55],CH        ;88 69 55
MOV [BX+DI+0x55],CL        ;88 49 55
MOV [BX+DI+0x55],CS        ;8c 49 55
MOV [BX+DI+0x55],CX        ;89 49 55
MOV [BX+DI+0x55],DH        ;88 71 55
MOV [BX+DI+0x55],DI        ;89 79 55
MOV [BX+DI+0x55],DL        ;88 51 55
MOV [BX+DI+0x55],DS        ;8c 59 55
MOV [BX+DI+0x55],DX        ;89 51 55
MOV [BX+DI+0x55],ES        ;8c 41 55
MOV [BX+DI+0x55],SI        ;89 71 55
MOV [BX+DI+0x55],SP        ;89 61 55
MOV [BX+DI+0x55],SS        ;8c 51 55
MOV [BX+DI],AH             ;88 21
MOV [BX+DI],AL             ;88 01
MOV [BX+DI],AX             ;89 01
MOV [BX+DI],BH             ;88 39
MOV [BX+DI],BL             ;88 19
MOV [BX+DI],BP             ;89 29
MOV [BX+DI],BX             ;89 19
MOV [BX+DI],CH             ;88 29
MOV [BX+DI],CL             ;88 09
MOV [BX+DI],CS             ;8c 09
MOV [BX+DI],CX             ;89 09
MOV [BX+DI],DH             ;88 31
MOV [BX+DI],DI             ;89 39
MOV [BX+DI],DL             ;88 11
MOV [BX+DI],DS             ;8c 19
MOV [BX+DI],DX             ;89 11
MOV [BX+DI],ES             ;8c 01
MOV [BX+DI],SI             ;89 31
MOV [BX+DI],SP             ;89 21
MOV [BX+DI],SS             ;8c 11
MOV [BX+SI+0x5566],AH      ;88 a0 66 55
MOV [BX+SI+0x5566],AL      ;88 80 66 55
MOV [BX+SI+0x5566],AX      ;89 80 66 55
MOV [BX+SI+0x5566],BH      ;88 b8 66 55
MOV [BX+SI+0x5566],BL      ;88 98 66 55
MOV [BX+SI+0x5566],BP      ;89 a8 66 55
MOV [BX+SI+0x5566],BX      ;89 98 66 55
MOV [BX+SI+0x5566],CH      ;88 a8 66 55

MOV [BX+SI+0x5566],CL      ;88 88 66 55
MOV [BX+SI+0x5566],CS      ;8c 88 66 55
MOV [BX+SI+0x5566],CX      ;89 88 66 55
MOV [BX+SI+0x5566],DH      ;88 b0 66 55
MOV [BX+SI+0x5566],DI      ;89 b8 66 55
MOV [BX+SI+0x5566],DL      ;88 90 66 55
MOV [BX+SI+0x5566],DS      ;8c 98 66 55
MOV [BX+SI+0x5566],DX      ;89 90 66 55
MOV [BX+SI+0x5566],ES      ;8c 80 66 55
MOV [BX+SI+0x5566],SI      ;89 b0 66 55
MOV [BX+SI+0x5566],SP      ;89 a0 66 55
MOV [BX+SI+0x5566],SS      ;8c 90 66 55
MOV [BX+SI+0x55],AH        ;88 60 55
MOV [BX+SI+0x55],AL        ;88 40 55
MOV [BX+SI+0x55],AX        ;89 40 55
MOV [BX+SI+0x55],BH        ;88 78 55
MOV [BX+SI+0x55],BL        ;88 58 55
MOV [BX+SI+0x55],BP        ;89 68 55
MOV [BX+SI+0x55],BX        ;89 58 55
MOV [BX+SI+0x55],CH        ;88 68 55
MOV [BX+SI+0x55],CL        ;88 48 55
MOV [BX+SI+0x55],CS        ;8c 48 55
MOV [BX+SI+0x55],CX        ;89 48 55
MOV [BX+SI+0x55],DH        ;88 70 55
MOV [BX+SI+0x55],DI        ;89 78 55
MOV [BX+SI+0x55],DL        ;88 50 55
MOV [BX+SI+0x55],DS        ;8c 58 55
MOV [BX+SI+0x55],DX        ;89 50 55
MOV [BX+SI+0x55],ES        ;8c 40 55
MOV [BX+SI+0x55],SI        ;89 70 55
MOV [BX+SI+0x55],SP        ;89 60 55
MOV [BX+SI+0x55],SS        ;8c 50 55
MOV [BX+SI],AH             ;88 20
MOV [BX+SI],AL             ;88 00
MOV [BX+SI],AX             ;89 00
MOV [BX+SI],BH             ;88 38
MOV [BX+SI],BL             ;88 18
MOV [BX+SI],BP             ;89 28
MOV [BX+SI],BX             ;89 18
MOV [BX+SI],CH             ;88 28
MOV [BX+SI],CL             ;88 08
MOV [BX+SI],CS             ;8c 08
MOV [BX+SI],CX             ;89 08
MOV [BX+SI],DH             ;88 30
MOV [BX+SI],DI             ;89 38
MOV [BX+SI],DL             ;88 10
MOV [BX+SI],DS             ;8c 18
MOV [BX+SI],DX             ;89 10
MOV [BX+SI],ES             ;8c 00
MOV [BX+SI],SI             ;89 30
MOV [BX+SI],SP             ;89 20
MOV [BX+SI],SS             ;8c 10
MOV [BX],AH                ;88 27
MOV [BX],AL                ;88 07
MOV [BX],AX                ;89 07
MOV [BX],BH                ;88 3f
MOV [BX],BL                ;88 1f
MOV [BX],BP                ;89 2f
MOV [BX],BX                ;89 1f
MOV [BX],CH                ;88 2f
MOV [BX],CL                ;88 0f
MOV [BX],CS                ;8c 0f
MOV [BX],CX                ;89 0f
MOV [BX],DH                ;88 37
MOV [BX],DI                ;89 3f
MOV [BX],DL                ;88 17
MOV [BX],DS                ;8c 1f
MOV [BX],DX                ;89 17
MOV [BX],ES                ;8c 07
MOV [BX],SI                ;89 37
MOV [BX],SP                ;89 27
MOV [BX],SS                ;8c 17
MOV [DI+0x5566],AH         ;88 a5 66 55
MOV [DI+0x5566],AL         ;88 85 66 55
MOV [DI+0x5566],AX         ;89 85 66 55
MOV [DI+0x5566],BH         ;88 bd 66 55
MOV [DI+0x5566],BL         ;88 9d 66 55
MOV [DI+0x5566],BP         ;89 ad 66 55
MOV [DI+0x5566],BX         ;89 9d 66 55
MOV [DI+0x5566],CH         ;88 ad 66 55
MOV [DI+0x5566],CL         ;88 8d 66 55
MOV [DI+0x5566],CS         ;8c 8d 66 55
MOV [DI+0x5566],CX         ;89 8d 66 55
MOV [DI+0x5566],DH         ;88 b5 66 55
MOV [DI+0x5566],DI         ;89 bd 66 55
MOV [DI+0x5566],DL         ;88 95 66 55
MOV [DI+0x5566],DS         ;8c 9d 66 55
MOV [DI+0x5566],DX         ;89 95 66 55
MOV [DI+0x5566],ES         ;8c 85 66 55
```

```
MOV [DI+0x5566],SI ..............;89 b5 66 55        MOV [SI],BX .....................;89 1c
MOV [DI+0x5566],SP ..............;89 a5 66 55        MOV [SI],CH .....................;88 2c
MOV [DI+0x5566],SS ..............;8c 95 66 55        MOV [SI],CL .....................;88 0c
MOV [DI+0x55],AH ................;88 65 55           MOV [SI],CS .....................;8c 0c
MOV [DI+0x55],AL ................;88 45 55           MOV [SI],CX .....................;89 0c
MOV [DI+0x55],AX ................;89 45 55           MOV [SI],DH .....................;88 34
MOV [DI+0x55],BH ................;88 7d 55           MOV [SI],DI .....................;89 3c
MOV [DI+0x55],BL ................;88 5d 55           MOV [SI],DL .....................;88 14
MOV [DI+0x55],BP ................;89 6d 55           MOV [SI],DS .....................;8c 1c
MOV [DI+0x55],BX ................;89 5d 55           MOV [SI],DX .....................;89 14
MOV [DI+0x55],CH ................;88 6d 55           MOV [SI],ES .....................;8c 04
MOV [DI+0x55],CL ................;88 4d 55           MOV [SI],SI .....................;89 34
MOV [DI+0x55],CS ................;8c 4d 55           MOV [SI],SP .....................;89 24
MOV [DI+0x55],CX ................;89 4d 55           MOV [SI],SS .....................;8c 14
MOV [DI+0x55],DH ................;88 75 55           MOVSB ...........................;a4
MOV [DI+0x55],DI ................;89 7d 55           MOVSW ...........................;a5
MOV [DI+0x55],DL ................;88 55 55           MUL AH ..........................;f6 e4
MOV [DI+0x55],DS ................;8c 5d 55           MUL AL ..........................;f6 e0
MOV [DI+0x55],DX ................;89 55 55           MUL AX ..........................;f7 e0
MOV [DI+0x55],ES ................;8c 45 55           MUL BH ..........................;f6 e7
MOV [DI+0x55],SI ................;89 75 55           MUL BL ..........................;f6 e3
MOV [DI+0x55],SP ................;89 65 55           MUL BP ..........................;f7 e5
MOV [DI+0x55],SS ................;8c 55 55           MUL BX ..........................;f7 e3
MOV [DI],AH .....................;88 25              MUL BYTE [0x5566] ...............;f6 26 66 55
MOV [DI],AL .....................;88 05              MUL BYTE [BP+0x5566] ............;f6 a6 66 55
MOV [DI],AX .....................;89 05              MUL BYTE [BP+0x55] ..............;f6 66 55
MOV [DI],BH .....................;88 3d              MUL BYTE [BP+DI+0x5566] .........;f6 a3 66 55
MOV [DI],BL .....................;88 1d              MUL BYTE [BP+DI+0x55] ...........;f6 63 55
MOV [DI],BP .....................;89 2d              MUL BYTE [BP+DI] ................;f6 23
MOV [DI],BX .....................;89 1d              MUL BYTE [BP+SI+0x5566] .........;f6 a2 66 55
MOV [DI],CH .....................;88 2d              MUL BYTE [BP+SI+0x55] ...........;f6 62 55
MOV [DI],CL .....................;88 0d              MUL BYTE [BP+SI] ................;f6 22
MOV [DI],CS .....................;8c 0d              MUL BYTE [BX+0x5566] ............;f6 a7 66 55
MOV [DI],CX .....................;89 0d              MUL BYTE [BX+0x55] ..............;f6 67 55
MOV [DI],DH .....................;88 35              MUL BYTE [BX+DI+0x5566] .........;f6 a1 66 55
MOV [DI],DI .....................;89 3d              MUL BYTE [BX+DI+0x55] ...........;f6 61 55
MOV [DI],DL .....................;88 15              MUL BYTE [BX+DI] ................;f6 21
MOV [DI],DS .....................;8c 1d              MUL BYTE [BX+SI+0x5566] .........;f6 a0 66 55
MOV [DI],DX .....................;89 15              MUL BYTE [BX+SI+0x55] ...........;f6 60 55
MOV [DI],ES .....................;8c 05              MUL BYTE [BX+SI] ................;f6 20
MOV [DI],SI .....................;89 35              MUL BYTE [BX] ...................;f6 27
MOV [DI],SP .....................;89 25              MUL BYTE [DI+0x5566] ............;f6 a5 66 55
MOV [DI],SS .....................;8c 15              MUL BYTE [DI+0x55] ..............;f6 65 55
MOV [SI+0x5566],AH ..............;88 a4 66 55        MUL BYTE [DI] ...................;f6 25
MOV [SI+0x5566],AL ..............;88 84 66 55        MUL BYTE [SI+0x5566] ............;f6 a4 66 55
MOV [SI+0x5566],AX ..............;89 84 66 55        MUL BYTE [SI+0x55] ..............;f6 64 55
MOV [SI+0x5566],BH ..............;88 bc 66 55        MUL BYTE [SI] ...................;f6 24
MOV [SI+0x5566],BL ..............;88 9c 66 55        MUL CH ..........................;f6 e5
MOV [SI+0x5566],BP ..............;89 ac 66 55        MUL CL ..........................;f6 e1
MOV [SI+0x5566],BX ..............;89 9c 66 55        MUL CX ..........................;f7 e1
MOV [SI+0x5566],CH ..............;88 ac 66 55        MUL DH ..........................;f6 e6
MOV [SI+0x5566],CL ..............;88 8c 66 55        MUL DI ..........................;f7 e7
MOV [SI+0x5566],CS ..............;8c 8c 66 55        MUL DL ..........................;f6 e2
MOV [SI+0x5566],CX ..............;89 8c 66 55        MUL DX ..........................;f7 e2
MOV [SI+0x5566],DH ..............;88 b4 66 55        MUL SI ..........................;f7 e6
MOV [SI+0x5566],DI ..............;89 bc 66 55        MUL SP ..........................;f7 e4
MOV [SI+0x5566],DL ..............;88 94 66 55        MUL WORD [0x5566] ...............;f7 26 66 55
MOV [SI+0x5566],DS ..............;8c 9c 66 55        MUL WORD [BP+0x5566] ............;f7 a6 66 55
MOV [SI+0x5566],DX ..............;89 94 66 55        MUL WORD [BP+0x55] ..............;f7 66 55
MOV [SI+0x5566],ES ..............;8c 84 66 55        MUL WORD [BP+DI+0x5566] .........;f7 a3 66 55
MOV [SI+0x5566],SI ..............;89 b4 66 55        MUL WORD [BP+DI+0x55] ...........;f7 63 55
MOV [SI+0x5566],SP ..............;89 a4 66 55        MUL WORD [BP+DI] ................;f7 23
MOV [SI+0x5566],SS ..............;8c 94 66 55        MUL WORD [BP+SI+0x5566] .........;f7 a2 66 55
MOV [SI+0x55],AH ................;88 64 55           MUL WORD [BP+SI+0x55] ...........;f7 62 55
MOV [SI+0x55],AL ................;88 44 55           MUL WORD [BP+SI] ................;f7 22
MOV [SI+0x55],AX ................;89 44 55           MUL WORD [BX+0x5566] ............;f7 a7 66 55
MOV [SI+0x55],BH ................;88 7c 55           MUL WORD [BX+0x55] ..............;f7 67 55
MOV [SI+0x55],BL ................;88 5c 55           MUL WORD [BX+DI+0x5566] .........;f7 a1 66 55
MOV [SI+0x55],BP ................;89 6c 55           MUL WORD [BX+DI+0x55] ...........;f7 61 55
MOV [SI+0x55],BX ................;89 5c 55           MUL WORD [BX+DI] ................;f7 21
MOV [SI+0x55],CH ................;88 6c 55           MUL WORD [BX+SI+0x5566] .........;f7 a0 66 55
MOV [SI+0x55],CL ................;88 4c 55           MUL WORD [BX+SI+0x55] ...........;f7 60 55
MOV [SI+0x55],CS ................;8c 4c 55           MUL WORD [BX+SI] ................;f7 20
MOV [SI+0x55],CX ................;89 4c 55           MUL WORD [BX] ...................;f7 27
MOV [SI+0x55],DH ................;88 74 55           MUL WORD [DI+0x5566] ............;f7 a5 66 55
MOV [SI+0x55],DI ................;89 7c 55           MUL WORD [DI+0x55] ..............;f7 65 55
MOV [SI+0x55],DL ................;88 54 55           MUL WORD [DI] ...................;f7 25
MOV [SI+0x55],DS ................;8c 5c 55           MUL WORD [SI+0x5566] ............;f7 a4 66 55
MOV [SI+0x55],DX ................;89 54 55           MUL WORD [SI+0x55] ..............;f7 64 55
MOV [SI+0x55],ES ................;8c 44 55           MUL WORD [SI] ...................;f7 24
MOV [SI+0x55],SI ................;89 74 55           NEG AH ..........................;f6 dc
MOV [SI+0x55],SP ................;89 64 55           NEG AL ..........................;f6 d8
MOV [SI+0x55],SS ................;8c 54 55           NEG AX ..........................;f7 d8
MOV [SI],AH .....................;88 24              NEG BH ..........................;f6 df
MOV [SI],AL .....................;88 04              NEG BL ..........................;f6 db
MOV [SI],AX .....................;89 04              NEG BP ..........................;f7 dd
MOV [SI],BH .....................;88 3c              NEG BX ..........................;f7 db
MOV [SI],BL .....................;88 1c              NEG BYTE [0x5566] ...............;f6 1e 66 55
MOV [SI],BP .....................;89 2c              NEG BYTE [BP+0x5566] ............;f6 9e 66 55
```

199

```
NEG BYTE [BP+0x55]              ;f6 5e 55
NEG BYTE [BP+DI+0x5566]         ;f6 9b 66 55
NEG BYTE [BP+DI+0x55]           ;f6 5b 55
NEG BYTE [BP+DI]                ;f6 1b
NEG BYTE [BP+SI+0x5566]         ;f6 9a 66 55
NEG BYTE [BP+SI+0x55]           ;f6 5a 55
NEG BYTE [BP+SI]                ;f6 1a
NEG BYTE [BX+0x5566]            ;f6 9f 66 55
NEG BYTE [BX+0x55]              ;f6 5f 55
NEG BYTE [BX+DI+0x5566]         ;f6 99 66 55
NEG BYTE [BX+DI+0x55]           ;f6 59 55
NEG BYTE [BX+DI]                ;f6 19
NEG BYTE [BX+SI+0x5566]         ;f6 98 66 55
NEG BYTE [BX+SI+0x55]           ;f6 58 55
NEG BYTE [BX+SI]                ;f6 18
NEG BYTE [BX]                   ;f6 1f
NEG BYTE [DI+0x5566]            ;f6 9d 66 55
NEG BYTE [DI+0x55]              ;f6 5d 55
NEG BYTE [DI]                   ;f6 1d
NEG BYTE [SI+0x5566]            ;f6 9c 66 55
NEG BYTE [SI+0x55]              ;f6 5c 55
NEG BYTE [SI]                   ;f6 1c
NEG CH                          ;f6 dd
NEG CL                          ;f6 d9
NEG CX                          ;f7 d9
NEG DH                          ;f6 de
NEG DI                          ;f7 df
NEG DL                          ;f6 da
NEG DX                          ;f7 da
NEG SI                          ;f7 de
NEG SP                          ;f7 dc
NEG WORD [0x5566]               ;f7 1e 66 55
NEG WORD [BP+0x5566]            ;f7 9e 66 55
NEG WORD [BP+0x55]              ;f7 5e 55
NEG WORD [BP+DI+0x5566]         ;f7 9b 66 55
NEG WORD [BP+DI+0x55]           ;f7 5b 55
NEG WORD [BP+DI]                ;f7 1b
NEG WORD [BP+SI+0x5566]         ;f7 9a 66 55
NEG WORD [BP+SI+0x55]           ;f7 5a 55
NEG WORD [BP+SI]                ;f7 1a
NEG WORD [BX+0x5566]            ;f7 9f 66 55
NEG WORD [BX+0x55]              ;f7 5f 55
NEG WORD [BX+DI+0x5566]         ;f7 99 66 55
NEG WORD [BX+DI+0x55]           ;f7 59 55
NEG WORD [BX+DI]                ;f7 19
NEG WORD [BX+SI+0x5566]         ;f7 98 66 55
NEG WORD [BX+SI+0x55]           ;f7 58 55
NEG WORD [BX+SI]                ;f7 18
NEG WORD [BX]                   ;f7 1f
NEG WORD [DI+0x5566]            ;f7 9d 66 55
NEG WORD [DI+0x55]              ;f7 5d 55
NEG WORD [DI]                   ;f7 1d
NEG WORD [SI+0x5566]            ;f7 9c 66 55
NEG WORD [SI+0x55]              ;f7 5c 55
NEG WORD [SI]                   ;f7 1c
NOP                             ;90
NOT AH                          ;f6 d4
NOT AL                          ;f6 d0
NOT AX                          ;f7 d0
NOT BH                          ;f6 d7
NOT BL                          ;f6 d3
NOT BP                          ;f7 d5
NOT BX                          ;f7 d3
NOT BYTE [0x5566]               ;f6 16 66 55
NOT BYTE [BP+0x5566]            ;f6 96 66 55
NOT BYTE [BP+0x55]              ;f6 56 55
NOT BYTE [BP+DI+0x5566]         ;f6 93 66 55
NOT BYTE [BP+DI+0x55]           ;f6 53 55
NOT BYTE [BP+DI]                ;f6 13
NOT BYTE [BP+SI+0x5566]         ;f6 92 66 55
NOT BYTE [BP+SI+0x55]           ;f6 52 55
NOT BYTE [BP+SI]                ;f6 12
NOT BYTE [BX+0x5566]            ;f6 97 66 55
NOT BYTE [BX+0x55]              ;f6 57 55
NOT BYTE [BX+DI+0x5566]         ;f6 91 66 55
NOT BYTE [BX+DI+0x55]           ;f6 51 55
NOT BYTE [BX+DI]                ;f6 11
NOT BYTE [BX+SI+0x5566]         ;f6 90 66 55
NOT BYTE [BX+SI+0x55]           ;f6 50 55
NOT BYTE [BX+SI]                ;f6 10
NOT BYTE [BX]                   ;f6 17
NOT BYTE [DI+0x5566]            ;f6 95 66 55
NOT BYTE [DI+0x55]              ;f6 55 55
NOT BYTE [DI]                   ;f6 15
NOT BYTE [SI+0x5566]            ;f6 94 66 55
NOT BYTE [SI+0x55]              ;f6 54 55
NOT BYTE [SI]                   ;f6 14
NOT CH                          ;f6 d5
NOT CL                          ;f6 d1
NOT CX                          ;f7 d1
NOT DH                          ;f6 d6
NOT DI                          ;f7 d7
NOT DL                          ;f6 d2
NOT DX                          ;f7 d2
NOT SI                          ;f7 d6
NOT SP                          ;f7 d4
NOT WORD [0x5566]               ;f7 16 66 55
NOT WORD [BP+0x5566]            ;f7 96 66 55
NOT WORD [BP+0x55]              ;f7 56 55
NOT WORD [BP+DI+0x5566]         ;f7 93 66 55
NOT WORD [BP+DI+0x55]           ;f7 53 55
NOT WORD [BP+DI]                ;f7 13
NOT WORD [BP+SI+0x5566]         ;f7 92 66 55
NOT WORD [BP+SI+0x55]           ;f7 52 55
NOT WORD [BP+SI]                ;f7 12
NOT WORD [BX+0x5566]            ;f7 97 66 55
NOT WORD [BX+0x55]              ;f7 57 55
NOT WORD [BX+DI+0x5566]         ;f7 91 66 55
NOT WORD [BX+DI+0x55]           ;f7 51 55
NOT WORD [BX+DI]                ;f7 11
NOT WORD [BX+SI+0x5566]         ;f7 90 66 55
NOT WORD [BX+SI+0x55]           ;f7 50 55
NOT WORD [BX+SI]                ;f7 10
NOT WORD [BX]                   ;f7 17
NOT WORD [DI+0x5566]            ;f7 95 66 55
NOT WORD [DI+0x55]              ;f7 55 55
NOT WORD [DI]                   ;f7 15
NOT WORD [SI+0x5566]            ;f7 94 66 55
NOT WORD [SI+0x55]              ;f7 54 55
NOT WORD [SI]                   ;f7 14
OR AH,0x88                      ;80 cc 88
OR AH,AH                        ;08 e4
OR AH,AL                        ;08 c4
OR AH,BH                        ;08 fc
OR AH,BL                        ;08 dc
OR AH,CH                        ;08 ec
OR AH,CL                        ;08 cc
OR AH,DH                        ;08 f4
OR AH,DL                        ;08 d4
OR AH,[0x5566]                  ;0a 26 66 55
OR AH,[BP+0x5566]               ;0a a6 66 55
OR AH,[BP+0x55]                 ;0a 66 55
OR AH,[BP+DI+0x5566]            ;0a a3 66 55
OR AH,[BP+DI+0x55]              ;0a 63 55
OR AH,[BP+DI]                   ;0a 23
OR AH,[BP+SI+0x5566]            ;0a a2 66 55
OR AH,[BP+SI+0x55]              ;0a 62 55
OR AH,[BP+SI]                   ;0a 22
OR AH,[BX+0x5566]               ;0a a7 66 55
OR AH,[BX+0x55]                 ;0a 67 55
OR AH,[BX+DI+0x5566]            ;0a a1 66 55
OR AH,[BX+DI+0x55]              ;0a 61 55
OR AH,[BX+DI]                   ;0a 21
OR AH,[BX+SI+0x5566]            ;0a a0 66 55
OR AH,[BX+SI+0x55]              ;0a 60 55
OR AH,[BX+SI]                   ;0a 20
OR AH,[BX]                      ;0a 27
OR AH,[DI+0x5566]               ;0a a5 66 55
OR AH,[DI+0x55]                 ;0a 65 55
OR AH,[DI]                      ;0a 25
OR AH,[SI+0x5566]               ;0a a4 66 55
OR AH,[SI+0x55]                 ;0a 64 55
OR AH,[SI]                      ;0a 24
OR AL,0x55                      ;0c 55
OR AL,0x88                      ;80 c8 88
OR AL,AH                        ;08 e0
OR AL,AL                        ;08 c0
OR AL,BH                        ;08 f8
OR AL,BL                        ;08 d8
OR AL,CH                        ;08 e8
OR AL,CL                        ;08 c8
OR AL,DH                        ;08 f0
OR AL,DL                        ;08 d0
OR AL,[0x5566]                  ;0a 06 66 55
OR AL,[BP+0x5566]               ;0a 86 66 55
OR AL,[BP+0x55]                 ;0a 46 55
OR AL,[BP+DI+0x5566]            ;0a 83 66 55
OR AL,[BP+DI+0x55]              ;0a 43 55
OR AL,[BP+DI]                   ;0a 03
OR AL,[BP+SI+0x5566]            ;0a 82 66 55
OR AL,[BP+SI+0x55]              ;0a 42 55
OR AL,[BP+SI]                   ;0a 02
OR AL,[BX+0x5566]               ;0a 87 66 55
OR AL,[BX+0x55]                 ;0a 47 55
OR AL,[BX+DI+0x5566]            ;0a 81 66 55
OR AL,[BX+DI+0x55]              ;0a 41 55
OR AL,[BX+DI]                   ;0a 01
OR AL,[BX+SI+0x5566]            ;0a 80 66 55
```

```
OR AL,[BX+SI+0x55] .............:0a 40 55
OR AL,[BX+SI] ..................:0a 00
OR AL,[BX] .....................:0a 07
OR AL,[DI+0x5566] ..............:0a 85 66 55
OR AL,[DI+0x55] ................:0a 45 55
OR AL,[DI] .....................:0a 05
OR AL,[SI+0x5566] ..............:0a 84 66 55
OR AL,[SI+0x55] ................:0a 44 55
OR AL,[SI] .....................:0a 04
OR AX,0x5566 ...................:0d 66 55
OR AX,0x77 .....................:83 c8 77
OR AX,0x7788 ...................:81 c8 88 77
OR AX,AX .......................:09 c0
OR AX,BP .......................:09 e8
OR AX,BX .......................:09 d8
OR AX,CX .......................:09 c8
OR AX,DI .......................:09 f8
OR AX,DX .......................:09 d0
OR AX,SI .......................:09 f0
OR AX,SP .......................:09 e0
OR AX,[0x5566] .................:0b 06 66 55
OR AX,[BP+0x5566] ..............:0b 86 66 55
OR AX,[BP+0x55] ................:0b 46 55
OR AX,[BP+DI+0x5566] ...........:0b 83 66 55
OR AX,[BP+DI+0x55] .............:0b 43 55
OR AX,[BP+DI] ..................:0b 03
OR AX,[BP+SI+0x5566] ...........:0b 82 66 55
OR AX,[BP+SI+0x55] .............:0b 42 55
OR AX,[BP+SI] ..................:0b 02
OR AX,[BX+0x5566] ..............:0b 87 66 55
OR AX,[BX+0x55] ................:0b 47 55
OR AX,[BX+DI+0x5566] ...........:0b 81 66 55
OR AX,[BX+DI+0x55] .............:0b 41 55
OR AX,[BX+DI] ..................:0b 01
OR AX,[BX+SI+0x5566] ...........:0b 80 66 55
OR AX,[BX+SI+0x55] .............:0b 40 55
OR AX,[BX+SI] ..................:0b 00
OR AX,[BX] .....................:0b 07
OR AX,[DI+0x5566] ..............:0b 85 66 55
OR AX,[DI+0x55] ................:0b 45 55
OR AX,[DI] .....................:0b 05
OR AX,[SI+0x5566] ..............:0b 84 66 55
OR AX,[SI+0x55] ................:0b 44 55
OR AX,[SI] .....................:0b 04
OR BH,0x88 .....................:80 cf 88
OR BH,AH .......................:08 e7
OR BH,AL .......................:08 c7
OR BH,BH .......................:08 ff
OR BH,BL .......................:08 df
OR BH,CH .......................:08 ef
OR BH,CL .......................:08 cf
OR BH,DH .......................:08 f7
OR BH,DL .......................:08 d7
OR BH,[0x5566] .................:0a 3e 66 55
OR BH,[BP+0x5566] ..............:0a be 66 55
OR BH,[BP+0x55] ................:0a 7e 55
OR BH,[BP+DI+0x5566] ...........:0a bb 66 55
OR BH,[BP+DI+0x55] .............:0a 7b 55
OR BH,[BP+DI] ..................:0a 3b
OR BH,[BP+SI+0x5566] ...........:0a ba 66 55
OR BH,[BP+SI+0x55] .............:0a 7a 55
OR BH,[BP+SI] ..................:0a 3a
OR BH,[BX+0x5566] ..............:0a bf 66 55
OR BH,[BX+0x55] ................:0a 7f 55
OR BH,[BX+DI+0x5566] ...........:0a b9 66 55
OR BH,[BX+DI+0x55] .............:0a 79 55
OR BH,[BX+DI] ..................:0a 39
OR BH,[BX+SI+0x5566] ...........:0a b8 66 55
OR BH,[BX+SI+0x55] .............:0a 78 55
OR BH,[BX+SI] ..................:0a 38
OR BH,[BX] .....................:0a 3f
OR BH,[DI+0x5566] ..............:0a bd 66 55
OR BH,[DI+0x55] ................:0a 7d 55
OR BH,[DI] .....................:0a 3d
OR BH,[SI+0x5566] ..............:0a bc 66 55
OR BH,[SI+0x55] ................:0a 7c 55
OR BH,[SI] .....................:0a 3c
OR BL,0x88 .....................:80 cb 88
OR BL,AH .......................:08 e3
OR BL,AL .......................:08 c3
OR BL,BH .......................:08 fb
OR BL,BL .......................:08 db
OR BL,CH .......................:08 eb
OR BL,CL .......................:08 cb
OR BL,DH .......................:08 f3
OR BL,DL .......................:08 d3
OR BL,[0x5566] .................:0a 1e 66 55
OR BL,[BP+0x5566] ..............:0a 9e 66 55
OR BL,[BP+0x55] ................:0a 5e 55
OR BL,[BP+DI+0x5566] ...........:0a 9b 66 55
OR BL,[BP+DI+0x55] .............:0a 5b 55
OR BL,[BP+DI] ..................:0a 1b
OR BL,[BP+SI+0x5566] ...........:0a 9a 66 55
OR BL,[BP+SI+0x55] .............:0a 5a 55
OR BL,[BP+SI] ..................:0a 1a
OR BL,[BX+0x5566] ..............:0a 9f 66 55
OR BL,[BX+0x55] ................:0a 5f 55
OR BL,[BX+DI+0x5566] ...........:0a 99 66 55
OR BL,[BX+DI+0x55] .............:0a 59 55
OR BL,[BX+DI] ..................:0a 19
OR BL,[BX+SI+0x5566] ...........:0a 98 66 55
OR BL,[BX+SI+0x55] .............:0a 58 55
OR BL,[BX+SI] ..................:0a 18
OR BL,[BX] .....................:0a 1f
OR BL,[DI+0x5566] ..............:0a 9d 66 55
OR BL,[DI+0x55] ................:0a 5d 55
OR BL,[DI] .....................:0a 1d
OR BL,[SI+0x5566] ..............:0a 9c 66 55
OR BL,[SI+0x55] ................:0a 5c 55
OR BL,[SI] .....................:0a 1c
OR BP,0x77 .....................:83 cd 77
OR BP,0x7788 ...................:81 cd 88 77
OR BP,AX .......................:09 c5
OR BP,BP .......................:09 ed
OR BP,BX .......................:09 dd
OR BP,CX .......................:09 cd
OR BP,DI .......................:09 fd
OR BP,DX .......................:09 d5
OR BP,SI .......................:09 f5
OR BP,SP .......................:09 e5
OR BP,[0x5566] .................:0b 2e 66 55
OR BP,[BP+0x5566] ..............:0b ae 66 55
OR BP,[BP+0x55] ................:0b 6e 55
OR BP,[BP+DI+0x5566] ...........:0b ab 66 55
OR BP,[BP+DI+0x55] .............:0b 6b 55
OR BP,[BP+DI] ..................:0b 2b
OR BP,[BP+SI+0x5566] ...........:0b aa 66 55
OR BP,[BP+SI+0x55] .............:0b 6a 55
OR BP,[BP+SI] ..................:0b 2a
OR BP,[BX+0x5566] ..............:0b af 66 55
OR BP,[BX+0x55] ................:0b 6f 55
OR BP,[BX+DI+0x5566] ...........:0b a9 66 55
OR BP,[BX+DI+0x55] .............:0b 69 55
OR BP,[BX+DI] ..................:0b 29
OR BP,[BX+SI+0x5566] ...........:0b a8 66 55
OR BP,[BX+SI+0x55] .............:0b 68 55
OR BP,[BX+SI] ..................:0b 28
OR BP,[BX] .....................:0b 2f
OR BP,[DI+0x5566] ..............:0b ad 66 55
OR BP,[DI+0x55] ................:0b 6d 55
OR BP,[DI] .....................:0b 2d
OR BP,[SI+0x5566] ..............:0b ac 66 55
OR BP,[SI+0x55] ................:0b 6c 55
OR BP,[SI] .....................:0b 2c
OR BX,0x77 .....................:83 cb 77
OR BX,0x7788 ...................:81 cb 88 77
OR BX,AX .......................:09 c3
OR BX,BP .......................:09 eb
OR BX,BX .......................:09 db
OR BX,CX .......................:09 cb
OR BX,DI .......................:09 fb
OR BX,DX .......................:09 d3
OR BX,SI .......................:09 f3
OR BX,SP .......................:09 e3
OR BX,[0x5566] .................:0b 1e 66 55
OR BX,[BP+0x5566] ..............:0b 9e 66 55
OR BX,[BP+0x55] ................:0b 5e 55
OR BX,[BP+DI+0x5566] ...........:0b 9b 66 55
OR BX,[BP+DI+0x55] .............:0b 5b 55
OR BX,[BP+DI] ..................:0b 1b
OR BX,[BP+SI+0x5566] ...........:0b 9a 66 55
OR BX,[BP+SI+0x55] .............:0b 5a 55
OR BX,[BP+SI] ..................:0b 1a
OR BX,[BX+0x5566] ..............:0b 9f 66 55
OR BX,[BX+0x55] ................:0b 5f 55
OR BX,[BX+DI+0x5566] ...........:0b 99 66 55
OR BX,[BX+DI+0x55] .............:0b 59 55
OR BX,[BX+DI] ..................:0b 19
OR BX,[BX+SI+0x5566] ...........:0b 98 66 55
OR BX,[BX+SI+0x55] .............:0b 58 55
OR BX,[BX+SI] ..................:0b 18
OR BX,[BX] .....................:0b 1f
OR BX,[DI+0x5566] ..............:0b 9d 66 55
OR BX,[DI+0x55] ................:0b 5d 55
OR BX,[DI] .....................:0b 1d
OR BX,[SI+0x5566] ..............:0b 9c 66 55
OR BX,[SI+0x55] ................:0b 5c 55
OR BX,[SI] .....................:0b 1c
```

```
OR BYTE [0x5566],0x88 ..........;80 0e 66 55 88        OR CL,[SI] ....................;0a 0c
OR BYTE [BP+0x5566],0x88 .......;80 8e 66 55 88        OR CX,0x77 ...................;83 c9 77
OR BYTE [BP+0x55],0x88 .........;80 4e 55 88           OR CX,0x7788 .................;81 c9 88 77
OR BYTE [BP+DI+0x5566],0x88 ....;80 8b 66 55 88        OR CX,AX .....................;09 c1
OR BYTE [BP+DI+0x55],0x88 ......;80 4b 55 88           OR CX,BP .....................;09 e9
OR BYTE [BP+DI],0x88 ...........;80 0b 88              OR CX,BX .....................;09 d9
OR BYTE [BP+SI+0x5566],0x88 ....;80 8a 66 55 88        OR CX,CX .....................;09 c9
OR BYTE [BP+SI+0x55],0x88 ......;80 4a 55 88           OR CX,DI .....................;09 f9
OR BYTE [BP+SI],0x88 ...........;80 0a 88              OR CX,DX .....................;09 d1
OR BYTE [BX+0x5566],0x88 .......;80 8f 66 55 88        OR CX,SI .....................;09 f1
OR BYTE [BX+0x55],0x88 .........;80 4f 55 88           OR CX,SP .....................;09 e1
OR BYTE [BX+DI+0x5566],0x88 ....;80 89 66 55 88        OR CX,[0x5566] ...............;0b 0e 66 55
OR BYTE [BX+DI+0x55],0x88 ......;80 49 55 88           OR CX,[BP+0x5566] ............;0b 8e 66 55
OR BYTE [BX+DI],0x88 ...........;80 09 88              OR CX,[BP+0x55] ..............;0b 4e 55
OR BYTE [BX+SI+0x5566],0x88 ....;80 88 66 55 88        OR CX,[BP+DI+0x5566] .........;0b 8b 66 55
OR BYTE [BX+SI+0x55],0x88 ......;80 48 55 88           OR CX,[BP+DI+0x55] ...........;0b 4b 55
OR BYTE [BX+SI],0x88 ...........;80 08 88              OR CX,[BP+DI] ................;0b 0b
OR BYTE [BX],0x88 ..............;80 0f 88              OR CX,[BP+SI+0x5566] .........;0b 8a 66 55
OR BYTE [DI+0x5566],0x88 .......;80 8d 66 55 88        OR CX,[BP+SI+0x55] ...........;0b 4a 55
OR BYTE [DI+0x55],0x88 .........;80 4d 55 88           OR CX,[BP+SI] ................;0b 0a
OR BYTE [DI],0x88 ..............;80 0d 88              OR CX,[BX+0x5566] ............;0b 8f 66 55
OR BYTE [SI+0x5566],0x88 .......;80 8c 66 55 88        OR CX,[BX+0x55] ..............;0b 4f 55
OR BYTE [SI+0x55],0x88 .........;80 4c 55 88           OR CX,[BX+DI+0x5566] .........;0b 89 66 55
OR BYTE [SI],0x88 ..............;80 0c 88              OR CX,[BX+DI+0x55] ...........;0b 49 55
OR CH,0x88 ....................;80 cd 88               OR CX,[BX+DI] ................;0b 09
OR CH,AH ......................;08 e5                  OR CX,[BX+SI+0x5566] .........;0b 88 66 55
OR CH,AL ......................;08 c5                  OR CX,[BX+SI+0x55] ...........;0b 48 55
OR CH,BH ......................;08 fd                  OR CX,[BX+SI] ................;0b 08
OR CH,BL ......................;08 dd                  OR CX,[BX] ...................;0b 0f
OR CH,CH ......................;08 ed                  OR CX,[DI+0x5566] ............;0b 8d 66 55
OR CH,CL ......................;08 cd                  OR CX,[DI+0x55] ..............;0b 4d 55
OR CH,DH ......................;08 f5                  OR CX,[DI] ...................;0b 0d
OR CH,DL ......................;08 d5                  OR CX,[SI+0x5566] ............;0b 8c 66 55
OR CH,[0x5566] ................;0a 2e 66 55            OR CX,[SI+0x55] ..............;0b 4c 55
OR CH,[BP+0x5566] .............;0a ae 66 55            OR CX,[SI] ...................;0b 0c
OR CH,[BP+0x55] ...............;0a 6e 55               OR DH,0x88 ...................;80 ce 88
OR CH,[BP+DI+0x5566] ..........;0a ab 66 55            OR DH,AH .....................;08 e6
OR CH,[BP+DI+0x55] ............;0a 6b 55               OR DH,AL .....................;08 c6
OR CH,[BP+DI] .................;0a 2b                  OR DH,BH .....................;08 fe
OR CH,[BP+SI+0x5566] ..........;0a aa 66 55            OR DH,BL .....................;08 de
OR CH,[BP+SI+0x55] ............;0a 6a 55               OR DH,CH .....................;08 ee
OR CH,[BP+SI] .................;0a 2a                  OR DH,CL .....................;08 ce
OR CH,[BX+0x5566] .............;0a af 66 55            OR DH,DH .....................;08 f6
OR CH,[BX+0x55] ...............;0a 6f 55               OR DH,DL .....................;08 d6
OR CH,[BX+DI+0x5566] ..........;0a a9 66 55            OR DH,[0x5566] ...............;0a 36 66 55
OR CH,[BX+DI+0x55] ............;0a 69 55               OR DH,[BP+0x5566] ............;0a b6 66 55
OR CH,[BX+DI] .................;0a 29                  OR DH,[BP+0x55] ..............;0a 76 55
OR CH,[BX+SI+0x5566] ..........;0a a8 66 55            OR DH,[BP+DI+0x5566] .........;0a b3 66 55
OR CH,[BX+SI+0x55] ............;0a 68 55               OR DH,[BP+DI+0x55] ...........;0a 73 55
OR CH,[BX+SI] .................;0a 28                  OR DH,[BP+DI] ................;0a 33
OR CH,[BX] ....................;0a 2f                  OR DH,[BP+SI+0x5566] .........;0a b2 66 55
OR CH,[DI+0x5566] .............;0a ad 66 55            OR DH,[BP+SI+0x55] ...........;0a 72 55
OR CH,[DI+0x55] ...............;0a 6d 55               OR DH,[BP+SI] ................;0a 32
OR CH,[DI] ....................;0a 2d                  OR DH,[BX+0x5566] ............;0a b7 66 55
OR CH,[SI+0x5566] .............;0a ac 66 55            OR DH,[BX+0x55] ..............;0a 77 55
OR CH,[SI+0x55] ...............;0a 6c 55               OR DH,[BX+DI+0x5566] .........;0a b1 66 55
OR CH,[SI] ....................;0a 2c                  OR DH,[BX+DI+0x55] ...........;0a 71 55
OR CL,0x88 ....................;80 c9 88               OR DH,[BX+DI] ................;0a 31
OR CL,AH ......................;08 e1                  OR DH,[BX+SI+0x5566] .........;0a b0 66 55
OR CL,AL ......................;08 c1                  OR DH,[BX+SI+0x55] ...........;0a 70 55
OR CL,BH ......................;08 f9                  OR DH,[BX+SI] ................;0a 30
OR CL,BL ......................;08 d9                  OR DH,[BX] ...................;0a 37
OR CL,CH ......................;08 e9                  OR DH,[DI+0x5566] ............;0a b5 66 55
OR CL,CL ......................;08 c9                  OR DH,[DI+0x55] ..............;0a 75 55
OR CL,DH ......................;08 f1                  OR DH,[DI] ...................;0a 35
OR CL,DL ......................;08 d1                  OR DH,[SI+0x5566] ............;0a b4 66 55
OR CL,[0x5566] ................;0a 0e 66 55            OR DH,[SI+0x55] ..............;0a 74 55
OR CL,[BP+0x5566] .............;0a 8e 66 55            OR DH,[SI] ...................;0a 34
OR CL,[BP+0x55] ...............;0a 4e 55               OR DI,0x77 ...................;83 cf 77
OR CL,[BP+DI+0x5566] ..........;0a 8b 66 55            OR DI,0x7788 .................;81 cf 88 77
OR CL,[BP+DI+0x55] ............;0a 4b 55               OR DI,AX .....................;09 c7
OR CL,[BP+DI] .................;0a 0b                  OR DI,BP .....................;09 ef
OR CL,[BP+SI+0x5566] ..........;0a 8a 66 55            OR DI,BX .....................;09 df
OR CL,[BP+SI+0x55] ............;0a 4a 55               OR DI,CX .....................;09 cf
OR CL,[BP+SI] .................;0a 0a                  OR DI,DI .....................;09 ff
OR CL,[BX+0x5566] .............;0a 8f 66 55            OR DI,DX .....................;09 d7
OR CL,[BX+0x55] ...............;0a 4f 55               OR DI,SI .....................;09 f7
OR CL,[BX+DI+0x5566] ..........;0a 89 66 55            OR DI,SP .....................;09 e7
OR CL,[BX+DI+0x55] ............;0a 49 55               OR DI,[0x5566] ...............;0b 3e 66 55
OR CL,[BX+DI] .................;0a 09                  OR DI,[BP+0x5566] ............;0b be 66 55
OR CL,[BX+SI+0x5566] ..........;0a 88 66 55            OR DI,[BP+0x55] ..............;0b 7e 55
OR CL,[BX+SI+0x55] ............;0a 48 55               OR DI,[BP+DI+0x5566] .........;0b bb 66 55
OR CL,[BX+SI] .................;0a 08                  OR DI,[BP+DI+0x55] ...........;0b 7b 55
OR CL,[BX] ....................;0a 0f                  OR DI,[BP+DI] ................;0b 3b
OR CL,[DI+0x5566] .............;0a 8d 66 55            OR DI,[BP+SI+0x5566] .........;0b ba 66 55
OR CL,[DI+0x55] ...............;0a 4d 55               OR DI,[BP+SI+0x55] ...........;0b 7a 55
OR CL,[DI] ....................;0a 0d                  OR DI,[BP+SI] ................;0b 3a
OR CL,[SI+0x5566] .............;0a 8c 66 55            OR DI,[BX+0x5566] ............;0b bf 66 55
OR CL,[SI+0x55] ...............;0a 4c 55               OR DI,[BX+0x55] ..............;0b 7f 55
```

```
OR DI,[BX+DI+0x5566] ...........;0b b9 66 55
OR DI,[BX+DI+0x55] ...........;0b 79 55
OR DI,[BX+DI] ...........;0b 39
OR DI,[BX+SI+0x5566] ...........;0b b8 66 55
OR DI,[BX+SI+0x55] ...........;0b 78 55
OR DI,[BX+SI] ...........;0b 38
OR DI,[BX] ...........;0b 3f
OR DI,[DI+0x5566] ...........;0b bd 66 55
OR DI,[DI+0x55] ...........;0b 7d 55
OR DI,[DI] ...........;0b 3d
OR DI,[SI+0x5566] ...........;0b bc 66 55
OR DI,[SI+0x55] ...........;0b 7c 55
OR DI,[SI] ...........;0b 3c
OR DL,0x88 ...........;80 ca 88
OR DL,AH ...........;08 e2
OR DL,AL ...........;08 c2
OR DL,BH ...........;08 fa
OR DL,BL ...........;08 da
OR DL,CH ...........;08 ea
OR DL,CL ...........;08 ca
OR DL,DH ...........;08 f2
OR DL,DL ...........;08 d2
OR DL,[0x5566] ...........;0a 16 66 55
OR DL,[BP+0x5566] ...........;0a 96 66 55
OR DL,[BP+0x55] ...........;0a 56 55
OR DL,[BP+DI+0x5566] ...........;0a 93 66 55
OR DL,[BP+DI+0x55] ...........;0a 53 55
OR DL,[BP+DI] ...........;0a 13
OR DL,[BP+SI+0x5566] ...........;0a 92 66 55
OR DL,[BP+SI+0x55] ...........;0a 52 55
OR DL,[BP+SI] ...........;0a 12
OR DL,[BX+0x5566] ...........;0a 97 66 55
OR DL,[BX+0x55] ...........;0a 57 55
OR DL,[BX+DI+0x5566] ...........;0a 91 66 55
OR DL,[BX+DI+0x55] ...........;0a 51 55
OR DL,[BX+DI] ...........;0a 11
OR DL,[BX+SI+0x5566] ...........;0a 90 66 55
OR DL,[BX+SI+0x55] ...........;0a 50 55
OR DL,[BX+SI] ...........;0a 10
OR DL,[BX] ...........;0a 17
OR DL,[DI+0x5566] ...........;0a 95 66 55
OR DL,[DI+0x55] ...........;0a 55 55
OR DL,[DI] ...........;0a 15
OR DL,[SI+0x5566] ...........;0a 94 66 55
OR DL,[SI+0x55] ...........;0a 54 55
OR DL,[SI] ...........;0a 14
OR DX,0x77 ...........;83 ca 77
OR DX,0x7788 ...........;81 ca 88 77
OR DX,AX ...........;09 c2
OR DX,BP ...........;09 ea
OR DX,BX ...........;09 da
OR DX,CX ...........;09 ca
OR DX,DI ...........;09 fa
OR DX,DX ...........;09 d2
OR DX,SI ...........;09 f2
OR DX,SP ...........;09 e2
OR DX,[0x5566] ...........;0b 16 66 55
OR DX,[BP+0x5566] ...........;0b 96 66 55
OR DX,[BP+0x55] ...........;0b 56 55
OR DX,[BP+DI+0x5566] ...........;0b 93 66 55
OR DX,[BP+DI+0x55] ...........;0b 53 55
OR DX,[BP+DI] ...........;0b 13
OR DX,[BP+SI+0x5566] ...........;0b 92 66 55
OR DX,[BP+SI+0x55] ...........;0b 52 55
OR DX,[BP+SI] ...........;0b 12
OR DX,[BX+0x5566] ...........;0b 97 66 55
OR DX,[BX+0x55] ...........;0b 57 55
OR DX,[BX+DI+0x5566] ...........;0b 91 66 55
OR DX,[BX+DI+0x55] ...........;0b 51 55
OR DX,[BX+DI] ...........;0b 11
OR DX,[BX+SI+0x5566] ...........;0b 90 66 55
OR DX,[BX+SI+0x55] ...........;0b 50 55
OR DX,[BX+SI] ...........;0b 10
OR DX,[BX] ...........;0b 17
OR DX,[DI+0x5566] ...........;0b 95 66 55
OR DX,[DI+0x55] ...........;0b 55 55
OR DX,[DI] ...........;0b 15
OR DX,[SI+0x5566] ...........;0b 94 66 55
OR DX,[SI+0x55] ...........;0b 54 55
OR DX,[SI] ...........;0b 14
OR SI,0x77 ...........;83 ce 77
OR SI,0x7788 ...........;81 ce 88 77
OR SI,AX ...........;09 c6
OR SI,BP ...........;09 ee
OR SI,BX ...........;09 de
OR SI,CX ...........;09 ce
OR SI,DI ...........;09 fe
OR SI,DX ...........;09 d6
OR SI,SI ...........;09 f6

OR SI,SP ...........;09 e6
OR SI,[0x5566] ...........;0b 36 66 55
OR SI,[BP+0x5566] ...........;0b b6 66 55
OR SI,[BP+0x55] ...........;0b 76 55
OR SI,[BP+DI+0x5566] ...........;0b b3 66 55
OR SI,[BP+DI+0x55] ...........;0b 73 55
OR SI,[BP+DI] ...........;0b 33
OR SI,[BP+SI+0x5566] ...........;0b b2 66 55
OR SI,[BP+SI+0x55] ...........;0b 72 55
OR SI,[BP+SI] ...........;0b 32
OR SI,[BX+0x5566] ...........;0b b7 66 55
OR SI,[BX+0x55] ...........;0b 77 55
OR SI,[BX+DI+0x5566] ...........;0b b1 66 55
OR SI,[BX+DI+0x55] ...........;0b 71 55
OR SI,[BX+DI] ...........;0b 31
OR SI,[BX+SI+0x5566] ...........;0b b0 66 55
OR SI,[BX+SI+0x55] ...........;0b 70 55
OR SI,[BX+SI] ...........;0b 30
OR SI,[BX] ...........;0b 37
OR SI,[DI+0x5566] ...........;0b b5 66 55
OR SI,[DI+0x55] ...........;0b 75 55
OR SI,[DI] ...........;0b 35
OR SI,[SI+0x5566] ...........;0b b4 66 55
OR SI,[SI+0x55] ...........;0b 74 55
OR SI,[SI] ...........;0b 34
OR SP,0x77 ...........;83 cc 77
OR SP,0x7788 ...........;81 cc 88 77
OR SP,AX ...........;09 c4
OR SP,BP ...........;09 ec
OR SP,BX ...........;09 dc
OR SP,CX ...........;09 cc
OR SP,DI ...........;09 fc
OR SP,DX ...........;09 d4
OR SP,SI ...........;09 f4
OR SP,SP ...........;09 e4
OR SP,[0x5566] ...........;0b 26 66 55
OR SP,[BP+0x5566] ...........;0b a6 66 55
OR SP,[BP+0x55] ...........;0b 66 55
OR SP,[BP+DI+0x5566] ...........;0b a3 66 55
OR SP,[BP+DI+0x55] ...........;0b 63 55
OR SP,[BP+DI] ...........;0b 23
OR SP,[BP+SI+0x5566] ...........;0b a2 66 55
OR SP,[BP+SI+0x55] ...........;0b 62 55
OR SP,[BP+SI] ...........;0b 22
OR SP,[BX+0x5566] ...........;0b a7 66 55
OR SP,[BX+0x55] ...........;0b 67 55
OR SP,[BX+DI+0x5566] ...........;0b a1 66 55
OR SP,[BX+DI+0x55] ...........;0b 61 55
OR SP,[BX+DI] ...........;0b 21
OR SP,[BX+SI+0x5566] ...........;0b a0 66 55
OR SP,[BX+SI+0x55] ...........;0b 60 55
OR SP,[BX+SI] ...........;0b 20
OR SP,[BX] ...........;0b 27
OR SP,[DI+0x5566] ...........;0b a5 66 55
OR SP,[DI+0x55] ...........;0b 65 55
OR SP,[DI] ...........;0b 25
OR SP,[SI+0x5566] ...........;0b a4 66 55
OR SP,[SI+0x55] ...........;0b 64 55
OR SP,[SI] ...........;0b 24
OR WORD [0x5566],0x77 ...........;83 0e 66 55 77
OR WORD [0x5566],0x7788 ...........;81 0e 66 55 88 77
OR WORD [BP+0x5566],0x77 ...........;83 8e 66 55 77
OR WORD [BP+0x5566],0x7788 ...........;81 8e 66 55 88 77
OR WORD [BP+0x55],0x77 ...........;83 4e 55 77
OR WORD [BP+0x55],0x7788 ...........;81 4e 55 88 77
OR WORD [BP+DI+0x5566],0x77 ...........;83 8b 66 55 77
OR WORD [BP+DI+0x5566],0x7788 ...........;81 8b 66 55 88 77
OR WORD [BP+DI+0x55],0x77 ...........;83 4b 55 77
OR WORD [BP+DI+0x55],0x7788 ...........;81 4b 55 88 77
OR WORD [BP+DI],0x77 ...........;83 0b 77
OR WORD [BP+DI],0x7788 ...........;81 0b 88 77
OR WORD [BP+SI+0x5566],0x77 ...........;83 8a 66 55 77
OR WORD [BP+SI+0x5566],0x7788 ...........;81 8a 66 55 88 77
OR WORD [BP+SI+0x55],0x77 ...........;83 4a 55 77
OR WORD [BP+SI+0x55],0x7788 ...........;81 4a 55 88 77
OR WORD [BP+SI],0x77 ...........;83 0a 77
OR WORD [BP+SI],0x7788 ...........;81 0a 88 77
OR WORD [BX+0x5566],0x77 ...........;83 8f 66 55 77
OR WORD [BX+0x5566],0x7788 ...........;81 8f 66 55 88 77
OR WORD [BX+0x55],0x77 ...........;83 4f 55 77
OR WORD [BX+0x55],0x7788 ...........;81 4f 55 88 77
OR WORD [BX+DI+0x5566],0x77 ...........;83 89 66 55 77
OR WORD [BX+DI+0x5566],0x7788 ...........;81 89 66 55 88 77
OR WORD [BX+DI+0x55],0x77 ...........;83 49 55 77
OR WORD [BX+DI+0x55],0x7788 ...........;81 49 55 88 77
OR WORD [BX+DI],0x77 ...........;83 09 77
OR WORD [BX+DI],0x7788 ...........;81 09 88 77
OR WORD [BX+SI+0x5566],0x77 ...........;83 88 66 55 77
OR WORD [BX+SI+0x5566],0x7788 ...........;81 88 66 55 88 77
```

```
OR WORD [BX+SI+0x55],0x77 ......;83 48 55 77
OR WORD [BX+SI+0x55],0x7788 ....;81 48 55 88 77
OR WORD [BX+SI],0x77 ..........;83 08 77
OR WORD [BX+SI],0x7788 .........;81 08 88 77
OR WORD [BX],0x77 .............;83 0f 77
OR WORD [BX],0x7788 ...........;81 0f 88 77
OR WORD [DI+0x5566],0x77 ......;83 8d 66 55 77
OR WORD [DI+0x5566],0x7788 ....;81 8d 66 55 88 77
OR WORD [DI+0x55],0x77 ........;83 4d 55 77
OR WORD [DI+0x55],0x7788 ......;81 4d 55 88 77
OR WORD [DI],0x77 .............;83 0d 77
OR WORD [DI],0x7788 ...........;81 0d 88 77
OR WORD [SI+0x5566],0x77 ......;83 8c 66 55 77
OR WORD [SI+0x5566],0x7788 ....;81 8c 66 55 88 77
OR WORD [SI+0x55],0x77 ........;83 4c 55 77
OR WORD [SI+0x55],0x7788 ......;81 4c 55 88 77
OR WORD [SI],0x77 .............;83 0c 77
OR WORD [SI],0x7788 ...........;81 0c 88 77
OR [0x5566],AH ................;08 26 66 55
OR [0x5566],AL ................;08 06 66 55
OR [0x5566],AX ................;09 06 66 55
OR [0x5566],BH ................;08 3e 66 55
OR [0x5566],BL ................;08 1e 66 55
OR [0x5566],BP ................;09 2e 66 55
OR [0x5566],BX ................;09 1e 66 55
OR [0x5566],CH ................;08 2e 66 55
OR [0x5566],CL ................;08 0e 66 55
OR [0x5566],CX ................;09 0e 66 55
OR [0x5566],DH ................;08 36 66 55
OR [0x5566],DI ................;09 3e 66 55
OR [0x5566],DL ................;08 16 66 55
OR [0x5566],DX ................;09 16 66 55
OR [0x5566],SI ................;09 36 66 55
OR [0x5566],SP ................;09 26 66 55
OR [BP+0x5566],AH .............;08 a6 66 55
OR [BP+0x5566],AL .............;08 86 66 55
OR [BP+0x5566],AX .............;09 86 66 55
OR [BP+0x5566],BH .............;08 be 66 55
OR [BP+0x5566],BL .............;08 9e 66 55
OR [BP+0x5566],BP .............;09 ae 66 55
OR [BP+0x5566],BX .............;09 9e 66 55
OR [BP+0x5566],CH .............;08 ae 66 55
OR [BP+0x5566],CL .............;08 8e 66 55
OR [BP+0x5566],CX .............;09 8e 66 55
OR [BP+0x5566],DH .............;08 b6 66 55
OR [BP+0x5566],DI .............;09 be 66 55
OR [BP+0x5566],DL .............;08 96 66 55
OR [BP+0x5566],DX .............;09 96 66 55
OR [BP+0x5566],SI .............;09 b6 66 55
OR [BP+0x5566],SP .............;09 a6 66 55
OR [BP+0x55],AH ...............;08 66 55
OR [BP+0x55],AL ...............;08 46 55
OR [BP+0x55],AX ...............;09 46 55
OR [BP+0x55],BH ...............;08 7e 55
OR [BP+0x55],BL ...............;08 5e 55
OR [BP+0x55],BP ...............;09 6e 55
OR [BP+0x55],BX ...............;09 5e 55
OR [BP+0x55],CH ...............;08 6e 55
OR [BP+0x55],CL ...............;08 4e 55
OR [BP+0x55],CX ...............;09 4e 55
OR [BP+0x55],DH ...............;08 76 55
OR [BP+0x55],DI ...............;09 7e 55
OR [BP+0x55],DL ...............;08 56 55
OR [BP+0x55],DX ...............;09 56 55
OR [BP+0x55],SI ...............;09 76 55
OR [BP+0x55],SP ...............;09 66 55
OR [BP+DI+0x5566],AH ..........;08 a3 66 55
OR [BP+DI+0x5566],AL ..........;08 83 66 55
OR [BP+DI+0x5566],AX ..........;09 83 66 55
OR [BP+DI+0x5566],BH ..........;08 bb 66 55
OR [BP+DI+0x5566],BL ..........;08 9b 66 55
OR [BP+DI+0x5566],BP ..........;09 ab 66 55
OR [BP+DI+0x5566],BX ..........;09 9b 66 55
OR [BP+DI+0x5566],CH ..........;08 ab 66 55
OR [BP+DI+0x5566],CL ..........;08 8b 66 55
OR [BP+DI+0x5566],CX ..........;09 8b 66 55
OR [BP+DI+0x5566],DH ..........;08 b3 66 55
OR [BP+DI+0x5566],DI ..........;09 bb 66 55
OR [BP+DI+0x5566],DL ..........;08 93 66 55
OR [BP+DI+0x5566],DX ..........;09 93 66 55
OR [BP+DI+0x5566],SI ..........;09 b3 66 55
OR [BP+DI+0x5566],SP ..........;09 a3 66 55
OR [BP+DI+0x55],AH ............;08 63 55
OR [BP+DI+0x55],AL ............;08 43 55
OR [BP+DI+0x55],AX ............;09 43 55
OR [BP+DI+0x55],BH ............;08 7b 55
OR [BP+DI+0x55],BL ............;08 5b 55
OR [BP+DI+0x55],BP ............;09 6b 55
OR [BP+DI+0x55],BX ............;09 5b 55

OR [BP+DI+0x55],CH ............;08 6b 55
OR [BP+DI+0x55],CL ............;08 4b 55
OR [BP+DI+0x55],CX ............;09 4b 55
OR [BP+DI+0x55],DH ............;08 73 55
OR [BP+DI+0x55],DI ............;09 7b 55
OR [BP+DI+0x55],DL ............;08 53 55
OR [BP+DI+0x55],DX ............;09 53 55
OR [BP+DI+0x55],SI ............;09 73 55
OR [BP+DI+0x55],SP ............;09 63 55
OR [BP+DI],AH .................;08 23
OR [BP+DI],AL .................;08 03
OR [BP+DI],AX .................;09 03
OR [BP+DI],BH .................;08 3b
OR [BP+DI],BL .................;08 1b
OR [BP+DI],BP .................;09 2b
OR [BP+DI],BX .................;09 1b
OR [BP+DI],CH .................;08 2b
OR [BP+DI],CL .................;08 0b
OR [BP+DI],CX .................;09 0b
OR [BP+DI],DH .................;08 33
OR [BP+DI],DI .................;09 3b
OR [BP+DI],DL .................;08 13
OR [BP+DI],DX .................;09 13
OR [BP+DI],SI .................;09 33
OR [BP+DI],SP .................;09 23
OR [BP+SI+0x5566],AH ..........;08 a2 66 55
OR [BP+SI+0x5566],AL ..........;08 82 66 55
OR [BP+SI+0x5566],AX ..........;09 82 66 55
OR [BP+SI+0x5566],BH ..........;08 ba 66 55
OR [BP+SI+0x5566],BL ..........;08 9a 66 55
OR [BP+SI+0x5566],BP ..........;09 aa 66 55
OR [BP+SI+0x5566],BX ..........;09 9a 66 55
OR [BP+SI+0x5566],CH ..........;08 aa 66 55
OR [BP+SI+0x5566],CL ..........;08 8a 66 55
OR [BP+SI+0x5566],CX ..........;09 8a 66 55
OR [BP+SI+0x5566],DH ..........;08 b2 66 55
OR [BP+SI+0x5566],DI ..........;09 ba 66 55
OR [BP+SI+0x5566],DL ..........;08 92 66 55
OR [BP+SI+0x5566],DX ..........;09 92 66 55
OR [BP+SI+0x5566],SI ..........;09 b2 66 55
OR [BP+SI+0x5566],SP ..........;09 a2 66 55
OR [BP+SI+0x55],AH ............;08 62 55
OR [BP+SI+0x55],AL ............;08 42 55
OR [BP+SI+0x55],AX ............;09 42 55
OR [BP+SI+0x55],BH ............;08 7a 55
OR [BP+SI+0x55],BL ............;08 5a 55
OR [BP+SI+0x55],BP ............;09 6a 55
OR [BP+SI+0x55],BX ............;09 5a 55
OR [BP+SI+0x55],CH ............;08 6a 55
OR [BP+SI+0x55],CL ............;08 4a 55
OR [BP+SI+0x55],CX ............;09 4a 55
OR [BP+SI+0x55],DH ............;08 72 55
OR [BP+SI+0x55],DI ............;09 7a 55
OR [BP+SI+0x55],DL ............;08 52 55
OR [BP+SI+0x55],DX ............;09 52 55
OR [BP+SI+0x55],SI ............;09 72 55
OR [BP+SI+0x55],SP ............;09 62 55
OR [BP+SI],AH .................;08 22
OR [BP+SI],AL .................;08 02
OR [BP+SI],AX .................;09 02
OR [BP+SI],BH .................;08 3a
OR [BP+SI],BL .................;08 1a
OR [BP+SI],BP .................;09 2a
OR [BP+SI],BX .................;09 1a
OR [BP+SI],CH .................;08 2a
OR [BP+SI],CL .................;08 0a
OR [BP+SI],CX .................;09 0a
OR [BP+SI],DH .................;08 32
OR [BP+SI],DI .................;09 3a
OR [BP+SI],DL .................;08 12
OR [BP+SI],DX .................;09 12
OR [BP+SI],SI .................;09 32
OR [BP+SI],SP .................;09 22
OR [BX+0x5566],AH .............;08 a7 66 55
OR [BX+0x5566],AL .............;08 87 66 55
OR [BX+0x5566],AX .............;09 87 66 55
OR [BX+0x5566],BH .............;08 bf 66 55
OR [BX+0x5566],BL .............;08 9f 66 55
OR [BX+0x5566],BP .............;09 af 66 55
OR [BX+0x5566],BX .............;09 9f 66 55
OR [BX+0x5566],CH .............;08 af 66 55
OR [BX+0x5566],CL .............;08 8f 66 55
OR [BX+0x5566],CX .............;09 8f 66 55
OR [BX+0x5566],DH .............;08 b7 66 55
OR [BX+0x5566],DI .............;09 bf 66 55
OR [BX+0x5566],DL .............;08 97 66 55
OR [BX+0x5566],DX .............;09 97 66 55
OR [BX+0x5566],SI .............;09 b7 66 55
OR [BX+0x5566],SP .............;09 a7 66 55
```

```
OR [BX+0x55],AH .................;08 67 55
OR [BX+0x55],AL .................;08 47 55
OR [BX+0x55],AX .................;09 47 55
OR [BX+0x55],BH .................;08 7f 55
OR [BX+0x55],BL .................;08 5f 55
OR [BX+0x55],BP .................;09 6f 55
OR [BX+0x55],BX .................;09 5f 55
OR [BX+0x55],CH .................;08 6f 55
OR [BX+0x55],CL .................;08 4f 55
OR [BX+0x55],CX .................;09 4f 55
OR [BX+0x55],DH .................;08 77 55
OR [BX+0x55],DI .................;09 7f 55
OR [BX+0x55],DL .................;08 57 55
OR [BX+0x55],DX .................;09 57 55
OR [BX+0x55],SI .................;09 77 55
OR [BX+0x55],SP .................;08 67 55
OR [BX+DI+0x5566],AH ...........;08 a1 66 55
OR [BX+DI+0x5566],AL ...........;08 81 66 55
OR [BX+DI+0x5566],AX ...........;09 81 66 55
OR [BX+DI+0x5566],BH ...........;08 b9 66 55
OR [BX+DI+0x5566],BL ...........;08 99 66 55
OR [BX+DI+0x5566],BP ...........;09 a9 66 55
OR [BX+DI+0x5566],BX ...........;09 99 66 55
OR [BX+DI+0x5566],CH ...........;08 a9 66 55
OR [BX+DI+0x5566],CL ...........;08 89 66 55
OR [BX+DI+0x5566],CX ...........;09 89 66 55
OR [BX+DI+0x5566],DH ...........;08 b1 66 55
OR [BX+DI+0x5566],DI ...........;09 b9 66 55
OR [BX+DI+0x5566],DL ...........;08 91 66 55
OR [BX+DI+0x5566],DX ...........;09 91 66 55
OR [BX+DI+0x5566],SI ...........;09 b1 66 55
OR [BX+DI+0x5566],SP ...........;09 a1 66 55
OR [BX+DI+0x55],AH .............;08 61 55
OR [BX+DI+0x55],AL .............;08 41 55
OR [BX+DI+0x55],AX .............;09 41 55
OR [BX+DI+0x55],BH .............;08 79 55
OR [BX+DI+0x55],BL .............;08 59 55
OR [BX+DI+0x55],BP .............;09 69 55
OR [BX+DI+0x55],BX .............;09 59 55
OR [BX+DI+0x55],CH .............;08 69 55
OR [BX+DI+0x55],CL .............;08 49 55
OR [BX+DI+0x55],CX .............;09 49 55
OR [BX+DI+0x55],DH .............;08 71 55
OR [BX+DI+0x55],DI .............;09 79 55
OR [BX+DI+0x55],DL .............;08 51 55
OR [BX+DI+0x55],DX .............;09 51 55
OR [BX+DI+0x55],SI .............;09 71 55
OR [BX+DI+0x55],SP .............;09 61 55
OR [BX+DI],AH ..................;08 21
OR [BX+DI],AL ..................;08 01
OR [BX+DI],AX ..................;09 01
OR [BX+DI],BH ..................;08 39
OR [BX+DI],BL ..................;08 19
OR [BX+DI],BP ..................;09 29
OR [BX+DI],BX ..................;09 19
OR [BX+DI],CH ..................;08 29
OR [BX+DI],CL ..................;08 09
OR [BX+DI],CX ..................;09 09
OR [BX+DI],DH ..................;08 31
OR [BX+DI],DI ..................;09 39
OR [BX+DI],DL ..................;08 11
OR [BX+DI],DX ..................;09 11
OR [BX+DI],SI ..................;09 31
OR [BX+DI],SP ..................;09 21
OR [BX+SI+0x5566],AH ...........;08 a0 66 55
OR [BX+SI+0x5566],AL ...........;08 80 66 55
OR [BX+SI+0x5566],AX ...........;09 80 66 55
OR [BX+SI+0x5566],BH ...........;08 b8 66 55
OR [BX+SI+0x5566],BL ...........;08 98 66 55
OR [BX+SI+0x5566],BP ...........;09 a8 66 55
OR [BX+SI+0x5566],BX ...........;09 98 66 55
OR [BX+SI+0x5566],CH ...........;08 a8 66 55
OR [BX+SI+0x5566],CL ...........;08 88 66 55
OR [BX+SI+0x5566],CX ...........;09 88 66 55
OR [BX+SI+0x5566],DH ...........;08 b0 66 55
OR [BX+SI+0x5566],DI ...........;09 b8 66 55
OR [BX+SI+0x5566],DL ...........;08 90 66 55
OR [BX+SI+0x5566],DX ...........;09 90 66 55
OR [BX+SI+0x5566],SI ...........;09 b0 66 55
OR [BX+SI+0x5566],SP ...........;09 a0 66 55
OR [BX+SI+0x55],AH .............;08 60 55
OR [BX+SI+0x55],AL .............;08 40 55
OR [BX+SI+0x55],AX .............;09 40 55
OR [BX+SI+0x55],BH .............;08 78 55
OR [BX+SI+0x55],BL .............;08 58 55
OR [BX+SI+0x55],BP .............;09 68 55
OR [BX+SI+0x55],BX .............;09 58 55
OR [BX+SI+0x55],CH .............;08 68 55
OR [BX+SI+0x55],CL .............;08 48 55
OR [BX+SI+0x55],CX .............;09 48 55
OR [BX+SI+0x55],DH .............;08 70 55
OR [BX+SI+0x55],DI .............;09 78 55
OR [BX+SI+0x55],DL .............;08 50 55
OR [BX+SI+0x55],DX .............;09 50 55
OR [BX+SI+0x55],SI .............;09 70 55
OR [BX+SI+0x55],SP .............;09 60 55
OR [BX+SI],AH ..................;08 20
OR [BX+SI],AL ..................;08 00
OR [BX+SI],AX ..................;09 00
OR [BX+SI],BH ..................;08 38
OR [BX+SI],BL ..................;08 18
OR [BX+SI],BP ..................;09 28
OR [BX+SI],BX ..................;09 18
OR [BX+SI],CH ..................;08 28
OR [BX+SI],CL ..................;08 08
OR [BX+SI],CX ..................;09 08
OR [BX+SI],DH ..................;08 30
OR [BX+SI],DI ..................;09 38
OR [BX+SI],DL ..................;08 10
OR [BX+SI],DX ..................;09 10
OR [BX+SI],SI ..................;09 30
OR [BX+SI],SP ..................;09 20
OR [BX],AH .....................;08 27
OR [BX],AL .....................;08 07
OR [BX],AX .....................;09 07
OR [BX],BH .....................;08 3f
OR [BX],BL .....................;08 1f
OR [BX],BP .....................;09 2f
OR [BX],BX .....................;09 1f
OR [BX],CH .....................;08 2f
OR [BX],CL .....................;08 0f
OR [BX],CX .....................;09 0f
OR [BX],DH .....................;08 37
OR [BX],DI .....................;09 3f
OR [BX],DL .....................;08 17
OR [BX],DX .....................;09 17
OR [BX],SI .....................;09 37
OR [BX],SP .....................;09 27
OR [DI+0x5566],AH ..............;08 a5 66 55
OR [DI+0x5566],AL ..............;08 85 66 55
OR [DI+0x5566],AX ..............;09 85 66 55
OR [DI+0x5566],BH ..............;08 bd 66 55
OR [DI+0x5566],BL ..............;08 9d 66 55
OR [DI+0x5566],BP ..............;09 ad 66 55
OR [DI+0x5566],BX ..............;09 9d 66 55
OR [DI+0x5566],CH ..............;08 ad 66 55
OR [DI+0x5566],CL ..............;08 8d 66 55
OR [DI+0x5566],CX ..............;09 8d 66 55
OR [DI+0x5566],DH ..............;08 b5 66 55
OR [DI+0x5566],DI ..............;09 bd 66 55
OR [DI+0x5566],DL ..............;08 95 66 55
OR [DI+0x5566],DX ..............;09 95 66 55
OR [DI+0x5566],SI ..............;09 b5 66 55
OR [DI+0x5566],SP ..............;09 a5 66 55
OR [DI+0x55],AH ................;08 65 55
OR [DI+0x55],AL ................;08 45 55
OR [DI+0x55],AX ................;09 45 55
OR [DI+0x55],BH ................;08 7d 55
OR [DI+0x55],BL ................;08 5d 55
OR [DI+0x55],BP ................;09 6d 55
OR [DI+0x55],BX ................;09 5d 55
OR [DI+0x55],CH ................;08 6d 55
OR [DI+0x55],CL ................;08 4d 55
OR [DI+0x55],CX ................;09 4d 55
OR [DI+0x55],DH ................;08 75 55
OR [DI+0x55],DI ................;09 7d 55
OR [DI+0x55],DL ................;08 55 55
OR [DI+0x55],DX ................;09 55 55
OR [DI+0x55],SI ................;09 75 55
OR [DI+0x55],SP ................;09 65 55
OR [DI],AH .....................;08 25
OR [DI],AL .....................;08 05
OR [DI],AX .....................;09 05
OR [DI],BH .....................;08 3d
OR [DI],BL .....................;08 1d
OR [DI],BP .....................;09 2d
OR [DI],BX .....................;09 1d
OR [DI],CH .....................;08 2d
OR [DI],CL .....................;08 0d
OR [DI],CX .....................;09 0d
OR [DI],DH .....................;08 35
OR [DI],DI .....................;09 3d
OR [DI],DL .....................;08 15
OR [DI],DX .....................;09 15
OR [DI],SI .....................;09 35
OR [DI],SP .....................;09 25
OR [SI+0x5566],AH ..............;08 a4 66 55
OR [SI+0x5566],AL ..............;08 84 66 55
```

205

```
OR [SI+0x5566],AX ................ ;09 84 66 55
OR [SI+0x5566],BH ................ ;08 bc 66 55
OR [SI+0x5566],BL ................ ;08 9c 66 55
OR [SI+0x5566],BP ................ ;09 ac 66 55
OR [SI+0x5566],BX ................ ;09 9c 66 55
OR [SI+0x5566],CH ................ ;08 ac 66 55
OR [SI+0x5566],CL ................ ;08 8c 66 55
OR [SI+0x5566],CX ................ ;09 8c 66 55
OR [SI+0x5566],DH ................ ;08 b4 66 55
OR [SI+0x5566],DI ................ ;09 bc 66 55
OR [SI+0x5566],DL ................ ;08 94 66 55
OR [SI+0x5566],DX ................ ;09 94 66 55
OR [SI+0x5566],SI ................ ;09 b4 66 55
OR [SI+0x5566],SP ................ ;09 a4 66 55
OR [SI+0x55],AH .................. ;08 64 55
OR [SI+0x55],AL .................. ;08 44 55
OR [SI+0x55],AX .................. ;09 44 55
OR [SI+0x55],BH .................. ;08 7c 55
OR [SI+0x55],BL .................. ;08 5c 55
OR [SI+0x55],BP .................. ;09 6c 55
OR [SI+0x55],BX .................. ;09 5c 55
OR [SI+0x55],CH .................. ;08 6c 55
OR [SI+0x55],CL .................. ;08 4c 55
OR [SI+0x55],CX .................. ;09 4c 55
OR [SI+0x55],DH .................. ;08 74 55
OR [SI+0x55],DI .................. ;09 7c 55
OR [SI+0x55],DL .................. ;08 54 55
OR [SI+0x55],DX .................. ;09 54 55
OR [SI+0x55],SI .................. ;09 74 55
OR [SI+0x55],SP .................. ;09 64 55
OR [SI],AH ....................... ;08 24
OR [SI],AL ....................... ;08 04
OR [SI],AX ....................... ;09 04
OR [SI],BH ....................... ;08 3c
OR [SI],BL ....................... ;08 1c
OR [SI],BP ....................... ;09 2c
OR [SI],BX ....................... ;09 1c
OR [SI],CH ....................... ;08 2c
OR [SI],CL ....................... ;08 0c
OR [SI],CX ....................... ;09 0c
OR [SI],DH ....................... ;08 34
OR [SI],DI ....................... ;09 3c
OR [SI],DL ....................... ;08 14
OR [SI],DX ....................... ;09 14
OR [SI],SI ....................... ;09 34
OR [SI],SP ....................... ;09 24
OUT (0x55),AL .................... ;e6 55
OUT (0x55),AX .................... ;e7 55
OUT DX,AL ........................ ;ee
OUT DX,AX ........................ ;ef
POP AX ........................... ;58
POP BP ........................... ;5d
POP BX ........................... ;5b
POP CX ........................... ;59
POP DI ........................... ;5f
POP DS ........................... ;1f
POP DX ........................... ;5a
POP ES ........................... ;07
POP SI ........................... ;5e
POP SP ........................... ;5c
POP SS ........................... ;17
POP WORD [0x5566] ................ ;8f 06 66 55
POP WORD [BP+0x5566] ............. ;8f 86 66 55
POP WORD [BP+0x55] ............... ;8f 46 55
POP WORD [BP+DI+0x5566] .......... ;8f 83 66 55
POP WORD [BP+DI+0x55] ............ ;8f 43 55
POP WORD [BP+DI] ................. ;8f 03
POP WORD [BP+SI+0x5566] .......... ;8f 82 66 55
POP WORD [BP+SI+0x55] ............ ;8f 42 55
POP WORD [BP+SI] ................. ;8f 02
POP WORD [BX+0x5566] ............. ;8f 87 66 55
POP WORD [BX+0x55] ............... ;8f 47 55
POP WORD [BX+DI+0x5566] .......... ;8f 81 66 55
POP WORD [BX+DI+0x55] ............ ;8f 41 55
POP WORD [BX+DI] ................. ;8f 01
POP WORD [BX+SI+0x5566] .......... ;8f 80 66 55
POP WORD [BX+SI+0x55] ............ ;8f 40 55
POP WORD [BX+SI] ................. ;8f 00
POP WORD [BX] .................... ;8f 07
POP WORD [DI+0x5566] ............. ;8f 85 66 55
POP WORD [DI+0x55] ............... ;8f 45 55
POP WORD [DI] .................... ;8f 05
POP WORD [SI+0x5566] ............. ;8f 84 66 55
POP WORD [SI+0x55] ............... ;8f 44 55
POP WORD [SI] .................... ;8f 04
POPF ............................. ;9d
PUSH AX .......................... ;50
PUSH BP .......................... ;55
PUSH BX .......................... ;53

PUSH CS .......................... ;0e
PUSH CX .......................... ;51
PUSH DI .......................... ;57
PUSH DS .......................... ;1e
PUSH DX .......................... ;52
PUSH ES .......................... ;06
PUSH SI .......................... ;56
PUSH SP .......................... ;54
PUSH SS .......................... ;16
PUSH WORD [0x5566] ............... ;ff 36 66 55
PUSH WORD [BP+0x5566] ............ ;ff b6 66 55
PUSH WORD [BP+0x55] .............. ;ff 76 55
PUSH WORD [BP+DI+0x5566] ......... ;ff b3 66 55
PUSH WORD [BP+DI+0x55] ........... ;ff 73 55
PUSH WORD [BP+DI] ................ ;ff 33
PUSH WORD [BP+SI+0x5566] ......... ;ff b2 66 55
PUSH WORD [BP+SI+0x55] ........... ;ff 72 55
PUSH WORD [BP+SI] ................ ;ff 32
PUSH WORD [BX+0x5566] ............ ;ff b7 66 55
PUSH WORD [BX+0x55] .............. ;ff 77 55
PUSH WORD [BX+DI+0x5566] ......... ;ff b1 66 55
PUSH WORD [BX+DI+0x55] ........... ;ff 71 55
PUSH WORD [BX+DI] ................ ;ff 31
PUSH WORD [BX+SI+0x5566] ......... ;ff b0 66 55
PUSH WORD [BX+SI+0x55] ........... ;ff 70 55
PUSH WORD [BX+SI] ................ ;ff 30
PUSH WORD [BX] ................... ;ff 37
PUSH WORD [DI+0x5566] ............ ;ff b5 66 55
PUSH WORD [DI+0x55] .............. ;ff 75 55
PUSH WORD [DI] ................... ;ff 35
PUSH WORD [SI+0x5566] ............ ;ff b4 66 55
PUSH WORD [SI+0x55] .............. ;ff 74 55
PUSH WORD [SI] ................... ;ff 34
PUSHF ............................ ;9c
RCL AH,1 ......................... ;d0 d4
RCL AH,CL ........................ ;d2 d4
RCL AL,1 ......................... ;d0 d0
RCL AL,CL ........................ ;d2 d0
RCL AX,1 ......................... ;d1 d0
RCL AX,CL ........................ ;d3 d0
RCL BH,1 ......................... ;d0 d7
RCL BH,CL ........................ ;d2 d7
RCL BL,1 ......................... ;d0 d3
RCL BL,CL ........................ ;d2 d3
RCL BP,1 ......................... ;d1 d5
RCL BP,CL ........................ ;d3 d5
RCL BX,1 ......................... ;d1 d3
RCL BX,CL ........................ ;d3 d3
RCL BYTE [0x5566],1 .............. ;d0 16 66 55
RCL BYTE [0x5566],CL ............. ;d2 16 66 55
RCL BYTE [BP+0x5566],1 ........... ;d0 96 66 55
RCL BYTE [BP+0x5566],CL .......... ;d2 96 66 55
RCL BYTE [BP+0x55],1 ............. ;d0 56 55
RCL BYTE [BP+0x55],CL ............ ;d2 56 55
RCL BYTE [BP+DI+0x5566],1 ........ ;d0 93 66 55
RCL BYTE [BP+DI+0x5566],CL ....... ;d2 93 66 55
RCL BYTE [BP+DI+0x55],1 .......... ;d0 53 55
RCL BYTE [BP+DI+0x55],CL ......... ;d2 53 55
RCL BYTE [BP+DI],1 ............... ;d0 13
RCL BYTE [BP+DI],CL .............. ;d2 13
RCL BYTE [BP+SI+0x5566],1 ........ ;d0 92 66 55
RCL BYTE [BP+SI+0x5566],CL ....... ;d2 92 66 55
RCL BYTE [BP+SI+0x55],1 .......... ;d0 52 55
RCL BYTE [BP+SI+0x55],CL ......... ;d2 52 55
RCL BYTE [BP+SI],1 ............... ;d0 12
RCL BYTE [BP+SI],CL .............. ;d2 12
RCL BYTE [BX+0x5566],1 ........... ;d0 97 66 55
RCL BYTE [BX+0x5566],CL .......... ;d2 97 66 55
RCL BYTE [BX+0x55],1 ............. ;d0 57 55
RCL BYTE [BX+0x55],CL ............ ;d2 57 55
RCL BYTE [BX+DI+0x5566],1 ........ ;d0 91 66 55
RCL BYTE [BX+DI+0x5566],CL ....... ;d2 91 66 55
RCL BYTE [BX+DI+0x55],1 .......... ;d0 51 55
RCL BYTE [BX+DI+0x55],CL ......... ;d2 51 55
RCL BYTE [BX+DI],1 ............... ;d0 11
RCL BYTE [BX+DI],CL .............. ;d2 11
RCL BYTE [BX+SI+0x5566],1 ........ ;d0 90 66 55
RCL BYTE [BX+SI+0x5566],CL ....... ;d2 90 66 55
RCL BYTE [BX+SI+0x55],1 .......... ;d0 50 55
RCL BYTE [BX+SI+0x55],CL ......... ;d2 50 55
RCL BYTE [BX+SI],1 ............... ;d0 10
RCL BYTE [BX+SI],CL .............. ;d2 10
RCL BYTE [BX],1 .................. ;d0 17
RCL BYTE [BX],CL ................. ;d2 17
RCL BYTE [DI+0x5566],1 ........... ;d0 95 66 55
RCL BYTE [DI+0x5566],CL .......... ;d2 95 66 55
RCL BYTE [DI+0x55],1 ............. ;d0 55 55
RCL BYTE [DI+0x55],CL ............ ;d2 55 55
RCL BYTE [DI],1 .................. ;d0 15
```

```
RCL BYTE [DI],CL .................;d2 15
RCL BYTE [SI+0x5566],1 ...........;d0 94 66 55
RCL BYTE [SI+0x5566],CL ..........;d2 94 66 55
RCL BYTE [SI+0x55],1 .............;d0 54 55
RCL BYTE [SI+0x55],CL ............;d2 54 55
RCL BYTE [SI],1 ..................;d0 14
RCL BYTE [SI],CL .................;d2 14
RCL CH,1 .........................;d0 d5
RCL CH,CL ........................;d2 d5
RCL CL,1 .........................;d0 d1
RCL CL,CL ........................;d2 d1
RCL CX,1 .........................;d1 d1
RCL CX,CL ........................;d3 d1
RCL DH,1 .........................;d0 d6
RCL DH,CL ........................;d2 d6
RCL DI,1 .........................;d1 d7
RCL DI,CL ........................;d3 d7
RCL DL,1 .........................;d0 d2
RCL DL,CL ........................;d2 d2
RCL DX,1 .........................;d1 d2
RCL DX,CL ........................;d3 d2
RCL SI,1 .........................;d1 d6
RCL SI,CL ........................;d3 d6
RCL SP,1 .........................;d1 d4
RCL SP,CL ........................;d3 d4
RCL WORD [0x5566],1 ..............;d1 16 66 55
RCL WORD [0x5566],CL .............;d3 16 66 55
RCL WORD [BP+0x5566],1 ...........;d1 96 66 55
RCL WORD [BP+0x5566],CL ..........;d3 96 66 55
RCL WORD [BP+0x55],1 .............;d1 56 55
RCL WORD [BP+0x55],CL ............;d3 56 55
RCL WORD [BP+DI+0x5566],1 ........;d1 93 66 55
RCL WORD [BP+DI+0x5566],CL .......;d3 93 66 55
RCL WORD [BP+DI+0x55],1 ..........;d1 53 55
RCL WORD [BP+DI+0x55],CL .........;d3 53 55
RCL WORD [BP+DI],1 ...............;d1 13
RCL WORD [BP+DI],CL ..............;d3 13
RCL WORD [BP+SI+0x5566],1 ........;d1 92 66 55
RCL WORD [BP+SI+0x5566],CL .......;d3 92 66 55
RCL WORD [BP+SI+0x55],1 ..........;d1 52 55
RCL WORD [BP+SI+0x55],CL .........;d3 52 55
RCL WORD [BP+SI],1 ...............;d1 12
RCL WORD [BP+SI],CL ..............;d3 12
RCL WORD [BX+0x5566],1 ...........;d1 97 66 55
RCL WORD [BX+0x5566],CL ..........;d3 97 66 55
RCL WORD [BX+0x55],1 .............;d1 57 55
RCL WORD [BX+0x55],CL ............;d3 57 55
RCL WORD [BX+DI+0x5566],1 ........;d1 91 66 55
RCL WORD [BX+DI+0x5566],CL .......;d3 91 66 55
RCL WORD [BX+DI+0x55],1 ..........;d1 51 55
RCL WORD [BX+DI+0x55],CL .........;d3 51 55
RCL WORD [BX+DI],1 ...............;d1 11
RCL WORD [BX+DI],CL ..............;d3 11
RCL WORD [BX+SI+0x5566],1 ........;d1 90 66 55
RCL WORD [BX+SI+0x5566],CL .......;d3 90 66 55
RCL WORD [BX+SI+0x55],1 ..........;d1 50 55
RCL WORD [BX+SI+0x55],CL .........;d3 50 55
RCL WORD [BX+SI],1 ...............;d1 10
RCL WORD [BX+SI],CL ..............;d3 10
RCL WORD [BX],1 ..................;d1 17
RCL WORD [BX],CL .................;d3 17
RCL WORD [DI+0x5566],1 ...........;d1 95 66 55
RCL WORD [DI+0x5566],CL ..........;d3 95 66 55
RCL WORD [DI+0x55],1 .............;d1 55 55
RCL WORD [DI+0x55],CL ............;d3 55 55
RCL WORD [DI],1 ..................;d1 15
RCL WORD [DI],CL .................;d3 15
RCL WORD [SI+0x5566],1 ...........;d1 94 66 55
RCL WORD [SI+0x5566],CL ..........;d3 94 66 55
RCL WORD [SI+0x55],1 .............;d1 54 55
RCL WORD [SI+0x55],CL ............;d3 54 55
RCL WORD [SI],1 ..................;d1 14
RCL WORD [SI],CL .................;d3 14
RCR AH,1 .........................;d0 dc
RCR AH,CL ........................;d2 dc
RCR AL,1 .........................;d0 d8
RCR AL,CL ........................;d2 d8
RCR AX,1 .........................;d1 d8
RCR AX,CL ........................;d3 d8
RCR BH,1 .........................;d0 df
RCR BH,CL ........................;d2 df
RCR BL,1 .........................;d0 db
RCR BL,CL ........................;d2 db
RCR BP,1 .........................;d1 dd
RCR BP,CL ........................;d3 dd
RCR BX,1 .........................;d1 db
RCR BX,CL ........................;d3 db
RCR BYTE [0x5566],1 ..............;d0 1e 66 55
RCR BYTE [0x5566],CL .............;d2 1e 66 55

RCR BYTE [BP+0x5566],1 ...........;d0 9e 66 55
RCR BYTE [BP+0x5566],CL ..........;d2 9e 66 55
RCR BYTE [BP+0x55],1 .............;d0 5e 55
RCR BYTE [BP+0x55],CL ............;d2 5e 55
RCR BYTE [BP+DI+0x5566],1 ........;d0 9b 66 55
RCR BYTE [BP+DI+0x5566],CL .......;d2 9b 66 55
RCR BYTE [BP+DI+0x55],1 ..........;d0 5b 55
RCR BYTE [BP+DI+0x55],CL .........;d2 5b 55
RCR BYTE [BP+DI],1 ...............;d0 1b
RCR BYTE [BP+DI],CL ..............;d2 1b
RCR BYTE [BP+SI+0x5566],1 ........;d0 9a 66 55
RCR BYTE [BP+SI+0x5566],CL .......;d2 9a 66 55
RCR BYTE [BP+SI+0x55],1 ..........;d0 5a 55
RCR BYTE [BP+SI+0x55],CL .........;d2 5a 55
RCR BYTE [BP+SI],1 ...............;d0 1a
RCR BYTE [BP+SI],CL ..............;d2 1a
RCR BYTE [BX+0x5566],1 ...........;d0 9f 66 55
RCR BYTE [BX+0x5566],CL ..........;d2 9f 66 55
RCR BYTE [BX+0x55],1 .............;d0 5f 55
RCR BYTE [BX+0x55],CL ............;d2 5f 55
RCR BYTE [BX+DI+0x5566],1 ........;d0 99 66 55
RCR BYTE [BX+DI+0x5566],CL .......;d2 99 66 55
RCR BYTE [BX+DI+0x55],1 ..........;d0 59 55
RCR BYTE [BX+DI+0x55],CL .........;d2 59 55
RCR BYTE [BX+DI],1 ...............;d0 19
RCR BYTE [BX+DI],CL ..............;d2 19
RCR BYTE [BX+SI+0x5566],1 ........;d0 98 66 55
RCR BYTE [BX+SI+0x5566],CL .......;d2 98 66 55
RCR BYTE [BX+SI+0x55],1 ..........;d0 58 55
RCR BYTE [BX+SI+0x55],CL .........;d2 58 55
RCR BYTE [BX+SI],1 ...............;d0 18
RCR BYTE [BX+SI],CL ..............;d2 18
RCR BYTE [BX],1 ..................;d0 1f
RCR BYTE [BX],CL .................;d2 1f
RCR BYTE [DI+0x5566],1 ...........;d0 9d 66 55
RCR BYTE [DI+0x5566],CL ..........;d2 9d 66 55
RCR BYTE [DI+0x55],1 .............;d0 5d 55
RCR BYTE [DI+0x55],CL ............;d2 5d 55
RCR BYTE [DI],1 ..................;d0 1d
RCR BYTE [DI],CL .................;d2 1d
RCR BYTE [SI+0x5566],1 ...........;d0 9c 66 55
RCR BYTE [SI+0x5566],CL ..........;d2 9c 66 55
RCR BYTE [SI+0x55],1 .............;d0 5c 55
RCR BYTE [SI+0x55],CL ............;d2 5c 55
RCR BYTE [SI],1 ..................;d0 1c
RCR BYTE [SI],CL .................;d2 1c
RCR CH,1 .........................;d0 dd
RCR CH,CL ........................;d2 dd
RCR CL,1 .........................;d0 d9
RCR CL,CL ........................;d2 d9
RCR CX,1 .........................;d1 d9
RCR CX,CL ........................;d3 d9
RCR DH,1 .........................;d0 de
RCR DH,CL ........................;d2 de
RCR DI,1 .........................;d1 df
RCR DI,CL ........................;d3 df
RCR DL,1 .........................;d0 da
RCR DL,CL ........................;d2 da
RCR DX,1 .........................;d1 da
RCR DX,CL ........................;d3 da
RCR SI,1 .........................;d1 de
RCR SI,CL ........................;d3 de
RCR SP,1 .........................;d1 dc
RCR SP,CL ........................;d3 dc
RCR WORD [0x5566],1 ..............;d1 1e 66 55
RCR WORD [0x5566],CL .............;d3 1e 66 55
RCR WORD [BP+0x5566],1 ...........;d1 9e 66 55
RCR WORD [BP+0x5566],CL ..........;d3 9e 66 55
RCR WORD [BP+0x55],1 .............;d1 5e 55
RCR WORD [BP+0x55],CL ............;d3 5e 55
RCR WORD [BP+DI+0x5566],1 ........;d1 9b 66 55
RCR WORD [BP+DI+0x5566],CL .......;d3 9b 66 55
RCR WORD [BP+DI+0x55],1 ..........;d1 5b 55
RCR WORD [BP+DI+0x55],CL .........;d3 5b 55
RCR WORD [BP+DI],1 ...............;d1 1b
RCR WORD [BP+DI],CL ..............;d3 1b
RCR WORD [BP+SI+0x5566],1 ........;d1 9a 66 55
RCR WORD [BP+SI+0x5566],CL .......;d3 9a 66 55
RCR WORD [BP+SI+0x55],1 ..........;d1 5a 55
RCR WORD [BP+SI+0x55],CL .........;d3 5a 55
RCR WORD [BP+SI],1 ...............;d1 1a
RCR WORD [BP+SI],CL ..............;d3 1a
RCR WORD [BX+0x5566],1 ...........;d1 9f 66 55
RCR WORD [BX+0x5566],CL ..........;d3 9f 66 55
RCR WORD [BX+0x55],1 .............;d1 5f 55
RCR WORD [BX+0x55],CL ............;d3 5f 55
RCR WORD [BX+DI+0x5566],1 ........;d1 99 66 55
RCR WORD [BX+DI+0x5566],CL .......;d3 99 66 55
RCR WORD [BX+DI+0x55],1 ..........;d1 59 55
```

```
RCR WORD [BX+DI+0x55],CL ...... ;d3 59 55
RCR WORD [BX+DI],1 ........... ;d1 19
RCR WORD [BX+DI],CL .......... ;d3 19
RCR WORD [BX+SI+0x5566],1 .... ;d1 98 66 55
RCR WORD [BX+SI+0x5566],CL ... ;d3 98 66 55
RCR WORD [BX+SI+0x55],1 ...... ;d1 58 55
RCR WORD [BX+SI+0x55],CL ..... ;d3 58 55
RCR WORD [BX+SI],1 ........... ;d1 18
RCR WORD [BX+SI],CL .......... ;d3 18
RCR WORD [BX],1 .............. ;d1 1f
RCR WORD [BX],CL ............. ;d3 1f
RCR WORD [DI+0x5566],1 ....... ;d1 9d 66 55
RCR WORD [DI+0x5566],CL ...... ;d3 9d 66 55
RCR WORD [DI+0x55],1 ......... ;d1 5d 55
RCR WORD [DI+0x55],CL ........ ;d3 5d 55
RCR WORD [DI],1 .............. ;d1 1d
RCR WORD [DI],CL ............. ;d3 1d
RCR WORD [SI+0x5566],1 ....... ;d1 9c 66 55
RCR WORD [SI+0x5566],CL ...... ;d3 9c 66 55
RCR WORD [SI+0x55],1 ......... ;d1 5c 55
RCR WORD [SI+0x55],CL ........ ;d3 5c 55
RCR WORD [SI],1 .............. ;d1 1c
RCR WORD [SI],CL ............. ;d3 1c
REPNZ ........................ ;f2
REPZ ......................... ;f3
RET .......................... ;c3
RET 0x5566 ................... ;c2 66 55
RETF ......................... ;cb
RETF 0x5566 .................. ;ca 66 55
ROL AH,1 ..................... ;d0 c4
ROL AH,CL .................... ;d2 c4
ROL AL,1 ..................... ;d0 c0
ROL AL,CL .................... ;d2 c0
ROL AX,1 ..................... ;d1 c0
ROL AX,CL .................... ;d3 c0
ROL BH,1 ..................... ;d0 c7
ROL BH,CL .................... ;d2 c7
ROL BL,1 ..................... ;d0 c3
ROL BL,CL .................... ;d2 c3
ROL BP,1 ..................... ;d1 c5
ROL BP,CL .................... ;d3 c5
ROL BX,1 ..................... ;d1 c3
ROL BX,CL .................... ;d3 c3
ROL BYTE [0x5566],1 .......... ;d0 06 66 55
ROL BYTE [0x5566],CL ......... ;d2 06 66 55
ROL BYTE [BP+0x5566],1 ....... ;d0 86 66 55
ROL BYTE [BP+0x5566],CL ...... ;d2 86 66 55
ROL BYTE [BP+0x55],1 ......... ;d0 46 55
ROL BYTE [BP+0x55],CL ........ ;d2 46 55
ROL BYTE [BP+DI+0x5566],1 .... ;d0 83 66 55
ROL BYTE [BP+DI+0x5566],CL ... ;d2 83 66 55
ROL BYTE [BP+DI+0x55],1 ...... ;d0 43 55
ROL BYTE [BP+DI+0x55],CL ..... ;d2 43 55
ROL BYTE [BP+DI],1 ........... ;d0 03
ROL BYTE [BP+DI],CL .......... ;d2 03
ROL BYTE [BP+SI+0x5566],1 .... ;d0 82 66 55
ROL BYTE [BP+SI+0x5566],CL ... ;d2 82 66 55
ROL BYTE [BP+SI+0x55],1 ...... ;d0 42 55
ROL BYTE [BP+SI+0x55],CL ..... ;d2 42 55
ROL BYTE [BP+SI],1 ........... ;d0 02
ROL BYTE [BP+SI],CL .......... ;d2 02
ROL BYTE [BX+0x5566],1 ....... ;d0 87 66 55
ROL BYTE [BX+0x5566],CL ...... ;d2 87 66 55
ROL BYTE [BX+0x55],1 ......... ;d0 47 55
ROL BYTE [BX+0x55],CL ........ ;d2 47 55
ROL BYTE [BX+DI+0x5566],1 .... ;d0 81 66 55
ROL BYTE [BX+DI+0x5566],CL ... ;d2 81 66 55
ROL BYTE [BX+DI+0x55],1 ...... ;d0 41 55
ROL BYTE [BX+DI+0x55],CL ..... ;d2 41 55
ROL BYTE [BX+DI],1 ........... ;d0 01
ROL BYTE [BX+DI],CL .......... ;d2 01
ROL BYTE [BX+SI+0x5566],1 .... ;d0 80 66 55
ROL BYTE [BX+SI+0x5566],CL ... ;d2 80 66 55
ROL BYTE [BX+SI+0x55],1 ...... ;d0 40 55
ROL BYTE [BX+SI+0x55],CL ..... ;d2 40 55
ROL BYTE [BX+SI],1 ........... ;d0 00
ROL BYTE [BX+SI],CL .......... ;d2 00
ROL BYTE [BX],1 .............. ;d0 07
ROL BYTE [BX],CL ............. ;d2 07
ROL BYTE [DI+0x5566],1 ....... ;d0 85 66 55
ROL BYTE [DI+0x5566],CL ...... ;d2 85 66 55
ROL BYTE [DI+0x55],1 ......... ;d0 45 55
ROL BYTE [DI+0x55],CL ........ ;d2 45 55
ROL BYTE [DI],1 .............. ;d0 05
ROL BYTE [DI],CL ............. ;d2 05
ROL BYTE [SI+0x5566],1 ....... ;d0 84 66 55
ROL BYTE [SI+0x5566],CL ...... ;d2 84 66 55
ROL BYTE [SI+0x55],1 ......... ;d0 44 55
ROL BYTE [SI+0x55],CL ........ ;d2 44 55

ROL BYTE [SI],1 .............. ;d0 04
ROL BYTE [SI],CL ............. ;d2 04
ROL CH,1 ..................... ;d0 c5
ROL CH,CL .................... ;d2 c5
ROL CL,1 ..................... ;d0 c1
ROL CL,CL .................... ;d2 c1
ROL CX,1 ..................... ;d1 c1
ROL CX,CL .................... ;d3 c1
ROL DH,1 ..................... ;d0 c6
ROL DH,CL .................... ;d2 c6
ROL DI,1 ..................... ;d1 c7
ROL DI,CL .................... ;d3 c7
ROL DL,1 ..................... ;d0 c2
ROL DL,CL .................... ;d2 c2
ROL DX,1 ..................... ;d1 c2
ROL DX,CL .................... ;d3 c2
ROL SI,1 ..................... ;d1 c6
ROL SI,CL .................... ;d3 c6
ROL SP,1 ..................... ;d1 c4
ROL SP,CL .................... ;d3 c4
ROL WORD [0x5566],1 .......... ;d1 06 66 55
ROL WORD [0x5566],CL ......... ;d3 06 66 55
ROL WORD [BP+0x5566],1 ....... ;d1 86 66 55
ROL WORD [BP+0x5566],CL ...... ;d3 86 66 55
ROL WORD [BP+0x55],1 ......... ;d1 46 55
ROL WORD [BP+0x55],CL ........ ;d3 46 55
ROL WORD [BP+DI+0x5566],1 .... ;d1 83 66 55
ROL WORD [BP+DI+0x5566],CL ... ;d3 83 66 55
ROL WORD [BP+DI+0x55],1 ...... ;d1 43 55
ROL WORD [BP+DI+0x55],CL ..... ;d3 43 55
ROL WORD [BP+DI],1 ........... ;d1 03
ROL WORD [BP+DI],CL .......... ;d3 03
ROL WORD [BP+SI+0x5566],1 .... ;d1 82 66 55
ROL WORD [BP+SI+0x5566],CL ... ;d3 82 66 55
ROL WORD [BP+SI+0x55],1 ...... ;d1 42 55
ROL WORD [BP+SI+0x55],CL ..... ;d3 42 55
ROL WORD [BP+SI],1 ........... ;d1 02
ROL WORD [BP+SI],CL .......... ;d3 02
ROL WORD [BX+0x5566],1 ....... ;d1 87 66 55
ROL WORD [BX+0x5566],CL ...... ;d3 87 66 55
ROL WORD [BX+0x55],1 ......... ;d1 47 55
ROL WORD [BX+0x55],CL ........ ;d3 47 55
ROL WORD [BX+DI+0x5566],1 .... ;d1 81 66 55
ROL WORD [BX+DI+0x5566],CL ... ;d3 81 66 55
ROL WORD [BX+DI+0x55],1 ...... ;d1 41 55
ROL WORD [BX+DI+0x55],CL ..... ;d3 41 55
ROL WORD [BX+DI],1 ........... ;d1 01
ROL WORD [BX+DI],CL .......... ;d3 01
ROL WORD [BX+SI+0x5566],1 .... ;d1 80 66 55
ROL WORD [BX+SI+0x5566],CL ... ;d3 80 66 55
ROL WORD [BX+SI+0x55],1 ...... ;d1 40 55
ROL WORD [BX+SI+0x55],CL ..... ;d3 40 55
ROL WORD [BX+SI],1 ........... ;d1 00
ROL WORD [BX+SI],CL .......... ;d3 00
ROL WORD [BX],1 .............. ;d1 07
ROL WORD [BX],CL ............. ;d3 07
ROL WORD [DI+0x5566],1 ....... ;d1 85 66 55
ROL WORD [DI+0x5566],CL ...... ;d3 85 66 55
ROL WORD [DI+0x55],1 ......... ;d1 45 55
ROL WORD [DI+0x55],CL ........ ;d3 45 55
ROL WORD [DI],1 .............. ;d1 05
ROL WORD [DI],CL ............. ;d3 05
ROL WORD [SI+0x5566],1 ....... ;d1 84 66 55
ROL WORD [SI+0x5566],CL ...... ;d3 84 66 55
ROL WORD [SI+0x55],1 ......... ;d1 44 55
ROL WORD [SI+0x55],CL ........ ;d3 44 55
ROL WORD [SI],1 .............. ;d1 04
ROL WORD [SI],CL ............. ;d3 04
ROR AH,1 ..................... ;d0 cc
ROR AH,CL .................... ;d2 cc
ROR AL,1 ..................... ;d0 c8
ROR AL,CL .................... ;d2 c8
ROR AX,1 ..................... ;d1 c8
ROR AX,CL .................... ;d3 c8
ROR BH,1 ..................... ;d0 cf
ROR BH,CL .................... ;d2 cf
ROR BL,1 ..................... ;d0 cb
ROR BL,CL .................... ;d2 cb
ROR BP,1 ..................... ;d1 cd
ROR BP,CL .................... ;d3 cd
ROR BX,1 ..................... ;d1 cb
ROR BX,CL .................... ;d3 cb
ROR BYTE [0x5566],1 .......... ;d0 0e 66 55
ROR BYTE [0x5566],CL ......... ;d2 0e 66 55
ROR BYTE [BP+0x5566],1 ....... ;d0 8e 66 55
ROR BYTE [BP+0x5566],CL ...... ;d2 8e 66 55
ROR BYTE [BP+0x55],1 ......... ;d0 4e 55
ROR BYTE [BP+0x55],CL ........ ;d2 4e 55
ROR BYTE [BP+DI+0x5566],1 .... ;d0 8b 66 55
```

```
ROR BYTE [BP+DI+0x5566],CL .....;d2 8b 66 55      ROR WORD [BX+SI+0x55],1 .........;d1 48 55
ROR BYTE [BP+DI+0x55],1 .........;d0 4b 55        ROR WORD [BX+SI+0x55],CL ........;d3 48 55
ROR BYTE [BP+DI+0x55],CL .......;d2 4b 55         ROR WORD [BX+SI],1 .............;d1 08
ROR BYTE [BP+DI],1 .............;d0 0b            ROR WORD [BX+SI],CL ............;d3 08
ROR BYTE [BP+DI],CL ............;d2 0b            ROR WORD [BX],1 ...............;d1 0f
ROR BYTE [BP+SI+0x5566],1 ......;d0 8a 66 55      ROR WORD [BX],CL ..............;d3 0f
ROR BYTE [BP+SI+0x5566],CL .....;d2 8a 66 55      ROR WORD [DI+0x5566],1 .........;d1 8d 66 55
ROR BYTE [BP+SI+0x55],1 .........;d0 4a 55        ROR WORD [DI+0x5566],CL ........;d3 8d 66 55
ROR BYTE [BP+SI+0x55],CL .......;d2 4a 55         ROR WORD [DI+0x55],1 ...........;d1 4d 55
ROR BYTE [BP+SI],1 .............;d0 0a            ROR WORD [DI+0x55],CL ..........;d3 4d 55
ROR BYTE [BP+SI],CL ............;d2 0a            ROR WORD [DI],1 ...............;d1 0d
ROR BYTE [BX+0x5566],1 .........;d0 8f 66 55      ROR WORD [DI],CL ..............;d3 0d
ROR BYTE [BX+0x5566],CL .......;d2 8f 66 55       ROR WORD [SI+0x5566],1 .........;d1 8c 66 55
ROR BYTE [BX+0x55],1 ...........;d0 4f 55         ROR WORD [SI+0x5566],CL ........;d3 8c 66 55
ROR BYTE [BX+0x55],CL ..........;d2 4f 55         ROR WORD [SI+0x55],1 ...........;d1 4c 55
ROR BYTE [BX+DI+0x5566],1 ......;d0 89 66 55      ROR WORD [SI+0x55],CL ..........;d3 4c 55
ROR BYTE [BX+DI+0x5566],CL .....;d2 89 66 55      ROR WORD [SI],1 ...............;d1 0c
ROR BYTE [BX+DI+0x55],1 .........;d0 49 55        ROR WORD [SI],CL ..............;d3 0c
ROR BYTE [BX+DI+0x55],CL .......;d2 49 55         SAHF .........................;9e
ROR BYTE [BX+DI],1 .............;d0 09            SAR AH,1 ......................;d0 fc
ROR BYTE [BX+DI],CL ............;d2 09            SAR AH,CL .....................;d2 fc
ROR BYTE [BX+SI+0x5566],1 ......;d0 88 66 55      SAR AL,1 ......................;d0 f8
ROR BYTE [BX+SI+0x5566],CL .....;d2 88 66 55      SAR AL,CL .....................;d2 f8
ROR BYTE [BX+SI+0x55],1 .........;d0 48 55        SAR AX,1 ......................;d1 f8
ROR BYTE [BX+SI+0x55],CL .......;d2 48 55         SAR AX,CL .....................;d3 f8
ROR BYTE [BX+SI],1 .............;d0 08            SAR BH,1 ......................;d0 ff
ROR BYTE [BX+SI],CL ............;d2 08            SAR BH,CL .....................;d2 ff
ROR BYTE [BX],1 ...............;d0 0f             SAR BL,1 ......................;d0 fb
ROR BYTE [BX],CL ..............;d2 0f             SAR BL,CL .....................;d2 fb
ROR BYTE [DI+0x5566],1 .........;d0 8d 66 55      SAR BP,1 ......................;d1 fd
ROR BYTE [DI+0x5566],CL .......;d2 8d 66 55       SAR BP,CL .....................;d3 fd
ROR BYTE [DI+0x55],1 ...........;d0 4d 55         SAR BX,1 ......................;d1 fb
ROR BYTE [DI+0x55],CL ..........;d2 4d 55         SAR BX,CL .....................;d3 fb
ROR BYTE [DI],1 ...............;d0 0d             SAR BYTE [0x5566],1 ...........;d0 3e 66 55
ROR BYTE [DI],CL ..............;d2 0d             SAR BYTE [0x5566],CL ..........;d2 3e 66 55
ROR BYTE [SI+0x5566],1 .........;d0 8c 66 55      SAR BYTE [BP+0x5566],1 .........;d0 be 66 55
ROR BYTE [SI+0x5566],CL ........;d2 8c 66 55      SAR BYTE [BP+0x5566],CL .......;d2 be 66 55
ROR BYTE [SI+0x55],1 ...........;d0 4c 55         SAR BYTE [BP+0x55],1 ..........;d0 7e 55
ROR BYTE [SI+0x55],CL ..........;d2 4c 55         SAR BYTE [BP+0x55],CL .........;d2 7e 55
ROR BYTE [SI],1 ...............;d0 0c             SAR BYTE [BP+DI+0x5566],1 ......;d0 bb 66 55
ROR BYTE [SI],CL ..............;d2 0c             SAR BYTE [BP+DI+0x5566],CL ....;d2 bb 66 55
ROR CH,1 ......................;d0 cd             SAR BYTE [BP+DI+0x55],1 ........;d0 7b 55
ROR CH,CL .....................;d2 cd             SAR BYTE [BP+DI+0x55],CL .......;d2 7b 55
ROR CL,1 ......................;d0 c9             SAR BYTE [BP+DI],1 .............;d0 3b
ROR CL,CL .....................;d2 c9             SAR BYTE [BP+DI],CL ............;d2 3b
ROR CX,1 ......................;d1 c9             SAR BYTE [BP+SI+0x5566],1 ......;d0 ba 66 55
ROR CX,CL .....................;d3 c9             SAR BYTE [BP+SI+0x5566],CL .....;d2 ba 66 55
ROR DH,1 ......................;d0 ce             SAR BYTE [BP+SI+0x55],1 ........;d0 7a 55
ROR DH,CL .....................;d2 ce             SAR BYTE [BP+SI+0x55],CL .......;d2 7a 55
ROR DI,1 ......................;d1 cf             SAR BYTE [BP+SI],1 .............;d0 3a
ROR DI,CL .....................;d3 cf             SAR BYTE [BP+SI],CL ............;d2 3a
ROR DL,1 ......................;d0 ca             SAR BYTE [BX+0x5566],1 .........;d0 bf 66 55
ROR DL,CL .....................;d2 ca             SAR BYTE [BX+0x5566],CL .......;d2 bf 66 55
ROR DX,1 ......................;d1 ca             SAR BYTE [BX+0x55],1 ..........;d0 7f 55
ROR DX,CL .....................;d3 ca             SAR BYTE [BX+0x55],CL .........;d2 7f 55
ROR SI,1 ......................;d1 ce             SAR BYTE [BX+DI+0x5566],1 ......;d0 b9 66 55
ROR SI,CL .....................;d3 ce             SAR BYTE [BX+DI+0x5566],CL ....;d2 b9 66 55
ROR SP,1 ......................;d1 cc             SAR BYTE [BX+DI+0x55],1 ........;d0 79 55
ROR SP,CL .....................;d3 cc             SAR BYTE [BX+DI+0x55],CL .......;d2 79 55
ROR WORD [0x5566],1 ...........;d1 0e 66 55       SAR BYTE [BX+DI],1 .............;d0 39
ROR WORD [0x5566],CL ..........;d3 0e 66 55       SAR BYTE [BX+DI],CL ............;d2 39
ROR WORD [BP+0x5566],1 .........;d1 8e 66 55      SAR BYTE [BX+SI+0x5566],1 ......;d0 b8 66 55
ROR WORD [BP+0x5566],CL .......;d3 8e 66 55       SAR BYTE [BX+SI+0x5566],CL .....;d2 b8 66 55
ROR WORD [BP+0x55],1 ...........;d1 4e 55         SAR BYTE [BX+SI+0x55],1 ........;d0 78 55
ROR WORD [BP+0x55],CL ..........;d3 4e 55         SAR BYTE [BX+SI+0x55],CL .......;d2 78 55
ROR WORD [BP+DI+0x5566],1 ......;d1 8b 66 55      SAR BYTE [BX+SI],1 .............;d0 38
ROR WORD [BP+DI+0x5566],CL ....;d3 8b 66 55       SAR BYTE [BX+SI],CL ............;d2 38
ROR WORD [BP+DI+0x55],1 .........;d1 4b 55        SAR BYTE [BX],1 ...............;d0 3f
ROR WORD [BP+DI+0x55],CL .......;d3 4b 55         SAR BYTE [BX],CL ..............;d2 3f
ROR WORD [BP+DI],1 .............;d1 0b            SAR BYTE [DI+0x5566],1 .........;d0 bd 66 55
ROR WORD [BP+DI],CL ............;d3 0b            SAR BYTE [DI+0x5566],CL .......;d2 bd 66 55
ROR WORD [BP+SI+0x5566],1 ......;d1 8a 66 55      SAR BYTE [DI+0x55],1 ...........;d0 7d 55
ROR WORD [BP+SI+0x5566],CL .....;d3 8a 66 55      SAR BYTE [DI+0x55],CL ..........;d2 7d 55
ROR WORD [BP+SI+0x55],1 .........;d1 4a 55        SAR BYTE [DI],1 ...............;d0 3d
ROR WORD [BP+SI+0x55],CL .......;d3 4a 55         SAR BYTE [DI],CL ..............;d2 3d
ROR WORD [BP+SI],1 .............;d1 0a            SAR BYTE [SI+0x5566],1 .........;d0 bc 66 55
ROR WORD [BP+SI],CL ............;d3 0a            SAR BYTE [SI+0x5566],CL ........;d2 bc 66 55
ROR WORD [BX+0x5566],1 .........;d1 8f 66 55      SAR BYTE [SI+0x55],1 ...........;d0 7c 55
ROR WORD [BX+0x5566],CL .......;d3 8f 66 55       SAR BYTE [SI+0x55],CL ..........;d2 7c 55
ROR WORD [BX+0x55],1 ...........;d1 4f 55         SAR BYTE [SI],1 ...............;d0 3c
ROR WORD [BX+0x55],CL ..........;d3 4f 55         SAR BYTE [SI],CL ..............;d2 3c
ROR WORD [BX+DI+0x5566],1 ......;d1 89 66 55      SAR CH,1 ......................;d0 fd
ROR WORD [BX+DI+0x5566],CL ....;d3 89 66 55       SAR CH,CL .....................;d2 fd
ROR WORD [BX+DI+0x55],1 .........;d1 49 55        SAR CL,1 ......................;d0 f9
ROR WORD [BX+DI+0x55],CL .......;d3 49 55         SAR CL,CL .....................;d2 f9
ROR WORD [BX+DI],1 .............;d1 09            SAR CX,1 ......................;d1 f9
ROR WORD [BX+DI],CL ............;d3 09            SAR CX,CL .....................;d3 f9
ROR WORD [BX+SI+0x5566],1 ......;d1 88 66 55      SAR DH,1 ......................;d0 fe
ROR WORD [BX+SI+0x5566],CL .....;d3 88 66 55      SAR DH,CL .....................;d2 fe
```

```
SAR DI,1 ........................;d1 ff
SAR DI,CL .......................;d3 ff
SAR DL,1 ........................;d0 fa
SAR DL,CL .......................;d2 fa
SAR DX,1 ........................;d1 fa
SAR DX,CL .......................;d3 fa
SAR SI,1 ........................;d1 fe
SAR SI,CL .......................;d3 fe
SAR SP,1 ........................;d1 fc
SAR SP,CL .......................;d3 fc
SAR WORD [0x5566],1 .............;d1 3e 66 55
SAR WORD [0x5566],CL ............;d3 3e 66 55
SAR WORD [BP+0x5566],1 ..........;d1 be 66 55
SAR WORD [BP+0x5566],CL .........;d3 be 66 55
SAR WORD [BP+0x55],1 ............;d1 7e 55
SAR WORD [BP+0x55],CL ...........;d3 7e 55
SAR WORD [BP+DI+0x5566],1 .......;d1 bb 66 55
SAR WORD [BP+DI+0x5566],CL ......;d3 bb 66 55
SAR WORD [BP+DI+0x55],1 .........;d1 7b 55
SAR WORD [BP+DI+0x55],CL ........;d3 7b 55
SAR WORD [BP+DI],1 ..............;d1 3b
SAR WORD [BP+DI],CL .............;d3 3b
SAR WORD [BP+SI+0x5566],1 .......;d1 ba 66 55
SAR WORD [BP+SI+0x5566],CL ......;d3 ba 66 55
SAR WORD [BP+SI+0x55],1 .........;d1 7a 55
SAR WORD [BP+SI+0x55],CL ........;d3 7a 55
SAR WORD [BP+SI],1 ..............;d1 3a
SAR WORD [BP+SI],CL .............;d3 3a
SAR WORD [BX+0x5566],1 ..........;d1 bf 66 55
SAR WORD [BX+0x5566],CL .........;d3 bf 66 55
SAR WORD [BX+0x55],1 ............;d1 7f 55
SAR WORD [BX+0x55],CL ...........;d3 7f 55
SAR WORD [BX+DI+0x5566],1 .......;d1 b9 66 55
SAR WORD [BX+DI+0x5566],CL ......;d3 b9 66 55
SAR WORD [BX+DI+0x55],1 .........;d1 79 55
SAR WORD [BX+DI+0x55],CL ........;d3 79 55
SAR WORD [BX+DI],1 ..............;d1 39
SAR WORD [BX+DI],CL .............;d3 39
SAR WORD [BX+SI+0x5566],1 .......;d1 b8 66 55
SAR WORD [BX+SI+0x5566],CL ......;d3 b8 66 55
SAR WORD [BX+SI+0x55],1 .........;d1 78 55
SAR WORD [BX+SI+0x55],CL ........;d3 78 55
SAR WORD [BX+SI],1 ..............;d1 38
SAR WORD [BX+SI],CL .............;d3 38
SAR WORD [BX],1 .................;d1 3f
SAR WORD [BX],CL ................;d3 3f
SAR WORD [DI+0x5566],1 ..........;d1 bd 66 55
SAR WORD [DI+0x5566],CL .........;d3 bd 66 55
SAR WORD [DI+0x55],1 ............;d1 7d 55
SAR WORD [DI+0x55],CL ...........;d3 7d 55
SAR WORD [DI],1 .................;d1 3d
SAR WORD [DI],CL ................;d3 3d
SAR WORD [SI+0x5566],1 ..........;d1 bc 66 55
SAR WORD [SI+0x5566],CL .........;d3 bc 66 55
SAR WORD [SI+0x55],1 ............;d1 7c 55
SAR WORD [SI+0x55],CL ...........;d3 7c 55
SAR WORD [SI],1 .................;d1 3c
SAR WORD [SI],CL ................;d3 3c
SBB AH,0x88 .....................;80 dc 88
SBB AH,AH .......................;18 e4
SBB AH,AL .......................;18 c4
SBB AH,BH .......................;18 fc
SBB AH,BL .......................;18 dc
SBB AH,CH .......................;18 ec
SBB AH,CL .......................;18 cc
SBB AH,DH .......................;18 f4
SBB AH,DL .......................;18 d4
SBB AH,[0x5566] .................;1a 26 66 55
SBB AH,[BP+0x5566] ..............;1a a6 66 55
SBB AH,[BP+0x55] ................;1a 66 55
SBB AH,[BP+DI+0x5566] ...........;1a a3 66 55
SBB AH,[BP+DI+0x55] .............;1a 63 55
SBB AH,[BP+DI] ..................;1a 23
SBB AH,[BP+SI+0x5566] ...........;1a a2 66 55
SBB AH,[BP+SI+0x55] .............;1a 62 55
SBB AH,[BP+SI] ..................;1a 22
SBB AH,[BX+0x5566] ..............;1a a7 66 55
SBB AH,[BX+0x55] ................;1a 67 55
SBB AH,[BX+DI+0x5566] ...........;1a a1 66 55
SBB AH,[BX+DI+0x55] .............;1a 61 55
SBB AH,[BX+DI] ..................;1a 21
SBB AH,[BX+SI+0x5566] ...........;1a a0 66 55
SBB AH,[BX+SI+0x55] .............;1a 60 55
SBB AH,[BX+SI] ..................;1a 20
SBB AH,[BX] .....................;1a 27
SBB AH,[DI+0x5566] ..............;1a a5 66 55
SBB AH,[DI+0x55] ................;1a 65 55
SBB AH,[DI] .....................;1a 25
SBB AH,[SI+0x5566] ..............;1a a4 66 55
```

```
SBB AH,[SI+0x55] ................;1a 64 55
SBB AH,[SI] .....................;1a 24
SBB AL,0x55 .....................;1c 55
SBB AL,0x88 .....................;80 d8 88
SBB AL,AH .......................;18 e0
SBB AL,AL .......................;18 c0
SBB AL,BH .......................;18 f8
SBB AL,BL .......................;18 d8
SBB AL,CH .......................;18 e8
SBB AL,CL .......................;18 c8
SBB AL,DH .......................;18 f0
SBB AL,DL .......................;18 d0
SBB AL,[0x5566] .................;1a 06 66 55
SBB AL,[BP+0x5566] ..............;1a 86 66 55
SBB AL,[BP+0x55] ................;1a 46 55
SBB AL,[BP+DI+0x5566] ...........;1a 83 66 55
SBB AL,[BP+DI+0x55] .............;1a 43 55
SBB AL,[BP+DI] ..................;1a 03
SBB AL,[BP+SI+0x5566] ...........;1a 82 66 55
SBB AL,[BP+SI+0x55] .............;1a 42 55
SBB AL,[BP+SI] ..................;1a 02
SBB AL,[BX+0x5566] ..............;1a 87 66 55
SBB AL,[BX+0x55] ................;1a 47 55
SBB AL,[BX+DI+0x5566] ...........;1a 81 66 55
SBB AL,[BX+DI+0x55] .............;1a 41 55
SBB AL,[BX+DI] ..................;1a 01
SBB AL,[BX+SI+0x5566] ...........;1a 80 66 55
SBB AL,[BX+SI+0x55] .............;1a 40 55
SBB AL,[BX+SI] ..................;1a 00
SBB AL,[BX] .....................;1a 07
SBB AL,[DI+0x5566] ..............;1a 85 66 55
SBB AL,[DI+0x55] ................;1a 45 55
SBB AL,[DI] .....................;1a 05
SBB AL,[SI+0x5566] ..............;1a 84 66 55
SBB AL,[SI+0x55] ................;1a 44 55
SBB AL,[SI] .....................;1a 04
SBB AX,0x5566 ...................;1d 66 55
SBB AX,0x77 .....................;83 d8 77
SBB AX,0x7788 ...................;81 d8 88 77
SBB AX,AX .......................;19 c0
SBB AX,BP .......................;19 e8
SBB AX,BX .......................;19 d8
SBB AX,CX .......................;19 c8
SBB AX,DI .......................;19 f8
SBB AX,DX .......................;19 d0
SBB AX,SI .......................;19 f0
SBB AX,SP .......................;19 e0
SBB AX,[0x5566] .................;1b 06 66 55
SBB AX,[BP+0x5566] ..............;1b 86 66 55
SBB AX,[BP+0x55] ................;1b 46 55
SBB AX,[BP+DI+0x5566] ...........;1b 83 66 55
SBB AX,[BP+DI+0x55] .............;1b 43 55
SBB AX,[BP+DI] ..................;1b 03
SBB AX,[BP+SI+0x5566] ...........;1b 82 66 55
SBB AX,[BP+SI+0x55] .............;1b 42 55
SBB AX,[BP+SI] ..................;1b 02
SBB AX,[BX+0x5566] ..............;1b 87 66 55
SBB AX,[BX+0x55] ................;1b 47 55
SBB AX,[BX+DI+0x5566] ...........;1b 81 66 55
SBB AX,[BX+DI+0x55] .............;1b 41 55
SBB AX,[BX+DI] ..................;1b 01
SBB AX,[BX+SI+0x5566] ...........;1b 80 66 55
SBB AX,[BX+SI+0x55] .............;1b 40 55
SBB AX,[BX+SI] ..................;1b 00
SBB AX,[BX] .....................;1b 07
SBB AX,[DI+0x5566] ..............;1b 85 66 55
SBB AX,[DI+0x55] ................;1b 45 55
SBB AX,[DI] .....................;1b 05
SBB AX,[SI+0x5566] ..............;1b 84 66 55
SBB AX,[SI+0x55] ................;1b 44 55
SBB AX,[SI] .....................;1b 04
SBB BH,0x88 .....................;80 df 88
SBB BH,AH .......................;18 e7
SBB BH,AL .......................;18 c7
SBB BH,BH .......................;18 ff
SBB BH,BL .......................;18 df
SBB BH,CH .......................;18 ef
SBB BH,CL .......................;18 cf
SBB BH,DH .......................;18 f7
SBB BH,DL .......................;18 d7
SBB BH,[0x5566] .................;1a 3e 66 55
SBB BH,[BP+0x5566] ..............;1a be 66 55
SBB BH,[BP+0x55] ................;1a 7e 55
SBB BH,[BP+DI+0x5566] ...........;1a bb 66 55
SBB BH,[BP+DI+0x55] .............;1a 7b 55
SBB BH,[BP+DI] ..................;1a 3b
SBB BH,[BP+SI+0x5566] ...........;1a ba 66 55
SBB BH,[BP+SI+0x55] .............;1a 7a 55
SBB BH,[BP+SI] ..................;1a 3a
```

210

```
SBB BH,[BX+0x5566] ............ ;1a bf 66 55      SBB BX,DX ..................... ;19 d3
SBB BH,[BX+55] ................ ;1a 7f 55         SBB BX,SI ..................... ;19 f3
SBB BH,[BX+DI+0x5566] ......... ;1a b9 66 55      SBB BX,SP ..................... ;19 e3
SBB BH,[BX+DI+0x55] ........... ;1a 79 55         SBB BX,[0x5566] .............. ;1b 1e 66 55
SBB BH,[BX+DI] ............... ;1a 39             SBB BX,[BP+0x5566] ........... ;1b 9e 66 55
SBB BH,[BX+SI+0x5566] ......... ;1a b8 66 55      SBB BX,[BP+0x55] ............. ;1b 5e 55
SBB BH,[BX+SI+0x55] ........... ;1a 78 55         SBB BX,[BP+DI+0x5566] ........ ;1b 9b 66 55
SBB BH,[BX+SI] ............... ;1a 38             SBB BX,[BP+DI+0x55] .......... ;1b 5b 55
SBB BH,[BX] .................. ;1a 3f             SBB BX,[BP+DI] ............... ;1b 1b
SBB BH,[DI+0x5566] ........... ;1a bd 66 55       SBB BX,[BP+SI+0x5566] ........ ;1b 9a 66 55
SBB BH,[DI+0x55] ............. ;1a 7d 55          SBB BX,[BP+SI+0x55] .......... ;1b 5a 55
SBB BH,[DI] .................. ;1a 3d             SBB BX,[BP+SI] ............... ;1b 1a
SBB BH,[SI+0x5566] ........... ;1a bc 66 55       SBB BX,[BX+0x5566] ........... ;1b 9f 66 55
SBB BH,[SI+0x55] ............. ;1a 7c 55          SBB BX,[BX+0x55] ............. ;1b 5f 55
SBB BH,[SI] .................. ;1a 3c             SBB BX,[BX+DI+0x5566] ........ ;1b 99 66 55
SBB BL,0x88 .................. ;80 db 88          SBB BX,[BX+DI+0x55] .......... ;1b 59 55
SBB BL,AH .................... ;18 e3             SBB BX,[BX+DI] ............... ;1b 19
SBB BL,AL .................... ;18 c3             SBB BX,[BX+SI+0x5566] ........ ;1b 98 66 55
SBB BL,BH .................... ;18 fb             SBB BX,[BX+SI+0x55] .......... ;1b 58 55
SBB BL,BL .................... ;18 db             SBB BX,[BX+SI] ............... ;1b 18
SBB BL,CH .................... ;18 eb             SBB BX,[BX] .................. ;1b 1f
SBB BL,CL .................... ;18 cb             SBB BX,[DI+0x5566] ........... ;1b 9d 66 55
SBB BL,DH .................... ;18 f3             SBB BX,[DI+0x55] ............. ;1b 5d 55
SBB BL,DL .................... ;18 d3             SBB BX,[DI] .................. ;1b 1d
SBB BL,[0x5566] .............. ;1a 1e 66 55       SBB BX,[SI+0x5566] ........... ;1b 9c 66 55
SBB BL,[BP+0x5566] ........... ;1a 9e 66 55       SBB BX,[SI+0x55] ............. ;1b 5c 55
SBB BL,[BP+0x55] ............. ;1a 5e 55          SBB BX,[SI] .................. ;1b 1c
SBB BL,[BP+DI+0x5566] ........ ;1a 9b 66 55       SBB BYTE [0x5566],0x88 ....... ;80 1e 66 55 88
SBB BL,[BP+DI+0x55] .......... ;1a 5b 55          SBB BYTE [BP+0x5566],0x88 .... ;80 9e 66 55 88
SBB BL,[BP+DI] ............... ;1a 1b             SBB BYTE [BP+0x55],0x88 ...... ;80 5e 55 88
SBB BL,[BP+SI+0x5566] ........ ;1a 9a 66 55       SBB BYTE [BP+DI+0x5566],0x88 . ;80 9b 66 55 88
SBB BL,[BP+SI+0x55] .......... ;1a 5a 55          SBB BYTE [BP+DI+0x55],0x88 ... ;80 5b 55 88
SBB BL,[BP+SI] ............... ;1a 1a             SBB BYTE [BP+DI],0x88 ........ ;80 1b 88
SBB BL,[BX+0x5566] ........... ;1a 9f 66 55       SBB BYTE [BP+SI+0x5566],0x88 . ;80 9a 66 55 88
SBB BL,[BX+0x55] ............. ;1a 5f 55          SBB BYTE [BP+SI+0x55],0x88 ... ;80 5a 55 88
SBB BL,[BX+DI+0x5566] ........ ;1a 99 66 55       SBB BYTE [BP+SI],0x88 ........ ;80 1a 88
SBB BL,[BX+DI+0x55] .......... ;1a 59 55          SBB BYTE [BX+0x5566],0x88 .... ;80 9f 66 55 88
SBB BL,[BX+DI] ............... ;1a 19             SBB BYTE [BX+0x55],0x88 ...... ;80 5f 55 88
SBB BL,[BX+SI+0x5566] ........ ;1a 98 66 55       SBB BYTE [BX+DI+0x5566],0x88 . ;80 99 66 55 88
SBB BL,[BX+SI+0x55] .......... ;1a 58 55          SBB BYTE [BX+DI+0x55],0x88 ... ;80 59 55 88
SBB BL,[BX+SI] ............... ;1a 18             SBB BYTE [BX+DI],0x88 ........ ;80 19 88
SBB BL,[BX] .................. ;1a 1f             SBB BYTE [BX+SI+0x5566],0x88 . ;80 98 66 55 88
SBB BL,[DI+0x5566] ........... ;1a 9d 66 55       SBB BYTE [BX+SI+0x55],0x88 ... ;80 58 55 88
SBB BL,[DI+0x55] ............. ;1a 5d 55          SBB BYTE [BX+SI],0x88 ........ ;80 18 88
SBB BL,[DI] .................. ;1a 1d             SBB BYTE [BX],0x88 ........... ;80 1f 88
SBB BL,[SI+0x5566] ........... ;1a 9c 66 55       SBB BYTE [DI+0x5566],0x88 .... ;80 9d 66 55 88
SBB BL,[SI+0x55] ............. ;1a 5c 55          SBB BYTE [DI+0x55],0x88 ...... ;80 5d 55 88
SBB BL,[SI] .................. ;1a 1c             SBB BYTE [DI],0x88 ........... ;80 1d 88
SBB BP,0x77 .................. ;83 dd 77          SBB BYTE [SI+0x5566],0x88 .... ;80 9c 66 55 88
SBB BP,0x7788 ................ ;81 dd 88 77       SBB BYTE [SI+0x55],0x88 ...... ;80 5c 55 88
SBB BP,AX .................... ;19 c5             SBB BYTE [SI],0x88 ........... ;80 1c 88
SBB BP,BP .................... ;19 ed             SBB CH,0x88 .................. ;80 dd 88
SBB BP,BX .................... ;19 dd             SBB CH,AH .................... ;18 e5
SBB BP,CX .................... ;19 cd             SBB CH,AL .................... ;18 c5
SBB BP,DI .................... ;19 fd             SBB CH,BH .................... ;18 fd
SBB BP,DX .................... ;19 d5             SBB CH,BL .................... ;18 dd
SBB BP,SI .................... ;19 f5             SBB CH,CH .................... ;18 ed
SBB BP,SP .................... ;19 e5             SBB CH,CL .................... ;18 cd
SBB BP,[0x5566] .............. ;1b 2e 66 55       SBB CH,DH .................... ;18 f5
SBB BP,[BP+0x5566] ........... ;1b ae 66 55       SBB CH,DL .................... ;18 d5
SBB BP,[BP+0x55] ............. ;1b 6e 55          SBB CH,[0x5566] .............. ;1a 2e 66 55
SBB BP,[BP+DI+0x5566] ........ ;1b ab 66 55       SBB CH,[BP+0x5566] ........... ;1a ae 66 55
SBB BP,[BP+DI+0x55] .......... ;1b 6b 55          SBB CH,[BP+0x55] ............. ;1a 6e 55
SBB BP,[BP+DI] ............... ;1b 2b             SBB CH,[BP+DI+0x5566] ........ ;1a ab 66 55
SBB BP,[BP+SI+0x5566] ........ ;1b aa 66 55       SBB CH,[BP+DI+0x55] .......... ;1a 6b 55
SBB BP,[BP+SI+0x55] .......... ;1b 6a 55          SBB CH,[BP+DI] ............... ;1a 2b
SBB BP,[BP+SI] ............... ;1b 2a             SBB CH,[BP+SI+0x5566] ........ ;1a aa 66 55
SBB BP,[BX+0x5566] ........... ;1b af 66 55       SBB CH,[BP+SI+0x55] .......... ;1a 6a 55
SBB BP,[BX+0x55] ............. ;1b 6f 55          SBB CH,[BP+SI] ............... ;1a 2a
SBB BP,[BX+DI+0x5566] ........ ;1b a9 66 55       SBB CH,[BX+0x5566] ........... ;1a af 66 55
SBB BP,[BX+DI+0x55] .......... ;1b 69 55          SBB CH,[BX+0x55] ............. ;1a 6f 55
SBB BP,[BX+DI] ............... ;1b 29             SBB CH,[BX+DI+0x5566] ........ ;1a a9 66 55
SBB BP,[BX+SI+0x5566] ........ ;1b a8 66 55       SBB CH,[BX+DI+0x55] .......... ;1a 69 55
SBB BP,[BX+SI+0x55] .......... ;1b 68 55          SBB CH,[BX+DI] ............... ;1a 29
SBB BP,[BX+SI] ............... ;1b 28             SBB CH,[BX+SI+0x5566] ........ ;1a a8 66 55
SBB BP,[BX] .................. ;1b 2f             SBB CH,[BX+SI+0x55] .......... ;1a 68 55
SBB BP,[DI+0x5566] ........... ;1b ad 66 55       SBB CH,[BX+SI] ............... ;1a 28
SBB BP,[DI+0x55] ............. ;1b 6d 55          SBB CH,[BX] .................. ;1a 2f
SBB BP,[DI] .................. ;1b 2d             SBB CH,[DI+0x5566] ........... ;1a ad 66 55
SBB BP,[SI+0x5566] ........... ;1b ac 66 55       SBB CH,[DI+0x55] ............. ;1a 6d 55
SBB BP,[SI+0x55] ............. ;1b 6c 55          SBB CH,[DI] .................. ;1a 2d
SBB BP,[SI] .................. ;1b 2c             SBB CH,[SI+0x5566] ........... ;1a ac 66 55
SBB BX,0x77 .................. ;83 db 77          SBB CH,[SI+0x55] ............. ;1a 6c 55
SBB BX,0x7788 ................ ;81 db 88 77       SBB CH,[SI] .................. ;1a 2c
SBB BX,AX .................... ;19 c3             SBB CL,0x88 .................. ;80 d9 88
SBB BX,BP .................... ;19 eb             SBB CL,AH .................... ;18 e1
SBB BX,BX .................... ;19 db             SBB CL,AL .................... ;18 c1
SBB BX,CX .................... ;19 cb             SBB CL,BH .................... ;18 f9
SBB BX,DI .................... ;19 fb             SBB CL,BL .................... ;18 d9
```

```
SBB CL,CH ......................;18 e9
SBB CL,CL ......................;18 c9
SBB CL,DH ......................;18 f1
SBB CL,DL ......................;18 d1
SBB CL,[0x5566] ................;1a 0e 66 55
SBB CL,[BP+0x5566] .............;1a 8e 66 55
SBB CL,[BP+0x55] ...............;1a 4e 55
SBB CL,[BP+DI+0x5566] ..........;1a 8b 66 55
SBB CL,[BP+DI+0x55] ............;1a 4b 55
SBB CL,[BP+DI] .................;1a 0b
SBB CL,[BP+SI+0x5566] ..........;1a 8a 66 55
SBB CL,[BP+SI+0x55] ............;1a 4a 55
SBB CL,[BP+SI] .................;1a 0a
SBB CL,[BX+0x5566] .............;1a 8f 66 55
SBB CL,[BX+0x55] ...............;1a 4f 55
SBB CL,[BX+DI+0x5566] ..........;1a 89 66 55
SBB CL,[BX+DI+0x55] ............;1a 49 55
SBB CL,[BX+DI] .................;1a 09
SBB CL,[BX+SI+0x5566] ..........;1a 88 66 55
SBB CL,[BX+SI+0x55] ............;1a 48 55
SBB CL,[BX+SI] .................;1a 08
SBB CL,[BX] ....................;1a 0f
SBB CL,[DI+0x5566] .............;1a 8d 66 55
SBB CL,[DI+0x55] ...............;1a 4d 55
SBB CL,[DI] ....................;1a 0d
SBB CL,[SI+0x5566] .............;1a 8c 66 55
SBB CL,[SI+0x55] ...............;1a 4c 55
SBB CL,[SI] ....................;1a 0c
SBB CX,0x77 ....................;83 d9 77
SBB CX,0x7788 ..................;81 d9 88 77
SBB CX,AX ......................;19 c1
SBB CX,BP ......................;19 e9
SBB CX,BX ......................;19 d9
SBB CX,CX ......................;19 c9
SBB CX,DI ......................;19 f9
SBB CX,DX ......................;19 d1
SBB CX,SI ......................;19 f1
SBB CX,SP ......................;19 e1
SBB CX,[0x5566] ................;1b 0e 66 55
SBB CX,[BP+0x5566] .............;1b 8e 66 55
SBB CX,[BP+0x55] ...............;1b 4e 55
SBB CX,[BP+DI+0x5566] ..........;1b 8b 66 55
SBB CX,[BP+DI+0x55] ............;1b 4b 55
SBB CX,[BP+DI] .................;1b 0b
SBB CX,[BP+SI+0x5566] ..........;1b 8a 66 55
SBB CX,[BP+SI+0x55] ............;1b 4a 55
SBB CX,[BP+SI] .................;1b 0a
SBB CX,[BX+0x5566] .............;1b 8f 66 55
SBB CX,[BX+0x55] ...............;1b 4f 55
SBB CX,[BX+DI+0x5566] ..........;1b 89 66 55
SBB CX,[BX+DI+0x55] ............;1b 49 55
SBB CX,[BX+DI] .................;1b 09
SBB CX,[BX+SI+0x5566] ..........;1b 88 66 55
SBB CX,[BX+SI+0x55] ............;1b 48 55
SBB CX,[BX+SI] .................;1b 08
SBB CX,[BX] ....................;1b 0f
SBB CX,[DI+0x5566] .............;1b 8d 66 55
SBB CX,[DI+0x55] ...............;1b 4d 55
SBB CX,[DI] ....................;1b 0d
SBB CX,[SI+0x5566] .............;1b 8c 66 55
SBB CX,[SI+0x55] ...............;1b 4c 55
SBB CX,[SI] ....................;1b 0c
SBB DH,0x88 ....................;80 de 88
SBB DH,AH ......................;18 e6
SBB DH,AL ......................;18 c6
SBB DH,BH ......................;18 fe
SBB DH,BL ......................;18 de
SBB DH,CH ......................;18 ee
SBB DH,CL ......................;18 ce
SBB DH,DH ......................;18 f6
SBB DH,DL ......................;18 d6
SBB DH,[0x5566] ................;1a 36 66 55
SBB DH,[BP+0x5566] .............;1a b6 66 55
SBB DH,[BP+0x55] ...............;1a 76 55
SBB DH,[BP+DI+0x5566] ..........;1a b3 66 55
SBB DH,[BP+DI+0x55] ............;1a 73 55
SBB DH,[BP+DI] .................;1a 33
SBB DH,[BP+SI+0x5566] ..........;1a b2 66 55
SBB DH,[BP+SI+0x55] ............;1a 72 55
SBB DH,[BP+SI] .................;1a 32
SBB DH,[BX+0x5566] .............;1a b7 66 55
SBB DH,[BX+0x55] ...............;1a 77 55
SBB DH,[BX+DI+0x5566] ..........;1a b1 66 55
SBB DH,[BX+DI+0x55] ............;1a 71 55
SBB DH,[BX+DI] .................;1a 31
SBB DH,[BX+SI+0x5566] ..........;1a b0 66 55
SBB DH,[BX+SI+0x55] ............;1a 70 55
SBB DH,[BX+SI] .................;1a 30
SBB DH,[BX] ....................;1a 37
```

```
SBB DH,[DI+0x5566] .............;1a b5 66 55
SBB DH,[DI+0x55] ...............;1a 75 55
SBB DH,[DI] ....................;1a 35
SBB DH,[SI+0x5566] .............;1a b4 66 55
SBB DH,[SI+0x55] ...............;1a 74 55
SBB DH,[SI] ....................;1a 34
SBB DI,0x77 ....................;83 df 77
SBB DI,0x7788 ..................;81 df 88 77
SBB DI,AX ......................;19 c7
SBB DI,BP ......................;19 ef
SBB DI,BX ......................;19 df
SBB DI,CX ......................;19 cf
SBB DI,DI ......................;19 ff
SBB DI,DX ......................;19 d7
SBB DI,SI ......................;19 f7
SBB DI,SP ......................;19 e7
SBB DI,[0x5566] ................;1b 3e 66 55
SBB DI,[BP+0x5566] .............;1b be 66 55
SBB DI,[BP+0x55] ...............;1b 7e 55
SBB DI,[BP+DI+0x5566] ..........;1b bb 66 55
SBB DI,[BP+DI+0x55] ............;1b 7b 55
SBB DI,[BP+DI] .................;1b 3b
SBB DI,[BP+SI+0x5566] ..........;1b ba 66 55
SBB DI,[BP+SI+0x55] ............;1b 7a 55
SBB DI,[BP+SI] .................;1b 3a
SBB DI,[BX+0x5566] .............;1b bf 66 55
SBB DI,[BX+0x55] ...............;1b 7f 55
SBB DI,[BX+DI+0x5566] ..........;1b b9 66 55
SBB DI,[BX+DI+0x55] ............;1b 79 55
SBB DI,[BX+DI] .................;1b 39
SBB DI,[BX+SI+0x5566] ..........;1b b8 66 55
SBB DI,[BX+SI+0x55] ............;1b 78 55
SBB DI,[BX+SI] .................;1b 38
SBB DI,[BX] ....................;1b 3f
SBB DI,[DI+0x5566] .............;1b bd 66 55
SBB DI,[DI+0x55] ...............;1b 7d 55
SBB DI,[DI] ....................;1b 3d
SBB DI,[SI+0x5566] .............;1b bc 66 55
SBB DI,[SI+0x55] ...............;1b 7c 55
SBB DI,[SI] ....................;1b 3c
SBB DL,0x88 ....................;80 da 88
SBB DL,AH ......................;18 e2
SBB DL,AL ......................;18 c2
SBB DL,BH ......................;18 fa
SBB DL,BL ......................;18 da
SBB DL,CH ......................;18 ea
SBB DL,CL ......................;18 ca
SBB DL,DH ......................;18 f2
SBB DL,DL ......................;18 d2
SBB DL,[0x5566] ................;1a 16 66 55
SBB DL,[BP+0x5566] .............;1a 96 66 55
SBB DL,[BP+0x55] ...............;1a 56 55
SBB DL,[BP+DI+0x5566] ..........;1a 93 66 55
SBB DL,[BP+DI+0x55] ............;1a 53 55
SBB DL,[BP+DI] .................;1a 13
SBB DL,[BP+SI+0x5566] ..........;1a 92 66 55
SBB DL,[BP+SI+0x55] ............;1a 52 55
SBB DL,[BP+SI] .................;1a 12
SBB DL,[BX+0x5566] .............;1a 97 66 55
SBB DL,[BX+0x55] ...............;1a 57 55
SBB DL,[BX+DI+0x5566] ..........;1a 91 66 55
SBB DL,[BX+DI+0x55] ............;1a 51 55
SBB DL,[BX+DI] .................;1a 11
SBB DL,[BX+SI+0x5566] ..........;1a 90 66 55
SBB DL,[BX+SI+0x55] ............;1a 50 55
SBB DL,[BX+SI] .................;1a 10
SBB DL,[BX] ....................;1a 17
SBB DL,[DI+0x5566] .............;1a 95 66 55
SBB DL,[DI+0x55] ...............;1a 55 55
SBB DL,[DI] ....................;1a 15
SBB DL,[SI+0x5566] .............;1a 94 66 55
SBB DL,[SI+0x55] ...............;1a 54 55
SBB DL,[SI] ....................;1a 14
SBB DX,0x77 ....................;83 da 77
SBB DX,0x7788 ..................;81 da 88 77
SBB DX,AX ......................;19 c2
SBB DX,BP ......................;19 ea
SBB DX,BX ......................;19 da
SBB DX,CX ......................;19 ca
SBB DX,DI ......................;19 fa
SBB DX,DX ......................;19 d2
SBB DX,SI ......................;19 f2
SBB DX,SP ......................;19 e2
SBB DX,[0x5566] ................;1b 16 66 55
SBB DX,[BP+0x5566] .............;1b 96 66 55
SBB DX,[BP+0x55] ...............;1b 56 55
SBB DX,[BP+DI+0x5566] ..........;1b 93 66 55
SBB DX,[BP+DI+0x55] ............;1b 53 55
SBB DX,[BP+DI] .................;1b 13
```

```
SBB DX,[BP+SI+0x5566] .........;1b 92 66 55
SBB DX,[BP+SI+0x55] ...........;1b 52 55
SBB DX,[BP+SI] ................;1b 12
SBB DX,[BX+0x5566] ............;1b 97 66 55
SBB DX,[BX+0x55] ..............;1b 57 55
SBB DX,[BX+DI+0x5566] .........;1b 91 66 55
SBB DX,[BX+DI+0x55] ...........;1b 51 55
SBB DX,[BX+DI] ................;1b 11
SBB DX,[BX+SI+0x5566] .........;1b 90 66 55
SBB DX,[BX+SI+0x55] ...........;1b 50 55
SBB DX,[BX+SI] ................;1b 10
SBB DX,[BX] ...................;1b 17
SBB DX,[DI+0x5566] ............;1b 95 66 55
SBB DX,[DI+0x55] ..............;1b 55 55
SBB DX,[DI] ...................;1b 15
SBB DX,[SI+0x5566] ............;1b 94 66 55
SBB DX,[SI+0x55] ..............;1b 54 55
SBB DX,[SI] ...................;1b 14
SBB SI,0x77 ...................;83 de 77
SBB SI,0x7788 .................;81 de 88 77
SBB SI,AX .....................;19 c6
SBB SI,BP .....................;19 ee
SBB SI,BX .....................;19 de
SBB SI,CX .....................;19 ce
SBB SI,DI .....................;19 fe
SBB SI,DX .....................;19 d6
SBB SI,SI .....................;19 f6
SBB SI,SP .....................;19 e6
SBB SI,[0x5566] ...............;1b 36 66 55
SBB SI,[BP+0x5566] ............;1b b6 66 55
SBB SI,[BP+0x55] ..............;1b 76 55
SBB SI,[BP+DI+0x5566] .........;1b b3 66 55
SBB SI,[BP+DI+0x55] ...........;1b 73 55
SBB SI,[BP+DI] ................;1b 33
SBB SI,[BP+SI+0x5566] .........;1b b2 66 55
SBB SI,[BP+SI+0x55] ...........;1b 72 55
SBB SI,[BP+SI] ................;1b 32
SBB SI,[BX+0x5566] ............;1b b7 66 55
SBB SI,[BX+0x55] ..............;1b 77 55
SBB SI,[BX+DI+0x5566] .........;1b b1 66 55
SBB SI,[BX+DI+0x55] ...........;1b 71 55
SBB SI,[BX+DI] ................;1b 31
SBB SI,[BX+SI+0x5566] .........;1b b0 66 55
SBB SI,[BX+SI+0x55] ...........;1b 70 55
SBB SI,[BX+SI] ................;1b 30
SBB SI,[BX] ...................;1b 37
SBB SI,[DI+0x5566] ............;1b b5 66 55
SBB SI,[DI+0x55] ..............;1b 75 55
SBB SI,[DI] ...................;1b 35
SBB SI,[SI+0x5566] ............;1b b4 66 55
SBB SI,[SI+0x55] ..............;1b 74 55
SBB SI,[SI] ...................;1b 34
SBB SP,0x77 ...................;83 dc 77
SBB SP,0x7788 .................;81 dc 88 77
SBB SP,AX .....................;19 c4
SBB SP,BP .....................;19 ec
SBB SP,BX .....................;19 dc
SBB SP,CX .....................;19 cc
SBB SP,DI .....................;19 fc
SBB SP,DX .....................;19 d4
SBB SP,SI .....................;19 f4
SBB SP,SP .....................;19 e4
SBB SP,[0x5566] ...............;1b 26 66 55
SBB SP,[BP+0x5566] ............;1b a6 66 55
SBB SP,[BP+0x55] ..............;1b 66 55
SBB SP,[BP+DI+0x5566] .........;1b a3 66 55
SBB SP,[BP+DI+0x55] ...........;1b 63 55
SBB SP,[BP+DI] ................;1b 23
SBB SP,[BP+SI+0x5566] .........;1b a2 66 55
SBB SP,[BP+SI+0x55] ...........;1b 62 55
SBB SP,[BP+SI] ................;1b 22
SBB SP,[BX+0x5566] ............;1b a7 66 55
SBB SP,[BX+0x55] ..............;1b 67 55
SBB SP,[BX+DI+0x5566] .........;1b a1 66 55
SBB SP,[BX+DI+0x55] ...........;1b 61 55
SBB SP,[BX+DI] ................;1b 21
SBB SP,[BX+SI+0x5566] .........;1b a0 66 55
SBB SP,[BX+SI+0x55] ...........;1b 60 55
SBB SP,[BX+SI] ................;1b 20
SBB SP,[BX] ...................;1b 27
SBB SP,[DI+0x5566] ............;1b a5 66 55
SBB SP,[DI+0x55] ..............;1b 65 55
SBB SP,[DI] ...................;1b 25
SBB SP,[SI+0x5566] ............;1b a4 66 55
SBB SP,[SI+0x55] ..............;1b 64 55
SBB SP,[SI] ...................;1b 24
SBB WORD [0x5566],0x77 ........;83 1e 66 55 77
SBB WORD [0x5566],0x7788 ......;81 1e 66 55 88 77
SBB WORD [BP+0x5566],0x77 .....;83 9e 66 55 77
```

```
SBB WORD [BP+0x5566],0x7788 ....;81 9e 66 55 88 77
SBB WORD [BP+0x55],0x77 ........;83 5e 55 77
SBB WORD [BP+0x55],0x7788 ......;81 5e 55 88 77
SBB WORD [BP+DI+0x5566],0x77 ...;83 9b 66 55 77
SBB WORD [BP+DI+0x5566],0x7788 .;81 9b 66 55 88 77
SBB WORD [BP+DI+0x55],0x77 .....;83 5b 55 77
SBB WORD [BP+DI+0x55],0x7788 ...;81 5b 55 88 77
SBB WORD [BP+DI],0x77 ..........;83 1b 77
SBB WORD [BP+DI],0x7788 ........;81 1b 88 77
SBB WORD [BP+SI+0x5566],0x77 ...;83 9a 66 55 77
SBB WORD [BP+SI+0x5566],0x7788 .;81 9a 66 55 88 77
SBB WORD [BP+SI+0x55],0x77 .....;83 5a 55 77
SBB WORD [BP+SI+0x55],0x7788 ...;81 5a 55 88 77
SBB WORD [BP+SI],0x77 ..........;83 1a 77
SBB WORD [BP+SI],0x7788 ........;81 1a 88 77
SBB WORD [BX+0x5566],0x77 ......;83 9f 66 55 77
SBB WORD [BX+0x5566],0x7788 ....;81 9f 66 55 88 77
SBB WORD [BX+0x55],0x77 ........;83 5f 55 77
SBB WORD [BX+0x55],0x7788 ......;81 5f 55 88 77
SBB WORD [BX+DI+0x5566],0x77 ...;83 99 66 55 77
SBB WORD [BX+DI+0x5566],0x7788 .;81 99 66 55 88 77
SBB WORD [BX+DI+0x55],0x77 .....;83 59 55 77
SBB WORD [BX+DI+0x55],0x7788 ...;81 59 55 88 77
SBB WORD [BX+DI],0x77 ..........;83 19 77
SBB WORD [BX+DI],0x7788 ........;81 19 88 77
SBB WORD [BX+SI+0x5566],0x77 ...;83 98 66 55 77
SBB WORD [BX+SI+0x5566],0x7788 .;81 98 66 55 88 77
SBB WORD [BX+SI+0x55],0x77 .....;83 58 55 77
SBB WORD [BX+SI+0x55],0x7788 ...;81 58 55 88 77
SBB WORD [BX+SI],0x77 ..........;83 18 77
SBB WORD [BX+SI],0x7788 ........;81 18 88 77
SBB WORD [BX],0x77 .............;83 1f 77
SBB WORD [BX],0x7788 ...........;81 1f 88 77
SBB WORD [DI+0x5566],0x77 ......;83 9d 66 55 77
SBB WORD [DI+0x5566],0x7788 ....;81 9d 66 55 88 77
SBB WORD [DI+0x55],0x77 ........;83 5d 55 77
SBB WORD [DI+0x55],0x7788 ......;81 5d 55 88 77
SBB WORD [DI],0x77 .............;83 1d 77
SBB WORD [DI],0x7788 ...........;81 1d 88 77
SBB WORD [SI+0x5566],0x77 ......;83 9c 66 55 77
SBB WORD [SI+0x5566],0x7788 ....;81 9c 66 55 88 77
SBB WORD [SI+0x55],0x77 ........;83 5c 55 77
SBB WORD [SI+0x55],0x7788 ......;81 5c 55 88 77
SBB WORD [SI],0x77 .............;83 1c 77
SBB WORD [SI],0x7788 ...........;81 1c 88 77
SBB [0x5566],AH ...............;18 26 66 55
SBB [0x5566],AL ...............;18 06 66 55
SBB [0x5566],AX ...............;19 06 66 55
SBB [0x5566],BH ...............;18 3e 66 55
SBB [0x5566],BL ...............;18 1e 66 55
SBB [0x5566],BP ...............;19 2e 66 55
SBB [0x5566],BX ...............;19 1e 66 55
SBB [0x5566],CH ...............;18 2e 66 55
SBB [0x5566],CL ...............;18 0e 66 55
SBB [0x5566],CX ...............;19 0e 66 55
SBB [0x5566],DH ...............;18 36 66 55
SBB [0x5566],DI ...............;19 3e 66 55
SBB [0x5566],DL ...............;18 16 66 55
SBB [0x5566],DX ...............;19 16 66 55
SBB [0x5566],SI ...............;19 36 66 55
SBB [0x5566],SP ...............;19 26 66 55
SBB [BP+0x5566],AH ............;18 a6 66 55
SBB [BP+0x5566],AL ............;18 86 66 55
SBB [BP+0x5566],AX ............;19 86 66 55
SBB [BP+0x5566],BH ............;18 be 66 55
SBB [BP+0x5566],BL ............;18 9e 66 55
SBB [BP+0x5566],BP ............;19 ae 66 55
SBB [BP+0x5566],BX ............;19 9e 66 55
SBB [BP+0x5566],CH ............;18 ae 66 55
SBB [BP+0x5566],CL ............;18 8e 66 55
SBB [BP+0x5566],CX ............;19 8e 66 55
SBB [BP+0x5566],DH ............;18 b6 66 55
SBB [BP+0x5566],DI ............;19 be 66 55
SBB [BP+0x5566],DL ............;18 96 66 55
SBB [BP+0x5566],DX ............;19 96 66 55
SBB [BP+0x5566],SI ............;19 b6 66 55
SBB [BP+0x5566],SP ............;19 a6 66 55
SBB [BP+0x55],AH ..............;18 66 55
SBB [BP+0x55],AL ..............;18 46 55
SBB [BP+0x55],AX ..............;19 46 55
SBB [BP+0x55],BH ..............;18 7e 55
SBB [BP+0x55],BL ..............;18 5e 55
SBB [BP+0x55],BP ..............;19 6e 55
SBB [BP+0x55],BX ..............;19 5e 55
SBB [BP+0x55],CH ..............;18 6e 55
SBB [BP+0x55],CL ..............;18 4e 55
SBB [BP+0x55],CX ..............;19 4e 55
SBB [BP+0x55],DH ..............;18 76 55
SBB [BP+0x55],DI ..............;19 7e 55
```

```
SBB [BP+0x55],DL .................;18 56 55
SBB [BP+0x55],DX .................;19 56 55
SBB [BP+0x55],SI .................;19 76 55
SBB [BP+0x55],SP .................;19 66 55
SBB [BP+DI+0x5566],AH ...........;18 a3 66 55
SBB [BP+DI+0x5566],AL ...........;18 83 66 55
SBB [BP+DI+0x5566],AX ...........;19 83 66 55
SBB [BP+DI+0x5566],BH ...........;18 bb 66 55
SBB [BP+DI+0x5566],BL ...........;18 9b 66 55
SBB [BP+DI+0x5566],BP ...........;19 ab 66 55
SBB [BP+DI+0x5566],BX ...........;19 9b 66 55
SBB [BP+DI+0x5566],CH ...........;18 ab 66 55
SBB [BP+DI+0x5566],CL ...........;18 8b 66 55
SBB [BP+DI+0x5566],CX ...........;19 8b 66 55
SBB [BP+DI+0x5566],DH ...........;18 b3 66 55
SBB [BP+DI+0x5566],DI ...........;19 bb 66 55
SBB [BP+DI+0x5566],DL ...........;18 93 66 55
SBB [BP+DI+0x5566],DX ...........;19 93 66 55
SBB [BP+DI+0x5566],SI ...........;19 b3 66 55
SBB [BP+DI+0x5566],SP ...........;19 a3 66 55
SBB [BP+DI+0x55],AH .............;18 63 55
SBB [BP+DI+0x55],AL .............;18 43 55
SBB [BP+DI+0x55],AX .............;19 43 55
SBB [BP+DI+0x55],BH .............;18 7b 55
SBB [BP+DI+0x55],BL .............;18 5b 55
SBB [BP+DI+0x55],BP .............;19 6b 55
SBB [BP+DI+0x55],BX .............;19 5b 55
SBB [BP+DI+0x55],CH .............;18 6b 55
SBB [BP+DI+0x55],CL .............;18 4b 55
SBB [BP+DI+0x55],CX .............;19 4b 55
SBB [BP+DI+0x55],DH .............;18 73 55
SBB [BP+DI+0x55],DI .............;19 7b 55
SBB [BP+DI+0x55],DL .............;18 53 55
SBB [BP+DI+0x55],DX .............;19 53 55
SBB [BP+DI+0x55],SI .............;19 73 55
SBB [BP+DI+0x55],SP .............;19 63 55
SBB [BP+DI],AH ..................;18 23
SBB [BP+DI],AL ..................;18 03
SBB [BP+DI],AX ..................;19 03
SBB [BP+DI],BH ..................;18 3b
SBB [BP+DI],BL ..................;18 1b
SBB [BP+DI],BP ..................;19 2b
SBB [BP+DI],BX ..................;19 1b
SBB [BP+DI],CH ..................;18 2b
SBB [BP+DI],CL ..................;18 0b
SBB [BP+DI],CX ..................;19 0b
SBB [BP+DI],DH ..................;18 33
SBB [BP+DI],DI ..................;19 3b
SBB [BP+DI],DL ..................;18 13
SBB [BP+DI],DX ..................;19 13
SBB [BP+DI],SI ..................;19 33
SBB [BP+DI],SP ..................;19 23
SBB [BP+SI+0x5566],AH ...........;18 a2 66 55
SBB [BP+SI+0x5566],AL ...........;18 82 66 55
SBB [BP+SI+0x5566],AX ...........;19 82 66 55
SBB [BP+SI+0x5566],BH ...........;18 ba 66 55
SBB [BP+SI+0x5566],BL ...........;18 9a 66 55
SBB [BP+SI+0x5566],BP ...........;19 aa 66 55
SBB [BP+SI+0x5566],BX ...........;19 9a 66 55
SBB [BP+SI+0x5566],CH ...........;18 aa 66 55
SBB [BP+SI+0x5566],CL ...........;18 8a 66 55
SBB [BP+SI+0x5566],CX ...........;19 8a 66 55
SBB [BP+SI+0x5566],DH ...........;18 b2 66 55
SBB [BP+SI+0x5566],DI ...........;19 ba 66 55
SBB [BP+SI+0x5566],DL ...........;18 92 66 55
SBB [BP+SI+0x5566],DX ...........;19 92 66 55
SBB [BP+SI+0x5566],SI ...........;19 b2 66 55
SBB [BP+SI+0x5566],SP ...........;19 a2 66 55
SBB [BP+SI+0x55],AH .............;18 62 55
SBB [BP+SI+0x55],AL .............;18 42 55
SBB [BP+SI+0x55],AX .............;19 42 55
SBB [BP+SI+0x55],BH .............;18 7a 55
SBB [BP+SI+0x55],BL .............;18 5a 55
SBB [BP+SI+0x55],BP .............;19 6a 55
SBB [BP+SI+0x55],BX .............;19 5a 55
SBB [BP+SI+0x55],CH .............;18 6a 55
SBB [BP+SI+0x55],CL .............;18 4a 55
SBB [BP+SI+0x55],CX .............;19 4a 55
SBB [BP+SI+0x55],DH .............;18 72 55
SBB [BP+SI+0x55],DI .............;19 7a 55
SBB [BP+SI+0x55],DL .............;18 52 55
SBB [BP+SI+0x55],DX .............;19 52 55
SBB [BP+SI+0x55],SI .............;19 72 55
SBB [BP+SI+0x55],SP .............;19 62 55
SBB [BP+SI],AH ..................;18 22
SBB [BP+SI],AL ..................;18 02
SBB [BP+SI],AX ..................;19 02
SBB [BP+SI],BH ..................;18 3a
SBB [BP+SI],BL ..................;18 1a

SBB [BP+SI],BP ..................;19 2a
SBB [BP+SI],BX ..................;19 1a
SBB [BP+SI],CH ..................;18 2a
SBB [BP+SI],CL ..................;18 0a
SBB [BP+SI],CX ..................;19 0a
SBB [BP+SI],DH ..................;18 32
SBB [BP+SI],DI ..................;19 3a
SBB [BP+SI],DL ..................;18 12
SBB [BP+SI],DX ..................;19 12
SBB [BP+SI],SI ..................;19 32
SBB [BP+SI],SP ..................;19 22
SBB [BX+0x5566],AH ..............;18 a7 66 55
SBB [BX+0x5566],AL ..............;18 87 66 55
SBB [BX+0x5566],AX ..............;19 87 66 55
SBB [BX+0x5566],BH ..............;18 bf 66 55
SBB [BX+0x5566],BL ..............;18 9f 66 55
SBB [BX+0x5566],BP ..............;19 af 66 55
SBB [BX+0x5566],BX ..............;19 9f 66 55
SBB [BX+0x5566],CH ..............;18 af 66 55
SBB [BX+0x5566],CL ..............;18 8f 66 55
SBB [BX+0x5566],CX ..............;19 8f 66 55
SBB [BX+0x5566],DH ..............;18 b7 66 55
SBB [BX+0x5566],DI ..............;19 bf 66 55
SBB [BX+0x5566],DL ..............;18 97 66 55
SBB [BX+0x5566],DX ..............;19 97 66 55
SBB [BX+0x5566],SI ..............;19 b7 66 55
SBB [BX+0x5566],SP ..............;19 a7 66 55
SBB [BX+0x55],AH ................;18 67 55
SBB [BX+0x55],AL ................;18 47 55
SBB [BX+0x55],AX ................;19 47 55
SBB [BX+0x55],BH ................;18 7f 55
SBB [BX+0x55],BL ................;18 5f 55
SBB [BX+0x55],BP ................;19 6f 55
SBB [BX+0x55],BX ................;19 5f 55
SBB [BX+0x55],CH ................;18 6f 55
SBB [BX+0x55],CL ................;18 4f 55
SBB [BX+0x55],CX ................;19 4f 55
SBB [BX+0x55],DH ................;18 77 55
SBB [BX+0x55],DI ................;19 7f 55
SBB [BX+0x55],DL ................;18 57 55
SBB [BX+0x55],DX ................;19 57 55
SBB [BX+0x55],SI ................;19 77 55
SBB [BX+0x55],SP ................;19 67 55
SBB [BX+DI+0x5566],AH ...........;18 a1 66 55
SBB [BX+DI+0x5566],AL ...........;18 81 66 55
SBB [BX+DI+0x5566],AX ...........;19 81 66 55
SBB [BX+DI+0x5566],BH ...........;18 b9 66 55
SBB [BX+DI+0x5566],BL ...........;18 99 66 55
SBB [BX+DI+0x5566],BP ...........;19 a9 66 55
SBB [BX+DI+0x5566],BX ...........;19 99 66 55
SBB [BX+DI+0x5566],CH ...........;18 a9 66 55
SBB [BX+DI+0x5566],CL ...........;18 89 66 55
SBB [BX+DI+0x5566],CX ...........;19 89 66 55
SBB [BX+DI+0x5566],DH ...........;18 b1 66 55
SBB [BX+DI+0x5566],DI ...........;19 b9 66 55
SBB [BX+DI+0x5566],DL ...........;18 91 66 55
SBB [BX+DI+0x5566],DX ...........;19 91 66 55
SBB [BX+DI+0x5566],SI ...........;19 b1 66 55
SBB [BX+DI+0x5566],SP ...........;19 a1 66 55
SBB [BX+DI+0x55],AH .............;18 61 55
SBB [BX+DI+0x55],AL .............;18 41 55
SBB [BX+DI+0x55],AX .............;19 41 55
SBB [BX+DI+0x55],BH .............;18 79 55
SBB [BX+DI+0x55],BL .............;18 59 55
SBB [BX+DI+0x55],BP .............;19 69 55
SBB [BX+DI+0x55],BX .............;19 59 55
SBB [BX+DI+0x55],CH .............;18 69 55
SBB [BX+DI+0x55],CL .............;18 49 55
SBB [BX+DI+0x55],CX .............;19 49 55
SBB [BX+DI+0x55],DH .............;18 71 55
SBB [BX+DI+0x55],DI .............;19 79 55
SBB [BX+DI+0x55],DL .............;18 51 55
SBB [BX+DI+0x55],DX .............;19 51 55
SBB [BX+DI+0x55],SI .............;19 71 55
SBB [BX+DI+0x55],SP .............;19 61 55
SBB [BX+DI],AH ..................;18 21
SBB [BX+DI],AL ..................;18 01
SBB [BX+DI],AX ..................;19 01
SBB [BX+DI],BH ..................;18 39
SBB [BX+DI],BL ..................;18 19
SBB [BX+DI],BP ..................;19 29
SBB [BX+DI],BX ..................;19 19
SBB [BX+DI],CH ..................;18 29
SBB [BX+DI],CL ..................;18 09
SBB [BX+DI],CX ..................;19 09
SBB [BX+DI],DH ..................;18 31
SBB [BX+DI],DI ..................;19 39
SBB [BX+DI],DL ..................;18 11
SBB [BX+DI],DX ..................;19 11
```

```
SBB [BX+DI],SI .................;19 31          SBB [DI+0x55],CH ..............;18 6d 55
SBB [BX+DI],SP .................;19 21          SBB [DI+0x55],CL ..............;18 4d 55
SBB [BX+SI+0x5566],AH .........;18 a0 66 55     SBB [DI+0x55],CX ..............;19 4d 55
SBB [BX+SI+0x5566],AL .........;18 80 66 55     SBB [DI+0x55],DH ..............;18 75 55
SBB [BX+SI+0x5566],AX .........;19 80 66 55     SBB [DI+0x55],DI ..............;19 7d 55
SBB [BX+SI+0x5566],BH .........;18 b8 66 55     SBB [DI+0x55],DL ..............;18 55 55
SBB [BX+SI+0x5566],BL .........;18 98 66 55     SBB [DI+0x55],DX ..............;19 55 55
SBB [BX+SI+0x5566],BP .........;19 a8 66 55     SBB [DI+0x55],SI ..............;19 75 55
SBB [BX+SI+0x5566],BX .........;19 98 66 55     SBB [DI+0x55],SP ..............;19 65 55
SBB [BX+SI+0x5566],CH .........;18 a8 66 55     SBB [DI],AH ...................;18 25
SBB [BX+SI+0x5566],CL .........;18 88 66 55     SBB [DI],AL ...................;18 05
SBB [BX+SI+0x5566],CX .........;19 88 66 55     SBB [DI],AX ...................;19 05
SBB [BX+SI+0x5566],DH .........;18 b0 66 55     SBB [DI],BH ...................;18 3d
SBB [BX+SI+0x5566],DI .........;19 b8 66 55     SBB [DI],BL ...................;18 1d
SBB [BX+SI+0x5566],DL .........;18 90 66 55     SBB [DI],BP ...................;19 2d
SBB [BX+SI+0x5566],DX .........;19 90 66 55     SBB [DI],BX ...................;19 1d
SBB [BX+SI+0x5566],SI .........;19 b0 66 55     SBB [DI],CH ...................;18 2d
SBB [BX+SI+0x5566],SP .........;19 a0 66 55     SBB [DI],CL ...................;18 0d
SBB [BX+SI+0x55],AH ...........;18 60 55        SBB [DI],CX ...................;19 0d
SBB [BX+SI+0x55],AL ...........;18 40 55        SBB [DI],DH ...................;18 35
SBB [BX+SI+0x55],AX ...........;19 40 55        SBB [DI],DI ...................;19 3d
SBB [BX+SI+0x55],BH ...........;18 78 55        SBB [DI],DL ...................;18 15
SBB [BX+SI+0x55],BL ...........;18 58 55        SBB [DI],DX ...................;19 15
SBB [BX+SI+0x55],BP ...........;19 68 55        SBB [DI],SI ...................;19 35
SBB [BX+SI+0x55],BX ...........;19 58 55        SBB [DI],SP ...................;19 25
SBB [BX+SI+0x55],CH ...........;18 68 55        SBB [SI+0x5566],AH ............;18 a4 66 55
SBB [BX+SI+0x55],CL ...........;18 48 55        SBB [SI+0x5566],AL ............;18 84 66 55
SBB [BX+SI+0x55],CX ...........;19 48 55        SBB [SI+0x5566],AX ............;19 84 66 55
SBB [BX+SI+0x55],DH ...........;18 70 55        SBB [SI+0x5566],BH ............;18 bc 66 55
SBB [BX+SI+0x55],DI ...........;19 78 55        SBB [SI+0x5566],BL ............;18 9c 66 55
SBB [BX+SI+0x55],DL ...........;18 50 55        SBB [SI+0x5566],BP ............;19 ac 66 55
SBB [BX+SI+0x55],DX ...........;19 50 55        SBB [SI+0x5566],BX ............;19 9c 66 55
SBB [BX+SI+0x55],SI ...........;19 70 55        SBB [SI+0x5566],CH ............;18 ac 66 55
SBB [BX+SI+0x55],SP ...........;19 60 55        SBB [SI+0x5566],CL ............;18 8c 66 55
SBB [BX+SI],AH .................;18 20          SBB [SI+0x5566],CX ............;19 8c 66 55
SBB [BX+SI],AL .................;18 00          SBB [SI+0x5566],DH ............;18 b4 66 55
SBB [BX+SI],AX .................;19 00          SBB [SI+0x5566],DI ............;19 bc 66 55
SBB [BX+SI],BH .................;18 38          SBB [SI+0x5566],DL ............;18 94 66 55
SBB [BX+SI],BL .................;18 18          SBB [SI+0x5566],DX ............;19 94 66 55
SBB [BX+SI],BP .................;19 28          SBB [SI+0x5566],SI ............;19 b4 66 55
SBB [BX+SI],BX .................;19 18          SBB [SI+0x5566],SP ............;19 a4 66 55
SBB [BX+SI],CH .................;18 28          SBB [SI+0x55],AH ..............;18 64 55
SBB [BX+SI],CL .................;18 08          SBB [SI+0x55],AL ..............;18 44 55
SBB [BX+SI],CX .................;19 08          SBB [SI+0x55],AX ..............;19 44 55
SBB [BX+SI],DH .................;18 30          SBB [SI+0x55],BH ..............;18 7c 55
SBB [BX+SI],DI .................;19 38          SBB [SI+0x55],BL ..............;18 5c 55
SBB [BX+SI],DL .................;18 10          SBB [SI+0x55],BP ..............;19 6c 55
SBB [BX+SI],DX .................;19 10          SBB [SI+0x55],BX ..............;19 5c 55
SBB [BX+SI],SI .................;19 30          SBB [SI+0x55],CH ..............;18 6c 55
SBB [BX+SI],SP .................;19 20          SBB [SI+0x55],CL ..............;18 4c 55
SBB [BX],AH ....................;18 27          SBB [SI+0x55],CX ..............;19 4c 55
SBB [BX],AL ....................;18 07          SBB [SI+0x55],DH ..............;18 74 55
SBB [BX],AX ....................;19 07          SBB [SI+0x55],DI ..............;19 7c 55
SBB [BX],BH ....................;18 3f          SBB [SI+0x55],DL ..............;18 54 55
SBB [BX],BL ....................;18 1f          SBB [SI+0x55],DX ..............;19 54 55
SBB [BX],BP ....................;19 2f          SBB [SI+0x55],SI ..............;19 74 55
SBB [BX],BX ....................;19 1f          SBB [SI+0x55],SP ..............;19 64 55
SBB [BX],CH ....................;18 2f          SBB [SI],AH ...................;18 24
SBB [BX],CL ....................;18 0f          SBB [SI],AL ...................;18 04
SBB [BX],CX ....................;19 0f          SBB [SI],AX ...................;19 04
SBB [BX],DH ....................;18 37          SBB [SI],BH ...................;18 3c
SBB [BX],DI ....................;19 3f          SBB [SI],BL ...................;18 1c
SBB [BX],DL ....................;18 17          SBB [SI],BP ...................;19 2c
SBB [BX],DX ....................;19 17          SBB [SI],BX ...................;19 1c
SBB [BX],SI ....................;19 37          SBB [SI],CH ...................;18 2c
SBB [BX],SP ....................;19 27          SBB [SI],CL ...................;18 0c
SBB [DI+0x5566],AH ............;18 a5 66 55     SBB [SI],CX ...................;19 0c
SBB [DI+0x5566],AL ............;18 85 66 55     SBB [SI],DH ...................;18 34
SBB [DI+0x5566],AX ............;19 85 66 55     SBB [SI],DI ...................;19 3c
SBB [DI+0x5566],BH ............;18 bd 66 55     SBB [SI],DL ...................;18 14
SBB [DI+0x5566],BL ............;18 9d 66 55     SBB [SI],DX ...................;19 14
SBB [DI+0x5566],BP ............;19 ad 66 55     SBB [SI],SI ...................;19 34
SBB [DI+0x5566],BX ............;19 9d 66 55     SBB [SI],SP ...................;19 24
SBB [DI+0x5566],CH ............;18 ad 66 55     SCASB .........................;ae
SBB [DI+0x5566],CL ............;18 8d 66 55     SCASW .........................;af
SBB [DI+0x5566],CX ............;19 8d 66 55     SHL AH,1 ......................;d0 e4
SBB [DI+0x5566],DH ............;18 b5 66 55     SHL AH,CL .....................;d2 e4
SBB [DI+0x5566],DI ............;19 bd 66 55     SHL AL,1 ......................;d0 e0
SBB [DI+0x5566],DL ............;18 95 66 55     SHL AL,CL .....................;d2 e0
SBB [DI+0x5566],DX ............;19 95 66 55     SHL AX,1 ......................;d1 e0
SBB [DI+0x5566],SI ............;19 b5 66 55     SHL AX,CL .....................;d3 e0
SBB [DI+0x5566],SP ............;19 a5 66 55     SHL BH,1 ......................;d0 e7
SBB [DI+0x55],AH ..............;18 65 55        SHL BH,CL .....................;d2 e7
SBB [DI+0x55],AL ..............;18 45 55        SHL BL,1 ......................;d0 e3
SBB [DI+0x55],AX ..............;19 45 55        SHL BL,CL .....................;d2 e3
SBB [DI+0x55],BH ..............;18 7d 55        SHL BP,1 ......................;d1 e5
SBB [DI+0x55],BL ..............;18 5d 55        SHL BP,CL .....................;d3 e5
SBB [DI+0x55],BP ..............;19 6d 55        SHL BX,1 ......................;d1 e3
SBB [DI+0x55],BX ..............;19 5d 55        SHL BX,CL .....................;d3 e3
```

```
SHL BYTE [0x5566],1 ...........;d0 26 66 55
SHL BYTE [0x5566],CL ..........;d2 26 66 55
SHL BYTE [BP+0x5566],1 ........;d0 a6 66 55
SHL BYTE [BP+0x5566],CL .......;d2 a6 66 55
SHL BYTE [BP+0x55],1 ..........;d0 66 55
SHL BYTE [BP+0x55],CL .........;d2 66 55
SHL BYTE [BP+DI+0x5566],1 .....;d0 a3 66 55
SHL BYTE [BP+DI+0x5566],CL ....;d2 a3 66 55
SHL BYTE [BP+DI+0x55],1 .......;d0 63 55
SHL BYTE [BP+DI+0x55],CL ......;d2 63 55
SHL BYTE [BP+DI],1 ............;d0 23
SHL BYTE [BP+DI],CL ...........;d2 23
SHL BYTE [BP+SI+0x5566],1 .....;d0 a2 66 55
SHL BYTE [BP+SI+0x5566],CL ....;d2 a2 66 55
SHL BYTE [BP+SI+0x55],1 .......;d0 62 55
SHL BYTE [BP+SI+0x55],CL ......;d2 62 55
SHL BYTE [BP+SI],1 ............;d0 22
SHL BYTE [BP+SI],CL ...........;d2 22
SHL BYTE [BX+0x5566],1 ........;d0 a7 66 55
SHL BYTE [BX+0x5566],CL .......;d2 a7 66 55
SHL BYTE [BX+0x55],1 ..........;d0 67 55
SHL BYTE [BX+0x55],CL .........;d2 67 55
SHL BYTE [BX+DI+0x5566],1 .....;d0 a1 66 55
SHL BYTE [BX+DI+0x5566],CL ....;d2 a1 66 55
SHL BYTE [BX+DI+0x55],1 .......;d0 61 55
SHL BYTE [BX+DI+0x55],CL ......;d2 61 55
SHL BYTE [BX+DI],1 ............;d0 21
SHL BYTE [BX+DI],CL ...........;d2 21
SHL BYTE [BX+SI+0x5566],1 .....;d0 a0 66 55
SHL BYTE [BX+SI+0x5566],CL ....;d2 a0 66 55
SHL BYTE [BX+SI+0x55],1 .......;d0 60 55
SHL BYTE [BX+SI+0x55],CL ......;d2 60 55
SHL BYTE [BX+SI],1 ............;d0 20
SHL BYTE [BX+SI],CL ...........;d2 20
SHL BYTE [BX],1 ...............;d0 27
SHL BYTE [BX],CL ..............;d2 27
SHL BYTE [DI+0x5566],1 ........;d0 a5 66 55
SHL BYTE [DI+0x5566],CL .......;d2 a5 66 55
SHL BYTE [DI+0x55],1 ..........;d0 65 55
SHL BYTE [DI+0x55],CL .........;d2 65 55
SHL BYTE [DI],1 ...............;d0 25
SHL BYTE [DI],CL ..............;d2 25
SHL BYTE [SI+0x5566],1 ........;d0 a4 66 55
SHL BYTE [SI+0x5566],CL .......;d2 a4 66 55
SHL BYTE [SI+0x55],1 ..........;d0 64 55
SHL BYTE [SI+0x55],CL .........;d2 64 55
SHL BYTE [SI],1 ...............;d0 24
SHL BYTE [SI],CL ..............;d2 24
SHL CH,1 .......................;d0 e5
SHL CH,CL .....................;d2 e5
SHL CL,1 .......................;d0 e1
SHL CL,CL .....................;d2 e1
SHL CX,1 .......................;d1 e1
SHL CX,CL .....................;d3 e1
SHL DH,1 .......................;d0 e6
SHL DH,CL .....................;d2 e6
SHL DI,1 .......................;d1 e7
SHL DI,CL .....................;d3 e7
SHL DL,1 .......................;d0 e2
SHL DL,CL .....................;d2 e2
SHL DX,1 .......................;d1 e2
SHL DX,CL .....................;d3 e2
SHL SI,1 .......................;d1 e6
SHL SI,CL .....................;d3 e6
SHL SP,1 .......................;d1 e4
SHL SP,CL .....................;d3 e4
SHL WORD [0x5566],1 ...........;d1 26 66 55
SHL WORD [0x5566],CL ..........;d3 26 66 55
SHL WORD [BP+0x5566],1 ........;d1 a6 66 55
SHL WORD [BP+0x5566],CL .......;d3 a6 66 55
SHL WORD [BP+0x55],1 ..........;d1 66 55
SHL WORD [BP+0x55],CL .........;d3 66 55
SHL WORD [BP+DI+0x5566],1 .....;d1 a3 66 55
SHL WORD [BP+DI+0x5566],CL ....;d3 a3 66 55
SHL WORD [BP+DI+0x55],1 .......;d1 63 55
SHL WORD [BP+DI+0x55],CL ......;d3 63 55
SHL WORD [BP+DI],1 ............;d1 23
SHL WORD [BP+DI],CL ...........;d3 23
SHL WORD [BP+SI+0x5566],1 .....;d1 a2 66 55
SHL WORD [BP+SI+0x5566],CL ....;d3 a2 66 55
SHL WORD [BP+SI+0x55],1 .......;d1 62 55
SHL WORD [BP+SI+0x55],CL ......;d3 62 55
SHL WORD [BP+SI],1 ............;d1 22
SHL WORD [BP+SI],CL ...........;d3 22
SHL WORD [BX+0x5566],1 ........;d1 a7 66 55
SHL WORD [BX+0x5566],CL .......;d3 a7 66 55
SHL WORD [BX+0x55],1 ..........;d1 67 55
SHL WORD [BX+0x55],CL .........;d3 67 55
SHL WORD [BX+DI+0x5566],1 .....;d1 a1 66 55

SHL WORD [BX+DI+0x5566],CL ....;d3 a1 66 55
SHL WORD [BX+DI+0x55],1 .......;d1 61 55
SHL WORD [BX+DI+0x55],CL ......;d3 61 55
SHL WORD [BX+DI],1 ............;d1 21
SHL WORD [BX+DI],CL ...........;d3 21
SHL WORD [BX+SI+0x5566],1 .....;d1 a0 66 55
SHL WORD [BX+SI+0x5566],CL ....;d3 a0 66 55
SHL WORD [BX+SI+0x55],1 .......;d1 60 55
SHL WORD [BX+SI+0x55],CL ......;d3 60 55
SHL WORD [BX+SI],1 ............;d1 20
SHL WORD [BX+SI],CL ...........;d3 20
SHL WORD [BX],1 ...............;d1 27
SHL WORD [BX],CL ..............;d3 27
SHL WORD [DI+0x5566],1 ........;d1 a5 66 55
SHL WORD [DI+0x5566],CL .......;d3 a5 66 55
SHL WORD [DI+0x55],1 ..........;d1 65 55
SHL WORD [DI+0x55],CL .........;d3 65 55
SHL WORD [DI],1 ...............;d1 25
SHL WORD [DI],CL ..............;d3 25
SHL WORD [SI+0x5566],1 ........;d1 a4 66 55
SHL WORD [SI+0x5566],CL .......;d3 a4 66 55
SHL WORD [SI+0x55],1 ..........;d1 64 55
SHL WORD [SI+0x55],CL .........;d3 64 55
SHL WORD [SI],1 ...............;d1 24
SHL WORD [SI],CL ..............;d3 24
SHR AH,1 .......................;d0 ec
SHR AH,CL .....................;d2 ec
SHR AL,1 .......................;d0 e8
SHR AL,CL .....................;d2 e8
SHR AX,1 .......................;d1 e8
SHR AX,CL .....................;d3 e8
SHR BH,1 .......................;d0 ef
SHR BH,CL .....................;d2 ef
SHR BL,1 .......................;d0 eb
SHR BL,CL .....................;d2 eb
SHR BP,1 .......................;d1 ed
SHR BP,CL .....................;d3 ed
SHR BX,1 .......................;d1 eb
SHR BX,CL .....................;d3 eb
SHR BYTE [0x5566],1 ...........;d0 2e 66 55
SHR BYTE [0x5566],CL ..........;d2 2e 66 55
SHR BYTE [BP+0x5566],1 ........;d0 ae 66 55
SHR BYTE [BP+0x5566],CL .......;d2 ae 66 55
SHR BYTE [BP+0x55],1 ..........;d0 6e 55
SHR BYTE [BP+0x55],CL .........;d2 6e 55
SHR BYTE [BP+DI+0x5566],1 .....;d0 ab 66 55
SHR BYTE [BP+DI+0x5566],CL ....;d2 ab 66 55
SHR BYTE [BP+DI+0x55],1 .......;d0 6b 55
SHR BYTE [BP+DI+0x55],CL ......;d2 6b 55
SHR BYTE [BP+DI],1 ............;d0 2b
SHR BYTE [BP+DI],CL ...........;d2 2b
SHR BYTE [BP+SI+0x5566],1 .....;d0 aa 66 55
SHR BYTE [BP+SI+0x5566],CL ....;d2 aa 66 55
SHR BYTE [BP+SI+0x55],1 .......;d0 6a 55
SHR BYTE [BP+SI+0x55],CL ......;d2 6a 55
SHR BYTE [BP+SI],1 ............;d0 2a
SHR BYTE [BP+SI],CL ...........;d2 2a
SHR BYTE [BX+0x5566],1 ........;d0 af 66 55
SHR BYTE [BX+0x5566],CL .......;d2 af 66 55
SHR BYTE [BX+0x55],1 ..........;d0 6f 55
SHR BYTE [BX+0x55],CL .........;d2 6f 55
SHR BYTE [BX+DI+0x5566],1 .....;d0 a9 66 55
SHR BYTE [BX+DI+0x5566],CL ....;d2 a9 66 55
SHR BYTE [BX+DI+0x55],1 .......;d0 69 55
SHR BYTE [BX+DI+0x55],CL ......;d2 69 55
SHR BYTE [BX+DI],1 ............;d0 29
SHR BYTE [BX+DI],CL ...........;d2 29
SHR BYTE [BX+SI+0x5566],1 .....;d0 a8 66 55
SHR BYTE [BX+SI+0x5566],CL ....;d2 a8 66 55
SHR BYTE [BX+SI+0x55],1 .......;d0 68 55
SHR BYTE [BX+SI+0x55],CL ......;d2 68 55
SHR BYTE [BX+SI],1 ............;d0 28
SHR BYTE [BX+SI],CL ...........;d2 28
SHR BYTE [BX],1 ...............;d0 2f
SHR BYTE [BX],CL ..............;d2 2f
SHR BYTE [DI+0x5566],1 ........;d0 ad 66 55
SHR BYTE [DI+0x5566],CL .......;d2 ad 66 55
SHR BYTE [DI+0x55],1 ..........;d0 6d 55
SHR BYTE [DI+0x55],CL .........;d2 6d 55
SHR BYTE [DI],1 ...............;d0 2d
SHR BYTE [DI],CL ..............;d2 2d
SHR BYTE [SI+0x5566],1 ........;d0 ac 66 55
SHR BYTE [SI+0x5566],CL .......;d2 ac 66 55
SHR BYTE [SI+0x55],1 ..........;d0 6c 55
SHR BYTE [SI+0x55],CL .........;d2 6c 55
SHR BYTE [SI],1 ...............;d0 2c
SHR BYTE [SI],CL ..............;d2 2c
SHR CH,1 .......................;d0 ed
SHR CH,CL .....................;d2 ed
```

SHR CL,1	;d0 e9
SHR CL,CL	;d2 e9
SHR CX,1	;d1 e9
SHR CX,CL	;d3 e9
SHR DH,1	;d0 ee
SHR DH,CL	;d2 ee
SHR DI,1	;d1 ef
SHR DI,CL	;d3 ef
SHR DL,1	;d0 ea
SHR DL,CL	;d2 ea
SHR DX,1	;d1 ea
SHR DX,CL	;d3 ea
SHR SI,1	;d1 ee
SHR SI,CL	;d3 ee
SHR SP,1	;d1 ec
SHR SP,CL	;d3 ec
SHR WORD [0x5566],1	;d1 2e 66 55
SHR WORD [0x5566],CL	;d3 2e 66 55
SHR WORD [BP+0x5566],1	;d1 ae 66 55
SHR WORD [BP+0x5566],CL	;d3 ae 66 55
SHR WORD [BP+0x55],1	;d1 6e 55
SHR WORD [BP+0x55],CL	;d3 6e 55
SHR WORD [BP+DI+0x5566],1	;d1 ab 66 55
SHR WORD [BP+DI+0x5566],CL	;d3 ab 66 55
SHR WORD [BP+DI+0x55],1	;d1 6b 55
SHR WORD [BP+DI+0x55],CL	;d3 6b 55
SHR WORD [BP+DI],1	;d1 2b
SHR WORD [BP+DI],CL	;d3 2b
SHR WORD [BP+SI+0x5566],1	;d1 aa 66 55
SHR WORD [BP+SI+0x5566],CL	;d3 aa 66 55
SHR WORD [BP+SI+0x55],1	;d1 6a 55
SHR WORD [BP+SI+0x55],CL	;d3 6a 55
SHR WORD [BP+SI],1	;d1 2a
SHR WORD [BP+SI],CL	;d3 2a
SHR WORD [BX+0x5566],1	;d1 af 66 55
SHR WORD [BX+0x5566],CL	;d3 af 66 55
SHR WORD [BX+0x55],1	;d1 6f 55
SHR WORD [BX+0x55],CL	;d3 6f 55
SHR WORD [BX+DI+0x5566],1	;d1 a9 66 55
SHR WORD [BX+DI+0x5566],CL	;d3 a9 66 55
SHR WORD [BX+DI+0x55],1	;d1 69 55
SHR WORD [BX+DI+0x55],CL	;d3 69 55
SHR WORD [BX+DI],1	;d1 29
SHR WORD [BX+DI],CL	;d3 29
SHR WORD [BX+SI+0x5566],1	;d1 a8 66 55
SHR WORD [BX+SI+0x5566],CL	;d3 a8 66 55
SHR WORD [BX+SI+0x55],1	;d1 68 55
SHR WORD [BX+SI+0x55],CL	;d3 68 55
SHR WORD [BX+SI],1	;d1 28
SHR WORD [BX+SI],CL	;d3 28
SHR WORD [BX],1	;d1 2f
SHR WORD [BX],CL	;d3 2f
SHR WORD [DI+0x5566],1	;d1 ad 66 55
SHR WORD [DI+0x5566],CL	;d3 ad 66 55
SHR WORD [DI+0x55],1	;d1 6d 55
SHR WORD [DI+0x55],CL	;d3 6d 55
SHR WORD [DI],1	;d1 2d
SHR WORD [DI],CL	;d3 2d
SHR WORD [SI+0x5566],1	;d1 ac 66 55
SHR WORD [SI+0x5566],CL	;d3 ac 66 55
SHR WORD [SI+0x55],1	;d1 6c 55
SHR WORD [SI+0x55],CL	;d3 6c 55
SHR WORD [SI],1	;d1 2c
SHR WORD [SI],CL	;d3 2c
SS	;36
STC	;f9
STD	;fd
STI	;fb
STOSB	;aa
STOSW	;ab
SUB AH,0x88	;80 ec 88
SUB AH,AH	;28 e4
SUB AH,AL	;28 c4
SUB AH,BH	;28 fc
SUB AH,BL	;28 dc
SUB AH,CH	;28 ec
SUB AH,CL	;28 cc
SUB AH,DH	;28 f4
SUB AH,DL	;28 d4
SUB AH,[0x5566]	;2a 26 66 55
SUB AH,[BP+0x5566]	;2a a6 66 55
SUB AH,[BP+0x55]	;2a 66 55
SUB AH,[BP+DI+0x5566]	;2a a3 66 55
SUB AH,[BP+DI+0x55]	;2a 63 55
SUB AH,[BP+DI]	;2a 23
SUB AH,[BP+SI+0x5566]	;2a a2 66 55
SUB AH,[BP+SI+0x55]	;2a 62 55
SUB AH,[BP+SI]	;2a 22
SUB AH,[BX+0x5566]	;2a a7 66 55
SUB AH,[BX+0x55]	;2a 67 55
SUB AH,[BX+DI+0x5566]	;2a a1 66 55
SUB AH,[BX+DI+0x55]	;2a 61 55
SUB AH,[BX+DI]	;2a 21
SUB AH,[BX+SI+0x5566]	;2a a0 66 55
SUB AH,[BX+SI+0x55]	;2a 60 55
SUB AH,[BX+SI]	;2a 20
SUB AH,[BX]	;2a 27
SUB AH,[DI+0x5566]	;2a a5 66 55
SUB AH,[DI+0x55]	;2a 65 55
SUB AH,[DI]	;2a 25
SUB AH,[SI+0x5566]	;2a a4 66 55
SUB AH,[SI+0x55]	;2a 64 55
SUB AH,[SI]	;2a 24
SUB AL,0x55	;2c 55
SUB AL,0x88	;80 e8 88
SUB AL,AH	;28 e0
SUB AL,AL	;28 c0
SUB AL,BH	;28 f8
SUB AL,BL	;28 d8
SUB AL,CH	;28 e8
SUB AL,CL	;28 c8
SUB AL,DH	;28 f0
SUB AL,DL	;28 d0
SUB AL,[0x5566]	;2a 06 66 55
SUB AL,[BP+0x5566]	;2a 86 66 55
SUB AL,[BP+0x55]	;2a 46 55
SUB AL,[BP+DI+0x5566]	;2a 83 66 55
SUB AL,[BP+DI+0x55]	;2a 43 55
SUB AL,[BP+DI]	;2a 03
SUB AL,[BP+SI+0x5566]	;2a 82 66 55
SUB AL,[BP+SI+0x55]	;2a 42 55
SUB AL,[BP+SI]	;2a 02
SUB AL,[BX+0x5566]	;2a 87 66 55
SUB AL,[BX+0x55]	;2a 47 55
SUB AL,[BX+DI+0x5566]	;2a 81 66 55
SUB AL,[BX+DI+0x55]	;2a 41 55
SUB AL,[BX+DI]	;2a 01
SUB AL,[BX+SI+0x5566]	;2a 80 66 55
SUB AL,[BX+SI+0x55]	;2a 40 55
SUB AL,[BX+SI]	;2a 00
SUB AL,[BX]	;2a 07
SUB AL,[DI+0x5566]	;2a 85 66 55
SUB AL,[DI+0x55]	;2a 45 55
SUB AL,[DI]	;2a 05
SUB AL,[SI+0x5566]	;2a 84 66 55
SUB AL,[SI+0x55]	;2a 44 55
SUB AL,[SI]	;2a 04
SUB AX,0x5566	;2d 66 55
SUB AX,0x77	;83 e8 77
SUB AX,0x7788	;81 e8 88 77
SUB AX,AX	;29 c0
SUB AX,BP	;29 e8
SUB AX,BX	;29 d8
SUB AX,CX	;29 c8
SUB AX,DI	;29 f8
SUB AX,DX	;29 d0
SUB AX,SI	;29 f0
SUB AX,SP	;29 e0
SUB AX,[0x5566]	;2b 06 66 55
SUB AX,[BP+0x5566]	;2b 86 66 55
SUB AX,[BP+0x55]	;2b 46 55
SUB AX,[BP+DI+0x5566]	;2b 83 66 55
SUB AX,[BP+DI+0x55]	;2b 43 55
SUB AX,[BP+DI]	;2b 03
SUB AX,[BP+SI+0x5566]	;2b 82 66 55
SUB AX,[BP+SI+0x55]	;2b 42 55
SUB AX,[BP+SI]	;2b 02
SUB AX,[BX+0x5566]	;2b 87 66 55
SUB AX,[BX+0x55]	;2b 47 55
SUB AX,[BX+DI+0x5566]	;2b 81 66 55
SUB AX,[BX+DI+0x55]	;2b 41 55
SUB AX,[BX+DI]	;2b 01
SUB AX,[BX+SI+0x5566]	;2b 80 66 55
SUB AX,[BX+SI+0x55]	;2b 40 55
SUB AX,[BX+SI]	;2b 00
SUB AX,[BX]	;2b 07
SUB AX,[DI+0x5566]	;2b 85 66 55
SUB AX,[DI+0x55]	;2b 45 55
SUB AX,[DI]	;2b 05
SUB AX,[SI+0x5566]	;2b 84 66 55
SUB AX,[SI+0x55]	;2b 44 55
SUB AX,[SI]	;2b 04
SUB BH,0x88	;80 ef 88
SUB BH,AH	;28 e7
SUB BH,AL	;28 c7
SUB BH,BH	;28 ff
SUB BH,BL	;28 df
SUB BH,CH	;28 ef

```
SUB BH,CL .......................;28 cf
SUB BH,DH .......................;28 f7
SUB BH,DL .......................;28 d7
SUB BH,[0x5566] .................;2a 3e 66 55
SUB BH,[BP+0x5566] ..............;2a be 66 55
SUB BH,[BP+0x55] ................;2a 7e 55
SUB BH,[BP+DI+0x5566] ...........;2a bb 66 55
SUB BH,[BP+DI+0x55] .............;2a 7b 55
SUB BH,[BP+DI] ..................;2a 3b
SUB BH,[BP+SI+0x5566] ...........;2a ba 66 55
SUB BH,[BP+SI+0x55] .............;2a 7a 55
SUB BH,[BP+SI] ..................;2a 3a
SUB BH,[BX+0x5566] ..............;2a bf 66 55
SUB BH,[BX+0x55] ................;2a 7f 55
SUB BH,[BX+DI+0x5566] ...........;2a b9 66 55
SUB BH,[BX+DI+0x55] .............;2a 79 55
SUB BH,[BX+DI] ..................;2a 39
SUB BH,[BX+SI+0x5566] ...........;2a b8 66 55
SUB BH,[BX+SI+0x55] .............;2a 78 55
SUB BH,[BX+SI] ..................;2a 38
SUB BH,[BX] .....................;2a 3f
SUB BH,[DI+0x5566] ..............;2a bd 66 55
SUB BH,[DI+0x55] ................;2a 7d 55
SUB BH,[DI] .....................;2a 3d
SUB BH,[SI+0x5566] ..............;2a bc 66 55
SUB BH,[SI+0x55] ................;2a 7c 55
SUB BH,[SI] .....................;2a 3c
SUB BL,0x88 .....................;80 eb 88
SUB BL,AH .......................;28 e3
SUB BL,AL .......................;28 c3
SUB BL,BH .......................;28 fb
SUB BL,BL .......................;28 db
SUB BL,CH .......................;28 eb
SUB BL,CL .......................;28 cb
SUB BL,DH .......................;28 f3
SUB BL,DL .......................;28 d3
SUB BL,[0x5566] .................;2a 1e 66 55
SUB BL,[BP+0x5566] ..............;2a 9e 66 55
SUB BL,[BP+0x55] ................;2a 5e 55
SUB BL,[BP+DI+0x5566] ...........;2a 9b 66 55
SUB BL,[BP+DI+0x55] .............;2a 5b 55
SUB BL,[BP+DI] ..................;2a 1b
SUB BL,[BP+SI+0x5566] ...........;2a 9a 66 55
SUB BL,[BP+SI+0x55] .............;2a 5a 55
SUB BL,[BP+SI] ..................;2a 1a
SUB BL,[BX+0x5566] ..............;2a 9f 66 55
SUB BL,[BX+0x55] ................;2a 5f 55
SUB BL,[BX+DI+0x5566] ...........;2a 99 66 55
SUB BL,[BX+DI+0x55] .............;2a 59 55
SUB BL,[BX+DI] ..................;2a 19
SUB BL,[BX+SI+0x5566] ...........;2a 98 66 55
SUB BL,[BX+SI+0x55] .............;2a 58 55
SUB BL,[BX+SI] ..................;2a 18
SUB BL,[BX] .....................;2a 1f
SUB BL,[DI+0x5566] ..............;2a 9d 66 55
SUB BL,[DI+0x55] ................;2a 5d 55
SUB BL,[DI] .....................;2a 1d
SUB BL,[SI+0x5566] ..............;2a 9c 66 55
SUB BL,[SI+0x55] ................;2a 5c 55
SUB BL,[SI] .....................;2a 1c
SUB BP,0x77 .....................;83 ed 77
SUB BP,0x7788 ...................;81 ed 88 77
SUB BP,AX .......................;29 c5
SUB BP,BP .......................;29 ed
SUB BP,BX .......................;29 dd
SUB BP,CX .......................;29 cd
SUB BP,DI .......................;29 fd
SUB BP,DX .......................;29 d5
SUB BP,SI .......................;29 f5
SUB BP,SP .......................;29 e5
SUB BP,[0x5566] .................;2b 2e 66 55
SUB BP,[BP+0x5566] ..............;2b ae 66 55
SUB BP,[BP+0x55] ................;2b 6e 55
SUB BP,[BP+DI+0x5566] ...........;2b ab 66 55
SUB BP,[BP+DI+0x55] .............;2b 6b 55
SUB BP,[BP+DI] ..................;2b 2b
SUB BP,[BP+SI+0x5566] ...........;2b aa 66 55
SUB BP,[BP+SI+0x55] .............;2b 6a 55
SUB BP,[BP+SI] ..................;2b 2a
SUB BP,[BX+0x5566] ..............;2b af 66 55
SUB BP,[BX+0x55] ................;2b 6f 55
SUB BP,[BX+DI+0x5566] ...........;2b a9 66 55
SUB BP,[BX+DI+0x55] .............;2b 69 55
SUB BP,[BX+DI] ..................;2b 29
SUB BP,[BX+SI+0x5566] ...........;2b a8 66 55
SUB BP,[BX+SI+0x55] .............;2b 68 55
SUB BP,[BX+SI] ..................;2b 28
SUB BP,[BX] .....................;2b 2f
SUB BP,[DI+0x5566] ..............;2b ad 66 55

SUB BP,[DI+0x55] ................;2b 6d 55
SUB BP,[DI] .....................;2b 2d
SUB BP,[SI+0x5566] ..............;2b ac 66 55
SUB BP,[SI+0x55] ................;2b 6c 55
SUB BP,[SI] .....................;2b 2c
SUB BX,0x77 .....................;83 eb 77
SUB BX,0x7788 ...................;81 eb 88 77
SUB BX,AX .......................;29 c3
SUB BX,BP .......................;29 eb
SUB BX,BX .......................;29 db
SUB BX,CX .......................;29 cb
SUB BX,DI .......................;29 fb
SUB BX,DX .......................;29 d3
SUB BX,SI .......................;29 f3
SUB BX,SP .......................;29 e3
SUB BX,[0x5566] .................;2b 1e 66 55
SUB BX,[BP+0x5566] ..............;2b 9e 66 55
SUB BX,[BP+0x55] ................;2b 5e 55
SUB BX,[BP+DI+0x5566] ...........;2b 9b 66 55
SUB BX,[BP+DI+0x55] .............;2b 5b 55
SUB BX,[BP+DI] ..................;2b 1b
SUB BX,[BP+SI+0x5566] ...........;2b 9a 66 55
SUB BX,[BP+SI+0x55] .............;2b 5a 55
SUB BX,[BP+SI] ..................;2b 1a
SUB BX,[BX+0x5566] ..............;2b 9f 66 55
SUB BX,[BX+0x55] ................;2b 5f 55
SUB BX,[BX+DI+0x5566] ...........;2b 99 66 55
SUB BX,[BX+DI+0x55] .............;2b 59 55
SUB BX,[BX+DI] ..................;2b 19
SUB BX,[BX+SI+0x5566] ...........;2b 98 66 55
SUB BX,[BX+SI+0x55] .............;2b 58 55
SUB BX,[BX+SI] ..................;2b 18
SUB BX,[BX] .....................;2b 1f
SUB BX,[DI+0x5566] ..............;2b 9d 66 55
SUB BX,[DI+0x55] ................;2b 5d 55
SUB BX,[DI] .....................;2b 1d
SUB BX,[SI+0x5566] ..............;2b 9c 66 55
SUB BX,[SI+0x55] ................;2b 5c 55
SUB BX,[SI] .....................;2b 1c
SUB BYTE [0x5566],0x88 .........;80 2e 66 55 88
SUB BYTE [BP+0x5566],0x88 ......;80 ae 66 55 88
SUB BYTE [BP+0x55],0x88 ........;80 6e 55 88
SUB BYTE [BP+DI+0x5566],0x88 ...;80 ab 66 55 88
SUB BYTE [BP+DI+0x55],0x88 .....;80 6b 55 88
SUB BYTE [BP+DI],0x88 ..........;80 2b 88
SUB BYTE [BP+SI+0x5566],0x88 ...;80 aa 66 55 88
SUB BYTE [BP+SI+0x55],0x88 .....;80 6a 55 88
SUB BYTE [BP+SI],0x88 ..........;80 2a 88
SUB BYTE [BX+0x5566],0x88 ......;80 af 66 55 88
SUB BYTE [BX+0x55],0x88 ........;80 6f 55 88
SUB BYTE [BX+DI+0x5566],0x88 ...;80 a9 66 55 88
SUB BYTE [BX+DI+0x55],0x88 .....;80 69 55 88
SUB BYTE [BX+DI],0x88 ..........;80 29 88
SUB BYTE [BX+SI+0x5566],0x88 ...;80 a8 66 55 88
SUB BYTE [BX+SI+0x55],0x88 .....;80 68 55 88
SUB BYTE [BX+SI],0x88 ..........;80 28 88
SUB BYTE [BX],0x88 .............;80 2f 88
SUB BYTE [DI+0x5566],0x88 ......;80 ad 66 55 88
SUB BYTE [DI+0x55],0x88 ........;80 6d 55 88
SUB BYTE [DI],0x88 .............;80 2d 88
SUB BYTE [SI+0x5566],0x88 ......;80 ac 66 55 88
SUB BYTE [SI+0x55],0x88 ........;80 6c 55 88
SUB BYTE [SI],0x88 .............;80 2c 88
SUB CH,0x88 .....................;80 ed 88
SUB CH,AH .......................;28 e5
SUB CH,AL .......................;28 c5
SUB CH,BH .......................;28 fd
SUB CH,BL .......................;28 dd
SUB CH,CH .......................;28 ed
SUB CH,CL .......................;28 cd
SUB CH,DH .......................;28 f5
SUB CH,DL .......................;28 d5
SUB CH,[0x5566] .................;2a 2e 66 55
SUB CH,[BP+0x5566] ..............;2a ae 66 55
SUB CH,[BP+0x55] ................;2a 6e 55
SUB CH,[BP+DI+0x5566] ...........;2a ab 66 55
SUB CH,[BP+DI+0x55] .............;2a 6b 55
SUB CH,[BP+DI] ..................;2a 2b
SUB CH,[BP+SI+0x5566] ...........;2a aa 66 55
SUB CH,[BP+SI+0x55] .............;2a 6a 55
SUB CH,[BP+SI] ..................;2a 2a
SUB CH,[BX+0x5566] ..............;2a af 66 55
SUB CH,[BX+0x55] ................;2a 6f 55
SUB CH,[BX+DI+0x5566] ...........;2a a9 66 55
SUB CH,[BX+DI+0x55] .............;2a 69 55
SUB CH,[BX+DI] ..................;2a 29
SUB CH,[BX+SI+0x5566] ...........;2a a8 66 55
SUB CH,[BX+SI+0x55] .............;2a 68 55
SUB CH,[BX+SI] ..................;2a 28
```

```
SUB CH,[BX] .....................;2a 2f
SUB CH,[DI+0x5566] .............;2a ad 66 55
SUB CH,[DI+0x55] ...............;2a 6d 55
SUB CH,[DI] ....................;2a 2d
SUB CH,[SI+0x5566] .............;2a ac 66 55
SUB CH,[SI+0x55] ...............;2a 6c 55
SUB CH,[SI] ....................;2a 2c
SUB CL,0x88 ....................;80 e9 88
SUB CL,AH ......................;28 e1
SUB CL,AL ......................;28 c1
SUB CL,BH ......................;28 f9
SUB CL,BL ......................;28 d9
SUB CL,CH ......................;28 e9
SUB CL,CL ......................;28 c9
SUB CL,DH ......................;28 f1
SUB CL,DL ......................;28 d1
SUB CL,[0x5566] ................;2a 0e 66 55
SUB CL,[BP+0x5566] .............;2a 8e 66 55
SUB CL,[BP+0x55] ...............;2a 4e 55
SUB CL,[BP+DI+0x5566] ..........;2a 8b 66 55
SUB CL,[BP+DI+0x55] ............;2a 4b 55
SUB CL,[BP+DI] .................;2a 0b
SUB CL,[BP+SI+0x5566] ..........;2a 8a 66 55
SUB CL,[BP+SI+0x55] ............;2a 4a 55
SUB CL,[BP+SI] .................;2a 0a
SUB CL,[BX+0x5566] .............;2a 8f 66 55
SUB CL,[BX+0x55] ...............;2a 4f 55
SUB CL,[BX+DI+0x5566] ..........;2a 89 66 55
SUB CL,[BX+DI+0x55] ............;2a 49 55
SUB CL,[BX+DI] .................;2a 09
SUB CL,[BX+SI+0x5566] ..........;2a 88 66 55
SUB CL,[BX+SI+0x55] ............;2a 48 55
SUB CL,[BX+SI] .................;2a 08
SUB CL,[BX] ....................;2a 0f
SUB CL,[DI+0x5566] .............;2a 8d 66 55
SUB CL,[DI+0x55] ...............;2a 4d 55
SUB CL,[DI] ....................;2a 0d
SUB CL,[SI+0x5566] .............;2a 8c 66 55
SUB CL,[SI+0x55] ...............;2a 4c 55
SUB CL,[SI] ....................;2a 0c
SUB CX,0x77 ....................;83 e9 77
SUB CX,0x7788 ..................;81 e9 88 77
SUB CX,AX ......................;29 c1
SUB CX,BP ......................;29 e9
SUB CX,BX ......................;29 d9
SUB CX,CX ......................;29 c9
SUB CX,DI ......................;29 f9
SUB CX,DX ......................;29 d1
SUB CX,SI ......................;29 f1
SUB CX,SP ......................;29 e1
SUB CX,[0x5566] ................;2b 0e 66 55
SUB CX,[BP+0x5566] .............;2b 8e 66 55
SUB CX,[BP+0x55] ...............;2b 4e 55
SUB CX,[BP+DI+0x5566] ..........;2b 8b 66 55
SUB CX,[BP+DI+0x55] ............;2b 4b 55
SUB CX,[BP+DI] .................;2b 0b
SUB CX,[BP+SI+0x5566] ..........;2b 8a 66 55
SUB CX,[BP+SI+0x55] ............;2b 4a 55
SUB CX,[BP+SI] .................;2b 0a
SUB CX,[BX+0x5566] .............;2b 8f 66 55
SUB CX,[BX+0x55] ...............;2b 4f 55
SUB CX,[BX+DI+0x5566] ..........;2b 89 66 55
SUB CX,[BX+DI+0x55] ............;2b 49 55
SUB CX,[BX+DI] .................;2b 09
SUB CX,[BX+SI+0x5566] ..........;2b 88 66 55
SUB CX,[BX+SI+0x55] ............;2b 48 55
SUB CX,[BX+SI] .................;2b 08
SUB CX,[BX] ....................;2b 0f
SUB CX,[DI+0x5566] .............;2b 8d 66 55
SUB CX,[DI+0x55] ...............;2b 4d 55
SUB CX,[DI] ....................;2b 0d
SUB CX,[SI+0x5566] .............;2b 8c 66 55
SUB CX,[SI+0x55] ...............;2b 4c 55
SUB CX,[SI] ....................;2b 0c
SUB DH,0x88 ....................;80 ee 88
SUB DH,AH ......................;28 e6
SUB DH,AL ......................;28 c6
SUB DH,BH ......................;28 fe
SUB DH,BL ......................;28 de
SUB DH,CH ......................;28 ee
SUB DH,CL ......................;28 ce
SUB DH,DH ......................;28 f6
SUB DH,DL ......................;28 d6
SUB DH,[0x5566] ................;2a 36 66 55
SUB DH,[BP+0x5566] .............;2a b6 66 55
SUB DH,[BP+0x55] ...............;2a 76 55
SUB DH,[BP+DI+0x5566] ..........;2a b3 66 55
SUB DH,[BP+DI+0x55] ............;2a 73 55
SUB DH,[BP+DI] .................;2a 33
SUB DH,[BP+SI+0x5566] ..........;2a b2 66 55
SUB DH,[BP+SI+0x55] ............;2a 72 55
SUB DH,[BP+SI] .................;2a 32
SUB DH,[BX+0x5566] .............;2a b7 66 55
SUB DH,[BX+0x55] ...............;2a 77 55
SUB DH,[BX+DI+0x5566] ..........;2a b1 66 55
SUB DH,[BX+DI+0x55] ............;2a 71 55
SUB DH,[BX+DI] .................;2a 31
SUB DH,[BX+SI+0x5566] ..........;2a b0 66 55
SUB DH,[BX+SI+0x55] ............;2a 70 55
SUB DH,[BX+SI] .................;2a 30
SUB DH,[BX] ....................;2a 37
SUB DH,[DI+0x5566] .............;2a b5 66 55
SUB DH,[DI+0x55] ...............;2a 75 55
SUB DH,[DI] ....................;2a 35
SUB DH,[SI+0x5566] .............;2a b4 66 55
SUB DH,[SI+0x55] ...............;2a 74 55
SUB DH,[SI] ....................;2a 34
SUB DI,0x77 ....................;83 ef 77
SUB DI,0x7788 ..................;81 ef 88 77
SUB DI,AX ......................;29 c7
SUB DI,BP ......................;29 ef
SUB DI,BX ......................;29 df
SUB DI,CX ......................;29 cf
SUB DI,DI ......................;29 ff
SUB DI,DX ......................;29 d7
SUB DI,SI ......................;29 f7
SUB DI,SP ......................;29 e7
SUB DI,[0x5566] ................;2b 3e 66 55
SUB DI,[BP+0x5566] .............;2b be 66 55
SUB DI,[BP+0x55] ...............;2b 7e 55
SUB DI,[BP+DI+0x5566] ..........;2b bb 66 55
SUB DI,[BP+DI+0x55] ............;2b 7b 55
SUB DI,[BP+DI] .................;2b 3b
SUB DI,[BP+SI+0x5566] ..........;2b ba 66 55
SUB DI,[BP+SI+0x55] ............;2b 7a 55
SUB DI,[BP+SI] .................;2b 3a
SUB DI,[BX+0x5566] .............;2b bf 66 55
SUB DI,[BX+0x55] ...............;2b 7f 55
SUB DI,[BX+DI+0x5566] ..........;2b b9 66 55
SUB DI,[BX+DI+0x55] ............;2b 79 55
SUB DI,[BX+DI] .................;2b 39
SUB DI,[BX+SI+0x5566] ..........;2b b8 66 55
SUB DI,[BX+SI+0x55] ............;2b 78 55
SUB DI,[BX+SI] .................;2b 38
SUB DI,[BX] ....................;2b 3f
SUB DI,[DI+0x5566] .............;2b bd 66 55
SUB DI,[DI+0x55] ...............;2b 7d 55
SUB DI,[DI] ....................;2b 3d
SUB DI,[SI+0x5566] .............;2b bc 66 55
SUB DI,[SI+0x55] ...............;2b 7c 55
SUB DI,[SI] ....................;2b 3c
SUB DL,0x88 ....................;80 ea 88
SUB DL,AH ......................;28 e2
SUB DL,AL ......................;28 c2
SUB DL,BH ......................;28 fa
SUB DL,BL ......................;28 da
SUB DL,CH ......................;28 ea
SUB DL,CL ......................;28 ca
SUB DL,DH ......................;28 f2
SUB DL,DL ......................;28 d2
SUB DL,[0x5566] ................;2a 16 66 55
SUB DL,[BP+0x5566] .............;2a 96 66 55
SUB DL,[BP+0x55] ...............;2a 56 55
SUB DL,[BP+DI+0x5566] ..........;2a 93 66 55
SUB DL,[BP+DI+0x55] ............;2a 53 55
SUB DL,[BP+DI] .................;2a 13
SUB DL,[BP+SI+0x5566] ..........;2a 92 66 55
SUB DL,[BP+SI+0x55] ............;2a 52 55
SUB DL,[BP+SI] .................;2a 12
SUB DL,[BX+0x5566] .............;2a 97 66 55
SUB DL,[BX+0x55] ...............;2a 57 55
SUB DL,[BX+DI+0x5566] ..........;2a 91 66 55
SUB DL,[BX+DI+0x55] ............;2a 51 55
SUB DL,[BX+DI] .................;2a 11
SUB DL,[BX+SI+0x5566] ..........;2a 90 66 55
SUB DL,[BX+SI+0x55] ............;2a 50 55
SUB DL,[BX+SI] .................;2a 10
SUB DL,[BX] ....................;2a 17
SUB DL,[DI+0x5566] .............;2a 95 66 55
SUB DL,[DI+0x55] ...............;2a 55 55
SUB DL,[DI] ....................;2a 15
SUB DL,[SI+0x5566] .............;2a 94 66 55
SUB DL,[SI+0x55] ...............;2a 54 55
SUB DL,[SI] ....................;2a 14
SUB DX,0x77 ....................;83 ea 77
SUB DX,0x7788 ..................;81 ea 88 77
SUB DX,AX ......................;29 c2
SUB DX,BP ......................;29 ea
```

```
SUB DX,BX .................;29 da              SUB SP,[BX+SI+0x55] ..........;2b 60 55
SUB DX,CX .................;29 ca              SUB SP,[BX+SI] ...............;2b 20
SUB DX,DI .................;29 fa              SUB SP,[BX] ..................;2b 27
SUB DX,DX .................;29 d2              SUB SP,[DI+0x5566] ...........;2b a5 66 55
SUB DX,SI .................;29 f2              SUB SP,[DI+0x55] .............;2b 65 55
SUB DX,SP .................;29 e2              SUB SP,[DI] ..................;2b 25
SUB DX,[0x5566] ...........;2b 16 66 55        SUB SP,[SI+0x5566] ...........;2b a4 66 55
SUB DX,[BP+0x5566] ........;2b 96 66 55        SUB SP,[SI+0x55] .............;2b 64 55
SUB DX,[BP+0x55] ..........;2b 56 55           SUB SP,[SI] ..................;2b 24
SUB DX,[BP+DI+0x5566] .....;2b 93 66 55        SUB WORD [0x5566],0x77 .......;83 2e 66 55 77
SUB DX,[BP+DI+0x55] .......;2b 53 55           SUB WORD [0x5566],0x7788 .....;81 2e 66 55 88 77
SUB DX,[BP+DI] ............;2b 13              SUB WORD [BP+0x5566],0x77 ....;83 ae 66 55 77
SUB DX,[BP+SI+0x5566] .....;2b 92 66 55        SUB WORD [BP+0x5566],0x7788 ..;81 ae 66 55 88 77
SUB DX,[BP+SI+0x55] .......;2b 52 55           SUB WORD [BP+0x55],0x77 ......;83 6e 55 77
SUB DX,[BP+SI] ............;2b 12              SUB WORD [BP+0x55],0x7788 ....;81 6e 55 88 77
SUB DX,[BX+0x5566] ........;2b 97 66 55        SUB WORD [BP+DI+0x5566],0x77 ..;83 ab 66 55 77
SUB DX,[BX+0x55] ..........;2b 57 55           SUB WORD [BP+DI+0x5566],0x7788 .;81 ab 66 55 88 77
SUB DX,[BX+DI+0x5566] .....;2b 91 66 55        SUB WORD [BP+DI+0x55],0x77 ...;83 6b 55 77
SUB DX,[BX+DI+0x55] .......;2b 51 55           SUB WORD [BP+DI+0x55],0x7788 .;81 6b 55 88 77
SUB DX,[BX+DI] ............;2b 11              SUB WORD [BP+DI],0x77 ........;83 2b 77
SUB DX,[BX+SI+0x5566] .....;2b 90 66 55        SUB WORD [BP+DI],0x7788 ......;81 2b 88 77
SUB DX,[BX+SI+0x55] .......;2b 50 55           SUB WORD [BP+SI+0x5566],0x77 ..;83 aa 66 55 77
SUB DX,[BX+SI] ............;2b 10              SUB WORD [BP+SI+0x5566],0x7788 .;81 aa 66 55 88 77
SUB DX,[BX] ...............;2b 17              SUB WORD [BP+SI+0x55],0x77 ...;83 6a 55 77
SUB DX,[DI+0x5566] ........;2b 95 66 55        SUB WORD [BP+SI+0x55],0x7788 .;81 6a 55 88 77
SUB DX,[DI+0x55] ..........;2b 55 55           SUB WORD [BP+SI],0x77 ........;83 2a 77
SUB DX,[DI] ...............;2b 15              SUB WORD [BP+SI],0x7788 ......;81 2a 88 77
SUB DX,[SI+0x5566] ........;2b 94 66 55        SUB WORD [BX+0x5566],0x77 ....;83 af 66 55 77
SUB DX,[SI+0x55] ..........;2b 54 55           SUB WORD [BX+0x5566],0x7788 ..;81 af 66 55 88 77
SUB DX,[SI] ...............;2b 14              SUB WORD [BX+0x55],0x77 ......;83 6f 55 77
SUB SI,0x77 ...............;83 ee 77           SUB WORD [BX+0x55],0x7788 ....;81 6f 55 88 77
SUB SI,0x7788 .............;81 ee 88 77        SUB WORD [BX+DI+0x5566],0x77 ..;83 a9 66 55 77
SUB SI,AX .................;29 c6              SUB WORD [BX+DI+0x5566],0x7788 .;81 a9 66 55 88 77
SUB SI,BP .................;29 ee              SUB WORD [BX+DI+0x55],0x77 ...;83 69 55 77
SUB SI,BX .................;29 de              SUB WORD [BX+DI+0x55],0x7788 .;81 69 55 88 77
SUB SI,CX .................;29 ce              SUB WORD [BX+DI],0x77 ........;83 29 77
SUB SI,DI .................;29 fe              SUB WORD [BX+DI],0x7788 ......;81 29 88 77
SUB SI,DX .................;29 d6              SUB WORD [BX+SI+0x5566],0x77 ..;83 a8 66 55 77
SUB SI,SI .................;29 f6              SUB WORD [BX+SI+0x5566],0x7788 .;81 a8 66 55 88 77
SUB SI,SP .................;29 e6              SUB WORD [BX+SI+0x55],0x77 ...;83 68 55 77
SUB SI,[0x5566] ...........;2b 36 66 55        SUB WORD [BX+SI+0x55],0x7788 .;81 68 55 88 77
SUB SI,[BP+0x5566] ........;2b b6 66 55        SUB WORD [BX+SI],0x77 ........;83 28 77
SUB SI,[BP+0x55] ..........;2b 76 55           SUB WORD [BX+SI],0x7788 ......;81 28 88 77
SUB SI,[BP+DI+0x5566] .....;2b b3 66 55        SUB WORD [BX],0x77 ...........;83 2f 77
SUB SI,[BP+DI+0x55] .......;2b 73 55           SUB WORD [BX],0x7788 .........;81 2f 88 77
SUB SI,[BP+DI] ............;2b 33              SUB WORD [DI+0x5566],0x77 ....;83 ad 66 55 77
SUB SI,[BP+SI+0x5566] .....;2b b2 66 55        SUB WORD [DI+0x5566],0x7788 ..;81 ad 66 55 88 77
SUB SI,[BP+SI+0x55] .......;2b 72 55           SUB WORD [DI+0x55],0x77 ......;83 6d 55 77
SUB SI,[BP+SI] ............;2b 32              SUB WORD [DI+0x55],0x7788 ....;81 6d 55 88 77
SUB SI,[BX+0x5566] ........;2b b7 66 55        SUB WORD [DI],0x77 ...........;83 2d 77
SUB SI,[BX+0x55] ..........;2b 77 55           SUB WORD [DI],0x7788 .........;81 2d 88 77
SUB SI,[BX+DI+0x5566] .....;2b b1 66 55        SUB WORD [SI+0x5566],0x77 ....;83 ac 66 55 77
SUB SI,[BX+DI+0x55] .......;2b 71 55           SUB WORD [SI+0x5566],0x7788 ..;81 ac 66 55 88 77
SUB SI,[BX+DI] ............;2b 31              SUB WORD [SI+0x55],0x77 ......;83 6c 55 77
SUB SI,[BX+SI+0x5566] .....;2b b0 66 55        SUB WORD [SI+0x55],0x7788 ....;81 6c 55 88 77
SUB SI,[BX+SI+0x55] .......;2b 70 55           SUB WORD [SI],0x77 ...........;83 2c 77
SUB SI,[BX+SI] ............;2b 30              SUB WORD [SI],0x7788 .........;81 2c 88 77
SUB SI,[BX] ...............;2b 37              SUB [0x5566],AH ..............;28 26 66 55
SUB SI,[DI+0x5566] ........;2b b5 66 55        SUB [0x5566],AL ..............;28 06 66 55
SUB SI,[DI+0x55] ..........;2b 75 55           SUB [0x5566],AX ..............;29 06 66 55
SUB SI,[DI] ...............;2b 35              SUB [0x5566],BH ..............;28 3e 66 55
SUB SI,[SI+0x5566] ........;2b b4 66 55        SUB [0x5566],BL ..............;28 1e 66 55
SUB SI,[SI+0x55] ..........;2b 74 55           SUB [0x5566],BP ..............;29 2e 66 55
SUB SI,[SI] ...............;2b 34              SUB [0x5566],BX ..............;29 1e 66 55
SUB SP,0x77 ...............;83 ec 77           SUB [0x5566],CH ..............;28 2e 66 55
SUB SP,0x7788 .............;81 ec 88 77        SUB [0x5566],CL ..............;28 0e 66 55
SUB SP,AX .................;29 c4              SUB [0x5566],CX ..............;29 0e 66 55
SUB SP,BP .................;29 ec              SUB [0x5566],DH ..............;28 36 66 55
SUB SP,BX .................;29 dc              SUB [0x5566],DI ..............;29 3e 66 55
SUB SP,CX .................;29 cc              SUB [0x5566],DL ..............;28 16 66 55
SUB SP,DI .................;29 fc              SUB [0x5566],DX ..............;29 16 66 55
SUB SP,DX .................;29 d4              SUB [0x5566],SI ..............;29 36 66 55
SUB SP,SI .................;29 f4              SUB [0x5566],SP ..............;29 26 66 55
SUB SP,SP .................;29 e4              SUB [BP+0x5566],AH ...........;28 a6 66 55
SUB SP,[0x5566] ...........;2b 26 66 55        SUB [BP+0x5566],AL ...........;28 86 66 55
SUB SP,[BP+0x5566] ........;2b a6 66 55        SUB [BP+0x5566],AX ...........;29 86 66 55
SUB SP,[BP+0x55] ..........;2b 66 55           SUB [BP+0x5566],BH ...........;28 be 66 55
SUB SP,[BP+DI+0x5566] .....;2b a3 66 55        SUB [BP+0x5566],BL ...........;28 9e 66 55
SUB SP,[BP+DI+0x55] .......;2b 63 55           SUB [BP+0x5566],BP ...........;29 ae 66 55
SUB SP,[BP+DI] ............;2b 23              SUB [BP+0x55GG],BX ...........;29 9e 66 55
SUB SP,[BP+SI+0x5566] .....;2b a2 66 55        SUB [BP+0x5566],CH ...........;28 ae 66 55
SUB SP,[BP+SI+0x55] .......;2b 62 55           SUB [BP+0x5566],CL ...........;28 8e 66 55
SUB SP,[BP+SI] ............;2b 22              SUB [BP+0x5566],CX ...........;29 8e 66 55
SUB SP,[BX+0x5566] ........;2b a7 66 55        SUB [BP+0x5566],DH ...........;28 b6 66 55
SUB SP,[BX+0x55] ..........;2b 67 55           SUB [BP+0x5566],DI ...........;29 be 66 55
SUB SP,[BX+DI+0x5566] .....;2b a1 66 55        SUB [BP+0x5566],DL ...........;28 96 66 55
SUB SP,[BX+DI+0x55] .......;2b 61 55           SUB [BP+0x5566],DX ...........;29 96 66 55
SUB SP,[BX+DI] ............;2b 21              SUB [BP+0x5566],SI ...........;29 b6 66 55
SUB SP,[BX+SI+0x5566] .....;2b a0 66 55        SUB [BP+0x5566],SP ...........;29 a6 66 55
```

```
SUB [BP+0x55],AH ...............;28 66 55      SUB [BP+SI+0x55],CX ...........;29 4a 55
SUB [BP+0x55],AL ...............;28 46 55      SUB [BP+SI+0x55],DH ...........;28 72 55
SUB [BP+0x55],AX ...............;29 46 55      SUB [BP+SI+0x55],DI ...........;29 7a 55
SUB [BP+0x55],BH ...............;28 7e 55      SUB [BP+SI+0x55],DL ...........;28 52 55
SUB [BP+0x55],BL ...............;28 5e 55      SUB [BP+SI+0x55],DX ...........;29 52 55
SUB [BP+0x55],BP ...............;29 6e 55      SUB [BP+SI+0x55],SI ...........;29 72 55
SUB [BP+0x55],BX ...............;29 5e 55      SUB [BP+SI+0x55],SP ...........;29 62 55
SUB [BP+0x55],CH ...............;28 6e 55      SUB [BP+SI],AH ................;28 22
SUB [BP+0x55],CL ...............;28 4e 55      SUB [BP+SI],AL ................;28 02
SUB [BP+0x55],CX ...............;29 4e 55      SUB [BP+SI],AX ................;29 02
SUB [BP+0x55],DH ...............;28 76 55      SUB [BP+SI],BH ................;28 3a
SUB [BP+0x55],DI ...............;29 7e 55      SUB [BP+SI],BL ................;28 1a
SUB [BP+0x55],DL ...............;28 56 55      SUB [BP+SI],BP ................;29 2a
SUB [BP+0x55],DX ...............;29 56 55      SUB [BP+SI],BX ................;29 1a
SUB [BP+0x55],SI ...............;29 76 55      SUB [BP+SI],CH ................;28 2a
SUB [BP+0x55],SP ...............;29 66 55      SUB [BP+SI],CL ................;28 0a
SUB [BP+DI+0x5566],AH .........;28 a3 66 55    SUB [BP+SI],CX ................;29 0a
SUB [BP+DI+0x5566],AL .........;28 83 66 55    SUB [BP+SI],DH ................;28 32
SUB [BP+DI+0x5566],AX .........;29 83 66 55    SUB [BP+SI],DI ................;29 3a
SUB [BP+DI+0x5566],BH .........;28 bb 66 55    SUB [BP+SI],DL ................;28 12
SUB [BP+DI+0x5566],BL .........;28 9b 66 55    SUB [BP+SI],DX ................;29 12
SUB [BP+DI+0x5566],BP .........;29 9b 66 55    SUB [BP+SI],SI ................;29 32
SUB [BP+DI+0x5566],BX .........;29 9b 66 55    SUB [BP+SI],SP ................;29 22
SUB [BP+DI+0x5566],CH .........;28 ab 66 55    SUB [BX+0x5566],AH ...........;28 a7 66 55
SUB [BP+DI+0x5566],CL .........;28 8b 66 55    SUB [BX+0x5566],AL ...........;28 87 66 55
SUB [BP+DI+0x5566],CX .........;29 8b 66 55    SUB [BX+0x5566],AX ...........;29 87 66 55
SUB [BP+DI+0x5566],DH .........;28 b3 66 55    SUB [BX+0x5566],BH ...........;28 bf 66 55
SUB [BP+DI+0x5566],DI .........;29 bb 66 55    SUB [BX+0x5566],BL ...........;28 9f 66 55
SUB [BP+DI+0x5566],DL .........;28 93 66 55    SUB [BX+0x5566],BP ...........;29 af 66 55
SUB [BP+DI+0x5566],DX .........;29 93 66 55    SUB [BX+0x5566],BX ...........;29 9f 66 55
SUB [BP+DI+0x5566],SI .........;29 b3 66 55    SUB [BX+0x5566],CH ...........;28 af 66 55
SUB [BP+DI+0x5566],SP .........;29 a3 66 55    SUB [BX+0x5566],CL ...........;28 8f 66 55
SUB [BP+DI+0x55],AH ...........;28 63 55       SUB [BX+0x5566],CX ...........;29 8f 66 55
SUB [BP+DI+0x55],AL ...........;28 43 55       SUB [BX+0x5566],DH ...........;28 b7 66 55
SUB [BP+DI+0x55],AX ...........;29 43 55       SUB [BX+0x5566],DI ...........;29 bf 66 55
SUB [BP+DI+0x55],BH ...........;28 7b 55       SUB [BX+0x5566],DL ...........;28 97 66 55
SUB [BP+DI+0x55],BL ...........;28 5b 55       SUB [BX+0x5566],DX ...........;29 97 66 55
SUB [BP+DI+0x55],BP ...........;29 6b 55       SUB [BX+0x5566],SI ...........;29 b7 66 55
SUB [BP+DI+0x55],BX ...........;29 5b 55       SUB [BX+0x5566],SP ...........;29 a7 66 55
SUB [BP+DI+0x55],CH ...........;28 6b 55       SUB [BX+0x55],AH .............;28 67 55
SUB [BP+DI+0x55],CL ...........;28 4b 55       SUB [BX+0x55],AL .............;28 47 55
SUB [BP+DI+0x55],CX ...........;29 4b 55       SUB [BX+0x55],AX .............;29 47 55
SUB [BP+DI+0x55],DH ...........;28 73 55       SUB [BX+0x55],BH .............;28 7f 55
SUB [BP+DI+0x55],DI ...........;29 7b 55       SUB [BX+0x55],BL .............;28 5f 55
SUB [BP+DI+0x55],DL ...........;28 53 55       SUB [BX+0x55],BP .............;29 6f 55
SUB [BP+DI+0x55],DX ...........;29 53 55       SUB [BX+0x55],BX .............;29 5f 55
SUB [BP+DI+0x55],SI ...........;29 73 55       SUB [BX+0x55],CH .............;28 6f 55
SUB [BP+DI+0x55],SP ...........;29 63 55       SUB [BX+0x55],CL .............;28 4f 55
SUB [BP+DI],AH ................;28 23          SUB [BX+0x55],CX .............;29 4f 55
SUB [BP+DI],AL ................;28 03          SUB [BX+0x55],DH .............;28 77 55
SUB [BP+DI],AX ................;29 03          SUB [BX+0x55],DI .............;29 7f 55
SUB [BP+DI],BH ................;28 3b          SUB [BX+0x55],DL .............;28 57 55
SUB [BP+DI],BL ................;28 1b          SUB [BX+0x55],DX .............;29 57 55
SUB [BP+DI],BP ................;29 2b          SUB [BX+0x55],SI .............;29 77 55
SUB [BP+DI],BX ................;29 1b          SUB [BX+0x55],SP .............;29 67 55
SUB [BP+DI],CH ................;28 2b          SUB [BX+DI+0x5566],AH ........;28 a1 66 55
SUB [BP+DI],CL ................;28 0b          SUB [BX+DI+0x5566],AL ........;28 81 66 55
SUB [BP+DI],CX ................;29 0b          SUB [BX+DI+0x5566],AX ........;29 81 66 55
SUB [BP+DI],DH ................;28 33          SUB [BX+DI+0x5566],BH ........;28 b9 66 55
SUB [BP+DI],DI ................;29 3b          SUB [BX+DI+0x5566],BL ........;28 99 66 55
SUB [BP+DI],DL ................;28 13          SUB [BX+DI+0x5566],BP ........;29 a9 66 55
SUB [BP+DI],DX ................;29 13          SUB [BX+DI+0x5566],BX ........;29 99 66 55
SUB [BP+DI],SI ................;29 33          SUB [BX+DI+0x5566],CH ........;28 a9 66 55
SUB [BP+DI],SP ................;29 23          SUB [BX+DI+0x5566],CL ........;28 89 66 55
SUB [BP+SI+0x5566],AH .........;28 a2 66 55    SUB [BX+DI+0x5566],CX ........;29 89 66 55
SUB [BP+SI+0x5566],AL .........;28 82 66 55    SUB [BX+DI+0x5566],DH ........;28 b1 66 55
SUB [BP+SI+0x5566],AX .........;29 82 66 55    SUB [BX+DI+0x5566],DI ........;29 b9 66 55
SUB [BP+SI+0x5566],BH .........;28 ba 66 55    SUB [BX+DI+0x5566],DL ........;28 91 66 55
SUB [BP+SI+0x5566],BL .........;28 9a 66 55    SUB [BX+DI+0x5566],DX ........;29 91 66 55
SUB [BP+SI+0x5566],BP .........;29 aa 66 55    SUB [BX+DI+0x5566],SI ........;29 b1 66 55
SUB [BP+SI+0x5566],BX .........;29 9a 66 55    SUB [BX+DI+0x5566],SP ........;29 a1 66 55
SUB [BP+SI+0x5566],CH .........;28 aa 66 55    SUB [BX+DI+0x55],AH ..........;28 61 55
SUB [BP+SI+0x5566],CL .........;28 8a 66 55    SUB [BX+DI+0x55],AL ..........;28 41 55
SUB [BP+SI+0x5566],CX .........;29 8a 66 55    SUB [BX+DI+0x55],AX ..........;29 41 55
SUB [BP+SI+0x5566],DH .........;28 b2 66 55    SUB [BX+DI+0x55],BH ..........;28 79 55
SUB [BP+SI+0x5566],DI .........;29 ba 66 55    SUB [BX+DI+0x55],BL ..........;28 59 55
SUB [BP+SI+0x5566],DL .........;28 92 66 55    SUB [BX+DI+0x55],BP ..........;29 69 55
SUB [BP+SI+0x5566],DX .........;29 92 66 55    SUB [BX+DI+0x55],BX ..........;29 59 55
SUB [BP+SI+0x5566],SI .........;29 b2 66 55    SUB [BX+DI+0x55],CH ..........;28 69 55
SUB [BP+SI+0x5566],SP .........;29 a2 66 55    SUB [BX+DI+0x55],CL ..........;28 49 55
SUB [BP+SI+0x55],AH ...........;28 62 55       SUB [BX+DI+0x55],CX ..........;29 49 55
SUB [BP+SI+0x55],AL ...........;28 42 55       SUB [BX+DI+0x55],DH ..........;28 71 55
SUB [BP+SI+0x55],AX ...........;29 42 55       SUB [BX+DI+0x55],DI ..........;29 79 55
SUB [BP+SI+0x55],BH ...........;28 7a 55       SUB [BX+DI+0x55],DL ..........;28 51 55
SUB [BP+SI+0x55],BL ...........;28 5a 55       SUB [BX+DI+0x55],DX ..........;29 51 55
SUB [BP+SI+0x55],BP ...........;29 6a 55       SUB [BX+DI+0x55],SI ..........;29 71 55
SUB [BP+SI+0x55],BX ...........;29 5a 55       SUB [BX+DI+0x55],SP ..........;29 61 55
SUB [BP+SI+0x55],CH ...........;28 6a 55       SUB [BX+DI],AH ...............;28 21
SUB [BP+SI+0x55],CL ...........;28 4a 55       SUB [BX+DI],AL ...............;28 01
```

```
SUB [BX+DI],AX .................;29 01
SUB [BX+DI],BH .................;28 39
SUB [BX+DI],BL .................;28 19
SUB [BX+DI],BP .................;29 29
SUB [BX+DI],BX .................;29 19
SUB [BX+DI],CH .................;28 29
SUB [BX+DI],CL .................;28 09
SUB [BX+DI],CX .................;29 09
SUB [BX+DI],DH .................;28 31
SUB [BX+DI],DI .................;29 39
SUB [BX+DI],DL .................;28 11
SUB [BX+DI],DX .................;29 11
SUB [BX+DI],SI .................;29 31
SUB [BX+DI],SP .................;29 21
SUB [BX+SI+0x5566],AH ..........;28 a0 66 55
SUB [BX+SI+0x5566],AL ..........;28 80 66 55
SUB [BX+SI+0x5566],AX ..........;29 80 66 55
SUB [BX+SI+0x5566],BH ..........;28 b8 66 55
SUB [BX+SI+0x5566],BL ..........;28 98 66 55
SUB [BX+SI+0x5566],BP ..........;29 a8 66 55
SUB [BX+SI+0x5566],BX ..........;29 98 66 55
SUB [BX+SI+0x5566],CH ..........;28 a8 66 55
SUB [BX+SI+0x5566],CL ..........;28 88 66 55
SUB [BX+SI+0x5566],CX ..........;29 88 66 55
SUB [BX+SI+0x5566],DH ..........;28 b0 66 55
SUB [BX+SI+0x5566],DI ..........;29 b8 66 55
SUB [BX+SI+0x5566],DL ..........;28 90 66 55
SUB [BX+SI+0x5566],DX ..........;29 90 66 55
SUB [BX+SI+0x5566],SI ..........;29 b0 66 55
SUB [BX+SI+0x5566],SP ..........;29 a0 66 55
SUB [BX+SI+0x55],AH ............;28 60 55
SUB [BX+SI+0x55],AL ............;28 40 55
SUB [BX+SI+0x55],AX ............;29 40 55
SUB [BX+SI+0x55],BH ............;28 78 55
SUB [BX+SI+0x55],BL ............;28 58 55
SUB [BX+SI+0x55],BP ............;29 68 55
SUB [BX+SI+0x55],BX ............;29 58 55
SUB [BX+SI+0x55],CH ............;28 68 55
SUB [BX+SI+0x55],CL ............;28 48 55
SUB [BX+SI+0x55],CX ............;29 48 55
SUB [BX+SI+0x55],DH ............;28 70 55
SUB [BX+SI+0x55],DI ............;29 78 55
SUB [BX+SI+0x55],DL ............;28 50 55
SUB [BX+SI+0x55],DX ............;29 50 55
SUB [BX+SI+0x55],SI ............;29 70 55
SUB [BX+SI+0x55],SP ............;29 60 55
SUB [BX+SI],AH .................;28 20
SUB [BX+SI],AL .................;28 00
SUB [BX+SI],AX .................;29 00
SUB [BX+SI],BH .................;28 38
SUB [BX+SI],BL .................;28 18
SUB [BX+SI],BP .................;29 28
SUB [BX+SI],BX .................;29 18
SUB [BX+SI],CH .................;28 28
SUB [BX+SI],CL .................;28 08
SUB [BX+SI],CX .................;29 08
SUB [BX+SI],DH .................;28 30
SUB [BX+SI],DI .................;29 38
SUB [BX+SI],DL .................;28 10
SUB [BX+SI],DX .................;29 10
SUB [BX+SI],SI .................;29 30
SUB [BX+SI],SP .................;29 20
SUB [BX],AH ....................;28 27
SUB [BX],AL ....................;28 07
SUB [BX],AX ....................;29 07
SUB [BX],BH ....................;28 3f
SUB [BX],BL ....................;28 1f
SUB [BX],BP ....................;29 2f
SUB [BX],BX ....................;29 1f
SUB [BX],CH ....................;28 2f
SUB [BX],CL ....................;28 0f
SUB [BX],CX ....................;29 0f
SUB [BX],DH ....................;28 37
SUB [BX],DI ....................;29 3f
SUB [BX],DL ....................;28 17
SUB [BX],DX ....................;29 17
SUB [BX],SI ....................;29 37
SUB [BX],SP ....................;29 27
SUB [DI+0x5566],AH .............;28 a5 66 55
SUB [DI+0x5566],AL .............;28 85 66 55
SUB [DI+0x5566],AX .............;29 85 66 55
SUB [DI+0x5566],BH .............;28 bd 66 55
SUB [DI+0x5566],BL .............;28 9d 66 55
SUB [DI+0x5566],BP .............;29 ad 66 55
SUB [DI+0x5566],BX .............;29 9d 66 55
SUB [DI+0x5566],CH .............;28 ad 66 55
SUB [DI+0x5566],CL .............;28 8d 66 55
SUB [DI+0x5566],CX .............;29 8d 66 55
SUB [DI+0x5566],DH .............;28 b5 66 55
```

```
SUB [DI+0x5566],DI .............;29 bd 66 55
SUB [DI+0x5566],DL .............;28 95 66 55
SUB [DI+0x5566],DX .............;29 95 66 55
SUB [DI+0x5566],SI .............;29 b5 66 55
SUB [DI+0x5566],SP .............;29 a5 66 55
SUB [DI+0x55],AH ...............;28 65 55
SUB [DI+0x55],AL ...............;28 45 55
SUB [DI+0x55],AX ...............;29 45 55
SUB [DI+0x55],BH ...............;28 7d 55
SUB [DI+0x55],BL ...............;28 5d 55
SUB [DI+0x55],BP ...............;29 6d 55
SUB [DI+0x55],BX ...............;29 5d 55
SUB [DI+0x55],CH ...............;28 6d 55
SUB [DI+0x55],CL ...............;28 4d 55
SUB [DI+0x55],CX ...............;29 4d 55
SUB [DI+0x55],DH ...............;28 75 55
SUB [DI+0x55],DI ...............;29 7d 55
SUB [DI+0x55],DL ...............;28 55 55
SUB [DI+0x55],DX ...............;29 55 55
SUB [DI+0x55],SI ...............;29 75 55
SUB [DI+0x55],SP ...............;29 65 55
SUB [DI],AH ....................;28 25
SUB [DI],AL ....................;28 05
SUB [DI],AX ....................;29 05
SUB [DI],BH ....................;28 3d
SUB [DI],BL ....................;28 1d
SUB [DI],BP ....................;29 2d
SUB [DI],BX ....................;29 1d
SUB [DI],CH ....................;28 2d
SUB [DI],CL ....................;28 0d
SUB [DI],CX ....................;29 0d
SUB [DI],DH ....................;28 35
SUB [DI],DI ....................;29 3d
SUB [DI],DL ....................;28 15
SUB [DI],DX ....................;29 15
SUB [DI],SI ....................;29 35
SUB [DI],SP ....................;29 25
SUB [SI+0x5566],AH .............;28 a4 66 55
SUB [SI+0x5566],AL .............;28 84 66 55
SUB [SI+0x5566],AX .............;29 84 66 55
SUB [SI+0x5566],BH .............;28 bc 66 55
SUB [SI+0x5566],BL .............;28 9c 66 55
SUB [SI+0x5566],BP .............;29 ac 66 55
SUB [SI+0x5566],BX .............;29 9c 66 55
SUB [SI+0x5566],CH .............;28 ac 66 55
SUB [SI+0x5566],CL .............;28 8c 66 55
SUB [SI+0x5566],CX .............;29 8c 66 55
SUB [SI+0x5566],DH .............;28 b4 66 55
SUB [SI+0x5566],DI .............;29 bc 66 55
SUB [SI+0x5566],DL .............;28 94 66 55
SUB [SI+0x5566],DX .............;29 94 66 55
SUB [SI+0x5566],SI .............;29 b4 66 55
SUB [SI+0x5566],SP .............;29 a4 66 55
SUB [SI+0x55],AH ...............;28 64 55
SUB [SI+0x55],AL ...............;28 44 55
SUB [SI+0x55],AX ...............;29 44 55
SUB [SI+0x55],BH ...............;28 7c 55
SUB [SI+0x55],BL ...............;28 5c 55
SUB [SI+0x55],BP ...............;29 6c 55
SUB [SI+0x55],BX ...............;29 5c 55
SUB [SI+0x55],CH ...............;28 6c 55
SUB [SI+0x55],CL ...............;28 4c 55
SUB [SI+0x55],CX ...............;29 4c 55
SUB [SI+0x55],DH ...............;28 74 55
SUB [SI+0x55],DI ...............;29 7c 55
SUB [SI+0x55],DL ...............;28 54 55
SUB [SI+0x55],DX ...............;29 54 55
SUB [SI+0x55],SI ...............;29 74 55
SUB [SI+0x55],SP ...............;29 64 55
SUB [SI],AH ....................;28 24
SUB [SI],AL ....................;28 04
SUB [SI],AX ....................;29 04
SUB [SI],BH ....................;28 3c
SUB [SI],BL ....................;28 1c
SUB [SI],BP ....................;29 2c
SUB [SI],BX ....................;29 1c
SUB [SI],CH ....................;28 2c
SUB [SI],CL ....................;28 0c
SUB [SI],CX ....................;29 0c
SUB [SI],DH ....................;28 34
SUB [SI],DI ....................;29 3c
SUB [SI],DL ....................;28 14
SUB [SI],DX ....................;29 14
SUB [SI],SI ....................;29 34
SUB [SI],SP ....................;29 24
TEST AH,0x77 ...................;f6 c4 77
TEST AH,AH .....................;84 e4
TEST AH,AL .....................;84 c4
TEST AH,BH .....................;84 fc
```

```
TEST AH,BL ...................... ;84 dc        TEST CH,BL ...................... ;84 dd
TEST AH,CH ...................... ;84 ec        TEST CH,CH ...................... ;84 ed
TEST AH,CL ...................... ;84 cc        TEST CH,CL ...................... ;84 cd
TEST AH,DH ...................... ;84 f4        TEST CH,DH ...................... ;84 f5
TEST AH,DL ...................... ;84 d4        TEST CH,DL ...................... ;84 d5
TEST AL,0x55 .................... ;a8 55        TEST CL,0x77 .................... ;f6 c1 77
TEST AL,0x77 .................... ;f6 c0 77     TEST CL,AH ...................... ;84 e1
TEST AL,AH ...................... ;84 e0        TEST CL,AL ...................... ;84 c1
TEST AL,AL ...................... ;84 c0        TEST CL,BH ...................... ;84 f9
TEST AL,BH ...................... ;84 f8        TEST CL,BL ...................... ;84 d9
TEST AL,BL ...................... ;84 d8        TEST CL,CH ...................... ;84 e9
TEST AL,CH ...................... ;84 e8        TEST CL,CL ...................... ;84 c9
TEST AL,CL ...................... ;84 c8        TEST CL,DH ...................... ;84 f1
TEST AL,DH ...................... ;84 f0        TEST CL,DL ...................... ;84 d1
TEST AL,DL ...................... ;84 d0        TEST CX,0x7788 ................. ;f7 c1 88 77
TEST AX,0x5566 ................. ;a9 66 55      TEST CX,AX ...................... ;85 c1
TEST AX,0x7788 ................. ;f7 c0 88 77   TEST CX,BP ...................... ;85 e9
TEST AX,AX ...................... ;85 c0        TEST CX,BX ...................... ;85 d9
TEST AX,BP ...................... ;85 e8        TEST CX,CX ...................... ;85 c9
TEST AX,BX ...................... ;85 d8        TEST CX,DI ...................... ;85 f9
TEST AX,CX ...................... ;85 c8        TEST CX,DX ...................... ;85 d1
TEST AX,DI ...................... ;85 f8        TEST CX,SI ...................... ;85 f1
TEST AX,DX ...................... ;85 d0        TEST CX,SP ...................... ;85 e1
TEST AX,SI ...................... ;85 f0        TEST DH,0x77 .................... ;f6 c6 77
TEST AX,SP ...................... ;85 e0        TEST DH,AH ...................... ;84 e6
TEST BH,0x77 .................... ;f6 c7 77     TEST DH,AL ...................... ;84 c6
TEST BH,AH ...................... ;84 e7        TEST DH,BH ...................... ;84 fe
TEST BH,AL ...................... ;84 c7        TEST DH,BL ...................... ;84 de
TEST BH,BH ...................... ;84 ff        TEST DH,CH ...................... ;84 ee
TEST BH,BL ...................... ;84 df        TEST DH,CL ...................... ;84 ce
TEST BH,CH ...................... ;84 ef        TEST DH,DH ...................... ;84 f6
TEST BH,CL ...................... ;84 cf        TEST DH,DL ...................... ;84 d6
TEST BH,DH ...................... ;84 f7        TEST DI,0x7788 ................. ;f7 c7 88 77
TEST BH,DL ...................... ;84 d7        TEST DI,AX ...................... ;85 c7
TEST BL,0x77 .................... ;f6 c3 77     TEST DI,BP ...................... ;85 ef
TEST BL,AH ...................... ;84 e3        TEST DI,BX ...................... ;85 df
TEST BL,AL ...................... ;84 c3        TEST DI,CX ...................... ;85 cf
TEST BL,BH ...................... ;84 fb        TEST DI,DI ...................... ;85 ff
TEST BL,BL ...................... ;84 db        TEST DI,DX ...................... ;85 d7
TEST BL,CH ...................... ;84 eb        TEST DI,SI ...................... ;85 f7
TEST BL,CL ...................... ;84 cb        TEST DI,SP ...................... ;85 e7
TEST BL,DH ...................... ;84 f3        TEST DL,0x77 .................... ;f6 c2 77
TEST BL,DL ...................... ;84 d3        TEST DL,AH ...................... ;84 e2
TEST BP,0x7788 ................. ;f7 c5 88 77   TEST DL,AL ...................... ;84 c2
TEST BP,AX ...................... ;85 c5        TEST DL,BH ...................... ;84 fa
TEST BP,BP ...................... ;85 ed        TEST DL,BL ...................... ;84 da
TEST BP,BX ...................... ;85 dd        TEST DL,CH ...................... ;84 ea
TEST BP,CX ...................... ;85 cd        TEST DL,CL ...................... ;84 ca
TEST BP,DI ...................... ;85 fd        TEST DL,DH ...................... ;84 f2
TEST BP,DX ...................... ;85 d5        TEST DL,DL ...................... ;84 d2
TEST BP,SI ...................... ;85 f5        TEST DX,0x7788 ................. ;f7 c2 88 77
TEST BP,SP ...................... ;85 e5        TEST DX,AX ...................... ;85 c2
TEST BX,0x7788 ................. ;f7 c3 88 77   TEST DX,BP ...................... ;85 ea
TEST BX,AX ...................... ;85 c3        TEST DX,BX ...................... ;85 da
TEST BX,BP ...................... ;85 eb        TEST DX,CX ...................... ;85 ca
TEST BX,BX ...................... ;85 db        TEST DX,DI ...................... ;85 fa
TEST BX,CX ...................... ;85 cb        TEST DX,DX ...................... ;85 d2
TEST BX,DI ...................... ;85 fb        TEST DX,SI ...................... ;85 f2
TEST BX,DX ...................... ;85 d3        TEST DX,SP ...................... ;85 e2
TEST BX,SI ...................... ;85 f3        TEST SI,0x7788 ................. ;f7 c6 88 77
TEST BX,SP ...................... ;85 e3        TEST SI,AX ...................... ;85 c6
TEST BYTE [0x5566],0x77 ...... ;f6 06 66 55 77  TEST SI,BP ...................... ;85 ee
TEST BYTE [BP+0x5566],0x77 ... ;f6 86 66 55 77  TEST SI,BX ...................... ;85 de
TEST BYTE [BP+0x55],0x77 ...... ;f6 46 55 77    TEST SI,CX ...................... ;85 ce
TEST BYTE [BP+DI+0x5566],0x77 ;f6 83 66 55 77   TEST SI,DI ...................... ;85 fe
TEST BYTE [BP+DI+0x55],0x77 .... ;f6 43 55 77   TEST SI,DX ...................... ;85 d6
TEST BYTE [BP+DI],0x77 ......... ;f6 03 77      TEST SI,SI ...................... ;85 f6
TEST BYTE [BP+SI+0x5566],0x77 ;f6 82 66 55 77   TEST SI,SP ...................... ;85 e6
TEST BYTE [BP+SI+0x55],0x77 .... ;f6 42 55 77   TEST SP,0x7788 ................. ;f7 c4 88 77
TEST BYTE [BP+SI],0x77 ......... ;f6 02 77      TEST SP,AX ...................... ;85 c4
TEST BYTE [BX+0x5566],0x77 ... ;f6 87 66 55 77  TEST SP,BP ...................... ;85 ec
TEST BYTE [BX+0x55],0x77 ...... ;f6 47 55 77    TEST SP,BX ...................... ;85 dc
TEST BYTE [BX+DI+0x5566],0x77 ;f6 81 66 55 77   TEST SP,CX ...................... ;85 cc
TEST BYTE [BX+DI+0x55],0x77 .... ;f6 41 55 77   TEST SP,DI ...................... ;85 fc
TEST BYTE [BX+DI],0x77 ......... ;f6 01 77      TEST SP,DX ...................... ;85 d4
TEST BYTE [BX+SI+0x5566],0x77 ;f6 80 66 55 77   TEST SP,SI ...................... ;85 f4
TEST BYTE [BX+SI+0x55],0x77 .... ;f6 40 55 77   TEST SP,SP ...................... ;85 e4
TEST BYTE [BX+SI],0x77 ......... ;f6 00 77      TEST WORD [0x5566],0x7788 ...... ;f7 06 66 55 88 77
TEST BYTE [BX],0x77 ............. ;f6 07 77     TEST WORD [BP+0x5566],0x7788 ... ;f7 86 66 55 88 77
TEST BYTE [DI+0x5566],0x77 ... ;f6 85 66 55 77  TEST WORD [BP+0x55],0x7788 .... ;f7 46 55 88 77
TEST BYTE [DI+0x55],0x77 ...... ;f6 45 55 77    TEST WORD [BP+DI+0x5566],0x7788 ;f7 83 66 55 88 77
TEST BYTE [DI],0x77 ............. ;f6 05 77     TEST WORD [BP+DI+0x55],0x7788 .. ;f7 43 55 88 77
TEST BYTE [SI+0x5566],0x77 ... ;f6 84 66 55 77  TEST WORD [BP+DI],0x7788 ...... ;f7 03 88 77
TEST BYTE [SI+0x55],0x77 ...... ;f6 44 55 77    TEST WORD [BP+SI+0x5566],0x7788 ;f7 82 66 55 88 77
TEST BYTE [SI],0x77 ............. ;f6 04 77     TEST WORD [BP+SI+0x55],0x7788 .. ;f7 42 55 88 77
TEST CH,0x77 .................... ;f6 c5 77     TEST WORD [BP+SI],0x7788 ...... ;f7 02 88 77
TEST CH,AH ...................... ;84 e5        TEST WORD [BX+0x5566],0x7788 ... ;f7 87 66 55 88 77
TEST CH,AL ...................... ;84 c5        TEST WORD [BX+0x55],0x7788 .... ;f7 47 55 88 77
TEST CH,BH ...................... ;84 fd        TEST WORD [BX+DI+0x5566],0x7788 ;f7 81 66 55 88 77
```

```
TEST WORD [BX+DI+0x55],0x7788 ..;f7 41 55 88 77
TEST WORD [BX+DI],0x7788 .......;f7 01 88 77
TEST WORD [BX+SI+0x5566],0x7788 ;f7 80 66 55 88 77
TEST WORD [BX+SI+0x55],0x7788 ..;f7 40 55 88 77
TEST WORD [BX+SI],0x7788 .......;f7 00 88 77
TEST WORD [BX],0x7788 ..........;f7 07 88 77
TEST WORD [DI+0x5566],0x7788 ...;f7 85 66 55 88 77
TEST WORD [DI+0x55],0x7788 .....;f7 45 55 88 77
TEST WORD [DI],0x7788 ..........;f7 05 88 77
TEST WORD [SI+0x5566],0x7788 ...;f7 84 66 55 88 77
TEST WORD [SI+0x55],0x7788 .....;f7 44 55 88 77
TEST WORD [SI],0x7788 ..........;f7 04 88 77
TEST [0x5566],AH ...............;84 26 66 55
TEST [0x5566],AL ...............;84 06 66 55
TEST [0x5566],AX ...............;85 06 66 55
TEST [0x5566],BH ...............;84 3e 66 55
TEST [0x5566],BL ...............;84 1e 66 55
TEST [0x5566],BP ...............;85 2e 66 55
TEST [0x5566],BX ...............;85 1e 66 55
TEST [0x5566],CH ...............;84 2e 66 55
TEST [0x5566],CL ...............;84 0e 66 55
TEST [0x5566],CX ...............;85 0e 66 55
TEST [0x5566],DH ...............;84 36 66 55
TEST [0x5566],DI ...............;85 3e 66 55
TEST [0x5566],DL ...............;84 16 66 55
TEST [0x5566],DX ...............;85 16 66 55
TEST [0x5566],SI ...............;85 36 66 55
TEST [0x5566],SP ...............;85 26 66 55
TEST [BP+0x5566],AH ............;84 a6 66 55
TEST [BP+0x5566],AL ............;84 86 66 55
TEST [BP+0x5566],AX ............;85 86 66 55
TEST [BP+0x5566],BH ............;84 be 66 55
TEST [BP+0x5566],BL ............;84 9e 66 55
TEST [BP+0x5566],BP ............;85 ae 66 55
TEST [BP+0x5566],BX ............;85 9e 66 55
TEST [BP+0x5566],CH ............;84 ae 66 55
TEST [BP+0x5566],CL ............;84 8e 66 55
TEST [BP+0x5566],CX ............;85 8e 66 55
TEST [BP+0x5566],DH ............;84 b6 66 55
TEST [BP+0x5566],DI ............;85 be 66 55
TEST [BP+0x5566],DL ............;84 96 66 55
TEST [BP+0x5566],DX ............;85 96 66 55
TEST [BP+0x5566],SI ............;85 b6 66 55
TEST [BP+0x5566],SP ............;85 a6 66 55
TEST [BP+0x55],AH ..............;84 66 55
TEST [BP+0x55],AL ..............;84 46 55
TEST [BP+0x55],AX ..............;85 46 55
TEST [BP+0x55],BH ..............;84 7e 55
TEST [BP+0x55],BL ..............;84 5e 55
TEST [BP+0x55],BP ..............;85 6e 55
TEST [BP+0x55],BX ..............;85 5e 55
TEST [BP+0x55],CH ..............;84 6e 55
TEST [BP+0x55],CL ..............;84 4e 55
TEST [BP+0x55],CX ..............;85 4e 55
TEST [BP+0x55],DH ..............;84 76 55
TEST [BP+0x55],DI ..............;85 7e 55
TEST [BP+0x55],DL ..............;84 56 55
TEST [BP+0x55],DX ..............;85 56 55
TEST [BP+0x55],SI ..............;85 76 55
TEST [BP+0x55],SP ..............;85 66 55
TEST [BP+DI+0x5566],AH ........;84 a3 66 55
TEST [BP+DI+0x5566],AL ........;84 83 66 55
TEST [BP+DI+0x5566],AX ........;85 83 66 55
TEST [BP+DI+0x5566],BH ........;84 bb 66 55
TEST [BP+DI+0x5566],BL ........;84 9b 66 55
TEST [BP+DI+0x5566],BP ........;85 ab 66 55
TEST [BP+DI+0x5566],BX ........;85 9b 66 55
TEST [BP+DI+0x5566],CH ........;84 ab 66 55
TEST [BP+DI+0x5566],CL ........;84 8b 66 55
TEST [BP+DI+0x5566],CX ........;85 8b 66 55
TEST [BP+DI+0x5566],DH ........;84 b3 66 55
TEST [BP+DI+0x5566],DI ........;85 bb 66 55
TEST [BP+DI+0x5566],DL ........;84 93 66 55
TEST [BP+DI+0x5566],DX ........;85 93 66 55
TEST [BP+DI+0x5566],SI ........;85 b3 66 55
TEST [BP+DI+0x5566],SP ........;85 a3 66 55
TEST [BP+DI+0x55],AH ...........;84 63 55
TEST [BP+DI+0x55],AL ...........;84 43 55
TEST [BP+DI+0x55],AX ...........;85 43 55
TEST [BP+DI+0x55],BH ...........;84 7b 55
TEST [BP+DI+0x55],BL ...........;84 5b 55
TEST [BP+DI+0x55],BP ...........;85 6b 55
TEST [BP+DI+0x55],BX ...........;85 5b 55
TEST [BP+DI+0x55],CH ...........;84 6b 55
TEST [BP+DI+0x55],CL ...........;84 4b 55
TEST [BP+DI+0x55],CX ...........;85 4b 55
TEST [BP+DI+0x55],DH ...........;84 73 55
TEST [BP+DI+0x55],DI ...........;85 7b 55
TEST [BP+DI+0x55],DL ...........;84 53 55

TEST [BP+DI+0x55],DX ...........;85 53 55
TEST [BP+DI+0x55],SI ...........;85 73 55
TEST [BP+DI+0x55],SP ...........;85 63 55
TEST [BP+DI],AH ................;84 23
TEST [BP+DI],AL ................;84 03
TEST [BP+DI],AX ................;85 03
TEST [BP+DI],BH ................;84 3b
TEST [BP+DI],BL ................;84 1b
TEST [BP+DI],BP ................;85 2b
TEST [BP+DI],BX ................;85 1b
TEST [BP+DI],CH ................;84 2b
TEST [BP+DI],CL ................;84 0b
TEST [BP+DI],CX ................;85 0b
TEST [BP+DI],DH ................;84 33
TEST [BP+DI],DI ................;85 3b
TEST [BP+DI],DL ................;84 13
TEST [BP+DI],DX ................;85 13
TEST [BP+DI],SI ................;85 33
TEST [BP+DI],SP ................;85 23
TEST [BP+SI+0x5566],AH .........;84 a2 66 55
TEST [BP+SI+0x5566],AL .........;84 82 66 55
TEST [BP+SI+0x5566],AX .........;85 82 66 55
TEST [BP+SI+0x5566],BH .........;84 ba 66 55
TEST [BP+SI+0x5566],BL .........;84 9a 66 55
TEST [BP+SI+0x5566],BP .........;85 aa 66 55
TEST [BP+SI+0x5566],BX .........;85 9a 66 55
TEST [BP+SI+0x5566],CH .........;84 aa 66 55
TEST [BP+SI+0x5566],CL .........;84 8a 66 55
TEST [BP+SI+0x5566],CX .........;85 8a 66 55
TEST [BP+SI+0x5566],DH .........;84 b2 66 55
TEST [BP+SI+0x5566],DI .........;85 ba 66 55
TEST [BP+SI+0x5566],DL .........;84 92 66 55
TEST [BP+SI+0x5566],DX .........;85 92 66 55
TEST [BP+SI+0x5566],SI .........;85 b2 66 55
TEST [BP+SI+0x5566],SP .........;85 a2 66 55
TEST [BP+SI+0x55],AH ...........;84 62 55
TEST [BP+SI+0x55],AL ...........;84 42 55
TEST [BP+SI+0x55],AX ...........;85 42 55
TEST [BP+SI+0x55],BH ...........;84 7a 55
TEST [BP+SI+0x55],BL ...........;84 5a 55
TEST [BP+SI+0x55],BP ...........;85 6a 55
TEST [BP+SI+0x55],BX ...........;85 5a 55
TEST [BP+SI+0x55],CH ...........;84 6a 55
TEST [BP+SI+0x55],CL ...........;84 4a 55
TEST [BP+SI+0x55],CX ...........;85 4a 55
TEST [BP+SI+0x55],DH ...........;84 72 55
TEST [BP+SI+0x55],DI ...........;85 7a 55
TEST [BP+SI+0x55],DL ...........;84 52 55
TEST [BP+SI+0x55],DX ...........;85 52 55
TEST [BP+SI+0x55],SI ...........;85 72 55
TEST [BP+SI+0x55],SP ...........;85 62 55
TEST [BP+SI],AH ................;84 22
TEST [BP+SI],AL ................;84 02
TEST [BP+SI],AX ................;85 02
TEST [BP+SI],BH ................;84 3a
TEST [BP+SI],BL ................;84 1a
TEST [BP+SI],BP ................;85 2a
TEST [BP+SI],BX ................;85 1a
TEST [BP+SI],CH ................;84 2a
TEST [BP+SI],CL ................;84 0a
TEST [BP+SI],CX ................;85 0a
TEST [BP+SI],DH ................;84 32
TEST [BP+SI],DI ................;85 3a
TEST [BP+SI],DL ................;84 12
TEST [BP+SI],DX ................;85 12
TEST [BP+SI],SI ................;85 32
TEST [BP+SI],SP ................;85 22
TEST [BX+0x5566],AH ............;84 a7 66 55
TEST [BX+0x5566],AL ............;84 87 66 55
TEST [BX+0x5566],AX ............;85 87 66 55
TEST [BX+0x5566],BH ............;84 bf 66 55
TEST [BX+0x5566],BL ............;84 9f 66 55
TEST [BX+0x5566],BP ............;85 af 66 55
TEST [BX+0x5566],BX ............;85 9f 66 55
TEST [BX+0x5566],CH ............;84 af 66 55
TEST [BX+0x5566],CL ............;84 8f 66 55
TEST [BX+0x5566],CX ............;85 8f 66 55
TEST [BX+0x5566],DH ............;84 b7 66 55
TEST [BX+0x5566],DI ............;85 bf 66 55
TEST [BX+0x5566],DL ............;84 97 66 55
TEST [BX+0x5566],DX ............;85 97 66 55
TEST [BX+0x5566],SI ............;85 b7 66 55
TEST [BX+0x5566],SP ............;85 a7 66 55
TEST [BX+0x55],AH ..............;84 67 55
TEST [BX+0x55],AL ..............;84 47 55
TEST [BX+0x55],AX ..............;85 47 55
TEST [BX+0x55],BH ..............;84 7f 55
TEST [BX+0x55],BL ..............;84 5f 55
TEST [BX+0x55],BP ..............;85 6f 55
```

```
TEST [BX+0x55],BX .............;85 5f 55        TEST [BX+SI+0x55],SP ..........;85 60 55
TEST [BX+0x55],CH .............;84 6f 55        TEST [BX+SI],AH ...............;84 20
TEST [BX+0x55],CL .............;84 4f 55        TEST [BX+SI],AL ...............;84 00
TEST [BX+0x55],CX .............;85 4f 55        TEST [BX+SI],AX ...............;85 00
TEST [BX+0x55],DH .............;84 77 55        TEST [BX+SI],BH ...............;84 38
TEST [BX+0x55],DI .............;85 7f 55        TEST [BX+SI],BL ...............;84 18
TEST [BX+0x55],DL .............;84 57 55        TEST [BX+SI],BP ...............;85 28
TEST [BX+0x55],DX .............;85 57 55        TEST [BX+SI],BX ...............;85 18
TEST [BX+0x55],SI .............;85 77 55        TEST [BX+SI],CH ...............;84 28
TEST [BX+0x55],SP .............;85 67 55        TEST [BX+SI],CL ...............;84 08
TEST [BX+DI+0x5566],AH ........;84 a1 66 55     TEST [BX+SI],CX ...............;85 08
TEST [BX+DI+0x5566],AL ........;84 81 66 55     TEST [BX+SI],DH ...............;84 30
TEST [BX+DI+0x5566],AX ........;85 a1 66 55     TEST [BX+SI],DI ...............;85 38
TEST [BX+DI+0x5566],BH ........;84 b9 66 55     TEST [BX+SI],DL ...............;84 10
TEST [BX+DI+0x5566],BL ........;84 99 66 55     TEST [BX+SI],DX ...............;85 10
TEST [BX+DI+0x5566],BP ........;85 a9 66 55     TEST [BX+SI],SI ...............;85 30
TEST [BX+DI+0x5566],BX ........;85 99 66 55     TEST [BX+SI],SP ...............;85 20
TEST [BX+DI+0x5566],CH ........;84 a9 66 55     TEST [BX],AH ..................;84 27
TEST [BX+DI+0x5566],CL ........;84 89 66 55     TEST [BX],AL ..................;84 07
TEST [BX+DI+0x5566],CX ........;85 89 66 55     TEST [BX],AX ..................;85 07
TEST [BX+DI+0x5566],DH ........;84 b1 66 55     TEST [BX],BH ..................;84 3f
TEST [BX+DI+0x5566],DI ........;85 b9 66 55     TEST [BX],BL ..................;84 1f
TEST [BX+DI+0x5566],DL ........;84 91 66 55     TEST [BX],BP ..................;85 2f
TEST [BX+DI+0x5566],DX ........;85 91 66 55     TEST [BX],BX ..................;85 1f
TEST [BX+DI+0x5566],SI ........;85 b1 66 55     TEST [BX],CH ..................;84 2f
TEST [BX+DI+0x5566],SP ........;85 a1 66 55     TEST [BX],CL ..................;84 0f
TEST [BX+DI+0x55],AH ..........;84 61 55        TEST [BX],CX ..................;85 0f
TEST [BX+DI+0x55],AL ..........;84 41 55        TEST [BX],DH ..................;84 37
TEST [BX+DI+0x55],AX ..........;85 41 55        TEST [BX],DI ..................;85 3f
TEST [BX+DI+0x55],BH ..........;84 79 55        TEST [BX],DL ..................;84 17
TEST [BX+DI+0x55],BL ..........;84 59 55        TEST [BX],DX ..................;85 17
TEST [BX+DI+0x55],BP ..........;85 69 55        TEST [BX],SI ..................;85 37
TEST [BX+DI+0x55],BX ..........;85 59 55        TEST [BX],SP ..................;85 27
TEST [BX+DI+0x55],CH ..........;84 69 55        TEST [DI+0x5566],AH ...........;84 a5 66 55
TEST [BX+DI+0x55],CL ..........;84 49 55        TEST [DI+0x5566],AL ...........;84 85 66 55
TEST [BX+DI+0x55],CX ..........;85 49 55        TEST [DI+0x5566],AX ...........;85 85 66 55
TEST [BX+DI+0x55],DH ..........;84 71 55        TEST [DI+0x5566],BH ...........;84 bd 66 55
TEST [BX+DI+0x55],DI ..........;85 79 55        TEST [DI+0x5566],BL ...........;84 9d 66 55
TEST [BX+DI+0x55],DL ..........;84 51 55        TEST [DI+0x5566],BP ...........;85 ad 66 55
TEST [BX+DI+0x55],DX ..........;85 51 55        TEST [DI+0x5566],BX ...........;85 9d 66 55
TEST [BX+DI+0x55],SI ..........;85 71 55        TEST [DI+0x5566],CH ...........;84 ad 66 55
TEST [BX+DI+0x55],SP ..........;85 61 55        TEST [DI+0x5566],CL ...........;84 8d 66 55
TEST [BX+DI],AH ...............;84 21           TEST [DI+0x5566],CX ...........;85 8d 66 55
TEST [BX+DI],AL ...............;84 01           TEST [DI+0x5566],DH ...........;84 b5 66 55
TEST [BX+DI],AX ...............;85 01           TEST [DI+0x5566],DI ...........;85 bd 66 55
TEST [BX+DI],BH ...............;84 39           TEST [DI+0x5566],DL ...........;84 95 66 55
TEST [BX+DI],BL ...............;84 19           TEST [DI+0x5566],DX ...........;85 95 66 55
TEST [BX+DI],BP ...............;85 29           TEST [DI+0x5566],SI ...........;85 b5 66 55
TEST [BX+DI],BX ...............;85 19           TEST [DI+0x5566],SP ...........;85 a5 66 55
TEST [BX+DI],CH ...............;84 29           TEST [DI+0x55],AH .............;84 65 55
TEST [BX+DI],CL ...............;84 09           TEST [DI+0x55],AL .............;84 45 55
TEST [BX+DI],CX ...............;85 09           TEST [DI+0x55],AX .............;85 45 55
TEST [BX+DI],DH ...............;84 31           TEST [DI+0x55],BH .............;84 7d 55
TEST [BX+DI],DI ...............;85 39           TEST [DI+0x55],BL .............;84 5d 55
TEST [BX+DI],DL ...............;84 11           TEST [DI+0x55],BP .............;85 6d 55
TEST [BX+DI],DX ...............;85 11           TEST [DI+0x55],BX .............;85 5d 55
TEST [BX+DI],SI ...............;85 31           TEST [DI+0x55],CH .............;84 6d 55
TEST [BX+DI],SP ...............;85 21           TEST [DI+0x55],CL .............;84 4d 55
TEST [BX+SI+0x5566],AH ........;84 a0 66 55     TEST [DI+0x55],CX .............;85 4d 55
TEST [BX+SI+0x5566],AL ........;84 80 66 55     TEST [DI+0x55],DH .............;84 75 55
TEST [BX+SI+0x5566],AX ........;85 80 66 55     TEST [DI+0x55],DI .............;85 7d 55
TEST [BX+SI+0x5566],BH ........;84 b8 66 55     TEST [DI+0x55],DL .............;84 55 55
TEST [BX+SI+0x5566],BL ........;84 98 66 55     TEST [DI+0x55],DX .............;85 55 55
TEST [BX+SI+0x5566],BP ........;85 a8 66 55     TEST [DI+0x55],SI .............;85 75 55
TEST [BX+SI+0x5566],BX ........;85 98 66 55     TEST [DI+0x55],SP .............;85 65 55
TEST [BX+SI+0x5566],CH ........;84 a8 66 55     TEST [DI],AH ..................;84 25
TEST [BX+SI+0x5566],CL ........;84 88 66 55     TEST [DI],AL ..................;84 05
TEST [BX+SI+0x5566],CX ........;85 88 66 55     TEST [DI],AX ..................;85 05
TEST [BX+SI+0x5566],DH ........;84 b0 66 55     TEST [DI],BH ..................;84 3d
TEST [BX+SI+0x5566],DI ........;85 b8 66 55     TEST [DI],BL ..................;84 1d
TEST [BX+SI+0x5566],DL ........;84 90 66 55     TEST [DI],BP ..................;85 2d
TEST [BX+SI+0x5566],DX ........;85 90 66 55     TEST [DI],BX ..................;85 1d
TEST [BX+SI+0x5566],SI ........;85 b0 66 55     TEST [DI],CH ..................;84 2d
TEST [BX+SI+0x5566],SP ........;85 a0 66 55     TEST [DI],CL ..................;84 0d
TEST [BX+SI+0x55],AH ..........;84 60 55        TEST [DI],CX ..................;85 0d
TEST [BX+SI+0x55],AL ..........;84 40 55        TEST [DI],DH ..................;84 35
TEST [BX+SI+0x55],AX ..........;85 40 55        TEST [DI],DI ..................;85 3d
TEST [BX+SI+0x55],BH ..........;84 78 55        TEST [DI],DL ..................;84 15
TEST [BX+SI+0x55],BL ..........;84 58 55        TEST [DI],DX ..................;85 15
TEST [BX+SI+0x55],BP ..........;85 68 55        TEST [DI],SI ..................;85 35
TEST [BX+SI+0x55],BX ..........;85 58 55        TEST [DI],SP ..................;85 25
TEST [BX+SI+0x55],CH ..........;84 68 55        TEST [SI+0x5566],AH ...........;84 a4 66 55
TEST [BX+SI+0x55],CL ..........;84 48 55        TEST [SI+0x5566],AL ...........;84 84 66 55
TEST [BX+SI+0x55],CX ..........;85 48 55        TEST [SI+0x5566],AX ...........;85 84 66 55
TEST [BX+SI+0x55],DH ..........;84 70 55        TEST [SI+0x5566],BH ...........;84 bc 66 55
TEST [BX+SI+0x55],DI ..........;85 78 55        TEST [SI+0x5566],BL ...........;84 9c 66 55
TEST [BX+SI+0x55],DL ..........;84 50 55        TEST [SI+0x5566],BP ...........;85 ac 66 55
TEST [BX+SI+0x55],DX ..........;85 50 55        TEST [SI+0x5566],BX ...........;85 9c 66 55
TEST [BX+SI+0x55],SI ..........;85 70 55        TEST [SI+0x5566],CH ...........;84 ac 66 55
```

```
TEST [SI+0x5566],CL .........;84 8c 66 55
TEST [SI+0x5566],CX .........;85 8c 66 55
TEST [SI+0x5566],DH .........;84 b4 66 55
TEST [SI+0x5566],DI .........;85 bc 66 55
TEST [SI+0x5566],DL .........;84 94 66 55
TEST [SI+0x5566],DX .........;85 94 66 55
TEST [SI+0x5566],SI .........;85 b4 66 55
TEST [SI+0x5566],SP .........;85 a4 66 55
TEST [SI+0x55],AH ...........;84 64 55
TEST [SI+0x55],AL ...........;84 44 55
TEST [SI+0x55],AX ...........;85 44 55
TEST [SI+0x55],BH ...........;84 7c 55
TEST [SI+0x55],BL ...........;84 5c 55
TEST [SI+0x55],BP ...........;85 6c 55
TEST [SI+0x55],BX ...........;85 5c 55
TEST [SI+0x55],CH ...........;84 6c 55
TEST [SI+0x55],CL ...........;84 4c 55
TEST [SI+0x55],CX ...........;85 4c 55
TEST [SI+0x55],DH ...........;84 74 55
TEST [SI+0x55],DI ...........;85 7c 55
TEST [SI+0x55],DL ...........;84 54 55
TEST [SI+0x55],DX ...........;85 54 55
TEST [SI+0x55],SI ...........;85 74 55
TEST [SI+0x55],SP ...........;85 64 55
TEST [SI],AH ................;84 24
TEST [SI],AL ................;84 04
TEST [SI],AX ................;85 04
TEST [SI],BH ................;84 3c
TEST [SI],BL ................;84 1c
TEST [SI],BP ................;85 2c
TEST [SI],BX ................;85 1c
TEST [SI],CH ................;84 2c
TEST [SI],CL ................;84 0c
TEST [SI],CX ................;85 0c
TEST [SI],DH ................;84 34
TEST [SI],DI ................;85 3c
TEST [SI],DL ................;84 14
TEST [SI],DX ................;85 14
TEST [SI],SI ................;85 34
TEST [SI],SP ................;85 24
WAIT ........................;9b
XCHG AH,AH ..................;86 e4
XCHG AH,AL ..................;86 c4
XCHG AH,BH ..................;86 fc
XCHG AH,BL ..................;86 dc
XCHG AH,CH ..................;86 ec
XCHG AH,CL ..................;86 cc
XCHG AH,DH ..................;86 f4
XCHG AH,DL ..................;86 d4
XCHG AL,AH ..................;86 e0
XCHG AL,AL ..................;86 c0
XCHG AL,BH ..................;86 f8
XCHG AL,BL ..................;86 d8
XCHG AL,CH ..................;86 e8
XCHG AL,CL ..................;86 c8
XCHG AL,DH ..................;86 f0
XCHG AL,DL ..................;86 d0
XCHG AX,AX ..................;87 c0
XCHG AX,BP ..................;87 e8
XCHG AX,BP ..................;95
XCHG AX,BX ..................;87 d8
XCHG AX,BX ..................;93
XCHG AX,CX ..................;87 c8
XCHG AX,CX ..................;91
XCHG AX,DI ..................;87 f8
XCHG AX,DI ..................;97
XCHG AX,DX ..................;87 d0
XCHG AX,DX ..................;92
XCHG AX,SI ..................;87 f0
XCHG AX,SI ..................;96
XCHG AX,SP ..................;87 e0
XCHG AX,SP ..................;94
XCHG BH,AH ..................;86 e7
XCHG BH,AL ..................;86 c7
XCHG BH,BH ..................;86 ff
XCHG BH,BL ..................;86 df
XCHG BH,CH ..................;86 ef
XCHG BH,CL ..................;86 cf
XCHG BH,DH ..................;86 f7
XCHG BH,DL ..................;86 d7
XCHG BL,AH ..................;86 e3
XCHG BL,AL ..................;86 c3
XCHG BL,BH ..................;86 fb
XCHG BL,BL ..................;86 db
XCHG BL,CH ..................;86 eb
XCHG BL,CL ..................;86 cb
XCHG BL,DH ..................;86 f3
XCHG BL,DL ..................;86 d3
XCHG BP,AX ..................;87 c5

XCHG BP,BP .................;87 ed
XCHG BP,BX .................;87 dd
XCHG BP,CX .................;87 cd
XCHG BP,DI .................;87 fd
XCHG BP,DX .................;87 d5
XCHG BP,SI .................;87 f5
XCHG BP,SP .................;87 e5
XCHG BX,AX .................;87 c3
XCHG BX,BP .................;87 eb
XCHG BX,BX .................;87 db
XCHG BX,CX .................;87 cb
XCHG BX,DI .................;87 fb
XCHG BX,DX .................;87 d3
XCHG BX,SI .................;87 f3
XCHG BX,SP .................;87 e3
XCHG CH,AH .................;86 e5
XCHG CH,AL .................;86 c5
XCHG CH,BH .................;86 fd
XCHG CH,BL .................;86 dd
XCHG CH,CH .................;86 ed
XCHG CH,CL .................;86 cd
XCHG CH,DH .................;86 f5
XCHG CH,DL .................;86 d5
XCHG CL,AH .................;86 e1
XCHG CL,AL .................;86 c1
XCHG CL,BH .................;86 f9
XCHG CL,BL .................;86 d9
XCHG CL,CH .................;86 e9
XCHG CL,CL .................;86 c9
XCHG CL,DH .................;86 f1
XCHG CL,DL .................;86 d1
XCHG CX,AX .................;87 c1
XCHG CX,BP .................;87 e9
XCHG CX,BX .................;87 d9
XCHG CX,CX .................;87 c9
XCHG CX,DI .................;87 f9
XCHG CX,DX .................;87 d1
XCHG CX,SI .................;87 f1
XCHG CX,SP .................;87 e1
XCHG DH,AH .................;86 e6
XCHG DH,AL .................;86 c6
XCHG DH,BH .................;86 fe
XCHG DH,BL .................;86 de
XCHG DH,CH .................;86 ee
XCHG DH,CL .................;86 ce
XCHG DH,DH .................;86 f6
XCHG DH,DL .................;86 d6
XCHG DI,AX .................;87 c7
XCHG DI,BP .................;87 ef
XCHG DI,BX .................;87 df
XCHG DI,CX .................;87 cf
XCHG DI,DI .................;87 ff
XCHG DI,DX .................;87 d7
XCHG DI,SI .................;87 f7
XCHG DI,SP .................;87 e7
XCHG DL,AH .................;86 e2
XCHG DL,AL .................;86 c2
XCHG DL,BH .................;86 fa
XCHG DL,BL .................;86 da
XCHG DL,CH .................;86 ea
XCHG DL,CL .................;86 ca
XCHG DL,DH .................;86 f2
XCHG DL,DL .................;86 d2
XCHG DX,AX .................;87 c2
XCHG DX,BP .................;87 ea
XCHG DX,BX .................;87 da
XCHG DX,CX .................;87 ca
XCHG DX,DI .................;87 fa
XCHG DX,DX .................;87 d2
XCHG DX,SI .................;87 f2
XCHG DX,SP .................;87 e2
XCHG SI,AX .................;87 c6
XCHG SI,BP .................;87 ee
XCHG SI,BX .................;87 de
XCHG SI,CX .................;87 ce
XCHG SI,DI .................;87 fe
XCHG SI,DX .................;87 d6
XCHG SI,SI .................;87 f6
XCHG SI,SP .................;87 e6
XCHG SP,AX .................;87 c4
XCHG SP,BP .................;87 ec
XCHG SP,BX .................;87 dc
XCHG SP,CX .................;87 cc
XCHG SP,DI .................;87 fc
XCHG SP,DX .................;87 d4
XCHG SP,SI .................;87 f4
XCHG SP,SP .................;87 e4
XCHG [0x5566],AH ..........;86 26 66 55
XCHG [0x5566],AL ..........;86 06 66 55
```

```
XCHG [0x5566],AX ............ ;87 06 66 55        XCHG [BP+DI],DI ............... ;87 3b
XCHG [0x5566],BH ............ ;86 3e 66 55        XCHG [BP+DI],DL ............... ;86 13
XCHG [0x5566],BL ............ ;86 1e 66 55        XCHG [BP+DI],DX ............... ;87 13
XCHG [0x5566],BP ............ ;87 2e 66 55        XCHG [BP+DI],SI ............... ;87 33
XCHG [0x5566],BX ............ ;87 1e 66 55        XCHG [BP+DI],SP ............... ;87 23
XCHG [0x5566],CH ............ ;86 2e 66 55        XCHG [BP+SI+0x5566],AH ........ ;86 a2 66 55
XCHG [0x5566],CL ............ ;86 0e 66 55        XCHG [BP+SI+0x5566],AL ........ ;86 82 66 55
XCHG [0x5566],CX ............ ;87 0e 66 55        XCHG [BP+SI+0x5566],AX ........ ;87 82 66 55
XCHG [0x5566],DH ............ ;86 36 66 55        XCHG [BP+SI+0x5566],BH ........ ;86 ba 66 55
XCHG [0x5566],DI ............ ;87 3e 66 55        XCHG [BP+SI+0x5566],BL ........ ;86 9a 66 55
XCHG [0x5566],DL ............ ;86 16 66 55        XCHG [BP+SI+0x5566],BP ........ ;87 aa 66 55
XCHG [0x5566],DX ............ ;87 16 66 55        XCHG [BP+SI+0x5566],BX ........ ;87 9a 66 55
XCHG [0x5566],SI ............ ;87 36 66 55        XCHG [BP+SI+0x5566],CH ........ ;86 aa 66 55
XCHG [0x5566],SP ............ ;87 26 66 55        XCHG [BP+SI+0x5566],CL ........ ;86 8a 66 55
XCHG [BP+0x5566],AH ......... ;86 a6 66 55        XCHG [BP+SI+0x5566],CX ........ ;87 8a 66 55
XCHG [BP+0x5566],AL ......... ;86 86 66 55        XCHG [BP+SI+0x5566],DH ........ ;86 b2 66 55
XCHG [BP+0x5566],AX ......... ;87 86 66 55        XCHG [BP+SI+0x5566],DI ........ ;87 ba 66 55
XCHG [BP+0x5566],BH ......... ;86 be 66 55        XCHG [BP+SI+0x5566],DL ........ ;86 92 66 55
XCHG [BP+0x5566],BL ......... ;86 9e 66 55        XCHG [BP+SI+0x5566],DX ........ ;87 92 66 55
XCHG [BP+0x5566],BP ......... ;87 ae 66 55        XCHG [BP+SI+0x5566],SI ........ ;87 b2 66 55
XCHG [BP+0x5566],BX ......... ;87 9e 66 55        XCHG [BP+SI+0x5566],SP ........ ;87 a2 66 55
XCHG [BP+0x5566],CH ......... ;86 ae 66 55        XCHG [BP+SI+0x55],AH .......... ;86 62 55
XCHG [BP+0x5566],CL ......... ;86 8e 66 55        XCHG [BP+SI+0x55],AL .......... ;86 42 55
XCHG [BP+0x5566],CX ......... ;87 8e 66 55        XCHG [BP+SI+0x55],AX .......... ;87 42 55
XCHG [BP+0x5566],DH ......... ;86 b6 66 55        XCHG [BP+SI+0x55],BH .......... ;86 7a 55
XCHG [BP+0x5566],DI ......... ;87 be 66 55        XCHG [BP+SI+0x55],BL .......... ;86 5a 55
XCHG [BP+0x5566],DL ......... ;86 96 66 55        XCHG [BP+SI+0x55],BP .......... ;87 6a 55
XCHG [BP+0x5566],DX ......... ;87 96 66 55        XCHG [BP+SI+0x55],BX .......... ;87 5a 55
XCHG [BP+0x5566],SI ......... ;87 b6 66 55        XCHG [BP+SI+0x55],CH .......... ;86 6a 55
XCHG [BP+0x5566],SP ......... ;87 a6 66 55        XCHG [BP+SI+0x55],CL .......... ;86 4a 55
XCHG [BP+0x55],AH ........... ;86 66 55           XCHG [BP+SI+0x55],CX .......... ;87 4a 55
XCHG [BP+0x55],AL ........... ;86 46 55           XCHG [BP+SI+0x55],DH .......... ;86 72 55
XCHG [BP+0x55],AX ........... ;87 46 55           XCHG [BP+SI+0x55],DI .......... ;87 7a 55
XCHG [BP+0x55],BH ........... ;86 7e 55           XCHG [BP+SI+0x55],DL .......... ;86 52 55
XCHG [BP+0x55],BL ........... ;86 5e 55           XCHG [BP+SI+0x55],DX .......... ;87 52 55
XCHG [BP+0x55],BP ........... ;87 6e 55           XCHG [BP+SI+0x55],SI .......... ;87 72 55
XCHG [BP+0x55],BX ........... ;87 5e 55           XCHG [BP+SI+0x55],SP .......... ;87 62 55
XCHG [BP+0x55],CH ........... ;86 6e 55           XCHG [BP+SI],AH ............... ;86 22
XCHG [BP+0x55],CL ........... ;86 4e 55           XCHG [BP+SI],AL ............... ;86 02
XCHG [BP+0x55],CX ........... ;87 4e 55           XCHG [BP+SI],AX ............... ;87 02
XCHG [BP+0x55],DH ........... ;86 76 55           XCHG [BP+SI],BH ............... ;86 3a
XCHG [BP+0x55],DI ........... ;87 7e 55           XCHG [BP+SI],BL ............... ;86 1a
XCHG [BP+0x55],DL ........... ;86 56 55           XCHG [BP+SI],BP ............... ;87 2a
XCHG [BP+0x55],DX ........... ;87 56 55           XCHG [BP+SI],BX ............... ;87 1a
XCHG [BP+0x55],SI ........... ;87 76 55           XCHG [BP+SI],CH ............... ;86 2a
XCHG [BP+0x55],SP ........... ;87 66 55           XCHG [BP+SI],CL ............... ;86 0a
XCHG [BP+DI+0x5566],AH ...... ;86 a3 66 55        XCHG [BP+SI],CX ............... ;87 0a
XCHG [BP+DI+0x5566],AL ...... ;86 83 66 55        XCHG [BP+SI],DH ............... ;86 32
XCHG [BP+DI+0x5566],AX ...... ;87 83 66 55        XCHG [BP+SI],DI ............... ;87 3a
XCHG [BP+DI+0x5566],BH ...... ;86 bb 66 55        XCHG [BP+SI],DL ............... ;86 12
XCHG [BP+DI+0x5566],BL ...... ;86 9b 66 55        XCHG [BP+SI],DX ............... ;87 12
XCHG [BP+DI+0x5566],BP ...... ;87 ab 66 55        XCHG [BP+SI],SI ............... ;87 32
XCHG [BP+DI+0x5566],BX ...... ;87 9b 66 55        XCHG [BP+SI],SP ............... ;87 22
XCHG [BP+DI+0x5566],CH ...... ;86 ab 66 55        XCHG [BX+0x5566],AH .......... ;86 a7 66 55
XCHG [BP+DI+0x5566],CL ...... ;86 8b 66 55        XCHG [BX+0x5566],AL .......... ;86 87 66 55
XCHG [BP+DI+0x5566],CX ...... ;87 8b 66 55        XCHG [BX+0x5566],AX .......... ;87 87 66 55
XCHG [BP+DI+0x5566],DH ...... ;86 b3 66 55        XCHG [BX+0x5566],BH .......... ;86 bf 66 55
XCHG [BP+DI+0x5566],DI ...... ;87 bb 66 55        XCHG [BX+0x5566],BL .......... ;86 9f 66 55
XCHG [BP+DI+0x5566],DL ...... ;86 93 66 55        XCHG [BX+0x5566],BP .......... ;87 af 66 55
XCHG [BP+DI+0x5566],DX ...... ;87 93 66 55        XCHG [BX+0x5566],BX .......... ;87 9f 66 55
XCHG [BP+DI+0x5566],SI ...... ;87 b3 66 55        XCHG [BX+0x5566],CH .......... ;86 af 66 55
XCHG [BP+DI+0x5566],SP ...... ;87 a3 66 55        XCHG [BX+0x5566],CL .......... ;86 8f 66 55
XCHG [BP+DI+0x55],AH ........ ;86 63 55           XCHG [BX+0x5566],CX .......... ;87 8f 66 55
XCHG [BP+DI+0x55],AL ........ ;86 43 55           XCHG [BX+0x5566],DH .......... ;86 b7 66 55
XCHG [BP+DI+0x55],AX ........ ;87 43 55           XCHG [BX+0x5566],DI .......... ;87 bf 66 55
XCHG [BP+DI+0x55],BH ........ ;86 7b 55           XCHG [BX+0x5566],DL .......... ;86 97 66 55
XCHG [BP+DI+0x55],BL ........ ;86 5b 55           XCHG [BX+0x5566],DX .......... ;87 97 66 55
XCHG [BP+DI+0x55],BP ........ ;87 6b 55           XCHG [BX+0x5566],SI .......... ;87 b7 66 55
XCHG [BP+DI+0x55],BX ........ ;87 5b 55           XCHG [BX+0x5566],SP .......... ;87 a7 66 55
XCHG [BP+DI+0x55],CH ........ ;86 6b 55           XCHG [BX+0x55],AH ............ ;86 67 55
XCHG [BP+DI+0x55],CL ........ ;86 4b 55           XCHG [BX+0x55],AL ............ ;86 47 55
XCHG [BP+DI+0x55],CX ........ ;87 4b 55           XCHG [BX+0x55],AX ............ ;87 47 55
XCHG [BP+DI+0x55],DH ........ ;86 73 55           XCHG [BX+0x55],BH ............ ;86 7f 55
XCHG [BP+DI+0x55],DI ........ ;87 7b 55           XCHG [BX+0x55],BL ............ ;86 5f 55
XCHG [BP+DI+0x55],DL ........ ;86 53 55           XCHG [BX+0x55],BP ............ ;87 6f 55
XCHG [BP+DI+0x55],DX ........ ;87 53 55           XCHG [BX+0x55],BX ............ ;87 5f 55
XCHG [BP+DI+0x55],SI ........ ;87 73 55           XCHG [BX+0x55],CH ............ ;86 6f 55
XCHG [BP+DI+0x55],SP ........ ;87 63 55           XCHG [BX+0x55],CL ............ ;86 4f 55
XCHG [BP+DI],AH .............. ;86 23             XCHG [BX+0x55],CX ............ ;87 4f 55
XCHG [BP+DI],AL .............. ;86 03             XCHG [BX+0x55],DH ............ ;86 77 55
XCHG [BP+DI],AX .............. ;87 03             XCHG [BX+0x55],DI ............ ;87 7f 55
XCHG [BP+DI],BH .............. ;86 3b             XCHG [BX+0x55],DL ............ ;86 57 55
XCHG [BP+DI],BL .............. ;86 1b             XCHG [BX+0x55],DX ............ ;87 57 55
XCHG [BP+DI],BP .............. ;87 2b             XCHG [BX+0x55],SI ............ ;87 77 55
XCHG [BP+DI],BX .............. ;87 1b             XCHG [BX+0x55],SP ............ ;87 67 55
XCHG [BP+DI],CH .............. ;86 2b             XCHG [BX+DI+0x5566],AH ....... ;86 a1 66 55
XCHG [BP+DI],CL .............. ;86 0b             XCHG [BX+DI+0x5566],AL ....... ;86 81 66 55
XCHG [BP+DI],CX .............. ;87 0b             XCHG [BX+DI+0x5566],AX ....... ;87 81 66 55
XCHG [BP+DI],DH .............. ;86 33             XCHG [BX+DI+0x5566],BH ....... ;86 b9 66 55
```

227

```
XCHG [BX+DI+0x5566],BL .........;86 99 66 55
XCHG [BX+DI+0x5566],BP .........;87 a9 66 55
XCHG [BX+DI+0x5566],BX .........;87 99 66 55
XCHG [BX+DI+0x5566],CH .........;86 a9 66 55
XCHG [BX+DI+0x5566],CL .........;86 89 66 55
XCHG [BX+DI+0x5566],CX .........;87 89 66 55
XCHG [BX+DI+0x5566],DH .........;86 b1 66 55
XCHG [BX+DI+0x5566],DI .........;87 b9 66 55
XCHG [BX+DI+0x5566],DL .........;86 91 66 55
XCHG [BX+DI+0x5566],DX .........;87 91 66 55
XCHG [BX+DI+0x5566],SI .........;87 b1 66 55
XCHG [BX+DI+0x5566],SP .........;87 a1 66 55
XCHG [BX+DI+0x55],AH ...........;86 61 55
XCHG [BX+DI+0x55],AL ...........;86 41 55
XCHG [BX+DI+0x55],AX ...........;87 41 55
XCHG [BX+DI+0x55],BH ...........;86 79 55
XCHG [BX+DI+0x55],BL ...........;86 59 55
XCHG [BX+DI+0x55],BP ...........;87 69 55
XCHG [BX+DI+0x55],BX ...........;87 59 55
XCHG [BX+DI+0x55],CH ...........;86 69 55
XCHG [BX+DI+0x55],CL ...........;86 49 55
XCHG [BX+DI+0x55],CX ...........;87 49 55
XCHG [BX+DI+0x55],DH ...........;86 71 55
XCHG [BX+DI+0x55],DI ...........;87 79 55
XCHG [BX+DI+0x55],DL ...........;86 51 55
XCHG [BX+DI+0x55],DX ...........;87 51 55
XCHG [BX+DI+0x55],SI ...........;87 71 55
XCHG [BX+DI+0x55],SP ...........;87 61 55
XCHG [BX+DI],AH ................;86 21
XCHG [BX+DI],AL ................;86 01
XCHG [BX+DI],AX ................;87 01
XCHG [BX+DI],BH ................;86 39
XCHG [BX+DI],BL ................;86 19
XCHG [BX+DI],BP ................;87 29
XCHG [BX+DI],BX ................;87 19
XCHG [BX+DI],CH ................;86 29
XCHG [BX+DI],CL ................;86 09
XCHG [BX+DI],CX ................;87 09
XCHG [BX+DI],DH ................;86 31
XCHG [BX+DI],DI ................;87 39
XCHG [BX+DI],DL ................;86 11
XCHG [BX+DI],DX ................;87 11
XCHG [BX+DI],SI ................;87 31
XCHG [BX+DI],SP ................;87 21
XCHG [BX+SI+0x5566],AH .........;86 a0 66 55
XCHG [BX+SI+0x5566],AL .........;86 80 66 55
XCHG [BX+SI+0x5566],AX .........;87 80 66 55
XCHG [BX+SI+0x5566],BH .........;86 b8 66 55
XCHG [BX+SI+0x5566],BL .........;86 98 66 55
XCHG [BX+SI+0x5566],BP .........;87 a8 66 55
XCHG [BX+SI+0x5566],BX .........;87 98 66 55
XCHG [BX+SI+0x5566],CH .........;86 a8 66 55
XCHG [BX+SI+0x5566],CL .........;86 88 66 55
XCHG [BX+SI+0x5566],CX .........;87 88 66 55
XCHG [BX+SI+0x5566],DH .........;86 b0 66 55
XCHG [BX+SI+0x5566],DI .........;87 b8 66 55
XCHG [BX+SI+0x5566],DL .........;86 90 66 55
XCHG [BX+SI+0x5566],DX .........;87 90 66 55
XCHG [BX+SI+0x5566],SI .........;87 b0 66 55
XCHG [BX+SI+0x5566],SP .........;87 a0 66 55
XCHG [BX+SI+0x55],AH ...........;86 60 55
XCHG [BX+SI+0x55],AL ...........;86 40 55
XCHG [BX+SI+0x55],AX ...........;87 40 55
XCHG [BX+SI+0x55],BH ...........;86 78 55
XCHG [BX+SI+0x55],BL ...........;86 58 55
XCHG [BX+SI+0x55],BP ...........;87 68 55
XCHG [BX+SI+0x55],BX ...........;87 58 55
XCHG [BX+SI+0x55],CH ...........;86 68 55
XCHG [BX+SI+0x55],CL ...........;86 48 55
XCHG [BX+SI+0x55],CX ...........;87 48 55
XCHG [BX+SI+0x55],DH ...........;86 70 55
XCHG [BX+SI+0x55],DI ...........;87 78 55
XCHG [BX+SI+0x55],DL ...........;86 50 55
XCHG [BX+SI+0x55],DX ...........;87 50 55
XCHG [BX+SI+0x55],SI ...........;87 70 55
XCHG [BX+SI+0x55],SP ...........;87 60 55
XCHG [BX+SI],AH ................;86 20
XCHG [BX+SI],AL ................;86 00
XCHG [BX+SI],AX ................;87 00
XCHG [BX+SI],BH ................;86 38
XCHG [BX+SI],BL ................;86 18
XCHG [BX+SI],BP ................;87 28
XCHG [BX+SI],BX ................;87 18
XCHG [BX+SI],CH ................;86 28
XCHG [BX+SI],CL ................;86 08
XCHG [BX+SI],CX ................;87 08
XCHG [BX+SI],DH ................;86 30
XCHG [BX+SI],DI ................;87 38
XCHG [BX+SI],DL ................;86 10

XCHG [BX+SI],DX ................;87 10
XCHG [BX+SI],SI ................;87 30
XCHG [BX+SI],SP ................;87 20
XCHG [BX],AH ...................;86 27
XCHG [BX],AL ...................;86 07
XCHG [BX],AX ...................;87 07
XCHG [BX],BH ...................;86 3f
XCHG [BX],BL ...................;86 1f
XCHG [BX],BP ...................;87 2f
XCHG [BX],BX ...................;87 1f
XCHG [BX],CH ...................;86 2f
XCHG [BX],CL ...................;86 0f
XCHG [BX],CX ...................;87 0f
XCHG [BX],DH ...................;86 37
XCHG [BX],DI ...................;87 3f
XCHG [BX],DL ...................;86 17
XCHG [BX],DX ...................;87 17
XCHG [BX],SI ...................;87 37
XCHG [BX],SP ...................;87 27
XCHG [DI+0x5566],AH ............;86 a5 66 55
XCHG [DI+0x5566],AL ............;86 85 66 55
XCHG [DI+0x5566],AX ............;87 85 66 55
XCHG [DI+0x5566],BH ............;86 bd 66 55
XCHG [DI+0x5566],BL ............;86 9d 66 55
XCHG [DI+0x5566],BP ............;87 ad 66 55
XCHG [DI+0x5566],BX ............;87 9d 66 55
XCHG [DI+0x5566],CH ............;86 ad 66 55
XCHG [DI+0x5566],CL ............;86 8d 66 55
XCHG [DI+0x5566],CX ............;87 8d 66 55
XCHG [DI+0x5566],DH ............;86 b5 66 55
XCHG [DI+0x5566],DI ............;87 bd 66 55
XCHG [DI+0x5566],DL ............;86 95 66 55
XCHG [DI+0x5566],DX ............;87 95 66 55
XCHG [DI+0x5566],SI ............;87 b5 66 55
XCHG [DI+0x5566],SP ............;87 a5 66 55
XCHG [DI+0x55],AH ..............;86 65 55
XCHG [DI+0x55],AL ..............;86 45 55
XCHG [DI+0x55],AX ..............;87 45 55
XCHG [DI+0x55],BH ..............;86 7d 55
XCHG [DI+0x55],BL ..............;86 5d 55
XCHG [DI+0x55],BP ..............;87 6d 55
XCHG [DI+0x55],BX ..............;87 5d 55
XCHG [DI+0x55],CH ..............;86 6d 55
XCHG [DI+0x55],CL ..............;86 4d 55
XCHG [DI+0x55],CX ..............;87 4d 55
XCHG [DI+0x55],DH ..............;86 75 55
XCHG [DI+0x55],DI ..............;87 7d 55
XCHG [DI+0x55],DL ..............;86 55 55
XCHG [DI+0x55],DX ..............;87 55 55
XCHG [DI+0x55],SI ..............;87 75 55
XCHG [DI+0x55],SP ..............;87 65 55
XCHG [DI],AH ...................;86 25
XCHG [DI],AL ...................;86 05
XCHG [DI],AX ...................;87 05
XCHG [DI],BH ...................;86 3d
XCHG [DI],BL ...................;86 1d
XCHG [DI],BP ...................;87 2d
XCHG [DI],BX ...................;87 1d
XCHG [DI],CH ...................;86 2d
XCHG [DI],CL ...................;86 0d
XCHG [DI],CX ...................;87 0d
XCHG [DI],DH ...................;86 35
XCHG [DI],DI ...................;87 3d
XCHG [DI],DL ...................;86 15
XCHG [DI],DX ...................;87 15
XCHG [DI],SI ...................;87 35
XCHG [DI],SP ...................;87 25
XCHG [SI+0x5566],AH ............;86 a4 66 55
XCHG [SI+0x5566],AL ............;86 84 66 55
XCHG [SI+0x5566],AX ............;87 84 66 55
XCHG [SI+0x5566],BH ............;86 bc 66 55
XCHG [SI+0x5566],BL ............;86 9c 66 55
XCHG [SI+0x5566],BP ............;87 ac 66 55
XCHG [SI+0x5566],BX ............;87 9c 66 55
XCHG [SI+0x5566],CH ............;86 ac 66 55
XCHG [SI+0x5566],CL ............;86 8c 66 55
XCHG [SI+0x5566],CX ............;87 8c 66 55
XCHG [SI+0x5566],DH ............;86 b4 66 55
XCHG [SI+0x5566],DI ............;87 bc 66 55
XCHG [SI+0x5566],DL ............;86 94 66 55
XCHG [SI+0x5566],DX ............;87 94 66 55
XCHG [SI+0x5566],SI ............;87 b4 66 55
XCHG [SI+0x5566],SP ............;87 a4 66 55
XCHG [SI+0x55],AH ..............;86 64 55
XCHG [SI+0x55],AL ..............;86 44 55
XCHG [SI+0x55],AX ..............;87 44 55
XCHG [SI+0x55],BH ..............;86 7c 55
XCHG [SI+0x55],BL ..............;86 5c 55
XCHG [SI+0x55],BP ..............;87 6c 55
```

```
XCHG [SI+0x55],BX .............. ;87 5c 55
XCHG [SI+0x55],CH .............. ;86 6c 55
XCHG [SI+0x55],CL .............. ;86 4c 55
XCHG [SI+0x55],CX .............. ;87 4c 55
XCHG [SI+0x55],DH .............. ;86 74 55
XCHG [SI+0x55],DI .............. ;87 7c 55
XCHG [SI+0x55],DL .............. ;86 54 55
XCHG [SI+0x55],DX .............. ;87 54 55
XCHG [SI+0x55],SI .............. ;87 74 55
XCHG [SI+0x55],SP .............. ;87 64 55
XCHG [SI],AH ................... ;86 24
XCHG [SI],AL ................... ;86 04
XCHG [SI],AX ................... ;87 04
XCHG [SI],BH ................... ;86 3c
XCHG [SI],BL ................... ;86 1c
XCHG [SI],BP ................... ;87 2c
XCHG [SI],BX ................... ;87 1c
XCHG [SI],CH ................... ;86 2c
XCHG [SI],CL ................... ;86 0c
XCHG [SI],CX ................... ;87 0c
XCHG [SI],DH ................... ;86 34
XCHG [SI],DI ................... ;87 3c
XCHG [SI],DL ................... ;86 14
XCHG [SI],DX ................... ;87 14
XCHG [SI],SI ................... ;87 34
XCHG [SI],SP ................... ;87 24
XLAT .......................... ;d7
XOR AH,0x88 ................... ;80 f4 88
XOR AH,AH ..................... ;30 e4
XOR AH,AL ..................... ;30 c4
XOR AH,BH ..................... ;30 fc
XOR AH,BL ..................... ;30 dc
XOR AH,CH ..................... ;30 ec
XOR AH,CL ..................... ;30 cc
XOR AH,DH ..................... ;30 f4
XOR AH,DL ..................... ;30 d4
XOR AH,[0x5566] ............... ;32 26 66 55
XOR AH,[BP+0x5566] ............ ;32 a6 66 55
XOR AH,[BP+0x55] .............. ;32 66 55
XOR AH,[BP+DI+0x5566] ......... ;32 a3 66 55
XOR AH,[BP+DI+0x55] ........... ;32 63 55
XOR AH,[BP+DI] ................ ;32 23
XOR AH,[BP+SI+0x5566] ......... ;32 a2 66 55
XOR AH,[BP+SI+0x55] ........... ;32 62 55
XOR AH,[BP+SI] ................ ;32 22
XOR AH,[BX+0x5566] ............ ;32 a7 66 55
XOR AH,[BX+0x55] .............. ;32 67 55
XOR AH,[BX+DI+0x5566] ......... ;32 a1 66 55
XOR AH,[BX+DI+0x55] ........... ;32 61 55
XOR AH,[BX+DI] ................ ;32 21
XOR AH,[BX+SI+0x5566] ......... ;32 a0 66 55
XOR AH,[BX+SI+0x55] ........... ;32 60 55
XOR AH,[BX+SI] ................ ;32 20
XOR AH,[BX] ................... ;32 27
XOR AH,[DI+0x5566] ............ ;32 a5 66 55
XOR AH,[DI+0x55] .............. ;32 65 55
XOR AH,[DI] ................... ;32 25
XOR AH,[SI+0x5566] ............ ;32 a4 66 55
XOR AH,[SI+0x55] .............. ;32 64 55
XOR AH,[SI] ................... ;32 24
XOR AL,0x55 ................... ;34 55
XOR AL,0x88 ................... ;80 f0 88
XOR AL,AH ..................... ;30 e0
XOR AL,AL ..................... ;30 c0
XOR AL,BH ..................... ;30 f8
XOR AL,BL ..................... ;30 d8
XOR AL,CH ..................... ;30 e8
XOR AL,CL ..................... ;30 c8
XOR AL,DH ..................... ;30 f0
XOR AL,DL ..................... ;30 d0
XOR AL,[0x5566] ............... ;32 06 66 55
XOR AL,[BP+0x5566] ............ ;32 86 66 55
XOR AL,[BP+0x55] .............. ;32 46 55
XOR AL,[BP+DI+0x5566] ......... ;32 83 66 55
XOR AL,[BP+DI+0x55] ........... ;32 43 55
XOR AL,[BP+DI] ................ ;32 03
XOR AL,[BP+SI+0x5566] ......... ;32 82 66 55
XOR AL,[BP+SI+0x55] ........... ;32 42 55
XOR AL,[BP+SI] ................ ;32 02
XOR AL,[BX+0x5566] ............ ;32 87 66 55
XOR AL,[BX+0x55] .............. ;32 47 55
XOR AL,[BX+DI+0x5566] ......... ;32 81 66 55
XOR AL,[BX+DI+0x55] ........... ;32 41 55
XOR AL,[BX+DI] ................ ;32 01
XOR AL,[BX+SI+0x5566] ......... ;32 80 66 55
XOR AL,[BX+SI+0x55] ........... ;32 40 55
XOR AL,[BX+SI] ................ ;32 00
XOR AL,[BX] ................... ;32 07
XOR AL,[DI+0x5566] ............ ;32 85 66 55

XOR AL,[DI+0x55] .............. ;32 45 55
XOR AL,[DI] ................... ;32 05
XOR AL,[SI+0x5566] ............ ;32 84 66 55
XOR AL,[SI+0x55] .............. ;32 44 55
XOR AL,[SI] ................... ;32 04
XOR AX,0x5566 ................. ;35 66 55
XOR AX,0x77 ................... ;83 f0 77
XOR AX,0x7788 ................. ;81 f0 88 77
XOR AX,AX ..................... ;31 c0
XOR AX,BP ..................... ;31 e8
XOR AX,BX ..................... ;31 d8
XOR AX,CX ..................... ;31 c8
XOR AX,DI ..................... ;31 f8
XOR AX,DX ..................... ;31 d0
XOR AX,SI ..................... ;31 f0
XOR AX,SP ..................... ;31 e0
XOR AX,[0x5566] ............... ;33 06 66 55
XOR AX,[BP+0x5566] ............ ;33 86 66 55
XOR AX,[BP+0x55] .............. ;33 46 55
XOR AX,[BP+DI+0x5566] ......... ;33 83 66 55
XOR AX,[BP+DI+0x55] ........... ;33 43 55
XOR AX,[BP+DI] ................ ;33 03
XOR AX,[BP+SI+0x5566] ......... ;33 82 66 55
XOR AX,[BP+SI+0x55] ........... ;33 42 55
XOR AX,[BP+SI] ................ ;33 02
XOR AX,[BX+0x5566] ............ ;33 87 66 55
XOR AX,[BX+0x55] .............. ;33 47 55
XOR AX,[BX+DI+0x5566] ......... ;33 81 66 55
XOR AX,[BX+DI+0x55] ........... ;33 41 55
XOR AX,[BX+DI] ................ ;33 01
XOR AX,[BX+SI+0x5566] ......... ;33 80 66 55
XOR AX,[BX+SI+0x55] ........... ;33 40 55
XOR AX,[BX+SI] ................ ;33 00
XOR AX,[BX] ................... ;33 07
XOR AX,[DI+0x5566] ............ ;33 85 66 55
XOR AX,[DI+0x55] .............. ;33 45 55
XOR AX,[DI] ................... ;33 05
XOR AX,[SI+0x5566] ............ ;33 84 66 55
XOR AX,[SI+0x55] .............. ;33 44 55
XOR AX,[SI] ................... ;33 04
XOR BH,0x88 ................... ;80 f7 88
XOR BH,AH ..................... ;30 e7
XOR BH,AL ..................... ;30 c7
XOR BH,BH ..................... ;30 ff
XOR BH,BL ..................... ;30 df
XOR BH,CH ..................... ;30 ef
XOR BH,CL ..................... ;30 cf
XOR BH,DH ..................... ;30 f7
XOR BH,DL ..................... ;30 d7
XOR BH,[0x5566] ............... ;32 3e 66 55
XOR BH,[BP+0x5566] ............ ;32 be 66 55
XOR BH,[BP+0x55] .............. ;32 7e 55
XOR BH,[BP+DI+0x5566] ......... ;32 bb 66 55
XOR BH,[BP+DI+0x55] ........... ;32 7b 55
XOR BH,[BP+DI] ................ ;32 3b
XOR BH,[BP+SI+0x5566] ......... ;32 ba 66 55
XOR BH,[BP+SI+0x55] ........... ;32 7a 55
XOR BH,[BP+SI] ................ ;32 3a
XOR BH,[BX+0x5566] ............ ;32 bf 66 55
XOR BH,[BX+0x55] .............. ;32 7f 55
XOR BH,[BX+DI+0x5566] ......... ;32 b9 66 55
XOR BH,[BX+DI+0x55] ........... ;32 79 55
XOR BH,[BX+DI] ................ ;32 39
XOR BH,[BX+SI+0x5566] ......... ;32 b8 66 55
XOR BH,[BX+SI+0x55] ........... ;32 78 55
XOR BH,[BX+SI] ................ ;32 38
XOR BH,[BX] ................... ;32 3f
XOR BH,[DI+0x5566] ............ ;32 bd 66 55
XOR BH,[DI+0x55] .............. ;32 7d 55
XOR BH,[DI] ................... ;32 3d
XOR BH,[SI+0x5566] ............ ;32 bc 66 55
XOR BH,[SI+0x55] .............. ;32 7c 55
XOR BH,[SI] ................... ;32 3c
XOR BL,0x88 ................... ;80 f3 88
XOR BL,AH ..................... ;30 e3
XOR BL,AL ..................... ;30 c3
XOR BL,BH ..................... ;30 fb
XOR BL,BL ..................... ;30 db
XOR BL,CH ..................... ;30 eb
XOR BL,CL ..................... ;30 cb
XOR BL,DH ..................... ;30 f3
XOR BL,DL ..................... ;30 d3
XOR BL,[0x5566] ............... ;32 1e 66 55
XOR BL,[BP+0x5566] ............ ;32 9e 66 55
XOR BL,[BP+0x55] .............. ;32 5e 55
XOR BL,[BP+DI+0x5566] ......... ;32 9b 66 55
XOR BL,[BP+DI+0x55] ........... ;32 5b 55
XOR BL,[BP+DI] ................ ;32 1b
XOR BL,[BP+SI+0x5566] ......... ;32 9a 66 55
```

```
XOR BL,[BP+SI+0x55] ...........;32 5a 55
XOR BL,[BP+SI] ...............;32 1a
XOR BL,[BX+0x5566] ...........;32 9f 66 55
XOR BL,[BX+0x55] .............;32 5f 55
XOR BL,[BX+DI+0x5566] ........;32 99 66 55
XOR BL,[BX+DI+0x55] ..........;32 59 55
XOR BL,[BX+DI] ...............;32 19
XOR BL,[BX+SI+0x5566] ........;32 98 66 55
XOR BL,[BX+SI+0x55] ..........;32 58 55
XOR BL,[BX+SI] ...............;32 18
XOR BL,[BX] ..................;32 1f
XOR BL,[DI+0x5566] ...........;32 9d 66 55
XOR BL,[DI+0x55] .............;32 5d 55
XOR BL,[DI] ..................;32 1d
XOR BL,[SI+0x5566] ...........;32 9c 66 55
XOR BL,[SI+0x55] .............;32 5c 55
XOR BL,[SI] ..................;32 1c
XOR BP,0x77 ..................;83 f5 77
XOR BP,0x7788 ................;81 f5 88 77
XOR BP,AX ....................;31 c5
XOR BP,BP ....................;31 ed
XOR BP,BX ....................;31 dd
XOR BP,CX ....................;31 cd
XOR BP,DI ....................;31 fd
XOR BP,DX ....................;31 d5
XOR BP,SI ....................;31 f5
XOR BP,SP ....................;31 e5
XOR BP,[0x5566] ..............;33 2e 66 55
XOR BP,[BP+0x5566] ...........;33 ae 66 55
XOR BP,[BP+0x55] .............;33 6e 55
XOR BP,[BP+DI+0x5566] ........;33 ab 66 55
XOR BP,[BP+DI+0x55] ..........;33 6b 55
XOR BP,[BP+DI] ...............;33 2b
XOR BP,[BP+SI+0x55] ..........;33 aa 66 55
XOR BP,[BP+SI+0x55] ..........;33 6a 55
XOR BP,[BP+SI] ...............;33 2a
XOR BP,[BX+0x5566] ...........;33 af 66 55
XOR BP,[BX+0x55] .............;33 6f 55
XOR BP,[BX+DI+0x5566] ........;33 a9 66 55
XOR BP,[BX+DI+0x55] ..........;33 69 55
XOR BP,[BX+DI] ...............;33 29
XOR BP,[BX+SI+0x5566] ........;33 a8 66 55
XOR BP,[BX+SI+0x55] ..........;33 68 55
XOR BP,[BX+SI] ...............;33 28
XOR BP,[BX] ..................;33 2f
XOR BP,[DI+0x5566] ...........;33 ad 66 55
XOR BP,[DI+0x55] .............;33 6d 55
XOR BP,[DI] ..................;33 2d
XOR BP,[SI+0x5566] ...........;33 ac 66 55
XOR BP,[SI+0x55] .............;33 6c 55
XOR BP,[SI] ..................;33 2c
XOR BX,0x77 ..................;83 f3 77
XOR BX,0x7788 ................;81 f3 88 77
XOR BX,AX ....................;31 c3
XOR BX,BP ....................;31 eb
XOR BX,BX ....................;31 db
XOR BX,CX ....................;31 cb
XOR BX,DI ....................;31 fb
XOR BX,DX ....................;31 d3
XOR BX,SI ....................;31 f3
XOR BX,SP ....................;31 e3
XOR BX,[0x5566] ..............;33 1e 66 55
XOR BX,[BP+0x5566] ...........;33 9e 66 55
XOR BX,[BP+0x55] .............;33 5e 55
XOR BX,[BP+DI+0x5566] ........;33 9b 66 55
XOR BX,[BP+DI+0x55] ..........;33 5b 55
XOR BX,[BP+DI] ...............;33 1b
XOR BX,[BP+SI+0x5566] ........;33 9a 66 55
XOR BX,[BP+SI+0x55] ..........;33 5a 55
XOR BX,[BP+SI] ...............;33 1a
XOR BX,[BX+0x5566] ...........;33 9f 66 55
XOR BX,[BX+0x55] .............;33 5f 55
XOR BX,[BX+DI+0x5566] ........;33 99 66 55
XOR BX,[BX+DI+0x55] ..........;33 59 55
XOR BX,[BX+DI] ...............;33 19
XOR BX,[BX+SI+0x5566] ........;33 98 66 55
XOR BX,[BX+SI+0x55] ..........;33 58 55
XOR BX,[BX+SI] ...............;33 18
XOR BX,[BX] ..................;33 1f
XOR BX,[DI+0x5566] ...........;33 9d 66 55
XOR BX,[DI+0x55] .............;33 5d 55
XOR BX,[DI] ..................;33 1d
XOR BX,[SI+0x5566] ...........;33 9c 66 55
XOR BX,[SI+0x55] .............;33 5c 55
XOR BX,[SI] ..................;33 1c
XOR BYTE [0x5566],0x88 .......;80 36 66 55 88
XOR BYTE [BP+0x5566],0x88 ....;80 b6 66 55 88
XOR BYTE [BP+0x55],0x88 ......;80 76 55 88
XOR BYTE [BP+DI+0x5566],0x88 .;80 b3 66 55 88

XOR BYTE [BP+DI+0x55],0x88 ....;80 73 55 88
XOR BYTE [BP+DI],0x88 .........;80 33 88
XOR BYTE [BP+SI+0x5566],0x88 ...;80 b2 66 55 88
XOR BYTE [BP+SI+0x55],0x88 ....;80 72 55 88
XOR BYTE [BP+SI],0x88 .........;80 32 88
XOR BYTE [BX+0x5566],0x88 .....;80 b7 66 55 88
XOR BYTE [BX+0x55],0x88 .......;80 77 55 88
XOR BYTE [BX+DI+0x5566],0x88 ...;80 b1 66 55 88
XOR BYTE [BX+DI+0x55],0x88 ....;80 71 55 88
XOR BYTE [BX+DI],0x88 .........;80 31 88
XOR BYTE [BX+SI+0x5566],0x88 ..;80 b0 66 55 88
XOR BYTE [BX+SI+0x55],0x88 ....;80 70 55 88
XOR BYTE [BX+SI],0x88 .........;80 30 88
XOR BYTE [BX],0x88 ............;80 37 88
XOR BYTE [DI+0x5566],0x88 .....;80 b5 66 55 88
XOR BYTE [DI+0x55],0x88 .......;80 75 55 88
XOR BYTE [DI],0x88 ............;80 35 88
XOR BYTE [SI+0x5566],0x88 .....;80 b4 66 55 88
XOR BYTE [SI+0x55],0x88 .......;80 74 55 88
XOR BYTE [SI],0x88 ............;80 34 88
XOR CH,0x88 ..................;80 f5 88
XOR CH,AH ....................;30 e5
XOR CH,AL ....................;30 c5
XOR CH,BH ....................;30 fd
XOR CH,BL ....................;30 dd
XOR CH,CH ....................;30 ed
XOR CH,CL ....................;30 cd
XOR CH,DH ....................;30 f5
XOR CH,DL ....................;30 d5
XOR CH,[0x5566] ..............;32 2e 66 55
XOR CH,[BP+0x5566] ...........;32 ae 66 55
XOR CH,[BP+0x55] .............;32 6e 55
XOR CH,[BP+DI+0x5566] ........;32 ab 66 55
XOR CH,[BP+DI+0x55] ..........;32 6b 55
XOR CH,[BP+DI] ...............;32 2b
XOR CH,[BP+SI+0x5566] ........;32 aa 66 55
XOR CH,[BP+SI+0x55] ..........;32 6a 55
XOR CH,[BP+SI] ...............;32 2a
XOR CH,[BX+0x5566] ...........;32 af 66 55
XOR CH,[BX+0x55] .............;32 6f 55
XOR CH,[BX+DI+0x5566] ........;32 a9 66 55
XOR CH,[BX+DI+0x55] ..........;32 69 55
XOR CH,[BX+DI] ...............;32 29
XOR CH,[BX+SI+0x5566] ........;32 a8 66 55
XOR CH,[BX+SI+0x55] ..........;32 68 55
XOR CH,[BX+SI] ...............;32 28
XOR CH,[BX] ..................;32 2f
XOR CH,[DI+0x5566] ...........;32 ad 66 55
XOR CH,[DI+0x55] .............;32 6d 55
XOR CH,[DI] ..................;32 2d
XOR CH,[SI+0x5566] ...........;32 ac 66 55
XOR CH,[SI+0x55] .............;32 6c 55
XOR CH,[SI] ..................;32 2c
XOR CL,0x88 ..................;80 f1 88
XOR CL,AH ....................;30 e1
XOR CL,AL ....................;30 c1
XOR CL,BH ....................;30 f9
XOR CL,BL ....................;30 d9
XOR CL,CH ....................;30 e9
XOR CL,CL ....................;30 c9
XOR CL,DH ....................;30 f1
XOR CL,DL ....................;30 d1
XOR CL,[0x5566] ..............;32 0e 66 55
XOR CL,[BP+0x5566] ...........;32 8e 66 55
XOR CL,[BP+0x55] .............;32 4e 55
XOR CL,[BP+DI+0x5566] ........;32 8b 66 55
XOR CL,[BP+DI+0x55] ..........;32 4b 55
XOR CL,[BP+DI] ...............;32 0b
XOR CL,[BP+SI+0x5566] ........;32 8a 66 55
XOR CL,[BP+SI+0x55] ..........;32 4a 55
XOR CL,[BP+SI] ...............;32 0a
XOR CL,[BX+0x5566] ...........;32 8f 66 55
XOR CL,[BX+0x55] .............;32 4f 55
XOR CL,[BX+DI+0x5566] ........;32 89 66 55
XOR CL,[BX+DI+0x55] ..........;32 49 55
XOR CL,[BX+DI] ...............;32 09
XOR CL,[BX+SI+0x5566] ........;32 88 66 55
XOR CL,[BX+SI+0x55] ..........;32 48 55
XOR CL,[BX+SI] ...............;32 08
XOR CL,[BX] ..................;32 0f
XOR CL,[DI+0x5566] ...........;32 8d 66 55
XOR CL,[DI+0x55] .............;32 4d 55
XOR CL,[DI] ..................;32 0d
XOR CL,[SI+0x5566] ...........;32 8c 66 55
XOR CL,[SI+0x55] .............;32 4c 55
XOR CL,[SI] ..................;32 0c
XOR CX,0x77 ..................;83 f1 77
XOR CX,0x7788 ................;81 f1 88 77
XOR CX,AX ....................;31 c1
```

230

```
XOR CX,BP .....................;31 e9
XOR CX,BX .....................;31 d9
XOR CX,CX .....................;31 c9
XOR CX,DI .....................;31 f9
XOR CX,DX .....................;31 d1
XOR CX,SI .....................;31 f1
XOR CX,SP .....................;31 e1
XOR CX,[0x5566] ...............;33 0e 66 55
XOR CX,[BP+0x5566] ............;33 8e 66 55
XOR CX,[BP+0x55] ..............;33 4e 55
XOR CX,[BP+DI+0x5566] .........;33 8b 66 55
XOR CX,[BP+DI+0x55] ...........;33 4b 55
XOR CX,[BP+DI] ................;33 0b
XOR CX,[BP+SI+0x5566] .........;33 8a 66 55
XOR CX,[BP+SI+0x55] ...........;33 4a 55
XOR CX,[BP+SI] ................;33 0a
XOR CX,[BX+0x5566] ............;33 8f 66 55
XOR CX,[BX+0x55] ..............;33 4f 55
XOR CX,[BX+DI+0x5566] .........;33 89 66 55
XOR CX,[BX+DI+0x55] ...........;33 49 55
XOR CX,[BX+DI] ................;33 09
XOR CX,[BX+SI+0x5566] .........;33 88 66 55
XOR CX,[BX+SI+0x55] ...........;33 48 55
XOR CX,[BX+SI] ................;33 08
XOR CX,[BX] ...................;33 0f
XOR CX,[DI+0x5566] ............;33 8d 66 55
XOR CX,[DI+0x55] ..............;33 4d 55
XOR CX,[DI] ...................;33 0d
XOR CX,[SI+0x5566] ............;33 8c 66 55
XOR CX,[SI+0x55] ..............;33 4c 55
XOR CX,[SI] ...................;33 0c
XOR DH,0x88 ...................;80 f6 88
XOR DH,AH .....................;30 e6
XOR DH,AL .....................;30 c6
XOR DH,BH .....................;30 fe
XOR DH,BL .....................;30 de
XOR DH,CH .....................;30 ee
XOR DH,CL .....................;30 ce
XOR DH,DH .....................;30 f6
XOR DH,DL .....................;30 d6
XOR DH,[0x5566] ...............;32 36 66 55
XOR DH,[BP+0x5566] ............;32 b6 66 55
XOR DH,[BP+0x55] ..............;32 76 55
XOR DH,[BP+DI+0x5566] .........;32 b3 66 55
XOR DH,[BP+DI+0x55] ...........;32 73 55
XOR DH,[BP+DI] ................;32 33
XOR DH,[BP+SI+0x5566] .........;32 b2 66 55
XOR DH,[BP+SI+0x55] ...........;32 72 55
XOR DH,[BP+SI] ................;32 32
XOR DH,[BX+0x5566] ............;32 b7 66 55
XOR DH,[BX+0x55] ..............;32 77 55
XOR DH,[BX+DI+0x5566] .........;32 b1 66 55
XOR DH,[BX+DI+0x55] ...........;32 71 55
XOR DH,[BX+DI] ................;32 31
XOR DH,[BX+SI+0x5566] .........;32 b0 66 55
XOR DH,[BX+SI+0x55] ...........;32 70 55
XOR DH,[BX+SI] ................;32 30
XOR DH,[BX] ...................;32 37
XOR DH,[DI+0x5566] ............;32 b5 66 55
XOR DH,[DI+0x55] ..............;32 75 55
XOR DH,[DI] ...................;32 35
XOR DH,[SI+0x5566] ............;32 b4 66 55
XOR DH,[SI+0x55] ..............;32 74 55
XOR DH,[SI] ...................;32 34
XOR DI,0x77 ...................;83 f7 77
XOR DI,0x7788 .................;81 f7 88 77
XOR DI,AX .....................;31 c7
XOR DI,BP .....................;31 ef
XOR DI,BX .....................;31 df
XOR DI,CX .....................;31 cf
XOR DI,DI .....................;31 ff
XOR DI,DX .....................;31 d7
XOR DI,SI .....................;31 f7
XOR DI,SP .....................;31 e7
XOR DI,[0x5566] ...............;33 3e 66 55
XOR DI,[BP+0x5566] ............;33 be 66 55
XOR DI,[BP+0x55] ..............;33 7e 55
XOR DI,[BP+DI+0x5566] .........;33 bb 66 55
XOR DI,[BP+DI+0x55] ...........;33 7b 55
XOR DI,[BP+DI] ................;33 3b
XOR DI,[BP+SI+0x5566] .........;33 ba 66 55
XOR DI,[BP+SI+0x55] ...........;33 7a 55
XOR DI,[BP+SI] ................;33 3a
XOR DI,[BX+0x5566] ............;33 bf 66 55
XOR DI,[BX+0x55] ..............;33 7f 55
XOR DI,[BX+DI+0x5566] .........;33 b9 66 55
XOR DI,[BX+DI+0x55] ...........;33 79 55
XOR DI,[BX+DI] ................;33 39
XOR DI,[BX+SI+0x5566] .........;33 b8 66 55

XOR DI,[BX+SI+0x55] ...........;33 78 55
XOR DI,[BX+SI] ................;33 38
XOR DI,[BX] ...................;33 3f
XOR DI,[DI+0x5566] ............;33 bd 66 55
XOR DI,[DI+0x55] ..............;33 7d 55
XOR DI,[DI] ...................;33 3d
XOR DI,[SI+0x5566] ............;33 bc 66 55
XOR DI,[SI+0x55] ..............;33 7c 55
XOR DI,[SI] ...................;33 3c
XOR DL,0x88 ...................;80 f2 88
XOR DL,AH .....................;30 e2
XOR DL,AL .....................;30 c2
XOR DL,BH .....................;30 fa
XOR DL,BL .....................;30 da
XOR DL,CH .....................;30 ea
XOR DL,CL .....................;30 ca
XOR DL,DH .....................;30 f2
XOR DL,DL .....................;30 d2
XOR DL,[0x5566] ...............;32 16 66 55
XOR DL,[BP+0x5566] ............;32 96 66 55
XOR DL,[BP+0x55] ..............;32 56 55
XOR DL,[BP+DI+0x5566] .........;32 93 66 55
XOR DL,[BP+DI+0x55] ...........;32 53 55
XOR DL,[BP+DI] ................;32 13
XOR DL,[BP+SI+0x5566] .........;32 92 66 55
XOR DL,[BP+SI+0x55] ...........;32 52 55
XOR DL,[BP+SI] ................;32 12
XOR DL,[BX+0x5566] ............;32 97 66 55
XOR DL,[BX+0x55] ..............;32 57 55
XOR DL,[BX+DI+0x5566] .........;32 91 66 55
XOR DL,[BX+DI+0x55] ...........;32 51 55
XOR DL,[BX+DI] ................;32 11
XOR DL,[BX+SI+0x5566] .........;32 90 66 55
XOR DL,[BX+SI+0x55] ...........;32 50 55
XOR DL,[BX+SI] ................;32 10
XOR DL,[BX] ...................;32 17
XOR DL,[DI+0x5566] ............;32 95 66 55
XOR DL,[DI+0x55] ..............;32 55 55
XOR DL,[DI] ...................;32 15
XOR DL,[SI+0x5566] ............;32 94 66 55
XOR DL,[SI+0x55] ..............;32 54 55
XOR DL,[SI] ...................;32 14
XOR DX,0x77 ...................;83 f2 77
XOR DX,0x7788 .................;81 f2 88 77
XOR DX,AX .....................;31 c2
XOR DX,BP .....................;31 ea
XOR DX,BX .....................;31 da
XOR DX,CX .....................;31 ca
XOR DX,DI .....................;31 fa
XOR DX,DX .....................;31 d2
XOR DX,SI .....................;31 f2
XOR DX,SP .....................;31 e2
XOR DX,[0x5566] ...............;33 16 66 55
XOR DX,[BP+0x5566] ............;33 96 66 55
XOR DX,[BP+0x55] ..............;33 56 55
XOR DX,[BP+DI+0x5566] .........;33 93 66 55
XOR DX,[BP+DI+0x55] ...........;33 53 55
XOR DX,[BP+DI] ................;33 13
XOR DX,[BP+SI+0x5566] .........;33 92 66 55
XOR DX,[BP+SI+0x55] ...........;33 52 55
XOR DX,[BP+SI] ................;33 12
XOR DX,[BX+0x5566] ............;33 97 66 55
XOR DX,[BX+0x55] ..............;33 57 55
XOR DX,[BX+DI+0x5566] .........;33 91 66 55
XOR DX,[BX+DI+0x55] ...........;33 51 55
XOR DX,[BX+DI] ................;33 11
XOR DX,[BX+SI+0x5566] .........;33 90 66 55
XOR DX,[BX+SI+0x55] ...........;33 50 55
XOR DX,[BX+SI] ................;33 10
XOR DX,[BX] ...................;33 17
XOR DX,[DI+0x5566] ............;33 95 66 55
XOR DX,[DI+0x55] ..............;33 55 55
XOR DX,[DI] ...................;33 15
XOR DX,[SI+0x5566] ............;33 94 66 55
XOR DX,[SI+0x55] ..............;33 54 55
XOR DX,[SI] ...................;33 14
XOR SI,0x77 ...................;83 f6 77
XOR SI,0x7788 .................;81 f6 88 77
XOR SI,AX .....................;31 c6
XOR SI,BP .....................;31 ee
XOR SI,BX .....................;31 de
XOR SI,CX .....................;31 ce
XOR SI,DI .....................;31 fe
XOR SI,DX .....................;31 d6
XOR SI,SI .....................;31 f6
XOR SI,SP .....................;31 e6
XOR SI,[0x5566] ...............;33 36 66 55
XOR SI,[BP+0x5566] ............;33 b6 66 55
XOR SI,[BP+0x55] ..............;33 76 55
```

```
XOR SI,[BP+DI+0x5566] ........;33 b3 66 55
XOR SI,[BP+DI+0x55] ...........;33 73 55
XOR SI,[BP+DI] ...............;33 33
XOR SI,[BP+SI+0x5566] ........;33 b2 66 55
XOR SI,[BP+SI+0x55] ...........;33 72 55
XOR SI,[BP+SI] ...............;33 32
XOR SI,[BX+0x5566] ...........;33 b7 66 55
XOR SI,[BX+0x55] .............;33 77 55
XOR SI,[BX+DI+0x5566] ........;33 b1 66 55
XOR SI,[BX+DI+0x55] ..........;33 71 55
XOR SI,[BX+DI] ...............;33 31
XOR SI,[BX+SI+0x5566] ........;33 b0 66 55
XOR SI,[BX+SI+0x55] ..........;33 70 55
XOR SI,[BX+SI] ...............;33 30
XOR SI,[BX] ..................;33 37
XOR SI,[DI+0x5566] ...........;33 b5 66 55
XOR SI,[DI+0x55] .............;33 75 55
XOR SI,[DI] ..................;33 35
XOR SI,[SI+0x5566] ...........;33 b4 66 55
XOR SI,[SI+0x55] .............;33 74 55
XOR SI,[SI] ..................;33 34
XOR SP,0x77 ..................;83 f4 77
XOR SP,0x7788 ................;81 f4 88 77
XOR SP,AX ....................;31 c4
XOR SP,BP ....................;31 ec
XOR SP,BX ....................;31 dc
XOR SP,CX ....................;31 cc
XOR SP,DI ....................;31 fc
XOR SP,DX ....................;31 d4
XOR SP,SI ....................;31 f4
XOR SP,SP ....................;31 e4
XOR SP,[0x5566] ..............;33 26 66 55
XOR SP,[BP+0x5566] ...........;33 a6 66 55
XOR SP,[BP+0x55] .............;33 66 55
XOR SP,[BP+DI+0x5566] ........;33 a3 66 55
XOR SP,[BP+DI+0x55] ..........;33 63 55
XOR SP,[BP+DI] ...............;33 23
XOR SP,[BP+SI+0x5566] ........;33 a2 66 55
XOR SP,[BP+SI+0x55] ..........;33 62 55
XOR SP,[BP+SI] ...............;33 22
XOR SP,[BX+0x5566] ...........;33 a7 66 55
XOR SP,[BX+0x55] .............;33 67 55
XOR SP,[BX+DI+0x5566] ........;33 a1 66 55
XOR SP,[BX+DI+0x55] ..........;33 61 55
XOR SP,[BX+DI] ...............;33 21
XOR SP,[BX+SI+0x5566] ........;33 a0 66 55
XOR SP,[BX+SI+0x55] ..........;33 60 55
XOR SP,[BX+SI] ...............;33 20
XOR SP,[BX] ..................;33 27
XOR SP,[DI+0x5566] ...........;33 a5 66 55
XOR SP,[DI+0x55] .............;33 65 55
XOR SP,[DI] ..................;33 25
XOR SP,[SI+0x5566] ...........;33 a4 66 55
XOR SP,[SI+0x55] .............;33 64 55
XOR SP,[SI] ..................;33 24
XOR WORD [0x5566],0x77 .......;83 36 66 55 77
XOR WORD [0x5566],0x7788 .....;81 36 66 55 88 77
XOR WORD [BP+0x5566],0x77 ....;83 b6 66 55 77
XOR WORD [BP+0x5566],0x7788 ..;81 b6 66 55 88 77
XOR WORD [BP+0x55],0x77 ......;83 76 55 77
XOR WORD [BP+0x55],0x7788 ....;81 76 55 88 77
XOR WORD [BP+DI+0x5566],0x77 .;83 b3 66 55 77
XOR WORD [BP+DI+0x5566],0x7788 :81 b3 66 55 88 77
XOR WORD [BP+DI+0x55],0x77 ...;83 73 55 77
XOR WORD [BP+DI+0x55],0x7788 .;81 73 55 88 77
XOR WORD [BP+DI],0x77 ........;83 33 77
XOR WORD [BP+DI],0x7788 ......;81 33 88 77
XOR WORD [BP+SI+0x5566],0x77 .;83 b2 66 55 77
XOR WORD [BP+SI+0x5566],0x7788 :81 b2 66 55 88 77
XOR WORD [BP+SI+0x55],0x77 ...;83 72 55 77
XOR WORD [BP+SI+0x55],0x7788 .;81 72 55 88 77
XOR WORD [BP+SI],0x77 ........;83 32 77
XOR WORD [BP+SI],0x7788 ......;81 32 88 77
XOR WORD [BX+0x5566],0x77 ....;83 b7 66 55 77
XOR WORD [BX+0x5566],0x7788 ..;81 b7 66 55 88 77
XOR WORD [BX+0x55],0x77 ......;83 77 55 77
XOR WORD [BX+0x55],0x7788 ....;81 77 55 88 77
XOR WORD [BX+DI+0x5566],0x77 .;83 b1 66 55 77
XOR WORD [BX+DI+0x5566],0x7788 :81 b1 66 55 88 77
XOR WORD [BX+DI+0x55],0x77 ...;83 71 55 77
XOR WORD [BX+DI+0x55],0x7788 .;81 71 55 88 77
XOR WORD [BX+DI],0x77 ........;83 31 77
XOR WORD [BX+DI],0x7788 ......;81 31 88 77
XOR WORD [BX+SI+0x5566],0x77 .;83 b0 66 55 77
XOR WORD [BX+SI+0x5566],0x7788 :81 b0 66 55 88 77
XOR WORD [BX+SI+0x55],0x77 ...;83 70 55 77
XOR WORD [BX+SI+0x55],0x7788 .;81 70 55 88 77
XOR WORD [BX+SI],0x77 ........;83 30 77
XOR WORD [BX+SI],0x7788 ......;81 30 88 77

XOR WORD [BX],0x77 ...........;83 37 77
XOR WORD [BX],0x7788 .........;81 37 88 77
XOR WORD [DI+0x5566],0x77 ....;83 b5 66 55 77
XOR WORD [DI+0x5566],0x7788 ..;81 b5 66 55 88 77
XOR WORD [DI+0x55],0x77 ......;83 75 55 77
XOR WORD [DI+0x55],0x7788 ....;81 75 55 88 77
XOR WORD [DI],0x77 ...........;83 35 77
XOR WORD [DI],0x7788 .........;81 35 88 77
XOR WORD [SI+0x5566],0x77 ....;83 b4 66 55 77
XOR WORD [SI+0x5566],0x7788 ..;81 b4 66 55 88 77
XOR WORD [SI+0x55],0x77 ......;83 74 55 77
XOR WORD [SI+0x55],0x7788 ....;81 74 55 88 77
XOR WORD [SI],0x77 ...........;83 34 77
XOR WORD [SI],0x7788 .........;81 34 88 77
XOR [0x5566],AH ..............;30 26 66 55
XOR [0x5566],AL ..............;30 06 66 55
XOR [0x5566],AX ..............;31 06 66 55
XOR [0x5566],BH ..............;30 3e 66 55
XOR [0x5566],BL ..............;30 1e 66 55
XOR [0x5566],BP ..............;31 2e 66 55
XOR [0x5566],BX ..............;31 1e 66 55
XOR [0x5566],CH ..............;30 2e 66 55
XOR [0x5566],CL ..............;30 0e 66 55
XOR [0x5566],CX ..............;31 0e 66 55
XOR [0x5566],DH ..............;30 36 66 55
XOR [0x5566],DI ..............;31 3e 66 55
XOR [0x5566],DL ..............;30 16 66 55
XOR [0x5566],DX ..............;31 16 66 55
XOR [0x5566],SI ..............;31 36 66 55
XOR [0x5566],SP ..............;31 26 66 55
XOR [BP+0x5566],AH ...........;30 a6 66 55
XOR [BP+0x5566],AL ...........;30 86 66 55
XOR [BP+0x5566],AX ...........;31 86 66 55
XOR [BP+0x5566],BH ...........;30 be 66 55
XOR [BP+0x5566],BL ...........;30 9e 66 55
XOR [BP+0x5566],BP ...........;31 ae 66 55
XOR [BP+0x5566],BX ...........;31 9e 66 55
XOR [BP+0x5566],CH ...........;30 ae 66 55
XOR [BP+0x5566],CL ...........;30 8e 66 55
XOR [BP+0x5566],CX ...........;31 8e 66 55
XOR [BP+0x5566],DH ...........;30 b6 66 55
XOR [BP+0x5566],DI ...........;31 be 66 55
XOR [BP+0x5566],DL ...........;30 96 66 55
XOR [BP+0x5566],DX ...........;31 96 66 55
XOR [BP+0x5566],SI ...........;31 b6 66 55
XOR [BP+0x5566],SP ...........;31 a6 66 55
XOR [BP+0x55],AH .............;30 66 55
XOR [BP+0x55],AL .............;30 46 55
XOR [BP+0x55],AX .............;31 46 55
XOR [BP+0x55],BH .............;30 7e 55
XOR [BP+0x55],BL .............;30 5e 55
XOR [BP+0x55],BP .............;31 6e 55
XOR [BP+0x55],BX .............;31 5e 55
XOR [BP+0x55],CH .............;30 6e 55
XOR [BP+0x55],CL .............;30 4e 55
XOR [BP+0x55],CX .............;31 4e 55
XOR [BP+0x55],DH .............;30 76 55
XOR [BP+0x55],DI .............;31 7e 55
XOR [BP+0x55],DL .............;30 56 55
XOR [BP+0x55],DX .............;31 56 55
XOR [BP+0x55],SI .............;31 76 55
XOR [BP+0x55],SP .............;31 66 55
XOR [BP+DI+0x5566],AH ........;30 a3 66 55
XOR [BP+DI+0x5566],AL ........;30 83 66 55
XOR [BP+DI+0x5566],AX ........;31 83 66 55
XOR [BP+DI+0x5566],BH ........;30 bb 66 55
XOR [BP+DI+0x5566],BL ........;30 9b 66 55
XOR [BP+DI+0x5566],BP ........;31 ab 66 55
XOR [BP+DI+0x5566],BX ........;31 9b 66 55
XOR [BP+DI+0x5566],CH ........;30 ab 66 55
XOR [BP+DI+0x5566],CL ........;30 8b 66 55
XOR [BP+DI+0x5566],CX ........;31 8b 66 55
XOR [BP+DI+0x5566],DH ........;30 b3 66 55
XOR [BP+DI+0x5566],DI ........;31 bb 66 55
XOR [BP+DI+0x5566],DL ........;30 93 66 55
XOR [BP+DI+0x5566],DX ........;31 93 66 55
XOR [BP+DI+0x5566],SI ........;31 b3 66 55
XOR [BP+DI+0x5566],SP ........;31 a3 66 55
XOR [BP+DI+0x55],AH ..........;30 63 55
XOR [BP+DI+0x55],AL ..........;30 43 55
XOR [BP+DI+0x55],AX ..........;31 43 55
XOR [BP+DI+0x55],BH ..........;30 7b 55
XOR [BP+DI+0x55],BL ..........;30 5b 55
XOR [BP+DI+0x55],BP ..........;31 6b 55
XOR [BP+DI+0x55],BX ..........;31 5b 55
XOR [BP+DI+0x55],CH ..........;30 6b 55
XOR [BP+DI+0x55],CL ..........;30 4b 55
XOR [BP+DI+0x55],CX ..........;31 4b 55
XOR [BP+DI+0x55],DH ..........;30 73 55
```

```
XOR [BP+DI+0x55],DI .............;31 7b 55
XOR [BP+DI+0x55],DL .............;30 53 55
XOR [BP+DI+0x55],DX .............;31 53 55
XOR [BP+DI+0x55],SI .............;31 73 55
XOR [BP+DI+0x55],SP .............;31 63 55
XOR [BP+DI],AH ..................;30 23
XOR [BP+DI],AL ..................;30 03
XOR [BP+DI],AX ..................;31 03
XOR [BP+DI],BH ..................;30 3b
XOR [BP+DI],BL ..................;30 1b
XOR [BP+DI],BP ..................;31 2b
XOR [BP+DI],BX ..................;31 1b
XOR [BP+DI],CH ..................;30 2b
XOR [BP+DI],CL ..................;30 0b
XOR [BP+DI],CX ..................;31 0b
XOR [BP+DI],DH ..................;30 33
XOR [BP+DI],DI ..................;31 3b
XOR [BP+DI],DL ..................;30 13
XOR [BP+DI],DX ..................;31 13
XOR [BP+DI],SI ..................;31 33
XOR [BP+DI],SP ..................;31 23
XOR [BP+SI+0x5566],AH ...........;30 a2 66 55
XOR [BP+SI+0x5566],AL ...........;30 82 66 55
XOR [BP+SI+0x5566],AX ...........;31 82 66 55
XOR [BP+SI+0x5566],BH ...........;30 ba 66 55
XOR [BP+SI+0x5566],BL ...........;30 9a 66 55
XOR [BP+SI+0x5566],BP ...........;31 aa 66 55
XOR [BP+SI+0x5566],BX ...........;31 9a 66 55
XOR [BP+SI+0x5566],CH ...........;30 aa 66 55
XOR [BP+SI+0x5566],CL ...........;30 8a 66 55
XOR [BP+SI+0x5566],CX ...........;31 8a 66 55
XOR [BP+SI+0x5566],DH ...........;30 b2 66 55
XOR [BP+SI+0x5566],DI ...........;31 ba 66 55
XOR [BP+SI+0x5566],DL ...........;30 92 66 55
XOR [BP+SI+0x5566],DX ...........;31 92 66 55
XOR [BP+SI+0x5566],SI ...........;31 b2 66 55
XOR [BP+SI+0x5566],SP ...........;31 a2 66 55
XOR [BP+SI+0x55],AH .............;30 62 55
XOR [BP+SI+0x55],AL .............;30 42 55
XOR [BP+SI+0x55],AX .............;31 42 55
XOR [BP+SI+0x55],BH .............;30 7a 55
XOR [BP+SI+0x55],BL .............;30 5a 55
XOR [BP+SI+0x55],BP .............;31 6a 55
XOR [BP+SI+0x55],BX .............;31 5a 55
XOR [BP+SI+0x55],CH .............;30 6a 55
XOR [BP+SI+0x55],CL .............;30 4a 55
XOR [BP+SI+0x55],CX .............;31 4a 55
XOR [BP+SI+0x55],DH .............;30 72 55
XOR [BP+SI+0x55],DI .............;31 7a 55
XOR [BP+SI+0x55],DL .............;30 52 55
XOR [BP+SI+0x55],DX .............;31 52 55
XOR [BP+SI+0x55],SI .............;31 72 55
XOR [BP+SI+0x55],SP .............;31 62 55
XOR [BP+SI],AH ..................;30 22
XOR [BP+SI],AL ..................;30 02
XOR [BP+SI],AX ..................;31 02
XOR [BP+SI],BH ..................;30 3a
XOR [BP+SI],BL ..................;30 1a
XOR [BP+SI],BP ..................;31 2a
XOR [BP+SI],BX ..................;31 1a
XOR [BP+SI],CH ..................;30 2a
XOR [BP+SI],CL ..................;30 0a
XOR [BP+SI],CX ..................;31 0a
XOR [BP+SI],DH ..................;30 32
XOR [BP+SI],DI ..................;31 3a
XOR [BP+SI],DL ..................;30 12
XOR [BP+SI],DX ..................;31 12
XOR [BP+SI],SI ..................;31 32
XOR [BP+SI],SP ..................;31 22
XOR [BX+0x5566],AH ..............;30 a7 66 55
XOR [BX+0x5566],AL ..............;30 87 66 55
XOR [BX+0x5566],AX ..............;31 87 66 55
XOR [BX+0x5566],BH ..............;30 bf 66 55
XOR [BX+0x5566],BL ..............;30 9f 66 55
XOR [BX+0x5566],BP ..............;31 af 66 55
XOR [BX+0x5566],BX ..............;31 9f 66 55
XOR [BX+0x5566],CH ..............;30 af 66 55
XOR [BX+0x5566],CL ..............;30 8f 66 55
XOR [BX+0x5566],CX ..............;31 8f 66 55
XOR [BX+0x5566],DH ..............;30 b7 66 55
XOR [BX+0x5566],DI ..............;31 bf 66 55
XOR [BX+0x5566],DL ..............;30 97 66 55
XOR [BX+0x5566],DX ..............;31 97 66 55
XOR [BX+0x5566],SI ..............;31 b7 66 55
XOR [BX+0x5566],SP ..............;31 a7 66 55
XOR [BX+0x55],AH ................;30 67 55
XOR [BX+0x55],AL ................;30 47 55
XOR [BX+0x55],AX ................;31 47 55
XOR [BX+0x55],BH ................;30 7f 55

XOR [BX+0x55],BL ................;30 5f 55
XOR [BX+0x55],BP ................;31 6f 55
XOR [BX+0x55],BX ................;31 5f 55
XOR [BX+0x55],CH ................;30 6f 55
XOR [BX+0x55],CL ................;30 4f 55
XOR [BX+0x55],CX ................;31 4f 55
XOR [BX+0x55],DH ................;30 77 55
XOR [BX+0x55],DI ................;31 7f 55
XOR [BX+0x55],DL ................;30 57 55
XOR [BX+0x55],DX ................;31 57 55
XOR [BX+0x55],SI ................;31 77 55
XOR [BX+0x55],SP ................;31 67 55
XOR [BX+DI+0x5566],AH ...........;30 a1 66 55
XOR [BX+DI+0x5566],AL ...........;30 81 66 55
XOR [BX+DI+0x5566],AX ...........;31 81 66 55
XOR [BX+DI+0x5566],BH ...........;30 b9 66 55
XOR [BX+DI+0x5566],BL ...........;30 99 66 55
XOR [BX+DI+0x5566],BP ...........;31 a9 66 55
XOR [BX+DI+0x5566],BX ...........;31 99 66 55
XOR [BX+DI+0x5566],CH ...........;30 a9 66 55
XOR [BX+DI+0x5566],CL ...........;30 89 66 55
XOR [BX+DI+0x5566],CX ...........;31 89 66 55
XOR [BX+DI+0x5566],DH ...........;30 b1 66 55
XOR [BX+DI+0x5566],DI ...........;31 b9 66 55
XOR [BX+DI+0x5566],DL ...........;30 91 66 55
XOR [BX+DI+0x5566],DX ...........;31 91 66 55
XOR [BX+DI+0x5566],SI ...........;31 b1 66 55
XOR [BX+DI+0x5566],SP ...........;31 a1 66 55
XOR [BX+DI+0x55],AH .............;30 61 55
XOR [BX+DI+0x55],AL .............;30 41 55
XOR [BX+DI+0x55],AX .............;31 41 55
XOR [BX+DI+0x55],BH .............;30 79 55
XOR [BX+DI+0x55],BL .............;30 59 55
XOR [BX+DI+0x55],BP .............;31 69 55
XOR [BX+DI+0x55],BX .............;31 59 55
XOR [BX+DI+0x55],CH .............;30 69 55
XOR [BX+DI+0x55],CL .............;30 49 55
XOR [BX+DI+0x55],CX .............;31 49 55
XOR [BX+DI+0x55],DH .............;30 71 55
XOR [BX+DI+0x55],DI .............;31 79 55
XOR [BX+DI+0x55],DL .............;30 51 55
XOR [BX+DI+0x55],DX .............;31 51 55
XOR [BX+DI+0x55],SI .............;31 71 55
XOR [BX+DI+0x55],SP .............;31 61 55
XOR [BX+DI],AH ..................;30 21
XOR [BX+DI],AL ..................;30 01
XOR [BX+DI],AX ..................;31 01
XOR [BX+DI],BH ..................;30 39
XOR [BX+DI],BL ..................;30 19
XOR [BX+DI],BP ..................;31 29
XOR [BX+DI],BX ..................;31 19
XOR [BX+DI],CH ..................;30 29
XOR [BX+DI],CL ..................;30 09
XOR [BX+DI],CX ..................;31 09
XOR [BX+DI],DH ..................;30 31
XOR [BX+DI],DI ..................;31 39
XOR [BX+DI],DL ..................;30 11
XOR [BX+DI],DX ..................;31 11
XOR [BX+DI],SI ..................;31 31
XOR [BX+DI],SP ..................;31 21
XOR [BX+SI+0x5566],AH ...........;30 a0 66 55
XOR [BX+SI+0x5566],AL ...........;30 80 66 55
XOR [BX+SI+0x5566],AX ...........;31 80 66 55
XOR [BX+SI+0x5566],BH ...........;30 b8 66 55
XOR [BX+SI+0x5566],BL ...........;30 98 66 55
XOR [BX+SI+0x5566],BP ...........;31 a8 66 55
XOR [BX+SI+0x5566],BX ...........;31 98 66 55
XOR [BX+SI+0x5566],CH ...........;30 a8 66 55
XOR [BX+SI+0x5566],CL ...........;30 88 66 55
XOR [BX+SI+0x5566],CX ...........;31 88 66 55
XOR [BX+SI+0x5566],DH ...........;30 b0 66 55
XOR [BX+SI+0x5566],DI ...........;31 b8 66 55
XOR [BX+SI+0x5566],DL ...........;30 90 66 55
XOR [BX+SI+0x5566],DX ...........;31 90 66 55
XOR [BX+SI+0x5566],SI ...........;31 b0 66 55
XOR [BX+SI+0x5566],SP ...........;31 a0 66 55
XOR [BX+SI+0x55],AH .............;30 60 55
XOR [BX+SI+0x55],AL .............;30 40 55
XOR [BX+SI+0x55],AX .............;31 40 55
XOR [BX+SI+0x55],BH .............;30 78 55
XOR [BX+SI+0x55],BL .............;30 58 55
XOR [BX+SI+0x55],BP .............;31 68 55
XOR [BX+SI+0x55],BX .............;31 58 55
XOR [BX+SI+0x55],CH .............;30 68 55
XOR [BX+SI+0x55],CL .............;30 48 55
XOR [BX+SI+0x55],CX .............;31 48 55
XOR [BX+SI+0x55],DH .............;30 70 55
XOR [BX+SI+0x55],DI .............;31 78 55
XOR [BX+SI+0x55],DL .............;30 50 55
```

```
XOR [BX+SI+0x55],DX ............;31 50 55        XOR [DI+0x55],SP ..............;31 65 55
XOR [BX+SI+0x55],SI ............;31 70 55        XOR [DI],AH ...................;30 25
XOR [BX+SI+0x55],SP ...........;31 60 55         XOR [DI],AL ...................;30 05
XOR [BX+SI],AH ................;30 20            XOR [DI],AX ...................;31 05
XOR [BX+SI],AL ................;30 00            XOR [DI],BH ...................;30 3d
XOR [BX+SI],AX ................;31 00            XOR [DI],BL ...................;30 1d
XOR [BX+SI],BH ................;30 38            XOR [DI],BP ...................;31 2d
XOR [BX+SI],BL ................;30 18            XOR [DI],BX ...................;31 1d
XOR [BX+SI],BP ................;31 28            XOR [DI],CH ...................;30 2d
XOR [BX+SI],BX ................;31 18            XOR [DI],CL ...................;30 0d
XOR [BX+SI],CH ................;30 28            XOR [DI],CX ...................;31 0d
XOR [BX+SI],CL ................;30 08            XOR [DI],DH ...................;30 35
XOR [BX+SI],CX ................;31 08            XOR [DI],DI ...................;31 3d
XOR [BX+SI],DH ................;30 30            XOR [DI],DL ...................;30 15
XOR [BX+SI],DI ................;31 38            XOR [DI],DX ...................;31 15
XOR [BX+SI],DL ................;30 10            XOR [DI],SI ...................;31 35
XOR [BX+SI],DX ................;31 10            XOR [DI],SP ...................;31 25
XOR [BX+SI],SI ................;31 30            XOR [SI+0x5566],AH ...........;30 a4 66 55
XOR [BX+SI],SP ................;31 20            XOR [SI+0x5566],AL ...........;30 84 66 55
XOR [BX],AH ...................;30 27            XOR [SI+0x5566],AX ...........;31 84 66 55
XOR [BX],AL ...................;30 07            XOR [SI+0x5566],BH ...........;30 bc 66 55
XOR [BX],AX ...................;31 07            XOR [SI+0x5566],BL ...........;30 9c 66 55
XOR [BX],BH ...................;30 3f            XOR [SI+0x5566],BP ...........;31 ac 66 55
XOR [BX],BL ...................;30 1f            XOR [SI+0x5566],BX ...........;31 9c 66 55
XOR [BX],BP ...................;31 2f            XOR [SI+0x5566],CH ...........;30 ac 66 55
XOR [BX],BX ...................;31 1f            XOR [SI+0x5566],CL ...........;30 8c 66 55
XOR [BX],CH ...................;30 2f            XOR [SI+0x5566],CX ...........;31 8c 66 55
XOR [BX],CL ...................;30 0f            XOR [SI+0x5566],DH ...........;30 b4 66 55
XOR [BX],CX ...................;31 0f            XOR [SI+0x5566],DI ...........;31 bc 66 55
XOR [BX],DH ...................;30 37            XOR [SI+0x5566],DL ...........;30 94 66 55
XOR [BX],DI ...................;31 3f            XOR [SI+0x5566],DX ...........;31 94 66 55
XOR [BX],DL ...................;30 17            XOR [SI+0x5566],SI ...........;31 b4 66 55
XOR [BX],DX ...................;31 17            XOR [SI+0x5566],SP ...........;31 a4 66 55
XOR [BX],SI ...................;31 37            XOR [SI+0x55],AH .............;30 64 55
XOR [BX],SP ...................;31 27            XOR [SI+0x55],AL .............;30 44 55
XOR [DI+0x5566],AH ...........;30 a5 66 55       XOR [SI+0x55],AX .............;31 44 55
XOR [DI+0x5566],AL ...........;30 85 66 55       XOR [SI+0x55],BH .............;30 7c 55
XOR [DI+0x5566],AX ...........;31 85 66 55       XOR [SI+0x55],BL .............;30 5c 55
XOR [DI+0x5566],BH ...........;30 bd 66 55       XOR [SI+0x55],BP .............;31 6c 55
XOR [DI+0x5566],BL ...........;30 9d 66 55       XOR [SI+0x55],BX .............;31 5c 55
XOR [DI+0x5566],BP ...........;31 ad 66 55       XOR [SI+0x55],CH .............;30 6c 55
XOR [DI+0x5566],BX ...........;31 9d 66 55       XOR [SI+0x55],CL .............;30 4c 55
XOR [DI+0x5566],CH ...........;30 ad 66 55       XOR [SI+0x55],CX .............;31 4c 55
XOR [DI+0x5566],CL ...........;30 8d 66 55       XOR [SI+0x55],DH .............;30 74 55
XOR [DI+0x5566],CX ...........;31 8d 66 55       XOR [SI+0x55],DI .............;31 7c 55
XOR [DI+0x5566],DH ...........;30 b5 66 55       XOR [SI+0x55],DL .............;30 54 55
XOR [DI+0x5566],DI ...........;31 bd 66 55       XOR [SI+0x55],DX .............;31 54 55
XOR [DI+0x5566],DL ...........;30 95 66 55       XOR [SI+0x55],SI .............;31 74 55
XOR [DI+0x5566],DX ...........;31 95 66 55       XOR [SI+0x55],SP .............;31 64 55
XOR [DI+0x5566],SI ...........;31 b5 66 55       XOR [SI],AH ...................;30 24
XOR [DI+0x5566],SP ...........;31 a5 66 55       XOR [SI],AL ...................;30 04
XOR [DI+0x55],AH .............;30 65 55          XOR [SI],AX ...................;31 04
XOR [DI+0x55],AL .............;30 45 55          XOR [SI],BH ...................;30 3c
XOR [DI+0x55],AX .............;31 45 55          XOR [SI],BL ...................;30 1c
XOR [DI+0x55],BH .............;30 7d 55          XOR [SI],BP ...................;31 2c
XOR [DI+0x55],BL .............;30 5d 55          XOR [SI],BX ...................;31 1c
XOR [DI+0x55],BP .............;31 6d 55          XOR [SI],CH ...................;30 2c
XOR [DI+0x55],BX .............;31 5d 55          XOR [SI],CL ...................;30 0c
XOR [DI+0x55],CH .............;30 6d 55          XOR [SI],CX ...................;31 0c
XOR [DI+0x55],CL .............;30 4d 55          XOR [SI],DH ...................;30 34
XOR [DI+0x55],CX .............;31 4d 55          XOR [SI],DI ...................;31 3c
XOR [DI+0x55],DH .............;30 75 55          XOR [SI],DL ...................;30 14
XOR [DI+0x55],DI .............;31 7d 55          XOR [SI],DX ...................;31 14
XOR [DI+0x55],DL .............;30 55 55          XOR [SI],SI ...................;31 34
XOR [DI+0x55],DX .............;31 55 55          XOR [SI],SP ...................;31 24
XOR [DI+0x55],SI .............;31 75 55
```

Appendix D

bootRogue utility

This small program in C language generates the valid values for small subsets of dungeon rooms connections.

```c
/*
** bootRogue: generate valid connection sets.
**
** by Oscar Toledo G.
**
** Creation date: Sep/23/2019.
*/

#include <stdio.h>

int map[9];           /* Each map has 9 cells */
char valid[65536];    /* Valid configs are marked here */
char valid2[65536];

/*
** Explore the map using the configuration value
*/
int explore(int conf, int cell)
{
  int exits;
  int err;

  if (map[cell])    /* Already visited? */
    return 0;

  map[cell] = 1;    /* Mark it as visited */

  exits = (conf >> (cell * 2)) & 3;
  if (exits & 1) {  /* Can go to right? */
```

```c
    /* Isn't valid to go right at these positions */
    if (cell == 2 || cell == 5 || cell == 8)
      return 1;
    err = explore(conf, cell + 1);
    if (err)
      return err;
  }
  if (exits & 2) {  /* Can go down? */
    /* Isn't valid to go down at these positions */
    if (cell >= 6)
      return 1;
    err = explore(conf, cell + 3);
    if (err)
      return err;
  }
  if (cell != 0 && cell != 3 && cell != 6) {  /* Can go left? */
    exits = (conf >> ((cell - 1) * 2)) & 3;
    if (exits & 1) {
      err = explore(conf, cell - 1);
      if (err)
        return err;
    }
  }
  if (cell >= 3) {  /* Can go up? */
    exits = (conf >> ((cell - 3) * 2)) & 3;
    if (exits & 2) {
      err = explore(conf, cell - 3);
      if (err)
        return err;
    }
  }
  return 0;
}

/*
** Main program
*/
int main(void)
{
  int c;
  int d;
  int e;
  int prev;
  int count = 0;
  int best;
  int current_c;
  int current_d;
  int current_best;
```

```c
  prev = -1;
  for (c = 0; c < 0x10000; c++) { /* All configurations */
    memset(map, 0, sizeof(map));
    d = explore(c, 4);
    if (d == 0) {    /* Valid? */

      /*
      ** Check for cells remaining unconnected
      */
      for (d = 0; d < 9; d++) {
        if (map[d] == 0)
          break;
      }
      if (d == 9) { /* All connected */
        if (prev != (c >> 8)) {
          prev = c >> 8;
          printf("\n$%02x - ", prev);
        }
        printf("$%02x ", c & 0xff);
        count++;
        valid[c] = 1;
      }
    }
  }
  printf("%d valid\n", count);

  /*
  ** Get the best AND/OR combination for a pseudorandom number
  ** that generates the greatest possible variation of cells.
  */
  current_best = 0;
  for (c = 0; c < 0x10000; c++) {
/*  printf("\r%04x...", c);*/
    for (d = 0; d < 0x10000; d++) {
      if ((c & ~d) == 0)
        continue;
      if ((d & c) != 0)
        continue;
      best = 0;
      for (e = 0; e < 0x10000; e++) {
        prev = (e & c) | d;
        if (valid[prev] == 0)
          break;

        if (best == 0) {
          memset(valid2, 0, sizeof(valid2));
        }
```

```
        if (valid2[prev] == 0)
          best++;
        valid2[prev] = 1;
      }
    if (e == 0x10000) {
      if (best >= current_best) {
        current_best = best;
        printf("AND 0x%04x\\nOR 0x%04x ; %d\n", c, d, best);
      }
    }
  }
 }
}
```

Appendix E

About the author

Óscar Toledo Gutiérrez (Mexico, 1978) is an experienced computer programmer.

He has written hundreds of programs in several programming languages, collaborates in the design of the Fenix Operating System and the Biyubi Internet Browser, gives talks at universities and does game design and programming consulting.

He is the creator of the world's smallest chess programs written in C, Java, Javascript, x86 and 6502 machine code, and also the first Mexican to win the IOCCC (International Obfuscated C Code Contest): Best Game (2005), Best of Show (2007), Best Small Program (2007), Most Portable Chess Set (2007) and Best Non-chess Game (2012), and 2nd place winner at the first JS1K contest (2010).

One of his hobbies is working on classic consoles. He has developed games for MSX, Colecovision, Intellivision, TI-99/4A, Atari 2600, PC, Sega Master System, Memotech, Spectravideo and Tatung Einstein. His games Princess Quest and Mecha-8 are included in the Colecovision Flashback retro console by AtGames and he created the IntyBASIC language for programming Intellivision consoles.

He is also the author of the books *Toledo Nanochess: The Commented Source Code*, *Programming Games for Intellivision*, *Programming Boot Sector Games*, and *ColecoVision Games Guide*, and tweetstar with short stories in Spanish published in @historiasmini and now collected in 3 books.